The Future
of Architecture.
Since 1889.
–
Jean-Louis
Cohen

Table of contents

Introduction
Architecture's expanded field

01
Sheds to rails: the dominion of steel

02
The search for modern form

03
Domestic innovation and tectonic expression

07
In search of a language: from classicism to Cubism

08
The Great War and its side effects

09
Expressionism in Weimar Germany and the Netherlands

13
Architecture and revolution in Russia

14
The architecture of social reform

15
Internationalization, its networks and spectacles

Architecture's expanded field

William Morris's *News from Nowhere* and H. G. Wells's *When the Sleeper Wakes*, published in 1890 and 1899 respectively, depict a future society – a socialist utopia in the former case, a capitalist dystopia in the latter – encountered by the novels' protagonists after a long period of sleep. If the contemporary inhabitants of the planet had awakened in the early twenty-first century, they would have been at a loss to recognize not just the cities constellating the world's surface, but also the buildings making them up. Both cities and buildings have undergone fundamental transformations, more so than at any time in the past. Likewise, the quantity of building stock produced since 1900 has surpassed the sum total of that which existed in all previous human history.

Not only did the population of urban areas exceed that of the countryside for the first time shortly after the year 2000, but also the very forms of human presence on the face of the earth reflected thoroughgoing changes. In the nineteenth century, the train station and department store joined the house, palace, and temple in the existing inventory of building types. In the twentieth century, office and apartment towers, large housing developments, vast hangars enclosing factories and shopping centers, and a wide variety of infrastructures ranging from dams to airports followed. Contradicting the British historian Nikolaus Pevsner, who famously wrote that "a bicycle shed is a building; Lincoln Cathedral is a piece of architecture," [1] the most prosaic programs came to be considered objects worthy of aesthetic attention. This unprecedented surge in construction was meager compensation for a previously unimaginable level of destruction of natural resources and cultural treasures, the effects of industrialization, urbanization, and war. Architecture's mutations were not limited to the invention of programs responding to the new demands of production and consumption. The field also expanded with the rise of new types and classes of users. Architecture ceased to be a discipline exclusively in the service of the wealthy and began to address broader constituencies, including municipalities, cooperatives, and a wide range of institutions and social groups. [2] It also responded to the breaking down of classical codes, the rejection of historical imitation, and the introduction of new materials. Its new relations to technology, the arts, and the city were affected by external conditions as well as by internal ones. At times it had recourse to sources outside the discipline, adopting metaphors based on biological organisms, machines, or language; at other times it found inspiration within its own disciplinary traditions. [3] In view of all these transformations, it has been impossible to limit architecture's definition in this book to realized constructions. Unbuilt designs, as well as books, journals, and public manifestations embodying the culture of architecture in its broadest sense, have also been taken into account. Indeed, realized buildings are always informed by ideas, narratives, and repressed memories of past projects.

Two thresholds in time

The very delimitation "twentieth century" is open to debate. Rejecting a strictly chronological definition, the present narrative begins with the period from 1880 to 1914. It finds its temporal brackets between the "short century" that the British historian Eric Hobsbawm condensed into the years from 1914 to 1991 [4] and a longer span that places the twentieth century's origins within a continuum that goes as far back as the Enlightenment. This initial moment is characterized by the convergence of industrialization and urbanization, the rise of social democracy throughout Europe, the emergence of the social sciences as disciplinary specializations, and the dissemination of the thought of important philosophers from Friedrich Nietzsche to Henri Bergson. It also coincides with the rise of revolutionary art movements such as Symbolism in poetry and the arts, and Cubism in painting. While the European powers were fighting a war for world domination and orchestrating the triumph of imperialism, designers, and the images of their work, also began to make inroads around the globe, thanks to the unprecedented acceleration of modes of transport and new networks of printed information, which disseminated the cultural norms of the leading nations.

A pair of almost contemporaneous events were crucial to this beginning: the Universal Exposition in Paris of 1889 and the World's Columbian Exposition in Chicago of 1893. The Paris fair coincided with the climactic moment of European colonialism, while the Chicago fair signaled the emergence of the New World on the international scene. Both events called the very definition of architecture into question, in its purpose – as its addressees became much broader social groups – as well as its forms. Mass production, of which Fordism became the most significant system of organization, led to the creation of a worldwide market and encouraged the most radical architects to search for new forms consonant with the machine aesthetic. At the same time, traditionalists, who were often no less engaged socially and no less hostile to eclecticism, sought to perpetuate the more comforting archetypes of the past by adjusting them to new demands.

Almost one century later – after decolonization, which culminated with Nelson Mandela's release from prison in 1990, and the end of the Cold War, which was marked by the West's triumph over the Soviet bloc in 1989 – the winding down of the second millennium appeared to signal the next radical break in the culture of architecture. It is this moment that provides the closing bracket for this book. The automation of processes in a digital age had the effect of modifying the division of professional labor as well as the relationship between the design studio and the building site. The Guggenheim Museum in Bilbao, Spain, completed by Frank Gehry in 1997, was a highly visible exemplar of these new practices while also a demonstration of the potential importance of architecture in urban planning and public policy; together with dozens of other surprising buildings, Gehry's museum called into question the traditional definition of the architectural object. With architecture firms, clients, and cultural organizations enjoying unprecedented mobility, the rise of a generation of designers hyped by the international media, but initially engaged in theoretical and critical activity and open to utopian discourse, coincided with a crisis in the social policies that had developed over the course of the twentieth century. Coming on the heels of several generations of architects who had nurtured high aspirations to social transformation, designers at the end of the twentieth century often relinquished to developers and politicians tools that they might have used to achieve substantive reforms.

The span from 1889 to 2000 does not divide easily into tidy, self-contained segments. Rather, it is necessary to take into account multiple, overlapping temporalities throughout the century, as suggested by the historian Fernand Braudel in his historical interpretation of the Mediterranean world. → 5 Braudel used the architectural metaphor of multidimensional "planes" to describe these multiple temporalities. In twentieth-century architecture they include state policies and their highly volatile configurations; life cycles of institutions and organizations as well as cities and regions, which undergo slow processes of

growth and decline; and, most simply, the construction of major buildings and the lives of architects, critics, clients, and historians. More fleeting temporalities, in which concepts and ideals appear and disappear only to resurface a few decades later, also play their part. The problem of writing a history of twentieth-century architecture is precisely that of relating these differential rates of temporal change to specific designs and built objects. Given this framework, I have resisted the temptation to write a history of what has been known as the "Modern Movement" ever since Nikolaus Pevsner made a rather partisan identification of its "pioneers" in 1936, celebrating Walter Gropius as its major figurehead. [6] I have also avoided perpetuating the rubric of the "International Style," formulated in 1932 in New York, [7] preferring instead to shape a broader definition of modernity that cannot be reduced to the fetish of *novitas*, of the new for newness's sake. From this point of view, it was essential not to disregard architectural interpretations of modernity based on conservative or traditionalist concepts, even if they were frequently rejected or ridiculed by militant critics acting, as is often the case, on behalf of the leading architects. Resurgences of classicism and the occasional subversive eruption of the vernacular are part of this bigger picture. Indeed, far from being a rigid category, and even less a sterile one, tradition – though sometimes wholly fabricated – has consistently served as an intellectual stimulant. [8]

An exploration of the shifting boundaries between architecture and the related fields of art, urban planning, and technology also proved indispensable for understanding the changing methods of form-giving. The elevated ideals with which radical architects have often identified themselves – such as the machine aesthetic or organicism – needed to be taken into account, along with the effects of the apparently most abstract

manifestoes, which have sometimes exerted their influence at a distance of several decades. An attempt has been made throughout the book to identify the visual documents allowing the clearest understanding of these resonances and reverberations. Together with images of completed buildings, sometimes within their urban contexts, pages of magazines, book covers, and architects' portraits help to reconstruct the complexity of continuously changing networks of signs and forms.

The carousel of hegemonies

In the following pages, the different national "scenes" of architecture have been treated as porous to international strategies and debates – as contexts in which the latter were subjected to discussion, modification, and adaption – rather than as territories with impermeable borders. The history of twentieth-century architecture could be written by following the thread – or, rather, untangling the knot – of consecutive systems of hegemony imposed on national and regional cultures. [9] The period under consideration was characterized in crucial ways by recurrent economic and political conflicts between dominant states, including their military consequences. These conflicts had tremendous impact on culture. In 1941 the media tycoon Henry Luce declared that the twentieth century was destined to be the "American Century," following centuries implicitly perceived as "French" and then "English." [10] There is no doubt that the United States exercised considerable influence on architecture – as on many other fields of culture – even before the massive increase in its power following victory over the Axis forces in 1945 and a second triumphal moment at the end of the Cold War. [11] The vocabulary of architecture faithfully reflected these shifts. After 1945 American terminology supplemented the Italian language of architecture that had emerged during the Renaissance and then was supplemented by French and British terms in the eighteenth and nineteenth centuries and by German terms in the early twentieth century. → 12

But the hegemony of this relatively new civilization was not the only thing to have an impact on global architecture. Considering each national scene as a porous rather than closed realm reveals systems of domination of varying types, intensity, and duration, from industrial modes of production to patterns of leisure. National scenes have remained open despite recurrent attempts by authoritarian or xenophobic regimes to shore up their borders. Far from giving way to a homogenizing internationalism, national systems have constantly redefined themselves, shaped by the interplay of internal and external forces. Long before the advent of air travel and new information technologies, the global circulation of ideas and images by way of the steamship, the telegraph, and the mechanical reproduction of pictures – all nineteenth-century inventions – shaped every local scene.

These patterns may also be detected within colonial empires, which both reached their apogee and underwent their final collapse in the twentieth century, then were partially perpetuated under postcolonial conditions after 1945. But the relationship of the colonizer to the colonized was never unidirectional, and the hybridization that characterized urban planning and architecture in many colonies, where local themes were assimilated into constructions built by the dominant power, also operated between colonizing nations. → 13 The general plan of Chandigarh, capital of the Punjab – initially entrusted to the American architect Albert Mayer, then to Paris-based Le Corbusier – was rooted in town-planning principles that had

been perfected by the British. The architecture of the Moroccan city of Casablanca was defined in relation not just to Paris but also to Berlin and Los Angeles, while Buenos Aires contained echoes of Madrid, Budapest, Milan, New York, and Paris.

The continuity of type

On each national scene, the groups competing for dominance in architecture at times indulged in exaggerated polemics in order to consolidate their own "symbolic capital," in sociologist Pierre Bourdieu's sense of the term. → 14 It was therefore impossible to limit a history of the relationships structuring twentieth-century architecture to a list of aesthetic "influences" – a term I have consciously avoided. Instead, following Hans Robert Jauss, I found it essential to analyze the reception met by works and ideas, as this often redefined the professional identity of architects, even those working at a considerable distance from the buildings they were interpreting and sometimes emulating. → 15 This book proposes to map the relationships established among theoretical systems, seminal concepts, urban plans, paper projects, and completed buildings. This last, however, along with individual architects, remains the central focus, although, once again, with their local and international reception taken into account. The connection between imagined spaces and built ones was particularly strong in the twentieth century, given that the principal types of structures were often developed in a kind of leap from the shelf of the "ideal project library," as identified by Bruno Fortier, → 16 to the reality of the construction site.

The glass towers imagined by Ludwig Mies van der Rohe in 1921, for example, were built only in the 1950s. They then became a tiresome cliché – an easy target for critics advocating "postmodernism" – before being reborn at the end of the century thanks to new technological advances. Likewise, the *immeuble-villa* conceived by Le Corbusier in 1922, a collective dwelling with individual living spaces, has continued to inspire projects in the third millennium. The machine-building that Antonio Sant'Elia envisioned just before World War I would appear in a modified form in the Centre Pompidou in Paris, while the contorted, biomorphic structures dreamed of by the Expressionists have finally become feasible today in an age when digital modeling has made it possible to break down complex shapes into components that can be calculated and industrially produced.

Historians versus architects, or the problem of inclusion

Until the 1970s the histories told by Sigfried Giedion, Bruno Zevi, Henry-Russell Hitchcock, and Leonardo Benevolo perpetuated a view of modern architecture that gave priority to the radical character of its innovations. Each narrative carried its own particular biases. [17] As early as 1929 Giedion was interested in observing "national constants." [18] By 1941 he spoke of the creation of a "new tradition," a notion Hitchcock had proposed in 1929. [19] In 1951 Zevi responded to Giedion by highlighting the historical relationship of architectural culture to politics and surveying a vast array of buildings. [20] In 1958 Hitchcock described the "reintegration" of the arts of the engineer and the architect; he also preferred to write about buildings that he had actually had the opportunity to visit. [21] As for Benevolo, he placed the development of modern architecture

within an optimistic picture of the encounter between formal and technological invention and social advances. [22] Twenty years later, but in a similar vein, Kenneth Frampton proposed a "critical history" of the Modern Movement, seeking to prolong its "incomplete project." [23] Soon after, William Curtis took into account the global expansion of modern architecture, a perspective rooted in his own experiences in Asia and Latin America. [24] In 2002, Alan Colquhoun published a concise survey no less committed to the celebration of modernism than Frampton's. [25]

Reyner Banham, who as early as 1960 saw roots of modern architectural strategies in both Italian Futurism and French Classicism, was among those to propose a more subversive reading. [26] Manfredo Tafuri and Francesco Dal Co also analyzed the relationship of aesthetics and politics in twentieth-century architecture, underlining the ideological forces that shaped the field, [27] which Tafuri had addressed previously in his enigmatic but magisterial *Architecture and Utopia* (1973). Several generations of biographical dictionaries and encyclopedias have allowed readings parallel to those offered by these historical narratives. Recently Adrian Forty attempted, in *Words and Buildings*, to define the semantic field of modern architecture by identifying some of its key terms, whereas Anthony Vidler unveiled the strategies determining many of these founding histories. [28] Yet few of these works have attempted to reveal the continuities that characterize modern architecture – an often broken thread, but one that runs throughout the episodes discussed in this book.

From Giedion to Tafuri to Frampton, these discourses of architectural history have revealed the fact that the supposed autonomy or objectivity of the author is a quasi-fiction. Many of these books originated from a commission by a particular architect

– in Giedion's case, by Le Corbusier and Walter Gropius – or reflected an intellectual position developed in close contact with architects – in Tafuri's case, with Aldo Rossi and Vittorio Gregotti. Through such relationships, architects have undeniably shaped historians' thinking and writing and at times biased their interpretations.

The following pages try to place less emphasis on the creativity of incontestable "masters" like Frank Lloyd Wright, Le Corbusier, and Mies [29] than on the sometimes unfairly neglected work of architects who had less heroic careers but have been rediscovered through the publication of a plethora of monographs during the last two decades. The importance of the "masters" of modern architecture needs to be assessed as much through a careful reconsideration of their ascendancy and period of domination as through a celebration of their work. From this point of view – and unlike many of the volumes named above – this book attempts to be as inclusive as possible, within the limits of its format and at the risk of occasionally oversimplifying complex trajectories. I have frequently devoted more attention to the experimental beginnings of architects' careers than to their late periods, when their work often regressed or was simply frozen in place by success and repetition.

In order to avoid reproducing the kind of epic narrative with which many previous histories have interpreted the theories and designs of the most innovative architects of the nineteenth century – reducing their immediate predecessors to the dubious status of "pioneers" – I have taken a broad view of the unfolding of architectural modernity. The continuity between the ideals and reform strategies forged during the first decades of the Industrial Revolution and those of the "mature" modernism of the 1920s cannot be denied. Indeed, a definition of modernity limited to the aesthetic and design precepts of high modernism

appears all the more obsolete thirty years after the eruption of the last of several short-lived postmodernisms. Without going so far as to extend the definition of the modern condition to the vast configurations of scientific and political thought explored by, for example, Bruno Latour, [30] I have ventured beyond the limits of the movements literally proclaiming their own modernity to consider changes brought about by the convergence of the Enlightenment, the Industrial Revolution, and the rise of the nation-state. The adjustment of conservative building codes to the functional requirements of modernization – the objective process of the material transformation of society – belongs to this chronicle as much as do innovations in building typology and form, even if the former respond more to the mandates of state power and capital than to ideals of social reform. It is difficult and perhaps impossible to communicate in a single narrative a spectrum of experiences that thousands of monographs, exhibition catalogs, doctoral theses, and thematic studies have not yet exhausted. Yet by alternating wide brushstrokes with specific details, I have endeavored to evoke a landscape of recurrent themes and at times to reveal different ways of thinking about the past. Among these recurrent themes is the passionate search by modern architects for an architecture considered to be "rational" – a term that has enjoyed much success over many decades – or in any case to be justified by a *ratio* related to construction, function, or economy. This search led in extreme cases to a reduction of the conception of "rational" building to little more than the implementation of principles like the provision of optimal ventilation or an alignment guaranteeing maximum sunlight. Another recurrent theme in twentieth-century architecture has been the relationship of architectural programs to the needs of exploited social classes – a subject taken into consideration by professional architects for the first time in history during this period. Throughout the twentieth century, diverse populist movements constantly addressed this subject, whether structurally – for example, in terms of social housing – or aesthetically, by drawing on vernacular rather than "pedigreed" forms.

I have aspired to trace projects, alongside the dazzling accomplishments of the "masters" and their trailblazing experiments that claimed to free architecture from the weight of history, that are more reflective of the slow, cumulative, and irresistible process of modernization. During the golden age of Hollywood cinema, the major studios and leading producers categorized their movies as "A," "B," or "C" according to their budget. This narrative, though most often focused on A buildings, was initially written with the intention not to neglect the relationship between the "major" architecture of the most spectacular works and the "minor" architecture of mass production, which constituted the urban backdrop for the monumental projects. The physical limitations of a single volume have constrained this ambition. But if the pages that follow cannot unravel all the mysteries of twentieth-century architecture, they aim first and foremost to be an invitation to discovery and to suggest a framework within which to understand its most characteristic features.

Sheds to rails: the dominion of steel

The historical cycle referred to by the Scottish urban planner Patrick Geddes and his American disciple Lewis Mumford as the "paleotechnic age" was symbolized by the invention of the steam engine, the diffusion of the telegraph, and the expansion of the railroads. → 1 As it unfolded, the crisis of rapidly growing cities and the erosion of historicist architectural languages provoked a late-nineteenth-century revision of ideals that had been formulated in response to the Industrial Revolution. Most of the theoretical positions and slogans of the following decades sprang from these precocious visions of a new culture based on industry. The effects of scientific discoveries combined with Romanticism and belated echoes of the Enlightenment to broaden the ambitions of new nation-states that rapidly came to both support and depend upon imperialism and colonial expansion. National and international economic growth heightened the demand for public policies that would satisfy the expectations of increasingly well-organized workers.

In 1889 an international exposition opened in Paris to commemorate the hundredth anniversary of the fall of the Bastille. With their Galerie des Machines, 11 Ferdinand Dutert and Victor Contamin sought to outdo Joseph Paxton's Crystal Palace at the London world exposition, which in 1851 had revealed the vast gap between the mechanical elegance of its prefabricated glass envelope and the eclectic ornamentation of the industrial objects it housed. → 2 The sight of these new products featuring mass-produced decoration had spurred John Ruskin to pen diatribes against the machines that were stripping workers of their role in handcrafting objects. But the "Caribbean hut" also on view at the 1851 fair inspired the ideas that would fuel Gottfried Semper's treatise *Der Stil in den technischen und tektonischen Künsten* (Style in the Technical and Tectonic Arts; 1860–3). → 3 4

The lamp of style

At a time when national identity was developing in parallel with a passion for history, Semper and his French contemporary Eugène Emmanuel Viollet-le-Duc shared the beliefs that architecture must free itself from the multiple styles inherited from the past and that the logic embedded in the history of architecture, when released from the baggage of historical styles, would give rise to the one true style of the contemporary age. Semper declared, "Style is the accord of an art object with its genesis and with all the preconditions and circumstances of its becoming." → 4 Viollet-le-Duc added in his *Lectures on Architecture* 5 that style was no longer merely the result of the will to create a form, but rather the logical outcome of a given set of conditions: "As long as we are used to proceeding by reasoning, as long as we have a principle, any compositional task is possible, if not easy, and follows an orderly, methodical path, the results of which, though they may not be masterpieces, are at the very least fine, acceptable pieces of work that can have style." → 5 Thus a locomotive or a steamboat could be *stylish* in the sense meant by Viollet-le-Duc so long as it did not imitate a stagecoach or a sailboat but embraced its own technical requirements. The bold gestures represented by the Galerie des Machines, in which three-hinged arches spanned 110 meters (360 feet), and by the 300-meter (986-foot) tower that would soon take the name of Gustave Eiffel, 13 the man responsible for its design and erection, were made possible by the use of iron, the preeminent material of nineteenth-century industry. Though clearly visible in both these emblematic edifices, iron was carefully disguised in other contexts, including most of the buildings erected in Europe and North America in the middle of the century. Architectural theorists therefore took particular interest in the question of how to sheathe metallic structures. → 6

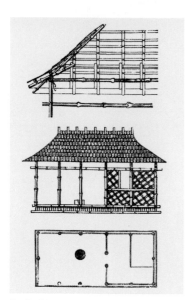

6 ▶ Firth of Forth Bridge, Benjamin Baker and John Fowler, Edinburgh, Inchgarvie and Fife, United Kingdom, 1880–90

4 Caribbean Hut, from *Der Stil in den technischen und tektonischen Künsten* (Style in the Technical and Tectonic Arts), Gottfried Semper, 1860–3

5 Vaulting of Large Spaces, from *Entretiens sur l'architecture* (Lectures on Architecture), Eugène Emmanuel Viollet-le-Duc, 1872

In his 1849 volume *The Seven Lamps of Architecture*, Ruskin had denounced "structural deceit" as inimical to architectural "truth." He wrote, "The architect is not *bound* [italics in original] to exhibit structure; nor are we to complain of him for concealing it, any more than we should regret that the outer surfaces of the human frame conceal much of its anatomy; nevertheless, that building will generally be the noblest, which to an intelligent eye discovers the great secrets of its structure, as an animal form does, although from a careless observer they may be concealed." →[7] In a similar vein, Semper – borrowing the notion of "tectonics," or the exterior expression of interior structure, from the historian Karl Bötticher – proposed to differentiate the *Kernform* (coreform) from the *Kunstform* (artform) in buildings. →[8] Fifty years later Walter Benjamin no longer resorted to these kinds of organic images to characterize nineteenth-century Parisian architecture but rather borrowed a figure from psychoanalysis. In a clarification of a statement by Giedion, he noted that the engineering structure of buildings played "the role of bodily processes – around which 'artistic' architectures gather, like dreams around the framework of physiological processes." →[9] He thus updated Semper's distinction between *Kernform* and *Kunstform* using a concept proposed by Sigmund Freud for the interpretation of dreams.

The eminence of the Beaux-Arts

The relationship of the outer skin to the internal structure remained a kind of mystery in the great Parisian buildings of the late nineteenth century, such as Charles Garnier's Opéra (1860–75) and Victor Laloux's Gare d'Orsay (1887–1900). The metal used in their construction was totally hidden by their facades, which, in the case of the Opéra, were expertly decorated with sculpture and architectural ornament. These two buildings epitomized the dominant status of the methods inculcated at the École des Beaux-Arts in Paris, which was uncontested as the leading school in Europe and much of the world. Among its student body were young Americans and Central and Eastern Europeans, whose adherence to its principles would vary widely after they returned home. The Beaux-Arts approach favored axial composition, symmetry, and hierarchy – above all in the context of the competitions in which its students engaged – and it neglected the relationship of buildings to the urban fabric in favor of an abstract vision that generally imposed them on empty sites. →[10] But as the New York architect and Beaux-Arts alumnus Ernest Flagg underlined in a lively article written upon his return from France, such an approach provided ballast against the hazards of professional practice. →[11]

The École was hardly characterized by complete unanimity, however; contradictory positions were often embraced even by those who adhered to its central principles. In contrast to the caricatures drawn by modernist critics, many exponents of eclecticism used the past not as a supermarket for historical ornaments but rather as a source for evaluating the "true" and "correct" language suited to each project; in this respect they differed from both the champions of a rigorous classicism and the hard-line rationalists. The Beaux-Arts "eclectics" often proclaimed their allegiance to Viollet-le-Duc, for whom a building's plan was a function of its purpose and its facade deduced from its plan. The Paris architect and critic Frantz Jourdain expressed this position by praising the architects of the 1889 exposition for having "put aside senile and dangerous formulas and understood that … social requirements cannot be subjected to the tyrannical rule of a style," and particularly for having understood that "it is the necessities of everyday life that have the right to dictate the structure and to demand that it provide rational exteriors, plans, and proportions." →[12]

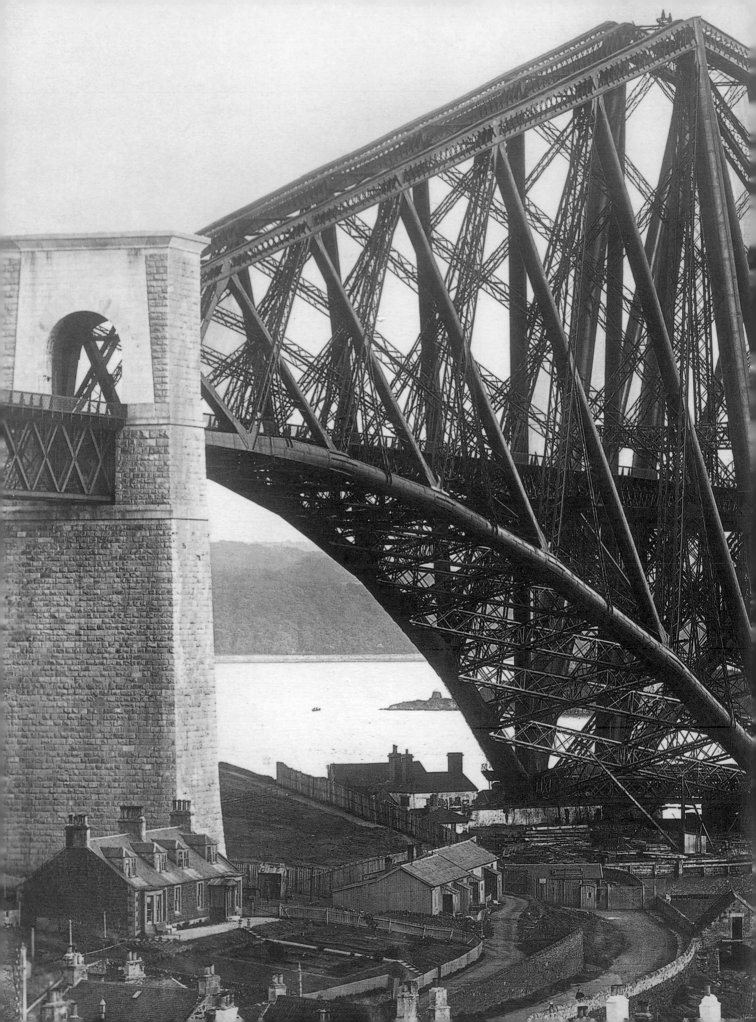

8 Page from *Moderne Architektur* (Modern Architecture), Otto Wagner, 1896

9 Postsparkasse, Otto Wagner, Vienna, Austria, 1903–6

10 ▶ *History of Human Habitation*, section at the Universal Exposition, Charles Garnier, Paris, France, 1889

Programs of modernization

The "everyday life" referred to by Jourdain had been radically transformed since the beginnings of industrialization. Increased manufacturing needs and expanded communication and distribution networks required more factories, train stations, markets, and department stores. The establishment of nation-states had stimulated the construction of palaces for the governing elites and large halls for parliamentary assemblies. New penal, healthcare, and education policies took material form in prisons, hospitals, schools, and universities. Above all, the dawn of the age of organization led to the proliferation of a new type of edifice, particularly in the United States: the large building devoted exclusively to offices. Traditional construction techniques relying on stone and brick masonry, though ingeniously reinforced with tie beams, girders, and iron frames, were reaching their limits, and the invention of new types of structures became crucial. Many contemporaries recognized the new horizons opened up by the great iron and glass halls built to serve the agendas of the Industrial Revolution and the nation-state. Decades earlier, the Russian writer Nikolai Gogol had put forward a vision of a new transparent, vertical architecture derived from his analysis of Gothic architecture and based on "one principal idea: height." → 13 Later in the century Émile Zola studied the concept of the new Parisian department stores in writing his novel *Au bonheur des dames* (The Ladies' Paradise; 1883) and solicited the advice of Jourdain, who would later design the Samaritaine Department Store in Paris. Zola's contemporary Joris-Karl Huysmans observed that the new iron edifices did not include "Greek, Gothic or Renaissance borrowings; they are a new, original form, unachievable with stone, possible only with the metallurgical products of our factories." → 14 As for Henry James, he returned to the United States after several years abroad and discovered the skyscrapers of New York with an admiration tinged with horror, writing in 1906 that they resembled "extravagant pins in a cushion already overplanted. → 15

The tension between civil engineering and architecture, so obvious in international exhibitions where historicist ornament contrasted sharply with structural innovations, was toned down somewhat in the great works of the engineers, often achieved without architects. Photographs of Eiffel's viaducts in Porto and Garabit (1876–7 and 1881–4, respectively) and of Benjamin Baker and John Fowler's spectacular bridge over the Firth of Forth (1880–90) **6** publicized the idea of an architecture based on the elasticity of the frame rather than the massiveness of the walls. Images of bridges, dams, locks, and other marvels of civil engineering free of any applied artistic forms inspired many careers in engineering and architecture. It is no coincidence that the illustration opening Le Corbusier's manifesto *Vers une architecture* (Toward an Architecture; 1923) is a view of the Garabit Viaduct. **12**

Networks of internationalization

Once travel by steamship and the rapid long-distance transmission and increasingly accurate reproduction of photographs encouraged the circulation of people and images, internationalization intensified. World's fairs became mass spectacles crowded with travelers from far-flung places, while professional architects hopped on trains and boats to go see their colleagues' work. → 16 Architectural periodicals provided plans and photographs of even the most distant structures, while a genuinely global market for architecture took shape through major competitions, such as the one in 1898 for the campus of the University of California, Berkeley, and those held between 1905 and 1914 for

11 Galerie des Machines, Ferdinand Dutert and Victor Contamin, Paris, France, 1889

12 Garabit Viaduct, Gustave Eiffel, Loubaresse/Ruynes-en-Margeride, France, 1881–4, page from Le Corbusier, *Vers une Architecture* (Towards an Architecture, 1923)

the design of new capital cities like Canberra and for extensions to Barcelona, Berlin, and Antwerp. Photography, already a widespread practice, became a powerful medium in the circulation of architectural forms and the study of urban environments. In fact, both architects and writers seized on the young medium and practiced it themselves: Émile Zola photographed the Crystal Palace as reconstructed in Sydenham, outside London, and Frank Lloyd Wright returned from his first trip to Japan with a collection of his own photographs of temples and gardens. [17] Artists' interpretations of modern life were no less significant. In Paris, Claude Monet painted memorable views of the Gare Saint-Lazare, the train station closest to his studio, while Gustave Caillebotte and Georges Seurat took an interest in the nearby Pont de l'Europe and the bridge in Asnières. [18] This acute attention to the metropolitan scenery would continue with the Expressionists and the Futurists. Though architects had a close working relationship with the practitioners of the decorative arts, it was the work of painters that especially transformed their sensibility. There were many domains of internationalization. The rapid growth of colonial empires, notably those of Great Britain and France, was accompanied by an assimilation and transformation of the visual languages of colonized peoples, which the European public encountered especially through the ephemeral extravaganzas of world's fairs. The Human Habitation pavilions built by Charles Garnier for the 1889 exposition **10** – and strongly criticized by the academy for their "lack of taste" – opened multiple cultures to observation. [19] Architects also had access to handbooks and portfolios containing examples of building designs and ornamental motifs from, for instance, the Far and Near East, which they could copy or adapt to their own purposes. The world's fair held in 1900 in Paris was something of a regression compared to its 1889 predecessor. Henri Deglane's Grand Palais and Charles Girault's Petit Palais

lacked the structural rigor of the Galerie des Machines. Rare were the pavilions displaying a new, more fluid aesthetic or even hinting at an organic life. The most remarkable contributions, such as the pavilion devoted to a novel evocation of a village church designed by Eliel Saarinen, who was representing Finland, served to crystallize the national forms for which the past century had constantly searched. From this time on, the most successful experiments were to take the form of houses and modest public buildings rather than the grand official architecture of nation-states and municipalities. The most coherent and revolutionary architectural hypothesis put forward during this period between the two Paris world's fairs was probably that of the Viennese architect Otto Wagner. In *Moderne Architektur* (1896), **8** written for his students at the Vienna Academy of Fine Arts, he advocated a *Nutzstil* (utilitarian style) that was free of historical references and that transposed the rhythms of industrial society to architecture: "One idea inspires the book, namely that the basis of today's predominant views on architecture must be shifted, and we must become fully aware that the sole departure point for our artistic work can only be modern life." [20] After his metropolitan railroad stations, which he began building in 1895, and the two buildings he erected on the Wienzeile in 1898, featuring bold floral decorations on ceramics and more conservative sculptural ornament, Wagner's designs underwent a spectacular transformation. The glazing of the main hall of his Postsparkasse (Post Office Savings Bank; 1903–6) **9** was free of any such decorative detail. On the exterior, the aluminum rivets attesting to the logic of the building's on-site assembly became the ornamentation, punctuating the still-symmetrical facade that the building turned to the Ringstraße. **7** These rivets, which affixed the stone building's cladding along the great monument-lined boulevard built in the last third of the nineteenth century, paradoxically pointed forward to an architecture freed from the weight of masonry.

The search for modern form

By the turn of the twentieth century, few progressive architects had failed to read the work of Friedrich Nietzsche. In *Thus Spoke Zarathustra*, the German philosopher had affirmed the role of "the creator" as an iconoclast, a "lawbreaker." [1] Equally rare were those architects ignorant of the writings of John Ruskin and William Morris, which called for artistic creation to be rooted in manual labor. A shared cult of youth drove architects and artists of the new generation to break with institutions that were now considered as outdated as they were tyrannical. The 1897 "secession" of Viennese artists and architects from the prevailing aesthetic culture in Austria – those who shared the realization that there were no longer any traditions left to reject – was the most spectacular example of this modern trend toward rupture with art and architecture's past. The movement included a group of young artists who, starting in 1898, gathered around the periodical *Ver sacrum* (Sacred Spring), its title an allusion to a poem by the Romantic writer Ludwig Uhland.

The unification between architecture and the decorative arts was a constant feature of the practice of these young professionals, who sought in different ways to turn each edifice into a "total work of art." The latter concept derived from the musical dramas of Richard Wagner, another figure venerated by European and North American intellectuals. [2] Stone, brick, metal, glass, wood, and ceramics became the instruments of a new orchestral composition in which the specific quality of each component was accentuated in a variety of design strategies known as Art Nouveau in France, Sezession in Austria, Jugendstil in Germany, Floreale or Liberty in Italy, and Modern in Russia.

Toward a "new art" from Paris to Berlin

The label "Art Nouveau" (new art) was borrowed from the eponymous Paris art gallery owned by Samuel Bing and designed by Louis Bonnier in 1895. It was applied to the experiments carried out in Paris by architects such as Hector Guimard and Jules Lavirotte. But the real starting point of the movement was found in a series of town houses that Victor Horta built in Brussels beginning in 1893. Here Horta followed the agenda that had been set forth in the first issue of the periodical *L'Art moderne* in 1881, which informed its readers: "The artist is not satisfied merely with building in the ideal, he is involved with everything that interests and touches us. Our monuments, houses, furniture, clothes, the slightest objects of everyday use are constantly revisited and transformed by Art, which combines with everything and constantly renews our entire life to make it more elegant and more noble, more cheerful and more social." [3] Horta followed Viollet-le-Duc's injunction to create rational and ethically "true" architecture. To do so, he devoted himself to the study of plant life, which inspired the motifs used in the columns and joists of his houses. He also conceived designs that allowed light to reach deep into the lots on which his houses were set. Horta's masterpiece, which made his vision legible to the working class, was the Maison du Peuple (People's House; 1898–9, demolished 1965) **16** in Brussels, a building that enclosed a meeting hall and a brasserie in a metallic cage. It would remain one of the clearest interpretations of this new type of building commissioned by workers' unions or cooperatives to serve as a proletarian alternative to bourgeois gathering places. French Socialist leader Jean Jaurès declared on the day of its opening: "Here dreams take the solidity of stone without losing their spiritual elevation." [4]

14 Sanatorium, Josef Hoffmann, Purkersdorf, Austria, 1904–5

15 Zacherlhaus, Jože Plečnik, Vienna, Austria, 1903–5

16 Maison du Peuple (People's House), Victor Horta, Brussels, Belgium, 1898–9, demolished 1965

17 Bloemenwerf House, Henry Van de Velde, Uccle, Belgium, 1895–6

18 Museum of Decorative Arts, Ödön Lechner, Budapest, Hungary, 1893–6

19 The Orchard, Charles F. A. Voysey, Chorleywood, United Kingdom, 1899

Horta's compatriot Henry van de Velde, born in Antwerp and trained as a painter, sought an aesthetic principle that would apply to every object of daily life. Looking back in 1916, he wrote, "Ruskin and Morris tried to chase ugliness from man's heart; I preached that we had to chase it from his mind." [5] His Bloemenwerf House (1895–6) **17** in Uccle, structured around a central double-height hall in the English fashion, and the residencies he built in Germany after 1900 were treated as creations in which "the ornamental motif becomes an organism." He proclaimed that "ornamentation is subject only to the laws of the goal it sets for itself: harmony and equilibrium. It is not expected to represent anything, it must be free to not represent anything since without this freedom it could not exist." [6] In Vienna a group of young architects from all over Central Europe gathered around Otto Wagner and saw their first works go up in the Austrian capital. Joseph Maria Olbrich built the Secession Building in 1898–9 to house the work of radical artists. Its pediment was inscribed with the slogan, "To the age its art, to art its freedom." He also built houses that aspired to provide an architectural interpretation of his clients' personalities. Josef Hoffmann undertook a search for a geometric language based on the square and on the interplay of black and white. With the Purkersdorf Sanatorium (1904–5) **14** near Vienna, he developed an orthogonal architecture with white surfaces, inspired by houses he had sketched on his travels in the south of Italy. The Slovenian native Jože Plečnik built the Zacherlhaus **15** in 1903–5 using prismatic shapes; this was a bold departure from the excessive subtleties that had quickly diminished the Secession's impact. Max Fabiani erected the Portois & Fix (1899–1900) and Artaria (1900) buildings, as well as the more classical Urania institute of popular science (1909–10). Wagner's students Jan Kotěra and Pavel Janák

disseminated their teacher's ideas in Bohemia. Wagner also had an impact in Budapest, where Ödön Lechner combined Wagner's approach with Hungarian ornamental themes in such buildings as the Museum of Decorative Arts (1893–6). **18** Having settled in Berlin, Van de Velde was invited by Count Harry Kessler to establish new art schools in Weimar, the capital of the Grand Duchy of Saxony. Van de Velde both designed buildings and put in place a curriculum based on a conception of form embodied in the "modern line," which he imagined to be as "expressive as the line that reveals the rush of blood beneath the epidermis, the breath that makes flesh rise, the energy that lifts our limbs." He added that the modern line had to transcribe the movements of life "whether we are devoting ourselves to practical daily chores or we are in a state of ecstasy, drunk or drawn into that divine dance, to which, as Zarathustra commands, man must constantly give himself over so as to escape the weight of life and material things." [7] For the industrialist Karl Ernst Osthaus, Van de Velde built in the small manufacturing town of Hagen first the Folkwang Museum (1900–2) then the large villa Hohenhof (1908), culminating a decade of work. While these developments were unfolding in Saxony, the Grand Duke Ernst Ludwig created the Darmstadt artists' colony. The outside world discovered it in 1901 on the occasion of an exposition there entitled *Ein Dokument deutscher Kunst* (A Document of German Art). Olbrich was the star of the show. Having completed the Secession Building in Vienna a few years before, he built the Ernst-Ludwig House **21** for the exposition, an artists' workshop that dominated the Darmstadt colony, as well as his own house, in which he conceived every detail, from textiles to cutlery. Peter Behrens, a painter-turned-architect from Hamburg with a more austere artistic language, followed suit by designing no less inclusively every feature of the house he built

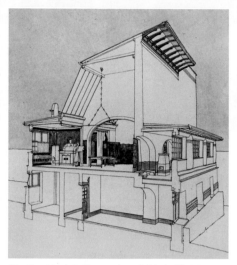

22 Elvira Photo Studio, August Endell, Munich, Germany, 1897, demolished 1944

23 ▶ Glasgow School of Art, Charles Rennie Mackintosh, Glasgow, United Kingdom, 1897–1908

21 Ernst-Ludwig House, Joseph Maria Olbrich, Darmstadt, Germany, 1899–1901

20 Behrens House, Peter Behrens, Darmstadt, Germany, 1899–1901

adjacent to Olbrich's. **20** Elsewhere other contemporary designs were more superficial, including the Elvira Photo Studio, (1897, demolished 1944), **22** in Munich realized by August Endell, with its decorative facade treatment. Familiar with Heinrich Wölfflin's psychology of art, Endell believed that a *Formgefühl* (form sense) was at the root of all architectural design. According to him, "The architect must be a form-artist; only the art of form leads the way to a new architecture." › 8

Great Britain after the Arts and Crafts

The close ties between Germany and Great Britain were exemplified by Charles Rennie Mackintosh's participation in the 1901 "House for an Art Lover" competition organized by the *Zeitschrift für Innendekoration* (Journal for Interior Decoration) and by his attention to Olbrich's work. Around this time, the Arts and Crafts movement, which had been centered on William Morris, began taking a new direction, and William A. Lethaby became its principal theorist. A former assistant to the architect Richard Norman Shaw, Lethaby founded the Central School of Arts and Crafts in 1888 in London, where he insisted on a socially generous curriculum. In his 1892 book *Architecture, Mysticism and Myth*, he called for architecture to be a "synthesis of the fine arts, the commune of all the crafts." › 9 But he also expressed a firm belief in the present, in agreement with his contemporaries. As Reyner Banham noted, an extension of Lethaby's position may be read in a 1905 article in *The Architectural Review*, which asks rhetorically: "Why should we architects live in perpetual rebellion with the present? … [I]f we could only think of our building as an entirely modern problem without precedent … just as the railway engine is, then, without doubt … the ruins of the past might crumble to dust but the

[true] architectural tradition would remain with us still." › 10
In practical terms, the Arts and Crafts heritage was represented principally by the houses of Charles Francis Annesley Voysey, whose puritanical approach resulted in what he called "modest country houses." His own residence, The Orchard (1899) **19**, in Chorleywood, Hertfordshire, was an example of such a house, with a rectangular layout designed for a middle-class, intellectually inclined owner. Although in Voysey's view "too much luxury is death to the artistic soul," › 11 his New Place, a residence commissioned by the publisher A. M. M. Stedman in Haslemere, Surrey (1899), certainly did not lack complexity. Several figures contributed to the modernization of the British scene during this period. The furniture designer Charles Robert Ashbee proposed to "reconstruct" the industrial system rather than rebel against it; he pointed out that in the "modern mechanical industry 'standard' is necessary, and 'standardization' is necessary," given that "the great social movement" of the Arts and Crafts had degenerated into "a narrow and tiresome little aristocracy working with great skill for the very rich." › 12 Following his design of the central hall of the Vienna Secession's exhibition in 1900, Ashbee's ideas were felt all the way to Chicago. There he met Frank Lloyd Wright, who drew on Ashbee's thinking in his 1901 book *The Arts and Crafts of the Machine*. Another English designer, Mackay Hugh Baillie Scott, focused on the interior space of houses, and his ideas met with such success in Germany that he was invited to join Ashbee in fitting out the Grand Duke of Hesse's palace in Darmstadt (1897–8).
More spectacular, Charles Rennie Mackintosh's activity centered on Glasgow, a city with a solid classical tradition. With Herbert McNair and the sisters Frances and Margaret Macdonald, who were close to the Symbolist movement on the Continent, he founded "The Four," also known as "The Mac Group." Their

24 Hill House, Charles Rennie Mackintosh, Helensburgh, United Kingdom, 1902–3

25 La Samaritaine Department Store, Frantz Jourdain, Paris, France, 1904–5

designs were shown in 1896 at the Arts and Crafts Exhibition Society. Mackintosh also designed several tearooms in Glasgow, including "The Willow" (1903–4), whose name was drawn from Dante Gabriel Rossetti's sonnet "The Willow Wood." Mackintosh scored the interior with a pattern of vertical lines that was echoed in the high backs of the chairs, while the use of white lacquer contrasted with natural oak. The stained-glass door panels and the lighting fixtures were especially inventive. Mackintosh built a handful of houses on hilly terrain, their prismatic volumes roofed with slates. Of these, Hill House, (1902–3), **24** publisher W. W. Blackie's home in Helensburgh, was particularly remarkable for the way its walls of stone and rough concrete recalled Scottish houses of the seventeenth century. For Windyhill, in Kilmacolm (1900), a house whose walls seem to embrace the garden of its owner, William Davidson, Mackintosh designed built-in furniture and white-lacquered chairs and decorated the walls with geometric motifs. But his major work, to which he devoted himself intermittently for more than ten years, was the Glasgow School of Art. **23** He first completed the east wing (1897–8), which opened large rectangular windows onto the street, incorporating allusions to Gothic religious buildings and medieval fortresses. Built considerably later, the west wing (1907–8) had a fundamentally different design. A gable structure with three vertical bow windows extending much of the height of the elevation, it was a revision of a scheme with small arched windows he had proposed initially. Mackintosh also designed two large glass boxes on the roof to serve as studios. But his major focus was on the library, which occupied two levels and included a balcony floating inside the building's masonry envelope. → 13 This warm composition of wooden elements, illuminated by light coming through

small cutouts, resembled a kind of sacred forest, especially when suffused with daylight from the glass roof. Mackintosh's work had considerable resonance on the Continent, and the orthogonal shapes of his library countered the preference there for more plantlike motifs.

Art Nouveau and the Paris–Nancy axis

On the other side of the Channel, Art Nouveau branched out into two principal centers: Paris and Nancy. In the capital city, critics derided the "noodle style" *(le style nouille)* of Hector Guimard, whose entrances to metro stations began to appear on Paris streets in 1900. The most remarkable of them looked like insects spreading diaphanous wings. The outcry by critics and the hostility of the conservative Commission for Old Paris prevented Guimard from realizing other such projects, including a kiosk he designed for the Place de l'Opéra in 1905. Inspired by his encounter with Horta's buildings, Guimard had become well known thanks to his Castel Béranger (1894–8), **28** a Paris building noted for its poetic assemblage of cast iron, brick, and rough and carved stone. Guimard densely covered the building's surfaces from its front gate, which opened onto an evocation of an underwater grotto, to the wainscoting of its apartments, with a vinelike web of lines. The building's facades revealed the interior articulation and abandoned any vertical or horizontal alignment.

It was rare for Guimard's houses, such as the one he designed for the ceramicist Louis Coillot in Lille (1898–1900), to sit quietly between parallel walls. Both the Castel Henriette in Sèvres (1899–1903, demolished 1969) and the Castel Orgeval in Villemoisson-sur-Orge (1900–3) extended the vocabulary of the Castel Béranger, displaying an acrobatic assembly of

26 Entrance Gate at the 1900 International Exposition, René Binet, Paris, France, 1900, as featured on a publicity blotting paper

27 Louis Majorelle House, Henri Sauvage, Nancy, France, 1898–1901

28 Castel Béranger, Hector Guimard, Paris, France, 1894–8

cylindrical turrets, elaborate windows, and conical roofs that enclosed ingenious plans and made no concession to symmetry. In 1929 Salvador Dalí interpreted Guimard's playful designs as "nothing but the cylindrical anamorphosis of hereditary symmetries." → 14 In fact, Guimard had already revealed his kinship with Viollet-le-Duc. He confirmed it with his École du Sacré-Coeur (1898) in Paris, where he constructed V-shaped cast-iron supports like the ones Viollet had included in an imaginary view in his *Entretiens sur l'architecture* (Lectures on Architecture) twenty-five years earlier. At the time, Guimard's largest building was the Humbert de Romans Concert Hall in Paris (1899–1901), the roof of which was held in place by branching wood columns that created the impression of a natural forest. Elsewhere in Paris only Jules Lavirotte's extravagantly decorated buildings, such as the Céramic Hôtel (1904) and his apartment building on Avenue Rapp, provoked outrage from contemporaries comparable to that elicited by Guimard's work.

Though dominated by eclecticism, the 1900 International Exposition in Paris did feature a few pavilions related to the new aesthetic, including the Bing pavilion by Bonnier, who also designed a stunning unbuilt giant globe for the geographer Élysée Reclus and who later built two elementary schools in Paris. Above all, the fair's entrance pavilion, **26** designed by René Binet, later the author of the new Printemps department stores (1907–10), reconnected with the organic sources of Art Nouveau. Binet's interpretation was inspired by the German biologist Ernst Haeckel, the author of a series of scientific investigations illustrated with brilliant color plates showing the structures of underwater organisms. As Binet wrote to Haeckel of his design: "Everything about it, from the general composition to the smallest details, has been inspired by your

studies." → 15 Another pavilion at the fair, designed by Francis Jourdain (the son of Frantz Jourdain) and Henri Sauvage for the American dancer Loïe Fuller, evoked the undulating fabrics she used in her performances.

Together with the ceramicist Alexandre Bigot and the glassmaker Jacques Gruber, Sauvage also built a house for the cabinetmaker Louis Majorelle (1898–1901) **27** in Nancy. Frantz Jourdain saw it as the culmination of Viollet-le-Duc's rationalist approach, a "mathematical solution to the problem posed," unencumbered by any concern for symmetry: "Sauvage applies this same respect for truth to his decorative work, which proves to be impeccably rational and which was conceived simultaneously with the structure, in one impulse, the consequence of an idea and the corollary of a theorem." → 16 In dialogue with the philosopher Paul Souriau, the bard of "rational beauty," the Nancy artists developed a body of work remarkable for its vitality and consistency, with Lucien Weissenburger's houses representing particularly elegant examples. → 17

Frantz Jourdain was more than a radical critic. In 1891 he became the first architect to join the Société Nationale des Beaux-Arts founded by Auguste Rodin, Eugène Carrière, and Pierre Puvis de Chavannes. He supported Alfred Dreyfus against his anti-Semitic accusers and was a friend of Émile Zola, whose funerary monument he designed in 1902. In 1903 he founded the Salon d'Automne, the principal showcase for Parisian innovation over the next twenty years.

His most brilliant architectural work was the Samaritaine Department Store **25** built between 1904–5 along the Seine in Paris. The exuberance of the wrought-iron decorations with floral motifs on its front contrasted with the rationality of its side facades, whose large rectangular windows evoked the office buildings of Chicago.

29 Riabushinsky House, Fiodor Shekhtel, Moscow, Russia, 1900–2

30 Botter House, Raimondo d'Aronco, Constantinople (Istanbul), Ottoman Empire (Turkey), 1900–1

From Italian "Floreale" to Russian "Modern"

At the turn of the century, the intellectual and aesthetic emancipation already underway in Austria and Belgium began to spread throughout Europe. In Italy the dominance of Viennese ideas manifested itself in the work of several architects. Raimondo d'Aronco was one of many Italian architects working in the Near East. Active in Istanbul from 1894 to 1909, he created, in the words of his Roman compatriot Marcello Piacentini, "a vast, variable, multifaceted body of work," characterized by an "exuberant, restless, impulsive" spirit. [18] His colorful houses on the Bosphorus and his designs in Pera, such as the Botter House (1900–1), 30 were characterized by the plasticity of their surfaces and the graphic effect of their metallic components.

Giuseppe Sommaruga and Ernesto Basile, active in Milan and Palermo, respectively, indulged in monumental and historicist imagery when designing public structures but used more flexible forms for their private commissions. Sommaruga's Palazzo Castiglione on Corso Venezia in Milan (1903–4) 31 caused a scandal – not because of its innovative concrete floors, which were invisible, but because of its rough facade and its anatomically explicit decor. Two voluptuous sculpted female figures on either side of the entrance were removed under pressure from critics and relocated to his Villa Romeo in Milan (1907–12). The latter was a sophisticated composition of materials and colors and probably the most apt example of an architecture described by the key terms "living organism, logic, function, constructed object." [19] Among Basile's abundant contributions to the city of Palermo, the Villino Florio (1900–2) and the Villa Igiea Hotel (1898–1900) stood out for their decorative whimsy. In Russia, which had been plunging headlong into industrial

development since the abolition of serfdom in 1861, the Muscovite bourgeoisie was quick to take hold of those themes gathered together by its architects under the banner of the "Modern" style. Though Viollet-le-Duc's reflections on a national style in his 1879 volume *L'art russe* (Russian Art) remained on everyone's mind, architects now turned to popular themes rather than those of religious structures. The leading protagonist of the Modern was Fiodor Shekhtel, the creator of the Russia Pavilion at the Glasgow World's Fair (1901), which was praised for its inventiveness and its coloration. In Moscow he organized the 1902 Exhibition of Architecture and Design in the New Style, displaying Viennese and Scottish works. Shekhtel built the Riabushinsky House in Moscow (1900–2), 29 with a sculptural staircase that ranks high as a realization of European Art Nouveau. He also built the Yaroslavl Train Station in Moscow (1902) for the industrialist Savva Mamontov, the patron of the Abramtsevo artists' colony, tapping into a repertory of popular and medieval Russian forms with the collaboration of the painter Konstantin Korovin. The Modern approach was not limited to big cities like Moscow and Saint Petersburg. It was also adopted in the rest of the Russian empire, as, for example, in Mikhail Eisenstein's buildings in Lvov and Riga. [20]

The Catalan renaissance

Catalonia presented what was probably the most remarkable European scene of the period, experiencing a *renaixensa*, or renaissance, rooted in its rediscovery of its own medieval history and the adoption of forms from the Orient. Several variations of Barcelona modernism are clearly visible on the Paseo de Gràcia, a wide bourgeois avenue in the city's extension planned in 1859 by Ildefonso Cerdà. Three buildings faced off

on the "Manzana de la Discordia" (its name meaning both "block of discord" and "apple of discord," playing on the double meaning of *manzana*). The Lleó Moreira Building (1902) by Lluís Domènech i Montañer is reminiscent of Parisian Art Nouveau. Farther along, the Amatller Building (1898–1900) by Josep Puig y Cadafalch, who was not only an architect but also an international traveler, archaeologist, and politician, featured medieval-style decoration and a stepped gable, evoking Hanseatic merchant houses and concealing its owner's photography studio. Next door, the Casa Battló by Antoni Gaudí (1906), a renovation of an older building, was nicknamed Casa de los Huesos (House of Bones) because of the bone-shaped columns along its front facade, which opens into a stairhall clad with blue ceramic tiles. The building is topped with a carapace of colored tiles.

The medievalizing features of Puig's Casa Terrades, also known as the Casa de les Punxes (House of Spikes) (1903–7), **33** express a clear nostalgia for Catalonia's golden age. Decorated with mosaics depicting nationalist motifs, the edifice caused a political scandal. A few blocks away, Domènech built the San Pau Hospital (1902–10), where the brick patterning is more playful. He combined an iron structure and wide glass openings with extraordinary sculptural inventiveness in the Palau de la Música Catalana (Palace of Catalan Music; 1905–8), **35** built for the Orféo Català choir as a symbol of the regional renaissance. The sense of imagination manifest in the decoration of the Palau is even more vivid in Gaudí's buildings. A genius inventor of structural and ornamental forms, this fervent Catholic was born into a family of craftsmen and, inspired by his readings of Ruskin and Viollet-le-Duc, retained a direct and permanent connection with his materials. → 21 After some initial buildings such as the Palacio Güell (1886–9), whose forms reflected

33 Casa Terrades (Casa de les Punxes; House of Spikes), Josep Puig y Cadafalch, Barcelona, Spain, 1903–7

strong neo-Gothic and neo-Moorish influences (the latter derived from a trip to Tangier), Gaudí pursued two parallel lines of research. On the one hand, he conceived structures based on slender frames and narrow arches, tested in innovative scale models that used strings to simulate the catenary curves distributing the structure's weight. On the other, he created an exuberant ornamental language with pieces of broken ceramic, wrought iron, and sculptures of his own invention.

Every facet of Gaudí's experimentation with structures is represented in the galleries and the cistern at Park Güell (1900–14), **34** while his investigation of residential types led him to the Paseo de Gràcia, where he built the Casa Milà (1906–10) **32** across from the Casa Battló. Known as the "Pedrera" (quarry), the Casa Milá evokes the rocky cliffs of the Pyrenees at Montserrat, a privileged site for Catalan regional identity. Inside, the steel column-and-beam structure supports the hanging stone facade, while the roof bristles with shapes covered in ceramic tiles and the underground level serves as a parking garage.

In the apartments, wavy ceilings were sculpted by Josep Maria Jujol, a collaborator of Gaudí who later carried on his research. Gaudí's most ambitious project was the Sagrada Familia Basilica, which he oversaw from 1883 until his death in 1926. He finished the crypt begun by his former employer, Juan Martorell Montells, as well as the walls of the apse and the eastern facade of the transept, which contains a stunning grouping of statues enmeshed in vines. Most importantly, he abandoned the Gothic system originally planned for the nave, replacing it with stable hyperboloids – surfaces with double curvatures – without a single flying buttress. The church's construction progressed episodically for a century and is still ongoing today.

Throughout Europe, most of the impulses initiated by the revolt of young architects and artists before 1900 persisted until 1914, and sometimes beyond. The rigidity of classical composition was fundamentally and successfully challenged thanks to strategies aimed at inventing a new urban picturesque and accommodating modern ways of life. The legacy of the Secession and Art Nouveau was also visible in the decorative elements that were soon to be mass produced – in direct contradiction to their movements' initially individualistic aims. Easily imitated and industrialized, these expressions were subject to both commercialization and the widest popular consumption, stretching to the farthest reaches of Latin America and Asia.

At the same time, the experiments undertaken from Vienna to Glasgow and from Moscow to Barcelona also led to the discovery of new geometries, from the experimental, lyrical language of Gaudí to the orthogonal, modular approach of Josef Hoffmann. This polarity between expressionism and functionalism, evident in their divergent directions, would come to the fore in the 1920s.

34 Park Güell, Antoni Gaudi, Barcelona, Spain, 1900–14

35 Palace of Catalan Music, Lluís Domènech i Montañer, Barcelona, Spain, 1905–8

Domestic innovation and tectonic expression

The collective search for a new "style" would never have begun without a more profound process of modernization underway. It operated on two distinct yet related planes: as a response to unprecedented social needs and as a dissemination of new construction technologies. The years between the Paris International Exposition of 1889 and World War I corresponded to the zenith of British and French imperialism, to Germany's belated but robust expansion, and to the emergence of the United States on the world stage. In this competitive environment, national hegemonies exercised contradictory effects on architects, reshaping their strategies and aesthetics.

The central place of Great Britain

The method of composition developed at the École des Beaux-Arts continued to dominate the design of public architecture, whereas a domestic architecture inspired by the Paris of Baron Georges-Eugène Haussmann spread to a wide array of cities, from Bucharest to Buenos Aires to New York. Yet the centrality of the role played by Great Britain in the sphere of domestic architecture was undeniable. The principles applied to British residential design in the last decade of the nineteenth century found enthusiasts among Parisians like Viollet-le-Duc and Paul Sédille, who praised them in 1890. → 1 The use of more open plans became widespread, and the double-height "English" hall became a common feature in French homes. → 2
At the beginning of the twentieth century, Edwin Lutyens inaugurated a break with the Arts and Crafts movement. He examined everyday dwellings and their close relationship to their gardens, which he was better able to understand after coming into contact with the landscape designer Gertrude Jekyll. Between 1889 and 1903 he designed in the English

countryside a series of stunning weekend houses – a new type of bourgeois residence characterized by a great number of guest rooms. Often nestled against stone walls and featuring striking contrasts between volumes and textures, these houses were laid out in conjunction with their gardens, generally designed by Jekyll. Their relative modesty was disguised by artifices, among them a play with perspective, that Lutyens used to exaggerate their scale. The apparent symmetry of L-shaped plans, as at Tigbourne Court in Witley, Surrey (1899–1901), **38** was no more than a visual illusion: the actual landscape is picturesque and irregular. At Deanery Garden in Sonning, Berkshire (1899–1902), built for Edward Hudson, founder of the popular periodical *Country Life*, a double-height entry hall illuminated by a large bay window contrasts with the solid walls enclosing it. At the Bois des Moutiers (1898) in Varengeville, on the French side of the Channel, commissioned by the banker Guillaume Mallet, the garden descends to the sea as if in an idyllic landscape painted by Claude Lorrain. These English houses were studied by critics eager to understand and replicate their essential features. One such observer, the Berlin architect Hermann Muthesius, published three volumes entitled *Das englische Haus* (The English House) **36** in 1908–11, which had a profound effect on German architecture. → 3 **37** The idealization of British material culture also dominated the thinking of critics of the established aesthetic order, among them Austrian Adolf Loos, who made it the pretext for his polemical project to "introduce Western culture into Austria." → 4 In the years leading up to World War I, Germany's rapid modernization and the close relationships established there between industry and the decorative arts diminished Britain's preeminence in the production of industrial objects. At the same time, relentless press coverage made both professionals

36　*Das Englische Haus* (The English House),
Hermann Muthesius, 1908–11

37　Freudenberg House, Hermann Muthesius, Berlin, Germany, 1907–8

38 ▶　Tigbourne Court, Edwin Lutyens, Witley, United Kingdom, 1899–1901

and the public in Germany aware of American urban and architectural developments. Mimicking Muthesius, F. Rudolf Vogel
published *Das amerikanische Haus* (The American House) in
1910, introducing the work of Henry Hobson Richardson and
his successors to a German readership. →5

Residential reform

Domestic architecture reflected the transformations in process. The reforms that took place in the United States, France,
England, and Germany were touched off by social, political,
technological, spatial, and aesthetic factors. At the social level,
architectural creativity was extended for the first time to a field
it had previously ignored: housing for the poor. As hygiene
became a fundamental concern in municipal and state policy,
government regulations were brought to bear on lower-class
housing projects, explicitly requiring the services of architects.
The entire sphere of residential architecture reflected the deep
changes in the living habits of most social classes. Bourgeois
residences became increasingly complex, with more rooms
devoted to receiving guests, larger and more numerous openings
to the outdoors, and the addition of bathrooms or, in the case
of France, less hospital-like *cabinets de toilette*. →6　The relative
amenity of different floors changed drastically with the installation
of electrical elevators, which replaced early hydraulic-powered
ones. These made upper levels – previously left to servants
and inhabitants of lesser means – and roof terraces more valu-
able and stimulated the construction of ever taller buildings. The
almost universal availability of electric lighting extended daytime
living into the night and modified the use of every type of room.
There was little uniformity. New building types augmented
established ones such as the town house and the apartment

building, whose layouts were already well defined. Structures
devoted to artist's studios, which had first appeared in Paris
during the Second Empire, were given new interpretations, as
with André Arfvidson's terra-cotta–clad reinforced-concrete
Studio Building (1912) **39** on Rue Campagne-Première in
Paris. Apartment or residential hotels, offering apartments with
in-house hotel services for bachelors and couples without
children, spread throughout the United States and occasionally grew to the size of skyscrapers. →7　The idea of collec-
tivizing domestic services engendered other types, such as
the *Einküchenhaus*, or communal-kitchen building; in 1909
Hermann Muthesius and Albert Geßner each built an example
in Berlin, at Friedenau and at Lichterfelde, respectively. →8

Unifying the urban landscape

It was no easy task to shape a harmonious urban landscape
composed of buildings by creators who individually aspired to
originality, particularly under the influence of Art Nouveau ideals. The question of how to regulate facades was hotly debated
in most European cities and some North American ones, sometimes at precisely the same time that competitions were reward-
ing the facades of the year's most original buildings. The unified
urban street wall, or *einheitliche Straßenfront*, found many
advocates in Germany, while in New York the demand for visual
continuity among buildings, based on the classicizing model
of Haussmann's Paris, often went under the name of "municipal improvement." →9　At the same time, the Paris building code
of 1902, **40** written by Louis Bonnier, encouraged a break with
what critics like Charles Baudelaire and Victor Hugo had
perceived as Haussmann's tyrannical horizontality. Thus the
question of uniformity generated divided opinions.

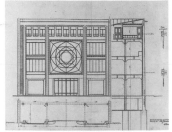

41 Automobile Garage, Auguste Perret, Paris, France, 1906–7, demolished 1971

39 Studio Building, André Arfvidson, Paris, France, 1912

40 Drawing illustrating the new Paris urban regulations, Louis Bonnier, 1902

The preoccupation with hygiene at the turn of the century had more far-reaching results than just increasing the number of apartments with bathrooms and toilets. It led to a reconceptualization of the very form that buildings should take. The building codes of major cities prescribed the enlargement of air shafts and courtyards for ventilation, while also aiming to broaden streets so as to space out housing blocks. For example, the New York State Tenement House Act of 1901 not only modified the facades of apartment blocks by requiring open spaces to be regularly placed along the street-facing walls, but also profoundly altered their floor plans by mandating larger courtyards. →10 The fear of tuberculosis led to a veritable obsession with sunlight. Projects by the Paris architect Adolphe-Augustin Rey, notably in his housing complex for the Rothschild Foundation (1905), where the open courtyard was adopted after wind-tunnel tests determined the optimal ventilation system for apartment buildings, clearly displayed this concern. →11 At the same time, the growing number of automobiles also had a direct effect on the design of domestic buildings. Initial solutions based on stables that had been used for horse-drawn carriages since the sixteenth century were quickly replaced by specialized garages, such as the one Auguste Perret designed on Rue de Ponthieu in Paris (1906–7, demolished 1971), **41** and by parking spaces constructed underneath new buildings. The automobile augured new ways of perceiving the urban landscape, blurring the perception of contrasts and thereby radically changing the very idea of the monument. In 1910 Peter Behrens declared, "Individual buildings no longer speak for themselves. The only architecture appropriate to such a way of viewing our surroundings, which has now become a habit, is one that produces surfaces as uniform and calm as possible, which in their simplicity present no obstacles." →12

If the nineteenth century saw the improvement of bank-financed housing projects, the early twentieth century was characterized by public programs benefiting white-collar employees as well as factory workers. The *Woningwet* (Housing Law) adopted in the Netherlands in 1901 called for public financing of dwellings built with municipal or cooperative sponsorship, mandating quality standards and imposing regulatory authority. Between 1894 and 1912 France passed a body of laws putting in place a program of low-cost housing that was guaranteed, and eventually financed, by the state. As a result, the number of housing projects increased through the initiatives of philanthropic societies such as the Rothschild Foundation and the Lebaudy Foundation, and subsequently through the work of specialized government agencies. The cooperative system was further developed in Germany, while in the UK the system combined municipal action with private philanthropy.

The advent of reinforced concrete

Construction was another field in which transformations took place at every level of architecture, particularly with the introduction of reinforced concrete. The effects of this new material on the planning and management of building construction were as profound as its impact on architectural theory. Produced by combining a mixture of cement, stone aggregates, and water with steel reinforcement, reinforced concrete was considered by Sigfried Giedion a "laboratory material," a direct result of progress in both chemistry and mathematics. →13 The few decades between the rediscovery of this material – originally used by the Romans – and its industrialization were marked by the invention of dependable methods to calculate the proportions of the concrete ingredients with

43 Hennebique Headquarters, Rue Danton, Edouard Arnaud, Paris, France, 1901

44 Church of Saint-Jean de Montmartre, Anatole de Baudot, Paris, France, 1894–1904

45 Baron Empain's "Hindu" Palace, Alexandre Marcel, Heliopolis, Egypt, 1907–10

rigorous precision and the development of patent-licensed construction systems. Engineers, contractors, and architects competed to master the techniques and to control a market that quickly became global. Just at the moment that iron structures seemed to have reached their limits, reinforced concrete offered new spatial possibilities to the constructive imagination. → 14

The French engineer François Hennebique's company became one of the first multinationals in the construction business, opening branches abroad in the 1890s to assist architects in adapting the new process of concrete construction to their projects. The Hennebique method, based on an apparently simple system of columns and beams, allowed for adventurous forms. → 15 The company built both historicist edifices, such as the "Hindu" palace designed by Alexandre Marcel for Baron Empain in Heliopolis (1907–10), **45** and totally utilitarian structures devoid of any ornamentation for its industrial clients. The building that Édouard Arnaud designed for the firm's Paris headquarters (1901) **43** appeared to be made of smooth carved stone, while Hennebique's own villa in Bourg-la-Reine (1903) explored all kinds of concrete surface treatments – washed, aggregated, striated, stuccoed – and provided an example of a roof terrace used as a garden, in this case for growing vegetables.

Other processes were experimented with. In one, the engineer Paul Cottancin poured concrete reinforced with wire into forms made of brick, which subsequently served as cladding for the building. The material was put to its most spectacular use by Anatole de Baudot in the Church of Saint-Jean de Montmartre (1894–1904). **44** With its arches seemingly suspended in midair, the building so terrified Parisians that the municipal authorities nearly forced the parish priest to raze it.

Alexandre Bigot's exposed brick and terra-cotta decorations gave the church a warmth that offset the cavernous nature of its interior. Until 1914 Baudot continued to develop numerous theoretical projects for concrete meeting or concert halls; in these he appeared to be striving to rediscover the power and light of the great Gothic naves and to realize what his mentor Viollet-le-Duc had envisioned in iron. In his posthumously published book *L'architecture, le passé, le présent* (Architecture: Past and Present; 1916), Baudot referred to iron as little more than a "step" toward "its successor, reinforced concrete, which has all of its advantages, and resolves with incontestable sureness the profound flaws found in the direct use of metal." → 16

It would fall to Auguste Perret to establish the primacy of concrete once and for all. → 17 An alumnus of the École des Beaux-Arts who had gone into business with his brothers Gustave and Claude, Perret broke the mold of Parisian urban architecture with his building on Rue Franklin (1903–4). **42** Its concrete structure was plainly visible from the street, barely clad by Bigot's ceramics. In 1908 the American critic Arthur C. David made no attempt to hide his contempt: "As an experiment in the frank treatment of a new material, this building has its interest; but the interest is assuredly not aesthetic. The architect has not made any attempt to give it a pleasing aspect; and it should be considered rather as the raw material of architecture than as the finished product." → 18 Full-fledged members of the Parisian art scene, the Perrets participated in the activities of the Passy circle, founded in July 1912, which also included the poets Guillaume Apollinaire and Paul Fort; the artists Francis Picabia, Albert Gleizes, and Raymond Duchamp-Villon; and the critic Sébastien Voirol. → 19

46 Woman's Club, Irving Gill, La Jolla, California, USA, 1912–13

In 1913 Auguste Perret made his name in Paris with the Champs Élysées Theater. **48** This "philharmonic palace" combining three separate halls, inspired by Louis Sullivan's Auditorium Building in Chicago, had first been entrusted to the Swiss architect Henri Fivaz, then to Henry van de Velde. When it came to its construction, however, the Belgian architect found himself competing with Perret, who had been consulted concerning the concrete structure. Though certain aspects of Van de Velde's conception were conserved in Perret's final design, they were worked into a concrete cage held by four bowstring arches of a type previously used exclusively for bridges. The outline of this structure is traceable on the facade in the design of the stone facing by the sculptor Antoine Bourdelle, who recruited the painters Maurice Denis, Edouard Vuillard, and Ker-Xavier Roussel in an exceptional collaboration. Nicknamed the "zeppelin of avenue Montaigne" by Germanophobe critics, this edifice hosted the world premiere of Igor Stravinsky's *Rite of Spring* in 1913. → 20

Perret was the most radical of the architects to explore the potential of concrete. His experiments quickly led him to erect factories and warehouses with slender vaults, the most widely publicized example of which was built for the Wallut agricultural supply company in Casablanca, a city that was a bridgehead for French colonization in Morocco. But Perret was not the only Parisian to experiment with the new material. François Le Coeur introduced concrete in public building with his extension to the Postal Administration Building in Paris (1907) and in telephone exchange buildings – a new type of program – on Rue du Faubourg-Poissonnière (1912) and Rue du Temple (1914). After the French state bought up private patents, concrete entered the public domain, and its use fascinated all types of innovators. In the United States, the prolific American inventor Thomas Alva Edison took an interest in concrete as early as

1902, and he laid the first concrete road, Route 57, in Warren County, New Jersey. But Edison's effort in 1906 to mold individual houses and all their furniture out of a single pour of concrete in Stewartville, New Jersey, was a commercial failure. The engineer Ernest L. Ransome had more success in developing concrete in the United States. Southern California turned out to be particularly fertile ground for research on the new material. Irving Gill invented a tilt-slab system of monolithic walls, poured on the ground, then hoisted to a vertical position; these were used in the La Jolla Woman's Club (1912–13). → 21 **46**

In New York the most interesting experiment in concrete was Grosvenor Atterbury's buildings at the Forest Hills Gardens complex in Queens (1909–13), which had a romantic touch. European civil engineers devoted themselves to inventing new processes and new forms adapted to the properties of the material. The Swiss engineer Robert Maillart designed unprecedentedly elegant works spanning Alpine rivers and ravines, beginning with the bridge over the Inn at Zuoz (1900) and the Tavanasa Bridge (1905). **47** His curved and taut forms went beyond the limits of the Hennebique method; as he explained in 1938, "Reinforced concrete does not grow like wood, is not rolled like steel, and has no joints like masonry. It is best compared with cast iron as a material that is cast in forms, and perhaps we can learn directly from the long development of the latter something about how, by avoiding rigidity in form, we can achieve a fluid continuity between members that serve different functions." → 22 The diaphanous shapes designed by the French civil engineer Eugène Freyssinet broke radically with the language of iron and stone structures. Freyssinet built a bridge in Ferrières-sur-Sichon (1906) and the Boutiron Bridge in Vichy (1913), among others, before going on to invent prestressed concrete in the 1920s. → 23

47 Concrete Bridge, Robert Maillart, Tavanasa, Switzerland, 1905

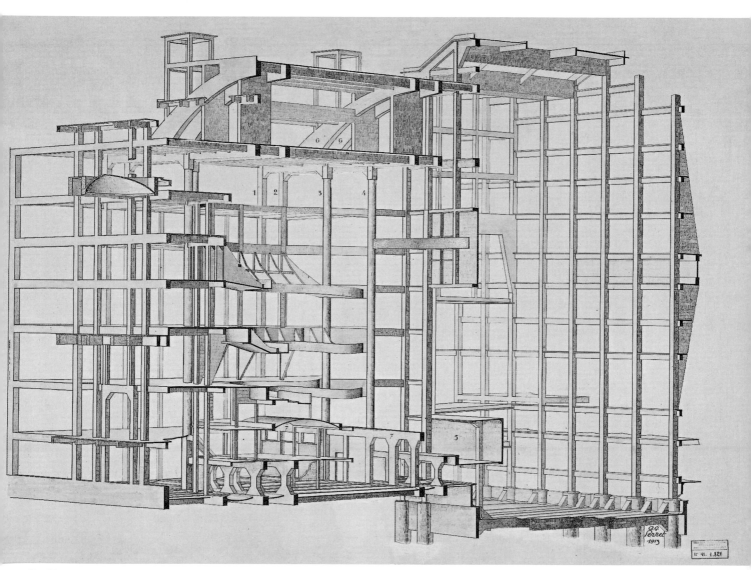

48 Champs-Elysées Theater, Auguste Perret, Paris, France, 1910–3

49 Seaplane Hangars, S. Schultz, K. N. Höjgaard and H. Forschammer, Reval (Tallinn), Russia (Estonia), 1917

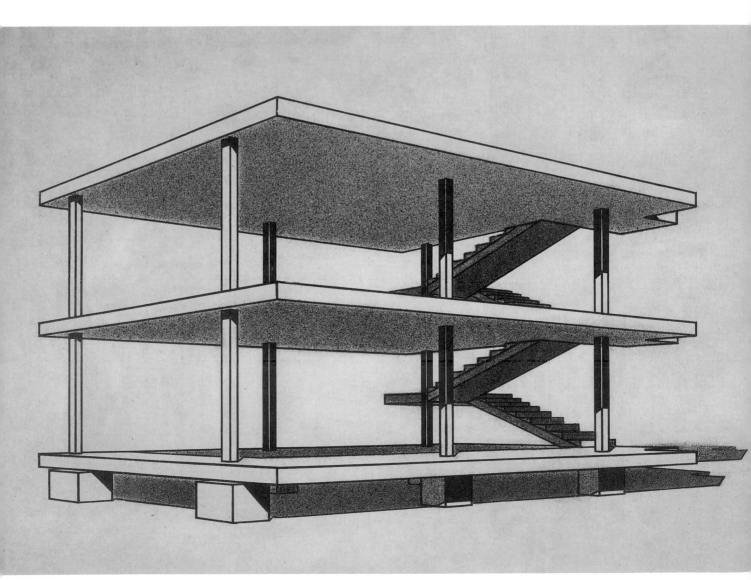

50 Dom-ino House, project, Charles-Édouard Jeanneret (Le Corbusier), France, 1914

Concrete nationalisms

Despite its apparent objectivity, concrete design was unavoidably animated by national characteristics. It was soon in use all over Europe, as in the stunning seaplane hangars **49** built in 1917 by the engineers S. Schultz and K. N. Höjgaard, and H. Forschammer for the Danish firm Christian & Nielsen in Reval (now Tallinn), Estonia. →[24] Though French in its earliest conception – a product of the research of Joseph Monier, whose name was long attached to the material in early German literature – and claimed by France for decades, concrete subsequently came to be considered "Germanic" by conservative critics who interpreted the "brutality" of certain buildings as an expression of Teutonic hardness. In fact, the Germans developed their own technologies. The Wayss & Freytag company devised techniques based on the Monier system, placing so much emphasis on methods of calculation that Hennebique declared his "horror at this hodgepodge of science" and his preference for the "plain old recipes" of the first concrete formulas. →[25] The most spectacular concrete building erected in the German empire was Max Berg's Jahrhunderthalle in what is now Wrocław (Centenary Hall; 1912–13), **51** which for a time was the most voluminous structure in the world. With a 65-meter (213-foot) diameter, the Jahrhunderthalle was the first building to outdo the Roman Pantheon's 43 meters (141 feet). The structure consisted of four large arches bearing thirty-two radial ribs plus additional concentric ones. Its exterior, with rather static stacks of window strips, did not hint at the spectacular, almost Piranesian space inside.

The ideas of the young Swiss architect Charles-Édouard Jeanneret – later to be known as Le Corbusier – had roots in both Germany and France. A friend of the engineer Max Du Bois, who had translated German handbooks on concrete into French, he was a draftsman in the Perret office from 1908 to 1909. In 1914 Jeanneret conceived a construction principle relying on columns and horizontal slabs to generate a potentially infinite number of configurations of plans and facades. The Dom-ino House **50** – its name combines references to the words *domus* (house) and *innovation* and also evokes the game of dominoes – was the most striking example of an architecture based on the building skeleton. →[26]

In just a few decades this material born of the research of chemists and engineers radically altered building practices and the conception of civil engineering works. It also changed the relationship between the load-bearing structure, the internal partitions, and the exterior of the building, leading to a break with the principles of both stone or brick masonry and wood or iron structures. Though they only partially met Viollet-le-Duc's expectations regarding the "truth" of the structure, the experimental constructions poured in concrete promised a new tectonic expression, in the sense given that term by Gottfried Semper, who saw tectonics as "a conscious attempt by the artisan to express cosmic laws and cosmic order when molding material." →[27] The tectonics of concrete heralded the fusion of *Kernform* and *Kunstform* of which Semper had dreamed.

America rediscovered, tall and wide

In *Democracy in America* (1835), Alexis de Tocqueville characterized the most ambitious men in democracies as being solely concerned with "the present moment": "They quickly achieve many endeavors, rather than erect a few particularly durable monuments." [1] For many decades this was exactly how Europeans perceived American architecture. Less impressed with grand public buildings like the Capitol in Washington, D.C., than with the nation's bridges, factories, and skyscrapers, they saw the latter as expressions of a technological sublime linked to the New World's economic power. [2] At the time, John and Washington Roebling's Brooklyn Bridge (1867–82) was probably the most renowned structure in the United States. After the U.S. census bureau officially confirmed the closing of the American frontier in 1890, a new epoch began that combined the end of westward territorial expansion with an imperialist thrust overseas. The development of great steel and transportation companies gave rise to projects of unprecedented scale. The architect Henry Hobson Richardson, who died in 1886, had anticipated such grand projects. He left an imaginative body of work that brilliantly deployed Romanesque models, as in his Trinity Church in Boston (1872–7). Richardson also recycled the tectonics of the Renaissance palazzo, as in his Marshall Field Warehouse in Chicago (1885–7, demolished 1930), with its austere stone walls.

Chicago in white and black

The 1893 World's Columbian Exposition **55** held in Chicago introduced American architecture both to a national audience and to the fair's many foreign visitors. Built under the authoritative direction of Daniel H. Burnham, with gardens designed by Frederick Law Olmsted, the fair centered on a complex of large buildings with classical exteriors. These inspired its nickname, the White City. The primary exception to the dominant classicism was the entrance to the Transportation Building, **56** designed by Louis Sullivan, which displayed an imaginative use of Turkish ornaments. Certain pavilions, such as the Japanese Ho-o-den, aroused visitors' curiosity. Yet for many travelers, the ultimate impression of Chicago was not that of Burnham's monumental yet ephemeral city, but the "black city" that had arisen since the great fire of 1871.

Chicago's giant slaughterhouses, most especially its conveyor-belt system, conceived for the dismembering of carcasses, served as models for many subsequent factories. [3] But even more vivid were Chicago's commercial buildings with their steel frames. People referred to them interchangeably as both "cloud-pressers" and "sky-scrapers," the latter name borrowed from that given to the tallest sail on a ship. The Parisian novelist Paul Bourget described these structures a year after the fair in his book *Outre-Mer: Impressions of America*, noting that the "simple power of necessity is to a certain degree a principle of beauty; and these structures so plainly manifest this necessity that you feel a strange emotion in contemplating them. It is the first draught of a new sort of art – an art of democracy made by the masses and for the masses." [4]

The buildings had begun to appear in Chicago's downtown Loop during the 1880s in response to the fourfold effect of urban concentration, the development of the steel frame, the elevator, and the telephone. William Le Baron Jenney built the Home Insurance Building (1885–6, demolished 1931) **52** and the second Leiter Building (1889–91) using a steel skeleton and partly non-bearing facades. Efficient organization and management made John Wellborn Root and Daniel H. Burnham's architectural firm the most modern in the world, to the point that the

52 Home Insurance Building, William Le Baron Jenney, Chicago, Illinois, USA, 1885–6, demolished 1931

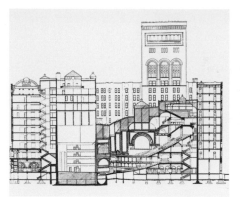

53 Auditorium Building, Dankmar Adler and Louis Sullivan, Chicago, Illinois, USA, 1886–9, section

54 Auditorium Building, Dankmar Adler and Louis Sullivan, Chicago, Illinois, USA, 1886–9, interior of opera house

55 ▶ World's Columbian Exposition, Daniel H. Burnham, Chicago, Illinois, USA, 1893

plan of its offices was published in the European press. ⇀ 5 Burnham and Root built the Rookery (1886–7), whose great courtyard covered in glass was clad in marble and reminiscent of Richardson's work; the Monadnock Building (1889–92), whose sixteen stories constituted the culminating achievement of load-bearing wall construction; the Masonic Temple (1890–2), briefly the tallest building in the world at twenty-two stories; and the Reliance Building (1890–4), whose terra-cotta facades were, for the first time in architectural history, entirely suspended from the steel skeleton rather than carrying their own load. These structures and those by the prolific firm of William Holabird and Martin Roche, such as the Tacoma Building (1888) and the Old Colony Building (1894), were largely clustered on LaSalle Street, a cradle of unprecedented innovation where the final break with the "dry goods box style" occurred as a result of the need for the best possible lighting for the offices. The first buildings were heterogeneous, with the street facades more elaborate than the side elevations, which were barely decorated. After Chicago promulgated its 1892 code, which limited buildings heights to 150 feet (45.7 meters), buildings with four identical facades became the rule. In any event, the economic crisis of the following years would stall their further rise. ⇀ 6

Sullivan's inventions

One of the structures most admired by visitors to Chicago in 1893 was Dankmar Adler and Louis Sullivan's Auditorium Building (1886–9). **53, 54** Covered in stone cladding that echoed the arches and rusticated walls of the Marshall Field Store and embellished with an almost symphonic orchestration of decorative surfaces and details, it combined an opera house

suspended within its metal skeleton with a hotel and offices. Its use of electricity was advanced, its ornamentation dense yet restrained. In 1892 Sullivan pronounced himself in favor of a moratorium on ornament, "in order that our thought might concentrate acutely upon the production of buildings well formed and comely in the nude." Yet this nudity was not to be total, and his "strong, athletic and simple forms" would be half-concealed "in a garment of poetic imagery." ⇀ 7 Sullivan was a reader of Ruskin and Viollet-le-Duc, whereas his partner Adler knew Semper well. Sullivan was also familiar with the French architect Victor Ruprich-Robert's *Flore ornementale* (Ornamental Flora; 1876), and he conceived his system of decoration, based on vegetal motifs, according to a metaphorical principle of growth. Sullivan continued to reflect on the theme of germination and proliferation until the end of his life. ⇀ 8

In an 1896 essay Sullivan proposed to examine the question of the tall office building "artistically considered." Some of his statements would imprint themselves upon the minds of his contemporaries: "It is the pervading law of all things organic and inorganic, of all things physical and metaphysical, of all things human and all things superhuman, of all true manifestations of the head, of the heart, of the soul, that the life is recognizable in its expression, that form follows function. This is the law." Referring to the "tall building," he wondered how to "proclaim from the dizzy height of this strange, weird, modern housetop the peaceful evangel of sentiment, of beauty, the cult of a higher life?" The solution was simple: "It must be tall, every inch of it tall. The force and power of altitude must be in it, the glory and pride of exaltation must be in it. It must be every inch a proud and soaring thing, rising in sheer exultation that from bottom to top it is a unit without a single dissenting line." He rejected the column as a useful model, with "the moulded [sic]

56 Transportation Building, World's Columbian Exposition, Louis Sullivan, Chicago, Illinois, USA, 1891–3

57 Schlesinger & Meyer Department Store (Carson, Pirie & Scott Store), Louis Sullivan, Chicago, Illinois, USA, 1899–1904

58 Guaranty Building, Dankmar Adler and Louis Sullivan, Buffalo, New York, USA, 1894–6

base of the column typical of the lower stories of our building, the plain or fluted shaft suggesting the monotonous, uninterrupted series of office-tiers, and the capital the completing power and luxuriance of the attic," counterposing the lessons of nature to the tyranny of the existing codes. → 9

With the Wainwright Building in Saint Louis (1890–1), the Guaranty Building in Buffalo (1894–6), **58** and the Bayard Building in New York (1897–9), Sullivan put his theories to the test. Perfectly legible in their vertical stacking, his structures read as prismatic volumes crowned with a thin cornice. The principal elements of their geometry were visible on their planar facades, which were covered in organic motifs. As autonomous structures, these buildings tended to fulfill the Neo-Grec ideal of the primitive temple. → 10 At the turn of the century, after the depression of the 1890s interrupted the construction of skyscrapers, Sullivan designed the Schlesinger & Meyer Department Store (1899–1904, renamed Carson, Pirie & Scott) **57** in Chicago, establishing a new equilibrium between the composite building's overall volume and the modular grid of the facade, which featured large rectangular bay windows. The repetitive nature of the rectilinear windows contrasted powerfully with the floral explosion of the cast-iron canopy at the building's corner. In Owatonna, Minnesota, where he built the National Farmers Bank (1906–7), and elsewhere in the Midwest, Sullivan subsequently designed boxlike structures clad in brick, the luxuriant decoration of which seemed to be compressed but barely contained by their geometric frames.

Wright and prairie architecture

Frank Lloyd Wright, another great American iconoclast, drafted two designs for his *lieber Meister* (beloved master) Sullivan

while employed in his office: part of the Auditorium Building and the Charnley House (1892), which featured remarkably playful interior volumes. But Wright was also taken by all things Japanese, particularly admiring the Pavilion of the Empire at the 1893 world's fair. Through his contacts with the Japan scholar Ernest Fenollosa, he discovered the writings of Edward Morse and Arthur Dow. → 11 For Wright, this culture offered a lesson in architecture, particularly with respect to the clear separation between the floor and the roof and the central place of the *tokonoma* – a niche for flower arrangements, which Wright replaced in his houses by the hearth or fireplace. Japan also provided lessons in graphics and in landscape. This would lead him from the gardens he saw on his first trip there in 1905 to the design of his Taliesin estate in Wisconsin in subsequent years. Wright established himself in the wealthy Protestant neighborhood of Oak Park, which he described as "a suburb which denies Chicago." → 12 There, influenced by social movements that approached the reform of domestic space as a way to reform moral behavior, he built his own house (1889–98). → 13 **59** Though symmetrical on the outside, the house has an interior that plays on the oppositions between two centers: the vaulted music room, symbolizing Oak Park's communal life, and the fireplace with "inglenooks," a private gathering place for the family. The house's collective aspect, reinforcing the importance of sociability and shared dinners, prevails over its individual spaces. Establishing his studio on the premises, Wright appended to the house a square office and an octagonal reading room (1895), which added complexity and fluidity to the overall structure.

His houses in Oak Park and nearby River Forest reveal Wright's extraordinary imagination. His success was rapid – he designed ninety buildings between 1901 and 1909. In 1900, an article in Boston's *Architectural Review* referred to Wright's

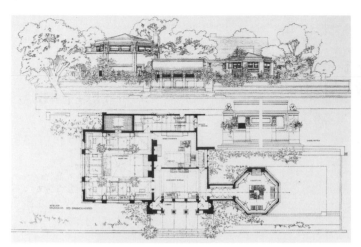

59 Frank Lloyd Wright House and Studio, Frank Lloyd Wright, Oak Park, Illinois, USA, 1889–98

60 William H. Winslow House and Stables, Frank Lloyd Wright, River Forest, Illinois, USA, 1893–4

"perpetual inspiration," contrasting it with the work of the "Great American *usines d'architecture*," the typical large factory-like American architecture offices; the author declared that "few architects have given us more poetic translations of materials into structure." [14] Influenced by reformers such as William C. Gannett, whose sermon "The House Beautiful" was typeset and reprinted by Wright in collaboration with his client William H. Winslow in 1897, the architect aimed for his houses, in Gannett's words, to serve the purpose of "dear togetherness," being "like a constant love-song without words, whose meaning is 'we are glad that we are alive together.' " [15] With its upper band of windows and overhanging roof, Winslow's house (1893–4) **60** in River Forest initiated Wright's exploration of horizontally extended forms. Though its relatively orderly, even solemn, street-side facade contrasts with the freer nature of the back, the entire building is striated with clearly articulated horizontal bands. The fireplace is the pivot of the structure. Here the housewife was to preside over a realm that extended to the entire interior. In 1901 Wright devised theoretical projects like "A Home in a Prairie Town" and "A Small House with 'Lots of Room in It' " for the *Ladies Home Journal*, positioning himself as the theorist of a new domestic architecture.

The architecture he elaborated was made to measure for the wide plains surrounding Chicago. In his 1908 article "In the Cause of Architecture," he wrote, "The Prairie has a beauty of its own, and we should recognize and accentuate this natural beauty, its quiet level. Hence, gently sloping roofs, low proportions, quiet skylines, suppressed heavyset chimneys and sheltering overhangs, low terraces and outreaching walls sequestering private gardens." [16] Starting with the Ward Willits House in Highland Park (1902), Wright developed ideas he had previously formulated for the Winslow House

and created a system based on a logic of growth and variation using a square-room module. [17] The continuity between the house and the landscape was made more intimate by the generous overhanging roofs, the low ceilings, and the horizontal juxtaposition of the windows. Wright's other realized projects of this period ranged from vast residences like the Susan L. Dana House (1902–4) **61** in Springfield, Illinois; the Darwin D. Martin House (1904) in Buffalo, New York; and the Avery Coonley House (1908) in Riverside, Illinois; to more modest buildings like the Frank Thomas and Edwin H. Cheney houses in Oak Park (1901 and 1904) and the Isabel Roberts House in River Forest (1908). Certain houses were located on spectacular terrain, like the Hardy House (1905), built on a cliff in Racine, Wisconsin. Among all of these, the Martin House is remarkable not only for its almost absolute absence of dividing walls and its use of free-standing supports, but also for the coherence of its geometry, which extends from objects and furniture to the rooms themselves and out into the garden. The continuity between the library, the living room, and the dining room is maintained by interstitial spaces that are like walls of air. Wright remained unlucky with his projects for major American industrialists. His former assistant Marion Mahony completed the house he designed for Henry Ford, and the project he proposed to Harold McCormick in Lake Forest (1907–9) was turned down. Yet the Frederick C. Robie House (1906–8) **62** in Chicago provided him with an opportunity to build a kind of spatial and technological manifesto, as Reyner Banham has noted. [18] The elongated house, extending along the street, is protected from rain and the noonday sun by projecting eaves. In the summer it is shaded by a courtyard on the north, which serves as a cool-air tank, while its horizontal windows help ventilate it. Inside, the passages are fluid between the

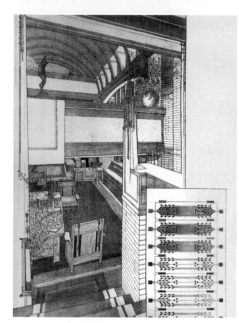

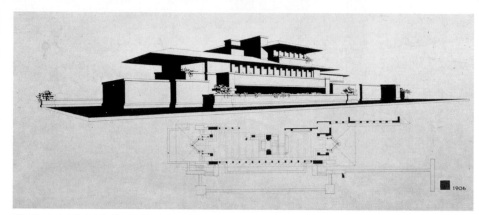

62 Frederick C. Robie House, Frank Lloyd Wright, Chicago, Illinois, USA, 1906–8, drawing made in the 1920s

63 ▶ Unity Temple, Frank Lloyd Wright, Oak Park, Illinois, USA, 1905–8

61 Susan L. Dana House, Frank Lloyd Wright, Springfield, Illinois, USA, 1902–4

second-floor living room and the dining room, which are separated by the chimney, and between the ground-floor billiard room and the children's game room. Radiators, heating tubes, and lighting devices are built into the walls. Unlike Sullivan, Wright had no interest in purely rational construction; instead he made ornament the starting point of his architectural configurations and adapted the structure to achieve his design goals. For example, the nearly 30-foot (10-meter) I-beams bearing the roof of the Robie House were installed lengthwise, once other motifs (like the repetitive rhythm of the ornamented windows) had been determined, without any reservations about this seemingly illogical solution.

Commissioned by Darwin Martin's brother John, the administrative building of the Larkin soap factory in Buffalo (1902–6, demolished 1950) **64** extended the principles of Wright's Prairie Houses to an office scheme. Despite its fortress-like appearance, the building was naturally illuminated by a glassed-in courtyard similar to the one at the Rookery, whose lobby Wright was remodeling at the time. He later described it as "a simple cliff of brick hermetically sealed (one of the first 'air-conditioned' buildings in the country) to keep the interior space clear of the poisonous gases in the smoke from the New York Central trains that puffed along beside it." → [19] The result of careful analysis of the building's intended use, Larkin combined Sullivan's organic conception of architecture with a strict orthogonal geometry. Most significantly, it represented a new type of open workplace, with steel furniture and lighting designed as integral to the whole and in keeping with the quasi-familial vision of the company.

Soon after this commission, Wright built Unity Temple in Oak Park (1905–8), **63** another monumental extension of the principles of his houses. The square masses of the church and the

Sunday school interact with one another like the formal components of Wright's domestic designs. The concrete mass of the walls, into which all the ducts and pipes were integrated, recalls the solid envelopes of Richardson's houses, while the church's interior recaptures the warm centrality of Wright's houses. Wright carefully studied the path leading into the house of worship from the street, and in his eyes it too became a "meeting place." The articulation of the basic structure and of the secondary elements, more complex than that in Buffalo, was part of a search for design unity that seemed to constitute a metaphor of the building's purpose. → [20]

Wright and Europe

Wright's principles were carried forward by a group of architects led by William Drummond, John Van Bergen, Marion Mahony, and Walter Burley Griffin and known collectively as the Prairie School. Their form of homage or excessive imitation aroused Wright's pique. Their inspirer spent 1909 and 1910 in Europe, having fled there with his client (and lover) Mamah Cheney. He visited Josef Hoffmann's and Joseph Maria Olbrich's buildings, which he already knew from photographs. He also studied architectural sculpture, taking particular interest in the work of Franz Metzner, who was responsible for the sculptural figures at Bruno Schmitz's Völkerschlachtdenkmal in Leipzig and Jože Plečnik's Zacherlhaus. From observing Metzner Wright developed a theory of "conventionalization," or the transformation of natural forms into abstract shapes, which he later used in his concrete construction units, or "textile blocks." Europe not only gave Wright an important geometry lesson in the interlocking squares and circles of the late Secession, but also led him to discover pre-Columbian America. → [21]

65 David B. Gamble House, Charles S. Greene and Henry M. Greene, Pasadena, California, USA, 1908

66 First Church of Christ Scientist, Bernard Maybeck, Berkeley, California, USA, 1910

The buildings he designed upon his return to the United States, such as Midway Gardens in Chicago (1914, demolished 1929), were visibly shaped by these discoveries.

Conversely, Europeans were becoming increasingly interested in Wright. The British architect Charles Robert Ashbee had met Wright in Chicago as early as 1900, but it was in Germany that Wright was now most recognized. He gave a lecture in Berlin at Bruno Möhring's invitation, and he saw his reputation grow greatly when the Wasmuth publishing house released a monograph on his buildings in 1911; this followed the release of a limited-edition large-size portfolio of his works and projects the year before. → 22 Richardson had long been the only American architect recognized in the Old World (notably in the Netherlands, Germany, and Finland), but Sullivan and Wright now took center stage in accounts by visitors to the United States such as Hendrik Petrus Berlage. At times their designs were reproduced in Europe almost exactly as in the model factory built by Walter Gropius and Adolf Meyer for the Cologne Werkbund Exhibition of 1914. → 23 California, though, remained largely unknown to Europeans, despite the significant works built there. It proved fertile ground for American followers of the Arts and Crafts movement, which cabinetmaker Gustave Stickley's periodical The Craftsman (1901) had served to disseminate. In Pasadena, the work of the brothers Charles S. and Henry M. Greene was best exemplified by their house for David B. Gamble (1908), 65 heir of a leading soap manufacturer – a skillful composition of solid wood elements on a masonry foundation. Like Wright's houses, but designed for a gentler climate, the Gamble House is largely open to the outdoors through a series of porches. The Greenes devoted the utmost care to the assembly of the wood frame and walls, using visible dowels that evoked the techniques of Japanese builders. The

first houses that Irving Gill designed in San Diego were also informed by the Arts and Crafts, while in Berkeley, Bernard Maybeck built the First Church of Christ Scientist (1910). 66 A large room on a square plan that extends to the outside with pergolas, it combines a wood and concrete structure with industrial steel sash for the glass wall in a manner reminiscent of Viollet-le-Duc's theoretical projects.

The skyscraper migrates to New York

After 1900 the experiments of East Coast architects focused on factories, silos, and, most conspicuously, skyscrapers. Unlike Chicago, New York did not pass any regulations limiting the height of new construction. In fact, vertical competition was unstoppable. The first batch of skyscrapers was built during the 1870s for newspapers, including Richard Morris Hunt's building for the New York Tribune (1873–5, demolished 1955). → 24 Beginning with the construction of the Tower Building by Bradford Lee Gilbert (1888–9, demolished 1914), the steel skeleton became the rule for skyscrapers. The completion of the Flatiron Building (1901–2) 69 – built for Chicago contractor George A. Fuller by Daniel H. Burnham – was an incontestable milestone. A 22-story vertical extrusion of its triangular site, the building was topped with a cornice evoking the capital of a column as in the ideal scheme contested by Sullivan. It could be the tip of a potentially gigantic imaginary Haussmannian block. Elevators and services were grouped in the building's core, allowing the window-lit areas of each floor to be entirely devoted to offices. Standing at the intersection of Broadway and Fifth Avenue, the Flatiron had such iconic power that the magazine Camera Work saw in it the promise of a new aesthetic, and one of its admirers, the photographer

69 Flatiron Building, Daniel H. Burnham, New York City, USA, 1901–2, photograph by Alfred Stieglitz

67 Woolworth Building, Cass Gilbert, New York City, USA, 1910–13

68 Equitable Building, Graham, Anderson and Probst, New York City, USA, 1913–15

Alfred Stieglitz, responded to the detractors of this "monster ocean steamer" that "it is not hideous, but the new America. The Flat Iron is to the United States what the Parthenon was to Greece." → 25 Other buildings, including the New York Times Building by Eidlitz and McKenzie (1903–5), soon further mined the potential of rare triangular sites in Manhattan's grid. With the 47-story, 594-foot (181-meter) Singer Building (1906–8, demolished 1968), Ernest Flagg responded to the Singer Company's explicit commission to create a definitive vertical structure. It was soon followed by the Metropolitan Life Insurance Company tower by Pierre L. Lebrun (1907–9), which was grafted to a larger block and made conscious reference to the campanile of Saint Mark's in Venice. Next came the Municipal Building by McKim, Mead and White (1909–14), which was likened to a modern Colossus of Rhodes in its straddling of Chambers Street. Built on an open U-plan, the Municipal Building symbolized the modernization of the city's administration. Popular Neo-Gothic themes found their place in the next victor in the ongoing race for height, the Woolworth Building (1910–13) **67** by Cass Gilbert. Though Frank W. Woolworth, founder of the dime-store chain, had insisted that his building be fifty feet taller than the Metropolitan Life building, the structure is remarkable primarily for the refinement of its elevators and interior circulation and the splendor of an entrance hall given a Byzantine atmosphere by gilt mosaics. The skyscraper's soaring appearance and the flamboyant Neo-Gothic decor of its terra-cotta exterior quickly led the public to refer to it as the "cathedral of commerce." → 26 Construction of the Equitable Building (1913–15) **68** by Burnham's successors Graham, Anderson and Probst served to crystallize gathering fears about the unrestrained individualism of high-rise structures. By 1913 Manhattan contained about a thousand

buildings between eleven and twenty stories high, and the problem of sunlight reaching the streets was much discussed. In 1916 the "menace" posed by the skyscraper was remedied by a zoning regulation that controlled the bulk of the tall building but did not restrict its height on up to 25 percent of the site. The new code also established sophisticated regulations to ensure ample light by requiring terraces and setbacks of upper floors. New York was therefore able to remain the "standing city" – as the novelist Louis-Ferdinand Céline put it → 27 – that would make such a strong impression on visitors between the world wars. Though his 1920 book *L'architecture aux États-Unis* (Architecture in the United States) included reproductions of these buildings, Jacques Gréber persisted in seeing American architecture as little more than a reflection of French "genius." His younger colleagues did not suffer from this superiority complex. On the contrary, they found the cross-Atlantic scene fascinating enough to launch a new path of migration, reversing that of the Americans still coming to Paris to study at the École des Beaux-Arts. The departure for Chicago of the Viennese architect Rudolf Schindler and his Prague colleague Antonin Raymond heralded a radical geographic shift in the centers of architecture.

The challenge
of the metropolis

In 1908 architect August Endell, a major proponent of the German Jugendstil forms, published a small book entitled *Die Schönheit der grossen Stadt* (The Beauty of the Metropolis). Though he did not turn a blind eye to urban problems such as poverty and congestion, Endell discovered a new aesthetic potential in the industrial landscape, transportation systems, and smoky city skies, much as the Impressionists had found inspiration in the Gare Saint-Lazare in Paris in the 1870s. Unlike Friedrich Nietzsche, who invited Zarathustra to "spit on the great city, which is the great swill room where all the swill spumes together," [1] Endell believed that the city "gathered in its streets a thousand beautiful things, innumerable marvels, infinite riches, accessible to all but seen by very few." [2] Though he regretted the absence of an elusive "intellectual beauty" with which scientific thinking might have endowed the city, he praised the beauty created by human organization and labor.

An explosion without precedent

The urban development that transformed much of the Western world had no precedent. It resulted in (and from) increasing industrialization, mass exodus from the countryside, and emigration to the Americas and the colonies. It also disrupted feudal institutions and encouraged the emergence of new forms of national citizenship. Vast territories were newly urbanized, and existing cities became denser, pushing municipal boundaries outward. The process of *Eingemeindung* (municipal integration) that originated in German urban areas became an international phenomenon with the creation in 1889 of the London County Council, the first metropolitan authority in world history, and in 1898 of Greater New York. As cities expanded, they were equipped with communication networks and public services. The resulting need to design dozens of new types of buildings, from suburban train stations to clinics and public baths, stimulated the architectural imagination. [3]

The dizzying growth in the populations of large cities deepened the housing crisis, which was already so serious in London, Paris, Berlin, and New York that it was becoming a threat to the social order. **70** Urban reforms related to housing, transportation, hygiene, education, and leisure were put in place during the last decade of the nineteenth century. During this era, municipalities became essential forces behind building projects that, in turn, reflected on a wide range of public policies and cooperative programs. Architects and engineers saw vast public commissions take shape. Meanwhile the nascent social sciences found the city to be an irresistible subject. The writings of sociologists such as Max Weber and Georg Simmel in Germany and Maurice Halbwachs in France and the research of their counterparts at the University of Chicago laid the foundations for a new critical approach to the study of social relationships based on systematic research and verifiable facts. [4]

Problems of hygiene were of primary significance. An issue first raised by physicians and scientists carrying out studies in Paris during the mid-eighteenth century, hygiene took a central place in philanthropic activities following devastating cholera epidemics a century later. The paradigm of the healthy city was applied not only to strategies related to urban design, but also to the design of individual structures. It would dominate architectural thought until almost the last third of the twentieth century. [5]

Concern for hygiene – initially focused on improving the circulation of air, then on sunlight, and finally on construction materials that would not deteriorate and facades that could be washed – transformed all of the thinking behind housing and public buildings. The low-cost Paris apartments designed by

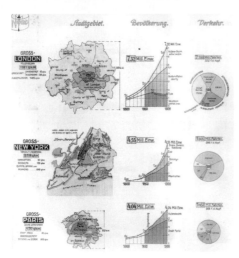

70 Compared growth of big cities c. 1910, from *Der Städtebau* (Town Planning), Werner Hegemann, 1910

71 Street layout, from *Town-Planning in Practice*, Raymond Unwin, 1909

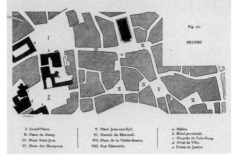

72 Streets in Bruges, from *City Planning According to Artistic Principles*, Camillo Sitte, 1889

73 ▶ "Hygienic" set-back housing, Henri Sauvage and Charles Sarrasin, Paris, France, 1912

Henri Sauvage and Charles Sarrasin **73** represent one example; they were advertised as "hygienic," even "athletic," thanks to their plans as well as to the white tiling of their facades and the provision of recreational areas for their users. → 6 Elsewhere, the concern to provide middle- and lower-class housing with adequate ventilation and access to sunlight led to the expansion and opening up of building courtyards.

The planners' toolbox

The very instruments used by architects, planners, and policy makers to calibrate the extension and modernization of cities were transformed by inputs from the natural and social sciences. Pressure from unions and political movements intensified the demands for a more democratic process of providing housing and advanced the emerging notion of "collective" needs. As a result, the discipline known in its parallel versions as *Städtebau* in Germany, town planning in Great Britain, and *urbanisme* in France took on new importance. → 7 The old method of creating roads and subdividing the land into lots without differentiating their use or their density was replaced by a complex approach to regulation and planning based on statistical data and public supervision of specialized stages of conception and construction. Planning became future oriented and prescriptive.
The notion of the urban plan became fundamental, symbolizing the hopes of professionals for the rational modernization and extension of cities. In the early twentieth century, expansion and beautification plans that had evolved over decades were replaced by regulations based on new, "scientific" methodologies, including measures to divide cities into zones – the term *zone* in both French and German was derived from military usage – and the elaboration of building regulations. → 8

In just a few years, urban planning became a world movement. The year 1910 witnessed the nearly simultaneous Town-Planning Conference in London and the *Allgemeine Städtebau-Ausstellung* (General Urban-Planning Exhibition) in Berlin, during which large cities had an opportunity to compare their plans of action. → 9 The challenge now was to anticipate growth and to regulate it not only by understanding real estate and technical systems but also by imagining the future architecture of large cities. Global networks of communication facilitated something resembling a collective, borderless think tank, bringing together policy makers, intellectuals, and technicians through field trips, conferences, and exhibitions. Periodicals such as *Der Städtebau* (founded in Berlin in 1904) and *The Town-Planning Review* (founded in London in 1909) began appearing, joining the handbooks edited by Josef Stübben and Raymond Unwin **71** as the basis of a library for an emergent international profession. → 10

Town, square, and monument

Yet the seeming unanimity of reformers and technicians was shattered the moment it came to putting a specific face on the cities of the future. Should the modern metropolis be designed by reinterpreting the picturesque beauty of historical sites; by expanding on the classical principles of monumentality, as represented by the Beaux-Arts obsession with axiality, hierarchy, and historicism; or by avoiding all nostalgia and designing a new framework for the future inspired by a modern mechanized and rationalized economy? The first position was fueled by the theories proposed in 1889 by the Viennese architect Camillo Sitte in his book *Der Städtebau nach seinen künstlerischen Grundsätzen* (City Planning according to Artistic Principles), **72**

75 World City, project, Ernest Hébrard, 1912

76 Future New York, Harvey Wiley Corbett, 1913

74 Plan of Chicago, Daniel H. Burnham and Edward H. Bennett, Chicago, Illinois, USA, 1909

which attracted a growing number of followers. Focusing on the city in its "Sunday best" – that is, on the city center – Sitte advocated studying the streets and squares of medieval and Renaissance towns as a basis for turning modern urban compositions into "total works of art" on the model of the Wagnerian opera he admired. → 11 An immediate bestseller, Sitte's book remained the bible of urban planners for decades, although they often reduced it to caricatural formulas based on imitation of medieval cities. No less successful, *Platz und Monument* (City Square and Monument), published by the art historian Albert Erich Brinckmann in 1908, reserved its praise for the Baroque and classical squares of Rome and Paris. → 12 The principles put forward for transforming Berlin, Paris, and Vienna were applied throughout the rest of Europe as new nation-states like Italy and Romania were established. They also found application in independent Latin American countries, including Brazil and Argentina; in Meiji Japan; in late Ottoman Turkey as it underwent modernization; and finally in colonial territories. Unlike the picturesque, contrasting forms to which Sitte was attracted, the massive schemes at the heart of these cities featured long axes and perspectives connecting vast esplanades dominated by colonnades and domes. Such "artistic" principles applied the Beaux-Arts model at the expanded scale of the grand urban structure. Daniel H. Burnham had used these principles in Chicago in 1893 to lay out his "White City," which was imitated at the International Exposition of 1900 in Paris and elsewhere.

The classicizing phantasmagoria of Chicago and other world's fairs and the grand urban compositions of Europe's historical cities provided the model for countless projects by American urban planners, who were committed to making the metropolis a "city beautiful," giving spatial form to the ideals of

the Progressive Era. → 13 As one of its most active agents, Burnham provided the movement with emblematic images such as the National Mall in Washington, D.C., which was renovated on the basis of his 1902 plan, and his plan for San Francisco, which remained unrealized after the 1906 earthquake despite, or perhaps because of, its ambitious scope. Even though the 1909 plan for Chicago **74** that he and Edward H. Bennett prepared at the request of local business associations was only partially implemented, it remained one of the most resonant images of the era. Its vision was of a large city divided into functional zones, crisscrossed with new streets and interconnected railways, refreshed by a system of parks linking it with the lake and surrounding prairies, and, most especially, crowned with a monumental city center that would have made it into a "Paris on Lake Michigan." → 14 Burnham's vocabulary was also adopted for certain projects with more humanistic intentions, such as the *Cité Mondiale* (World City) **75** designed in 1912 by the French architect Ernest Hébrard for the Norwegian sculptor and philanthropist Hendrik Christian Andersen. → 15 During this same brief but fertile period extending from 1890 to World War I, engineers, architects, landscape designers, and social reformers who were committed to solving the problems of the big city put forward a third set of principles that avoided both backward-looking imitation and grandiose rhetoric. The rapid spread of the automobile and the development of metropolitan railroads spurred a vision of the city as a gigantic machine for traffic. The architect Eugène Hénard's "Street of the Future," **77** presented at the London Town-Planning Conference in 1910, elaborated the ideas he had outlined in his *Études sur les transformations de Paris* (Studies on the Transformations of Paris; 1903), in which he proposed to set buildings back from the street through a system of *redents* (alternating indents). Hénard's

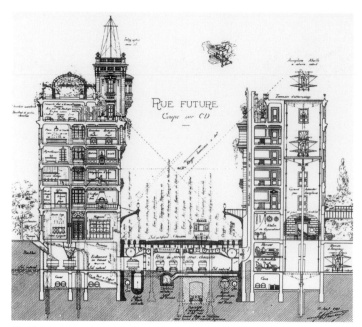

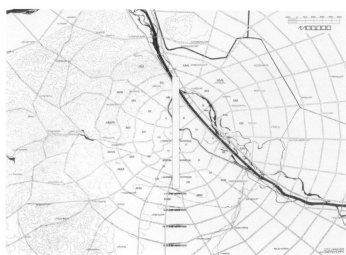

78 Vienna as an unlimited metropolis, from *Die Großstadt, eine Studie über diese* (The Development of a Great City), Otto Wagner, 1911

77 Street of the Future, Eugène Hénard, 1910

future street was entirely determined by traffic – whether automobile or airplane – and amounted to a series of great monuments surrounded by roads. The streets had multiple levels, allowing for the stacking of mass transit, automobiles, and pedestrians. → 16 In 1913 Hénard's New York counterpart Harvey Wiley Corbett took the fantasy a step further and imagined the streets of a future New York **76** as a network of dizzying canyons lined with fast lanes and suspended sidewalks, with levitating subways connecting to skyscrapers at the fortieth floor. Widely reproduced in popular newspapers, these images soon fascinated the Italian Futurists.

Not every city-planning proposal was so enthusiastic for the mechanical. Otto Wagner accepted the fact that the modern metropolis was no longer defined by its principal monuments or by the visual rules of the picturesque that had been applicable to the cities of antiquity. But he argued that the city must not be confused with the traffic systems serving it. In *Moderne Architektur*, he wrote that a city where anonymity was the rule would become a "conglomerate of cells" governed by monotonous repetition. Speculating on Vienna's future, he proposed in 1911 a new *Großstadt* (metropolis) **78** of potentially unlimited growth, meant to spread out like a spider's web. Composed of homologous neighborhoods in compact orthogonal blocks, it was to be arranged in a checkerboard pattern around evenly distributed public spaces and services. → 17

The idyll of the garden city

The "tentacular cities" that the Belgian poet Émile Verhaeren described in apocalyptic verses in 1895 seemed to many reformers to be places of perdition from which nothing good could come. → 18 Even the park systems designed by Frederick

Law Olmsted in Boston and other American cities – which found European advocates in the French landscape designer Jean Claude Nicolas Forestier and the German architect Fritz Schumacher, creator of Hamburg's Stadtpark – were deemed insufficient sources of fresh air. The Spanish engineer Arturo Soria y Mata's project of 1894 for a *ciudad lineal* (linear city) **79** suggested an alternative pattern for the growth of Madrid. The new suburbs were to extend longitudinally along either side of a streetcar making a loop around the city. Only a segment was built, but Soria expanded the concept to the regional scale with a scheme of continuous ribbons connecting cities. → 19 The German architect Theodor Fritsch and the British social reformer Ebenezer Howard reacted with proposals for broadscale decentralization. The latest in a long line of writers hostile to the city, encompassing Jean-Jacques Rousseau and Thomas Jefferson, → 20 Howard had developed his ideas out of the theories of the Americans Henry George and Edward Bellamy. He didactically expressed his opposition to both the malevolent "magnet" of the big city and the debilitating one of the countryside in a triangular diagram, touting instead the attraction of the "garden city." **80** This last would combine the advantages of the two other alternatives to become, in his view, the type of habitat most likely to appeal to people. In his 1898 book *To-Morrow: A Peaceful Path to Real Reform*, he described the broad outlines of a program intended to replace the creeping metropolis with a cluster of garden cities linked to the city center by railroad, each with a population whose size would be strictly limited. → 21 Meant to be funded by philanthropic capitalists or cooperatives, the garden city drew on American experiments such as Olmsted's Garden Suburb in Riverside, near Chicago, where Howard had lived. His clever oxymoron "garden city" – which for several decades had been one

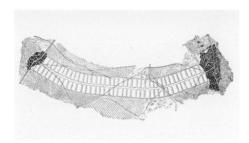

79 Linear City, Arturo Soria y Mata, 1894

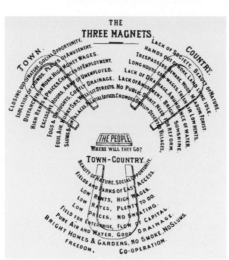

80 The Three Magnets, from *To-Morrow: A Peaceful Path to Real Reform*, Ebenezer Howard, 1902

81 Hampstead Garden Suburb, Raymond Unwin, London, United Kingdom, 1905–7

82 ▶ Page from *Une Cité Industrielle*, Tony Garnier, France, 1917

of Chicago's nicknames – quickly became a slogan that galvanized associations, municipalities, cooperatives, reformers, and also real-estate speculators around the world. Following the founding of the Garden-City Association in Great Britain in 1901, similar organizations devoted to promoting such experimental ventures cropped up in Germany and France and reached all the way to Russia. Articles on the subject were published as far away as Japan. → 22

The garden city quickly became more than a slogan. Expanding on the principles developed by Camillo Sitte, Raymond Unwin gave it canonical form with his designs for the first English garden city, which was sponsored by Howard himself, built in Letchworth beginning in 1903; and for Hampstead Garden Suburb (1905–7), **81** a private commission in London for Dame Henrietta Barnett. These refined urban compositions were based on Unwin's observations of English and Norman villages. Soon after, Richard Riemerschmid and Heinrich Tessenow conceived the garden city of Hellerau around the Deutsche Werkstätten factory near Dresden (1909–12). Meanwhile, ground was broken on the largest garden city in Europe, Wekerle in Budapest (1909–26). In Russia, Vladimir Semyonov adopted the British experiments in his design for the city of Prozorovskoe (1913), while Georges Benoit-Lévy drummed up interest in the movement in France. None of these projects fully met Howard's requirements; they contributed in most cases to the spread of nostalgic regionalist forms and responded to different political agendas, ranging from the paternalistic to the Social Democratic. By imitating the space of the village, they counterposed the reassuring context of the small community to the threats posed by modern society, following the arguments made by the German sociologist Ferdinand Tönnies in 1887. → 23 A rare exception to this rule was the Cité Industrielle project **82** of the Lyons

architect Tony Garnier, designs of which were published in 1917. → 24 An autonomous entity in opposition to the big city, it was secular and progressive, a more modern version of a 1901 sketch Garnier had based on a plan described in Émile Zola's novel *Travail* (Work).

Zoning for the colonies and for Europe's metropoles

The reform of existing cities was another goal. Alongside attempts to improve the appearance of city centers by creating more visually harmonious streets, such as the Boulevard Raspail in Paris and the southern extension of Seventh Avenue in New York, programs were implemented to replace slums with hygienic housing. The first attempts at urban renovation were launched in London at the municipality's initiative. Berlin soon followed. In Paris "insalubrious blocks" were earmarked in 1913 and included in the Extension Commission Report written that year by the architect Louis Bonnier and the historian Marcel Poëte. → 25 To a certain extent the "conservative surgery" advocated by Patrick Geddes, a visionary Scottish biologist who was influenced by sociology and turned to a career as an urban planner, was somewhat similar to these projects in its careful attention to social transformations in the city and to the relationships between "place, work, and folk," illustrated in his diagram of the "Valley Section." **83** Geddes differentiated between what he saw as the "Utopia" of the garden cities and a "Eutopia" that could result from patient modification of existing cities. → 26 Geddes tried but failed to apply his ideas in India, at a time when the colonized territories were becoming places for urban planners to experiment. In 1914 the European empires were at the height of their power, and the dominant nations set about

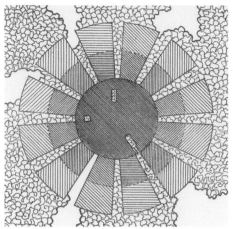

84 Extension plan for Berlin competition project, Bruno Möhring, Rudolf Eberstadt and Richard Petersen, 1910

85 Plan for Rabat, Henri Prost, Rabat, Morocco, 1914

creating new capitals. These were sometimes situated near historical urban areas, as was the case with Edwin Lutyens and Herbert Baker's New Delhi, which began to be planned in 1912 following Baker's design of the Union buildings in the South African capital of Pretoria (1909–13). It evolved into a scheme combining major roads and a hexagonal plan that culminated in Luytens's Viceroy's Palace. → 27 **86** In Rabat, the political capital of the French protectorate in Morocco, the Beaux-Arts graduate Henri Prost designed an administrative neighborhood that applied the characteristics of the garden city. **85** Other capitals were erected on new sites, such as Australia's Canberra. The 1911 international competition to build Canberra resulted in the selection of the American Walter Burley Griffin over the Finnish architect Eliel Saarinen and the French planner Donat-Alfred Agache. In Griffin's winning scheme, **87** the city encroached on the surrounding areas, making repeated use of elements borrowed from the Prairie Houses that Griffin had drafted as an employee in Frank Lloyd Wright's office. → 28

Following the competition for the expansion of Barcelona – won in 1905 by the French architect Léon Jaussely, one of the first advocates of zoning – the 1910 competition for Greater Berlin yielded what were probably the most complex strategies of the day. The submitted proposals spanned the entire gamut of ideas then being discussed on both sides of the Atlantic. Grandiose monumental avenues, giant train stations, and garden cities were the basic building blocks advanced by the competitors. Some proposals were truly revolutionary: Bruno Möhring's team integrated the surrounding region with the city through great cones of vegetation reaching into the city center, **84** an approach that later met with considerable success. In 1912 the Berlin critic Karl Scheffler, asking what "the architecture of the metropolis" should be, determined that it was only in the very large city that

a new architecture could appear. Echoing Max Weber's sociological analysis of bureaucracy, he linked the metropolis to the increasing degree of organization in society, with the clearest example being the American skyscraper stacking up thousands of clerical workers. → 29 For German urban planners, Chicago and New York were now points of reference as pertinent as London and Paris had been for previous generations. Site of the mass production of manufactured goods but also of the concentration of service jobs and services, the metropolis was more than a technical challenge for urban planners. As Endell had already sensed, the urban landscape, having been revolutionized by the arrival of the automobile, was also becoming the milieu and the raw material for the avant-gardes of modernism.

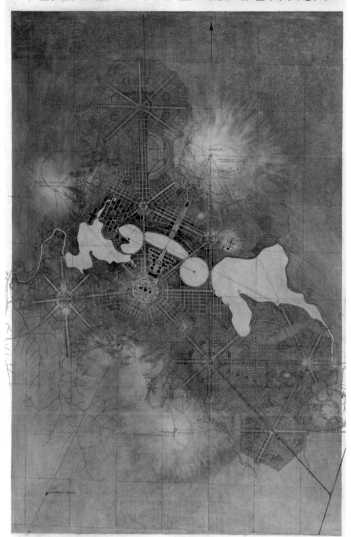

CITY AND ENVIRONS·

87 Plan for Canberra, Walter Burley Griffin, Canberra, Australia, 1911

IMPERIAL DELHI

86 Viceroy Palace and its surroundings, Edwin Lutyens, New Delhi, India, 1912–31

New production, new aesthetic

With the invention of the automobile, the spread of electricity, advances in scientific research – especially in chemistry and physics – and the increasing unification of the world's markets, architecture became both a factor for increasing industrial productivity and a key component of new visual strategies developed by big business. Concurrently, and to a certain degree in response, artists and architects devoted themselves to interpreting a new stage in the machine age's evolutionary advancement. Patrick Geddes and Lewis Mumford described it as "neotechnic" in opposition to the "paleotechnic" age of coal and steam power. →1 A variety of relationships between architects and industry began taking shape, ranging from the complete integration of architects into major corporations, to architects' efforts to promote the creative coordination of art and industry at all levels, to – last but not least – architects' independent and at times critical activities within building programs and cultural institutions.

The AEG model in Berlin

The emerging power and imperialism of Wilhelmine Germany, where industrialization had taken hold later than in Great Britain and France, found its economic strength in the rapid development of giant companies in the fields of steel, chemistry, and electricity. At a time when Britain dominated world commerce, the "made in Germany" label was seen as second-rate and derivative. German companies were thus driven to technical and aesthetic innovation in order to improve the image of their products at home and abroad. The most remarkable example of such a strategy was that of the Allgemeine Elektrizitätsgesellschaft (General Electricity Company, known as AEG), founded by Emil Rathenau in Berlin. Rathenau's son Walther, on whom the

character of Dr. Arnheim in Robert Musil's novel *The Man without Qualities* is based, eventually succeeded his father and played a leading role in German public life. The Rathenaus retained Peter Behrens, whose fame had spread following the design of his own house in Darmstadt as well as of his Exhibition Pavilion in Oldenburg (1905) and the Crematorium (1906–7) **88** that he designed in a Florentine manner in Hagen. The large design office Behrens established quickly became involved in all the AEG's activities. It created electric products for mass consumption – fans, toasters, teakettles, and other devices – with designs so definitive that they remain practically unchanged to this day. The company's visual communications, from posters to all types of printed matter, were carried out according to Behrens's specifications. →2 At a more monumental scale, Behrens was involved in the design of all the AEG buildings throughout Berlin, from factories to housing estates. Indeed, each product line called for a specific building, particularly if its components required highly specialized handling. The first building to be constructed was the Turbine Factory (1908–9), **89** which Behrens designed with the engineer Karl Bernhard. Its great form resembles a temple, as if to maintain a link between the industry-minded "Chicago on the Spree" – which Rathenau saw as replacing the Prussian monarchs' art-oriented "Athens on the Spree" – and the models of antiquity. →3 Flanked by a lower building with a wall consisting of a large plane of glass rhythmically divided by steel frames, the factory features a 25-meter (82-foot) triple-hinged frame, beneath which a crane moved the massive rotors and stators. On the front facade, the polygonal shape of the pediment evokes the contour of a bolt head at giant scale. Most interesting, Behrens played with a paradoxical contrast between mass and transparency. The corner pylons, which look like stone piers, are made

88 Crematorium, Peter Behrens, Hagen, Germany, 1906–7

89 Turbine Factory, Peter Behrens and Karl Bernhard, Berlin, Germany, 1908–9

90 The staff at the Behrens office, Neubabelsberg, Germany, 1910

of concrete yet carry only their own weight, leaning inward as they rise. The glass plane, on the other hand, tips at an angle to the exterior edge of the frame, as if bearing the heavy load of the giant roof, which in fact is supported by the underlying steel-frame structure.

Behrens also built the Kleinmotorenfabrik (Small Motor Factory; 1910–13), the front of which is distinguished by a series of dark brick columns without capitals standing five stories tall. The Hochspannungswerk (High Voltage Factory; 1909–10) is a more complex structure, in which the main halls were sandwiched between two taller volumes containing additional work areas. Here the study, coordination, and control of production clearly were integral to the manufacturing process: the era of organization was at hand. Like Charles Garnier's firm during the design of the Paris Opéra in the previous century, Behrens's firm attracted ambitious young architects from all over Germany and neighboring countries. **90** From 1908 to 1911 he recruited Walter Gropius, Adolf Meyer, Ludwig Mies (later known as Mies van der Rohe), and Charles-Édouard Jeanneret (later known as Le Corbusier), who constantly complained about the tyrannical rule of the "bear Behrens." Having recently read *Thus Spoke Zarathustra* for the first time, Jeanneret identified Behrens with the formidable Nietzschean superman. → 4

Behrens's success as the AEG's lead architect brought him projects for other industrialists and for the state, in which he explored the archetype of the Renaissance palace. In Düsseldorf he built the administrative offices of the steel manufacturing firm Mannesmann (1911–12), an ally of AEG, basing the entire complex, with its repetitive, apparently modular facade bays, on the basic unit of the office. With its metal structure covered in stone, the building reflected Behrens's interest in Jacob Burckhardt's *The Civilization of the Renaissance in Italy* (1860),

which he referred to in discussions of the design. → 5 In Saint Petersburg, Behrens enlisted Mies to help him build the German embassy (1912), a palace with a red granite colonnade reminiscent of the Kleinmotorenfabrik for the AEG but with a far more luxurious interior featuring black Doric columns.

Factory as inspiration

Walter Gropius and Adolf Meyer strove to follow the example set by their mentor, Behrens, in building the Fagus Factory in Alfeld an der Leine (1911–13). **91** Designed to produce beechwood shoe lasts, the factory was begun by the architect Eduard Werner in a Neo-Gothic style. Gropius and Meyer preserved Werner's masonry foundations, but used them as the base and frame for a light steel-and-glass curtain-wall facade. In contrast to the piers at Behrens's Turbine Factory, Gropius and Meyer's transparent corners contributed to dematerializing the building, and the image of a modular structure with razor-sharp outlines echoed the processes taking place inside the building. This heralded a new era in industrial architecture: factories were no longer reminiscent of castles and temples; instead, their design became an allusion to the precise handling of materials and to the sleekness of the products manufactured within them.

The owner of the Fagus Factory, Carl Benscheid, had shown Gropius photographs of another industrial world, North America, and in a 1913 essay, "The Development of Modern Industrial Architecture," **92** Gropius enthusiastically presented the grain silos and factories built in the "motherland of industry." In his eyes, "The compelling monumentality of the Canadian and South American grain silos, the coal silos built for the large railway companies, and the totally modern workshops of the North American firms almost bear comparison

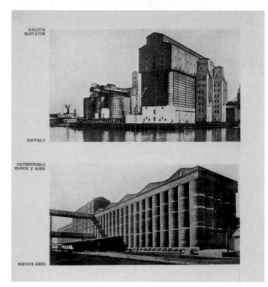

92 Page from "The Development of Modern Industrial
Architecture" in the Deutscher Werkbund annual,
Walter Gropius, 1913

with the buildings of ancient Egypt. Their individuality is so
unmistakable that the meaning of the structure becomes over-
whelmingly clear to the passer-by." → 6

Though Gropius and his successors knew little of the techniques
used to operate silos, structures deeply rooted in the American
agricultural economy, they grasped the aesthetic qualities
of those concrete cylinders and boxes. The automobile factories of Detroit also captivated Gropius. There is no doubt that
he studied them while preparing his project for Fagus. Albert
Kahn had erected a large concrete frame building in Highland
Park for the Ford Motor Company, achieving the ideal of the
"daylight factory." → 7 More than the skyscraper, which was
still beyond the reach of German designers, these factories
seemed to open the way to an architecture of pure economic
rationality. Not all German architects were ready to embrace
them, though. Paul Bonatz, a student of Theodor Fischer's studio in Munich, chose to evoke a Roman basilica in his Stuttgart
Railway Station (1912–30), **94** a reinforced-concrete building
clad in stone, implicitly asserting that modern networks like railroads demanded a monumentality that went beyond a rather
fetishistic reliance on steel and glass.

The prominent Berlin architect Hans Poelzig adopted a significantly different approach to building form and design during the same period. His Chemical Factory (1911–12) **95** in Luban
(Luboń), near Poznan in Silesia, evoked the brick attics of buildings in Hanseatic cities like Bremen and Hamburg in the north of
Germany as well as medieval fortifications and Roman aqueducts.
Far removed from Behrens's rhetoric of transparency in structures like the Turbine Factory, these buildings flaunted their
physical mass while their richly patterned brick surfaces revealed
to the attentive observer the difference between the supporting
and supported parts of the masonry. → 8

The Deutscher Werkbund

Other connections existing within institutional networks paralleled personal relationships between architects and industrial figures. Early twentieth-century German art reformers
seeking an aesthetic transformation of daily life longed for
a mutually beneficial alliance with industry. To this end,
they founded the Verband des deutschen Kunstgewerbes
(Association of German Arts and Crafts), presided over by
Hermann Muthesius. The movement's central organ was the
journal *Der Kunstwart* (The Guardian of Art), which was somewhat nationalistic in its orientation. → 9 The success of the
1906 *Kunstgewerbeausstellung* (Arts and Crafts Exhibition) in
Dresden led to the creation in Munich the following year of the
Deutscher Werkbund (German Work Union), a federation of
industrialists, state officials, architects, artists, and critics. While
the positions within this organization frequently conflicted,
the architect Fritz Schumacher, then a professor in Dresden,
defined the Werkbund's objective in his inaugural speech as
"overcoming the alienation between the executive and the
inventive spirit, in order to bridge the existing divide." → 10
Unlike their British predecessors in the Arts and Crafts movement,
with whom the supporters of the Kunstgewerbe identified, the
founders of the Werkbund were not opposed to the leading
capitalist firms of the day. Instead, they tried to figure out a way
to cooperate with industry so as to achieve the desired reform
of material culture. The inspiration for the organization came
primarily from Muthesius, who had become a professor of architecture at the Handelshochschule (Higher Trade School) in
Berlin, and from the reformer Friedrich Naumann, an advocate
of Christian Socialism and a deputy in the Reichstag. In 1908
Naumann outlined a theory advocating quality production as

93 *Ingenieur-äesthetik* (Engineering Aesthetics), Joseph August Lux, 1910

94 Railway Station, Paul Bonatz, Stuttgart, Germany, 1912–30

95 Chemical Factory, Hans Poelzig, Luban (Luboń), Germany (Poland), 1911–12

well as durability and premised on class collaboration: "The social needs of the working class can be united with the need for art of the progressive part of the population by replacing a theory based on attrition with one based on durability." → 11 The same year Naumann drew up most of the Werkbund statutes. The organization grew quickly. By the time it moved its headquarters to Berlin in 1912, it had nearly a thousand members, among them a growing number of businesses. Its activities expanded further with the spread of local groups (forty-five by 1914), the publication of its *Jahrbücher* (yearbooks), conferences, and exhibitions. The Werkbund worked indirectly through the Deutsches Museum für Kunst in Handel und Gewerbe (German Museum for Art in Trade and Industry), founded in Hagen by Karl Ernst Osthaus, another of its principal leaders, who organized many traveling exhibitions. At the instigation of the Werkbund and in imitation of the AEG model, companies recruited architects to design their office buildings and manufacturing facilities. The Norddeutsche Lloyd hired Paul Ludwig Troost and Bruno Paul, who designed four ships, while the Hamburg-Amerika-Linc worked with Muthesius. → 12 Though the Werkbund's primary goals were to raise the "artistic" level of German industrial production and to modernize consumer taste, the organization also devoted itself to promoting a form of aesthetic expression unique to technical objects and civil engineering structures. This *ingenieur-äesthetik* (engineering aesthetics), opposed to both classicism and Art Nouveau, provided the title for a 1910 book by Joseph August Lux, → 13 93 who described the aesthetic effects of machines in a discourse similar to that of Paul Souriau in France. While trying to dispel the German inferiority complex with respect to British industrial production, Lux and his acolytes also sought to combat German anxieties regarding the domination of French

"taste." → 14 They portrayed French culture as a holdover from an outdated *Zivilisation* that stood in opposition to the progressive *Kultur* of industry. This distinction operated on many levels. → 15 The extent of the Werkbund's success may be gauged by its 1914 exhibition in Cologne. The decision to hold the exhibition in a city so close to France was indicative of the association's increasingly nationalistic stance. At this point the Werkbund had 1,870 members and a constantly growing number of industrial sponsors. Yet the exhibition buildings hardly conveyed a sense of unanimity. → 16 Van de Velde pursued his ideal of linear form with a theater whose principal innovation was a tripartite stage. Gropius and Meyer's administration building continued the experiments they had initiated in Alfeld, with exterior staircases housed in glass cylinders. Their building was also reminiscent in many ways of the City National Bank and Hotel built by Frank Lloyd Wright in Mason City, Iowa (1909), particularly in its symmetrical composition and overhanging roof.

In July 1914 the Werkbund organized a conference to coincide with the exhibition. It was marked by a heated confrontation over the notion of *Typisierung* – the creation of type, or standardized objects. Muthesius believed that standardization was inevitable: "More than any other art, architecture strives toward the typical. Only in this can it find fulfillment. Only in the all-embracing and continuous pursuit of this aim can it regain that effectiveness and undoubted assurance that we admire in the works of past times that marched along the road of homogeneity." → 17 Van de Velde, on the other hand, was strictly opposed to the notion of *Typisierung*, just as he was hostile to any *Kulturpolitik* (cultural policy) – a somewhat paradoxical stance given that he was in the employ of the Grand Duke of Saxony – and he was supported in his argument by Gropius and by the individualistic positions of August Endell and

96 Glass Pavilion at the Werkbund Exposition, Bruno Taut, Cologne, Germany, 1914, exterior

97 Glass Pavilion at the Werkbund Exposition, Bruno Taut, Cologne, Germany, 1914, interior

Hermann Obrist. The conflict revealed an inherent contradiction within the Werkbund between the upholders of *Kunstgewerbe*, or the applied arts, and those who wished to place design in the service of production, a concept at the heart of industrial design. The most original building at the Cologne exhibition was by Bruno Taut, one of the young Werkbund rebels hostile to Muthesius. A prismatic polyhedral dome on a circular base, his Glass Pavilion **96, 97** aimed to demonstrate all the possibilities of glass by incorporating this material in the form of windows, glass bricks, and polychrome glass mosaics. [18] A frieze running around the building's fourteen-facet perimeter was inscribed with slogans such as "Happiness without glass, how crass!"; "Colored glass destroys hatred"; "Glass opens up a new age"; and "Brick building only does harm." Their author was the poet and novelist Paul Scheerbart, whom Taut had befriended in 1913. [19] In an aphorism-filled publication entitled *Glasarchitektur* (1914), Scheerbart expressed similar ideas, enumerating potential types of glass buildings while promising a new world based on colored-glass sensations and declaring that glass had the potential to be the salvation of society and individuals.

In his novel *Das graue Tuch* (The Gray Cloth), published the same year, Scheerbart related the exploits of a demiurge architect flying over the world in an airship, building observatories on glaciers and glass sanatoriums on lakeshores. [20] The nature of the relationship between architects and glass, which in the nineteenth century had centered on train stations and exhibition halls, and more recently on model factories like the Fagus, now shifted. By celebrating the utopian possibilities of glass, Scheerbart and Taut emphasized the experiences promised by an architecture no longer obsessed with structure and tectonics or with its place in stone cities. They heralded an architecture open to daydreams, with glass as an instrument of both reform and redemption.

Futurist mechanization

The Italian Futurists based their efforts to found a new artistic discourse and a new architectural style on the sensations produced by motion and speed. Just as Behrens came to distance himself from the Jugendstil – even if critics still spoke of a *Behrensstil* (Behrens style) – and Perret from the Art Nouveau, so the artists gathered around the poet and provocateur Filippo Tommaso Marinetti revolted against the Stile Liberty, the Italian version of Art Nouveau (also known as Floreale). This literary and artistic uprising was a response to the transformations provoked by industrialization and the growth of metropoles such as Milan and Turin. Marinetti's "Manifesto of Futurism" appeared in the Paris daily *Le Figaro* in 1909. Declaring war on historical cities, Marinetti wrote: "We will sing of the multicolored and polyphonic tides of revolution in the modern capitals; we will sing of the vibrant nightly fervor of arsenals and shipyards blazing with violent electric moons; greedy stations that devour smoke-plumed serpents; factories hung on clouds by the crooked lines of their smoke; bridges that stride the rivers like giant gymnasts, flashing in the sun with a glitter of knives." [21]

In 1910 the painter and sculptor Umberto Boccioni began expressing in his paintings the simultaneity of urban events, exalting the movement of crowds and the agitation of the streets. In his unpublished "Architettura futurista, manifesto" (1914), he evoked the possibility of an "architectural impressionism," an architecture of pure necessity, in which "the spaces of an edifice would provide the maximum performance,

98　The New City, project, Antonio Sant'Elia, 1914

99　Electric Power Plant, project, Antonio Sant'Elia, 1914

like a motor." He announced that the "dynamic needs of modern life will necessarily give rise to an evolving architecture" and noted that "the more ships, automobiles, and railroad stations have subordinated their architecture to the needs they have encountered, the more they have gained in artistic expression." Regrettably, in his view, "Processes as deeply informed as those employed by mechanics have been completely neglected in the construction of housing, roads, etc." The elevator, followed by the airplane, allowed for the conquest of the vertical dimension: "The future will progressively increase the architectural possibilities with regard to height and depth. Thus life will slice through the age-old horizontal line of the terrestrial surface, the infinite verticality of the elevator … and the spirals of the airplane and the dirigible." → 22
The young architect Antonio Sant'Elia repeated Boccioni's prophetic reflections almost literally in his July 1914 manifesto "L'architettura futurista." A cofounder with the critic Ugo Nebbia, the artist Leonardo Dudreville, and the architect Mario Chiattone of the Nuove Tendenze (New Tendencies) group, which had exhibited its work two months earlier at the Famiglia Artistica gallery in Milan, Sant'Elia had previously been inspired by the aesthetics of Otto Wagner. He had also undertaken a series of theoretical projects for monuments and industrial structures like electric power plants. 99
Impressed by images of such American constructions as the Brooklyn Bridge and Grand Central Station, and even more by Harvey Wiley Corbett's "Future New York" – which was reproduced in L'illustrazione italiana in 1913 – he imagined cities designed like an "immense, tumultuous, agile, mobile building site, dynamic in every part," and proclaimed: "Roofs must be exploited, basements utilized, the importance of facades diminished."

In the manifesto he published in August 1914, Sant'Elia described the Futurist house as "similar to a gigantic machine" made of "cement, glass, and iron, without painting and without sculpture, rich only in the innate beauty of its lines and reliefs." He called for a radical alteration of the organization of buildings: "Elevators must not be hidden in stair corners like solitary worms; rather, having become useless, staircases must be abolished, and elevators must climb like iron and glass snakes along the fronts of buildings." → 23 He also expressed his ideas in watercolor drawings for La Città Nuova (The New City), 98 shown in the Nuove Tendenze exhibition. Yet these ideas would long remain unknown. Only the illustrations accompanying his manifesto, published in Lacerba, had wide circulation. After the Second World War, the Communist philosopher Antonio Gramsci described Futurism, by then discredited by its alliance with Fascism, as nothing more than a kind of "Fordist fanfare" based on the "exaltation of big cities." → 24
Yet the attention the Futurists drew to machines and to the industrial milieu of modernization constituted a precedent without which the most refined new architecture of the 1920s would not have emerged.

In search of a language: from Classicism to Cubism

Some architects sought a source of renewal not in new technologies and responses to industrial production but rather in the discipline of architecture itself. Their preferences ranged from nostalgia for the classical to a radical rupture with all existing codes and forms of representation, even those focused on the machine, in order to return to the more abstract dimensions of design. Yet despite many attempts to overturn it, the architecture taught at the École des Beaux-Arts in Paris remained the dominant paradigm for the first two decades of the twentieth century. In fact, the École was responsible for the spread of a genuine "international style" years before this term was coined. [→ 1] Its dissemination was a belated expression of French dominance in matters of taste, continuing a pattern that had developed in the eighteenth century and was reinforced by the school's location in a city that was still the cultural capital of the world. [→ 2] The growing number of foreign students enrolling at the Beaux-Arts beginning in the last third of the nineteenth century, the international activities of major French academics and professionals, and the emigration of Beaux-Arts instructors also helped propagate the school's curriculum. The ongoing success of the Beaux-Arts method was due largely to its ability to integrate the functional requirements of modernization. The analytical approach taught in Julien-Azaïs Guadet's *Éléments et théorie de l'architecture* (Elements and Theory of Architecture; 1905), the school's principal design treatise, prepared students to evaluate new types of buildings that were more complex and less grandiloquent than the great palaces studied in pursuit of the Grand Prix de Rome, **100** with which the Beaux-Arts curriculum has too often been associated. [→ 3] The historicist elements applied to nineteenth-century buildings slowly disappeared, while the principles of symmetry and hierarchy were adjusted to new functional and symbolic requirements – sometimes with a great deal of imagination – until the late 1940s.

Anglo-American classicisms

The center of gravity of monumental classicism had largely shifted from Paris to the United States by the end of the nineteenth century. The scale of American commissions, whether funded by big business, the government, or philanthropists, resulted in buildings – and architectural firms – of unprecedented size. For instance, the development of railroads and of alliances among rail companies led Daniel H. Burnham to build Union Station in Washington, D.C., as a marble edifice that could be visually identified with the Capitol and the White House. In New York, Whitney Warren and Charles Wetmore with Charles Reed and Allen Stern built Grand Central Station (1903–13). Based on a spatial concept evoking the Roman baths, its giant concourse was erected over a network of underground tracks while a neighborhood took shape on top of these sunken spaces. The Gare d'Orsay in Paris, built on an identical principle, was the work of Victor Laloux, the Beaux-Arts professor who, not coincidentally, was the mentor to most of the school's American students. Another monumental New York train station was designed by the firm of Charles F. McKim, William R. Mead, and Stanford White: Pennsylvania Station (1905–10, demolished 1964), which featured a waiting room inspired by Rome's Baths of Caracalla and remarkable for its powerful exposed steel structure. McKim and White had previously worked with Henry Hobson Richardson. In fact, their first significant commission had been the Boston Public Library (1885–95), which stood across the street from their mentor's Trinity Church. Between 1870 and 1919 their firm constructed nearly a thousand buildings. They explored the principle of the Italian Renaissance palazzo in a variety of New York buildings, including the University Club (1900), a grandiose pile on Fifth Avenue, and the more delicate

100 Grand Prix de Rome project at the École des Beaux-Arts, Charles Lemaresquier, Paris, France, 1900

101 Low Memorial Library, McKim, Mead and White, New York City, USA, 1895–7

102 Heathcote, Edwin Lutyens, Ikley, United Kingdom, 1906

103 Page from *Um 1800* (Around 1800), Paul Mebes, 1908

Morgan Library (1906). On an urban scale, they designed the campus of Columbia University in upper Manhattan, an axial composition dominated by the dome of Low Memorial Library (1895–7). **101** Following in the footsteps of several hundred other architects, John M. Carrère and Thomas Hastings did their professional apprenticeship in McKim, Mead and White's office, having previously studied in Paris. They went on to design extravagant hotels and homes from Florida to the New York metropolitan area, as well as the New York Public Library (1897–1911), an example of civic magnificence in the service of delivering culture to the masses.

A classical resurgence was also underway in England. Beginning in 1904, Edwin Lutyens set about countering the vanity of "villa-dom," launching what he referred to, with characteristic humor, as a "Wrenaissance," a return to Christopher Wren. But Lutyens's frame of reference extended beyond the architect who had rebuilt Saint Paul's. A self-conscious reference to Andrea Palladio – "Palladio is the game," he wrote in 1903 → 4 – was evident in his designs for houses such as Heathcote (1906) **102** in Ilkley, Yorkshire and Nashdom, the residence of Prince and Princess Alexis Dolgorouki in Taplow, Buckinghamshire (1904–9). Erected on a terraced site, the latter had two different facades – one in exposed stone, the other in stuccoed brick – creating contrasts of rhythm and texture that extended the sense of counterpoint he had previously displayed, but now within less of a classical straitjacket.

German nostalgia

There was no shortage of proponents of classicism in Germany, though some slowly freed themselves from its tenets. The Munich architect Theodor Fischer, who had worked with Paul Wallot on the Reichstag in Berlin, invented new forms by using concrete in buildings such as the Garrison Church in Ulm (1905–10). **107** Fischer taught Camillo Sitte's picturesque urban precepts along with his own reflections on new building types, first in Stuttgart and later in Munich. Some architects diverged from the prevailing fixation on antiquity and, even more often, the Renaissance, idealizing instead other moments in the history of architecture. One of the books most widely used by German and Austrian designers prior to 1914 was *Um 1800* (Around 1800) **103** by the Berlin architect Paul Mebes. → 5 In this popular collection of nostalgic images of eighteenth-century building types, Mebes celebrated the honesty and formal restraint found in Germany's rural and bourgeois constructions at the turn of the previous century. He particularly emphasized the harmony between buildings and their gardens, as well as the stylistic unity of architectural elements, decoration, and furniture.

In some ways this vernacular and bourgeois traditionalism was an expression of the *Großstadtfeindlichkeit* (hostility toward the big city) that took hold among the German intelligentsia distressed about the erosion of cultural values brought on by urbanization and internationalization. This anxiety led to the idealization of a carefully edited past. The tendency was exemplified by Julius Langbehn's book *Rembrandt als Erzieher* (Rembrandt as Educator; 1890), which the author published anonymously. Its purpose was to denounce the problems affecting modern Germany and proclaim art the only possible force for resistance and renewal. The Dürerbund (Dürer Association), organized by the publisher and critic Ferdinand Avenarius (1902), and the Bund deutscher Heimatschutz (Society for the Preservation of the German Homeland), founded in 1904 by the teacher Ernst Rudorff, became the

104 School of Rhythmical Gymnastics, Heinrich Tessenow, Dresden, Germany, 1910–12

105 Drawing from *Hausbau und Dergleichen* (House Building and the Like), Heinrich Tessenow, 1916

106 Cover of *Das Andere* (The Other), Adolf Loos, 1903

principal mediators between these ideas and architecture. The Bund fought not only for the preservation of endangered landscapes, but also for forms that were altogether modern yet informed by tradition. It worked for the conservation of monuments as well as of rural structures, plant and animal life, and traditional practices, customs, holidays, and dress. The architect Paul Schultze-Naumburg – a frequent contributor to *Der Kunstwart*, a journal founded by Ferdinand Avenarius in 1887 – was the most effective propagandist for the principles of *Heimatschutz*. After the success of his book *Häusliche Kunstpflege* (Domestic Artistic Care; 1898), in which he argued for a refined and traditionalist culture of domestic architecture, the nine volumes of his *Kulturarbeiten* (Culture Works), published from 1901 to 1917, presented a binary vision of German housing, urban landscapes, and gardens, opposing "examples" and "counterexamples." This editorial device, which the radical moderns would later put to good use, buttressed his argument for a thoughtful replication of small, preindustrial cities, which he considered the only legitimate answer to the question of metropolitan expansion. It is telling that Schultze-Naumburg was among the many members of the Bund deutscher Heimatschutz who went on to found the Deutscher Werkbund: in his eyes and those of his colleagues, there was no contradiction between the fight for good industrial form and a taste for harmony. →6 The most elegant yet rigorous reading of the traditional German architecture produced during the period "around 1800" was provided by Heinrich Tessenow. In the garden city of Hellerau, which was closely associated with the Werkbund, he built several sets of houses that achieved an ideal of functionality and simplicity through a geometric and abstract rendition of traditional house types. He also provided Hellerau with its culminating achievement and central edifice, the School for

Rhythmic Gymnastics (1910–12), 104 which was built for the Swiss musician Émile Jacques-Dalcroze and the reformer Wolf Dohrn. Here, Tessenow successfully melded the archetypes of the classical temple and the bourgeois house. Thanks to his poetic pen-and-ink drawings, Tessenow's architectural language became widely accessible in books such as *Der Wohnungsbau* (Building Houses; 1909) and *Hausbau und dergleichen* (House Building and the Like; 1916). →7 105

Loos and the lure of "Western culture"

Adolf Loos was another architect focused on the early architecture of the nineteenth century, particularly on the Viennese buildings of Joseph Kornhäusel. Praising American technical objects he had discovered on a three-year stay in the United States, and combating both the outdated approaches of his contemporaries and the arbitrary aestheticism of the Secession, Loos set about introducing "Western culture," especially its clothing and plumbing, into Vienna. As publisher and author of the ephemeral broadsheet *Das Andere* (The Other; 1903), 106 he wrote essays in the spirit of the satirist Karl Kraus. *Das Andere* offered a radical critique of the Potemkin city erected around Vienna's Ringstraße in the 1860s, which Loos considered a monumental lie, and bitingly attacked the fashionable styles of Joseph Maria Olbrich and Henry van de Velde. Despite the title of his famous lecture "Ornament and Crime" (delivered in 1908, but first published in 1913 in Paris), →8 Loos was not categorically opposed to decoration. On the contrary, he espoused an appropriate, judicious use of ornament in which each material was used for what it was, without pretense. In an earlier article, "Das Prinzip der Bekleidung" (The Principle of Cladding; 1898), he used metaphors borrowed from fashion to

108   Goldmann and Salatsch Department Store, Adolf Loos, Vienna, Austria, 1909–11

109 Kärntner Bar, Adolf Loos, Vienna, Austria, 1907   **110** Steiner House, Adolf Loos, Vienna, Austria, 1910

discuss architecture, and in "Damenmode" (Ladies' Fashion; 1898), asserting that women were less attractive when they were naked, he praised the anonymous qualities of English fashion, the ideal of which was to make the wearer totally invisible in the middle of Piccadilly Circus. → 9

Loos's attachment to certain classical themes was clear in his use of Doric columns at the entry of the Villa Karma in Montreux, Switzerland (1903–6), and the Goldmann and Salatsch Department Store (1909–11) **108** on the Michaelerplatz in Vienna. The latter building provoked a scandal because of the bareness of its facade on the upper levels, a quality all the more striking since it was located across from the entrance to the Imperial Palace and Saint Michael's Church. Soon nicknamed the "Looshaus," the building has a facade that is divided into three bands beneath its cornice line: the upper stories, containing apartments, are based on a principle of sobriety and anonymity; the two lower levels, easily visible to passersby, are clad in green marble. The Doric columns, also in green marble, do not actually bear the weight of the facade. This differentiation on the facade echoes Louis Sullivan's similar treatment at the Carson, Pirie & Scott Department Store, and it also continues an architectural dialogue with Gottfried Semper.

Loos's work consisted primarily of fitting out residential and commercial interiors. The Kärntner Bar (1907) **109** in Vienna is a boxlike space just 7 meters deep, 3.5 meters tall, and 3.5 wide (23 by 11 by 11 feet). Loos combined Skyros marble, onyx, and wood with mirrors intended to enlarge the sense of the space; the effect was also meant to intensify customers' sense of tension and disorientation. Loos became involved in designing houses. Yet he did not consider the house to qualify as "art." In his essay "Architektur" (1910), he wrote: "Only a very small part of architecture belongs to art: the tomb and the monument.

Everything else, everything which serves a purpose, should be excluded from the realm of art." → 10

Many of Loos's houses, which often consist of cubic volumes with white surfaces and understated openings, appear to have been inspired by houses in London. They were embodiments of the argument in his essay "Heimatkunst" (Homeland Art; 1914): "The building should be dumb on the outside and reveal its wealth only on the inside." → 11 The exterior, in other words, was meant to belong to society and the interior to the individual. Differentiating the height of rooms according to their function and creating complex interpenetrations of levels and split-levels, Loos invented the *Raumplan*, or spatial plan, which revolutionized the conventional vertical superimposition of floors. In the Steiner House (1910) **110** in Vienna, local regulations limited Loos to only a single story on the street, so he developed the house toward the garden, deeming its centrifugal aspect "Japanese." Also in Vienna, his house for Dr. Gustav Scheu (1911–13) seemed to confirm the analysis of his work by another Viennese artist, the composer Arnold Schönberg, who saw it as "a non-composite, immediate, three-dimensional conception," in which "everything is thought out, imagined, composed and molded in space without any expedient, without auxiliary plans, without interruptions and breaks; directly, as if all the structures were transparent; as if the eye of the spirit were confronted by space in all its parts and as a totality simultaneously." → 12

Berlage and the question of proportions

Trained at the Zurich Polytechnic Institute, the Dutch architect Hendrik Petrus Berlage was a reader of Viollet-le-Duc and Semper, in whom he found the basis for a practical aesthetic: the only aesthetic capable of yielding style as such,

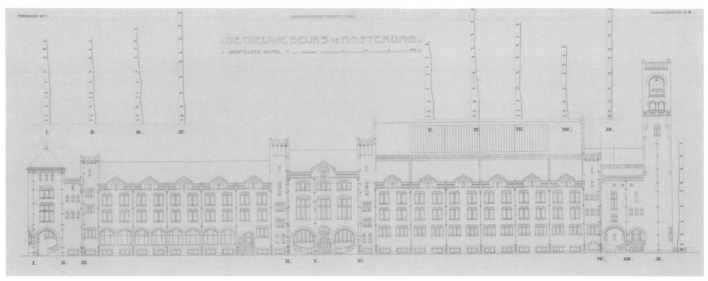

111   Stock Exchange, Hendrik Petrus Berlage, Amsterdam, Netherlands, 1896–1903, elevation

112   Stock Exchange, Hendrik Petrus Berlage, Amsterdam, Netherlands, 1896–1903, interior

113 Sint Hubertus Hunting Lodge, Hendrik Petrus Berlage and Bart Van der Leck, Hoenderloo, Netherlands, 1914–19

in opposition to the many styles of the past. In this, Berlage was quite close to such French architects as Frantz Jourdain. Visiting North America fifteen years after Loos, he returned to Europe full of enthusiasm for Louis Sullivan's and Frank Lloyd Wright's buildings. Like his Viennese contemporary Loos, he rejected the ephemerality of fashion, borrowing an aphorism from Thomas Sheraton's 1794 *Cabinet Maker*: "Time alters fashion … but what is founded on geometry and real science will remain unalterable." → 13

After constructing his first buildings in a Neo-Renaissance vein, Berlage began to explore systems of proportions in the Henny House in The Hague (1898) – in this case, square proportions. His major project at this date, his third project overall, was the Amsterdam Stock Exchange, **111, 112** designed with a Neo-Gothic plan in 1885 and built in 1896–1903. This enormous 143-by-55-meter (469-by-180-foot) edifice was based entirely on a modular grid and the "Egyptian triangle" system of proportions, with a height-to-base ratio of eight to five. He drew on the research of his compatriots Jan H. de Groot, J. L. M. Lauweriks, and K. P. C. de Bazel, who had developed this system three dimensionally in competition proposals that Berlage had the opportunity to study. He asserted: "I have become convinced that geometry, the mathematical science, is not only of great usefulness in the creation of artistic form but is also an absolute necessity." He hazarded a comparison: "Why should architecture – the art most frequently compared to music – something that led Schlegel to the well-known expression 'frozen music' – be composed without rhythmic, that is to say, geometrical laws?" → 14 In keeping with the rationalist credo that the plan should determine the elevation, the silhouette and especially the fenestration pattern of the Stock Exchange reveal the building's interior organization. While there is a rhythmic quality to

the principal facade on the Damrak, the eastern facade is more sedate and respects the scale of the neighboring blocks. The principal room is the commodity exchange, which features a large steel structural frame. The grain exchange is topped by horizontal beams, while the stock exchange, at the rear of the building, has lighter trusses. The difference in the spatial qualities of these three rooms expressed Berlage's belief that architecture "resides in the creation of spaces, not in the design of facades." → 15 The rooms were enclosed by walls whose solidity was punctuated by the indispensable structural bracing elements of brackets, keystones, and lintels.

The principal quality of the Stock Exchange is its serenity. Berlage said that he aimed to achieve an effect of "repose," by which he meant both serenity and rest: "In the smaller works of the ancients [there] is a charming repose. In contrast, our present-day architecture gives a very restless impression. I would almost say that the two words 'style' and 'repose' are synonymous; that repose is the same as style and style the same as repose." → 16 The Italian architect Aldo Rossi stressed that the Stock Exchange "does not seem to have the typical appearance of the cathedral of capital, of the temple of cash, which its name calls to mind," and that strangely, in its mysterious richness, it "seems instead like a market, a store, a gymnasium; it is devoid of the glorification of bourgeois wealth." → 17 The building had considerable impact throughout Europe, notably on the young Berlin architect Ludwig Mies, who was in competition with Berlage for the commission for the Kröller-Müller House. Though the Dutch architect failed to realize that project, he would design others for this rich family from The Hague: the Sint Hubertus Hunting Lodge (1914–19) **113** in Hoenderloo and the Holland House in London (1914). In the latter he most clearly put his observations of Sullivan's work to use.

114 "Cubist House" at the Salon d'Automne, Raymond Duchamp-Villon, Paris, France, 1912

Cubism and cubistics

Certain opponents to the idea of renewing architecture by means of its own linguistic codes turned in the direction of new art movements like Cubism, which for a time seemed to promise the geometric rationality sought by Berlage and others. Initial attempts at incorporating the devices of early Cubist painting into architecture were rather ineffective, though. In 1912, the sculptor Raymond Duchamp-Villon exhibited the facade and ground floor of a rather strange "Cubist House" **114** at the Salon d'Automne in Paris. Its floor plan was conventional and its Cubist touches mostly ornamental. → [18] Yet Duchamp-Villon had major ambitions, if a 1916 letter is any evidence: "We must establish a new decor of architecture, not only in the characteristic lines of our times, which would be but a transposition of these lines and forms in other materials, and which is an error. Rather, we must penetrate the relation of these objects among themselves, in order to interpret, in lines, planes, and synthetic volumes, which are balanced, in their place, in rhythms analogous to those of the life surrounding us." → [19] His ensemble at the Salon, undertaken on the initiative of the painter André Mare, essentially remained a showcase for his own work and that of his brother, Marcel Duchamp, as well as of his friends Roger de La Fresnaye, Jean Metzinger, Albert Gleizes, Fernand Léger, and Marie Laurencin. Cubism here was used not to challenge the spatiality of the living room or bedroom, but to create cornices and pediments whose polygonal shapes were essentially just an ornamental theme.

The most fruitful encounter between architecture and Cubism took place in Prague. At the time, Czech architectural culture was dominated by Otto Wagner, whose message was propagated by Jan Kotěra, the designer of a pavilion built for the Auguste Rodin exhibition in 1902 – a prime example of Prague's focus on Paris. As a student of Wagner, Kotěra favored linear patterns, as in his designs for the Urbánek Building in Prague (1911–13) and the house of the music publisher Jan Laichter (1908–9). He displayed a more dynamic conception of space in the Hradec Králové Museum (1909–12). His colleague Pavel Janák found a different precedent for Czech Cubism in the sculptural forms of the Bohemian Baroque, which he updated in his work. In 1910 Janák criticized Wagner: "It is possible to predict the future direction of architecture: creation. Artistic *thinking* and *abstraction* will predominate over practicality, which will recede, and the pursuit of *plastic form*, of the plastic realization of architectural concepts, will come to the fore." → [20] Janák proposed a complete program for the renewal of architecture and particularly of the facade, propounding the idea that a building should look like the result of a process of crystallization.

Groups in Prague such as the Association of Visual Artists and the Mánes Society carried on heated architectural debates over this idea. Janák's ideas were realized by Josef Gočár, notably in his orthogonal glass facade for the Wenke Department Store in Jaroměř (1909–10) and the House of the Black Madonna in Prague (1912), **115** whose facade combines the dark solids of its structural members with the crystalline prisms of its windows. The house introduced into Prague's old city the idea that a break with the existing codes of eclecticism and the Czech Sezession could lead to a unified aesthetic capable of rivaling the Gothic or the Bohemian Baroque. Gočár's approach was radicalized by Josef Chochol with a house in the Prague district of Vyšehrad (1911–12) **116** and a building on Neklanova Street in the same city (1913). Both were angular structures in which the building's entire volume contributed to highly contrasting

115 House of the Black Madonna, Josef Gočár, Prague, Bohemia (Czech Republic), 1912

116 House in Vyšehrad, Josef Chochol, Prague, Bohemia (Czech Republic), 1911–12

prismatic effects. Chochol displayed almost Futurist leanings in his declarations regarding an architecture of connections with daily life: "We first and always demand and need the fresh excitement of new artistic intensities, springing from the tumultuous and glowing mass of contemporary life." [21]

In 1930 the functionalist critic Karel Teige denounced "the basic, almost absurd misunderstanding of the fundamental and specific postulates of architecture" [22] exemplified by these Czech buildings. Nonetheless, they constituted an original and intense effort to replace classical certainties with the search for a new code, using Cubism as a formula in a paradoxical effort to distinguish the individual work.

The Great War and its side effects

Instead of disrupting the pattern of transformation in which architecture was engaged worldwide, the first industrial war in history had the opposite effect: by accelerating modernization, World War I revealed and challenged the nationalist leanings that had characterized the emerging architectural cultures. Some reformers of the prewar era had indeed expressed a certain admiration for aesthetic aspects of the technology of war. Members of the Deutscher Werkbund, whose buildings in Cologne were promptly converted into barracks in 1914, were attracted to the extraordinary rationality of German imperial navy vessels. [1] The Italian Futurists, for their part, hoped Italy would enter the war on the side of the Allies. As early as his 1909 manifesto Marinetti had declared, "We will glorify war – the only true hygiene of the world – militarism, patriotism, the destructive gesture of anarchists, the beautiful ideas which kill." [2] Several members of the movement joined the Lombard Battalion of Volunteer Cyclists and Automobilists. They would pay a heavy price in the war: Umberto Boccioni died in 1916 after falling off a horse, and Antonio Sant'Elia was killed the same year by a bullet to the head.

A triple mobilization

At first, architects were mobilized only for battle. The time they spent in the trenches would be the determining experience for a generation of young European architects, shaping their view of the world for decades to come. [3] On the Russian front, Erich Mendelsohn filled his sketchbooks **118** with visions of an architecture that would express the dynamism of industry. Architects and painters on the front lines were enlisted in the earliest efforts to create camouflage. Among those involved in this effort were Franz Marc, Fernand Léger, and André Mare,

whose watercolors depicted the operations of their own French team of *camoufleurs*. [4]

The second, more indirect mobilization was that of architecture itself, which was called upon to give shape to construction programs for a war that had quickly become "total." Though the design of fortifications, which spread across unprecedented expanses of territory, remained essentially a military task, programs related to aerial forces, the war's great novelty, were sometimes conceived by architects or civil engineers. Auguste Perret designed concrete and steel airplane hangars and shelters for dirigibles, while Eugène Freyssinet built airship hangars in Avord and Istres in 1916 and 1917. Continuing on from his war work after peace came, Freyssinet built gigantic parabolic dirigible hangars at Orly Airfield (1921–3, bombed 1944). **119** These 300-meter-long and 50-meter-high (985-foot by 364-foot) vaults were made rigid by the wavelike configuration of their arches, which were built from precast components.

The third mobilization was even more diffuse: it had to do with the industrial nature of a total war, in which human and material resources are deployed under the direction of state organizations run by industrialists – men like Walther Rathenau in Germany and socialists like Albert Thomas in France. Throughout Europe and the United States, the creation of major munitions and aviation factories and shipyards necessitated the hasty construction of housing developments to shelter the growing workforce. Architects took advantage of such projects to continue their pre-war research. Paul Schmitthenner's Staaken Garden City (1914–18) **117** near the munitions factory in Spandau, west of Berlin, realized the village ideal of *Heimatschutz* by using the architectural language of the eighteenth-century Dutch quarter in Potsdam. Schmitthenner organized the houses according to five given types and standardized elements like doors and windows. [5]

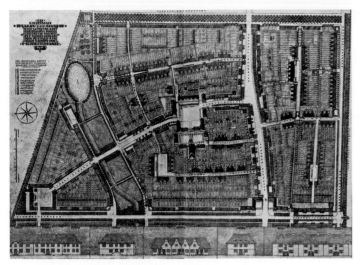

117 Garden City, Paul Schmitthenner, Staaken, Germany, 1914–18

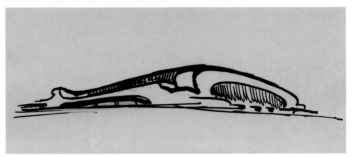

118 Industrial Building, from a sketchbook, Erich Mendelsohn, 1917

119 ▶ Dirigible Hangars, Eugène Freyssinet, Orly, France, 1921–3, demolished

The spread of Taylorism

In all the warring nations, production was transformed by
new concepts related to the scientific organization of labor.
Conceived in the United States by the engineer Frederick
Winslow Taylor and described in his *Principles of Scientific
Management* (1911), [6] these concepts were known in Europe
even before the war. At the time, socialist critics had denounced
the "organization of overwork." But the war-driven need to
make do with a reduced workforce and to incorporate women
into industrial production led to the introduction of a rigid hierarchy of management in the factory and to strict control over
workers' movements. [7] Manufactured products, particularly
munitions, had to meet new standards of quality, reliability, consistency, and compatibility. Standardization, which had been
initiated during the American Civil War, became a general
requirement and soon permeated architecture. In Germany
the engineer Heinrich Schaechterle, head of the Königliche
Fabrikationsbüro (Royal Manufacturing Office), known as Fabo,
prompted the founding of the Deutsche Industrie-Normen, or
DIN (German Industrial Norms), which eventually regulated
the entirety of production. The Americans also intensified their
efforts to make manufacturing processes as rational as possible. After the war, French architects studied their approach in
order to make reconstruction more efficient. [8]
The degree of organization needed to conduct a war that
mobilized millions of combatants and even more workers led
to the widespread dissemination of the concept of "planning."
The conduct of military operations and the organization of
industrial production required a continuous effort to prepare
the transformation of the territory. Wartime propaganda promoting planning led to the nearly universal adoption of this
concept after 1918 by politicians and economists, and its
metaphorical use by architects.

Commemoration and reconstruction

The first effect of the war, even before it was over, was an unprecedented increase in the number and size of military cemeteries.
Groups such as the Deutscher Werkbund set to work designing
them, playing a role in shaping a genuine cult of the warrior. [9]
In Great Britain, the Imperial War Graves Commission, founded
in 1917 by Fabian Ware, developed burial places in France and
Belgium for the bodies of soldiers left on the battlefield. To assist
him, Ware hired the writer Rudyard Kipling and the architects
Reginald Blomfield and Edwin Lutyens. They designed many
commemorative projects, including the cemetery of Étaples,
overlooking the English Channel near Le Touquet (1918–20),
and the Thiepval Memorial to the Missing of the Somme
(1927–32) **120** – a giant brick and stone arch that is supported by
several similar arches and suggests a type of classical abstraction. [10] In contrast to these serene memorial landscapes, the
ossuary built in Douaumont by Léon Azéma to commemorate the
bloody battle of Verdun (1920–32), **122** featuring a long concrete
vault, resembles a military structure grafted onto a neo-Romanesque steeple. There was no shortage of references to the architectural past in memorials such as Tannenberg (1924–7) **121** in
Hohenstein, Eastern Prussia; its series of towers arranged in a
circle, built by Johannes and Walter Krüger, evoke the Castel
del Monte built by the Hohenstaufens in Apulia. One exception to this nostalgic approach was the Monumento ai Caduti
(Monument to the Fallen; 1932–3) in Como, built by Giuseppe
Terragni, which took an aerodynamic form based on a Futurist
sketch made by Sant'Elia twenty years earlier.

120 Memorial to the Missing of the Somme, Edwin Lutyens, Thiepval, France, 1927–32

121 Tannenberg Memorial, Johannes Krüger and Walter Krüger, Hohenstein, Germany, 1924–7, destroyed

122 Douaumont Ossuary, Léon Azéma, Fleury-devant-Douaumont, France, 1920–32

Even cities far from the front lines felt the weight of a war that turned them into arsenals and impoverished them. [11] The reconstruction of destroyed urban areas soon became a high-stakes enterprise. Urban planners and architects rallied to rebuild even before the hostilities had come to an end, sometimes working in an international context. In France the American relief effort was not just military and economic. Beginning in 1917, the American urban planner George Burdett Ford assisted the association La Renaissance des Cités (The Renascence of the Cities) in the reconstruction of Rheims, **123** a city considered "martyred" since the German shelling of its cathedral in 1914. Ford's zoning-based plan for that city would be the first reconstruction plan approved in France after the war. [12] While the most advanced French and Belgian urban planners were involved in projects for re-creating destroyed cities, their realizations were far more conservative. In many cases they represented the triumph of regionalist ideals. The sole reconstruction effort in Germany – where innovative architects were careful to adhere to the principles of *Heimatschutz* – was in western Prussia. The showcase of this reconstruction was the city of Goldap, rebuilt by Fritz Schophol in 1919–21. [13] Prussian urban centers seemed to follow to the letter the traditionalist recommendations of Paul Mebes and Paul Schultze-Naumburg, which were codified in the work of the architect Friedrich Ostendorf. [14]

On the other side of the front, following the exhibition *La Cité Reconstituée* (The Reconstituted City) **124** in 1917 – in which studies of village buildings in the regions ruined by the war were exhibited alongside Tony Garnier's *Cité Industrielle* – the forms of traditional rural architecture were widely used as a basis for reconstructing urban areas. [15] But to see these rebuilt structures as no more than an expression of conservative taste would be an oversimplification. Though the

inhabitants' desire for recognizable forms was certainly a common concern among the rebuilders, it led them to propose interpretations that were far from literal. These were occasionally combined with authentic technological revolutions in construction. Notwithstanding the fact that iconoclastic systems such as Le Corbusier's Dom-ino project had little success, the immediate postwar period saw the triumph of reinforced concrete in northeast France, particularly for industrial structures and civilian buildings. At the same time, certain impressive structural feats, such as the rebuilding of the concrete frame of Rheims Cathedral by Henri Deneux (1924–6), had to be clad in stone to preserve an idealized vision of "reconstitution." This was certainly also the case with the Grand'Place in Arras, which was re-created from scratch. **125**

A careful look at complexes such as the garden cities of Rheims and the railroad towns of Lille-Délivrance, Douai, and Tergniers, built for the Compagnie du Nord under the direction of the engineer Raoul Dautry, reveals that regionalism worked hand in hand with standardization and rationalization.

In addition to these projects in areas affected by combat, postwar programs included housing for veterans, who soon became a considerable force on the European political scene. In German cities, housing developments for veterans figured into urban expansion plans. In Great Britain, the government's interventions during the war years in the sphere of social policy continued with the British Housing Act of 1919, which had the specific goal of providing "homes fit for heroes to live in." [16]

Postwar recomposition

Though the damage caused by World War I was unprecedented, the consequences of war went far beyond mere destruction.

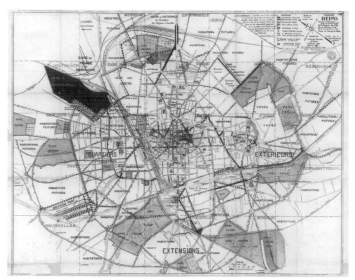

123 Plan for the reconstruction of Rheims, George Burdett Ford, Rheims, France, 1917

124 Farm buildings shown at the *La Cité Reconstituée* exhibition, Epieds, France, 1917

The new political geography that took shape had a direct impact on urban planning and architecture, beginning with the intense exchanges that developed among the defeated nations and lasted until the early 1930s. The relationships between Weimar Germany and the Soviet Union and between Germany and Turkey were as significant as the initial inroads of Americanization in Germany. During this same period, forced migrations, such as that of one million Greeks evicted from Turkey, had drastic effects on cities, quadrupling the population of Athens in just a few years. After the collapse of the German and Austrian empires, Czarist Russia and the Ottoman Empire gave way to new nationalist divisions and emerging nation-states such as Czechoslovakia, Finland, and Turkey, which used architecture to affirm their identities. Territories placed under French and British mandates in the Middle East – Lebanon, Palestine, Iraq – were transformed by modern plans and construction.

As nations dissolved and re-formed, professional organizations were also transformed and relocated according to new political borders. They were run by men who had been profoundly changed by war, and in some cases even displaced. The emigration of thousands of Russian architects and engineers as a consequence of the Bolshevik Revolution reconfigured professional circles in parts of Europe, while other groups were faced with forced relocation. Above all, their experience on the front lines made young architects eager to contribute to building a different society. Shortly after returning to civilian life, architects in Germany and Russia established utopian work collectives and devoted themselves to translating the need for social change into new experimental forms.

New architects between science and propaganda

After being "under fire" and experiencing the "storm of steel" – to borrow the titles of firsthand accounts of the front lines by Henri Barbusse (1916) and Ernst Jünger (1920) → 17 – the rising generation was faced with contradictory aspirations. The aspiration to a classical "return to order," as announced in Jean Cocteau's pamphlet *Le coq et l'arlequin* (Cock and Harlequin; 1918), reflected an anxiety stemming from the loss of cultural reference points. This anxiety was the basis of Oswald Spengler's reactionary diatribe *Der Untergang des Abendlandes* (The Decline of the West; 1917–22), which became compulsory reading for many architects. → 18 For many intellectuals and architects such disquietude coexisted with the desire for an uncompromised modernity, to be achieved through a radical break with the outdated world that had led to the war. Faith in the potential of science to enable humanity to transcend conflict led to the notion of experimental, scientific, or "laboratory" architecture of the 1920s and 1930s. In this work the authority accorded to the natural sciences was evident.

During the decade between the armistice of 1918 and the stock market crash of 1929, a postwar economy boosted by the spread of Fordism seemed to promise both affordable, durable consumer goods and high wages. The rise of newly founded organizations like the League of Nations and the International Labour Organization promised to ensure a peaceful world. The development of the illustrated press, the motion picture industry, and the grand spectacles of the world's fairs provided fertile ground for the activities of the professional elites. Like political groups – but also in imitation of the strategies of public relations and advertising firms, whose growth accompanied the spread

125 Grand'Place, Arras, France, rebuilt 1919–34

126 *Portrait of an Architect,* Wilhelm Schnarrenberger, 1923

127 *The Architect,* Mario Sironi, 1922

of Fordism and consumerism – architects succumbed to the seduction of using slogans to sum up their working methods and, more often, their aesthetic positions. → 19

Le Corbusier thus identified his "Cinq points d'une architecture moderne" (Five Points of a Modern Architecture; 1927), while Henry-Russell Hitchcock and Philip Johnson enumerated the "three principles" of the International Style (1932). In Athens the Congrès internationaux d'architecture moderne (International Congresses of Modern Architecture), or CIAM, boiled down urban planning to "four functions" (1933). The predilection for such quantifiable formulations and the proliferation of architectural periodicals revealed to what extent architecture had become a mass medium in its own right, particularly now that photographic reproduction had become easier to achieve and disseminate. → 20

Architects became the heroes of modern times in paintings by Wilhelm Schnarrenberger 126 and Mario Sironi. 127 The struggles and passions of the interwar architect later inspired Ayn Rand's 1943 novel *The Fountainhead*, whose protagonist was played by Gary Cooper in King Vidor's film adaptation. In 1924 the Dada artist Hans Richter described the "new architect" as operating in an "internationally organized" space. According to Richter he had to possess both a "new sensuousness" and the ability to respond to a society that was "more practical and less sentimental" in a world of "rapid mobility" and "precise calculations." → 21 The architect attuned to his era soon became, as the Russian Constructivist architect Moisei Ginzburg noted two years later with respect to Le Corbusier, "the very figure of the new man, full of energy and perseverance in the propaganda which he deploys in defense of his ideas." → 22

Expressionism in Weimar Germany and the Netherlands

No nation was more deeply affected by the trauma of World War I than Germany. The caste-bound society of the Hohenzollern Empire was replaced by the democratic Weimar Republic and its highly decentralized political structure. Architectural policies began to be shaped principally by municipal administrations, though some national organizations contributed to financing them. After the assassination of the leftist leaders Karl Liebknecht and Rosa Luxemburg in 1919 and the repression of the Spartacist League, their revolutionary party, the new Social Democratic-dominated government abandoned any serious or radical attempt to transform the modes of production. This left on the agenda only the utopia of a progressive "socialization," notably in the field of construction, where the model of the *Bauhütte* – or medieval guild – proved seductive. For a few years the unions considered having the *Bauhütten* participate directly in the reconstruction of the war-damaged north of France as part of reparations. These political and economic strategies found a cultural and architectural response in Expressionism, an aesthetic orientation born in poetry and in painting, which favored dynamic forms that embodied the psychological torment of wartime Germany.

The Arbeitsrat für Kunst

Following the empire's collapse, demobilized architects organized events intended to reveal new conceptions of architectural space. In late 1918, with a growing number of workers' and soldiers' councils being organized, the Arbeitsrat für Kunst (Work Council for the Arts) was established in Berlin under the direction of Walter Gropius, Cesar Klein, and Adolf Behne. Though the council was composed of a minority of architects – including Otto Bartning, and Bruno and Max Taut

– and a majority of artists – including Georg Kolbe, Ludwig Meidner, Max Pechstein, and Karl Schmitt-Rottluff – the former were clearly in control. In its "Architektur-Program," the Arbeitsrat put forward the idea of the *Gesamtkunstwerk* – total work of art – "under the wing of a great architecture." Written by Bruno Taut, this programmatic statement featured slogans such as "Art and people must form a unity" and "Art shall no longer be the enjoyment of the few but the life and happiness of the masses." [1]

The Arbeitsrat program laid out the new republic's strategies by insisting on the "public character of all building activity," the "unitary supervision of whole urban districts, streets, and residential estates," and the creation of "permanent experimental sites for testing and perfecting new architectural effects." It demanded the dissolution of all academies and of all monuments, including war memorials, that required an excessive quantity of materials, as well as the creation of a "national center to ensure the fostering of the arts within the framework of future law-making." [2]

In April 1919 members of the Arbeitsrat organized the *Ausstellung für unbekannte Architekten* (Exhibition for Unknown Architects). In the catalog Gropius wrote that architecture was "the crystalline expression of man's noblest thoughts, his ardor, his humanity, his faith, his religion! … There *are* no architects today, we are all of us merely preparing the way for him who will once again deserve the name of architect, for that means, *lord of art*, who will build gardens out of deserts and pile up wonders to the sky. [italics in original]" [3] Taut affirmed in the same leaflet that the desire for the future was architecture in the making: "One day there will be a *Weltanschauung* [world-view], and then there will also be its sign, its crystal – architecture." [4]

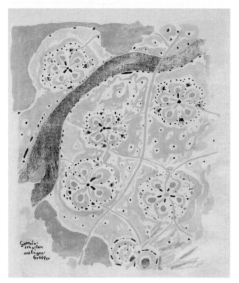

128 Illustration from *Die Auflösung der Städte, oder die Erde eine gute Wohnung* (The Dissolution of Cities, or the Earth as a Good Dwelling), Bruno Taut, 1920

129 Illustration from *Architekturentwürfe* (Architectural Projects), Hermann Finsterlin, 1919–20

130 ▶ Plate from *Alpine Architektur* (Alpine Architecture), Bruno Taut, 1919

Such a crystalline architecture had been prophesied by Paul Scheerbart, to whom the Arbeitsrat's manifesto *Ruf zum Bauen* (Call to Build; 1920) was dedicated. In 1919 Taut published his book *Die Stadtkrone* (The City Crown), **131** an urban vision full of references to pagodas and temples, proposing to place at the center of the future city a soaring tower that would embody its spiritual aspirations. The stunning plates of his *Alpine Architektur*, **130** published the same year, provided the most systematic expression of the new architecture to which the Arbeitsrat aspired, while expressing the ideal of brotherhood among the peoples of Europe. Indeed, his depictions of the multicolored glass cupolas of this architecture suspended above the Alps seemed a response to the pacifist texts by the French writer Romain Rolland and an anticipation of his German compatriot Thomas Mann's 1924 novel *Der Zauberberg* (The Magic Mountain). The origins of these images lie both in Scheerbart's writings and in the plates published by Ernst Haeckel in his *Kunstformen der Natur* (Art Forms in Nature) and *Kristallseelen* (Crystal Souls). → 5

From late 1919 to late 1920, in another exaltation of crystalline transparency, the utopian correspondence known as the *Gläserne Kette* (Glass chain) brought together the Taut brothers, Wenzel Hablik, Hans and Wassili Luckhardt, and Hans Scharoun. The pseudonyms adopted by the authors of this series of chain letters – among them Anfang (beginning), Mass, Stellarius, Prometh, and Angkor – allude to the reconciliation of man and the cosmos, an aspiration typical of the immediate postwar period. Bruno Taut rounded out this series of utopian pronouncements with *Die Auflösung der Städte, oder die Erde eine gute Wohnung* (The Dissolution of Cities, or the Earth as a Good Dwelling; 1920), **128** in which he imagined a great migration from the corrupted cities to the redemptive countryside,

adopting as his own the anti-urban arguments of Piotr Kropotkin and other anarchist and socialist theorists. Taut also founded the periodical *Frühlicht* (Dawn) and from 1921 to 1923 devoted his services to the city of Magdeburg in an effort to bring about the social program prescribed by the Arbeitsrat.

Some of the participants in the Gläserne Kette exchanges prudently avoided putting their words into action on the building site. This was the case with Hablik and with Hermann Finsterlin, whose projects, despite their apparently realistic programs, were mainly situated in an imaginary world. Hablik's *Ausstellungsbauten* (Exhibition Constructions; 1921) consisted of pyramidal superimpositions of prisms, while Finsterlin's *Architekturentwürfe* (Architectural Projects; 1919–20) **129** were unmistakably zoomorphic, evoking snails, seashells, and sea urchins.

Dynamism in architecture

The fluid and indeed elusive Expressionist movement in architecture that was embodied in these projects shared with contemporary pictorial experiments a world of fractured but dynamic forms. It also attracted older architects like Peter Behrens, who designed several new structures that transformed his former architectural language. → 6 His headquarters for Höchst in Frankfurt am Main (1920–4) was a more lyrical version of his classic prewar buildings. By reflecting the vertical light coming through glass roofs onto multicolored enameled-brick walls, he created one of the most striking interiors associated with Expressionism.

Hans Poelzig's new projects responded to Taut's call for transparency by playing with solid masses. In his contribution to the competition for the Haus der Freundschaft (House of

DAS BAUGEBIET, VOM MONTE
GENEROSO GESEHEN

Bergbekrönungen, -bearbeitungen, Täler ausgebaut — wie
im Vorigen. Die Hochfläche am Lugano-See
mit gestaffelter, von oben mosaikartig wirkender
Glasarchitektur bebaut.

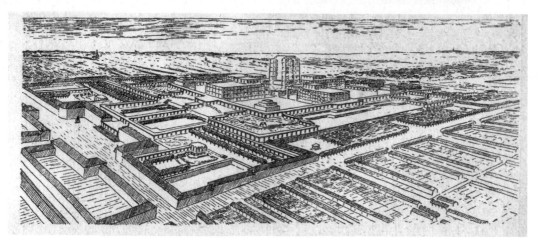

131 Illustration from *Die Stadtkrone* (The City Crown), Bruno Taut, 1919

Friendship; 1916) in Constantinople; the magical grotto he devised within the Große Schauspielhaus (Great Playhouse; 1918–19) **132** in Berlin, where Max Reinhardt staged his musical performances; and the successive variants of his Festspielhaus (Festival Hall; 1920–1) in Salzburg, he introduced a new world of imposing and mysterious forms. In 1919, apropos of the post-war resurrection of the German Werkbund, Poelzig declared: "True understanding of architecture is so unspeakably important because it determines the appearance of our homeland, which has been so disfigured by the half-hearted architecture of recent decades. … But it is not possible to reinstate architecture as a major art overnight. This will be possible only when a coherent major revolution of souls has taken place, when the conviction that we must create things for eternity has gained general recognition." → 7 As an architect with close ties to film and theater, Poelzig designed the set representing medieval Prague in Paul Wegener's *The Golem* (1923), creating an atmosphere as disturbing as that in films like Robert Wiene's *Cabinet of Doctor Caligari* (1920) and Friedrich Murnau's *Nosferatu* (1922). Poelzig continued to use his Expressionist language of stalactites and stalagmites throughout the 1920s, including in his studies of permanent buildings for the Berlin Fair of 1928.

The Expressionist aesthetic of the immediate postwar period also affected young architects whose initial works had been of a more rationalist bent. Gropius, for instance, echoed the engravings of Max Pechstein and Lyonel Feininger in his Märzgefällenen-Denkmal (Monument to the March Dead; 1920–1) in Weimar, with its jagged thrust to the sky. Gropius designed Adolf Sommerfeld's wooden house in Berlin-Steglitz (1920–1), in the same realm of angles and interrupted lines, but with a calmer symmetry. The house's construction was expedited by Sommerfeld's business as a commercial dealer in lumber.

In 1919 Erich Mendelsohn exhibited his wartime sketches from the front lines at the Paul Cassirer Gallery in Berlin. These consisted of very small India-ink perspectives of factories, warehouses, and hangars. He associated the dynamism of their strikingly sculptural forms, which appeared to be frozen in motion, with the "elastic qualities" of new materials: "The living quality of architecture depends upon sensuous seizure by means of touch and sight: upon the terrestrial cohesion of mass, upon the super-terrestrial liberty of light. … Out of its own laws, architecture lays down the conditions that govern its active masses." → 8 Mendelsohn's social connections in Berlin's bourgeois Jewish establishment allowed him to put his ideas into action more quickly than other architects, and his projects had an impact in the United States as early as 1921. → 9 For the newspaper publisher Rudolf Mosse, Mendelsohn, assisted by the young Viennese architect Richard Neutra, built a super-structure on top of the Berliner Tageblatt Building (1921–3) transforming the corner of the block into a kind of ship's prow, with forceful horizontal lines that overpowered the original facade. His Hat Factory complex in Luckenwalde, Germany, (1923) featured concrete buildings with oblique roofs that resembled folds of paper, creating a spectacular sculptural landscape.

Mendelsohn's most powerful building was the laboratory erected for Albert Einstein within the compound of the Potsdam Observatory (1919–21). **133** Intended for experiments with the solar spectrum, the lab combined two distinct elements: a tower topped by a cupola, and a horizontal volume into which light beams from above were guided and collected for analysis. The two elements were integrated in a plastic sculptural mass whose continuous surface made it look as if it were made of concrete rather than stuccoed brick. Though the name

GUT GARKAU

134 Schocken Department Store, Erich Mendelsohn, Chemnitz, Germany, 1926–8

133 Einstein Tower, Erich Mendelsohn, Potsdam, Germany, 1919–21

135 Garkau Farm, Hugo Häring, Scharbeutz-Klingberg, Germany, 1922–6

Einsteinturm (Einstein Tower) is an unmistakable reference to the series of Bismarcktürme (Bismarck Towers) built in many cities throughout Germany before 1914, this structure erected for scientific purposes high above the city was intended, more profoundly, as a kind of urban crown, responding to Taut's ideas. The forward motion that this brick sphinx seems to imply might be a materialization of the *élan vital* described by Henri Bergson in his *L'évolution créatrice* (Creative Evolution; 1907), which was translated into German in 1912. In any case, it suggests a completely different approach to organic form than the mollusklike shapes Finsterlin was drawing at the time.

In 1924 Mendelsohn crossed the ocean with the filmmaker Fritz Lang and discovered the United States. The experience revolutionized his way of thinking. He visited Frank Lloyd Wright and, most importantly, absorbed a new visual culture that he would report on in *Amerika, das Bilderbuch eines Architekten* (America, an Architect's Picture Book; 1926). → 10 After confronting the spectacle of the streets and skyscrapers of New York and Chicago, Mendelsohn transformed his own architecture: the Schocken department stores he built in Chemnitz (1926–8) **134** and Stuttgart (1929) took on almost aerodynamic forms and accentuated the play of light. In Berlin, the WOGA Leisure Complex on the Kufürstendamm (1928–9), dominated by the Universum Movie Theater, integrated contradictory programs into a single aesthetic entity, reflecting an aspiration to harmonious urban design, the absence of which Mendelsohn had deplored in the United States. → 11

Hanseatic Expressionism

The young Expressionists alternated between theorizing and, more episodically, building. Hans Scharoun, a contributor to

the Gläserne Kette, took part in the reconstruction of western Prussia until 1925. Hugo Häring, a member of the Novembergruppe – founded in 1918 by Bruno Beye, Cesar Klein, Moritz Meltzer, Max Pechstein, and Heinrich Richter – built the Garkau Farm in Scharbeutz-Klingberg, near Lübeck (1922–6). **135** The barn and cowshed featured both angular and curved shapes, adhering to the Expressionist ideal of dynamic form. They were covered in exposed brick and boards, concealing their concrete structure and latticelike wood framing, which bore a striking modernity little visible from the outside. The farm's plan was determined by its utilitarian purpose – to house and feed cattle – and faithfully respected the functional requirements that its lyrical exterior seemed to deny. The Hanseatic cities of northern Germany were particularly fertile ground for architectural research; their Gothic brick structures seemed to anticipate the vertical massing of the shipping company offices built in the 1920s. In Hamburg, Fritz Höger designed the Chilehaus (1922–3), **138** a large block with curved, surging facades clad in dark brick and ornamented with medieval motifs. The acute angle of the building's prow seemed a response to New York's Flatiron Building, toward which the vessels of the Hamburg-Amerika Line sailed. Reflecting Hamburg's dominion over the Baltic, the Estonian architect Robert Natus replicated the Chilehaus in miniature in Tallinn in 1936. → 12 The brothers Hans and Oskar Gerson, associated with Höger in the construction of the Sprinkenhof (1926–9), built the Ballinhaus Office Building (1926–9) using a more conventionally orthogonal geometry. Bernhard Hoetger's designs broke loose from the constraints of the office building. His houses (1922) and café (1924–5) in Worpswede, a colony for radical artists, revisited the vocabulary of the north's rural architecture. Perhaps most notable were his buildings

136 Plan for Amsterdam-South, Hendrik Petrus Berlage, 1914–17

137 De Dageraad Housing, Michel de Klerk and Piet Kramer, Amsterdam, Netherlands, 1918–23

138 Chilehaus, Fritz Höger, Hamburg, Germany, 1922–3

on Böttcherstraße in Bremen, which resembled sculptural collages. These, particularly the house for the painter Paula Modersohn-Becker (1923–7) **141** where a rough exterior accompanied an oneiric layout of oddly convoluted rooms, fully exploited the resources of brick.

De Klerk and the Amsterdam School

The obvious parallels between these buildings in Hamburg and Bremen and those erected in Amsterdam by Michel de Klerk beginning in 1915 were not coincidental. Though partly attributable to a shared culture of brick construction, the correspondences went deeper. To some extent, Weimar policies were a continuation of Dutch housing legislation, notably the Woningwet of 1901, which had guaranteed public financing for working-class housing. Regulated by a system of controls and standards, Dutch housing was built through municipal or cooperative programs. The neutrality of the Netherlands during the war allowed the country to launch programs more advanced than those of the combatant nations. While German cities were struggling to reactivate their construction industry, Amsterdam was already flush with building sites. → 13

But the German and Dutch projects also originated in a shared architectural matrix that incorporated the Theosophical theories of J. L. M. Lauweriks and the teaching of Hendrik Petrus Berlage, which had widely circulated in Germany. Meetings of Architectura et amicitia (Architecture and Friendship), a society of Amsterdam professionals established in 1855, hosted an intense debate on the question of *Gemeenschapkunst*, or social art. → 14 Johan Melchior van der Mey's Scheepvaarthuis (House of Shipping Companies; 1911–16) in Amsterdam, which deconstructed and recomposed elements of traditional architectural

language, also seems to anticipate Hoetger's buildings of the 1920s. Among the assistants on the Scheepvaarthuis was the young de Klerk, who designed many competition projects before building the Hillehuis (1912), an apartment house echoing the complex vertical organization of Van der Mey's building. Most significantly, de Klerk's three projects for the Eigen Haard (Own Hearth) cooperative in Amsterdam, built from 1922 to 1926, created a neighborhood in which urban form was absorbed into a continuum of interrelated sculptural effects. The play of the bricks' colors, which range from crimson to orange; the way they are laid both horizontally and vertically; and their diverse shapes, which vary from rectilinear to convex to concave, combine to create a rich world in which the modest size of the housing units is partly compensated for by the buildings' sensuous opulence. The facade is an undulating spectacle with unusual-shaped openings that call to mind woven and embroidered textiles. For the third building, nicknamed "The Ship," (1917–21) **140** de Klerk combined a village theme with a mechanical motif. The housing wraps around a courtyard in which the meeting hall plays the role of rural church while the post office serves as a locomotive pulling the entire complex, which in fact stood alongside the city's main railroad tracks. Next de Klerk collaborated with Piet Kramer on the housing scheme of De Dageraad (The Dawn; 1918–23), **137** a cooperative built as a component of Berlage's plan for Amsterdam-South (1914–17). **136** Here de Klerk presented a clear, open image of low-income housing. He aligned the houses along the street in a continuous wave in which each unit appears to be woven together with its neighbor. Once again he created the illusion of a village community by grouping the units two by two on a central square to form large houses separated by tall chimneys. → 15

139 Cover of *Wendingen* (Turning Points), Issue 2, cover designed by Michel de Klerk, 1918

140 "The Ship," Eigen Haard Housing Cooperative, Michel de Klerk, Amsterdam, Netherlands, 1917–21

141 Paula Modersohn-Becker House, Bernard Hoetger, Bremen, Germany, 1923–7

142 ▶ Second Goetheanum, Rudolf Steiner, Dornach, Switzerland, 1924–8

De Klerk was the most brilliant member of a group that included Dirk Greiner, Margaret Kropholler, and Jan Frederik Staal, all of whom were committed to the genuinely collective effort required to realize the different stages of Berlage's plan. The main activist behind what would soon come to be known as the Amsterdam School, Hendricus Theodorus Wijdeveld, was responsible for its publicity organ, *Wendingen* (Turning Points), **139** a large-format architecture magazine. He edited the magazine from 1918 to 1931, opening it to both experiments that had taken place in Russia since 1917 and new directions in Frank Lloyd Wright's work. In combination with the Expressionist accents latent in de Klerk's work, Wright's forms were sometimes detectable in the new buildings in Amsterdam.

Like many of the Dutch architects, the Austrian Rudolf Steiner had a background in the Theosophical movement. In 1912 he founded the Anthroposophical Society, formulating a secular doctrine inspired by Nietzsche and Goethe. For the community he established in Dornach, near Basel, he erected the Goetheanum (1913–20), a building with two wood domes surrounded by houses in the shape of rocks. This edifice burned down and was replaced by the second Goetheanum (1924–8), **142** a sculptural concrete volume that held an auditorium, a library, and meeting rooms. The large faceted volume inserted into the pastoral Swiss landscape majestically conveyed the aspiration to the total work of art that was one of the founding precepts of Expressionism.

Return to order in Paris

In 1924, seven years after his permanent move to Paris, Le Corbusier diagnosed a case of "acute neurasthenia" and the symptoms of a "breakdown" in the drawings that Bruno Taut had published four years earlier in his book *Die Auflösung der Städte*. [1] Well informed about the art and architecture of imperial Germany, Le Corbusier had turned his back on his youthful experiences there in the first months of World War I. French artists, though strongly in support of the war effort against Germany, had generally resisted the condemnations of Cubism voiced in more chauvinist circles in Paris, where the style had become associated with certain important German-owned collections and galleries and branded a *boche* ("kraut") art form. Yet they also sought during these years to rediscover the threads of a national tradition often identified with classicism, whether rendered literally or as a guiding principle open to multiple interpretations. [2]

Purist forms and urban compositions

In 1913, in his book *Les peintres cubistes*, Guillaume Apollinaire challenged architects to reclaim the torch of innovation from artists and to "construct with sublime intentions." [3] In 1917 a fellow poet, Pierre Reverdy, published an essay by yet another poet Paul Dermée in the first issue of his periodical *Nord-Sud* (North-South). In it Dermée wrote, "After a period of exuberance and force must follow a period of organization, of arrangement, of science – that is to say, a classic age." [4] Such calls to order were heard all the way to the Netherlands and Russia, and they were also picked up by Le Corbusier (still known at this time as Charles-Édouard Jeanneret) and the painter Amédée Ozenfant. In 1920, together with Dermée, Jeanneret and Ozenfant founded *L'Esprit nouveau* (The New Spirit), a multidisciplinary journal that served as the major platform for their theories and critiques until 1925.

In 1918 Jeanneret and Ozenfant published their Purist manifesto *Après le cubisme* (After Cubism). It reflected their equal interest in Greek temples and in the machines introduced into everyday life by the war. The new term "purism" was intended to "express in an intelligible word the character of the modern spirit." In stressing the "invariable," Jeanneret and Ozenfant were not "unmoved by the intelligence that governs certain machines." [5] *L'Esprit nouveau* likewise displayed a keen sense of history and an acute attention to the products of technology. It described itself as an "illustrated international review of contemporary activity," open to experimental psychology, psychoanalysis, and economics. Politically, it supported Bolshevik Russia and Franco-German reconciliation. [6] In a series of controversial essays Le Corbusier reminded "Messrs. les architectes" to "open eyes that do not see" to ships, cars, and airplanes. These provocative articles became the chapters of the book *Vers une architecture* (Toward an Architecture; 1923) **143**, a manifesto that celebrated mechanization, affirmed the necessity of using "regulating lines" to proportion buildings, and advised the study of ancient and Baroque architecture in order to absorb the "lesson of Rome." [7] The impact of Le Corbusier's writings was reinforced by the power of his theoretical projects. His Contemporary City for Three Million Inhabitants, exhibited at the Salon d'Automne (1922), and his Plan Voisin for Paris **144**, shown at the *Exposition Internationale des Arts Décoratifs et Industriels Modernes* (International Exposition of Modern Industrial and Decorative Arts, 1925), described a new metropolitan organism crisscrossed by highways and dominated by the glass towers of a "city of business" – a capitalist version of Taut's Stadtkrone. Le Corbusier surrounded the city with redent housing inspired by Eugène Hénard and with *immeuble-villas* (villa apartments) consisting of double-height dwellings with individual gardens, creating a radically new urban landscape.

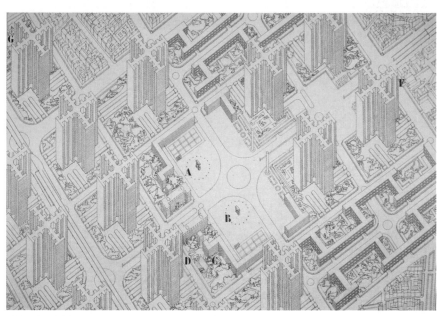

143 Page from *Vers une architecture* (Towards an Architecture), Le Corbusier, 1923

144 Plan Voisin, project, Le Corbusier, Paris, France, 1925

145 La Roche House, Le Corbusier and Pierre Jeanneret, Paris, France, 1923–4

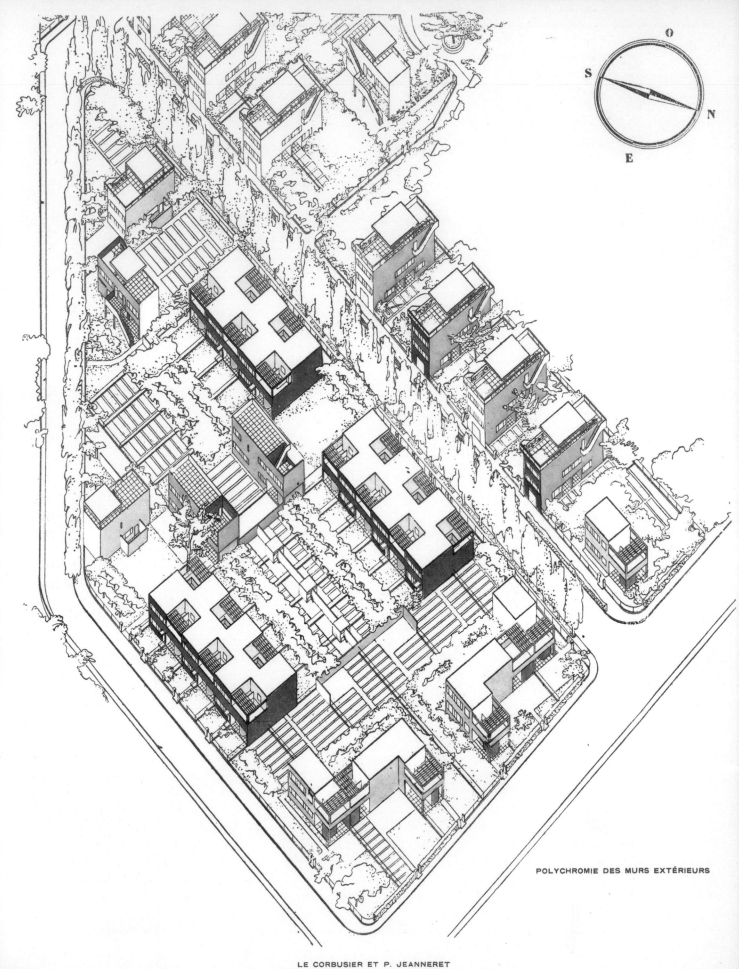

POLYCHROMIE DES MURS EXTÉRIEURS

LE CORBUSIER ET P. JEANNERET
QUARTIERS MODERNES FRUGES, A PESSAC-BORDEAUX - 1927

146 Workers' Houses
(Quartiers modernes Frugès),
Le Corbusier and Pierre Jeanneret,
Pessac, France, 1924–6

147 Stein/de Monzie House, Le Corbusier and Pierre Jeanneret, Garches, France, 1926–7

Le Corbusier and the modern house

During this period Le Corbusier injected the latest developments in painting into two domestic projects: a studio for Ozenfant (1922–3) and, particularly, a house for the Basel-born banker Raoul La Roche (1923–4) **145**. In the latter he radically modified his design after seeing an exhibition of architecture by the De Stijl group at a Paris gallery, which caused him to reconfigure the conventional arrangement of windows on the facade as a composition of opaque planes and glass walls. →[8] Inside, he conceived the house's circulation as a *promenade architecturale*, inspired by the descriptions of processions on the Acropolis in ancient Greece that Auguste Choisy had recounted in his 1899 *Histoire de l'architecture*. Le Corbusier's promenade governs the entire interior of the house from the entrance hall to the painting gallery, which he hung with Cubist canvases that he purchased for La Roche at sales of the Kahnweiler and Uhde collections. Around the same time, he built a home for his parents in the Swiss village of Corseaux on the shore of Lake Geneva (1923–6). A single horizontal window provides this modest dwelling with a view of the mountains and access to the light of the lake. The unshadowed luminosity inside the residence differs from the chiaroscuro of typical interiors just as the brightness of factories differs from the half-light of churches.

Despite his tireless courting of automobile and aviation industrialists, Le Corbusier, who established a professional partnership with his cousin Pierre Jeanneret in 1922, succeeded in building only a single workers' housing complex. **146** This was realized in 1924–6 in Pessac, near Bordeaux, for the industrialist Henri Frugès. Here he brought together the theoretical models he had been working on for ten years, including the Dom-ino

skeletal system and the Maison Citrohan three-story layout; the double-height living room of the latter was inspired by Paris artists' studios. For the Parisian elite he designed large houses, the most complex of which was built in the suburb of Garches for Michael Stein (brother of the writer Gertrude Stein), his wife Sarah Stein, and Gabrielle de Monzie (1926–7) **147**. →[9] The house's interplay of planar elements and cylindrical stairwells seems to transpose the geometry of Purist paintings into space, while the "regulating lines" of the facade draw on the ancient proportions of the golden section. Twenty years later, the architect-critic Colin Rowe found another precedent, detecting a similarity between the proportions of the villa's plan and those of Palladio's villas, which Le Corbusier knew well. →[10]

The weekend house that Le Corbusier built in 1929–31 for Pierre Savoye, a client in the insurance business, in Poissy, near Paris, is one of the canonical buildings of the twentieth century. The villa sits in the middle of a meadow like a flying machine that has just barely touched down. The boxlike structure features three levels interconnected by a ramp that guides the *promenade architecturale*. Wedged between the ground-floor *pilotis* (stilts), through which automobiles could slip in and out, and the top-floor solarium is the main level, an L-shaped floor built around a patio and illuminated by a horizontal strip of windows overlooking the landscape. The vast living room is basically doubled in surface by the patio, while the bedrooms and bathroom echo the floor plans of eighteenth-century Paris apartments.

These houses demonstrated the "Five Points" with which Le Corbusier summed up his contribution to a new architecture in 1927, alluding transparently to Vignola's five classical orders: *pilotis*, freeing up the ground plane; roof terrace, affording sunlight and communion with the skyline; free plan, replacing the "paralyzed plan" of load-bearing structures; ribbon

148 League of Nations competition project, Le Corbusier and Pierre Jeanneret, Geneva, Switzerland, 1927

149 Centrosoyuz (Central Union of Consumer Cooperatives), Le Corbusier and Pierre Jeanneret, Moscow, USSR (Russia), 1928–36

window, offering horizontal vistas; and free facade, whose openings were no longer dependent on traditional structural mechanics. All these points were made possible by the use of reinforced concrete. → 11

Grand vessels in Paris and Geneva

But domestic programs did not satisfy Le Corbusier's ambitions; he aimed for more important commissions. His failure to win the 1927 competition for the headquarters of the League of Nations in Geneva 148 was a personal trauma. His project elevated the principle of *pilotis* and terraces to the scale of a grand public edifice, making the site seem to flow beneath the building and merge with the Alpine landscape. → 12 Despite the publicity campaign mounted by his friends throughout Europe to protest the rejection of his project, the conservative jury remained unswayed. Le Corbusier was also thwarted in his efforts to erect a Mundanéum, or World City, in Geneva; a cultural complex in the spirit of Hendrik Christian Andersen's World City, the project was designed for the philanthropist Paul Otlet using a plan based on the golden section. Le Corbusier's invocation of classical proportions and his ziggurat-shaped museum – to be the centerpiece of the project – spurred attacks from radical architects like the Russian El Lissitzky. Lissitzky's criticism of Le Corbusier's excessive historicism and monumentality was echoed by the Prague critic Karel Teige, who scorned the "puzzling, archaic impression" made by this "metaphysical architecture." → 13 Nonetheless, it was in Moscow that Le Corbusier won his first major commission, for the Centrosoyuz (1928–36) 149, the headquarters of the Central Union of Consumer Cooperatives. Here he greatly amplified the principle of the *promenade architecturale*, designing ramps that rose six stories above a

ground floor punctuated by *pilotis*. As in his League of Nations project, the building combined a curvilinear auditorium volume with orthogonal office wings. But the innovative project – which included a forerunner of central air conditioning based on a system of "neutralizing walls" and "exact respiration" – was too technically advanced for the Soviet Union at this date. Material shortages caused the building's construction to drag on for many years. → 14

In the meantime, the Salvation Army commissioned Le Corbusier to design its City of Refuge in Paris. Realized in 1929–31, the building is a large concrete vessel whose purpose is to house the homeless. With this project, Le Corbusier was finally able to incorporate his fascination with ships into his architecture: he placed the apartment of the project's American patron, Winaretta Singer-Polignac, at the top of the building and arranged the communal spaces on the ground floor like the first-class lounges of a transatlantic liner. Though his "exact respiration" system for circulating air was rendered totally ineffectual by the lack of any device to extract the used air from the building, the Salvation Army hostel remained a didactic example of Le Corbusier's precepts of large-scale construction. So did another important realization in Paris of this period, the Swiss Pavilion at the Cité Universitaire (1929–33).

Perret and the "sovereign shelter"

No other architect on the Paris scene was able to scandalize people with innovations as much as Le Corbusier, although others tried. In a city where architects frequently formulated and implemented their modern ideals in direct competition with one another, there was no such thing as a united front. Le Corbusier's mentor, Auguste Perret, opposed the younger

150 Pavilion of *L'Esprit nouveau*, Le Corbusier and Pierre Jeanneret, Paris, France, 1924–5

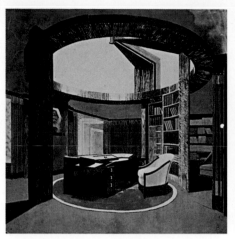

151 Study for a French Embassy, project, Pierre Chareau, Paris, France, 1925

152 Cortot Hall, École Normale de Musique, Auguste Perret, Paris, France, 1928–9

architect's use of the ribbon window, insisting that only "the vertical window frames man [and] agrees with his silhouette." → 15 In Le Raincy, east of Paris, Perret built Notre-Dame de la Consolation (1922) **153**, a church commemorating World War I fighters. Its vaulted nave of reinforced concrete held up by slender columns is illuminated by walls of concrete-framed stained glass. Perret's application of methods developed for factories and other secular structures to a religious edifice caused critics to describe it as "the holy chapel of reinforced concrete" and scorn it as a vulgar "prayer hangar." At the time, Perret's thinking was close to that of the poet Paul Valéry, whose Socratic dialogue *Eupalinos, ou l'architecte* (Eupalinos, or the Architect; 1921), suggested a revived classicism with nationalist accents. → 16 Using the concrete skeleton to emulate Greek monumentality in his public commissions, Perret tirelessly sought to implement his definition of the large building as "a vessel, a framework, a sovereign shelter capable of housing in its unity the variety of organs necessary to fulfill its function." → 17 In 1924 Perret opened an off-site studio of the École des Beaux-Arts near the Bois de Boulogne. It was known as the Palais de Bois (Wood Palace). Contradicting the school's official stance, he encouraged his followers – including Paul Nelson, Ernö Goldfinger, Oscar Nitzchké, and Denis Honegger – to practice an architecture featuring exposed structural elements made expressive by the interplay of light and shadow and the differentiation of finishes. In 1925 he designed the theater at the *Exposition Internationale des Arts Décoratifs et Industriels Modernes*; its three-part stage recalled the one built by Henry van de Velde in Cologne eleven years before. Next he built the stunning Cortot Hall (1928–9) **152**, a dizzyingly steep concert hall that, by using concrete cantilevers, he was able to squeeze into the middle of a tight Paris block.

Paris Art Deco

The 1925 exposition gave Le Corbusier the opportunity to build his Pavilion of *L'Esprit nouveau*. **150** In it he displayed dioramas of his Ville Contemporaine and Plan Voisin and, most significantly, a unit of his *immeuble-villas* outfitted with typical furniture bought from manufacturers' catalogs and a prototype of his standard cabinets. The pavilion was an implicit critique of the program of the exposition, whose directors, Charles Plumet and Louis Bonnier, sought to reassert French supremacy in the applied arts in the face of prewar competition from Germany. The latter's belated invitation to participate was a *de facto* exclusion.

Organized by the Union centrale des arts décoratifs and the Société des artistes décorateurs, or SAD, the 1925 exposition gave pride of place to the successful interior decorators who designed the "ensembles" of furniture associated with department stores as well as to the interior designers who merged art and commerce. They included Émile-Jacques Ruhlmann and the team of Louis Süe and André Mare. → 18 Two designers stood out from the crowd for work that was as elegant as it was cautiously modern: Francis Jourdain, who carefully created unadorned interiors that were in the spirit of Adolf Loos but affordable to all **154**; and Pierre Chareau, whose convertible furniture pieces – notably his cylindrical desk-bookshelf for the SAD pavilion's exhibit "A French Embassy" **151** – contrasted with the static nature of the main contributions. In the same pavilion Robert (Rob) Mallet-Stevens designed a lobby with a linear, abstract geometry that was similar in spirit to his Tourism Pavilion, also at the exposition. Four years later, he, Jourdain, and Chareau were among the founders of the Union des artistes modernes, or UAM, a group devoted to applying the

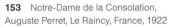

153 Notre-Dame de la Consolation,
Auguste Perret, Le Raincy, France, 1922

154 Smoking Room for a French Embassy, project, Francis Jourdain, Paris, France, 1925

155 Grand Hôtel Métropole, project, Henri Sauvage, Paris, France, 1928

radical modern aesthetic favored by the elite to the needs of a larger populace; it held its first exhibition in 1930. →19
One of the most prolific architects involved in the 1925 exhibition was Henri Sauvage, who created several pavilions for department stores. Sauvage had worked on the development of setback terraced buildings in Paris since before the war. After the war he built both a popular version – a low-income residence on Rue des Amiraux (1922), with a swimming pool at its center – and a bourgeois version called the Studio Building (1926), inspired by ocean liners. He also designed a megalomaniac version for a hotel on the bank of the Seine (1928) **155**. In Nantes, Sauvage built the imposing glass structure of the Decré Department Store (1931, bombed 1944). He also worked on the extension of the Samaritaine Department Store (1928, with Frantz Jourdain) in Paris, where he took a less radical approach since he had to comply with urban-planning regulations.

Mallet-Stevens, or elegant modernism

In 1927 Robert Mallet-Stevens received a unique honor for a living architect: he had a Paris street named after him. →20 He would build six houses on the new Rue Mallet-Stevens (1926–7) **158**. His own, featuring a double-height reception room, stands at the entry to the street. Next to it is the studio and residence of sculptors Jan and Joël Martel, whose quarters are clustered around the vertical cylinder of a staircase that leads to a belvedere topped by a circular "lid." Also on the street is a town house with a 150-seat screening room, built for the film director Eric Allatini, and a house for Madame Reifenberg, a pianist, featuring open living spaces extended by terraces, which offer a full panorama of the other cubistic houses on the block. Many artists and craftsmen, including the glass artist Louis Barillet and the young ironsmith

Jean Prouvé, were involved in building rue Mallet-Stevens. The construction site was headed by Gabriel Guevrekian, an Iranian architect of Armenian descent trained in Vienna.
In 1923 Mallet-Stevens began working on a large villa in Hyères for the art patrons Charles and Marie-Laure de Noailles **156**, who in 1930 would finance Jean Cocteau's film *Blood of a Poet* and Luis Buñuel's *L'âge d'or*. For this house, devoted to pleasure and entertainment, he designed a cubic structure hovering above the city and extended by terraces. He wrote: "It is no longer just some moldings that catch the light, it is the entire facade. The architect sculpts an enormous block, the house." →21 Erected in sections between 1924 and 1928, the house included a room devoted to flowers, the design of which was entrusted to Theo van Doesburg, and it overlooked a Cubist-inspired triangular garden by Guevrekian. In 1929 the American artist Man Ray declared that the "cubic forms" of the château "brought to mind the title of a poem by Mallarmé." →22 He used it as the setting for his disturbing film *Les mystères du château du Dé* (The Mysteries of the Château of Dice), a tableau vivant performed by masked guests. Having designed the sets for Marcel L'Herbier's *L'inhumaine* (The Inhuman Woman; 1923–4) **157**, a film intended to promote French fashion abroad, Mallet-Stevens began building a castle in Mézy for the couturier Paul Poiret (1921–3), but the project was never completed. In Paris he built the Alfa Romeo Garage on Rue Marbeuf (1927), which has a structure supported by concrete arches reminiscent of those in Perret's Théâtre des Champs-Élysées, and an apartment building on Rue Méchain (1928–9), which is a kind of vertical extrusion of the Rue Mallet-Stevens massing system. His largest project was a casino in Saint-Jean de Luz on the Basque coast (1927–8), a large reinforced-concrete building with interiors that make use of motifs first seen at the 1925 exposition.

156 Villa de Noailles, Robert Mallet-Stevens, Hyères, France, 1923–8

157 *L'inhumaine* film set, Robert Mallet-Stevens, 1923–4, for Marcel L' Herbier (director)

159 ► Hotel Nord-Sud, André Lurçat, Calvi, France, 1929–30

158 Houses on Rue Mallet-Stevens, Robert Mallet-Stevens, Paris, France, 1926–7

160 E 1027, Eileen Gray, Roquebrune Cap-Martin, France, 1929

The extent of French modernism

Having made his reputation as a member of Mallet-Stevens's circle, Gabriel Guevrekian received a commission through the painter Sonia Delaunay to design a town house for the couturier Jacques Heim in Neuilly (1927), reinforcing the significant link between architecture and fashion. No less close to Mallet-Stevens was the engineer and architect Georges-Henri Pingusson, who remodelled the facade and neon marquee of the Théâtre des Menus-Plaisirs (1926–9) and built the Paul Arrighi power plant in Vitry-sur-Seine (1926–32), a rare French example of modern aesthetics intersecting with a full-fledged industrial program.

At the initiative of his brother Jean, at that time a painter with ties to Surrealism, André Lurçat built the Villa Seurat (1925–7), an alley of artist studios in Paris begun two years before Rue Mallet-Stevens. The scheme consists of a sequence of six buildings made of cubic volumes with corner window openings. There are clear Loosian accents and above all a play with the continuity of the street wall. Across from Parc Montsouris, Lurçat built a house for the painter Walter Guggenbühl (1927). A cube set on a trapezoidal base extended by a bow window and a pergola, its simplified geometry and the repetitive configuration of openings on its planar surfaces had nothing to do with the underlying structural skeleton. This led the critic Marie Dormoy justly to contrast Lurçat's "fake concrete" to Perret's use of the material. → 23 The purest expression of Lurçat's approach may be seen in the linear and prismatic architecture of the small Hôtel Nord-Sud (1929–30) **159**, near the Corsican city of Calvi, which resembles a ship run aground on a reef.

While the most radical faction of French architecture managed to consolidate its positions during the 1920s, it occupied a small field. Large public and private projects continued to be awarded to more conservative firms. One notable exception was Tony Garnier's work

for the Radical-Socialist mayor of Lyons, Édouard Herriot. → 24 After completing the La Mouche Cattle Market and Slaughterhouse (1906–14), which featured a great market hall constructed of steel trusses and inspired by the Galerie des Machines, Garnier continued his work in Lyons with the États-Unis low-income housing development (1921–34), a suburban complex of airy concrete blocks, and the Grange-Blanche hospital (1910–34), a series of pavilions connected by a network of underground passages. The structural clarity of Garnier's work was increasingly inflected by classical nostalgia, however. A more monumental aspect of his work was visible in his many designs for memorials, while Mediterranean accents surfaced in his more intimate patio houses.

Trained in Lyons as part of Garnier's circle, Michel Roux-Spitz combined the smooth geometry of the moderns with more static modes of composition in his Paris apartment buildings, such as the ones on Rue Guynemer (1925–8) **161** and Avenue Henri Martin (1930–1). In the latter he incorporated features borrowed from naval architecture, with a certain heaviness. Pol Abraham and Charles Siclis provided their own interpretations, whether more tectonic or more spectacular, of the passion for structural expression that had spread in the 1920s. Eileen Gray, an Irish designer active in Paris, was the only woman to see her contribution acknowledged, with E 1027 (1929), **160** a villa she built on the Riviera for and with Jean Badovici, the editor of *L'Architecture vivante*. While the end of the decade saw an international alliance of radical architects throughout Europe, French architecture seemed to have two faces. The first was embodied in the experimental, sometimes provocative work that came out of the circle around Le Corbusier. Also innovative but more commercial, the second face, initially revealed in the *Exposition Internationale des Arts Décoratifs et Industriels Modernes*, produced reverberations that would be felt in North America and Britain as well as in colonial settings.

Dada, De Stijl, and Mies: from subversiveness to elementarism

By the final months of World War I there were already conflicting attempts to overthrow the dominant forces in art and architecture. Among the new movements, Expressionism had roots in prewar Europe, but other contenders, which appeared even before the German surrender, lacked such antecedents, instead emerging from the deep crisis provoked by battles among intellectuals and artists.

The Dada blast

Dada, the most destructive of these movements, had its moment between 1915 and 1923. It was characterized by the subversion of traditional representation, a preference for the new technique of montage, and a bluntly asserted nihilism. A nomadic phenomenon that changed according to its setting, it was founded in Zurich, then gravitated to New York and Germany, and finally settled in Paris. → 1 The evenings organized at Zurich's Cabaret Voltaire by the Germans Hugo Ball, Hans Richter, and Richard Huelsenbeck; the Alsatian Hans (Jean) Arp; and the Romanians Tristan Tzara and Marcel Janco were the opening act of a collective revolt against the very concept of art. The arrival of Francis Picabia and Marcel Duchamp in New York marked another distinctive Dada phase, particularly after they met Man Ray. Picabia's collages of mechanical parts and Duchamp's *Fountain*, a urinal that served as a "ready-made" art object, exhibited in 1917, signaled the Dadaists' interest in anonymous production and machines, which they derisively parodied and destroyed. Leaving Zurich for Berlin, Ball and Huelsenbeck expanded their activities after meeting George Grosz, Raoul Hausmann **162**, and John Heartfield, combining an ironic play on the icons of American civilization with an exploration of photomontage techniques. The Dadaists' involvement with architecture was not

well developed, although they had a longstanding interest in the "machine art" announced by Vladimir Tatlin's first constructions in Russia. From Berlin, Dada scattered to Cologne with Arp and Max Ernst, and to Hanover with Kurt Schwitters, until Picabia and Tzara finally shifted the movement's center of gravity to Paris, where it led to the birth of Surrealism in 1924. The legacy of these intense years was a vigorous impulse to challenge the traditional categories of art and architecture. It would have widespread and lasting effects, especially in Weimar Germany. The network connecting the members of the Dada galaxy to architectural movements branched out across the map; artists and architects at the edges of the movement went on to play important roles in less radical groups like the Arbeitsrat für Kunst and the German Werkbund.

The new forms of De Stijl

In the Netherlands, the Expressionism of the Amsterdam School was still the dominant force. But beginning in 1916 a radical movement took shape under the name De Stijl, a term that may be traced back to both Gottfried Semper's treatise *Der Stil* (Style) and Viollet-le-Duc's call to architects to define "the" style for modern architecture and construction (as opposed to choosing among a range of competing historical styles). Hendrik Petrus Berlage advanced both these ideas in the Dutch context. De Stijl never became a structured movement; its unstable and dynamic sphere of influence was centered around a monthly journal and a slogan. This irregularity seemed to contradict its main objective: for the artist to connect visual experience to metaphysical ideas, thereby creating harmonic works of art and reclaiming a central place in society. The search for a *nieuwe beelding* or *neue Gestaltung* – a Neo-Plasticism of a highly metaphysical order – was at odds

162 *Tatlin at Home*, Raoul Hausmann, 1920

164 ▶ *Les Architectes du Groupe De Stijl, Theo van Doesburg and Cornelis van Eesteren* exhibition, Galerie de l'effort moderne, Paris, France, 1923

163 Germany Pavilion (Barcelona Pavilion), Ludwig Mies van der Rohe, Barcelona, Spain, 1929, rebuilt 1983–6

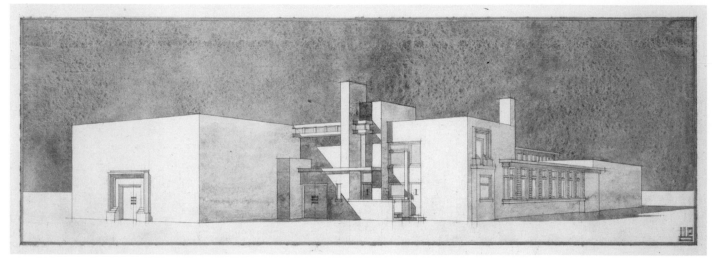

165 Factory, project, J. J. P. Oud, Pomerand, Netherlands, 1919

with Dada's biting irony. The members of the De Stijl circle ultimately aspired to positive creation, even if they first had to go through a phase of destroying conventions.

The initial issues of the journal *De Stijl* appeared in mid-1917 in Leiden under the editorship of the painter Theo van Doesburg. Contributors included the painters Piet Mondrian, Bart van der Leck, and Gino Severini; the architect J. J. P. Oud; and Vilmos Huszár, who designed the journal's logo. The group that assembled around *De Stijl* had already shared several experiences. Van der Leck had collaborated with Berlage in building the Sint Hubertus Hunting Lodge in Hondersloo for the Kröller-Müller family (1919). Van Doesburg and Oud had collaborated on the creation of a colorful, rhythmic interior for the De Vonk Vacation House in Noordwijkerhout (1917) and on the Allegonda Villa in Katwijk aan Zee (1917). Oud and Van Doesburg later went their separate ways following disputes over a project for the Spangen Low-Income Housing Development in Rotterdam, where the architect insisted on respecting economic limitations that the painter could not tolerate. → 2

Van Docsburg and Jan Wils together built the De Lange House in Alkmaar (1916–17), and Huszár and P. J. C. Klaarhamer, a friend of Berlage, joined efforts on the De Arendshoeve House in Voorburg (1916–19). During this initial phase, each member of De Stijl sought to establish his place in a collective endeavor. But starting in 1921, each participant began trying to achieve his own synthesis of painting, sculpture, and architecture. → 3 In this new phase, Van Doesburg became so domineering that by the time Mondrian and Oud left the group, he had totally isolated himself. Nonetheless, he was able to establish a European network by associating with El Lissitzky and Kurt Schwitters, and he lived for a period in Weimar, where he was unsuccessful in securing a teaching position at the Bauhaus.

In purely architectural terms, the founders of De Stijl followed distinct paths, with their production taking very different shapes. Van Doesburg was more theoretical and experimental, while Oud, Wils, and Gerrit Rietveld, an associate of the group beginning in 1919, were more professionally oriented. Mondrian also experimented in three dimensions, notably on the interior of his studio on Rue du Départ in Paris (1921–36) **166** and on his project for the Salon de Madame B. in Dresden (1926).

Van Doesburg's involvement in architectural projects began in 1917 and developed with the interior of the De Ligt House in Katwijk (1919), furnished by Rietveld. Van Doesburg told Oud that the house was "a painting in three dimensions." → 4 In 1923 he collaborated with the young architect Cornelis van Eesteren, whom he had met in Weimar, on the design of a concourse for the University of Amsterdam (1923). The stained-glass ceiling and the flat planes of colors painted on the walls conflicted with the orthogonal geometry of the plan, as if the chromatic and the spatial aspects of the project were totally unconnected. He also realized in collaboration with Van Eesteren three models shown in October and November 1923 at the exhibition *Les Architectes du Groupe De Stijl* at the Galerie de l'effort moderne in Paris **164**. This exhibition marked a crucial turning point in postwar architecture. The models were genuine three-dimensional objects in their own right, but their vertical and horizontal planes of color entirely dispensed with conventional notions of the window. The least radical of the three was a town house project supposedly intended for Léonce Rosenberg, the gallery's owner, which had a realistic-looking setting. The second model, a project for an artist's house, had welded-lead frames and planar color surfaces and recalled Mondrian's painted compositions with black lines. The third, a project for a private house **169**, was the most complex, and provided the

166 Mondrian Studio, Piet Mondrian, Paris, France, 1921–36

167 The Aubette Cinema and Dance Hall, Theo van Doesburg, Strasbourg, France, 1926–8, recontruction 1990–4 and 2006–8

168 ▶ Schröder House, Gerrit Rietveld, Utrecht, Netherlands, 1924

basis for Van Doesburg's subsequent "counter-constructions," in which "plane, line, and mass [were] freely arranged in a three-dimensional relationship." → 5 The models offered as synthetic a representation of three-dimensional space as the axonometrics drawn by Auguste Choisy in his 1899 *Histoire de l'architecture*. They had a strong impact on architects in Paris like Robert Mallet-Stevens and Le Corbusier. In turn, De Stijl annexed the French architects' work in the issue of its journal published in 1927 commemorating the group's tenth anniversary.

On the occasion of the 1923 exhibition, Van Doesburg attempted to provide a theoretical context for his work with a manifesto entitled "Vers une construction collective" (Toward a Collective Construction). Published the following year, it declared: "The idea that art is an *illusion divorced* from real life must be abandoned. The word 'Art' means nothing to us. We demand that it be replaced by the *construction of our environment according to creative laws* derived from well-defined principles. These laws, which are akin to those of economics, mathematics, technology, hygiene, and so forth, encourage a new plastic unity." → 6

Van Doesburg builds

The only large-scale project realized by Van Doesburg was the Aubette **167**, a dance hall, cinema, and restaurant on Place Kléber in Strasbourg (1926–8, restored 2008). The diagonal composition of his addition totally upturned the orthogonality of Jacques-François Blondel's existing building of 1778. The disconnection intensified by the use of color in the University of Amsterdam concourse characterized the project in Strasbourg as well. As Van Doesburg asserted, the principle of diagonal "counter-construction" called into question the horizontality and verticality of the architectural box: "Since the architectonic

elements were based upon orthogonal relationships, this room had to accommodate itself to a diagonal arrangement of colors, to a counter-composition which, by its nature, was to resist all the tensions of architecture. … If I were asked what I had in mind when I constructed this room, I should be able to reply: to oppose to the material room in three dimensions a supermaterial and pictorial, diagonal space." → 7 The originality of Van Doesburg's design, which was executed by Oscar Nitzchké and Denis Honegger, two students of Perret, was reinforced by comparisons with the undulating forms of Jean Arp's dance hall in the Aubette's cellar and Sophie Taueber-Arp's two-dimensional work in its tearoom. Van Doesburg ventured into the realm of urban planning with his City of Circulation project (1924–9), a complex of square eleven-story towers supported at their corners by sturdy piers that opened the ground level to automobiles. Finally, with the help of the young Dutch architect Abraham Elzas, he built his own house-studio in Meudon Val-Fleury, south of Paris (1927–30). Both in its details and in the use of *pilotis* to accommodate a small car, it was closer to Le Corbusier's villas than to his own more geometric work of 1923. A hyperactive figure, Van Doesburg used numerous pseudonyms to cloak his identity, which allowed him both to put forward quasi-Constructivist ideas and to indulge in Dadaist games. He founded the Concrete Art movement and later participated in establishing the Abstraction-Création group, and he continued to pursue a central role on the European scene until he died in 1931.

Oud and Rietveld, from furniture to house design

At the Paris exhibition of 1923, Oud showed his Purmerend Factory (1919) **165**, a project that dated from the early, more

170 Housing Development, J. J. P. Oud, Hoek van Holland, Netherlands, 1924–7

171 Kiefhoek Housing Development, J. J. P. Oud, Rotterdam, Netherlands, 1925–9

172 Schröder House, Gerrit Rietveld, Utrecht, Netherlands, 1924, axonometic of the second floor

169 Private House, project, Theo van Doesburg and Cornelis van Eesteren, 1923

collective phase of De Stijl and contained echoes of Frank Lloyd Wright. In his essay "Kunst en machine" (Art and Machine; 1917), Oud denounced "romantic" approaches, describing style as the result of two different trends: "the one, the technically industrial, which one might call the positive trend, aims at the aesthetic representation of products of a technical ingenuity. The second, which one might, in comparison, call the negative trend (although it is equally positive in its expression!) – i.e., art – aims to arrive at objectivity by reduction (abstraction). The unity of these two trends forms the essence of the new style." [8]
After a series of visually powerful theoretical projects, such as his seaside apartments of 1917, Oud built several significant housing developments. In the design of the Oud-Mathenesse Garden Suburb in Rotterdam (1922–3) he had to follow existing design guidelines, and his contribution was limited to selecting color schemes for the doors. Only in the superintendent's house, with its vivid colors and orthogonal shapes, was he able to implement the ideal of formal balance prescribed by De Stijl. Two years later Oud's facade for the Café De Unie (1925, bombed 1940) brought the new aesthetic to the very heart of Rotterdam.
With his next housing developments, Oud introduced new elements – for instance, the treatment of his buildings' exterior walls simply as skin rather than as load-bearing structures. His Hoek van Holland Housing Development (1924–7) **170** is the most lyrical. Built near the estuary of the Maas River, the development has rounded end-units, and the uniform line of balconies reflects Oud's interpretation of Le Corbusier's "reminder" about ocean liners. Though the Kiefhoek Development (1925–9) **171** in Rotterdam was far larger, Oud treated it in a more elemental manner. He abandoned the symmetry still in use in Hoek van Holland, instead aligning the parallel rectangular blocks of the two-story houses as if they formed part of a fabric that could be

infinitely expanded on all sides. Tellingly, the church built in 1929 for the development was a rigidly rectangular, factory-like box. Other architects explored ideas similar to those of De Stijl. Robert van 't Hoff was the most literal of the many Dutch architects who used a vocabulary derived from Frank Lloyd Wright's houses, notably in his Henny House in Huis ter Heide (1915–19), where he emulated a Prairie House exterior. Wright's hold on the imagination of Dutch architects was equally evident in Wils's design for the De Dubbele Sleutel (The Double Key) Restaurant (1918), where the exterior of the building clearly expressed its interior volumes. The sculptural aspects of Wils's Papaverhof Residential Development (1919–22) in The Hague contrasted with the more industrial leanings of Oud's developments.
The cabinetmaker Gerrit Rietveld, who had briefly made copies of Frank Lloyd Wright's furniture for Robert van 't Hoff, was involved with De Stijl's activities from the beginning. He conceived furniture prototypes composed of basic shapes – wood planes and standard profiles – sliced in ways that visually extended the volume of the objects. His most provocative piece from this period was the Red and Blue Armchair of 1918, which he later explained "was made to the end of showing that a thing of beauty, e.g., a spatial object, could be made of nothing but straight, machined materials." [9]
Rietveld, who rejected the inhibiting patronage of Van Doesburg, gave the most convincing interpretation of De Stijl's longing for a synthesis of the arts with his Schröder House (1924) **168, 172** in Utrecht. Located at the end of a row of banal brick buildings, the house plays with vertical and horizontal planes in three dimensions. Individually, the rooms are very small but flow into each other. Sliding partitions make it possible to modify the floor plans of the two main levels, which are partly lit by a small skylight. The intersection of planes and linear elements and the

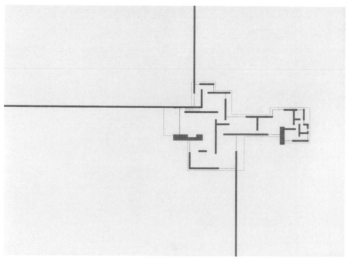

174 Concrete Office Building, project, Ludwig Mies van der Rohe, Berlin, Germany, 1923

175 Office Building, Friedrichstraße competition project, Ludwig Mies van der Rohe, Berlin, Germany, 1921

173 Brick Country House, project, Ludwig Mies van der Rohe, Berlin, Germany, 1923

articulation of joints and railings make the house's interior spaces as difficult to grasp from the inside as they are from the outside. Walls are no longer the single determining factor of space. Actually very compact, the house was not intended to be a manifesto for an aesthetic reinterpretation of domestic functions but rather, according to Rietveld, to create formal clarity and intensify the experience of space. [10] Projects by the Vienna-based artist and architect Friederich Kiesler, invited in 1923 to join De Stijl, seem to echo Rietveld's furniture and to transform it into broader, more inclusive spatial systems: the *Leger- und Trägersystem*, a flexible and independent hanging system for gallery displays, and the *Raumbühne*, or space stage, were constructed at the *Ausstellung neuer Theatertechnik* (Exhibition of New Theater Technology) in Vienna in 1924; while the "City in Space" appeared at the 1925 *Exposition Internationale des Arts Décoratifs et Industriels Modernes* in Paris. [11]

Mies van der Rohe's theoretical projects

Van Doesburg forged a close connection between the Netherlands and Germany not only through his presence on the doorstep of the Bauhaus but also through his participation in the Congress of Revolutionary Artists held in Düsseldorf in 1922. There he founded a short-lived "Constructivist International" together with Hans Richter and El Lissitzky. [12] In July 1923 Richter, Lissitzky, and Werner Gräff, who had attended Van Doesburg's lectures at the Bauhaus, published the first issue of the journal *G*, subtitled *Material zur elementare Gestaltung* (Materials for Elemental Form-Creation). Its program was to disseminate images of the technological world and to propose an architecture based on the *Sachlichkeit*, or objectivity, of construction systems. Van Doesburg published his own manifesto

"Zur elementaren Gestaltung" (On Elemental Form-Creation) in *G*. One of the principal supporters of and contributors to *G* was Ludwig Mies van der Rohe, who published his theoretical project for a Concrete Office Building **174** in the same issue that carried Van Doesburg's manifesto. It was accompanied by his own manifesto "Bürohaus" (Office Block), a first expression of his theoretical positions, in which he declared that "Architecture is the spatially apprehended will of the epoch," drawing on the ideas of Berlage, the precursor he most admired, and Behrens, who had considered architecture the "rhythmic incorporation of the spirit of the time." [13] A few months later, Van Doesburg invited Mies to participate in the De Stijl exhibition at the Galerie de l'Effort moderne.

Beginning in 1921, Mies conceived several iconoclastic projects. In a competition entry for a glass office building **175** on the Friedrichstraße in Berlin, he submitted a design for a glass prism with a triangular plan. The angular volume consisted entirely of a curtain wall, without base or cornice, which appeared to extend the glazing of the nearby train station over the entirety of its 80-meter (260-foot) structure. A radical response to New York's Flatiron Building – which the Berlin Dadaists had illustrated in their journal – Mies's project seemed to materialize Alfred Stieglitz's photos of Manhattan construction sites. Access to the upper floors was provided by a central elevator core, while narrow canyons lined with glass allowed light to penetrate to the interior of the site. The transparent facades revealing stacks of offices called to mind a beehive – a metaphorical term Mies used to identify the building in the competition. [14] In 1922 he elaborated a second version of the project in which the angular facades gave way to a more fluid and sinuous outline, praised by critics for its "Gothic power." [15]

176 Monument to Karl Liebknecht and Rosa Luxemburg, Ludwig Mies van der Rohe, Berlin, Germany, 1926, demolished 1935

177 Hermann Lange House, Ludwig Mies van der Rohe, Krefeld, Germany, 1928–9

After his Concrete Office project, which was an abstract interpretation of the palazzo block that Peter Behrens had built earlier for Mannesmann, Mies conceived a concrete "Country House" (1923), about which he would declare, "We know no forms, only problems of construction." → 16 The house extended horizontally across the site and reflected Mies's awareness of Wright's houses. His Brick Country House **173**, designed the same year, was more provocative. An assemblage of brick elements, the house consisted of orthogonal volumes joined in a free-flowing continuum. For Mies, this "series of spatial effects" was the result of "the wall [losing] its enclosing character and [serving] only to articulate the house organism." → 17

Up to this point, Mies's only real commissions were for bourgeois houses, for which he employed a traditionalist language. He was able to impose more radical views upon his clients only after 1925. Initially, he used brick in an aesthetic, expressive way, as in the Wolf House in Guben and especially in the Monument to Karl Liebknecht and Rosa Luxemburg (1926) **176** in Berlin, a sculptural interpretation of a wall evoking the execution of the two Spartacist leaders. Beginning with his houses for the textile industrialists Hermann Lange (1928–9) **177** and Josef Esters (1928) in Krefeld, his use of brick ceased to be load bearing. These two opulent homes, whose facades brought to mind the factories of the neighboring Ruhr region, had steel structures, which made it possible to superimpose very different floor plans on two different levels: large rooms to display the owners' collections on the ground floor, bedrooms above. Mies soon applied himself to a more radical annihilation of traditional domestic space. The first building to undergo such treatment, the Germany Pavilion at the 1929 Barcelona International Exposition **163**, did not have much of a program beyond its ceremonial purpose. The latent fluidity of his Brick

Country House began to be palpable in this sequence of open rooms resting on a podium and evoking the garden structures of Karl Friedrich Schinkel, which Mies admired. Its stone and glass partitions defined a free-flowing space and were clearly distinct from the load-bearing steel frame – despite a few invisible compromises. The dominant element was a wall of golden onyx, intended as a backdrop for the king of Spain's reception by German officials. In this space – unregulated by any axial system, open to diagonal views, and designed to accommodate visitors' movements – the only perceptible symmetry was the horizontal one between floor and ceiling, making the vertical space of the pavilion practically reversible. → 18

The promise of a new type of domestic space first glimpsed in Barcelona was brought to fruition in the house of Fritz and Grete Tugendhat (1928–30) **178, 179** in Brno, Czechoslovakia. Perched on a hill overlooking the city, the house reproduced the fluid floor plan of the Barcelona Pavilion, but this time areas had well-defined purposes, as if the partitions between rooms had been erased once the plan was completed. According to the critic Paul Westheim, Mies conceived the house as "a circulation route leading from room to room according to [the owners'] style of living." Westheim continued: "[T]he home must be considered entirely as a kind of business that, like any other business, is based on the principle of an articulation of various functions. No room should be isolated and cut off from the others. Even more, continuity between the rooms is to be pursued. The entire space is to be arranged organically, according to its envisaged uses." → 19 As at Barcelona, the living room, which overlooked the city, was backed with an onyx wall. The dining room was defined by a cylindrical partition of rosewood. In 1930, thanks to his very public success in Barcelona, Mies was named director of the Bauhaus in Dessau, where he would radically change the pedagogy of architecture.

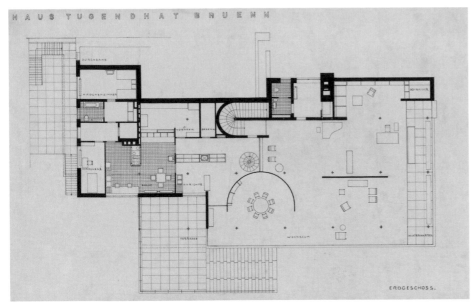

178, 179   Tugendhat House, Ludwig Mies van der Rohe, Brno, Czechoslovakia (Czech Republic), 1928–30

Architectural education in turmoil

World War I had contradictory effects on architectural schools. A number of innovations shook them to their very core during the 1920s, yet in most countries education remained staunchly conservative and the established centers did not relinquish their privileged position. At the same time, students in the postwar era moved more easily between schools, gravitating to the new polarities represented by pedagogical programs in Germany, Russia, and America, in search of learning that conveyed both the excitement of modern technologies and the energy of the radical movements that had appeared in the wake of the war.

The Beaux-Arts and the alternatives

At the École des Beaux-Arts in Paris, the memorial to hundreds of students who had died in the war served as a powerful reminder of the recent bloodbath. After the Allied victory, the school fell back on established routines, **180** and attempts at renewal that had emerged before the war were shelved. [1] Nonetheless, the school retained its worldwide prestige for a while, and, despite weaker enrollment by students from the United States, it continued to attract Latin Americans, including the Venezuelan Carlos Raúl Villanueva, and East Europeans like the Romanian Horia Creangă. A reversal of sorts took place when French graduates, including Marcel Chappey, Robert Camelot, and Raymond Lopez, received the Delano grants created after the war by the American Institute of Architects to draw the most brilliant young professionals to North America, thus inaugurating a modern *grand tour* in which Chicago and New York replaced Athens and Rome. [2]

In Paris, all alternatives to the official mode of architectural training failed. The atelier opened by Robert Mallet-Stevens in 1925 at the École Spéciale d'Architecture **181** closed after a few months. Even though Auguste Perret's atelier at the Palais de Bois was officially associated with the École des Beaux-Arts, his students consistently received failing grades in the École's project reviews and sometimes even had to disguise their affiliation with the atelier to have any chance of passing. In 1934 André Lurçat set up an autonomous atelier, where the Marxist art historian Max Raphaël gave a few lectures, but this effort was also short lived. [3]

In the United States, where the teaching of architecture was universally based on the Beaux-Arts model, teachers who had been trained in Paris but were aware of new trends initiated attempts at modernization in the early 1920s. Paul Philippe Cret, who had been a student in Jean-Louis Pascal's atelier at the Beaux-Arts, became a professor at the University of Pennsylvania in 1903, adjusting Julien-Azaïs Guadet's doctrine of composition to modern programs. In 1927 Jean Labatut, one of Victor Laloux's former students, began teaching at the American summer school in Fontainebleau, France, which had been founded by his master in 1923. The following year Labatut was hired to teach at Princeton University, where he would remain until the 1960s. [4] Another former student of Laloux and an instructor at Fontainebleau, Jacques Carlu, started teaching at the Massachusetts Institute of Technology in 1924 and remained there as head professor of architecture until 1933. Jean-Jacques Haffner, who had been at Harvard since 1922, was appointed to Carlu's position in 1938.

Yet by the mid-1920s, the French were beginning to lose their preeminence in American universities. The 1922 *Chicago Tribune* Tower competition brought new design concepts to the attention of academic institutions. Eliel Saarinen, winner of the competition's second prize, was recruited by Emil Lorch to teach at the University of Michigan Architecture School in Ann Arbor.

180 Grand Prix de Rome project, École des Beaux-Arts, Bernard Zehrfuss, 1939

181 Le Corbusier, Robert Mallet-Stevens and Auguste Perret at the École Spéciale d'Architecture, Paris, France, c. 1939

There he implemented a new curriculum with his Danish colleague, Knud Lonberg-Holm, who had designed, but not submitted, a radically modernist entry to the Tribune Tower contest. In 1925 Saarinen designed the campus of the Cranbrook Kingswood School (later the Cranbrook Academy of Art), and he became director there in 1932.

The Weimar Bauhaus

The most intense search for new educational methods took place in Germany, often picking up where prewar efforts had left off. Didactic programs were developed in accord with the conception of architecture as an experimental discipline for which knowledge of modern art, psychology, and industry was necessary. Apart from art schools like the Kunstschule Debschitz in Munich, the Frankfurter Kunstschule, the Akademie für Kunst und Kunstgewerbe in Breslau, and the Reimann-Schule in Berlin, by far the most innovative program was launched in Weimar in 1919. →[5] Five years earlier, the Belgian Henry van de Velde, who had founded a school there, had resigned under pressure from nationalist attacks. He recommended that it be entrusted to Walter Gropius, August Endell, or Hermann Obrist. Though the youngest of the three, Gropius was chosen, and it was through his initiative that the Kunstgewerbeschule (Arts and Crafts School) and the Hochschule für Bildende Kunst (Higher School of Fine Arts) were united in April 1919 under the name of the Staatliches Bauhaus (State Bauhaus). →[6]
In his founding program, Gropius described the goal of the new school: "to bring together all creative efforts into one whole, to reunify all the disciplines of practical art – sculpture, painting, handicrafts, and the crafts – which are inseparable components of a new architecture." He continued, "The

ultimate, if distant aim of the Bauhaus is the unified work of art – the great building – in which there is no distinction between monumental and decorative art." →[7] Initially this program was steeped in a mystical, Expressionist mood. The original faculty consisted primarily of artists: Lyonel Feininger, Johannes Itten, Paul Klee, Wassily Kandinsky, and Oskar Schlemmer. Within a few years László Moholy-Nagy replaced Itten. The Bauhaus curriculum began with a *Vorkurs*, an introductory course developed by Itten dedicated to the exploration of drawing, color, and materials. It continued in workshops geared to producing designs for actual clients. Architecture, although not taught as such until 1927, was the ultimate goal of the curriculum, which aimed for "mutual planning of extensive, utopian structural designs – public buildings and buildings for worship – aimed at the future." →[8]
Europe discovered Gropius's ambitious program at an exhibition held in Weimar in 1923. **183** Its aim was to maintain an ongoing relationship between the school and the public, an objective specifically set out in the 1919 manifesto. An integral part of the exhibition, the Haus am Horn, **185** designed by Georg Muche, provided an idea of the Bauhaus's architectural orientation. Built on a square plan, this experimental house with a central room suggested a family life without any servants; the kitchen was treated as a workstation and, with its panoptic view, a site of visual control over the household. Bauhaus students, including Marcel Breuer, furnished the Haus am Horn's interiors. The exhibit at the Bauhaus, entitled *Kunst und Technik – eine neue Einheit* (Art and Technology: A New Unity), made clear the school's new orientation toward industrial production, while the projects gathered under the title "Internationale Architektur" clearly positioned its experiments at the forefront of the European avant-garde. →[9]

183 Bauhaus exhibition, Walter Gropius, Weimar, Germany, 1923

182 Staatliches Bauhaus, Walter Gropius, Dessau, Germany, 1925–6

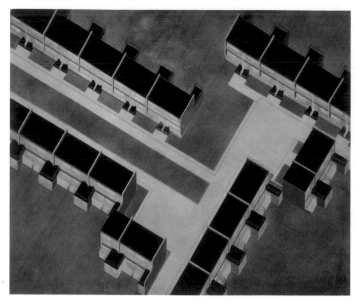

184 Törten Housing Estate, Walter Gropius, Dessau, Germany, 1926–8

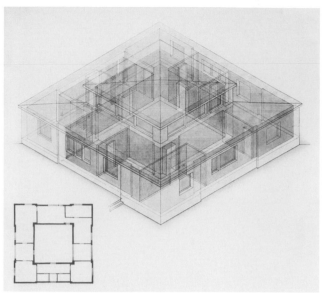

185 Haus am Horn, Georg Muche, Weimar, Germany, 1923

The Bauhaus in Dessau and Berlin

In 1924 the local government in Saxony rejected Gropius's program, forcing him to move the school to a new building in Dessau, **182** a manufacturing center closer to Berlin. Opened in 1926, the new facility, which Gropius designed, exemplified the principles of functional clarity and modularity now taught in its studios. Each element of the pinwheel-plan structure was conceived to supply the space and light needed for its specific functions. The workshops, for example, had glass roofs, while the students' living quarters had vertical windows and balconies. Gropius also built houses for the faculty nearby, providing his staff **188** with ample dwellings designed for artistic work and for entertaining. → 10 With the experimental Törten Housing Estate (1926–8), **184** commissioned by the municipality of Dessau, the school was able to address architectural questions at an urban scale. In conceiving these modest modules for working-class tenants in buildings made of precast concrete components, Gropius emulated the automobile assembly line, down to his linear organization of the construction site. Also built in Törten was a prefabricated Steel House by Muche and Richard Paulick, another example of the Bauhaus's effort to emulate factory production. → 11

In 1928 Gropius stepped down as director and was succeeded by Hannes Meyer. Under the left-wing Swiss architect the teaching of architecture became more structured. Meyer's functionalist agenda was encapsulated in a manifesto entitled "bauen" ("to build"), which stated, "All things in this world are a product of the formula: (function times economy) … building is nothing but organization: social, technical, economic, psychological organization." → 12 Ludwig Hilberseimer began offering courses in urban planning, and preliminary research on functional data and the

siting of buildings became an important component of the curriculum. The students built an apartment house in Dessau (1930) during Meyer's tenure, while the school became increasingly receptive to its director's communist ideas.

Meyer's political activism and his conflict-ridden relationships with many of the other Bauhaus *Meister* (masters) led to his being fired and replaced by Mies van der Rohe in 1930. With the support of his friend Lilly Reich, an interiors architect, Mies accentuated the shift of the Bauhaus toward architecture that had begun under Meyer and strove to make the school more professional. Exercises ceased to be utopian, and students focused instead on designing courtyard houses and studying the extended urban fabrics that interested Hilberseimer. → 13

In 1932 the municipality of Dessau, which had been taken over by the Nazis, evicted the Bauhaus. Mies reconstituted the school as a private institution based in an abandoned factory in Berlin-Steglitz until pressure from the Nazis forced him to close it down in the summer of 1933. This triggered a diaspora that would have lasting effects on schools around the world.

The Vkhutemas in Moscow

Though its reverberations were felt less on an international scale, an equally significant experiment took place in Moscow during the same years. Like the Bauhaus, it was based on an impulse to synthesize art and architecture, and therefore on interaction – at least during the initial phase of the curriculum – among painters, sculptors, and builders. The Vkhutemas, or Higher Art and Technical Studios, **186** resulted from a merger in 1920 between the School of Painting and Sculpture and the Stroganov School of Applied Arts. The most original of the initial two departments was the Rabfak, or Workers' Faculty,

186 Studio work at Vkhutemas, Moscow, USSR (Russia), 1928

188 ▶ Bauhaus staff on the roof at the opening of Walter Gropius's Bauhaus building, Dessau, Germany, 1926. From left: Josef Albers, Hinnerk Scheper, Georg Muche, László Moholy-Nagy, Herbert Bayer, Joost Schmidt, Walter Gropius, Marcel Breuer, Wassily Kandinsky, Paul Klee, Lyonel Feininger, Gunta Stölzl and Oskar Schlemmer.

187 A studio at the Institut Supérieur des Arts Décoratifs, Abbaye de la Cambre, Brussels, Belgium, 1930

189 Student project at Vkhutemas, Moscow, USSR (Russia), 1923

190 Lenin Institute, project, Ivan Leonidov, Moscow, USSR (Russia), 1927

191 Student project, Jean de Maisonseul, Algiers, Algeria, 1931

which offered accelerated remedial classes to workers without a high school education. At first glance the school's foundation course appears similar to the Bauhaus's *Vorkurs*. Its students carried out exercises in four basic disciplines taught by often ideologically opposed instructors: "graphics," with neoclassicist Vladimir Favorsky and Constructivist Alexander Rodchenko; "surface/color," with Alexander Vesnin and Lyubov Popova, both also active Constructivists; "volume," which gradually became little more than an introduction to sculpture; and "space," which was devoted to the study and assembly of basic volumes, under the direction of Nikolai Ladovsky, Nikolai Dokuchaev, and Vladimir Krinsky, the future founders of the rationalist group ASNOVA. → 14

After one or two years at the school, students were divided among faculties specializing in painting, typography, sculpture, textiles, ceramics, wood, metal, and architecture. In 1923 departments devoted to music and theater were introduced; in 1924 a department devoted to literature opened. The vertical integration of individual disciplines was thus more pronounced than at the Bauhaus, where specialization took place later. Studio work remained central in faculties such as the Metfak, which specialized in metalwork. Inspired by Vladimir Tatlin and headed by Rodchenko, it emphasized projects of a collective and functional nature. The school's more politicized, highly production-oriented students frequently came into head-on confrontation with colleagues they considered to be either "pure" or decorative artists. Students of the Arkhfak, or architecture studio, were divided into clear-cut camps: the conservatives, under professors Ivan Zholtovsky and Alexei Shchusev; the "New Academy," under Ilya Golosov and Konstantin Melnikov; and the remainder split between two directly competing movements: the "Rationalists," gathered around the trio of Ladovsky,

Dokuchaev, and Krinsky, and the Constructivists, around Vesnin. Ladovsky was the most active in developing an experimental method of teaching through his "psychotechnical laboratory," in which he perfected a battery of tests and techniques derived from Hugo Münsterberg's research in applied psychology at Harvard University; his aim was to measure the "psychotechnic qualities of architects" and their ability to perceive forms in space. In 1922–3 students also began to participate in the constantly increasing number of architecture competitions taking place in Moscow. **189** In 1924–5 all of the school's thesis projects were included in the "New Moscow" plan designed by Shchusev. Students next turned their attention to new programs for stadiums, workers' palaces, and communal housing. Specialization by individual workshops – in residential architecture, public buildings, urban planning, and so on – began to take shape in 1925. During this phase, the school developed projects for aviation factories, industrial facilities, film studios, and apartment and office buildings.

The projects for skyscrapers that were common before 1925 were no longer the order of the day. Nonetheless, certain thesis projects still explored radical hypotheses for public buildings. Ivan Leonidov designed a Lenin Institute (1927) **190** with a prophetic structure made of cables and futuristic electronic technology; Georgei Krutikov designed a Flying City (1928). After visiting the Vkhutemas in 1928, Le Corbusier described the school in his journal as an "extraordinary demonstration of the modern credo," adding: "Here a new world is being rebuilt" out of a "mystique which gives rise to a pure technique." → 15 During the 1930s, methods developed in the school's foundation course continued to be used, but traditional methods derived from the Beaux-Arts were gradually reinstated and the school's utopian passions died out.

192 New Bauhaus, Chicago, Illinois, USA, c. 1938

193 School of Architecture,
Liang Ssu Ch'eng, Nanjing, China, c. 1930

Innovative schools in the new and old worlds

The new schools in Europe at times favored conflicting approaches. In 1927 Henry van de Velde founded the Institut Supérieur des Arts Décoratifs at the Abbaye de la Cambre in Brussels, **187** which he would head until 1936, recruiting the modern architects Huib Hoste and Victor Bourgeois and the urban planner Louis Van der Swaelmen. In Italy a national reform led to the creation in 1924 of independent architecture faculties in the academies of fine art, but these remained solidly under the control of conservative architects. In Turkey, Bruno Taut, who resettled there after an initial exile in Japan, taught from 1936 until his death in 1938 at the Istanbul Academy of Fine Arts, where he pursued the reform of the school's curriculum begun by the Austrian Ernst Egli.

The 1930s were characterized by the establishment of a growing number of architecture schools outside Europe. Modest ateliers were opened in connection with the School of Fine Arts in Algiers by Léon Claro, **191** and in Casablanca by Marius Boyer. The Beaux-Arts model, diffracted through the prism of Paul Philippe Cret's teaching, served as the foundation for Chinese schools. The first of these, largely inspired by the Japanese, was founded in Suzhou in 1923, then taken over by the Central University in Nanjing **193** four years later and staffed with professors who had studied with Cret at the University of Pennsylvania. The following year a school was opened in Mukden (Shenyang) by Liang Ssu Ch'eng, another former student of Cret. [16] In Rio de Janeiro, Le Corbusier's 1929 lectures so inspired Lucio Costa that he was moved to modernize the curriculum of a school that had been founded by the French in the early nineteenth century.

The most consequential migration was the one that drove many of the Bauhaus teachers to the United States. A few American students had attended the Bauhaus in Berlin, [17] but the German experience did not bear fruit in American schools until the wave of emigration provoked by Nazism in the 1930s. Seven years after a first exhibition organized at the Chicago Art Club, an exhibition at the Museum of Modern Art in 1938, *Bauhaus 1918–1928*, firmly established the version of the school's history propagated by its founder. [18] Gropius had been recruited by Harvard as chair of the architecture department two years earlier and tasked by the school's dean, Joseph Hudnut, with the revision of the design curriculum. Under Gropius the school de-emphasized the teaching of architectural history and focused on analytical and collective approaches to design as well as on the modernization of studio programs. In 1938 Mies van der Rohe was hired to head the architecture program at the Armour Institute of Chicago, which two years later merged with the Lewis Institute to become the Illinois Institute of Technology. [19] Other Bauhaus *Meister* also took up places in new institutions. Josef Albers headed the program at Black Mountain College in North Carolina, while László Moholy-Nagy founded the New Bauhaus, later renamed the Institute of Design, in Chicago. **192** In 1933 Richard Paulick, who had been an assistant to Gropius in Dessau, landed in Shanghai, where he worked as an urban planner and taught at the university from 1940 to 1949. [20] In a single decade the scattering of Beaux-Arts alumni around the world had been largely superseded by the diaspora of the Bauhaus.

Architecture and revolution in Russia

During the fifteen years between the 1917 Bolshevik Revolution and Joseph Stalin's 1932 campaign to consolidate intellectual and artistic organizations under strict party rule, Russia was a laboratory for an astonishing range of urban and architectural invention. Prior to 1914 the Czarist empire had kept up to date with transformations in European architectural culture, and certain of the empire's territories, such as Finland and the Baltic states, had developed their own innovative architecture. Western theories were studied with great attention: John Ruskin's works were popular, and Russian readers had access to translations of books by Auguste Choisy and Heinrich Wölfflin. But developments in Russia's own architecture had been glimpsed outside its borders only at world's fairs such as the 1900 Paris exposition and, especially, the 1901 fair in Glasgow, where Fyodor Shekhtel's Russia Pavilion made a strong impression.

Before 1914, the experiments of architects like Shekhtel operating under the "modern" banner had developed contemporaneously with research on tensile-steel structures undertaken by the civil engineer Vladimir Shukhov and the first use of reinforced concrete by Russian builders. [1] But the social reforms that had come to the fore in Western Europe had been only marginally implemented following the revolution of 1905, and the comprehensive plans that had stimulated the creation of new building types in Germany and farther west were lacking, largely owing to the weakness of municipal governments.

The shock of revolution

The effects of the October 1917 revolution were as immediate as they were manifold. The civil war and then the Bolshevik repression sent thousands of professionals into exile, while the nationalization of land and the rise to power of new local councils known as "soviets" changed the circumstances for those who remained – including architects graduating from the new schools. The launch of a monumental propaganda plan in 1918 stimulated designs for the ephemeral transformation of streets and squares as part of the celebration of the revolution and May Day. Initially limited to a display of banners and the erection of isolated sculptures, these spectacles eventually transfigured vast public spaces such as Palace Square in Petrograd and provided a glimpse of how an "emancipated" workers' city might look. The most ambitious of these projects was artist Vladimir Tatlin's Monument to the Third International (1919), **194** which explicitly competed with the Eiffel Tower through its projected height of 400 meters (1,312 feet) and steel skeleton. Built of "steel, glass, and revolution," in the words of the critic Nikolai Punin, the tower was designed to hold within its spiraling framework a cube, a pyramid, a cylinder, and a half-sphere whose rotation was intended to represent the frequency of meetings of the Communist International's various steering committees. [2]

Until 1920, conflicts between the Red and White armies led to widespread destruction, which was intensified by Bolshevik campaigns against the Russian Orthodox Church. During these uncertain years before the Reds' power was consolidated, Sinskulptarkh, a group dedicated to the synthesis of sculpture and architecture (which became the Zhivskulptarkh once painters joined its ranks), tried to promote cooperation between various disciplines. They worked together on theoretical schemes for "people's houses" like those built in Western Europe before 1914, for communal houses, **196** and for "temples of friendship" that paralleled the utopian programs of German Expressionism. Nikolai Ladovsky and Vladimir Krinsky, who designed the most evocative of these projects, also helped

194 Monument to the Third International, project, Vladimir Tatlin, Petrograd (Saint Petersburg), Russia, 1919

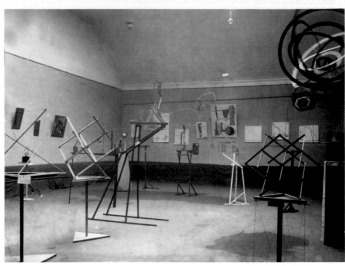

196 Communal House, project, Nikolai Ladovski, 1920

197 Obmokhu (Society of Young Artists) exhibition, Moscow, Russia, 1921

195 Komintern Radio Tower, Vladimir Shukhov, Moscow, Russia, 1922

transform pre-revolutionary art schools into the Vkhutemas. Concurrent discussions within the state-supported Inkhuk (Institute of Artistic Culture), where creative methods grounded in construction and inspired by engineering were opposed to those based on artistic "composition" and anchored in academic tradition, clearly revealed the differences separating Ladovsky and Krinsky from the supporters of Constructivism. The former aspired to create dynamic forms but were uninterested in their relationship with materials, while the latter insisted on adapting the model of engineering design to the sphere of art and architecture. The Constructivists exhibited sculptures made out of metal and inspired by engineering structures at the Obmokhu (Society of Young Artists) exhibition **197** in 1921. Already a teacher at the Vkhutemas, the artist Alexander Rodchenko played a crucial role in these formative stages. → 3

In 1920 the Bolsheviks launched the GOELRO plan (named for the State Comission for the Electrification of Russia) to build a network of power plants, and embarked on their New Economic Policy (NEP), which loosened restrictions on commerce. New types of architectural commissions – including factories, workers' housing, and electric power plants such as Ivan Zholtovsky's MOGES – were generated by needs related to this national electrification plan. There was also demand for more office buildings in connection with revived business activity and new trading companies such as Arcos and Mosselprom. Local soviets and social-action groups created within various companies initiated projects to build housing and create workers' clubs.

A profession renewed

Architecture in the USSR was shaped by constant competitions in which members of different professional associations and a few mavericks regularly participated. Several architects who had had successful careers before 1914 – such as Ivan Fomin, a Saint Petersburg neoclassicist; Zholtovsky, a Moscow neo-Palladian; and Alexei Shchusev, an opportunist who in 1923 reconstituted the MAO (Society of Moscow Architects) – continued to receive significant commissions. Two groups were formed in reaction to this old guard. The ASNOVA (Association of New Architects) **198** included Ladovsky, Krinsky, Dokuchaev, and, for a time, El Lissitzky. **200** This group was very influential among young people. It stood for strong tectonic expression of the building's structure and visual exaltation of its function. The second group, whose members were Constructivists, was formally launched with the creation of the OSA (Union of Contemporary Architects) in 1925. It was no coincidence that neither group's name included the term "modern," which had been discredited by its association with the Russian version of Art Nouveau. Chaired by Alexander Vesnin, the OSA was largely run by Moisei Ginzburg, whose book-manifesto *Stil i Epokha* (Style and Epoch; 1924) echoed Le Corbusier's theories by suggesting that a new design method should be based on the study of machines and the application of their systems to architecture. → 4 The periodical *Sovremennaia Arkhitektura* (Contemporary [i.e., Modern] Architecture), or *SA*, published under Ginzburg's direction from 1926 to 1930, presented OSA's new projects, as well as numerous Western examples, in a radically new graphic form. → 5

Independent architects such as Ilya Golosov, a proponent of a colorful, formally striking architecture, and especially Konstantin Melnikov rose to prominence through competitions. Melnikov created a sensation with his Makhorka Tobacco Pavilion at the Agricultural Exhibition held in Moscow in 1923 and, two years later, with the pavilion he designed to represent the USSR at

198 *Izvestia ASNOVA* (News of the Association of New Architects), layout by El Lissitzky, 1926

199 USSR Pavilion, Konstantin Melnikov, Paris, France, 1925

200 Skyhook, project, El Lissitzky, Moscow, USSR (Russia), 1925

201 Zuev Workers' Club, Ilya Golosov, Moscow, USSR (Russia), 1928

202 ▶ Rusakov Workers' Club, Konstantin Melnikov, Moscow, USSR (Russia), 1927–9

the *Exposition Internationale des Arts Décoratifs et Industriels Modernes*. **199** Composed of two glazed triangular volumes bisected diagonally by a staircase, it was the most conspicuous structure at the Paris exhibition. →⁶ It revealed to the West the existence of a new Russian architecture, which was further confirmed by the presentation elsewhere at the fair of over one hundred projects conceived in the USSR since 1920.
The commissions emanating from the new regime's institutions began to generate buildings. Among them was Grigory Barkhin's design for new headquarters for *Izvestia*, the Moscow daily newspaper, which reached back to classical architecture for its large metope-like oculi. Alexander Vesnin and his brothers Leonid and Victor failed to realize their 1924 project for the Moscow office of *Pravda*, a cage inspired by the metal chassis of the newspaper's printing presses, which was to have functioned as a base for billboards, megaphones, and projectors inscribing slogans on the clouds. But the three brothers did succeed in building the Mostorg Department Store (1927–9), which was wrapped in a glass facade, as was Boris Velikovsky's Gostorg Office Building (1926). In addition to newly built traditional apartment buildings, many new types of complexes sprang up, including Shchusev and Nikolai Markovnikov's Sokol Garden Suburb, inspired by the planning of Raymond Unwin. There were also workers' housing blocks on Usacheva Street and in the Shabolovka area, which Nikolai Travin erected near the Komintern Radio Tower (1922). **195** The latter, a lattice of stacked-up hyperboloids designed by Shukhov, seemed to be the real materialization of Tatlin's tower. Shukhov was also responsible for the roof structure of two bus depots built by Melnikov. Workers, the "victors" of the revolution, were at the heart of the new urban policies. Prosperous companies such as the Ivanovo textile mills, Sverdlovsk steelworks, and Baku oil firms used their income to provide social services and housing for their labor forces, as in the Armenikend neighborhood by Alexander Ivanitsky in Baku (1925–8). A fully equipped model district of collective housing was established in Leningrad near the Putilov Factory; the schools, communal kitchens, and workers' clubs around Alexander Gegello's housing on Tractor Street (1925–7) formed something like a small autonomous city centered on the collective workforce. →⁷

The "social condensers"

In the second half of the 1920s, neighborhoods multiplied according to the model of collectivized life – in strong distinction to their counterparts in Germany and Austria. Each Soviet building type was subjected to elaborate and specific research. In order to transform the population's daily habits as quickly as possible, buildings became what the Constructivists referred to as "social condensers," which were meant to accelerate changes in the everyday life of the working class. An unacknowledged successor to the pre-1914 "people's houses," the workers' club became the principal place of acculturation and the site where the confrontation between different architectural ideas proved most fruitful. The clubs retained the auditoriums, restaurants, and sometimes the athletic equipment of the people's houses, but libraries were given more prominence, with a strong emphasis on literacy campaigns. Above all, the buildings themselves were meant to serve as a new and more enduring form of monumental propaganda. The Zuev Workers' Club, **201** built by Golosov in Moscow, pivots expressively on a glass cylinder that houses a staircase connecting the different parts of the building. Located at the intersection of two streets, it appears as the hinge of the whole block.

203 Burevestnik Workers' Club, Konstantin Melnikov, Moscow, USSR (Russia), 1927–9

204 Narkomfin Communal House, Moisei Ginzburg and Ignati Milinis, Moscow, USSR (Russia), 1928–30

The five clubs in Moscow that Melnikov built practically simultaneously in 1927–9 were a testament both to this architect's inexhaustible imagination and to the potential of a building type that was in a perpetual state of experimentation. The three balconies of the theater of the Rusakov Workers' Club **202** cantilever over the street, while inside the seats face a stage wedged into a triangular plan. The Burevestnik Workers' Club **203** was remarkable for its large convertible theater and flanking tower, with a floor plan in the shape of a flower. Between the Kauchuk Workers' Club, a rather static vertical cylinder, and the Svoboda Workers' Club, a horizontal cylinder with mobile walls, Melnikov's forms evolved from an almost conventional monumentality to a search for kineticism, an approach he had pursued in his proposal for the Pravda Building competition in 1924 and would further develop in his project for a theater with a rotating stage in 1931.

The second type of "social condenser" was the "communal house," a residential complex with integrated services that was a direct descendant of the phalanstery, a utopian community inspired by the early socialist Charles Fourier in nineteenth-century France. Like the "garden city," the "communal house" was more a slogan than a well-defined concept. The term was used to describe a wide variety of installations, from the barely equipped dormitory recalling the dreariest workers' residences of the pre-1914 period to Moscow apartment buildings with standards that seem almost luxurious given the difficult conditions during the NEP. In the second half of the 1920s, full-scale experiments were carried out in an attempt to "reconstruct" everyday life through the collectivization of food services and reduction in the size of apartments; the provision of new, shared facilities was intended to offset the small living unit. The most productive of these experiments, the Narkomfin Communal

House, **204** was carried out under the aegis of Nikolai Miliutin, head of the People's Commissariat for Finance. A veteran Bolshevik who had studied architecture, Miliutin commissioned Ginzburg and Ignati Milinis to design a project to house his employees in the heart of Moscow. Using a vocabulary explicitly taken from Le Corbusier – *pilotis*, ribbon windows, and roof terraces – the project combined a glazed unit for communal services with a long housing block. Most of the living quarters were two- or three-level "cells" whose spatial complexity compensated somewhat for their cramped dimensions. Described as a "transition" between traditional apartments, which had now all become "domestic communes" shared by several tenants, and a new, still undefined form of totally collectivized dwelling, the building was remarkable for its precise design and careful execution. →⁸ Ginzburg followed it with another such building in Sverdlovsk, **206** while Mikhail Barshch and Alexander Pasternak built a more compact communal house in Moscow. All these buildings were based on the model dwelling schemes developed by Stroikom, or the State Building Committee of the Russian Republic, which carried out studies on how to reduce the size of rooms and integrate services based on German and American examples. But radical projects such as Ivan Nikolaev's dormitory for students at the Moscow Textile Institute and the extremist ideas of young Constructivists such as Sergei Kuzmin, who insisted that life be regulated down to the minute, quickly discredited the very idea of the communal house. Moscow also became the site of residential buildings with less ambitious ideological programs but powerful monumental presence. These included the Dynamo Building by Fomin (1928–9), which explored the potential of a "proletarian Doric," and the House on the Embankment by Boris Iofan (1930), a huge apartment block built on the Moskva River across from the Kremlin.

205 Melnikov House, Konstantin Melnikov, Moscow, USSR (Russia), 1927–9

206 Communal House, Moisei Ginzburg, Sverdlovsk (Yekaterinburg), USSR (Russia), 1930

The private house that Melnikov built for himself 205 with the fees he earned from his workers' clubs commissions remains unique, as individual residences were unauthorized: it consists of two interlocking cylindrical towers with stuccoed brick walls and lozenge-shaped windows that are reminiscent of peasant houses and the towers of Russian fortresses.

Polemics and rivalries

With the launch of the USSR's first Five Year Plan in 1927, the forced march toward industrialization spurred the construction of thousands of factories and hundreds of new cities. The assistance of Western architects was solicited. Thus Erich Mendelsohn built the Krasnoe Znamia (Red Banner) Textile Factory in Leningrad in 1926–8, and in the period leading up to 1932 Albert Kahn's firm built several hundred factories with components shipped from the United States. The brutal industrialization and collectivization of rural areas raised the question of what form the country's urban planning should take. In 1929 and 1930 those who supported the creation of a dense network of medium-sized cities – the "urbanists" – faced off against the "disurbanists," who sprang from the OSA and were proponents of a radical decentralization leading to the total eradication of cities. Formulated on the occasion of competitions held in 1929 for a "green city" near Moscow and in 1930 for the plan of the industrial city of Magnitogorsk, the dis-urbanist position – as theorized by the sociologist Mikhail Okhitovich – may be understood as a self-critical reaction to the communal house projects they had previously supported. →9 Miliutin proposed a third option: the "linear city," 208 based on the late nineteenth-century concept of the Spanish planner Soria y Mata.

The disurbanist model of a territory dotted with individual houses reached by automobiles was impracticable in the USSR of the time. In 1931 the Communist Party called to account the "irresponsible" architects who had proposed such plans, decreeing the "socialist reconstruction" of existing cities. This policy would be carried out with the participation of hundreds of architects and engineers from Germany, who had been led to emigrate either by the economic crisis in Germany, as was the case with Ernst May, or by an attraction to the USSR's revolutionary ideals, as with Hannes Meyer. From 1930 to 1935 these foreigners designed most of the new neighborhoods and defined the standards that would be applied to Soviet planning and housing for decades to come.

The 1931 decision in favor of socialist urban planning was made at a time when disagreements between ASNOVA and OSA – which had steadily escalated through the 1920s – had become particularly bitter, with young architects who defined themselves as "proletarians" politicizing the architectural discourse. The competing factions radicalized their positions, and campaigns targeted several architects. Leonidov, for one, was harshly criticized for the "lack of realism" of his glass prisms, while Melnikov was taken to task for his relentless individualism. The work of the Leningrad architect Iakov Chernikhov, whose boundless visual imagination took shape in unbuildable "architectural fantasies" 207 based on machine forms, further contributed to the characterization of the Constructivists as complete utopians. →10

The Palace of the Soviets competition

The project for a Palace of the Soviets, intended to symbolize the return of the Russian capital to Moscow after two centuries

207 Architectural Fantasy, Iakov Chernikhov, 1931

and the establishment of a new proletarian state, served as a pretext for the Communist Party – which up till then had cautiously avoided taking sides in the rival currents of revolutionary fervor – to formulate an official position on architecture. An initial competition for a Palace of Labor had been held in 1923. Though the Vesnin brothers' proposal for a composition of volumes featuring allusions to Auguste Perret made the biggest impact, Noa Trotsky won that competition with a neo-Byzantine project that was soon abandoned.

In 1931 an ambitious international competition, launched as if in emulation of those for the Tribune Building in Chicago and the League of Nations in Geneva, called for a project to be built on a site along the Moskva River across from the Kremlin. After a first round restricted to Soviet teams, notable Western architects, including Gropius, Poelzig, Perret, and Le Corbusier, were invited to submit proposals so as to give the proceedings a veneer of impartiality and openness. "Workers' collectives" were also asked to contribute their own naive designs. In early 1932, three of the 272 projects received were selected: those by Zholtovsky, Iofan, **210** and an unknown young American named Hector Hamilton. After another round, Iofan was awarded the commission, with Vladimir Shchuko and Vladimir Gelfreikh named as his collaborators. Iofan's initial project combined the requested 15,000- and 5,000-seat auditoriums with a statue of Vladimir Lenin standing on a tall base. Directly intervening in the design process, Stalin made many architectural "suggestions." →11 One of them resulted in the statue being placed atop one of the auditoriums, thereby making the project virtually unbuildable, as was inevitably recognized in the late 1940s.

The competition coincided with a 1932 decision by the Communist Party regarding the "reorganization of literary and artistic unions." All existing groups were dissolved – to the relief of some – and architects were invited to join a centralized union. Projects already underway were carried through in a climate that remained pluralistic for a few more years. But the decision in the Palace of the Soviets competition set a new direction for public architecture, which soon became the only option available, moving it in the direction of historicist monumentality. While the Vesnin brothers were still able to realize their Palace of Culture for the ZIL Automobile Factory in Moscow **209** unhampered – without doubt the largest workers' club ever built – Le Corbusier was able to finish his Centrosoyuz Building in 1936 only in the face of violent attacks on its radical modernity. The trends of the 1920s, beginning with Constructivism, were now rejected and their most radical proponents marginalized, as was the case with Leonidov, or killed, as with Okhitovich, who died in a Gulag camp in 1937. Stigmatized for his impenitent idiosyncratic gestures, Melnikov was forced into retirement at the age of fifty. →12

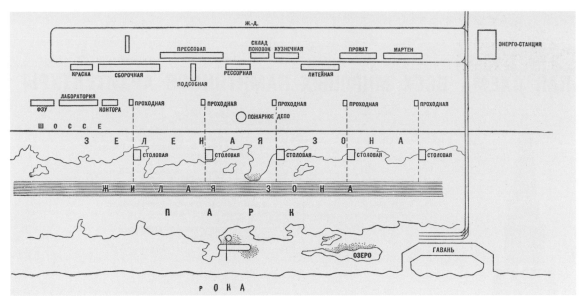

208　Linear City, project, Nikolai Miliutin, Nizhny Novgorod, USSR (Russia), 1930

210 ▶　Palace of Soviets, project, Boris Iofan, 1931–4

209　Palace of Culture for the ZIL Automobile Factory, Alexander Vesnin, Leonid Vesnin and Viktor Vesnin, Moscow, USSR (Russia), 1931–6

СРАВНИТЕЛЬНАЯ СХЕМА ВСЕХ МИРОВЫХ ПАМЯТНИКОВ АРХИТЕКТУРЫ И

1 Кельнский собор—160 м.
2. Пирамида Хеопса—137 м.
3. Штрассбуогский собор—142 м.
4. Церковь Стефана в Вене—139 м.
5. Церковь Мартина в Ландсхуте—137 м.
6. Собор Петра в Риме—143 м.
7. Антверпенский собор—130 м.
8. Церковь Михаила в Гамбурге—143 м.
9. Амьенский собор—126 м.
10. Фрайбургский собор—126 м.
11. Хефренская пирамида—126 м.
12. Руанский Собор (Колокольня)—151 м.
13. Собор в Шартре—122 м.
14. Собор в Метце—118 м.
15. Шпиц Петропавловской крепости
    в Ленинграде—109 м.

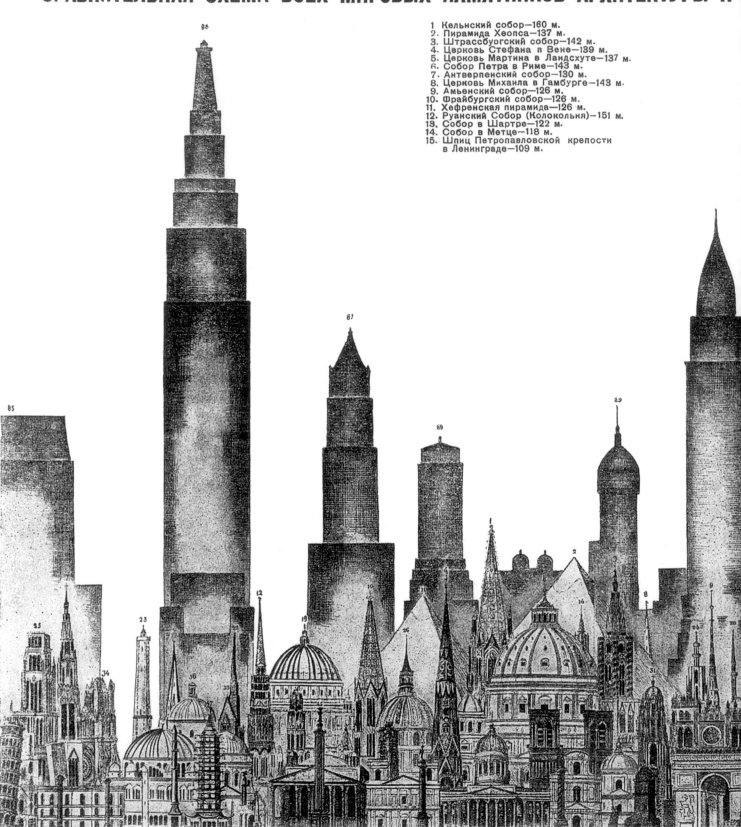

19. Церковь Павла в Лондоне—109 м.
20. Миланский собор—108 м.
21. Ульмский собор (незакончен.) ныне—161 м.
22. Ратуша в Брюсселе—90 м.
23. Башня Азинелли в Болонье—98 м.
24. Собор в Малинье—107 м.
25. Орлеанский собор—105 м.
26. Дворец инвалидов в Париже—104 м.
29. Исаакиевский собор в Ленинграде—97 м.
31. Франкфуртский собор—84 м.
33. Колокольня Ивана Великого в Москве—97 м.
34. Реймский собор—81 м.
35. Базельский собор—64 м.
36. Пантеон в Париже—79 м.
37. Башня Кутб—Минар в Дели—73 м.
38. Церковь Театинеров в Мюнхене—78 м.
39. Руанский собор—75 м.

40. Вестминстерское Аббатство в Лондоне—68 м.
44. Собор Нотрдам в Париже—66 м.
45. Монумент в Лондоне—61 м.
47. Фарфоровая башня в Нанкине (разрушена)—64 м.
49. Айя София в Константинополе—58 м.
51. Башня в Пизе - 55 м.
57. Акведук в Ниме—47 м.
60. Башня Антония в Риме—44 м.
85. Здание телефонной станции в Нью-Иорке—215 м.
86. Эмпайр Стэт Билдинг в Нью-Иорке (318) 407 м.
87. Вульворт Стэт Билдинг в Нью-Иорке—(233) 255 м.
88. Транспортешен Стэт Билдинг в Нью-Иорке—(165) 203 м.
89. Зингер Стэт Билдинг в Нью-Иорке—(186) 209 м.
90. Крайслер Стэт Билдинг в Нью-Иорке—(262) 330 м.
91. Эйфелева башня—300 м.
92. Принятый в основу проекта Дворца Советов проект арх. Б. Иофан—220 м.

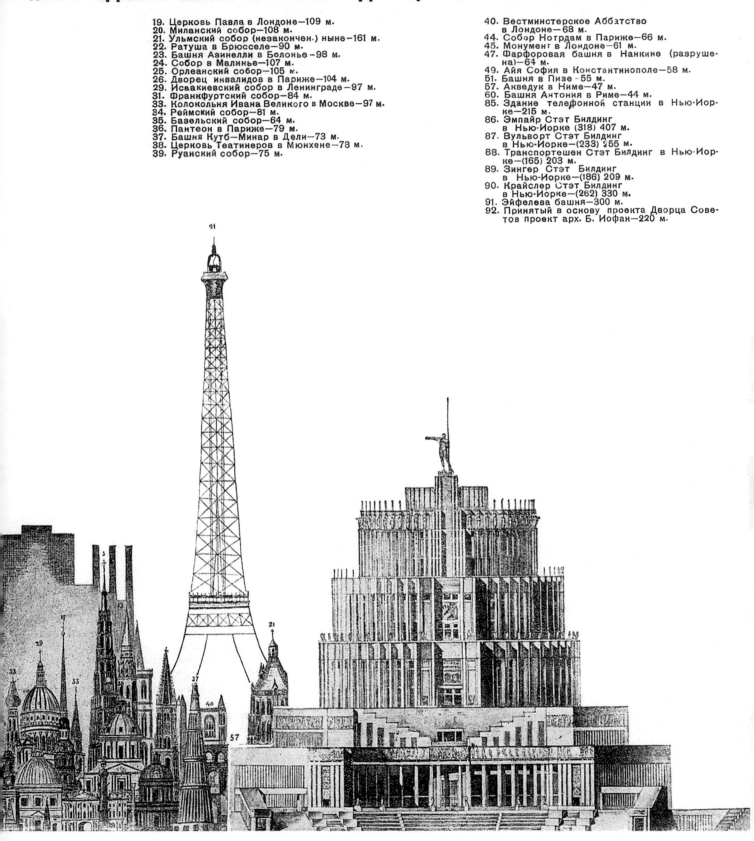

The architecture
of social reform

During the interwar period, transformations in architectural culture combined with a new emphasis on social reforms to yield a new type of urban entity: the *Siedlung* – to use the German term – or autonomous housing development. These complexes, which incorporated collective facilities, clearly had their origins in the village-inspired garden city, but after World War I, the somewhat nostalgic ideal of the first prototypes became only one of several models.

The steadfast commitment of public authorities and cooperatives not only to housing but also to educational, health, athletic, and civic facilities opened a vast market for architects, who no longer depended exclusively on face-to-face relationships with a bourgeois clientele. Harnessing these programs to realize the *Wohlfahrtsstadt*, or city of well-being – to which an exhibition was dedicated in Stuttgart in 1927 – required a solid alliance with the new decision makers and a significant change in architects' ways of working. Unlike the radical measures of collectivization adopted in the USSR, the change promised by these reforms was gradual. It was geared more to the growing mass of white-collar employees than to factory workers and was rooted in the doctrine of John Maynard Keynes, who advocated government intervention to solve economic problems. → 1

A wide spectrum of social and political reforms pertained to education and domestic life, notably in the kitchen, and led to new types of construction, such as housing projects with standardized building materials and kitchens, municipal swimming pools, and open-air schools. The postwar housing shortage and, a decade later, the economic crash of 1929 generated new building methods based on a reduction in kinds of buildings through the narrowing of typological variation and the mass production of building components through standardization and industrialization. Thorough, efficient policies for creating an architecture based on industrial production modes remained extremely rare, but efforts to achieve this objective despite the lack of policy initiatives were as common as attempts to give traditional construction the look of industrial products.

Modernizing cities

With the end of World War I, Europe became the setting for a vast transnational effort to expand metropolitan areas and reduce slums in existing urban centers. But modernization did not operate solely in the sphere of what Karl Marx had defined as the reproduction of labor power. In the era of Taylorism and Fordism, cities played a decisive role in organizing industrial production, market exchanges, and economic management, which increased pressure on city centers to make room for offices and infrastructures.

Questions of zoning extended to the scale of cities and even entire regions, such as the Ruhr in Germany, where the Ruhr Coal Region Settlement Association was founded in 1920. Both Le Corbusier and Ludwig Hilberseimer had an interest in reimagining the form of the business center, which led to their developing provocative projects. Le Corbusier's Ville Contemporaine and Plan Voisin presented an urban vision in which the city center was exclusively dedicated to business and controlled by private enterprise, while the periphery depended on public initiative. The same was true of the Berlin architect's projects: Hilberseimer's Hochhausstadt (1924) **212**, or high-rise city, was a capitalist business center that incorporated housing blocks built above vertically stacked streets. His 1930 Mischbebauung project, or mixed-height housing development, combined housing blocks with courtyard housing; intended for the city outskirts, it seemed to require greater public intervention. → 2

213 Winarskyhof, Peter Behrens, Josef Frank, Adolf Loos et al., Vienna, Austria, 1924–8

214 Westhausen Siedlung, Ernst May, Frankfurt am Main, Germany, 1929–31

The strengthening of the powers of local governments also led to another form of *Stadtkrone*: the civic center. The most striking of these reform-oriented public buildings were city halls designed to project municipal authority, whether in suburban neighborhoods, as with the one built by Tony Garnier and Jacques Debat-Ponsan in Boulogne (1931–4), or in ambitious midsize cities such as Hilversum in the Netherlands, **211** where Willem Marinus Dudok devoted sixteen years (1915–31) to translating motifs from Frank Lloyd Wright's domestic architecture to a monumental scale.

Red Vienna

Public projects were far from identical from one city to the next. While the model of a continuous city in which center and periphery had a comparable density was dominant in Amsterdam, Vienna's policy was based on consolidating distinct focal points in and around the city. In Berlin and Frankfurt, different housing solutions were explored in peripheries serviced by rail networks. New types of urban areas were developed in most of these cities, guaranteeing certain minimal standards of living space within public housing schemes that limited private property and added parkland to create a harmonious urban landscape.

Vienna was a unique case. Not only were its housing projects incorporated into the heart of the city, but they also achieved an ambitious scale. As the capital of an Austria considerably reduced from the time of the Hapsburg Empire, Vienna remained home to 1.8 million of the country's 8 million inhabitants. Between 1920 and 1934, when Austria was annexed by Nazi Germany, Vienna was governed by the Social Democrats, who levied a tax on rents. This new tax and the city's purchase of sizable plots of land allowed for the creation of 64,000 housing units – approximately 11 percent of the city's available housing. → 3

The *Hof* (courtyard apartment complex) was established as the dominant model, in emulation of the large Viennese housing blocks that had been built around courtyards since the seventeenth century. The first such project to be constructed was Robert Kalesa's Margaretengürtel (1919–20, subsequently expanded by Hubert Geßner to become the Metzleinstalerhof). Most typical of this original batch of housing developments was the Winarskyhof (1924–8), **213** which combined buildings by Peter Behrens, Josef Hoffmann, Oskar Strnad, Josef Frank, and Oskar Wlach. Earlier projects designed in 1922–3 under the direction of Adolf Loos, head architect of Vienna's Housing Authority, were never built. Large housing blocks containing communal facilities – schools, daycare centers, laundries, shops – became the dominant model, although some low-density projects such as Lockerwiese by Karl Schartelmüller (1928) and Am Wasserturm by Franz Schuster and Franz Schacherl (1928) continued to go up in the city's suburbs.

The plans for the housing units were established by municipal offices. Various teams of designers, many of them trained in Otto Wagner's studio, were responsible for the urban form and monumental aspects of the developments and the design of their architectural features. They usually incorporated representational elements emphasizing entrances or axes. The young architect Grete Schütte-Lihotzky designed the units' compact kitchens. Heinrich Schmid and Hermann Aichinger put up the Am Fuchsenfeld (1924–5), Rabenhof (1925), and Matteottihof complexes (1926–8); Emil Hoppe, Otto Schönthal, Franz Matuschek, and others built the Sandleitenhof (1924). Hubert Geßner was responsible for the expanded Metzleinstalerhof (1922–3), the Reumannhof (1924–6) and the Karl-Seitz-Hof (1926–7), the latter built in a semicircle around a large square, establishing a benchmark for the expansive scale of the new urban spaces.

215 Römerstadt Siedlung, Ernst May, Frankfurt am Main, Germany, 1927–8

The final housing developments incorporated a grand configuration of towers and arches on what was to be a "Ringstraße of the proletariat," designed in reaction to the bourgeois avenue that ringed the city's center. Rudolf Perco's Friedrich-Engels-Platz (1930–3) exemplifies one such project. At the same time, a linear, more abstract aesthetic appeared in buildings such as the one designed by Fritz Judtmann and Egon Riss on the Diehlgasse (1928–9). Karl Ehn's Karl-Marx-Hof (1925–30) **216** was both the most ambitious and the largest of Vienna's housing complexes. It extended over 1.3 km (three quarters of a mile), lining two sides of a vast rectangular square with a series of large courtyards containing communal facilities. The central building was surmounted by six towers that framed four large entrance arches, evoking the image of stout warriors guarding this bastion of the working class. A play of red and ocher stucco accentuated the strong relief of the facades. The fall of this "red fortress" to artillery fire from rightist forces in 1934 marked the end of the Social Democratic municipality and of a program exceptional for its scale and monumentality.

The New Frankfurt

The garden city was initially the most popular model adopted in the European suburbs, but Ebenezer Howard's original vision of it – according to which each garden city was meant to contain exactly 32,000 inhabitants and be totally autonomous – was rapidly scaled back. Those projects that were actually carried out, such as Le Logis and Floréal by Louis Van der Swaelmen in Watermael-Boitsfort near Brussels (1922), Sokol Garden Suburb in Moscow, and the first Parisian garden cities in Arcueil and Genevilliers, were far more modest in size, and their morphology gradually shifted away from Raymond Unwin's model. But the

garden city also led to the *Trabantenprinzip*, or "satellite city principle," which was the basis for the policies put into practice by Ernst May for the municipality of Frankfurt am Main from 1925 to 1930. Recruited by the mayor Ludwig Landmann – a member of the Democratic party – to merge the city's urban planning and building services, May created a public architecture office that, over a period of five years, directed a highly consequential municipal program, using building components standardized to specific norms and establishing widespread uniformity in housing units. [4] He applied the *Trabantenprinzip*, initially developed in Breslau following Unwin's ideas, and concentrated the city's investment on a crown of *Siedlungen* encircling Frankfurt that provided a starting point for substantial developments. Their structure quickly evolved from initial complexes such as the "zigzag" Bruchfeldstraße estate (1926–7), built around a courtyard but still displaying an unbroken urban facade; to developments like Praunheim (1926), with its housing aligned along the street; finally to identical apartment houses built parallel to one another, such as those of the Westhausen Estate (1929–31). This transition from the closed courtyard housing block to north-south–oriented parallel housing slabs based on the *Zeilenbau* principle – an arrangement of buildings in parallel lines – took place over just a few years. [5] The vast scale of the developments allowed builders to experiment with prefabricated construction systems, notably in Praunheim and Westhausen **214**, where increasingly large precast concrete panels were used. May's team worked to rationalize the construction and components of the dwelling according to Taylorist principles. Grete Schütte-Lihotzky established the model of the "Frankfurt Kitchen," **217** specifically conceived as a workstation for the housewife, now recast as a domestic producer. An extensive educational program was offered to instruct women in the new

218 Britz Großsiedlung, Bruno Taut, with Leberecht Migge and Martin Wagner, Berlin, Germany, 1925–30

219 Onkel-Toms-Hütte Waldsiedlung, Bruno Taut, Berlin, Germany, 1926–32

217 Frankfurt Kitchen, Grete Schütte-Lihotsky, Frankfurt am Main, Germany, 1926

domestic practices that went with the new dwellings. Certain of the developments like Römerstadt, **215** which was built on the Nidda River (1927–8), made careful use of topography to create a total environment, with landscaping as an integral factor. The work of the garden designer Leberecht Migge, who installed a network of vegetable gardens as a complement to the large collective spaces, was notable. → 6 The profusely illustrated journal *Das neue Frankfurt* (The New Frankfurt; 1926–30) accompanied this innovative body of work with propaganda aimed at the rest of Europe. But the housing units were often too expensive for the poorest members of society, and they tended to be rented to white-collar workers and the petite bourgeoisie rather than to factory workers.

Taut's housing developments in Berlin

During the same period, Bruno Taut built a significant series of *Siedlungen* for the GEHAG, an employees' cooperative in Berlin. Keeping in mind the principle of the "dissolution of cities" he had elaborated in 1920 in his unrealized Expressionist projects, Taut built the Britz *Großsiedlung*, **218** or large housing development, with Migge and Martin Wagner in 1925–30. Its dominant element was a band of housing built in a horseshoe configuration around a garden and pond, harking back to the *Anger*, a shared open space characteristic of colonial *Siedlungen* built during Prussia's seventeenth- and eighteenth-century campaigns to colonize Eastern Europe. Most notably, Britz featured a diverse series of outdoor public spaces lined with blue, ocher, and red houses. These colors recalled the hues Taut had seen in villages around the Venetian lagoon, where the inhabitants painted their dwellings; in Taut's view, the colorful houses symbolized the spirit of community. → 7 With the Onkel-Toms-Hütte Waldsiedlung, **219** or forest estate in western Berlin (1926–32), Taut experimented

with standardized components for doors and windows, though without compromising the variety and poetic composition of his building and facade types, which formed a vivid neighborhood in the pine-forest setting. Designed to contribute to the making of a tranquil landscape, each of Taut's developments had a unique form, giving its inhabitants a sense of local identity on the margins of the Berlin metropolis.

The explicitly experimental aspect of May's and Taut's housing complexes was also evident in the Dammerstock Development that Walter Gropius built in Karlsruhe. Some of these projects were funded by the Reichsforschungsgesellschaft für Wirtschaftlichkeit in Bau- und Wohnungswesen (State Research Society for Economy in Building and Housing), which was active in encouraging research into new solutions for mass housing in Weimar Germany from 1927 to 1931. But modernists were not the only ones to promote technical innovation and to find economical solutions. Commissioned by a more conservative authority, Heinrich Tessenow and Alexander Klein built the experimental houses of the small Am Fischtal Development (1928–9) next to Taut's Onkel-Toms-Hütte. → 8 Other large cities also launched ambitious housing programs for the working class. The municipality of Hamburg, Germany's second largest city, was particularly active. Fritz Schumacher, its city planner, built a large park (1908–20) and installed a ring of *Siedlungen*, including Dulsberg (1928–33), for which he himself designed many of the school facilities. → 9 This network of green areas combining broad community grounds and small parks took on decisive importance in transforming the urban space into an extended *Stadtlandschaft*, or citywide landscape – one of the goals of the sozialer *Städtebau* (social city-planning) movement. The most elegantly designed housing units to come out of this movement were by Karl Schneider, in Jarrestadt (1926–8), Barmbeck (1926–7), and Winterhude (1926–7). → 10

220 Butte Rouge Housing Development, Joseph Bassompierre, Paul de Rutté and Paul Sirvin, Châtenay-Malabry, France, 1929–34

221 Villeurbanne Skyscrapers, Môrice Leroux, Villeurbanne, France, 1930–4

French suburbs

In France, an active social housing policy was pursued most intensively in the Paris region. Within Paris itself, the Office public des HBM (Public Office for Low-Cost Housing) implemented projects whose forms remained conservative. These large housing blocks with open courtyards created a belt of red-brick apartment buildings on the site of the city's former fortifications, which had been demolished in 1919. In the suburbs, projects carried out by the departmental office headed by Henri Sellier, mayor of Suresnes, dotted the region with garden cities that followed Unwin's model and sometimes combined individual houses with collective dwellings. In the late 1920s these were replaced by larger housing developments, such as the one by Maurice Payret-Dortail in Plessis-Robinson (1923–32), consisting of large, repetitive concrete blocks. In Châtenay-Malabry, Joseph Bassompierre, Paul de Rutté, and Paul Sirvin built the Butte Rouge complex (1929–34), **220** inspired by Frankfurt's *Siedlungen*. It was remarkable for its sensitive relationship to its topography and the variety of its streets and squares. Although it drew on the basic systems of the garden city, the Butte Rouge made no concession to a picturesque neo-village style. Built along the edge of the forest of Verrières, it was dominated by a residential tower, undeniably its central element. In Sellier's opinion, "A group of low houses without a salient point, without architectural excitement, without any elevation to serve as a rallying point" was merely "a subdivision without soul or character." [11] He was clearly cognizant of the need for a visible sign of community to replace the traditional belfries and clock towers and to indicate that the residential community now predominated over other categories of urban collectivity, like the parish or municipality.

Unlike these housing developments built along forests and fields, the skyscrapers in Villeurbanne (1930–4), **221** a Socialist municipality adjacent to Lyons, were remarkable for their verticality. At the far end of an avenue lined by setback buildings with metal skeletons, the towers built by Môrice Leroux were intended to constitute an alternative center to the historical heart of the Lyons metropolitan area, affirming the autonomy of the suburban city. His city hall and people's house asserted this autonomy on a grand scale, turning the neighborhood into a symbolic landmark and site of collective enterprise, in opposition to the bourgeois city. [12]

Echoes overseas

European social housing models found an echo in Japan, where the garden city had already begun to be imported in 1907 under the name "pastoral city." Near Tokyo, the architect Kintaro Yabe, working for the philanthropic developer Eiichi Shibusawa, built the Denenchōfu Garden City on a radial plan oriented inward to the train station at its center. [13] Following the earthquake that destroyed much of Tokyo in 1923, the Dojunkai Corporation built rows of reinforced-concrete housing units, which were similar to European public housing, in Omotesando **222** (demolished 2003) and Daikanyama over the next decade. [14]

In her 1934 book *Modern Housing* the American reformer Catherine Bauer noted that the United States possessed some exemplary suburban housing developments – most frequently built at the initiative of cooperatives – that could compete with those in Europe. [15] The most widely touted was Sunnyside Gardens, **223** a complex in Queens, New York, constructed in 1924–6 by Clarence Stein, Henry Wright, and Frederick Ackerman. Its rather austere brick architecture was enlivened by gardens designed by Marjorie Sewell Cautley.

222 Dojunkai Apartments, Omotesando, Tokyo, Japan, 1924–6, demolished

Sunnyside
A Step
toward
Better
Housing

223 Sunnyside Gardens, Frederick Ackermann, Clarence Stein and Henry Wright, Queens, New York, USA, 1924–6

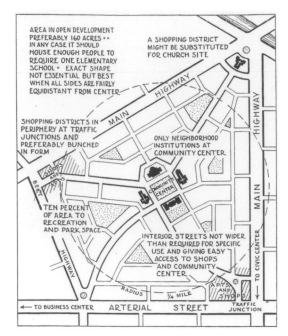

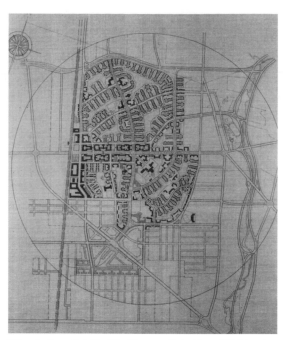

224 The Neighborhood Unit, illustration from *Neighborhood and Community Planning,* Clarence A. Perry, 1929

225 Radburn Satellite City, Clarence Stein, Henry Wright and Frederick Ackerman, Radburn, New Jersey, USA, 1927–9

226 Karl Marx School, André Lurçat, Villejuif, France, 1930–3

227 Open-air School, Eugène Beaudouin and Marcel Lods, Suresnes, France, 1934

228 Zonnestraal Sanatorium, Johannes Duiker, Hilversum, Netherlands, 1926–8

The same team was responsible for the Hillside Homes in the Bronx (1935). In both cases, New York's ubiquitous housing blocks were replaced by "superblocks" featuring generous playgrounds and gardens at their centers. With the satellite city of Radburn, New Jersey (1927–9), **225** the Stein/Wright/Ackerman/Cautley team introduced a fundamental modification to the garden-city model – which had already been reformulated in the context of the German *Siedlungen* – by systematically taking the automobile into account. Automobile and foot traffic flowed through separate public spaces, sometimes on different levels. Left unfinished owing to the stock market crash in 1929, the Radburn project inspired scores of later American schemes. [16] In Philadelphia, Oscar Storonov and Alfred Kastner built the Carl Mackley Houses (1932) for the local branch of the American Federation of Full-Fashioned Hosiery Workers. The vocabulary they used was closer to that of André Lurçat – for whom Storonov had worked – than of Le Corbusier, although they did borrow the element of indented massing from him. In the same period, the American economist Clarence A. Perry, who was employed by the Regional Plan of New York, dedicated himself to defining social norms and quantifying the size of residential areas. Basing his research on sociological studies, he developed the concept of the "neighborhood unit" **224** to define the structure and scale of the smallest urban-residential unit that would permit an optimal collective life. [17] Integrated into plans for American projects of the 1930s, this concept spread to the rest of the world following World War II.

Equipping the suburbs

Housing schemes built in the 1920s incorporated an unprecedented variety and density of public facilities. People's houses – or clubs dedicated to sports and leisure – became increasingly common, while buildings for education were the most characteristic. Progressive pedagogical models combined with architectural experimentation to produce a new type of school building that was luminous, open to outdoor spaces, and geared to positive learning. Open-air schools such as those by Johannes Duiker in Amsterdam (1926–8) and by Eugène Beaudouin and Marcel Lods in Suresnes (1934) **227** were among the most notable of these types of projects. They borrowed the idea of terraces facing the sun from tuberculosis sanatoriums such as Duiker's in Hilversum (1926–8), **228** turning the school building into a hygienic machine in which children's everyday lives were closely monitored. [18]

Between 1930 and 1933 André Lurçat built a school named after Karl Marx **226** for the Communist municipality of Villejuif, a suburb of Paris. It stood as a manifesto of modernity among the shoddy local housing divisions. The school's *pilotis*, ribbon windows, and terraces were arranged according to a precise geometry, in a kind of exaggerated version of Le Corbusier's key concepts. A total environment in which furniture, signage, and building details shared a single aesthetic, the school seemed to promise children in the suburbs access to a level of luxurious equipment previously unknown in the area's bare-bones neighborhoods. [19] In the late 1930s the unprecedented building effort carried out on the peripheries of Paris could be seen on a European and even a global scale. [20] It represented a new dimension of urban structuring – the neighborhood equipped with an infrastructure of community life and with modern amenities both inside and out. The result of an alliance of architects, landscape gardeners, and public authorities, its forms were not only a response to the new suburban conditions but a prefiguration of new kinds of dense urban centers to come.

Internationalization, its networks and spectacles

A flourishing worldwide network of interactions among modern architects existed long before New York's Museum of Modern Art heralded the so-called International Style in its fifteenth exhibition (1932), picking up on a slogan Walter Gropius had originated in Weimar in 1923. → 1 Architects were now engaging with one another in new and diverse ways: through participation in conferences, congresses, and other events; through the circulation of periodicals covering architectural trends; and through the creation of organizations both ephemeral and long lasting, from subversive to pompously official and stodgy. Far from being limited to the circulation of styles, the internationalization of architecture manifested itself in a variety of formats, ranging from publications to exhibitions to durable associations modeled on workers' internationals or on new postwar institutions.

The journal as printed stage

Photographs of new buildings and of the objects and structures that inspired them, such as machines and engineering works, became widely available between the wars. The international dissemination of images had begun before the end of World War I with the journal *De Stijl*, and it continued until it was interrupted by the authoritarian measures instituted by the Soviets and the Nazis, which extended to most of Europe under German occupation after 1940. In Paris, discord between Le Corbusier and Amédée Ozenfant led to the closing of *L'Esprit nouveau* in 1925, but Jean Badovici's *L'Architecture vivante* (Living Architecture), founded in 1923, continued to illustrate innovative work throughout Europe, including Russia, until 1932. *L'Architecture d'aujourd'hui* (Architecture of Today), founded in 1930 by the engineer

André Bloc, provided a platform for enlightened – or simply opportunistic – conservatives such as Albert Laprade. → 2 In Germany, after the short-lived *Frühlicht* and *G* disappeared, trade periodicals such as *Bauwelt* (Building World) continued to provide a mouthpiece for innovative positions until 1933, while *Wasmuths Monatshefte* (Wasmuth's Monthly), edited by Werner Hegemann, and *Moderne Bauformen* (Modern Building Forms) favored modern traditionalists. In Basel the functionalists Emil Roth, Hans Schmidt, and Mart Stam published the radical broadsheet *ABC, Beiträge zum Bauen* (ABC, Contributions to Building) **229** from 1924 to 1928, while in Zurich the critic Peter Meyer expressed his opinions in *Das Werk* (The Work), the journal of the Swiss Werkbund. The creation in Milan of both *Domus* and *La Casa Bella* (later *Casabella*) opened a dialogue between the more artistic perceptions of the former and the clearly social focus of the latter. In Moscow the Constructivist review *Sovremennaia Arkhitektura*, or *SA*, first published in 1926, disappeared in 1930, the year *Sovetskaia Arkhitektura* (Soviet Architecture) was launched; it then turned into the party-controlled *Arkhitektura SSSR* (USSR's Architecture) in 1933. Yet the periodical *Arkhitektura za rubezhom* (Architecture Abroad) continued publishing images of Western projects from 1934 to 1936. Reviews like *Stavba* (Construction) **230** in Prague, *Tér és Forma* (Space and Form) in Budapest, and *Blok* (Block) in Warsaw had a significant effect on the architectural culture of Central and Eastern Europe. A wide variety of publications proliferated, many of them graphically innovative. Periodicals such as *Al-'Imara* (The Architecture) in Cairo, *Mimar* (The Architect) in Istanbul, *Réalisations* in Morocco, and *Kokusai Kenchiku* (The Modern Architect) **231** in Japan suggest the extent to which architectural publishing had become a global phenomenon.

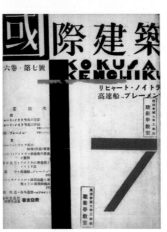

232 ▶ *Modern Architecture: International Exhibition*, curators Henry-Russell Hitchcock and Philip Johnson, New York City, USA, 1932

230 Cover of *Stavba* (Construction), Karel Teige, Prague, Czechoslovakia (Czech Republic), 1931

231 Cover of *Kokusai Kenchiku* (The Modern Architect), Japan, 1930

229 Cover of *ABC, Beiträge zum Bauen* (ABC, Contributions to Building), Basel, Switzerland, 1927–8

Model cities and open-air exhibitions

In addition to such publications, in which illustrations played an increasingly important role, exhibitions became an essential medium for disseminating new forms. Official international expositions in the nineteenth-century mold were still dependent on promoters, sponsors, and patrons, which circumscribed the opportunities they offered for presenting innovative ideas. Nonetheless, these events regularly featured high-profile pavilions that had a significant impact on the public's perception of modern architecture. The most striking examples include Le Corbusier's contributions to the Paris expositions of 1925 and 1937, particularly his Temps Nouveaux (New Times) pavilion of 1937; Mies van der Rohe's projects for the 1929 International Exposition in Barcelona and the 1931 Berlin Building Exhibition; the Czechoslovakia and Japan pavilions at the 1937 Paris exposition; and Lucio Costa and Oscar Niemeyer's Brazil Pavilion and Alvar Aalto's Finland Pavilion at the 1939 New York World's Fair. In the realm of national shows, the Stockholm Exposition of 1930 promoted functionalist architecture in Sweden, in what Alvar Aalto perceived at the time as a "language of pure, spontaneous joy." → 3

Like the villages constructed for nineteenth-century world's fairs, several experimental housing developments between the wars served as showcases for alternative concepts. Individual projects such as Georg Muche's 1923 Haus am Horn in Weimar and Le Corbusier's 1925 Pavilion of *L'Esprit nouveau* in Paris alternated with collective endeavors, the most spectacular being the housing exposition at the Weißenhof in Stuttgart. Built under the aegis of the Deutsche Werkbund for the *Die neue Wohnung* (The New Home) exhibition in 1927, the Weißenhof comprised some twenty buildings constructed according to

a master plan by Ludwig Mies van der Rohe. Mies invited his mentor Peter Behrens along with Walter Gropius, Bruno and Max Taut, J. J. P. Oud, Mart Stam, Hans Scharoun, Ludwig Hilberseimer, and Le Corbusier to contribute to this life-size demonstration of the principles of the *Neues Bauen*, or new building policy. (His exclusion of Heinrich Tessenow, Erich Mendelsohn, and Hugo Häring caused Adolf Loos to refuse to participate.) The critic Walter Curt Behrendt, the co-organizer of the exhibition, heralded the fact that the various buildings shared a common vocabulary of architectural traits, marking the triumph of a "new style." → 4 Dominated by an apartment block with a steel frame and movable partitions designed by Mies himself – one of the first experiments in flexible interiors – the buildings showcased the aesthetic of the flat roof, among other architectural principles, and of building methods like dry assembly with ready-made panels, the latter used by Gropius. The Stuttgart *Siedlung* met with plenty of ironic reactions. One of them, a postcard showing stereotypical "Oriental" figures and camels, **233** mocked the white, cubic development as an "Arab village." Yet the Weißenhof model inspired similar initiatives throughout Central Europe, including the *Nový Dům* (New Dwelling) exhibition in Brno (1928) and the *Wohnung und Werkraum* (Living and Work Space) exhibition in Breslau (1929). Unlike the relative luxury of the Stuttgart development, the Austrian *Werkbund Siedlung* exhibition in Vienna **236** had a clear-cut social agenda. The Baba Development in Prague (1931-2) **237** and the Neubühl Development in Zurich (1932) were less spectacular, more pragmatic versions of the same phenomenon. → 5 Often glaringly white and always photogenic, these developments demonstrated that a new way of living in sunlight and fresh air, in spaces stripped of old-fashioned furnishings, was not only desirable but also accessible to most

233 Weißenhofsiedlung, Ludwig Mies van der Rohe, Stuttgart, Germany, 1927, postcard mocking the exposition as an "Arab village"

234 Gruppo 7 section of the Third Monza Biennial, Monza, Italy, 1927

people. → 6 So strong were these convictions that the German traditionalists, who had been excluded from the 1927 exhibition, were compelled to return to Stuttgart in 1933 to take their revenge. Their conservative *Siedlung* at the Kochenhof consisted of wood houses with sloping roofs, but made out of prefabricated components.

Modern architecture enters the museums

Apart from these full-scale, open-air presentations, trade and industrial exhibitions regularly featured new ideas, beginning with the 1922 Salon d'Automne in Paris. In Berlin, the annual Große Berliner Kunstausstellung (Great Berlin Art Exhibition) gave Mies several opportunities to present his theoretical projects. In Italy, starting in 1927, the general public was offered an overview of the latest developments in the country's architecture at the biennials in Monza, near Milan, **234** later to be continued as the Milan triennials. Organizations such as the Union des artistes modernes in Paris seem to have been founded largely to ensure that their members were invited to participate in decorative-arts exhibitions. Meanwhile, art galleries remained receptive places to display the latest trends. For instance, the Russian avant-garde exhibition at the Van Diemen Gallery in Berlin (1922), the 1923 De Stijl show at the Galerie de l'effort moderne in Paris, the *Machine-Age Exposition* at Jane Heap's Little Gallery in New York (1927), **235** and the *Arts Primitifs dans la Maison d'Aujourd'hui* (Primitive Arts in the Contemporary Home) exhibition organized in Le Corbusier's own Paris apartment by the art dealer Louis Carré (1935) were milestones in circulating ideas and fostering the relationship between art and architecture. Museums played a relatively marginal role with the exception of certain German institutions such as the Provinzialmuseum in

Hanover, directed by Alexander Dorner; the ephemeral Museum of Contemporary Western Art in Moscow; and especially the Museum of Modern Art in New York. MoMA opened in 1929 on the twelfth floor of a building on Fifth Avenue and moved into its permanent home designed by Philip Goodwin and Edward Durell Stone ten years later. During this first decade the architecture department, founded by Philip Johnson, held several exhibitions. The one with most repercussions was the 1932 *Modern Architecture: International Exhibition*, **232** which focused on Gropius, Oud, Le Corbusier, and Wright and excluded both the Expressionists and the Constructivists. It was accompanied by a book in which Henry-Russell Hitchcock and Johnson put forth the principles of what they described as the "International Style": volume was to replace mass, ornament was to be eliminated, and regularity and flexibility were to supplant the academic obsession with symmetry. → 7 The exhibition's impact was intensified by its tour of sixteen American cities, where it was displayed in museums and department stores.

Following the success of this show – whose impact would nonetheless remain limited to the United States for decades – MoMA held monographic exhibitions devoted to Le Corbusier (1935) and Wright (1940). Architecture had only a discreet presence in the *Machine Art* exhibition of 1934, but was far more important in *Cubism and Abstract Art* (1936) and in *Bauhaus 1919–1928* (1938). Picking up on the housing section at MoMA's *Modern Architecture* show, which had been organized by Lewis Mumford, → 8 was *America Can't Have Housing*, a 1934 exhibition that dealt with social issues otherwise mostly absent from the museum's galleries. After World War II the MoMA model of a cultural institution with a designated place for architecture and design spread throughout the United States and the world.

237 Baba Housing Development catalog cover, Prague, Czechoslovakia (Czech Republic), 1931–2,

235 Cover for the catalog of *Machine-Age Exposition*, designed by Fernand Léger, New York City, USA, 1927

236 Poster for the Werkbund Siedlung exposition, Josef Frank et al., Vienna, Austria, 1931

The International Congresses of Modern Architecture (CIAM)

The public success of the Weißenhof housing exhibition in 1927 could not compensate for the failure of the modern projects submitted to the League of Nations competition the same year. Le Corbusier's proposal was rejected, as were a more radical project by Hannes Meyer and Hans Wittwer and one by Auguste Perret. To sustain the success of the Stuttgart exhibition and to heal the wound inflicted by rejection in Geneva, a group of architects gathered at the Château de La Sarraz in Switzerland in June 1928 and founded the Congrès Internationaux d'Architecture Moderne (International Congresses of Modern Architecture) or CIAM. **238** The Zurich art historian Sigfried Giedion was elected general secretary. By creating an international brotherhood on the model of the Social Democratic or Communist internationals, and by including groups from every country, this elite association of radical architects, backed by the elder figure of Hendrik Petrus Berlage, sought to use CIAM to make their voices heard by heads of state and industry. Although wracked by violent disagreements between Le Corbusier and May, Meyer, and Lurçat, the participants at the first meeting adopted a declaration affirming the "unity of their views on the fundamental conceptions of architecture and on their professional obligations" and proclaiming that "urbanism can no longer submit exclusively to the rules of a gratuitous aestheticism. It is functional by its very nature." [9]

The second congress was held in Frankfurt am Main in 1929. It inaugurated the practice that would continue at subsequent conferences of presenting exhibits in the form of graphic displays in a homogeneous format facilitating comparisons. **239** In Le Corbusier's absence, the discussion – dedicated to "Existenzminimum," or subsistence-level housing, and thus to compact,

economical dwelling units – was dominated by Gropius and May's architectural team from Germany, who were responsible for that year's exhibition. Yet with the government of Weimar Germany paralyzed by economic crisis, the social program formulated at the Frankfurt congress was only partly heeded. The third congress, held in Brussels in 1930, addressed urban form with a focus on hygiene and mass production. Participants discussed the theme of the rational development of the housing schemes, evaluating the advantages and disadvantages of high-rise constructions. Unlike the garden city – that "generous movement" that, in Le Corbusier's words, "led to the scattering of homes and the complete alienation of certain inhabited areas" – the aim was not so much the dispersal of the elements of the city but their "aeration." [10]

The fourth congress, devoted to the "functional city," was intended to examine the principles involved in expanding and renovating cities, and it was planned to be held in Moscow in an effort to expand CIAM's territory still farther. However, the aggressive campaign against modern architecture in the USSR led the organizers to relocate the 1933 meeting to Athens. The participants sailed there from Marseilles aboard the *Patris II*, a ship belonging to a relative of Christian Zervos, publisher of the magazine *Cahiers d'art*. In the absence of most German members, the group shifted perspective and focused on a more methodological and normative approach to the city. Discussions revolved around a graphic display that addressed the urban situation of some thirty cities, the plans of which featured standardized grids underscoring the similarity of problems from one city to the next. **240** The use of a system of universal codification developed by the Viennese philosopher Otto Neurath for presenting statistical information **241** – plus a statement expressing regret that the congress could not conduct

238 Participants in the First International Congress of Modern Architecture (CIAM), La Sarraz, Switzerland, 1928. From left to right, standing: Richard Dupierre, Mart Stam, Pierre Chareau, Victor Bourgeois, Max Ernst Haefeli, Pierre Jeanneret, Gerrit Rietveld, Rudolf Steiger, Ernst May, Alberto Sartoris, Gabriel Guevrékian, Hans Schmidt, Hugo Häring, Zavala, Lucienne Fiorentin, Le Corbusier, Paul Artaria, Hélène de Mandrot, Friedrich Gubler, Rochat, André Lurçat, Henri-Robert von der Mühll, Gino Maggioni, Huib Hoste, Sigfried Giedion, Werner Moser and Josef Frank; seated: Fernando García Mercadal, Molly Weber and Tadevossian.

239 Exhibition at the Second International Congress for Modern Architecture, Frankfurt am Main, Germany, 1929

240 Plan of Zurich, exhibited at the Fourth International Congress for Modern Architecture, Athens, Greece, 1933

its business in Esperanto – indicated the participants' desire to build a core of principles with universal application. → 11 After lively debates engaged by Cornelis van Eesteren, Le Corbusier, Fernand Léger, and others, the meeting resulted in a text defining all cities as composites of four urban "functions": living, working, recreation, and (especially) circulation. Ignoring Léger's exhortation to the architects to "put your plans in your pocket, go out in the street!" → 12 the participants agreed on a set of "observations" that were reductive but would nonetheless have significant consequences.

The emigration of CIAM's principal German founders after 1933 reinforced the group's leadership by a Zurich-Amsterdam axis. Nonetheless, Le Corbusier managed to control the fifth congress, which took place in 1937 in Paris and dealt with "housing and recreation." Most significantly, he produced a document he called *La charte d'Athènes* (The Athens Charter), an expanded version of CIAM's 1933 "observations." This litany of requirements, which Le Corbusier published anonymously during the German occupation of France, first in a small edition of 1942 and then in a larger one in 1943, has often been viewed as an "anti-idea" of the city, geared to the creation of homogenized and isotropic urban spaces. → 13 But it was also a composite of principles that had been set out by town planners since the beginning of the century, and it may be considered a simple reiteration of the concept of functional zoning established decades earlier in Germany and the United States. The charter set forth a critique of the "prevailing condition of the cities" under five headings, each containing "observations" followed by "requirements," or remedial measures, that the public was invited to demand. In terms of housing – and in reaction against suburbanization – "residential districts were to occupy the best locations within the urban space … having the best exposure

to sunshine with accessible verdant areas at their disposal." In terms of recreation, "High buildings, set far apart from one another" were to "free the ground for broad verdant areas." In terms of work, "distances between places of work and places of residence must be reduced to a minimum," and "industrial areas must be independent of the residential areas and separated from one another by a zone of vegetation." Finally, in terms of circulation, it was obvious that a dedicated traffic system would be essential to connect these isolated urban components; "Roads must be differentiated according to their purposes" and earmarked for pedestrian or more or less rapid car transit, reflecting Le Corbusier's hatred of the "corridor street." → 14

Contrary to what has sometimes been stated, the *Athens Charter* did not completely repudiate the heritage of the city; in fact, under a fifth heading, it called for elements of the historic city to be preserved as "architectural assets." Yet by tearing down the shoddy buildings surrounding them, "the vestiges of the past [would] be bathed in a new and possibly unexpected ambience, but certainly a tolerable one." → 15

Networks of influence and historical narratives

Although CIAM's ambitious program for the transformation of cities as reflected in the *Athens Charter* remained virtually unknown to the public until 1945, its founding premise – that architects and urban planners should make a decisive contribution to technical and social modernization – led to other strategies of persuasion beyond mere manifestos. Political networks and personal relationships were far more decisive in determining these contributions than the dialogue between the existing architectural elite and the political and economic leadership.

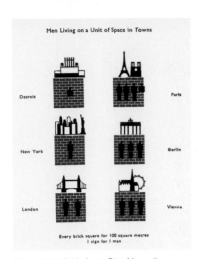

241 Analytical chart, Otto Neurath, exhibited at the Fourth International Congress for Modern Architecture, Athens, Greece, 1933

242 *Pioneers of the Modern Movement*, Nikolaus Pevsner, 1936, title page

243 *Space, Time and Architecture: The Growth of a New Tradition*, Sigfried Giedion, 1941, dust jacket

The allies of the moderns ranged from nations to municipalities, from cooperatives to unions, and they were also found in the business world, where the AEG model remained powerful. While certainly not the only architect to court the heads of the most significant industrial companies, Le Corbusier was probably the most persistent. After failing to seduce the leading French automobile manufacturers with his ideas – with the exception of the marginal Gabriel Voisin – he turned to Fiat and Olivetti in Italy. For nearly two years he also managed to maintain a close relationship with the shoe manufacturer Baťa, whose factory, located in the Moravian city of Zlín, had been designed by the company's architects according to a functional plan. Yet Le Corbusier's efforts to build a housing complex for the company in Hellocourt in eastern France, to design its stores, and to construct its pavilion at the Paris exposition of 1937 came to naught. → 16

Inspired by the mobilization of architects, urban reformers founded their own organizations. Expanding on the activities of the garden-city movement, which had been established worldwide by Ebenezer Howard's architectural heirs, the International Housing and Town Planning Federation, founded in 1926 in Frankfurt, attempted to coordinate efforts to build salubrious cities accessible to the working classes by organizing conferences that brought together administrators, economists, and professionals. As for architects, CIAM's rapid rise did not interrupt the regular gatherings of official professional congresses, which dated back to the previous century, nor did it prevent a few pathetically ineffective attempts to mediate between the position of the radicals and the reactionaries. The most notable example of the latter was a series of international meetings launched by Pierre Vago in 1932 under the aegis of *L'Architecture d'aujourd'hui* in hopes of creating a "third way"

between CIAM and conservative practitioners. After a memorable visit by French architects to Moscow in 1932, the meetings moved successively to Italy, Czechoslovakia, and Paris, increasing in attendance and creating lasting relationships among enlightened professionals. → 17

A final factor in the internationalization of architecture between the wars was the "up to the minute" documentation of the history of the various movements after 1920. As early as 1927, articles appeared emphasizing the geographic extent of the new architecture while various syntheses, more or less doctrinaire, described their genesis and locational inflections. Significant early books included Gustav-Adolf Platz's *Baukunst der neuesten Zeit* (Architecture of the Latest Times; 1927) and Henry-Russell Hitchcock's *Modern Architecture: Romanticism and Reintegration* (1929). These were followed by *Pioneers of the Modern Movement from William Morris to Walter Gropius* (1936) **242** by Nikolaus Pevsner, a German art historian who had emigrated to England. The title of Pevsner's book had even greater impact than the volume published by MoMA in 1932. → 18 With its dynamic connotations, the image of a "modern movement" – a term Otto Wagner had used forty years earlier – proved more successful than that of an international "style," a notion with which the moderns had an ambiguous relationship. The critic Sigfried Giedion, who had close ties to Gropius and Le Corbusier, gave the movement its gospel – or its catechism – by publishing the series of lectures he delivered in the late 1930s at Harvard, on Gropius's invitation, under the title *Space, Time and Architecture* (1941). → 19 **243**

Futurism and Rationalism in Fascist Italy

In Italy the proposals of modern architects seemed to find receptive partners for a short period among both industrialists and the political leaders of the new Fascist government, established in 1922. For the following fifteen years, a regime otherwise split by conflicts between modern-leaning and conservative ideologues supported the modernization of Italian architecture. Although relatively late in rallying to modern ideals, that architecture would make a notable and original contribution to European culture in the 1930s.

A second Futurism

While some leading Futurists were facing danger on the front lines of World War I, echoes of the movement reverberated in the engineer Giacomo Mattè-Trucco's gigantic Fiat Factory in Lingotto in Turin (1916–23). **245** Later, in their 1935 "Manifesto of Aerial Architecture," Filippo Tommaso Marinetti, Angiolo Mazzoni, and Mino Somenzi would call the Fiat Factory "the first constructive Futurist invention." Mattè-Trucco's plant was explicitly based on the Ford factory buildings in the United States, which various Italian engineers had visited in order to learn how to create "a new establishment in the American style." A modular structure composed of 8-by-8-meter (26-by-26-foot) units, the factory was erected by the Porcheddu reinforced-concrete company, which owned the Italian rights to the Hennebique system. → 1 The automobile assembly line ended on the roof, which served as a track to test new cars. Le Corbusier praised the 800 meters (2,600 feet) of this industrial "vessel" for its "clear form," "simplicity," "order," and "moral tension," and reproduced it in *L'Esprit nouveau* before personally taking a turn on the test track in 1934. The poet Blaise Cendrars had already imagined such a building in his 1917 poem about Fiat: "I envy the way you lie there/Big steamship of factories/At anchor/On the outskirts of town." → 2

Antonio Sant'Elia's ideas on the new industrial city were further developed during this period by Mario Chiattone, an architect from Bergamo, and by his Roman colleague Virgilio Marchi, whose images of urban schemes were expressive and lyrical. → 3 In 1924 Marchi declared that architecture should become "pure sculptural abstraction." → 4 Among the most notable members of the second wave of Futurism active in architecture were Enrico Prampolini, designer of the Futurist pavilion at the Turin International Exposition (1928) and Fortunato Depero, one of the authors of the 1915 manifesto "Ricostruzione futurista dell'universo" (Futurist Reconstruction of the Universe). The manifesto evoked an "edifice in a transformable noise style," an idea inspired by "clouds flying in a storm." A graphics and set designer, Depero built pavilions for the Monza Biennial (1927) in which he integrated typography with architecture. Among an abundance of Futurist theoretical projects, the most remarkable were a skyscraper by the Turin-based Bulgarian Nicolaj Diulgheroff (1927), a monument to sailors in the shape of a ship by Quirino De Giorgio (1930), an airplane-house by Alessandro Marinelli (1936), and a summer camp with buildings in the shape of trains by Clemente Busiri-Vici (c. 1930). → 5 Even more radical were projects by the painter-architect Tullio Crali, the proponent of an *aeropittura* (aeropainting) depicting views from diving airplanes; in 1931 he proposed spectacular combinations of contradictory elements such as a *porta-belvedere* (belvedere-door) and an *aeroporto-stazione* (airport–railroad station).

Muzio and the Novecento

Immediately after World War I, the "return to order" that was emerging elsewhere in Europe also manifested itself in Italy. Its proponents vigorously opposed Futurism and made a radical

244 *Gare Montparnasse (The Melancholy of Departure)*, Giorgio de Chirico, 1914

245 Fiat Factory, Giacomo Mattè-Trucco, Turin, Italy, 1916–23

246 Ca' Brutta, Giovanni Muzio, Milan, Italy, 1920–2

247 Santa Maria Novella Station, Giovanni Michelucci and Gruppo Toscano, Florence, Italy, 1933–4

break with both Stile Liberty and the eclecticism that had triumphed at the *Jubilee of Unity* exposition in Rome in 1911. The painter Giorgio de Chirico **244** set the tone in 1919 in the periodical *Valori plastici* (Plastic Values), founded the year before by Manlio Broglio and oriented primarily toward Paris. It was in "the construction of the city, the architectural form of houses, public squares, gardens, and passages, of gates and train stations, etc.," De Chirico wrote, that "the foundation of a great metaphysical aesthetic" would be discovered; "a day may come," he hoped, "when this aesthetic, currently left to the whims of chance, will become a law and a necessity for the upper classes and the directors of the public good." [6] The first exhibition of artists gathered under the name *Novecento* (Twentieth Century) was inaugurated in March 1923 by Benito Mussolini himself, whose lover at the time, the journalist and critic Margherita Sarfatti, was a supporter of the movement. In Mussolini's view at this date, the Novecento "would not encourage anything like an Art of the State," for "Art belongs to the domain of the individual." [7] The leading Novecento architects were Giovanni Muzio and Gio Ponti. Muzio, who was fully engaged in Milanese cultural life but also aware of the latest developments in Germany, France, and England, was one of the founders of the Associazione artistica fra i cultori di architettura (Artistic Association of the Amateurs of Architecture) and the Club degli urbanisti (Urban Planners Club). He aspired to a new "quadrant of the spirit" with an architectural order rooted in history. His Ca' Brutta (Ugly House; 1920–2) **246** on via Moscova in Milan offered the clearest refutation of Futurism, though he embraced modern technology enough to incorporate a garage underneath the building. Articulating the house's facades with a system of geometrically simplified niches and moldings, he divided its two adjacent blocks into three horizontal bands differentiated in surface treatment: rusticated stone

on the lowest level, marmorino stucco on the top, and plaster in between. Described as a "grim, ornery, unfriendly house" by the writer Alberto Savinio (Giorgio de Chirico's brother), [8] Ca' Brutta also came in for criticism from the architect Paolo Mezzanotte, who concluded that while lacking "the pompous vulgarity and the banal stupidity of so much concrete architecture," the classically inspired building displayed a "torment of lines and moldings [that] seems to be lacking precisely that asset peculiar to classical architecture: serenity." [9] After designing the Sala dei Marmi (Hall of Marbles) at the 1930 Monza Triennale with the painter Mario Sironi, Muzio declared: "When the building must be a work of art then calculations are not enough. Another, I would say metaphysical, order must govern the work. Therefore, the spirit that guides artists must be a uniform one, and this discipline cannot but be classical." [10] For the new campus of the Catholic University of Milan (1929–30), which had been founded in a former hospital by the priest and scientific researcher Agostino Gemelli, Muzio enclosed state-of-the-art facilities in brick walls dominated by a granite entrance portico. In the Palazzo dell'Arte (1933), **248** for the Milan Triennale, he built a machine for exhibiting, contrasting white interiors and staircases housed in glass cylinders with a facade regulated by a line of brick pilasters.

The Milan landscape was dotted with many other notable new structures, including the enigmatic Palazzo Fidia by Aldo Andreani (1930) and the Casa della Meridiana (1924–5) by Giuseppe De Finetti, a former student of Adolf Loos and an early anti-Fascist. The Milanese bourgeoisie commissioned elegant apartment buildings by Piero Portaluppi and an even greater number by Gio Ponti. Ponti launched the first issue of his magazine *Domus* in 1928, with a plea for a *casa all'italiana* (Italian-style house) that would put comfort first and not be reduced to

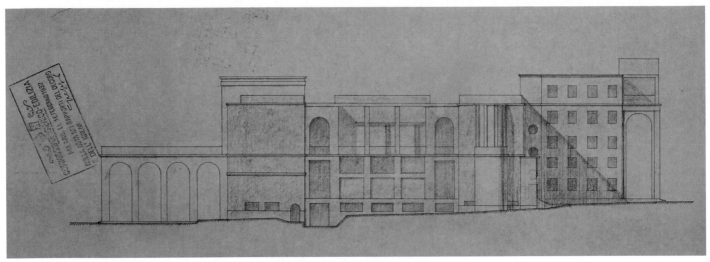

248 Palazzo dell'Arte for the Triennale, Giovanni Muzio, Milan, Italy, 1933

249 Casa Elettrica at the Triennale, Luigi Figini and Gino Pollini, Milan, Italy, 1930

250 Rustici Apartment Building, Giuseppe Terragni and Pietro Lingeri, Milan, Italy, 1933–6

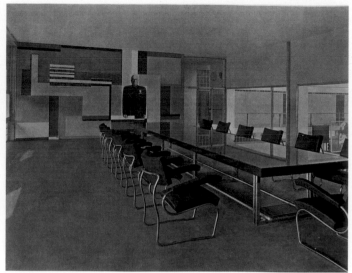

251 Casa del Fascio, Giuseppe Terragni, Como, Italy, 1932–6, interior with mural by Mario Radice

252 Casa del Fascio, Giuseppe Terragni, Como, Italy, 1932–6, photomontage of exterior with crowd

a mere "machine for living." → 11 Ponti's conception of the house as a "second set of clothes" owed much to his admiration for Palladio but without resorting to classical clichés. His designs for apartment towers and for the Palazzo Montecatini (1936) created an image of Milan as a city both opulent and modern.

The regime and Rationalism

Operating within Italy's polycentric culture, Mussolini's regime took a variety of approaches to urban planning and architecture, treating every movement and generation with equal attention, to the point that no single approach can be described unequivocally as Fascist. This was so despite the fact that the Duce directly interceded in Italian architecture during the early 1930s. → 12 During these years he announced his support for a project by Giovanni Michelucci and his Gruppo Toscano, thereby enabling him to win the competition to build the Santa Maria Novella Station in Florence (1933–4). 247 Michelucci's design called for a structure with long horizontal lines of concrete, brick, and glass – worlds apart from Ulisse Stacchini's overbearing Milan Station completed two years earlier after two decades of work. → 13 Mussolini issued statements encouraging the young architects who were responsible for the emergence of the movement known as *razionalismo* in the latter half of the 1920s. The first signs of their existence were four articles signed "Gruppo 7" published in 1926 in the *Rassegna italiana* (Italian Review). Following in Le Corbusier's footsteps, the group proclaimed that "a new spirit was born," initiating a heated debate with both the Futurists and the Novecento architects. → 14 The seven members – Luigi Figini, Gino Pollini, Guido Frette, Sebastiano Larco, Enrico Rava, Giuseppe Terragni, and Ubaldo Castagnoli (the last soon replaced by Adalberto Libera) – exhibited their projects at the

Monza Biennial of 1927 and, most importantly, at the first and second *Mostre di architettura razionale* (Exhibitions of Rational Architecture) in Rome in 1928 and 1931. In the meantime, they created MIAR, or the Movimento italiano per l'architettura razionale (Italian Movement for Rational Architecture). The young Milanese critic and gallery owner Pietro Maria Bardi, an ally of the Rationalists, spearheaded their attack. Denouncing "culturalist" excesses, he exhibited the *Tavolo degli orrori* (Panel of Horrors; 1931), 255 a collage showing buildings by Marcello Piacentini and others, in his gallery, and gave Il Duce a copy of his "Rapporto sull'architettura (per Mussolini)." The propaganda campaign was so successful that the conservatives hurried to found their own movement, RAMI, or the Raggruppamento architetti moderni italiani (Assembly of Modern Italian Architects). The major exhibitions of the 1930s kept pace with the development of new ideas. Libera designed the *Mostra della rivoluzione fascista* (Exhibition of the Fascist Revolution; 1932), whose main gate featured an impressive trio of fasces. In 1930, the Milan Triennial had offered the public its first glimpse of a complex of pavilions that were modern in both their technology and their form. The press pavilion by Luciano Baldessari, who also built the Bar Craja in Milan (1930), had the clarity of a factory. Figini and Pollini's Casa Elettrica 249 explored new domestic spaces. At the 1933 triennial, the Casa del Sabato per gli sposi (Saturday House for Spouses) by the BBPR group (Gian Luigi Banfi, Lodovico Belgiojoso, Enrico Peressutti, and Ernesto Nathan Rogers) suggested playful forms to accommodate leisure activities. At the same exhibition, Giuseppe Pagano demonstrated with his Casa a struttura di acciaio (House with a Steel Structure) that formal strategies previously put forward by Le Corbusier could take on new meaning when allied with northern Italy's expanding industry.

253   Post Office, Giuseppe Franzi Vaccaro, Naples, Italy, 1928–36

254   Tuberculosis Clinic, Ignazio Gardella, Alessandria, Italy, 1933–8

255 *Tavolo Degli Orrori* (Panel of Horrors), Pietro Maria Bardi, 1931

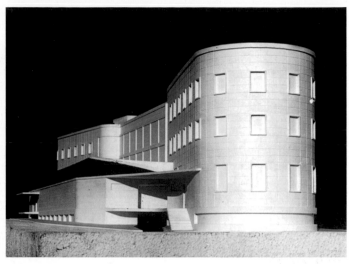

256 Post Office, Mario Ridolfi, Rome, Italy, 1933

A state program to construct post offices diffused these ideas into public architecture. Mario Ridolfi's Post Office (1933) **256** in Rome's Nomentana quarter has a fluid brick facade while Libera's on the Aventine Hill (also 1933) is an assemblage of marble prisms surrounding the glass roof of the main hall. As part of an effort to clean up the center of Naples, Giuseppe Vaccaro built a Palazzo delle Poste (Post Office; 1928–36) **253** with a curved roof hovering above the old neighboring buildings. Jean-Paul Sartre dryly described it as "a huge black-and-gray fake-marble structure," containing "huge halls with masses of service windows." [15] The Mussolini regime was willing to risk hiring young architects to design some of its other public projects as well. Luigi Moretti built Casa della GIL (House of the GIL, or Gioventú italiano del littorio, the Fascist youth organization) in Rome's Trastevere district (1933), while Agnoldomenico Pica built one in Narni (1937). In the public health sector, the BBPR group built the Colonia Elioterapeutica (Heliotherapy Sanatorium) in Legnano (1937–8), and Ignazio Gardella built a tuberculosis clinic in Alessandria, using vernacular brick screens inserted into a concrete framework (1933–8). **254**

Terragni's geometries

The most fruitful encounter between the regime and the new architecture took place in Como with Giuseppe Terragni's Casa del Fascio (House of Fasces; 1932–6). **252** A member of Gruppo 7, Terragni relied somewhat on Russian Constructivism for his first projects. His Officina per la Produzione del Gas (Gas Factory; 1927) combines basic volumes and metal latticework, while his Novocomum Apartment Building (1927–9), a large housing block with naval references, was bookended by glazed cylinders similar to those of Ilya Golosov's Zuev Workers' Club.

Like most intellectuals of his generation, Terragni was a true believer in Fascism, blinded to the regime's authoritarian nature by its early embrace of modern culture. In 1932 he contributed a dramatic photomontage to the *Mostra della rivoluzione fascista* depicting a dense crowd of people raising their arms in the Fascist salute. [16]

Standing directly across from the east end of the Como Cathedral, the Casa del Fascio was the headquarters for the local branch of Italy's sole political party. Its structure, a half-cube, is divided into four wings surrounding a central atrium that allows light to stream in. The facade on the piazza is a concrete frame faced with stone, protecting an inner layer of glass, which inspired Terragni to state, "Here the Mussolinian concept that fascism is a glass house into which all can look gives rise to this interpretation … no encumbrance, no barrier, no obstacle between the political leaders and the people." [17] Its proportions – precisely based on the golden section – and its geometrically determined elements may be viewed as a strict application of Le Corbusier's principle of "regulating lines." The building's interior **251** was also furnished by Terragni and featured abstract decorations painted by Mario Radice. This elegant and restrained integration of the arts helped make the Casa del Fascio a comprehensive alternative to the neoclassical edifices built by the regime elsewhere in Italy, which were decorated to excess with frescoes and sculptures.

Also in Como, Terragni built a nursery school in 1936–7 named after Antonio Sant'Elia. The local hero's memory was frequently invoked by the northern Rationalists, who exalted his sacrifice on the battlefield and, in publications like *Dopo Sant'Elia* (After Sant'Elia; 1935), contrasted his rigor with the more mannered neo-Futurist projects. [18] Terragni's design for the nursery school explored innovations by the French (André

257 Villa Oro, Luigi Cosenza and Bernard Rudofsky, Naples, Italy, 1934–7

258 Sabaudia New Town, Gino Cancellotti, Eugenio Montuori, Luigi Piccinato and Alfredo Scalpelli, Sabaudia, Italy, 1934

Lurçat, for one) and the Germans. Separated into wings corresponding to different functions of the institution, the building, with its suspended concrete slab and retractable awnings, is a device for catching light, and every room is doubled by an outside space. Terragni collaborated with Pietro Lingeri to build five residential buildings, all of which tried out novel approaches in terms of both typology, breaking with conservative domestic arrangements, and tectonics, offering a frank expression of structure. The Rustici Apartment Building (1933–6) **250** in Milan transcended the conflict between the unbroken urban facade and the *Zeilenbau* principle. Its system integrated the balconies that connected the housing blocks with the streetscape of buildings on the Corso Sempione. Terragni's Giuliani Frigerio Building in Como (1939) was the result of an extraordinarily rigorous exploration of proportions, materiality, and profiles. [19] He developed an unbuilt project with Lingeri for a Danteum in Rome (1938–40), which was a celebration less of the author of the *Divine Comedy* than of that literary work, used as a script for the building's spatial sequence. In a complex combination of rooms delimited by marble walls and planned according to the golden section, the visitor was programmed to move through "inferno" and "purgatory" to a final hall containing thirty-three glass columns of "paradise."

An ambiguous "Mediterraneanism"

Radice and Terragni were among the founders of the review *Quadrante*, which was headed by Pietro Maria Bardi and Massimo Bontempelli. Over three years, from 1933 to 1936, *Quadrante* set out a rigorous program and declared its support for a modern *mediterraneità* (Mediterraneanism), of which the Casa del Fascio was the paradigm and Le Corbusier's Purism a useful precedent. In 1931 MIAR had pointed out that "the tendency to exalt this Latin quality, which has allowed this architecture to define itself as Mediterranean, is becoming ever more pronounced." [20] Enrico Peressutti suggested that the new architecture had a source different from the purely platonic modern architecture from the north, namely in popular culture: "Architectures of white walls that are rectangular or square, horizontal or vertical; architectures of solids and voids, forms and colors, geometry and proportion … a geometry that speaks, an architecture whose walls ring out with the sound of life and song." [21] The Villa Oro (1934–7) **257** built on the Gulf of Naples by Luigi Cosenza and the Viennese émigré Bernard Rudofsky, a protégé of Ponti, perfectly illustrates this position. Here, Loos's *Raumplan* was combined with the cubic volumes of the architecture of the Campania. [22] Located a few miles away, the home of the writer Curzio Malaparte (1938–42) **261** has a more metaphysical aspect. The rectangular volume perches on the rocky promontory of the Punta Masullo in Capri, with a rooftop terrace connected to the ground by a single staircase spanning the width of the building – recalling the entrance to the Annunziata Church on the island of Lipari where the writer had once been deported. Malaparte was directly involved in the design of his house, whose preliminary plan was designed by Adalberto Libera. [23] It later served as the unforgettable setting of Jean-Luc Godard's film *Le Mépris* (Contempt; 1963). Founded in 1928 by Guido Marangoni, *Casabella* became, under the guidance of Giuseppe Pagano, the most sophisticated and thoughtful periodical in Europe. It was in *Casabella* that the anti-Fascist critic Edoardo Persico published his subtle evaluations of European architecture, countering the ingenuous or ideological celebration of *mediterraneità* with a discussion

259 Olivetti Factory, Luigi Figini and Gino Pollini, Ivrea, Italy, 1939–40

260 Plan for Milano Verde, Franco Albini, Ignazio Gardella, Giuseppe Minoletti, Giuseppe Pagano et al., Milan, Italy, 1938

261 ▶ Casa Malaparte, preliminary project Adalberto Libera, Capri, Italy, 1938–42

of modern European taste. Pagano was a determining force in the 1936 Milan Triennial, which gave evidence of the power of modern architecture in Italy and offered new views. It opened with a Salone d'Onore (Hall of Honor) conceived by Persico and Marcello Nizzoli and included a Sala della Coerenza (Room of Coherence) by BBPR. At the center of the exhibition park stood an abstract fountain by Carlo Cattaneo and Radice, which would be re-created in Como in 1960. Agnoldomenico Pica's *Architettura moderna in Italia* exhibition displayed the full range of national production, while *Architettura Rurale Italiana*, curated by Pagano and the German architect Guarniero (Werner) Daniel, convincingly revealed the vernacular sources of *mediterraneità* cited earlier by Peressutti. [→ 24]

New territories

During the 1930s, the Italian program of modernization was concentrated in part on the creation of new cities. The state lavished its greatest attention on developments built by the National Veterans' Organization in the Agro Pontino; these served as both outposts for Rome and centers of agricultural colonization. The administrative center of Littoria (now Latina) was designed by Oriolo Frezzotti (1932) according to a simplified radial plan. The Fascist mise-en-scène most effectively tapped into the sources of modern architecture in Sabaudia (1934), with a project by the Gruppo urbanisti romani (Roman Urban Planning Group) – Luigi Piccinato, Gino Cancellotti, Eugenio Montuori, and Alfredo Scalpelli. The plan for Sabaudia's city center, **258** with its asymmetrical piazzas dominated by the city hall tower, was a successful interpretation of Camillo Sitte's precepts, while the residential neighborhoods drew on German social housing.

The Fascist state and its organizations were not alone in determining planning policy at the regional scale. The industrialist Adriano Olivetti played an essential role in shaping modern industrial and design culture, both through products like the Lettera 42 typewriter, designed by the former Bauhaus teacher Xanti Schawinsky in 1935, and through his financing of architectural programs. [→ 25] Luigi Figini and Gino Pollini built the Olivetti Factory in Ivrea in 1939–40, **259** which had vast plate-glass windows and included housing and a daycare center for the employees' children. Olivetti hired the same architects to collaborate with BBPR and Piero Bottoni on a regional plan for the Aosta Valley (1936–40). The ancient Roman town of Aosta was redesigned according to functionalist zoning precepts based on its original layout and integrated into an overall plan with the ski resorts of Courmayeur and Sauze d'Oulx; the team's strategy is best represented in its designs for long linear buildings in scale with the Alpine landscape.

The clarity of these Olivetti-funded but unbuilt projects, and of the plan by Franco Albini, Ignazio Gardella, Giuseppe Minoletti, and Giuseppe Pagano for Milano Verde (Green Milan; 1938), **260** based on the German *Zeilenbau* principle, should not overshadow the fact that until Italy entered the war in 1940 the institutions and markets of Italian architecture were controlled neither by the regime nor by modern architects. Decisions and commissions were largely in the hands of a single architect, Marcello Piacentini, an all-powerful official who operated both in the public sphere and behind the scenes. [→ 26] A determined opportunist, he knew how to exploit the modernist discourse while remaining first and foremost a proponent of a reinvented classicism. Elsewhere in Europe, too, depending on the country, devotion to classical principles either remained in full force or was in the process of being revived.

The spectrum of classicisms and traditionalisms

The path to modernity was a winding one, and strategies based on selective readings of historical forms contributed as much as ones proposing new spatial and plastic languages. Architects who were committed to more or less critical interpretations of tradition maintained their power and networks of influence around the world, whether they clung to the dominant design methods of the nineteenth century or reacted to the pressure from experimental movements with a sort of precocious postmodernism. Even the political and economic forces most firmly attached to the use of classicism to express the durability of their power relied on other formal languages as well – with the possible exception of the Soviet Union, where the imposition of the Communist Party line left no room for irony or even mild subversion. Classicism could be either latent or manifest. Neither Bruno Zevi's definition of classicism as a series of "invariant" features, like symmetry and harmony, nor John Summerson's, which equated it with the permanence of the orders inherited from antiquity and the Renaissance, is relevant in this context. [1] Nor are geographical distinctions definitive. The relationships that different regimes maintained with competing architectural currents are best understood by examining them across borders rather than according to a country-by-country reading.

Literal classicism

Rooted in historical antecedents – whether Greek, Roman, or Palladian – literal classicism reached beyond the capitals of totalitarian regimes to all nations. [2] Cass Gilbert's Supreme Court Building in Washington, D.C. (1935), is a Greek temple hybridized with a rectangular box, while John Russell Pope's nearby National Gallery of Art (1937–41) **262** is a Pantheon

wrapped in a white stone sarcophagus. Edwin Luytens's designs for the Catholic cathedral of Liverpool (1929–40) were in the vein of his beloved "Wrenaissance," with a clear articulation of structural elements, while E. Vincent Harris's City Hall in Sheffield, England (1929–32), is evidence of a rather tepid classicism.

Following the 1933 Nazi takeover in Germany, the architects hired to design buildings representing National Socialism adopted Roman-inspired orders. Paul Ludwig Troost, who was much admired by Hitler, used a Tuscan order to conceal the steel structure of his Haus der Deutschen Kunst (House of German Art) **264** in Munich, built in 1933–7. His Ehrentempel (Honor Temple), built in 1933–5 and his Führerbau (Führer's Building), built in 1935–7, explicitly responded to Leo von Klenze's buildings on the Königsplatz, which were of a more elegant and flexible neoclassicism. After Troost's death, Albert Speer, a student of Heinrich Tessenow, was recruited by the Minister of Propaganda Josef Goebbels following his staging of Nazi events such as the 1935 Nuremberg rally, where he created *Lichtdomen* (cathedrals of light) with Flak projectors. Speer's theatrical settings for the regime's parades on the Zeppelinfeld and the Märzfeld in Nuremberg (1939) inflated the use of classical orders to an enormous scale.

Speer also built Hitler's Chancellery **263** on Voßstraße in Berlin in 1936–9, an assemblage of vacuous reception halls that Charlie Chaplin's film *The Great Dictator* (1940) does not exaggerate. [3] In 1937 Speer was appointed General Building Inspector for the Transformation of the Capital of the Reich, and he initiated a development plan for Berlin on the scale of the Nazis' imperial ambitions. The plan had a two-part structure. The bombastic city center was divided by a north-south axis perpendicular to the Avenue Unter den Linden, in accord

262 National Gallery of Art, John Russell Pope, Washington, DC, USA, 1937–41

263 Chancellery, Albert Speer, Berlin, Germany, 1936–9

265 Hartford County Building, Paul-Philippe Cret, Hartford, Connecticut, USA, 1926–9

264 House of German Art, Paul Ludwig Troost, Munich, Germany, 1933–7

266 House on Mokhovaia Street, Ivan Zholtovsky, Moscow, USSR (Russia), 1934

with an idea that had been formulated as early as 1910 by the city planner Martin Mächler. The axis connected a triumphal arch – reputedly based on a sketch by Hitler himself – and a Volkshalle (People's Hall) large enough to hold Saint Peter's Basilica in Rome. The city's periphery was occupied by a series of *Siedlungen*, while its avenues were incorporated into a network of ultramodern motorways.

In Moscow, literal classicism took a variety of shapes. In addition to Ivan Fomin's "proletarian Doric," whose simplified but athletic forms seem to illustrate the Vitruvian theory of the orders, there was the Bolshevik Palladianism that Ivan Zholtovsky used for his House on Mokhovaia Street (1934). **266** Zholtovsky's house proved to be the starting point for Stalinist classicism – probably the most theoretically complex form of classicism because it was founded on the principle of "critical assimilation" of the cultural heritage, a notion originally formulated in relation to literature and endorsed by the novelist Maxim Gorky. Roman references were excluded but the Renaissance, a period when the bourgeoisie had played a "progressive" role, was acceptable. The exercise of the "people's right to columns" was regulated by very precise stylistic requirements. →4

Modern classicism

Proponents of a modern classicism, despite the apparent oxymoron, made up a dominant but more diverse group. The parallel careers of two former students at the École des Beaux-Arts in Paris illustrate the difference particularly clearly. Paul-Philippe Cret, who was active in Philadelphia starting in 1903, built several notable public buildings in an increasingly abstract classical style that he eventually reduced to an almost ritual game of abstract signs evoking absent orders. His County Building

in Hartford, Connecticut (1926–9), **265** was rimmed by colossal pilasters. Yet he built the Folger Shakespeare Library in Washington, D.C. (1929–32), without capitals and designed pilasters whose fluting had more in common with Josef Hoffmann's constructions than with the Greek columns at Paestum. Cret incorporated some of Le Corbusier's ideas, but he remained skeptical about modern architecture's ability to fulfill its symbolic brief in the context of federal buildings. →5 Cret's former schoolmate Auguste Perret based his practice on totally different premises. He stayed true to the regulating idea of the classical orders in his buildings, but totally redefined it. For instance, his Musée des Travaux Publics in Paris (Museum of Public Works; 1936–46) **267** inverted the taper of the columns and reinvented their capitals to prolong the shaft fluidly and evoke the steel skeleton embedded in the concrete. Yet he kept the classical spirit of a double articulation of the colossal and secondary orders, both on the facade and inside the concrete-columned forest of the big hall, thereby illustrating his theory of the "sovereign shelter." In addition to his twist on the principle of the classical orders, Perret also used architectural types drawn from French classicism. The composition of his storehouse for the Mobilier National in Paris (1934–6), for instance, was similar to that of an eighteenth-century town house.

Although Perret designed a plan for a Cité des Musées (City of Museums) on the hill of Chaillot, on the Right Bank of the Seine, in 1934, the Musée des Travaux Publics was his only realized commission in the neighborhood. The jury for the competition to "camouflage" the Palais du Trocadéro, which had been erected for the 1878 international exposition, instead selected Louis-Hyppolite Boileau, Jacques Carlu, and Léon Azéma to build its successor, the Palais de Chaillot. Their

267 Musée des Travaux Publics, Auguste Perret, Paris, France, 1936–46

268 Academy of Sciences competition project, André Lurçat, Moscow, USSR (Russia), 1934–5

design brilliantly replaced the original Palais du Trocadéro with a belvedere that, unfortunately, was framed by two uninspired facades with mediocre details. Jean-Claude Dondel, Albéric Aubert, Paul Viard, and Marcel Dastugue won a competition held to design the adjacent Palais de Tokyo at the 1937 exposition; this building housed the modern art museums of the city of Paris and of the French state in symmetrical galleries standing on either side of a portico supported by cylindrical columns without capitals. The earlier Musée des Colonies, designed by Albert Laprade, Léon Jaussely, and Léon Bazin, was more inventive. This building, a legacy of the 1931 *Exposition Coloniale Internationale* in Paris, featured a loggia that had a portico with square pillars and a projecting thin, flat roof, below which ran an astonishing bas-relief sculpted by Alfred Janniot. Its modern interpretation of the colonnade was replicated more or less literally in 1936 by Timothy L. Pflueger in his Federal Building for the *Golden Gate International Exposition* in San Francisco and, fifteen years later, by Edward Durell Stone in his American Embassy in Delhi (1954).

Traditionalism and self-critical modernism

The obsession with classicism was not shared by traditionalist architects, who had recourse to other precedents. Ragnar Östberg's design for the Stockholm City Hall, **269** built from 1904 to 1923, made this alternative approach clear, evoking the brick architecture of Italian civic palaces and rejecting any overall classical composition. Echoing Paul Mebes and Paul Schultze-Naumburg, Paul Schmitthenner fashioned a familiar architecture of elegant proportions, which in some cases effectively incorporated prefabricated elements. The archetype for Schmitthenner's work was Goethe's garden

house in Weimar, a simple late-seventeenth-century structure with a steeply sloping roof. [6] The Stuttgart School, headed by Schmitthenner and Paul Bonatz, contributed a certain softness to German architectural production, in contrast to the grandiloquence of party and state buildings and public works like motorway viaducts. [7] The sphere of influence for modern traditionalists was particularly vast, extending all the way to Scandinavia and Baltic states like Estonia.

Some architects who had been prominent advocates of a radical modernism in the 1920s modified their work in the 1930s to integrate classical elements. André Lurçat, who was under Stalinist ideological pressure at the time, allowed symmetry and monumental hierarchy into his project for the Moscow Academy of Sciences competition (1934–5). [8] **268** J. J. P. Oud's classical composition for the Shell Headquarters (1938–42) **274** in The Hague, while not under such pressure, was the result of similar thinking; Oud had come to regard modernism as overly ascetic. The building drew heated criticism from Philip Johnson, who had been an early American supporter of Oud. [9] The work of the "renegade" moderns converged with that of architects who in a sense followed the reverse course, arriving at similar compromises through the gradual transformation of the methods they had learned at the Beaux-Arts and comparable institutions. In the USSR, repentance was clearly imposed. In the second half of the 1930s and early 1940s, former Constructivists could build only projects that respected the canons of Socialist Realism, starting with the symmetry and vertical hierarchy of classicism. This was the case with Moisei Ginzburg's sanatorium in Kislovodsk (1935–8), to which Ivan Leonidov contributed a staircase for an outdoor amphitheater, and Andrei Burov's House of the Architect in Moscow (1940). **270**

269 Stockholm City Hall, Ragnar Östberg, Stockholm, Sweden, 1904–23

270 House of the Architect, Andrei Burov, Moscow, USSR (Russia), 1940

Opportunism without borders

Those who might be called opportunists – or, at best, eclectics – had an entirely different approach, applying different styles to whatever type of structure was called for. After designing the People's Commissariat for Agriculture in a completely modern style (1928–33) and applying Art Deco touches to his Hotel Moskva (1930–5), the Russian architect Alexei Shchusev used an Eastern-influenced classicism for the Navoi Opera and Ballet Theater in Tashkent (1933–45), and drew inspiration from Vignola's Villa Farnese in Caprarola for his forbidding headquarters for the NKVD (state police; 1940–6) **276** on Lubyanka Square in Moscow. → [10] In Brescia, in the Torre della Rivoluzione (Tower of the Revolution; 1929–32), Marcello Piacentini combined the portico and Romanesque arcades of the Loggia dei Mercanti with an Art Deco entablature. → [11] The reactive – arguably postmodern or antimodern – classicism of younger architects may be attributed to a fear or denial of modernism that was sometimes also due to a reaction against the leaders of the innovative factions. In Russia this phenomenon informed the eclectic classicist designs of Boris Iofan for the Palace of the Soviets – Iofan was forced by the authorities to collaborate with the more experienced Vladimir Shchuko and Vladimir Gelfreikh, who had designed Moscow's Lenin Library (1928–41) – and of Karo Alabian, with Vladimir Simbirtsev, for the Theater of the Red Army (1934–40). Alabian was the most insidious enemy of Constructivism among the younger architects. To a certain extent, Giovanni Muzio evaded these different categories. His Milanese designs oscillated between more modern principles, as with the Bonaiti Apartment Building on Piazza Fiume (1935), an expression of classicism free of any literalism. This was the case as well with his government commissions, such as the Palazzo dei Giornali (1938–40) and the Palazzo dell'Amministrazione Provinciale (1936), in which materials played an expressive role, with marble used for the buildings' more representative front facades and brick for their more prosaic parts.

Islands of coexistence

There were also zones of compromise and coexistence. The Paris exposition of 1937 **277** featured a particularly diverse collection of structures erected on either side of a central axis connecting the Eiffel Tower to the new Palais de Chaillot and bookended by the German and Soviet pavilions, designed by Speer and Iofan respectively. The selection included innovative buildings such as Jaromír Krejcar's Czechoslovak pavilion and Junzo Sakakura's Japan pavilion, regionalist structures assembled to create the image of a rural center, as well as the French Republic's palaces with classical porticoes. → [12]

One of the major occasions for demonstrating this coexistence was the Città Universitaria in Rome (1932–40). Piacentini, the Fascist regime's most powerful architect, invited Giuseppe Pagano to collaborate with him on the project. → [13] Inserted into a rigid axial plan with a neoclassical sequence leading to the Piacentini-designed office of the university president, **272** Pagano's Institute for Hygiene and Physics was not hierarchal in the least. The rest of the campus was occupied by more modern buildings, including ones designed by Gio Ponti (the School of Mathematics, featuring expressive amphitheaters), **271** Giovanni Michelucci (the Histology Institute, with an austere stone facade), and Giuseppe Capponi (the Mineralogy Institute, with projecting glazed staircases). While the regime's ability to mediate between different styles had proved effective in

272 Rectorate of the Città Universitaria, Marcello Piacentini, Rome, Italy, 1932–40

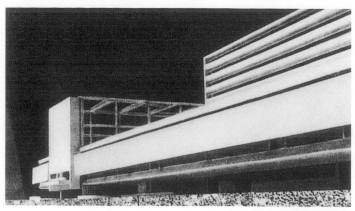

273 Palazzo del Littorio competition project, Antonio Carminati, Pietro Lingeri, Ernesto Saliva, Giuseppe Terragni and Luigi Vietti, Rome, Italy, 1933

274 Shell Headquarters, J. J. P. Oud, The Hague, Netherlands, 1938–42

Chapter 17 | The spectrum of classicisms and traditionalisms

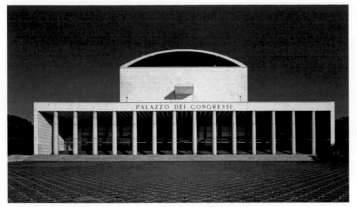

276 NKVD Headquarters, Alexei Shchusev, Moscow, USSR (Russia), 1940–6

275 Palazzo dei Congressi at the EUR, Adalberto Libera, Rome, Italy, 1938–54

277 ▶ *International Exposition of Art and Technology in Modern Life*, Paris, France, 1937, with Palais de Chaillot, designed by Jacques Carlu, Louis-Hippolyte Boileau and Léon Azéma, center; USSR Pavilion, designed by Boris Iofan, left; and Germany Pavilion, designed by Albert Speer, right

this case, the great competition for the design of the Palazzo del Littorio in 1933 **273** was a failure. During the competition's two rounds, the initial one for a site near the Roman Forum, the second for a site at the Porta San Paolo, designs by Antonio Carminati, Pietro Lingeri, Ernesto Saliva, Giuseppe Terragni, Luigi Vietti, Adalberto Libera, and BBPR clearly stood out. Yet it was the team of Vittorio Ballio Morpurgo, Enrico del Debbio, and Arnaldo Foschini that was selected to build a graceless edifice on a third, more remote site near the Mussolini Forum. In Rome the projected *Esposizione universale*, or EUR, planned for 1942, provided a final opportunity for stylistic coexistence. Once again the overall plan was entrusted to Piacentini. Competitions were held for the individual structures, giving rise to projects that were realized despite the cancellation of the exposition itself due to the war. They ranged from buildings firmly anchored in classical nostalgia to ones that were subtly modern. Among the former was the Palazzo della Civiltà Italiana (Palace of Italian Civilization; 1937–40) by Ernesto La Padula, Mario Romano, and Giovanni Guerrini; this large square coliseum overlooking the Tiber Valley was the symbol of the exposition. At the other end of the cross-axis was a prominent example of the latter approach: Libera's Palazzo dei Congressi (1938–54), **275** a boxy convention center volume topped by a concrete shell, featuring interior staircases that stood out against the building's glass walls. BBPR's post office, also on the site, displayed an elegant exploration of the tectonics of the facade. ⁓ 14

The urban ordering – or staging – of the 1930s thus exploited different types of classicism, whatever the ideological or political premise. In general, the ideal of the city as a total work of art centered on monumental complexes and allowed for collaboration with sculptors and painters, and it was shared

from Washington to Moscow, Rome to Paris, and London to Berlin. ⁓ 15 Nowhere, however, did the various strands of 1930s classicism correspond to a single language or finite corpus of invariant forms. Instead, they constituted a dynamic system, a field onto which the conflicts and contradictions of the decade were projected.

North American modernities

278 Imperial Hotel, Frank Lloyd
Wright, Tokyo, Japan, 1916–22

279 John Storer House, Frank
Lloyd Wright, Hollywood, California,
USA, 1923–4

If classicism had a promised land, it was the United States. Up
until World War II, the civic centers built in cities like Cleveland
and San Francisco testified to the persistence of the Beaux-Arts
model, although with regional inflections. Yet American architecture between the wars was also profoundly transformed by
individuals who came from diverse origins and contradictory
ambitions and belonged to several generations. The geography
of American architecture shifted westward with the appearance
in California of a professional environment and modern production methods. The economic situation and resulting federal policies also had an impact. Initially, the Great Depression brought
the construction of new buildings to a halt, but following the
election of Franklin Delano Roosevelt in 1932 and the launch of
the New Deal the following year, an unprecedented amount of
construction related to social programs got underway throughout the land of free enterprise.

Wright, the return

Although classicism was still dominant in the architectural production of the United States during the early 1920s, the most
remarkable professional figure there, Frank Lloyd Wright, was
hostile to it. Wright, who had refused in the 1890s to study at the
École des Beaux-Arts, had resurfaced after the tragic events that
burned down his home, Taliesin, and took the life of his lover,
Mamah Cheney, in 1914. After six years of work, he completed
the Imperial Hotel in Tokyo (1916–22, demolished 1968). 278
Although the complex was not destroyed in the 1923 earthquake – a fact Wright proudly pointed out for years to come
– it probably owed its survival less to its concrete, brick, and
limestone construction than to its distance from the quake's
epicenter. The hotel's spacious and symmetrical composition
included several decorative devices Wright had used previously
but brought together here with extraordinary virtuosity. He also
built the Jyu Gakuen School in Tokyo (1921), in which he
returned to the vocabulary of his Prairie Houses.

During the same period Wright designed the Hollyhock House
in Hollywood (1916–21) for a visionary client, the heiress Aline
Barnsdall. It inaugurated a new approach in his work. Both the
massing and ornamentation of the house reflected his interest
in Mexico's Mayan monuments – notably the Governor's Palace
in Uxmal, casts of which he had seen at the Chicago world's
fair in 1893 – while at the same time it retained the spatial
fluidity of his Prairie Houses. Wright was unable to realize his
project for the Doheny Ranch in the Sierra Madre (1921), which
responded to the vegetation and rock formations of the local
landscape, but he found California a welcoming context for his
"textile blocks" cast in cement and held together by steel rods.
He used these to build the Ennis, Storer, 279 Freeman, and
Millard houses in 1923–4. [1]

After several fallow years with no significant commissions,
Wright once again rethought his approach, and in the 1930s
he created a sensation with new buildings and a major urban
project. Energized by modern European architecture, particularly since he could recognize the impact of his own work on
it, he strove to reclaim the position of centrality he had once
held. [2] A first comeback effort failed when his project for
glass towers for St. Mark's in-the-Bouwerie in New York (1929)
was canceled. Several years later, his country house for Edgar
Kaufmann in Bear Run, Pennsylvania (1935–6), 280 featuring
concrete cantilevers and terraces suspended over the stream
that gave the house its name, Fallingwater, revealed a previously unknown facet of his work. Through the contrast between
the painted concrete structure and the stone walls, the extension

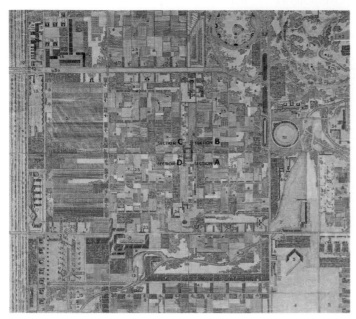

281 Broadacre City, project, Frank Lloyd Wright, 1932–5

of the horizontal windows, and the house's carefully plotted transparencies, Fallingwater brilliantly combined the Prairie themes with those of European modern architects ranging from Mies van der Rohe to Le Corbusier.

Well aware of how many of his younger colleagues had benefited from the aura surrounding radical projects of urban design, Wright exhibited a large urban model at the *Industrial Arts Exposition* held in 1935 at Rockefeller Center in New York. The scheme for Broadacre City **281** had been anticipated in his book *The Disappearing City* of 1932 and was his summary vision of America as a great, egalitarian composite of small property holdings. Decentralized industrial, educational, and administrative facilities were linked to houses by highways organized according to Henry Ford's scheme for a linear city in Muscle Shoals, Alabama, along the Mississippi River. Wright's vision of Broadacre City contained echoes of such theories as C. H. Douglas's Social Credit, Henry George's idea of common property, and Edward Bellamy's demand that scientific advances benefit the general public rather than remain in the hands of vested interests and driven by profit. Wright called for "*little* farms, *little* homes for industry, *little* factories, *little* schools, a *little* university and *little* laboratories on their own ground for professional men." The project linked ideas of decentralization, "architectural reintegration of all units into one fabric," and "free use of the ground held only by use and improvement." [italics in original] → 3

Far from trying to implement this project, however, which anticipated the suburban sprawl of the 1950s, Wright began building dwellings that were more affordable than his luxurious Prairie Houses. He called them "Usonian" houses, with that term evoking a vision of the United States put forward in Samuel Butler's novel *Erewhon* (1917). The social, economic, territorial, and technological context for these houses was different from that

of Chicago's wealthy suburbs. Usonian houses were intended for academics, engineers, and others with modest resources, as well as for professional women. They had smaller spaces and were often built of modular plywood panels. The great theater of the dining room disappeared, although the houses were still laid out horizontally, according to a variety of plan types. The Herbert Jacobs (1936) and John C. Pew (1938–40) **282** houses in Madison, Wisconsin, and the Alma Goetsch and Katherine Winckler House (1939) in Okemos, Michigan, were linear. The Paul R. Hanna House (1937), in Palo Alto, California, was built on a triangular plan, while other Usonian houses had square or circular plans. The Suntop Homes (1939) in Ardmore, Pennsylvania, were among those with multiple dwelling units, in this case an assemblage of four.

Wright's inventiveness was embodied in other projects as well. The exterior of the Johnson Wax Administrative Building (1936–9) **283** in Racine, Wisconsin, was brick-clad, but its interior evoked a forest of concrete columns whose mushroom capitals gave a distinct form to the ceiling. The light flooded into the building through clerestory bands containing special glass tubes. Thirty years after completing the Larkin Building, Wright continued to transform the very definition of the workplace at Johnson Wax, down to the metal furniture of his own design. In 1938 he began the construction of Taliesin West, a permanent structure on a campsite in Scottsdale, Arizona, where he and his "apprentices" had been spending winters since 1932. The frugal workshops and lodgings resembled a heap of rocks belonging to the natural site; their roof structures remained close to the spirit of the tents of the original encampment. Both in Wisconsin and in the Southwest, Wright gathered a changing group of disciples who would prove more effective in disseminating the design features of his projects than in spreading his theories.

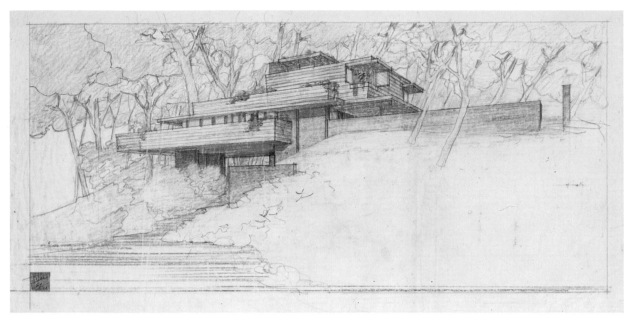

282 John C. Pew House, Frank Lloyd Wright, Madison, Wisconsin, USA, 1938–40

283 Johnson Wax Administrative Building, Frank Lloyd Wright, Racine, Wisconsin, USA, 1936–9

284 Horatio West Court, Irving Gill, Santa Monica, California, USA, 1919

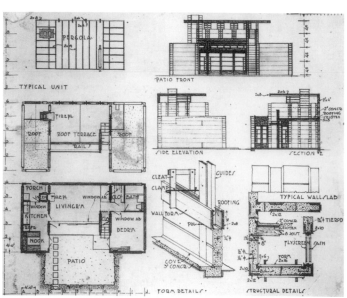

285 Pueblo Ribera Apartments, Rudolf Schindler, La Jolla, California, USA, 1923–5

286 Lovell Beach House, Rudolf Schindler, Newport Beach, California, USA, 1922–6

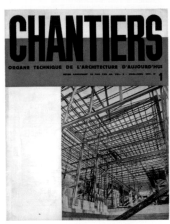

288 Dunsmuir Apartments, Gregory Ain, Los Angeles, California, USA, 1937

289 Landfair Apartments, Richard Neutra, Los Angeles, California, USA, 1938

287 Lovell House, Richard Neutra, Hollywood, California, USA, 1928–9, as shown on the cover of *Chantiers* magazine in 1934

Los Angeles – fertile ground

Wright left significant traces in Los Angeles thanks to work there by his son Lloyd Wright and by two of his former draftsmen, both trained in Vienna: Rudolf Schindler, who arrived in 1920 to coordinate Wright's Hollyhock House, and Richard Neutra, who joined his Austrian compatriot in 1925 after two years in Wright's Chicago studio. [4] Here they discovered the buildings of Irving Gill, who had been, like Wright, a draftsman for Louis Sullivan. Initially active in San Diego, Gill designed a series of concrete buildings in the city of Torrance. He also built the Walter Dodge House in Hollywood (1914–16, demolished 1970), a cubistic assemblage with Spanish touches, uncannily akin to Adolf Loos's residences in Vienna. Gill's Horatio West Court complex (1919) **284** in Santa Monica, with contrasting white volumes and thin window frames, was closer to the approach of Gerrit Rietveld. [5]

Schindler built his own house in Hollywood in 1921–2, combining wood components reminiscent of Japanese screens with prefabricated concrete panels separated by narrow slits to allow in light. Built on a single level, the house was conceived entirely in relation to the garden and geared to an open-air lifestyle, with exposed bedrooms providing a fitting setting for a Californian utopia. In La Jolla, he built the Pueblo Ribera Apartments (1923–5), **285** evoking the designs of Otto Wagner's disciples in Vienna with orthogonal structures in wood and poured concrete covered by Mediterranean vegetation. Most striking was the beach house for Dr. Philip Lovell in Newport Beach (1922–6), **286** in which Schindler used reinforced concrete to create a sequence of freestanding frames into which the rooms were placed like suspended wooden boxes. The double-height living room was articulated by the orthogonal

geometry of the glass facades, which, like the rest of the building, had slender wood mullions. Schindler would go on to combine the building vocabulary of these first houses with inventive variants in the many projects he built, often for leftist intellectuals, throughout Southern California. [6] The spectacular Charles H. Wolfe House, planted on the slope of Catalina Island (1928–31, demolished in 2002), and the low-rise John J. Buck House, on Genesee Avenue in Los Angeles (1934), explored a wide range of geometric configurations.

Schindler collaborated with Neutra on a project for the League of Nations competition. But their partnership came to an unhappy end when Neutra accepted a commission to build Philip Lovell's Hollywood home on his own. The "Health House," **287** completed in 1929, served as both a residence for this politically committed physician and hygienist and a nursery school. Built on a hill and standing on thin *pilotis*, it was the first American domestic structure to utilize a steel frame, which made it possible to wrap the building in an envelope of lightweight panels and windows. Its long living room was a more ascetic version of Wright's interiors. Thanks to Neutra's flair for publicity, the Lovell House had an immediate impact in Europe. With his books *Wie baut Amerika?* (How Does America Build?; 1927) and *Amerika* (1930), Neutra called attention both to his own work and to southern California architecture in general throughout German-speaking Europe and all the way to Soviet Russia. [7] The house Neutra built for himself in Silver Lake (1932; partly destroyed by fire 1963), named the Van der Leeuw Research House in honor of the Dutch industrialist who sponsored it, enabled him to further his experiments with metal structures. He also used metal in the film director Josef von Sternberg's house in Northridge (1935), which was later occupied by the novelist Ayn Rand. The patio of the Northridge house was encircled

290 Tabernacle Church of Christ, Eliel Saarinen, Columbus, Ohio, USA, 1939–42

292 Chicago Tribune Building, Raymond Hood and John M. Howells, Chicago, Illinois, USA, 1922–4

291 Chicago Tribune competition project, Eliel Saarinen, Chicago, Illinois, USA, 1922

by an aluminum wall that bordered the pool. Throughout this period Neutra was constantly refining a theoretical project for a mechanized city called "Rush City Reformed," on which he had worked since 1926. He also designed several Los Angeles apartment buildings, such as the Landfair 289 and the Strathmore (both 1938), in which the influence of European experiments can clearly be felt.

Although the Depression interrupted construction on the East Coast for several years, Los Angeles partially escaped the adverse economic effects and continued to develop as a thriving architectural center. → 8 Visitors to California discovered a seductive scene there revolving around Neutra, whose California "exile" seemed to certain European critics in the 1930s to be a metaphor of their own uncertain fate. Meanwhile Los Angeles promised "landscape marvels" to the traveler, as the architect Giuseppe Pagano wrote in *Casabella* after returning from a 1937 trip. → 9 But Neutra's effectiveness at self-promotion should not be allowed to overshadow the work of other architects active in transforming California architecture. Lloyd Wright, who was intensely active and often worked with the movie studios, made lyrical use of cement blocks in his John Sowden (1926) and Samuel Navarro (1928) houses. Some structures explored new geometric shapes on difficult terrain: the Entenza House (1937) by Harwell Hamilton Harris, a former employee of Neutra, played with a circular plan, while the Dunsmuir Apartments (1937) 288 by Gregory Ain, also trained by Neutra, played with volumes stacked on a hilly site typical of the Los Angeles landscape. Eliel Saarinen's immigrant experience was quite different. After designing ambitious urban development projects for the Chicago lakefront (1923) and for Detroit, he focused from 1925 until 1943 on expanding the Cranbrook campus in Bloomfield Hills, Michigan. As work progressed, the initial model of the English

college was replaced by a more rigorous and abstract interplay of structure and landscape, and the buildings became increasingly geometrical and austere. Built toward the end of this process, his Tabernacle Church of Christ (now the First Christian Church; 1939–42), 290 in Columbus, Indiana consisted simply of a plain rectangular box with a brick exterior through which natural light was ingeniously directed. → 10

The skyscraper reloaded

The transformation of the American skyscraper had been heralded by the Chicago Tribune competition in 1922, 291 and its significance could be observed in New York in the late 1920s. After a momentary pause, the race for height resumed in Manhattan with the competition between the Empire State Building and the Chrysler Building. Once New York City's 1916 zoning regulation had abolished height limitations on 25 percent of the building lot, the only constraints on verticality were a function of the potential profitability of the real estate. Buildings rose to increasingly gigantic proportions, urged upward by investors' narcissism. → 11 William Van Alen's Chrysler Building (1928–30) – at seventy-seven stories briefly the tallest building in the world – was notable for its beautiful lobby and its stainless steel crown. Shreve, Lamb and Harmon's 102-story Empire State Building (1931) outstripped the Chrysler Building in height but utterly failed to transform a banal application of the zoning rules into an original – or even appealing – form.

Although the suggestive phantasmagorias that Hugh Ferriss drew in his book *The Metropolis of To-Morrow* (1929), featuring visions of sky-high clusters of towers, remained unbuilt, more effective experiments were carried out by Raymond Hood. Trained at the École des Beaux-Arts in Paris, Hood was the

293 Crystal House, George F. Keck, at the *Century of Progress* exhibition, Chicago, Illinois, USA, 1933

294 Manhattan 1950, project, Raymond Hood, New York City, USA, 1929

295 Philadelphia Savings Fund Society Building, George Howe and William Lescaze, Philadelphia, Pennsylvania, USA, 1929–32

winner (with John M. Howells) of the Chicago Tribune competition with a project whose crown reproduced the Tour du Beurre in Rouen, a masterpiece of the French Gothic. **292** Hood's American Radiator Building in New York, designed with Frederick A. Godley and Jacques-André Fouilhoux (1924), was more striking for its facade with gilded ornamentation on black walls than for its overall architectural vocabulary. The *Daily News* Building (with Howells and Fouilhoux, 1929) explored new solutions, accentuating the building's upward thrust with vertical bands. The McGraw-Hill Building (with Godley, Fouilhoux, and Kenneth M. Murchison, 1928–31), which faced onto 42nd Street rather than one of Manhattan's avenues, asserted its presence in a seedy neighborhood west of Midtown with a bold use of green glazed terra-cotta. In 1929 Hood elaborated a theoretical project called "Manhattan 1950," **294** in which he proposed to rationalize distribution of the city's skyscrapers by concentrating them at the intersection of major streets and avenues and on the piers of bridges. → 12 This nearly spectral vision of a profoundly dense city, evocatively rendered by Ferriss, was never realized.

Hood's research bore further fruit with the construction of Rockefeller Center, which was finished under the direction of Wallace K. Harrison (with L. Andrew Reinhard, Henry Hofmeister, Godley, and Fouilhoux in 1930–40). Located in the heart of Manhattan, facing the shops of Fifth Avenue and backing onto Sixth Avenue (still a rather rough area at this time), the development was the first to implement the idea of a complex vertical city, combining offices with space for retail businesses and theaters. The basement shopping galleries were grouped around a sunken plaza, while the facades were cleverly set back to take best advantage of the constraints of the 1916 regulation. → 13 The dominant skyscraper of the Rockefeller

Center complex, the RCA Building, appears conservative when compared to the headquarters of the Philadelphia Saving Fund Society in Philadelphia, designed by George Howe and William Lescaze in 1929–32. **295** With its office tower rising atop a second-story banking hall, the building eschews the common strategy of housing the elevators in a central core. Rather, the elevators and services are grouped in a perpendicular block at the back of the building, giving the overall structure a T-shaped plan. PSFS may be said to be the first completely modern skyscraper, not least for the clear expression of verticals on its facade and for the Futurist-like device of displaying the bank's initials as a crown.

Industrial products: between factory and market

The banks and major companies that used skyscrapers to assert their presence in urban centers seemed to be of two minds when commissioning other facilities. Albert Kahn's firm built both the gigantic General Motors Headquarters in Detroit (1917–21) – a ponderous building with indents and cornices – and the factories that became such admired elements of the modern industrial landscape, among them Ford's River Rouge complex (1922–6) in Dearborn, Michigan. Images of the latter were circulated widely, with Charles Sheeler's paintings and photographs of the plant published all over the world. Meanwhile the factory's spatial solutions and the structures of its glassworks and furnaces served as fertile source material for other architects. With the Chrysler Half-Ton Truck Plant in Detroit (1937), Kahn developed a lighter architecture, making greater use of glass walls, while his Glenn Martin Airplane Factory (also 1937) **297** in Middle River, Maryland, was remarkable for the unprecedented span of its steel trusses. → 14

297   Glenn Martin Airplane Factory, Albert Kahn, Middle River, Maryland, USA, 1937

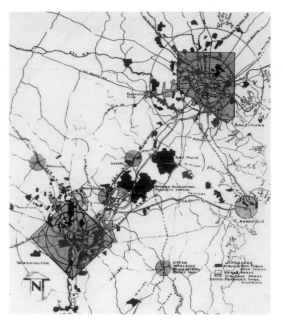

298   Greenbelt New Town, Clarence Stein, located between Washington, DC, and Baltimore, Maryland, USA, 1935–40

But the American economy was not solely dedicated to production, however deep the inroads made by Fordism. Businesses sought to combat the Great Depression by stimulating consumption, which required rethinking the visual appeal of consumer products and encouraged the active use of marketing techniques. → 15 New alliances were formed among architects, artists, and industrialists to make everyday products more desirable by redesigning them. These new relationships were influenced by the aesthetic established at the 1925 *Exposition Internationale des Arts Décoratifs et Industriels Modernes* in Paris. Americans had not contributed to the show for lack of having any products that had a "unique character" or "special expression." → 16 Yet the new field of "industrial design" – a term coined in 1926 – would quickly draw theater designers like Norman Bel Geddes and his disciple Henry Dreyfuss and graphic artists like Walter Dorwin Teague and Raymond Loewy to rethink the look of buildings and objects. This new cadre of professionals was hired by companies like Bell, Kodak, Chrysler, and General Electric to reconceptualize their products. → 17

The aerodynamic lines of automobiles, planes, and trains gave rise to the aesthetic practice of streamlining in the design of buildings and everyday objects. Its tremendous popularity was achieved in two major stages. The 1933 *Century of Progress* exhibition, held to commemorate Chicago's centennial, had a general plan devised by Hood. While hinting at what was to come in a post-Depression economy, its architecture was hardly revolutionary. Paul Philippe Cret built the Hall of Science, a relatively dynamic building. More audacious were two pavilions by George F. Keck – the entirely transparent Crystal House, **293** illuminated like a lantern at night, and the House of Tomorrow, built on a circular plan on top of a hangar for private planes.

Both these buildings boasted air conditioning, an invention that would radically alter architecture after World War II. The New York World's Fair of 1939 had a far greater impact. Organized by the City Parks Commissioner Robert Moses, it was dominated by Harrison and Fouilhoux's Trylon and Perisphere. Beyond the juxtaposition of national pavilions, the spectacular displays by American automobile manufacturers attracted the greatest attention, presenting visions of a society transformed by the automobile. Dreyfuss's model of "Democracity," exhibited in the Perisphere, proposed a new interaction among the classes comprising the American citizenry. Loewy designed the Chrysler Motors Pavilion, which featured a rocket launchpad. Bel Geddes's Futurama, **296** the star attraction of the General Motors Pavilion he designed with Albert Kahn, allowed visitors to "fly" over the city of the future, which had miraculously developed into the total design its creator had envisioned in 1932 in his book *Horizons*. → 18 The journalist and critic Walter Lippmann noted, "General Motors has spent a small fortune to convince the American Public that if it wishes to enjoy the full benefit of private enterprise in motor manufacturing it will have to rebuild its cities and its highways by public enterprise." → 19

The New Deal's housing reform and the European immigration

The New Deal's public policies represented another strategy for bringing the Depression to an end. These were based, in part, on ideas promoted by the Regional Planning Association of America, founded in 1923 by Clarence Stein, Benton MacKaye, Lewis Mumford, Alexander Bing, and Henry Wright. The RPAA aspired to integrate the natural landscape

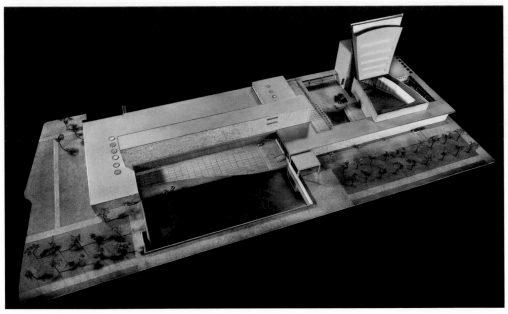

299 Smithsonian Gallery of Modern Art competition project, Eliel Saarinen and Eero Saarinen, Washington DC, USA, 1939

with a new infrastructure of roads. → 20 The Housing Study Guild, created in 1932 by Wright, Mumford, and Albert Mayer, focused more on housing issues. It was led by Catherine Bauer, whose book *Modern Housing* (1934) became its gospel. This militant approach transformed the discourse of the garden city into policy recommendations for greenbelt cities, which expanded on the Radburn experiment of a few years earlier. Roosevelt's adviser Rexford Guy Tugwell, who headed the Federal Resettlement Administration and was responsible for several social modernization laws, coordinated the creation of three autonomous new developments supported by federal financing: Greenbelt, Maryland; **298** Greenhills, Ohio; and Greendale, Wisconsin. Ground was broken on all three in 1935. Bauer's activism led to passage the same year of the Housing Act, which guaranteed the permanence of the Roosevelt administration programs. → 21 In 1939, with the creation of the Telesis Group – a term invented by the sociologist Lester Ward Frank to refer to scientifically based reform policies – the network of housing reform organizations extended to the West Coast. The group was headed by the San Francisco architect William Wurster, Bauer, and the landscape architect Garrett Eckbo, among others. → 22 Wurster's regionalist approach to modern architecture would resonate throughout the country.

Concurrent with the activities of the American reformers, a wave of emigrants fleeing Nazi Germany brought important European architects to the United States. Among them were two directors of the Bauhaus, Walter Gropius and Ludwig Mies van der Rohe, as well as the Bauhaus *Meister* László Moholy-Nagy, Josef Albers, and Ludwig Hilberseimer, all of whom embarked on second careers once in America. Gropius built a house for himself in Lincoln, Massachusetts, while Mies began designing a new campus for Illinois Institute of Technology. Other equally active

émigrés came from Hamburg: Oskar Gerson and Karl Schneider, who designed domestic equipment and stores for Sears, Roebuck; from Vienna: Victor Gruenbaum (later Gruen), whose modern boutiques soon attracted attention; and from Berlin: Werner Hegemann, who taught urban planning at Columbia University until his premature death in 1936.

Despite pressure from these groups and a gradual change in the public's expectations, public institutions were still extremely reluctant to accept modern architecture. The most obvious example of this resistance was the decision not to build an art gallery for the Smithsonian Institution in Washington, D.C., after a 1939 competition awarded the commission to Eliel and Eero Saarinen for a project based on a composition of abstract rectangular prisms. **299** The Saarinen design would have provided a fine counterbalance to John Russell Pope's National Gallery of Art, whose icy neoclassicism remained the only game in town.

Functionalism and machine aesthetics

Streamline Moderne, the commercial style in which American architects and designers borrowed formal motifs from the shapes of machines, was only the most superficial manifestation of the complex relationship between architecture and technology between the wars. In 1925 the Swiss functionalist periodical *ABC* declared that machines were beautiful "because they work, move, function" – unlike buildings, which were "sluggish, undynamic, pretentious." The editors went on to stake out seemingly a middle ground, stating that "the machine [was] neither the future paradise of the technical accomplishment of all our bourgeois wishes, nor the imminent abyss causing the annihilation of all human development." The machine was simply "the inflexible dictator of the possibilities and duties of our daily life." → 1

Rather than the impact of any one individual machine, it was the practically universal adoption of industrial manufacturing and management methods that transformed architecture. The typification and standardization of buildings and their components, and the rationalization of the construction site, were indicative of the full-scale transfer of industrial methods such as Fordism and Taylorism to the sphere of building. These advancements were advocated in nearly all the developed countries, though only Germany succeeded in establishing a coherent, government-regulated building policy before 1933. In addition to the rationalization of building processes, architects subscribed to the concept of *Sachlichkeit*, or objectivity, and asserted the primacy of "function" through conceptual methods and rhetoric that formally alluded to industry, emphasizing the scientific character of the new architecture. → 2 Functionalism was thus both an operational and a purely visual response to the changes wrought by modernity.

The notion of the functional had been in use since the nineteenth century. Louis Sullivan, much like Henri Labrouste earlier, had notably stated in 1896 that "form follows function," and this axiom indeed became a rallying cry, probably because of its useful ambiguity. Sullivan's notion of function, derived from the American sculptor Horatio Greenough, was framed in biological terms. In the 1920s it took on a more mathematical meaning, denoting the rigorous adjustment of architectural spaces to their use through quantitative data and calculations. In Germany the term *Zweck*, meaning "purpose" or "use," was adopted by Adolf Behne in his 1923 book *Der moderne Zweckbau* (The Modern Functional Building). → 3 In opposition, Henry-Russell Hitchcock and Philip Johnson rejected in 1932 the notion that "building is science and not art, [a conception] developed as an exaggeration of the idea of functionalism." → 4 At the same time, the Swiss architect Alberto Sartoris enlisted Filippo Tommaso Marinetti's support to publish his book *Gli elementi dell'architettura funzionale* (The Elements of Functionalist Architecture; 1932), → 5 in which he gathered most of modern architecture under the banner of functionalism. The most extreme confusion developed in the late 1920s over the justification of functionalism in the name of aesthetics. The term degenerated into a slogan, a blanket characterization under which many sorts of architecture were pursued, for the most part only implicitly related to the progress of technological modernity and its machine basis. → 6

Taylorism and architecture

The application of Frederick Winslow Taylor's scientific organization of labor to architecture was spurred by studies of domestic space carried out in the United States by his partners Lillian and Frank Gilbreth and by the home management reformer Christine

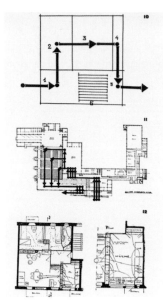

301 Stroikom housing studies, Mikhail Barshch and Vyacheslav Vladimirov, USSR, 1929, view of a refectory

300 The Functional Design Method, illustration in *Sovremennaia arkhitektura*, Moisei Ginzburg, 1927

302 ADGB Trade Union School, Hannes Meyer, Bernau, Germany, 1928–30

Frederick. Frederick's diagrams, published in her book *The New Housekeeping* in 1913 [7] were reproduced in Bruno Taut's *Die neue Wohnung* (The New Dwelling; 1924). The Russian architect Moisei Ginzburg based his "functional design method" **300** on his analysis of the configuration of factories as described by Henry Ford in his best-selling autobiography, *My Life and Work* (1922). Ginzburg's method combined Ford's system of movement – "the path of the assembly line, encompassing the entire process from beginning to end, from machine to machine" – with his system of equipment – "a system of different machines and tools that make it possible to realize the different stages of the production process." [8] All of the new building programs for housing and for educational and cultural facilities were to be treated as production sites. Taylorist ideas underwrote the recommendations of the Russian state building agency, Stroikom, for the construction of model housing units (1929), and Ginzburg, Mikhail Barshch, and Vyacheslav Vladimirov proposed minimal units and kitchens inspired by Ernst May's work in Frankfurt, as well as communal facilities based on the industrial concept of economy of means and an understanding of users' movements. Particularly noteworthy was their refectory, **301** with a conveyor belt delivering bread and soup – looking forward to the one in Charlie Chaplin's *Modern Times* (1936) – which was probably intended to familiarize the inhabitants with assembly lines, at that time a novelty in the USSR.

In Dessau, motion studies informed Walter Gropius's differentiation of the functions of buildings in projects at the Bauhaus. The city's labor exchange (1928), built in the shape of a semicircle, had a radial plan designed to regulate the paths of the unemployed workers who frequented the building, leading them from the waiting lines outside into counselors' offices either to a job interview or (depending on the case) directly to the exit.

Gropius's successor at the Dessau Bauhaus, Hannes Meyer, reinforced the "scientific" study of programs and projects. The school he built in 1928–30 **302** in Bernau, north of Berlin, for the ADGB trade union expanded on the method he had adopted for a project designed with Hans Wittwer for the League of Nations, where offices and meeting halls were articulated as separate functional volumes. The Bernau school stretched along a pond and all the classrooms and residences had the benefit of sunlight and a view. The massing and facades of each component of the scheme were differentiated, and the corridor leading from the amphitheater to the classrooms, which served as the spine of the long building, was also perfectly identifiable from the outside as a separate functional element. The tectonic expression of this complex, deemed "Spartan" by Adolf Behne, revealed but did not make a fetish of its concrete weight-bearing elements, glass block walls, and brick infill. [9]

From ergonomics to standard dimensions

Modernist architects were not alone in studying the circulation paths by which people traverse buildings. The traditionalist Alexander Klein, a Russian émigré to Germany, also analyzed patterns of movement inside dwellings, taking into account obstructions caused by furniture. His diagrams **303** served to chart the utility of different building types. [10] A tendency to simplify movement and reduce "excess" floor surface generally characterized the research into minimal dwelling standards in Germany and introduced the notion of economy not only into construction but also into the entire design process.

Klein's analysis and classification constituted only one episode in a collective endeavor that culminated in what remains probably the best-selling architecture book of all time: Ernst Neufert's

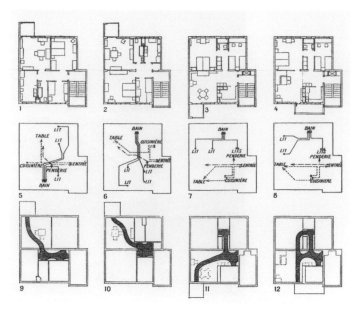

303 Comparative house plan studies, Alexander Klein, 1939

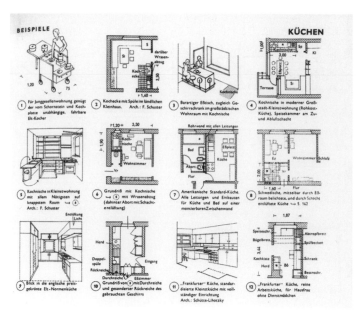

304 Examples of modern kitchens in *Bauentwurfslehre* (Building Design Handbook), Ernst Neufert, 1936

Bauentwurfslehre (Building Design Handbook; 1936). **304**
Authored by a former student at the Weimar Bauhaus who had become Gropius's office manager, the book compiled typical plans, construction details, and, most significantly, diagrams of human beings at rest and in motion. Its ergonomic principles made it possible to measure any type of space precisely, from residence to office, from dirigible cabin to grave. Although the representative buildings of the Nazi party and government favored classicism and a traditionalist *Heimatstil*, or picturesque indigenous style, Neufert's book introduced a functionalist model that would become a reference for many new buildings worldwide. → 11 Adopting functionalism did not always mean ignoring aesthetic or semantic concerns. For instance, the linguist Jan Mukařovský, a member of the Prague Linguistic Circle (along with Roman Jakobson, Sergei Karchevsky, and N. S. Trubetskoy), offered an expanded understanding of the notion of function. To the three basic functions of language – the cognitive function, related to transmission of information; the expressive function, related to the speaker, and the conative or receptive function, related to the listener – he added an aesthetic function, which took in the poetic dimension of language and art. In his view, "aesthetic function is not a mere, practically unimportant, epiphenomenon of other functions, but is a co-determinant of human reaction to reality." → 12 This extension of thinking about function was partially inspired by Mukařovský's knowledge of architecture through the writings of the Prague architect and critic Karel Teige.

Poetic functionalism: Chareau and Nelson

The situation of modern architecture in Paris in the late 1920s clearly demonstrated that the lessons gleaned from industrial processes did not all lead to "objective," scientific-minded design methods. While Taylor's and Ford's writings were translated into French, and Christine Frederick's work inspired the French domestic reformer Paulette Bernège, who wrote pamphlets that extended the discourse of "household organization," → 13 **305** alternative strategies developed as well. Pierre Chareau's 1920s designs for furniture made of steel and precious wood exemplified a more poetic approach. His pieces had movable and convertible components like those of machines and they seemed to achieve a perfect combination of industrial processes and cabinetry. A "poet and inventor," according to Frantz Jourdain, and more an "engineer-constructor" than a "colorist-decorator," in the words of the critic Marie Dormoy, → 14 Chareau fitted out apartments for a circle of enlightened clients and designed furniture and lamps in collaboration with the wrought-iron craftsman Louis Dalbet.

In Paris, Chareau and Bernard Bijvoet built the Maison de Verre (Glass House; 1927–31) **307** for Dr. Jean Dalsace and his wife, Annie Bernheim. This project involved an unprecedented level of complexity. Because of a tenant who refused to move out, it had to be built in between the ground-floor courtyard and garden and the building's uppermost floor. At night the glass-brick facades, supported by steel structural elements, make it look like a Chinese lantern. The house derives from the machine the expression of both its construction, featuring exposed rivets and anti-rust paints, and motion, from the movable partitions that can change the configuration of rooms and their components to the play of staircases. A kind of oversized mechanical toy, the architecture determines its occupants' circulation paths while providing a stark contrast with the owners' art collection. Most impressive is the way the variety of views and the direct, indirect, and diffused

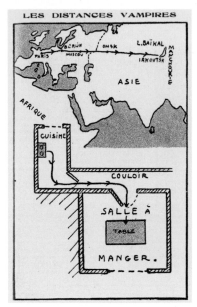

305 Vampire Distances, illustration in *Si les femmes faisaient les maisons* (If Women Built Houses), Paulette Bernège, 1928

illumination filtering through the translucent walls turn this introverted building into a theater of light. → 15

To some extent, Paul Nelson's Maison Suspendue (Suspended House; 1936–8) **306** was a response to Chareau's work. Designed for a theoretical site, this glass cage, nearly cubic in volume, hung from an arched steel frame and was penetrated by a helical ramp. It contrasted with the orthogonal language of Chareau, who only occasionally employed cylindrical forms in his designs, and its geometry was more organic than mechanical, thanks largely to contributions by the artists Jean Arp, Alexander Calder, and, later, Fernand Léger. Nelson, who previously designed a project for a vertical hospital campus in the city of Lille based on a rigorous analysis of its uses (1932), collaborated with Frantz-Philippe Jourdain and Oscar Nitzchké, his former classmate in Perret's atelier, to fashion a project for the Palais de la Découverte (Palace of Discovery; 1938) in Paris. A vast science museum sheltered under a bicycle-wheel-shaped roof, the building had a structure that evoked an airplane hangar. → 16

Working on his own, Nitzchké designed the Maison de la Publicité (House of Advertising; 1936–8) **308** on the Champs-Élysées, an unbuilt project that broke with Perret's emphasis of the frame on the building's exterior. Instead he created for the front facade a three-dimensional light display that was intended to be convertible and mobile. The facade structure consisted of a thin, three-dimensional metal grid held in place by cross-bracing, making it possible to insert a wide variety of components. Advertising slogans, images, and projection devices could be suspended from the openwork floor within the grid. Nitzchké's exploration of the idea of the building's continuous, instantaneous readjustment to changing usage would prove prescient of later architecture. → 17

Dynamic functionalism in France and the United States

A similarly dynamic functionalism was pursued by the team of Eugène Beaudouin and Marcel Lods, working in collaboration with the engineer Vladimir Bodiansky and the ironsmith Jean Prouvé. Their first joint project was the Cité de la Muette housing development in Drancy, France (1934–40, largely demolished 1977). **311** Its 14-story residential towers had steel structures on which concrete panels were dry-mounted. An assembly line, as in an automobile plant, was set up to move prefabricated panels across the construction site. In 1935 the team's contribution to the competition for an exhibition hall in the La Défense area west of Paris was remarkable for the audacious span of its steel arches and its kinetic aspect. Cars gained access to its circular roof through ramps inserted into the facade, which also contained huge sliding-glass doors rising the full height of the building.

For the Buc Aviation Club (1936; demolished 1944), the team designed a building of folded and stamped steel components, which were completely dry-mounted without the use of a crane. Its design and production were similar to the process employed for stressed-skin cars like Citroën's newly introduced front-wheel drive. Their architectural machine for the Maison du Peuple (People's House; 1936–40) **312** in Clichy may be taken as the first truly convertible multifunctional building, thanks to the sophisticated combination of mechanical systems designed by Bodiansky, an aeronautical engineer, and the metal components of Prouvé, an inventive manipulator of sheet metal and aluminum. Prouvé covered the building's steel structure with lightweight steel panels containing insulation held in tension between two thin sheets by prosaic mattress springs.

306 Suspended House, project, Paul Nelson, 1936–8

308 House of Advertising, project, Oscar Nitzchké, Paris, France, 1936–8

307 Glass House, Pierre Chareau and Bernard Bijvoet, Paris, France, 1927–31

Chapter 19 | Functionalism and machine aesthetics

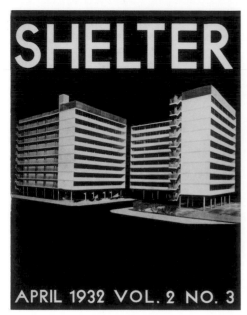

309 *Shelter* magazine, 1932

Enclosing a large open rectangular court that served as the heart of the building, the structure supported at the roof level sliding panels that could be retracted to expose the interior to the open air and floors that could be folded to do away with the separation between the second-story rooms and street-level market. Additional sliding partitions allowed for the building's interior to be reorganized into a series of independent spaces. The building's dynamic and modifiable design thus accommodated varying uses. [18]

Experiments carried out across the Atlantic explored similar territory. At the very moment the curators at New York's Museum of Modern Art were propagating a mythic simplification of modern architecture under the rubric "International Style," the founders of the Structural Studies Associates – R. Buckminster Fuller, Knud Lonberg-Holm, Theodore Larson, and a few others – took a more radical approach. In 1932 they set out their ideas in the five issues of the short-lived *Shelter*, **309** a magazine that they described as a "correlating medium for the forces of architecture." Reacting against MoMA's formalistic approach, they argued for a lighter, transportable, and easily demountable architecture that was derived from aeronautical technology and designed in collaboration with scientists. [19] Whereas MoMA offered modernism as a style, the *Shelter* group looked for a continued engagement with technology.

A prolific inventor, Fuller designed the Dymaxion House, an autonomous, prefabricated dwelling unit based on a hexagonal plan. Accompanying his global vision of a world colonized by an architecture contained in a kit of parts was a transportation system that used dirigibles to deliver his houses. Enlisting in his schemes young architects like Simon Breines, he managed to build three teardrop-shaped aerodynamic cars based on models built by the sculptor Isamu Noguchi and refined in a wind tunnel. Fuller's work was radically opposed to the purely style-focused work of conventional designers. The Dymaxion Bathroom (1936) **310** exemplified his research. A self-contained unit made of welded and stamped metal, this experimental design incorporated a built-in sink and tub into its continuous surfaces. A prototype was installed in Windshield, a house built by Richard Neutra for Anne and John Nicholas Brown on Fishers Island, New York (1938; destroyed by fire 1973). [20] Meanwhile Lonberg-Holm, who was an employee of the F. W. Dodge Corporation (publisher of the magazine *Architectural Record* and *Sweet's Catalog* of building supplies) and also a member of the American CIAM group, devised a "Time Zoning" system. It extended to an urban scale ideas of the obsolescence of buildings and their replacement, to an urban scale, a scale that was different than the one the architects in Clichy had taken into account on the other side of the Atlantic. [21]

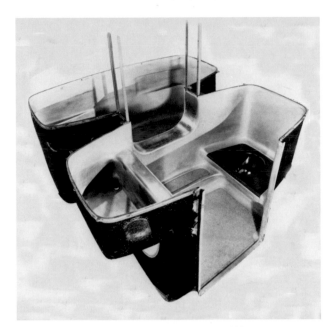

310 Dymaxion Bathroom, R. Buckminster Fuller, 1936

312 ▶ Maison du peuple (People's House), Eugène Beaudouin, Marcel Lods, Vladimir Bodiansky and Jean Prouvé, Clichy, France, 1936–40

311 Cité de la Muette Housing Development, Eugène Beaudouin and Marcel Lods, Drancy, France, 1934–40

Modern languages conquer the world

After World War I, the global spread of the new architecture that Buckminster Fuller had envisioned taking place through innovative technology was in fact propelled by a wider variety of forces. Programs for elite clients and for governments and institutions committed to modernization gave rise to concurrent but radically different types of projects. Luxury villas and social housing, shop interiors and urban plans, and model factories and primary schools all appeared side by side in periodicals whose rapid circulation carried architectural forms from one continent to another. Yet local and national contexts were so diverse that there was no real homogeneity internally, even if parallels can be drawn.

In his 1948 *Encyclopédie de l'architecture nouvelle* (Encyclopedia of New Architecture), Alberto Sartoris classified architectural production according to distinct "orders and climates": Mediterranean, Nordic, and American. →[1] While such differences were significant, other factors affected both the originality and the migration of forms. Geography certainly must be factored into any consideration of politics and poetics. After the fall of the Central Powers in World War I, for instance, the redrawing of Europe's map led to the formation or reconstitution of states such as Czechoslovakia, for which architecture sometimes became a way of asserting national identity. Among other phenomena was the move away from both academic eclecticism and Art Nouveau, which can be seen in a variety of contexts. Such an epistemological break – to use Gaston Bachelard's concept – was exemplified by the work of Northern European architects previously working in the spirit of neoclassicism, including Alvar Aalto and Erik Gunnar Asplund. No less significant was the catalytic effect of visiting architects, such as the shock resulting from Le Corbusier's 1929 lectures in Brazil, or the education of elites from Japan and elsewhere in nations where modernism had emerged earlier.

British reticence defeated

The case of Great Britain after the war is paradoxical. In this cradle of late-nineteenth-century reformist thinking, the response to new ideas, whether Continental or American, was largely skeptical. →[2] The Art Deco idiom did not cross the Channel from France until the late 1920s, taking form in London in monumental structures like the Battersea Power Station (1934) by Giles Gilbert Scott and buildings like the Hays Wharf (1932) by H. S. Goodhart-Rendel. The first spectacular British projects were commissions from the industrial sector, one example being the Wets Building of the Boots Factory (1930–2), **315** in Beeston with a gigantic concrete frame designed by the engineer Owen Williams. Its transparent exterior walls and roof made of glass bricks transformed it into a light box. Williams, who was responsible for the most modern aspects of the British Empire exhibition in Wembley in 1924–5, also built the Daily Express Building in London (1929–31), which he enveloped in a glass curtain wall that makes it a beacon at night.

The architect Wells Coates built the Lawn Road Flats in London in 1933–4, probably the first residential buildings in England to use an explicitly modern vocabulary, and the Embassy Court in Brighton in 1934. In 1931 he founded a company producing modern furniture, Isokon, for which Marcel Breuer began designing in 1935. In fact, émigré architects were decisive in formulating a new architecture in Britain. The Russian Berthold Lubetkin arrived in London in 1931 after attending the Vkhutemas in Moscow and subsequently collaborating with Jean Ginsberg in Paris on a remarkable modern apartment building on Avenue de Versailles (1928–31). With young architects including Francis Skinner and Denys Lasdun,

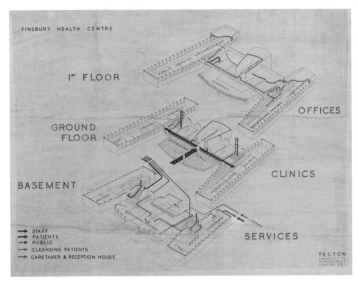

313 Finsbury Health Centre, Berthold Lubetkin and Tecton, London, United Kingdom, 1935–8

314 De La Warr Pavilion, Erich Mendelsohn and Serge Chermayeff, Bexhill-on-Sea, United Kingdom, 1934–5

316 ▶ Penguin Pool, London Zoo, Berthold Lubetkin and Tecton, London, United Kingdom, 1933–4

315 Wets Building, Boots Factory, Owen Williams, Beeston, United Kingdom, 1930–2

318 Addition to the Göteborg Courthouse, Erik Gunnar Asplund, Göteborg, Sweden, 1918–33

317 Restaurant at the Stockholm Exposition, Erik Gunnar Asplund, Stockholm, Sweden, 1930

319 Way of the Cross, Woodland Cemetery, Erik Gunnar Asplund, Stockholm, Sweden, 1933–40

Lubetkin founded the Tecton Group (short for "Architecton"), for which he designed two striking structures at the London Zoo. The Gorilla House (1932–3), a half-closed concrete cylinder designed with the young Danish engineer Ove Arup, is reminiscent of the private house in Moscow of Konstantin Melnikov, with whom Lubetkin had briefly collaborated. The Penguin Pool (1933–4) **316** is an inhabitable sculpture whose double-helix ramp evokes sculptor Naum Gabo's curved surfaces.

Turning their attention to human dwellings, Lubetkin and Tecton built two apartment blocks in London, both of which were architectural manifestos. Highpoint One (1933–5) made clever use of Le Corbusier's vocabulary, while Highpoint Two (1937–8) provided a more opulent elaboration, introducing brick to the facade and ironically recalling the imagery of *Vers une architecture* by slipping Greek caryatids under the concrete canopy. The Finsbury Health Centre, (1935–8) **313** which Tecton built for the Labour municipality of Finsbury, was even more ambitious. This interpretation of the "social condenser" – a concept that Lubetkin knew well from the Soviet context – was functionalist in its basic inspiration and in the way its interior spaces were closely related to the paths of the patients and visitors, while in the clarity of its construction and deployment of its mechanical systems it drew on principles of structural rationalism. [3]

Hungarian-born Ernö Goldfinger had studied with Perret before arriving in London in 1934. He designed several shops, a country house in Broxted (1937), and his own house in Hampstead (1937–8) – a reinterpretation of typical London houses, made of concrete and brick assembled with a subtle tectonic sensibility. [4] The German political situation precipitated the flight of many other refugees to London, most of whom just made brief stopovers before moving on. Walter

Gropius, Marcel Breuer, and László Moholy-Nagy left only faint traces of their presence, but Erich Mendelsohn and Serge Chermayeff's De La Warr Pavilion (1934–5) **314** in Bexhill-on-Sea, which resembled a maritime version of Mendelsohn's Berlin stores, was a large entertainment center with terraces overlooking the water. [5] During this period, the Modern Architecture Research Society, or MARS, founded by Coates in 1933 as a British wing of CIAM, developed into a forum for meetings between British architects and émigrés, whose interest in urban planning intensified as war became imminent.

Northern European modernisms

The transformations taking place in the no-less-ancient kingdom of Sweden were of a different order. [6] Here, the dominant figure was Erik Gunnar Asplund, who initially reacted against the National Romanticism of Ragnar Östberg and his own mentor, Ivar Tengbom, with neoclassical projects inflected by Mediterranean accents, such as the Snellmann House in Djursholm (1917–18). With Sigurd Lewerentz, he built the Woodland Cemetery Chapel in Stockholm (1918–20), whose compact volume and truncated pyramidical roof covering a domed interior evoked the popular classicism of the Swedish eighteenth century. Asplund also used domes in the Lister County Courthouse in Sölvesborg (1917–21) and notably in the Stockholm City Library (1918–28), where echoes of theoretical projects by Claude-Nicolas Ledoux and Étienne-Louis Boullée may be felt. The library's central component is a cylindrical reading room, its interior completely lined with books, with rectangular windows modulating the light. The spatial experience is that of following a path of initiation toward light and knowledge.

321 Viipuri Library, Alvar Aalto, Viipuri (Vyborg), Finland (Russia), 1927–35

322 Villa Mairea, Alvar Aalto, Noormarkku, Finland, 1938–9

320 Paimio Sanatorium, Alvar Aalto, Paimio, Finland, 1929–30

Asplund appeared to change his approach radically at the 1930 Stockholm Exposition. **317** There he built a complex of lightweight buildings with visible frames – an optimistic symbol of a modern architecture open to the outside, enlivened by color and banners. The tremendous popular success of these buildings served as a launchpad for *Funkis*, the functionalist approach to design embraced by Swedish architects linked to Asplund. The latter included such figures as Sven Markelius and Uno Ahrén, whose progressive social stance matched that of the *Neues Bauen* architects in Germany. Markelius and Ahrén designed the first building in Sweden embodying the radical *Funkis* ideas, a student center for the Stockholm Technical School (1930), in which they developed modern themes derived from French and German precedents; they then moved on to design public buildings and housing. → 7
Asplund's own projects continued to evolve. Although their overall plans retained a certain organic quality, their vocabulary became more geometric. The complexity and inventiveness of Asplund's work are nowhere more evident than in his addition to the Göteborg Courthouse, **318** a project initiated in 1918 but not carried out until 1933. The exterior transposes the Doric order of the original classical building into an elegant combination of load-bearing elements and infill panels, providing an analogue to the classical plinth and entablatures, while the great hall, surrounded by galleries, is covered in light-colored wood. Asplund returned to the site of the Woodland Cemetery to install a Way of the Cross (1933–40), **319** a route through open and closed spaces culminating in a stone-clad portico structure leading to his solemn but serene chapel. → 8
Among the new postwar states created in 1918 was Finland, freshly emancipated from Russian rule. It was the setting for the work of Alvar Aalto, which the world would discover at the

Paris and New York expositions of 1937 and 1939. Aalto's first buildings, among them the Jyväskylä Workers' Club (1924–5) and the Muurame Church (1926–9), are in a neoclassical vein close to that of Asplund. But after becoming acquainted with Le Corbusier's and Lurçat's Parisian buildings and comparable structures by German architects, he built the Turun Sanomat Newspaper Building in Turku (1928–9). → 9 Its long horizontal windows – Aalto did not hesitate to draw on Le Corbusier's lexicon – opened up space on the facade for a projection of the daily's front page, which was printed inside in a large white room with flaring concrete columns. The open-air stage that Aalto designed for the Seventh Centenary of Turku (1929) displayed his sculptural use of wood as a plastic medium. His first large project, the Paimio Sanatorium (1929–30), **320** developed in a more fluid manner the centrifugal configuration of the Dessau Bauhaus, differentiating each of its wings. He grouped the service and collective areas of the facility opposite the south facade, which he reserved for the tuberculosis patients, who took in the sun lying on the open balcony of the uppermost floor. Aalto designed all the sanatorium's furniture, including its innovative molded-plywood armchairs. Two buildings definitively established Aalto's originality. The first was the Viipuri (now Vyborg) Library of 1927–35, **321** which combined two rectangular boxes, the higher of which contains the reading rooms and is lit only by circular skylights. The library's most striking element is its sunken reading room, in which the reader is completely surrounded by books. The sense of warmth brought to the room by the books lining the white walls is carried over into the auditorium thanks to an undulating wood ceiling providing excellent acoustics. The second was Villa Mairea (1938–9), **322** where Aalto continued to explore the interplay between white surfaces and wood textures. It was built in Noormarkku for

324 Czechoslovakia Pavilion, Jaromír Krejcar, Paris Exposition, Paris, France, 1937, photo by Hugo Herdeg

323 French School, Jan Gillar, Prague, Czechoslovakia (Czech Republic), 1930–2

Harry Gullichsen and his wife, Maire, heir to the fortune of a lumber industrialist, and with whom he created the Artek furniture manufacturing company. The house is an assemblage of volumes that conform to an L-shaped plan, with a fluid sequence of large interior rooms converging at an open staircase that rises through a "grove" of thin wood poles echoing the nearby forest. Aalto also used wood as his primary material for the exterior of the Finland Pavilion at the Paris Exposition (1937) and for the large wavy wall he built to represent forest products inside the Finland Pavilion at the New York World's Fair (1939).

The modern as Czechoslovakia's national brand

In Central Europe, the success of functionalism and other architectural movements was intertwined with the establishment of the new Czechoslovak state. Culturally and linguistically Slavic, the republic founded in 1918 by Tomàš Masaryk sought to construct an identity free from references to Vienna's earlier domination. For the Czechoslovak elite, modern forms were an expression of the industrial values on which their prosperity was based. As the phase of Czech Cubism came to an end, its final manifestations in Prague – buildings like Josef Gočár's Bank of the Czechoslovak Legion (1923–4) and Pavel Janák's Riunione Adriatica (1922–4) – took on a belated monumentality, while the new architecture of modernism became the young state's self-conscious style. → 10 It was promoted by organizations such as the Devětsil association of intellectuals, the Czech Werkbund, and the Levá Fronta, which brought together the pro-Communist Left. The Czech avant-garde architects incessantly united and diverged within the ranks of these organizations under the tireless critical eye of Karel Teige. → 11

In Prague, prewar figures such as Janák relinquished Cubism for a calmer modernism. This is evident in his Julis Hotel (1932) and especially in the site plan of the Baba Development (1932), a collective project built by the city's modern architects. Ambitious public programs allowed Jaroslav Fragner to put up the Eastern Bohemia Power Plant in Kolín (1929–31), a large cubic composition on the banks of the Elbe, and Josef Havlíček and Karel Honzík to build the Prague Pensions Institute (1929–34). The Institute was probably the largest modern building in all of Europe save perhaps Oldřich Tyl and Josef Fuchs's Trade Fair Palace, also in Prague (1924–9), whose awesome scale provoked Le Corbusier's envy on a visit in 1930. Jan Gillar's French School in Prague (1930–2) **323** and Jaromír Krejcar's sanatorium in Trenčianské Teplice in Slovakia (1929–32) introduced ingenious and lucidly composed structures into the European discussion of new public buildings, which led the government to commission Krejcar to built the country's pavilion at the 1937 Paris Exposition. **324**

Thanks to municipal and industrial commissions, ambitious developments were built along with individual residences for Prague's and Brno's elites. These included Gočár's public complex in Hradec Kralové, and most especially, the urban plan of Zlín (1925–35), a genuine example of the rational city, designed by František Gahura, Vladimir Karfík, and Jiři Voženilek. Zlín was home to the Taylorized factories of the powerful international shoe manufacturer Baťa, whose company policies determined the development of the surrounding area. These policies were exported to several other Baťa sites elsewhere in Europe as well. Karfík's Baťa Office Tower (1938), **325** with the director's office designed as an exterior elevator moving vertically from one department to the next, was an emblem of the firm's architectural ambition. → 12

325 Baťa Office Tower, Vladimir Karfík, Zlín, Czechoslovakia (Czech Republic), 1938

326 Café Avion, Bohuslav Fuchs, Brno, Czechoslovakia (Czech Republic), 1927

327 *Blok*, cover of first issue, Mieczyslaw Szczuka graphic designer, published in Warsaw, Poland, 1924

A number of other industrial and commercial companies also adopted the modern vocabulary. Ludvík Kysela built retail establishments for the Lindt Department Store (1926–8) as well as for Baťa (1928–9) on Václavské Náměstí, the Champs-Élysées of Prague, with steel skeletons and glass facades. Punctuating Prague's center with remarkable retail spaces, Tyl designed the concrete and glass-block vault of the Černá Ruže Gallery (1932), and Josef Kittrich and Josef Hrubý were responsible for the glass facade of the Bílá Labut Department Store (1941). In Brno, the *Nový Dům* (New Dwelling) exhibition of 1928 proved that Czech architects could propose their own range of model constructions. Arnošt Wiesner's crematorium (1926–9) and commercial building (1926–7) bore witness to the vitality of Perret's ideas in Czechoslovakia, while the designs of Bohuslav Fuchs, including his Café Avion of 1927, **326** with its mezzanine café, and his municipal bathhouse of 1929–30 displayed a particularly elegant form of functionalism. Leftist architects who explored communal housing in the 1930s were clearly influenced by the research of Moisei Ginzburg and other Soviet colleagues. These architectural structures based on pure geometric forms, together with the aerodynamic Tatra automobiles designed by Hans Ledwinka, came to represent Czech industrial culture as a whole. Although modernist experiments largely came to an end in the Soviet Union and Germany in 1932 and 1933, they continued to be hotly debated in Czechoslovak journals such as *Stavba* (Construction) and *Stavitel* (The Architect).

The moderns in Hungary and Poland

Before 1914 Hungary's architecture had largely been shaped by the Secession and by Otto Wagner's teachings. Following the war, a neo-Baroque manner flourished in the work of Hungarian architects like Gyula Wälder, while dictator Miklós Horthy's appreciation of Mussolini assured a positive reception for Italian Novecento forms. → [13] The defeat of Béla Kun and his revolutionaries in 1919 led to a mass emigration of artists and intellectuals to Germany. This drain of creative workers was reinforced by the restricted admission of Jews into Hungarian universities. László Moholy-Nagy – who had contributed to the avant-garde journal *Mà* (Today), edited from 1916 by Lajos Kassák – left for Germany, along with Farkas Molnár, Ernst Kállai, Andor Weininger, Gyulia Papp, and Fred Forbat. Sandor Bortnyik opened his own art school, the Mühely, or workshop (1928–38), in Budapest based on the Bauhaus model. The Hungarian moderns joined CIAM in 1929 and published the review *Tér és Forma* (Space and Form) from 1928 to 1948. In 1931 and 1932, they organized exhibitions where Molnár and József Fischer presented their project for a *Kolház*, or communal house, though their commissions actually came from the enlightened bourgeoisie.

Upon his return to Hungary in 1927, Molnár built houses in Budapest on Cserje Street (1931) and Lejtö Street (1932). **329** The more sculptural touch found in the Lejtö Street house was also evident in Fischer's house on Szépvölgyi Avenue (1935), which echoed Lurçat's experiments. Notable among the city's apartment buildings was an elegant variation on the modern facade with horizontal windows, here decorated with travertine; it was built on Régiposta Street in 1933 by Lajos Kozma, a lapsed National Romantic architect. When construction finally picked up again in Budapest after Hungary suffered the effects of a comparatively mild economic depression, Béla Hofstätter and Ferenc Domán built a complex on Margit Boulevard (1937) featuring a rather lyrical and sinuous volume with several loggias. Oszkár Winkler's Berlin-inspired apartment house in Sopron

328 Zoliborz Cooperative Housing Estate, Barbara Brukalska and Stanislaw Brukalski, Warsaw, Poland, 1930–4

329 Dálnoky-Kováts Villa, Farkas Molnár, Budapest, Hungary, 1932

(1935) demonstrated the spread of new ideas to the provinces. Prior to 1914, the architecture of the territories that Poland would reclaim after the war had been divided between the influences of Vienna and Saint Petersburg, as may be seen, for instance, in the Cooperative Bank by Jan Heurich, Jr., in Warsaw (1912–17). After 1918 the Warsaw architects' neoclassicism stood in sharp contrast to the expressionism, or *Formizm* (Formism), favored in Krakow's ateliers. Even more evident, though, was the impact of Constructivism, as exemplified by the experiments of Katarzyna Kobro and Wladislaw Stzreminski, who had spent time in Moscow. Periodicals played a fundamental role in defining Poland's new culture and awareness of the rest of Europe. In 1924 Mieczyslaw Szczuka founded *Blok* (Block) **327** to encourage "utilitarian beauty." The following year Romuald Miller launched *Architektura i budownictwo* (Architecture and Construction), to which the younger generation responded in 1926 with *Praesens* (Presence). → 14 Among the contributors to these periodicals, Szymon Syrkus stood out for his European experience, acquired in Vienna, Moscow, and Berlin in 1922–4. He participated in the League of Nations competition and founded the Polish section of CIAM with Józef Szanajca. His Fertilizer Pavilion at the 1929 National Exhibition in Poznań evoked both Mallet-Stevens and Kazimir Malevich, while the Construction Pavilion by Bohdan Lachert and Szanajca leaned toward Futurism. With his wife, Helena, Syrkus built an apartment building on Jaworynska Street in Warsaw (1937) and row houses with double-height living rooms in Lódz-Marysin (1935). His plan for a "functional Warsaw," presented at CIAM's 1933 meeting, would remain an essential reference point for later reflections on the urbanism of the Polish capital. After 1930 an upswing following the economic depression made it possible to build new housing complexes, often based on

German models. Barbara Brukalska and Stanislaw Brukalski's Zoliborz Cooperative Housing Estate (1930–4) **328** in Warsaw featured large curvilinear balconies, while buildings such as Tadeusz Michejda's on Slowackiego Street in Katowice (1931) transformed the housing block with the use of open courtyards. There were also attempts to perpetuate a linear, modernized version of classicism, as in the case of the Krakow National Museum (1936–9) by Boleslav Szmidt, Juliusz Dumicki, and Janusz Juraczynski. Adolf Szyszko-Bohusz developed a regionalized variant of modernism with his surprising concrete and exposed-stone château built in Wisla-Kubalonka (1930–1) for the Polish president. → 15

Balkan figures

While Belgrade, the capital of the newly founded Yugoslavia, saw the emergence of scores of modern buildings, → 16 Ljubljana was the most remarkable center of innovation in the southern Slavic region. In two decades Jože Plečnik transformed the city. He was also active in Prague, where President Masaryk had invited him to remodel the gardens, courtyards, staircases, and apartments of Prague Castle (1920–35), the royal seat and symbolic heart of Bohemia. Plečnik built the Church of the Sacred Heart (1928–31) in Prague's Vinohrady quarter, a large rectangular volume enclosed by a brick wall that appears to be woven rather than constructed. The bell tower, containing a ramp illuminated by two large circular windows, appears as a taut homage to modernism, even from an architect increasingly drawn to playing with classical elements. In Ljubljana Plečnik taught architecture from 1921 on while building numerous churches and other structures that combined reinterpretations of the classical orders with Secessionist details, as in his

330 National and University Library, Jože Plečnik, Ljubljana, Yugoslavia (Slovenia), 1938–41

Vzajemna Insurance Building (1928–30). In a plan of 1928–9 for the Slovenian capital, he developed the banks of the Ljubljanica River by erecting three bridges that ingeniously connected its embankment to the street level. Later he designed the National and University Library (1938–41), **330** using luxurious materials that attest to his spatial and decorative inventiveness. A two-color stone palace, the library includes colonnaded halls sheathed in granite and a reading room paneled in wood. → 17 In Bucharest, where the influence of Paris remained prevalent and construction developed at an intense pace, the ex-Dadaist and former Beaux-Arts student Marcel Janco built a series of houses with cubic shapes, including the Florica Reich Villa (1936–7). The most prolific of the city's architects was Horia Creangă, another Beaux-Arts alumnus, who erected some of the large modern buildings that transformed the capital while maintaining a system of continuous blocks, as in the Building for the Asigurarea Românească or ARO (1929–31) **331** on Magheru Boulevard, a collection of provocative buildings, and the Burileanu-Malaxa Apartment Complex (1935–7). → 18 Greece, another nation-state that emerged strengthened from World War I, was flooded with mass immigration from the shores of the Aegean after the Turkish victory in the 1923 war. The French architect Ernest Hébrard rebuilt Thessaloniki, which had been destroyed by fire in 1917, with grand urban forms lined by classical arcades. A program of building primary schools in response to the influx of refugees introduced modern architecture to Athens. The program's most successful building was the Pefkakia School (1931–2) **332** by Dimitris Pikionis, who had trained in Munich and Paris. The Pefkakia's classrooms stepped down in terraces along the city's Lycabettus Hill. Other contributors to the program included Nikos Mitsakis and Kyriakos Panayotakos. The children's villages by Panos Dzelepis grew

out of the same policy, while Le Corbusier's ideas clearly had an impact on buildings like Stamo Papadaki's house in Glyfada (1932–3). The Heraklion Archaeological Museum (1933–58), built in Crete by Patroklos Karantinos, a former student of Perret, remains probably the most complex of these projects; in it the modern aesthetic meets with some of its antique sources. → 19

Iberian modernization

On the western shores of the Mediterranean, Spanish architecture was characterized by the persistence of classical culture, with isolated instances reflecting alternative approaches. → 20 Fernando García Mercadal, one of the founders of CIAM, built the Rincón de Goya in Zaragoza (1926–8), a founding statement of the new Spanish architecture, as was the Futurist-inspired San Sebastián Nautical Club in Basque country (1929), by José María Aizpurúa and Joaquín Labayén. The transformation of Madrid, with American-inspired high-rise buildings lining the Gran Vía, was accompanied by the creation of a university campus in the Moncloa district under the direction of Modesto López Otero. It was the period's defining project. The campus plan was modeled after American examples, but the buildings by Manuel Sánchez Arcas, Luis Lacasa, Agustín Aguirre, and Pascual Bravo were designed in a more innovative language of brick and concrete. Secundino Zuazo collaborated with the German Hermann Jansen on the plan for the Paseo de la Castellana and built the vast Casa de las Flores housing block (1930–1), an interpretation of the Viennese *Höfe*. He also designed the Recoletos Indoor Pelota Court (1935) with the engineer Eduardo Torroja. Torroja received enormous attention for the thin concrete shell he built for the stands of the Zarzuela Hippodrome (1935–6).

331 Asigurarea Românească Building, Horia Creangă, Bucharest, Romania, 1929–31

332 Pefkakia School, Dimitris Pikionis, Athens, Greece, 1931–2

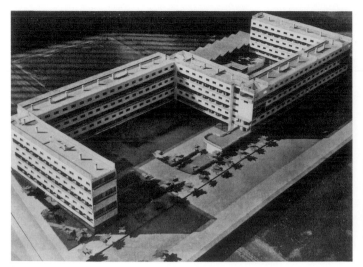

333 Casa Bloc, José Luís Sert, Joan Bautista Subirana and Josep Torres Clavé, Barcelona, Spain, 1932–6

334 Shirokiya Department Store, Kikuji Ishimoto and Bunzo Yamaguchi, Tokyo, Japan, 1928–31

The buildings by Miguel Martin Fernández de la Torre introduced the modern idiom to Las Palmas, in the Canary Islands. But in terms of architectural innovation, Barcelona remained the most important place in Spain, even as Gaudí's influence was waning. José Luís Sert introduced elements of Le Corbusier's vocabulary into his Carrer Muntaner Building (1929–31), in which double-height apartments define a facade with pronounced horizontals. In collaboration with Joan Bautista Subirana and Josep Torres Clavé, Sert designed the Casa Bloc (1932–6), **333** a housing complex whose plan is a fragment of the *redent* pattern invented by Le Corbusier. The tuberculosis clinic (1934–8) designed by the same team was probably the most radical and elegant structure in the entire Iberian peninsula. In 1937 Sert and Lacasa built the Spain Pavilion for the Paris international exposition.

Seven years earlier, Sert and Torres Clavé joined forces with García Mercadal and Antoni Bonet Castellana to found a Spanish branch of CIAM, GATEPAC, or Grupo de artistas y técnicos españoles para la arquitectura contemporánea (Group of Spanish Artists and Technicians for Contemporary Architecture). The Catalan branch, GATCPAC, or Grup d'arquitectes i tècnics catalans per al progrés de l'arquitectura contemporània (Group of Catalan Architects and Technicians for the Advancement of Contemporary Architecture), published the journal *Actividad contemporánea,* or *AC* (Contemporary Activity; 1931–7), which used manifestos and photomontages to express its support for social housing, the elimination of slums, and collective facilities. [21] GATCPAC's members collaborated on a design for a "city of leisure" near Barcelona (1931–5). They fought on the Republican side in the Civil War, and Torres Clavé died at the front, while Sert and Bonet were forced into exile by Franco's victory in 1939. Reconstruction

under Franco ushered in a period of widespread architectural regression, manifested in both new ministries built in Madrid and several new villages built in the rural areas.

Japanese experiments

The initial Japanese path to new architecture went by way of an assimilation of Western approaches. [22] The Czech architect Antonin Raymond, who had arrived in Tokyo with Frank Lloyd Wright in 1919, played a key role in this process, appropriating a great variety of architectural styles over two decades of work. He copied from Wright in the Rachel Reid House in Azabu (1924), while inserting architectonic elements derived from Cubism and De Stijl into the Reinanzaka House built in the same neighborhood (1923–4). Le Corbusier dismissed Raymond's summer house (1933) in Karuizawa, near Nagano, as a pastiche of his own design for the Errazuris House in Chile, whose V-shaped roof Raymond imitated. But Perret did not protest Raymond's borrowing the tectonics of Le Raincy in his Church of the Women's Christian College of Tokyo (1934). The Asaka Golf Club (1932) **336** in Saitama Prefecture mixes modern, orthogonal, and sinuous forms at a large scale. Raymond eventually designed more personal and mature projects, notably the Kawasaki House in Azabu (1934). [23] Sutemi Horiguchi and Mamoru Yamada, founders of the Japanese Secession, also searched for ways to mediate between the principles of traditional Japanese architecture and Western modernism, in both residences like Horiguchi's Okada House (1933–4) and public buildings that were part of larger modernization programs. Buildings by Kikuji Ishimoto, one of the Secessionist architects and, briefly, a student at the Weimar Bauhaus, clearly reflected their German sources. The

336 Asaka Golf Club, Antonin Raymond, Asaka, Japan, 1932

337 ▶ Casa Modernista 1, Grigori Warchavchik, São Paulo, Brazil, 1930

335 Nakayama House, Togo Murano, Kobe, Japan, 1934

offices he built for the newspaper *Asahi* in Sukyabashi, Tokyo (1927, demolished), featured a facade with rounded angles and openings reminiscent of Hans Poelzig's factory in Luban. His nearby Shirokiya Department Store (1928–31) **334** were obviously inspired by Erich Mendelsohn's Stuttgart and Chemnitz buildings. → [24] Tetsuro Yoshida also spent time in Germany, where he attended the second CIAM meeting in 1929. His design for Tokyo's Central Post Office (1927–31) is reminiscent of the school buildings he discovered there. His Osaka Post Office (1931), lit by a curved and glazed facade, is less monumental. Horiguchi later built the Oshima Island Weather Station (1938) in a similar spirit, incorporating German accents. Bunzo Yamaguchi, a student at the Bauhaus from 1930 to 1932, built a modest *Siedlung* in Bancho, Tokyo (1933), then replicated the basic design of Richard Neutra's Lovell House in his Migishi and Yamada houses (1934). Togo Murano, a more rebellious thinker educated at Waseda University, drew on the zigzag system of Ernst May's Bruchfeldstraße *Siedlung* in Frankfurt for his Osaka Pantheon (1933), but attempted to combine Japanese and Western spatial concepts in the luxurious Nakayama House (1934) **335** near Kobe, where he strove to fulfill the expectations of the Kansai region's upper bourgeoisie.

Junzo Sakakura, a former Beaux-Arts student and a draftsman in Le Corbusier's studio, undertook to devise an architecture that synthesized modernist currents with traditional elements of the Kyoto tea house and garden architecture. With this combination he won the competition to build the Japan Pavilion at the 1937 Paris exposition, triumphing over his predecessor in Le Corbusier's studio, Kunio Maekawa, who submitted a proposal apparently based on Asplund's designs for the 1930 Stockholm Exhibition and was passed over. Maekawa's 1931 project for the Imperial Museum in Ueno Park in Tokyo – clearly influenced by

his Paris master – was also rejected. The winner of that competition, Jin Watanabe, built a rather overbearing symmetrical composition that was completed in 1937, full of historicizing details and bringing together all the characteristics of state architecture. Watanabe's Imperial Museum signaled the end of the first age of modernist experiments in Japan. Around this time, probably anticipating the outbreak of the war, Raymond went to India to build the city of Auroville in Pondicherry. Japanese architects of the period clearly absorbed many Western approaches, but Japan's structures and building methods had a reciprocal impact on certain Westerners, including not only Wright but also Bruno Taut. Taut lived in the Japanese archipelago between 1933 and 1936 and, on his departure for Turkey, published a book declaring his unequivocal admiration for Japanese culture. → [25] Another example of this East-West cross-fertilization was the arrival in Tokyo in 1940 of Charlotte Perriand, at the invitation of the Ministry of Commerce and Industry. Rather than importing her Parisian experience to Japan, she reshaped her methods in response to its spaces and objects of everyday life.

Brazilian curves

Unknown to most observers of the period, an original architecture was flourishing in Brazil. Lucio Costa and Oscar Niemeyer's Brazil Pavilion at the 1939 New York World's Fair provided the international audience with its first glimpse of Brazilian innovations. Four years later, the Museum of Modern Art offered a broader survey with the exhibition *Brazil Builds*. → [26] Almost two decades had passed since Brazilian artists and intellectuals, most of them based in Paris, organized the *Semana de Arte Moderna* (Modern Art Week) in São Paulo, an arts festival held

338 Museum of the Missions, Lucio Costa, São Miguel das Missões,
Brazil, 1937–40

in 1922 on the initiative of the poet Mário de Andrade. The first
full-fledged Brazilian architectural event was organized in 1930
in the same city by Grigori Warchavchik, a native of Odessa and
former student at the Accademia di belle arti in Rome, where
he had worked for Marcello Piacentini. → 27 Warchavchik introduced São Paulo to modernism in 1928 with his house on Rua
Santa Cruz, then made a broader statement when he opened to
the public his Casa Modernista 1 (1930) **337** on Rua Itàpolis, a
compact construction whose cubic volume is extended by two
L-shaped porticoes. His next project was the larger Norschild
House in Rio de Janeiro (1931, demolished), with long balconies
that gave it a more sculptural appearance. The garden of the
house was created by Roberto Burle Marx, a painter who had
recently returned from Germany and was beginning to imagine
a specifically Brazilian approach to landscape design informed
by the patterns of modern abstract art.

Warchavchik also built an apartment building in São Paulo
(1939), the rectilinear facade of which ended in a curve. His collaborator, Lucio Costa, who was educated at Rio's Academia de
Bellas Artes, was at the time engaged in a battle against neo-
colonial architecture and played a fundamental role in the
decision by the Minister of Education Gustavo Capanema to
commission Le Corbusier to design the Ministry of Education
and Health (1936–43) **340** in Rio. Costa became one of the most
active members of SPHAN, or Serviço do patrimônio histórico
e artístico nacional (Service for the National Historical and
Artistic Heritage), founded by President Getúlio Vargas in 1937
and headed by Rodrigo Melo Franco de Andrade. Incorporating
architectural fragments from the eighteenth century, Costa
erected a museum facing the ruins of the Indian mission built
by the Jesuits in São Miguel das Missões (1937–40) **338** in Rio
Grande do Sul. The three white boxes of the galleries beneath a
large tile roof evoke Le Corbusier's Parisian houses.

The ministry in Rio was the incubator of modern architecture
in Brazil. The young architects Carlos Leão, Jorge Machado
Moreira, Affonso Eduardo Reidy, and Ernani Vasconcellos all
got their start there, as did the team's youngest member, Oscar
Niemeyer, who revealed his virtuosity. Niemeyer soon embarked
on a brilliant career, beginning with the Obra do Berço
Orphanage in Rio (1937), his first use of Le Corbusier's *brise-
soleil*, and with the Brazil Pavilion for the New York World's Fair.
Soon after, Juscelino Kubitschek, mayor of Belo Horizonte, capital of the state of Minas Gerais, hired Niemeyer to design a leisure complex around Pampulha Lake (1940–3), which became
the manifesto of a free and lyrical architecture. While the casino
depended on Corbusian themes, Niemeyer transcended these
influences in a yacht club whose V-shaped roof takes off from
the principle of the Paris architect's Errazuris House project.
The Casa do Baile, another building in the complex, is a simple
open-air dance hall on the lakeshore, delimited by a sinuous
concrete awning. The most impressive of Niemeyer's structures
at Pampulha is the Church of St. Francis of Assisi (1940–3), **339**
whose roof is held up by four thin concrete parabolic arches
and is lined with wood. The painter Cándido Portinari designed
the blue-and-white *azulejos* tiles on the exterior of the church,
as well as the fresco inside. Although the local church authorities refused to consecrate the unorthodox house of worship,
the publicity generated by both Niemeyer's world's fair pavilion
and the publication of the Pampulha complex immediately after
World War II gave the church an international impact greater
than that of any other Brazilian structure.

The principles of modern architecture made their mark in other
Latin American countries as well. In Mexico City's neighborhood
of Coyoacán, Juan O'Gorman, a painter and architect educated

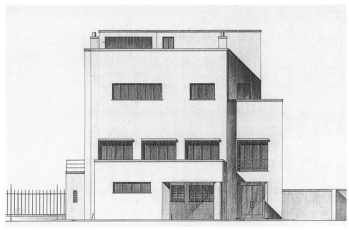

342 Ocampo House, Alejandro Bustillo, Buenos Aires, Argentina, 1929

341 Diego Rivera and Frida Kahlo Houses, Juan O'Gorman, Mexico City, Mexico, 1931–2

340 Ministry of Education and Health, Le Corbusier, Lucio Costa, Carlos Leão, Oscar Niemeyer, Jorge Moreira, Affonso Eduardo Reidy and Ernani Vasconcellos, Rio de Janeiro, Brazil, 1936–43

at the Academia de San Carlos, built two cubic studios on *pilotis* for the painters Diego Rivera and Frida Kahlo (1931–2). **341** Familiar with Adolf Loos's theories and Le Corbusier's buildings – and also with the French landscape designer Ferdinand Bac's Mediterranean gardens – Luis Barragán built the Emiliano Robles León House in Guadalajara. Mexico's modern architecture was consolidated in the late 1930s with the arrival of the Spanish architect Félix Candela and the German Max Cetto, as well as the presence of Hannes Meyer (1939–49) as a guest of the nationalist president Lazaro Cardenas. In Caracas, Venezuela, Carlos Raúl Villanueva, who had been trained in Paris, broke with accepted teachings by building two definitive modern statements: the Los Manolos House (1934) and the Gran Colombia School (1939–42).

Finally, in Argentina, where Beaux-Arts French culture was equally dominant, Alejandro Bustillo built two houses for Victoria Ocampo, the patron of Buenos Aires intellectuals: one was in Mar del Plata (1927), the other in the capital (1929). **342** Though more conventional than the house Le Corbusier designed for her, these houses clearly illustrated the compromises negotiated by architects throughout the Latin American continent between the initial forms of modern architecture and their locally acceptable applications. The urban landscape of Buenos Aires was also transformed with buildings by Andrés Kálnay and by Alberto Prebisch, including the Gran Rex movie theater (1936). → 28 While Mario Palanti's ornate Palacio Barolo Office Building on Avenida de Mayo (1922) deferred to the dominance of concrete as a building material, the Kavanagh Apartment Building by Gregorio Sánchez, Ernesto Lagos, and Luis M. de la Torre (1936) revealed a new direction opened up by the North American steel-frame building. → 29

Colonial experiences and new nationalisms

During the interwar decades colonial territories and outposts of former empires, where ruthless domination continued, offered fertile ground for experimentation by European architects before giving way to the emancipated cultures of the postcolonial states. Architectural policies and forms at times circulated "horizontally," moving back and forth between colonies and protectorates. For instance, France's practices in Morocco, which were partly inspired by British policies in India, eventually carried over to the Near East, where France had a mandate over Syria and Lebanon, but they were also felt in certain Italian colonies. Other influences were more indirect, such as a certain pervasive Americanism and the influence of German urban planning, which persisted even after Germany's loss of its colonies following World War I. Modernization in the colonial empires did not express itself in a single architectural language, however, and developments in the 1920s and 1930s were marked by contradictory phenomena. Although hygiene became a dominant concern in both housing and public policy, attention to it did not automatically generate either Cubist or functionalist forms, as was often the case in Europe. The development of tourism was also a significant factor. The demand for "local color" was based not just on notions of cultural identity as applied to public edifices and occasionally entire neighborhoods, with each city expected to have a distinctive aspect, but also on the allure of the exotic. [1] The colonies and certain emerging states were therefore shaped by complex systems of hybridization beyond what was experienced in Europe and North America. In some cases, modernist forms were embellished with historicist ornamentation; in others, historical forms were filtered through the prism of abstract modern geometries.

From Arabizing to modernizing in North Africa

Nowhere was this complexity more evident than in North Africa. In Algeria, Governor General Charles Jonnard's policy of "Arabizing" at the turn of the century had led to the construction of public buildings with facade schemes and decorative motifs drawn from an Islamic vocabulary, often reduced to Moorish themes. [2] During the interwar period, local architects and professionals from the northern Mediterranean introduced new approaches. The Boulevard Laferrière, built where Algiers's old ramparts had stood, was originally defined by edifices in the Arabizing style, such as Jules Voinot and Denis-Marius Toudoire's Central Post Office (1910–13) and Henri Petit's Dépêche Algérienne Building (1906). The boulevard acquired a new and dominant feature with the Palais du Gouvernement Général (Algerian Government Building; 1930–3), **345** designed by Jacques Guiauchain and built by the Perret brothers at its upper edge. This vast, concrete-framed rectangular box was equipped with movable partitions that could adjust to the government's changing configurations. Le Corbusier admired the way its "smooth and firm facade imposed itself," but the writer Georges Duhamel deemed it "completely foreign to its landscape," insisting that "the ground accepts it so poorly that it looks exactly as if it were expelling it, catapulting it out over the stunned city toward the sea." [3] The Perret office received an increasing number of commissions in Algiers, even though steel framing was common in the city, and exerted considerable influence there. The celebration of the centennial of French rule in 1930 launched the construction of projects such as Léon Claro and Albert Cès's civic center, or Maison du Peuple (People's House; 1935).

343 Obus Plan, Le Corbusier, Algiers, Algeria, 1931–2

344 Asayag Building, Marius Boyer, Casablanca, Morocco, 1930

345 Algerian Government Building, Jacques Guiauchain and the Perret brothers, Algiers, Algeria, 1930–3

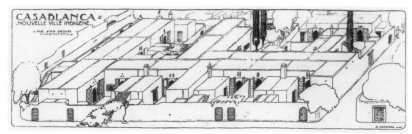

347 New Indigenous Town, Edmond Brion, Auguste Cadet and Albert Laprade, Casablanca, Morocco, 1917–22

346 Bendahan Apartment Building, Edmond Brion, Casablanca, Morocco, 1935

The building's main facade replicated the decorative theme of Perret's Théâtre des Champs-Élysées in Paris, while its side facades featured horizontal windows and *pilotis*. In 1936, three years after their *Exposition d'architecture et d'urbanisme*, the Association des Amis d'Alger (Association of the Friends of Algiers) chose the civic center as the site for their *Cité moderne* exhibition. This association, led by followers of Le Corbusier such as Jean-Pierre Faure and Pierre-André Emery, had invited the Paris architect to Algiers in 1931 to analyze the urban situation. Le Corbusier responded with his 1931–2 Obus Plan. **343** Meaning "explosive shell," Obus utilized ideas the architect had developed a few years earlier in Rio de Janeiro, mapping out a system of highways to run above the city and incorporating a ribbon of housing to serve a new business district located between the Casbah and the port. "The loftiest theoretical hypothesis of modern urban planning," according to Manfredo Tafuri, [4] the plan integrated arabesque forms from Le Corbusier's paintings with the turning radius of fast cars to produce an overall urban vision. It was, in its promoter's view, a civilizing volley fired from France toward Africa. Imposing a colonial image of modernization upon a partly demolished Casbah, the plan led to the conception, in 1938, of a skyscraper whose facade represented a crucial refinement of the principle of the *brise-soleil*. [5] Le Corbusier repeatedly revised the plan until 1942, but in vain. West of Algiers, another configuration of modern architecture evolved in Casablanca, the economic capital of France's Moroccan protectorate. The city's public buildings were all designed in an Arabizing vein by architects working for the Resident General Hubert Lyautey, who was personally responsible for giving the "Moroccan" touch to Adrien Laforgue's post office (1918–20) that served to set the pattern. But

Casablanca was a city that mixed hard work with hedonism, and the real monuments there were movie theaters such as Marius Boyer's Vox (1935), parking garages such as Pierre Bousquet's Auto-Hall (1930), and apartment buildings. Without any legislation limiting the height of new construction – and in this regard unlike Paris – Casablanca saw the erection of apartment buildings combining Le Corbusier's cruciform plans with Henri Sauvage's setback terraces. One such structure was the Asayag Building (1930) **344** by Boyer, whose work dotted the city center. Other notable buildings by Boyer included the Glaoui Arcade (1922), in a neo-Moroccan vein, and the Levy Bendayan Building (1928), with its spectacular portal opening into a courtyard. The fourteen-story Moretti-Milone Building (1934–5) by Pierre Jabin, Edmond Brion's ocean liner-shaped Bendahan Apartment Building **346** (1935), and various ambitious projects by Marcel Desmet all contributed to creating an urban landscape more modern than that of any city in metropolitan France. [6]

On the periphery of Casablanca's dense city center, the villas lining the residential streets were soon equipped with the latest furnishings. But the other remarkable aspect of the protectorate's program was the creation of a "new indigenous city" in the context of an explicit policy of social and ethnic segregation. The urban plan for this settlement intended for Muslim people arriving from the country's interior was sketched by Albert Laprade, a sharp observer of the ancient cities of Morocco and Andalusia, who laid out a labyrinth of streets bordered by the mute facades of introverted courtyard housing (1917–22). **347** Designed by Brion and Auguste Cadet and intended for families of various sizes, these dwellings so skillfully reproduced their historical precedents that they are often mistaken for pre-colonial buildings. Administered by the Habous, or religious

348 Hôtel Saint-Georges, Antoine Tabet with Georges Bordes, André Lotte and Jacques Poirrier, Beirut, Lebanon, 1930–2

349 Place de l'Étoile, Beirut, Lebanon, 1931–2, with Lebanese Parliament by Mardiros Altounian at left

foundations, this exemplary but spatially restricted development was insufficient to house the new rural migrants, who overflowed into bulging *bidonvilles* – a term coined locally to describe ramshackle housing areas, later to become standard French vocabulary for shantytowns anywhere.

Near Eastern and African endeavors

The advanced planning legislation that Lyautey implemented in Morocco served as the model for laws passed by the French during their mandates in Syria and Lebanon between 1920 and 1946. The development plans of brothers Réne and Raymon Danger for Aleppo, Damascus, Tripoli, and Beirut all borrowed features conceived by Henri Prost, such as functional zoning and arcaded streets, but their urban compositions were more conventional. The Place de l'Étoile **349** in Beirut had a clock tower at its center and was the site of Mardiros Altounian's Lebanese Parliament (1931–2); although not an innovative building, it provided the city with a monumental center. The modernization of Beirut's apartment buildings was directly inspired by architectural types that had been prevalent locally during the nineteenth century. [7] The Hôtel Saint-Georges (1930–2) **348** – built on the coast by Antoine Tabet with Jacques Poirrier, Georges Bordes, and André Lotte – was one of several adaptations of Auguste Perret's design strategies; [8] the Roxy Cinema (1932) by the engineer Ilyas Murr, a graduate of Massachusetts Institute of Technology, introduced American Art Deco forms into the area.

Overall, the architecture in French, Belgian, and British sub-Saharan colonies remained conservative. Only South Africa, then a British dominion, gave rise to innovative approaches, notably in the work of Rex Martienssen and his group of architects based in the Transvaal. In 1933 Martienssen, who established direct contact with Le Corbusier, published the only issue of the avant-garde review *zerohour*. He collaborated with John Fassler and Bernard Cooke on the Peterhouse and the Stern House in Johannesburg (1934–5). [9]

In Indonesia, controlled by the Dutch since the eighteenth century, the colonizers essentially produced a regionalist architecture modernized by architects such as Thomas Karsten, H. Maclaine Pont, and Wolff Schoemaker. The Surabaya City Hall by Cornelis Citroen (1920) combined a locally inspired sloping roof with the geometry espoused by Hendrik Petrus Berlage (who visited Indonesia in 1923) and Robert van't Hoff. In the 1930s the architectural vocabulary of Willem Marinus Dudok reigned supreme, and bolder buildings began to appear. These included Albert Frederik Aalbers's DENIS Bank (1935) and the Hotel Savoy Homann (1939) **351** in Bandung, whose lyrical aerodynamics were fully justified by the need for ventilation in that tropical climate. [10]

Italian architects played a notable role in Egypt, erecting many urban buildings in Alexandria. [11] In Cairo, where Baron Édouard Empain had created the new city of Heliopolis, architectural diversity prevailed. [12] Designers of residential buildings and public edifices moved away from Orientalist imagery to explore architectural forms similar to those found in European cities. [13]

Italian cities around the Mediterranean

The spirit of the Italian Novecento found an ideal proving ground in Libya. [14] Denouncing excessive use of the Moorish style, Giuseppe Volpi, Libya's governor during the early 1920s, turned to modern architecture. The Rationalist planner Luigi Piccinato answered the call to work in the Italian colony, as did Adalberto

351 Hotel Savoy Homann, Albert Frederick Aalbers, Bandung, Indonesia, 1939

350 Tagliero Service Station, Giuseppe Pettazzi, Asmara, Eritrea, 1938

352 Cathedral Square, project, Adalberto Libera, Tripoli, Libya, 1930

Libera, whose modern project submitted to the competition for the Cathedral Square in Tripoli (1930) **352** clashed with conservative entries. Italo Balbo's governorship (1934–40) brought a return to eclecticism. Ottavio Cabiati, the designer of a plan for Tripoli focused on precolonial elements (1931–5), stated that "every building that is not private but public or religious, erected by a colonial power in a country it rules, should use a clear stylistic vocabulary that is instantly comprehensible by both the local population and the visiting foreigners." He continued, "As the Italian language is spoken in Tripoli and Benghazi, so Italian architecture should be used there as well." → 15 Nostalgia resurfaced in structures like Guido Ferrazza's Banca d'Italia in Benghazi (1938), while Florestano Di Fausto's Hotel Al Mehari in Tripoli (1934) negotiated a compromise between Oriental cupolas and modern volumes.

Di Fausto, who had worked in Albania on a plan for Tirana (1929–31) with Armando Brasini, a designer of grandiloquent Libyan projects, was also active in the Dodecanese Islands, which had been annexed by Italy in 1912. Governor Mario Lago, who held office there from 1924 to 1936 and was committed to restoring the islands' "Latin" character, commissioned Di Fausto to design a plan for Rhodes (1926) centered on a Foro Italico (Italian Forum); **353** it included an Administrative Building (1926–7) and was ornamented with Gothic accents that evoked the Crusades. Di Fausto used similar elements for an Administrative Building on the island of Kos (1927–9). Adopting a more abstract idiom, Armando Bernabiti built a Casa del Fascio in Kos and an aquarium in Rhodes (both 1934–5). The clear, robust volumes of his Teatro Puccini in Rhodes (1936–7) responded to a new policy laid down by Governor Cesare Maria de Vecchi in 1936–41 that called for a "purification" of architecture. With Rodolfo Petracco, Bernabiti conceived the

small new city of Porto Lago on the island of Leros (1933–8). Asmara, the capital of Eritrea, colonized by Italy in 1895, became the object of an ambitious modern plan in 1935. Under the direction of chief engineer Guido Ferrazza, the plan turned the city into a genuine showcase for a monumentalized Rationalism, which was displayed in every type of structure from cinemas and apartment buildings to service stations. → 16 **350** There was no shortage of candidates to plan the cities of neighboring Ethiopia following its invasion by the Fascists in 1936. Marcello Piacentini directly approached Mussolini to secure commissions, while Le Corbusier prepared an unsolicited scheme for Addis Ababa that remained unpublished until 1987, long after his death. → 17 The city's plan was eventually designed by Ignazio Guidi and Cesare Valle (1936–8). The cathedral (1938) and city hall (1939) were built by Cesare Bazzani and Plinio Marconi respectively.

The modernization of Turkey and Iran

European architects played a significant role in modernizing states whose boundaries and governments were reshaped by World War I. In Turkey, Istanbul was the object of a development plan by Prost in the 1930s, but it was in Ankara, Mustafa Kemal Atatürk's chosen capital for the new nation, that the most monumental efforts were concentrated. → 18 The city plan was designed by the German Hermann Jansen, whose proposal had been selected over Léon Jaussely's in an international competition held in 1927–9. Bruno Taut, having arrived from Japan in 1936 and a professor in Istanbul until his death in 1938, built a high school in Trabzon as well as one in Ankara and designed the Faculty of Letters at the University of Ankara (1937–40), **354** integrating blue ceramics with Sassanid motifs. → 19

353 Administrative Building, Florestano di Fausto, Rhodes, Greece, 1926–7

354 Faculty of Letters, University of Ankara, Bruno Taut, Ankara, Turkey, 1937–40

355 Sümer Bank, Martin Elsaesser, Ankara, Turkey, 1935–8

356 Medical School, Tehran University, André Godard and Maxime Siroux, Tehran, Iran, 1934–6

357 ▶ Sun Yat-sen Mausoleum, Lu Yanzhi, Nanjing, China, 1925–9

He also designed a temporary catafalque for Atatürk's remains. In 1938 an international competition was held for a permanent Atatürk mausoleum in Ankara; it was eventually built after World War II by Emin Onat and Orhan Arda. Among other significant new structures in Ankara were a variety of ministerial buildings, including those by the Austrian Clemens Holzmeister, the Eytam and Emlak Bank (1931) by the Swiss-Austrian architect Ernst Egli, and the Sümer Bank (1935–8) by the Frankfurt architect Martin Elsaesser. **355** Close ties between Atatürk's Turkey and the USSR opened the road for the Constructivist architects Ivan Nikolaev, Ignati Milinis, and Alexander Pasternak to build a textile complex in Kayseri (1929–32), which had a plan derived from Le Corbusier's Mundanéum. At the same time, Turkish architects such as Seyfettin Nasih Arkan and Sedad Hakki Eldem developed their own mediation between Western design strategies and the patterns found in local domestic structures.

In 1926 Reza Shah Pahlavi launched neighboring Persia on a policy of modernization. It extended to semantics — the country was renamed Iran, a term emphasizing its Aryan roots, in 1935. Tehran's public buildings were conceived by foreigners like the Russian Nikolai Marcoff and the French architect-archaeologist André Godard, whose National Museum (1936) borrowed the motif of the Sassanid arch. Godard's Tehran University, (1934–6) **356** built out of concrete in collaboration with Maxime Siroux, displayed a modernized classicism free of any national accents. Certain émigrés found opportunities to return. After working in Vienna and Paris, Gabriel Guevrekian was invited to become city architect of Tehran, where from 1933 to 1937 he built several villas, trying to adjust his modernist language to local references. During these intensely productive years he also designed the Ministry of War and Ministry of Industry, the military school, the officers' club, and a theater. Trained at the École des Beaux-Arts in Paris, Mohsen Foroughi became the first Iranian dean of the country's school of architecture, which Godard founded in 1940. → 20

Chinese pluralism

In the 1920s, the first generation of architects with professional diplomas began to work in the universities and cities of a China that was plagued throughout the 1920s and 1930s by battles between warlords and between Nationalists and Communists. The most important of the young republic's memorial complexes was the mausoleum of its first president, Sun Yat-sen, (1925–9) **357** built by Lu Yanzhi on the slopes of Mount Zijing outside Nanjing. Although the mausoleum was a fundamental step in the return to historical Chinese forms, Western classicism was used at the same time on the city's university campus. Sun Yat-sen's son Sun Ke, a city planner who had studied in the United States, played an essential role in developing Guangzhou on the model of the garden city. Meanwhile the city center was transformed by the construction of buildings with Art Deco arcades.

The American presence in China was particularly notable. In industrial construction the Austin Company was active, while in urban planning Richard Murphy was responsible for the plan of Nanjing (1928). In the late 1920s Americans drew up plans for Shanghai. → 21 Skyscrapers in Shanghai were erected to serve as hotel and office buildings. In 1934 the Slovakian architect László Hudec put up the Joint Savings Society Building (later the Park Hotel) on Nanjing Lu, with a metal framework produced by the Union Brückenbau-AG

359 Salman Schocken Library, Erich Mendelsohn, Jerusalem, Palestine (Israel), 1934–6

of Dortmund, while Palmer and Turner built Sassoon House, (1926–9) **358** a hotel that was the dominant vertical structure along the urban riverfront of the Huangpu. The same firm was responsible for the neo-classical headquarters of the nearby Hong Kong and Shanghai Bank (1921–3). Western firms remained active until the Japanese invasion in 1937, building modest-size Art Deco skyscrapers and large American-style apartment blocks, such as Embankment House (1933) and the Broadway Mansions (1935) on the banks of the Suzhou Creek, both also by Palmer and Turner.

Modern hegemony in Palestine

During this period a unique architectural development took place in another location on the Mediterranean coastline. Under British mandate since 1920, Palestine had become a center of Jewish immigration and renaissance. Several cultures and generations converged there to form what remains probably the most comprehensive manifestation of modernist architecture outside Europe. In Jerusalem, new Jewish neighborhoods like Talpiot and Rehavia were planned by the German Richard Kauffmann. A student of Theodor Fischer, Kauffmann, who had worked on the Margarethenhöhe in Essen, also designed the stunning circular-plan settlement of Kfar Nahalal (1921). → 22

In 1934, Erich Mendelsohn, who a decade earlier had already designed projects in Haifa with Richard Neutra that strove "to achieve a union between Prussianism and the life-cycle of the Muezzin, between anti-nature and harmony with nature," → 23 opened an office in that city. He built the Anglo-Palestinian Bank (1937–9) and the Salman Schocken Library (1934–6), **359** a vast space lined with books and pierced with a bow window

that flooded the reading room with Mediterranean light, which Mendelsohn referred to as "Rembrandt's light." His largest building was the Hadassah Hospital on Mount Scopus (1940–1), a sequence of porticoes and domes on which the play of shadow and light was particularly powerful. Patrick Geddes, who had been invited to design the Hebrew University of Jerusalem, was responsible for the master plan for the new city of Tel Aviv in 1925, reworking an initial project by Kauffmann. The city was erected on farmland near Jaffa, combining thoroughfares planted with vegetation and blocks centered on small squares. It was a nearly literal illustration of Theodor Herzl's Zionist utopia, as described in his book *Altneuland* (Old New Land) of 1902. Beginning in 1934, Tel Aviv's central square, eventually named after its visionary mayor Meier Dizengoff, was surrounded by modern horizontal buildings. These were planned by Genia Averbuch, a graduate of the Académie de Bruxelles, who built the panoramic Galina Café, the dominant building at the 1934 Levant fair. Lining the streets of Tel Aviv were exalted interpretations of Le Corbusier's principles, most of them on *pilotis*. They included the Engel Building by Zeev Rechter (1935); **360** housing blocks such as the cooperative residences by the former Dessau Bauhaus student Arieh Sharon (1935–9), derived from similar projects in Weimar; and hundreds of small apartment buildings and terrace houses engaged in a volumetric play with prisms and cylinders. → 24

Pilotis exposing the ground floors of buildings to the refreshing sea breezes and defining covered outdoor spaces were among the examples of the surprisingly wide diffusion of the emblematic symbols of architectural modernity. In a new city unique for its scale and coherence, and also for its diversity of approaches, Tel Aviv's steel-frame buildings were particularly

360 Engel Building, Zeev Rechter, Tel Aviv, Palestine (Israel), 1935

notable. These included Carl Rubin's Hadar (Citrus) House (1936–8) **361** and Dov Karmi's Max Liebling House (1936), with its horizontal balconies casting deep shadows. In Rehovot, southeast of Tel Aviv, Mendelsohn designed a house for Chaim Weizmann, the physicist and future president of Israel – a U-shaped structure wrapped around a courtyard featuring a linear pool (1936) and pivoting on a cylindrical staircase. In Tel Aviv the ideal of the garden city met an "autonomous" architecture of pure volumes such as that which the historian Emil Kaufmann saw as marking the modernist encounter between Le Corbusier and Claude-Nicolas Ledoux. → 25 Tel Aviv also represented a unique case of private construction seizing without hesitation on the new aesthetic of the 1920s. Yet the Jewish settlements were not limited to neighborhoods of crisp white buildings. The pioneers' settlements in Palestine often resembled fortified polygons, revealing the colonial aspect of the Zionist enterprise. → 26

Dismissed by its critics for its resemblance to North African Casbahs, and lampooned as looking like "Arabic" villages, the new architecture that appeared in Europe in the early 1920s became a worldwide phenomenon within two decades. Yet despite its experimentation with mass housing, it largely remained a product intended for an urban elite clientele. In Europe and North America, it would take six years of war to transform modern architecture from an experimental practice into a state-endorsed public policy.

Architecture of a total war

World War II was a catalyst in the transformation of architectural theory and practice. While most historical analyses suggest that the war was a time of cultural stasis, in fact it was a significant phase in the acceleration of modernization, as World War I had been → [1] and was greeted as such by some. Just as the first Futurists had glorified war, in 1937 Filippo Tommaso Marinetti again greeted the Fascist invasion of Ethiopia by declaring, "War is beautiful because it creates new architecture, like that of the big tanks, the geometrical flight formations, the smoke spirals from burning villages …" → [2] Yet for the committed anti-Fascist Walter Benjamin, who saw militarism as a direct consequence of capitalist production, war was nothing more than "a rebellion of technology." → [3]

Front lines and home fronts

In a war that really began in Spain in July 1936 and did not end until after the atomic bombing of Hiroshima in August 1945, architects were called upon to be active in many more fields than just architecture. They participated in every aspect and experience of war, and everywhere from the front lines to the home front. Fortifications, for instance, although generally designed by military engineers, nonetheless took on architectural status, as Paul Virilio has pointed out in his analysis of the aesthetic aspects of the massive Nazi ramparts erected primarily along the Atlantic coast of Western Europe. → [4] These structures lacked the underground complexity of the bunkers of the French Maginot Line and the Czech fortifications that inspired them. But prophets of underground cities like the Paris architect Édouard Utudjian perceived them as the realization of their goals: housing, work, and leisure, divided into specific facilities, were connected by mechanized transport and reduced to

a spartan spatial economy. The building of such fortifications before 1939 – German submarine bases, for instance – and during the occupation of Europe mobilized construction companies and architectural firms, including that of the Perret brothers in France. → [5]

Even though numerous architects avoided direct combat by working for the war effort, many others became firsthand witnesses and were affected by traumatic experiences on the front lines. Their sketchbooks became documents of trenches and shelters, advances and retreats, destructions and conquests. Some were able to work on competition projects while being held in prisoner-of-war camps. French detainees even had their projects exhibited in Paris salons organized by the Vichy government. But above all, the total militarization of the home front linked architects into a complex production chain. Even before 1939, the need for factories to accommodate mass production of tanks, cannons, and planes launched gigantic American construction programs such as those carried out by the Austin Company and Albert Kahn Associates. Kahn's firm built, among other installations, the Chrysler Tank Arsenal (1941) **362** in Warren Township, Michigan, wrapped in a massive glass curtain wall; the Curtiss-Wright Factory in Buffalo, New York (1941); and the Dodge Factory in Chicago, Illinois (1941–2). These construction programs were accelerated by the attack on Pearl Harbor, leading Kahn Associates in 1942 to build the Ford Factory for the B-24 Liberator bomber in Willow Run, Michigan, in record time. To meet the demands of military commissions, the firm, then described as a "producer of production lines," was organized like a Taylorized assembly line. → [6] Kahn rejected the officially mandated military policy of building "windowless factories" to protect plants from nocturnal air raids. Yet the completely impermeable factory – built with a skeleton

362 Chrysler Tank Arsenal, Albert Kahn Associates, Warren Township, Michigan, USA, 1941

363 Heinkel Aircraft Factory, Herbert Rimpl, Oranienburg, Germany, 1936–8

of steel or laminated wood, hermetically sealed with light cladding, air conditioned, and lit twenty-four hours a day by fluorescent tubes – led to a new type of structure destined for a useful future in commerce, namely the "big box" structure that punctuates today's suburban landscapes. [7]

The construction of factories in Germany and its occupied territories was equally intense, although Allied bombings led to their eventual shift underground. Herbert Rimpl's Heinkel Aircraft Factory (1936–8) **363** in Oranienburg, his steelworks in Salzgitter (c. 1938), and Egon Eiermann's Märkischer Metallbau in the same city (1939–41) were notable products of an industrial policy wholly comparable to American methods, down to such details as the use of steel trusses and glass walls. [8] Although on a more limited scale and using less advanced finishes, the elegant and efficient designs of Rudolf Lodders and Bernhard Hermkes, for instance, testified to the persistence of functionalist culture within the Nazi militarized economy. War conditions also seemed propitious for modern architecture to Le Corbusier, who designed a munitions factory in Lannemezan, in southwestern France. "[Many] of our war factories, those which good fortune has placed upon a favourable site, can become the factories of the 'green belt,' places where work (with tools or machines) will be completely changed," he anticipated. "We can pass at one bound from the dismal surroundings of the past, into gay factories which make work seem friendly." [9]

Extreme scales

Wartime architecture was marked by the appearance of projects on extreme new scales. On the macro level, the structures erected for industrial production, for managing the war, and for processing masses of people were of unprecedented size. On the micro level, the quasi-scientific manner in which bodies were packed into regimented environments such as air raid shelters and barracks demanded an equally innovative approach to scale. Along with setting up assembly lines, housing factory workers became an urgent priority and led to ambitious American projects developed through the Lanham Act of 1940, which dedicated federal funding to wartime housing programs. Frank Lloyd Wright designed without success a variant of his Usonian houses for the Cloverleaf Housing Development in Pittsfield, Massachusetts, in 1942. In California, thousands of homes were built near the airplane factories in the Westchester neighborhood of Los Angeles. Richard Neutra, after participating in the Avion Village development in Grand Prairie, Texas (1940–1), built four sets of prefabricated houses in the state's metropolitan areas. The most significant was Channel Heights in San Pedro, where some two hundred two-story wood-frame houses with pitched roofs were arranged in terraces on a slope overlooking the Pacific. [10]

On the East Coast, Walter Gropius and Marcel Breuer designed and partially completed the Aluminum City development in New Kensington, Pennsylvania, filtering Weimar-era principles of German urban planning into wood-frame buildings and exhibiting a keen feeling for the landscape. The firm of Skidmore, Owings and Merrill, which got its start at the 1939 New York World's Fair, grew exponentially, thanks to a 1942 commission to build a 47,000-inhabitant city in Oak Ridge, Tennessee, to house one of the sites of the Manhattan Project, where the atomic bomb was being developed. To handle the job, SOM opened a new office staffed with 450 employees. [11] Both in the United States and abroad, the mobilization of male architects led to an unprecedented influx of women into the workforce.

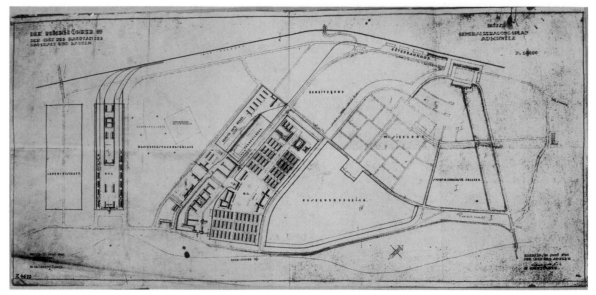

364 Auschwitz Concentration Camp, first master plan, Oświęcim (Auschwitz), Poland, 1941

Megaprojects such as the master planning of Oak Ridge and the construction of its uranium-separating factory were typical of wartime work, as were standardized military bases. Even though the latter had to accommodate extremely varied programs, they shared a common function: all were intended to organize, control, and move large groups of human beings. The Nazi extermination camps were extreme examples of panoptic rationalism. They were designed by modern architects like the Bauhaus graduate Fritz Ertl, who was recruited by the SS team that conceived the plan for Auschwitz **364** and its outbuildings, including a traditionalist *Siedlung* for the workers of the nearby chemical factory. → 12 The ambiguities of the regime's architectural policy found their most vivid illustration in the contrast between the sinister barracks and industrial crematoria of the concentration camps and the picturesque layout of the guards' houses. Another, less covert megaproject was the Pentagon (1941–3), **365** an office complex built in Washington, D.C., in just eleven months by G. Edwin Bergstrom and David Witmer to accommodate 32,000 Army employees. The largest office building in the world, it was able to be constructed so quickly because its assembly was reduced to the repetition of individual concrete components. → 13

Air raid protection

Supported by vast bureaucracies housed in purpose-built temporary structures all over the map, the actual fighting affected the civilian population as much as, if not more than, the military. → 14 Far from bringing universal peace, as Paul Scheerbart and other early proponents of aeronautics had imagined, the air war dissolved the very notion of a front line. Only the most remote areas remained safe from bombardment. In the 1920s

the lessons of World War I and the theories of the Italian general Giulio Douhet regarding the strategic importance of aviation had led planners to reflect on the best way of developing cities to protect them from air raids. Lieutenant Colonel Paul Vauthier considered Le Corbusier's approach the most efficient. The set-backs in his Ville Radieuse project, he theorized, would result in bombs falling between buildings; moreover, their terraces could be reinforced against "aerial torpedoes" while their *pilotis* would speed the dispersion of gas. → 15 While Le Corbusier and Vauthier embarked on a prolonged dialogue, the German engineer Hans Schoszberger evaluated the potential of different cities to survive strategic bombings in 1934, likewise praising Le Corbusier's schemes as well as Nikolai Miliutin's linear city. → 16

As the war drew closer, cities were put in a state of readiness to withstand air raids, and architects committed to a double effort: the protection of populations and the camouflaging of cities and strategic targets. This "passive defense," or air-raid protection, required professionals to examine and fortify existing buildings by strengthening their basements, by using sandbags to protect statues, fountains, and small buildings, and by turning sewage tunnels and subway stations into bomb shelters. → 17 Gigantic underground shelters in London in the shape of large spiral galleries were designed by Berthold Lubetkin and Tecton working together with the engineer Ove Arup, and proposed for the protection of the borough of Finsbury. → 18 **366** Working above ground, Konstanty Gutschow built numerous towers to serve as air-raid shelters in Hamburg. The urban landscape became studded with massive structures, some of which came to be used for active defense, such as the Flak towers built in Vienna and Berlin and those designed by Friedrich Tamms in Hamburg (1943). Creating fake landscapes became one of the more common wartime activities for architects. The use of camouflage

365 War Department Building (Pentagon), G. Edwin Bergstrom and David Witmer, Arlington, Virginia, USA, 1941–3

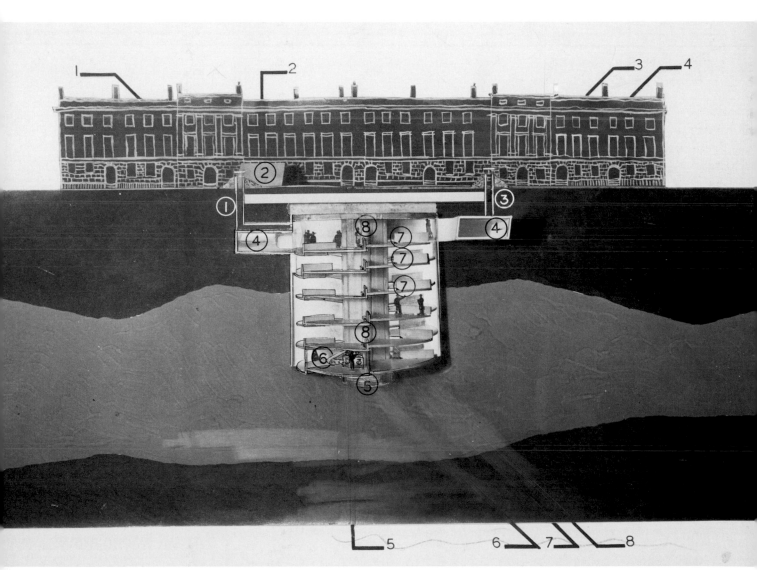

366 Air Raid Shelter, project, Berthold Lubetkin and Tecton, Finsbury, London, United Kingdom, 1939

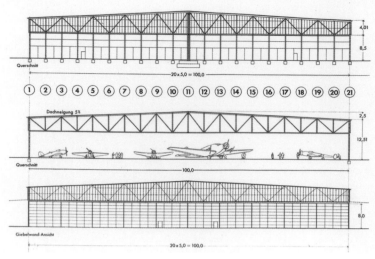

367 *Bauordnungslehre* (Building Ordering Handbook), Ernst Neufert, 1943

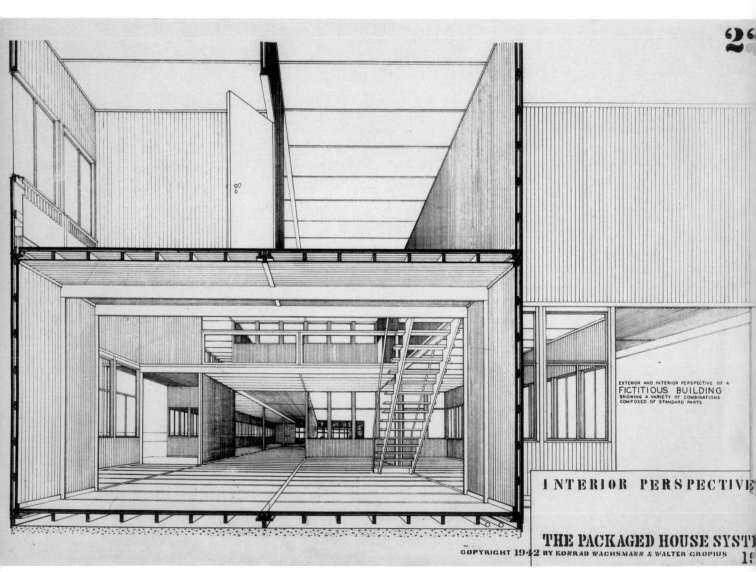

368 The Packaged House System, Konrad Wachsmann and Walter Gropius, 1941–6

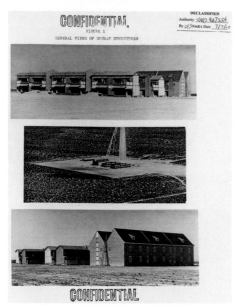

369 German and Japanese villages, Dugway
Proving Ground, Utah, USA, 1943

on both the front lines and the home front was a continuation
of the work of painters, who had participated in specialized
detachments during World War I. → [19] In late 1939 the Royal
Aeronautical Establishment in Farnborough mobilized many
British architects and artists to carry out a new policy of camouflaging the most vulnerable industrial targets. In the United
States the major universities offered courses in camouflage,
and at the Institute of Design in Chicago, László Moholy-Nagy
and György Kepes borrowed concepts from the psychology
of form to conduct research into its theoretical and practical
applications. → [20] Soviet architects designed a landscape of
decorated nets and screens for the *maskirovka* (camouflage)
of the Kremlin in Moscow and monuments in Leningrad.

Constructive and destructive techniques

The wartime commandeering of steel, aluminum, and certain
types of wood by the weapons industry and of cement for fortifications led to changes in the production of buildings. Scarce
materials were used sparingly, new composite materials were
invented, and small components were joined together to cover
large areas. One new product was laminated wood, a
technique made possible by advances in the chemistry of
adhesives. The rediscovery of wood as a favored material and
especially the industrialization of plastics, which grew out of
research undertaken by the DuPont Company in the 1930s,
were among the most important effects of the war effort on
new construction techniques.

But the war economy also required a paring down of housing
and industrial projects. Standardization spread across the board,
exemplified by new state policies on the normalization of
construction, such as those issued in France in 1941. In

Germany, Ernst Neufert – who assisted Albert Speer when
he replaced Fritz Todt as Reich Minister for Weapons and
Munitions in February 1942 – drew up dimensional norms
adapted to industrial construction, which he published under
the title *Bauordnungslehre* (Building Ordering Handbook;
1943). → [21] **367** Dividing the meter into eight 12.5-cm modules, he redefined the dimensions of all building components
for hangars, factories, and housing, even jokingly purporting to rewrite the proportions of the Doric temples of ancient
Greece. The Luftwaffe, one of the main sponsors of Neufert's
research, employed many modern architects, including Sergius
Ruegenberg, the former manager of Mies van der Rohe's office.
The direct involvement of architects in scientific experiments
related to weapons of destruction cannot be overlooked. For
example, the American army and the Standard Oil Corporation
tested the incendiary capacity of Napalm bombs in 1943 at
the Dugway Proving Ground **369** in Utah under conditions of
total architectural realism: Antonin Raymond built replicas
of Japanese dwellings, while Erich Mendelsohn and Konrad
Wachsmann, both having relocated to the United States, built
"German" houses in wood and stone that were fully furnished
by Hollywood set designers. → [22]

Mobility and flexibility

World War II was both mechanized and on the move, and
architecture participated in its perpetual mobility. Countless
strategies were devised for producing transportable structures
that could easily be picked up and relocated. During the 1930s
Jean Prouvé designed a house that could be dismantled and
reassembled. Although his design offered a vast range of
possibilities, initially it was adapted only to conventional

370 "Planning on a Clean Slate," caricature, United Kingdom, c. 1944

building types. Wartime research on both sides of the Atlantic developed systems with wider application. The most durable was the MERO system designed by the German engineer Max Mengeringhausen, who received a commission in 1940 from the technical director of the Luftwaffe, Ernst Udet, to research structures that could be assembled almost instantaneously. By 1942, Mengeringhausen perfected a system of polyhedral nodes that could connect up to eighteen steel tubes and be used for transportable hangars, office towers, and any kind of shelter. → 23 In the United States, Gropius teamed with Wachsmann, who had helped produce wood houses for the German firm of Christoph and Unmack in the 1920s, to design the Packaged House System in 1941–6. **368** It was based on a system of modular weight-bearing panels assembled by means of an ingenious "universal connector." With reluctant backing from industry, Wachsmann founded the General Panel Corporation to mass-produce the design in response to the urgent demand for cheap housing. → 24 Martin Wagner, now on the faculty at Harvard's architecture school, designed the Igloo House, constructed of sheets of steel. Meanwhile, a U.S. Navy team designed and put into mass production 170,000 Quonset huts. → 25 Similarly, in Great Britain, an ambitious program of research on prefabrication led to the design of mass-produced houses. → 26 Some architects considered military barracks and temporary housing to offer lessons in function and efficiency. Among them was Le Corbusier, who opposed the domestic notion of "furniture" to the military or industrial concept of "equipment": "Our war-time hutments, properly understood, might well be interpreted in terms of a predisposed plan which would lead us without any fuss to a speedy development of the social services. And it is because they are ready to hand in such abundance that an immediate social revival could be achieved." → 27

Architecture of military occupation

As the nineteenth-century military theorist Carl von Clausewitz famously wrote, war is simply "a continuation of politics by other means." → 28 World War II continued the annexation and enslavement of territories, partly accomplishing this end through their symbolic transformation and appropriation by means of architecture and urban planning. In certain cases these policies required deleting explicit signs of modernity; the Nazis "purified" Poland's squares and the streets of Alsace. But in Belgium they made use of the services of certain local modern architects and planners, including Raphaël Verwilghen, under the authority of Henry van de Velde. Several teams of modern architects were also put to work during the German occupation of Lorraine: Rudolf Schwarz designed the plan of Thionville, Emil Steffann constructed stone buildings interpreting local modes of construction, and Richard Döcker designed industrialized farms for the SS. In Alsace, Neufert applied his dimensional norms to the building of the Rhinau Electronics Plant (1943). → 29
The Japanese side of the Axis made use of modern architects as well. In 1942 Kenzo Tange won the competition to design the Japanese Cultural Center in Bangkok, coming in ahead of his mentor Kunio Maekawa, whose proposal was modern but called for a traditional roof. The same year Maekawa built a cultural center in Mukden, Manchuria, an area in which he had previously worked after winning the competition for the Dalian City Hall in 1938.

Imagining the postwar world

Both official organizations and architects – whether politically committed or involuntarily out of work – began designing the

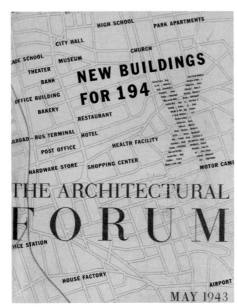

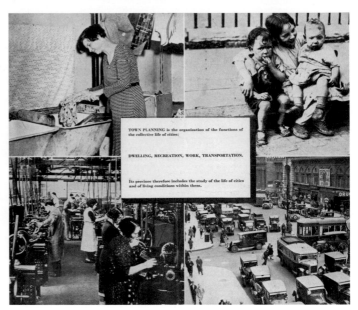

371 "New Buildings for 194X," *Architectural Forum*, May 1943

372 The Four Functions, illustration in *Can Our Cities Survive?*, José Luis Sert, 1942

postwar world well before the war was over. The Nazis hired Hans Hubert Leufgen and Friedrich Pabst in 1943 to prepare plans for the Germanization of Warsaw. →[30] In France and the Netherlands designs for reconstructing destroyed cities were drawn up by 1940 and in Russia by 1942. In France, the Vichy government applied a double process of legislative modernization and urban transformation in the earliest cities to be demolished, notably those in the valleys of the Seine and the Loire. In the Netherlands, the city architect W. G. Witteveen drafted a first plan for the reconstruction of Rotterdam immediately after it was razed by the Nazis in 1940, sensing that it would be an ideal site for the application of functionalist theories. Urban planners throughout Europe experienced a certain schadenfreude at the destruction of neighborhoods they considered "insalubrious" and saw the war as providing an ideal opportunity to replace them with modern urban forms. **370** The broad outlines of the projects developed by Speer's reconstruction team – a group of planners assigned mostly to the modernization of German cities – would be put to frequent use after the war. →[31]

Even in countries that escaped destruction, architects used the question of what the postwar world should look like to imagine new urban orientations and architectural types. One of the most remarkable initiatives was taken in 1943 by the American magazine *Architectural Forum*. A widely read issue entitled "New Buildings for 194X" **371** invited contributors to devise an architecture using "advanced but not stratospheric" technologies to describe an America of the future. Pietro Belluschi suggested new methods of air conditioning for offices; Victor Gruen proposed a prototypical version of the shopping center; Louis Kahn and Oscar Storonov presented their vision for the postwar house; William Lescaze designed a new type of gas station; and Mies van der Rohe described his Museum for a Small City, an open space in which partitions could be moved freely. →[32]

CIAM essentially remained dormant during the war years. Only the initially very small American group, headed by Neutra and William Wurster, undertook to meet. Its activities centered in New York around the CIAM Chapter for Relief and Postwar Planning, which was founded in 1944 by Knud Lonberg-Holm, Ernest Weissmann, and others. →[33] The publication of the book *Can Our Cities Survive?* (1942), **372** edited by José Luis Sert, expressed CIAM's fundamental positions. To some extent, it was the official "book of the Congress" in Athens, as Le Corbusier announced in his contemporaneous publication of the Athens Charter, an earlier edition of which Sert had prepared prior to 1939 in collaboration with Charlotte Perriand and Weissmann. Also in the United States, a significant change in CIAM's positions was set in motion in 1943 by Sert, Fernand Léger, and Sigfried Giedion, the secretary general of CIAM, in their joint position statement, "Nine Points on Monumentality." Their approach to monumentality – a subject heretofore virtually taboo in the discourse of modern architects, monuments being identified with historicism and the Beaux-Arts – was explicitly related to reconstruction. Now, they argued, citizens wanted "the buildings that represent their social and community life to give more than functional fulfillment," more than mere satisfaction of material needs. The *tabula rasa* seemed to be an indispensable precondition: only in "vast open spaces" in urban centers would "monumental architecture find its appropriate setting." "Monumental buildings [would] then be able to stand in space, for like trees or plants, [they] cannot be crowded in," →[34] the authors declared, suggesting that blighted parts of old cities would need to be demolished to achieve such an objective.

374 Memorial to the Victims of the Concentration Camps, BPR (Lodovico Belgiojoso, Enrico Peressutti and Ernesto Nathan Rogers), Milan, Italy, 1946

373 Dymaxion Dwelling Machine, R. Buckminster Fuller, Wichita, Kansas, USA, 1944–6

Converting to peace

The end of the conflict in 1945 brought an urgent need to retool the massive war machine built by the Allies, as well as any factories left undamaged in the Axis countries. The repurposing of military production methods not only focused on the building of houses for returning veterans and displaced populations, but also addressed numerous materials, instruments, and components of wartime technology now in surplus. The British effort seemed to be the most coherent. It was marked, among other things, by the exhibition *Britain Can Make It*, held in London in 1946, which included a "War to Peace" section displaying a vast range of military materials from plastic wrapping to waterproof fabrics to aluminum containers altered to serve peacetime needs, and paving the way for a transition "from Spitfires to saucepans." → 35

R. Buckminster Fuller undertook one of the most extraordinary campaigns to convince government officials to reuse military assembly lines for a completely new purpose. In 1940 he had applied the construction techniques used to make corrugated-metal grain silos to his Dymaxion Deployment Unit, a temporary circular dwelling of which not more than several hundred were produced. At the end of the war, he proposed converting the facilities of the Beech Aircraft Factory in Wichita, Kansas, to the production of his Dymaxion Dwelling Machine (1944–6). **373** More spacious than the Deployment Unit, the Dwelling Machine was also circular in plan, with a structure consisting of steel cables in tension radiated around a central mast. A horizontal window ran along the house's circumference. → 36 The dwelling, which could fit into a cylindrical case and be transported on a truck, attracted tremendous publicity, but only two prototypes were built – one of them is now on display at the Henry Ford

Museum in Dearborn, Michigan – and the Cold War quickly returned the airplane factory to its original function.

Although war production facilities were rarely successfully converted to peacetime use, innovative technologies and materials developed for the war did find major commercial markets. The new markets coincided with the return to civilian life of citizens whose outlook had been transformed by their encounters with wartime technology, preparing them for a postwar era of automobiles and electronics. The massive introduction of women into the workforce, an indirect effect of the mobilization, had a significant impact on domestic space, both because women were exposed to modern technology at work and because they were busier and therefore required their homes to be more efficient. Faced with these new expectations, a transformed architectural profession emerged in 1945 ready to shape the reconstruction and pursue modernization hand in hand with the building industry. Having been reorganized during the war, the building industry was able to make a smooth transition from running giant construction sites for munitions production to devoting itself to reconstruction and rehousing.

Memory and memorials

Well before the capitulation of Japan and the publication of Sert, Léger, and Giedion's "Nine Points," the need for remembrance and commemoration inspired countless projects for memorials. Wilhelm Kreis designed gigantic monuments to celebrate the Nazi victories in the USSR and Africa, which were rendered moot by the outcome of the war. → 37 In the immediate postwar period, the victors frequently dynamited the evidence of the Nazi past, while the Russians erected vast rhetorical monuments at home and abroad, among them the Victory

375 Hiroshima Peace Center,
Kenzo Tange, Hiroshima, Japan,
1949–56

Monument in Stalingrad and the Treptow Soviet War Memorial
in Berlin. In Hiroshima, Kenzo Tange built the Hiroshima Peace
Center (1949–56), **375** whose two raised, linear buildings are
sited near a concrete vault that alludes to traditional Japanese
burial mounds. Searching for a relationship to ancient Japanese
architecture, Tange found inspiration and evocative imagery in
photographs published by his professor Hideto Kishida. [→ 38]
Yet the most moving memorials were not the largest or most
bombastic. Among the most poignant was the monument by
Mario Fiorentino, Nello Aprile, Cino Calcaprina, and others to the
victims of the Ardeatine Caves massacre carried out by the Nazis
in Rome. Built in 1944–9, it stands on the very site of the crime,
leading visitors through the location where the martyrs' massacre
took place to their mass grave, marked with a 25-by-46 meter
(82-by-151-foot) horizontal slab. [→ 39] Designed shortly after, the
Memorial to the Victims of the Concentration Camps (1946) **374**
by BPR (Lodovico Belgiojoso, Enrico Peressutti, and Ernesto
Nathan Rogers) in Milan's Cimetero Monumentale, was a three-
dimensional Constructivist grid, in the interior of which were suspended marble plaques and relics from the camps. Referring to
prewar structures by the anti-Fascist Edoardo Persico, the memorial by the three remaining members of the BBPR partnership – the
fourth, Gian Luigi Banfi, perished in Mauthausen – was intended to
reflect humanistic values while suggesting a way for the project of
modernity to move on from the devastation of the war. [→ 40] In contrast to the solidity of the Roman memorial, the delicacy of the monument in Milan was a commentary on the fragility of democracy.
What remained of the most intense period of fighting in human
history besides ruins was a broadscale technological modernization that lent credibility to architectural modernism and
helped to coalesce a widespread aspiration to create a new
world of everyday modern forms out of the interwar tropes.

Tabula rasa to horror vacui: reconstruction and renaissance

From Coventry to Osaka, from Caen to Minsk, from Hamburg to Dresden to Milan, the postwar desolation was on a scale without historical precedent. Although modern urban planners had dreamed of seeing the world's slums disappear, they had never imagined destruction of this magnitude. Thanks to a sort of reversal in the relationship between war and production, the industrialization of destruction that had been achieved through aviation and advances in science now led to a changed approach to the design and construction of buildings. The consequence was the application on a massive scale of experimental solutions that had been proposed in the 1920s and 1930s. In the face of postwar misery, architectural principles that had been primarily in the theoretical sphere before the war quickly found their way into mass production. Through public programs, and in response to a transformed market, modern architecture found a new audience. But its apparent triumph in this widespread alliance with industrial production would sooner or later lead to a revolt among younger architects reluctant to lose touch with popular culture.

An American age

Once the April 1945 encounter of the Soviet and American troops on the Elbe was forgotten, the political configuration of the postwar world was quickly and radically altered by the showdown between the newly established Western and Eastern blocs. [1] This face-off would be embodied in the architecture of reconstruction projects and new cities built on both sides of the Iron Curtain in the decade following the Prague coup of 1948. After the war, disseminating American culture became an affair of state, made easier by the prestige of such technological triumphs as the Jeep, the Sherman tank, and the Flying Fortress, as well as by the ubiquity of Hollywood movies. The Museum of Modern Art's exhibitions, like the 1947 *Built in USA, 1932–1944*, **376** toured the world with the support of American government agencies. [2] The Department of State and the Department of Labor organized "productivity missions," or study trips, for professionals invited to the United States. For the first time, the predominant direction of flow of students across the Atlantic was reversed, with hundreds of grants being awarded to foreign students through programs such as the Delano-Aldrich Grants for French students and the Rockefeller Foundation's Harkness Fellowships, which allowed many British and German students to study in the United States. A de facto American dominance now became deliberate policy as the slow but inexorable process of the Americanization of European territories began. [3]

From 1948 to 1951 the European Recovery Program, which took the name of Secretary of State George C. Marshall, was implemented in Western Europe. Thirteen billion dollars – more than 100 billion in 2010 currency – was spent essentially to enable European states to acquire American hardware. But Europeans invested nine times more on their own economies, spurring the fastest period of growth in the Continent's history. After Russia and Eastern Europe rejected the Marshall Plan, the need for "containment" of the Soviet Bloc, to use a term proposed by the American diplomat George F. Kennan in 1946, legitimized not only the creation of the Atlantic Alliance in 1949, but also subsequent policies related to production and consumption – including the production and consumption of culture. [4] As soon as heavy industry was back up and running, Fordism took root in the Old World and the spread of the automobile began to modify urban space.

376 Cover to the German edition of the catalog for the Museum of Modern Art traveling exhibition *Built in USA 1932–1944*, 1947

377 Reconstruction project, Jan Knothe, Warsaw, Poland, 1950

Mirroring the Americanization process, "socialist" realism was promulgated in territories ranging from the Baltic to the Pacific after 1949. A policy of cultural imperialism put in place by the Soviets, it called for an architecture that was supposedly socialist in content and nationalist in form. More or less imposing itself on the modern design strategies that had appeared between the wars, it was applied – often in the face of outspoken resistance – to extremely diverse architectural cultures, sometimes provoking fruitful reflection on the relationship between intellectualized, abstract schemes and historical or vernacular motifs.

Literal reconstruction or radical modernization?

Urban rebuilding in Western Europe cannot be understood in terms of a univocal model. [5] Despite the hopes of the Swiss architect and artist Max Bill for a new age of urban planning – which he expressed in 1945 in what may have been the first attempt to present an overall vision of reconstruction [6] – architectural production from the wartime into the mid-1950s did not represent a coherent program. Instead, the postwar projects and buildings tended toward two diametric poles: on the one hand, total reconstitution; on the other, total eradication of historical traces. Examples of the former were actually quite rare. The reconstruction of Warsaw's old city **377** was the most spectacular because it conformed so well to the idea of a national renaissance. After being razed by the Germans, the old city became the object of a grandiloquent project by Matthew (Maciej) Nowicki, and then of an archaeologically precise restoration plan by Zygmunt Skibniewski. [7] A comparable German example on a much smaller scale was the restoration of the small medieval city of Rothenburg ob der Tauber. **378**

These reconstitutions corresponded to the idea – formulated by Jean-Charles Moreux during the occupation of France – of creating "museum neighborhoods" in parts of cities; in these places historical architecture was to be entirely conserved. This preservationist policy implied a change in the city's social makeup and was partly responsible for the expulsion of the working class from city centers, which were in due course reappropriated by the enlightened bourgeoisie. [8]

The other pole of the European approach to reconstruction was radical modernization on a regional scale, at the cost of a near-total disappearance of city centers. The master plan for London devised by the MARS group (Modern Architectural Research Society) **380** in 1942 integrated Westminster and the City into a central zone dedicated to government and cultural facilities along a linear east-west axis extending over several miles. This zone was encircled by a highway connecting the "legs" of the principal residential areas, giving the overall plan an insectlike shape. The *Kollektivplan* (collective plan) for Berlin, **379** designed under Hans Scharoun's direction in 1946, borrowed the MARS idea of an axial zone, in this case following the Spree rather than the Thames. Berlin was meant to remain a center of production, serviced by a denser grid of motorways than the one that had been suggested by Albert Speer's plan. A "cultural center" was created around the city's Museum Island. The Zehlendorf Plan of 1947 put even more emphasis on automobile traffic. But following the blockade and partition of Berlin in 1948, any overall plan for the divided city had to be abandoned. [9]

In France, the Ministry of Reconstruction and Urban Planning, founded in 1944 to oversee the French reconstruction effort, entrusted few projects to modern architects. [10] Le Corbusier designed a plan for the bombed-out city of Saint-Dié, **381**

378 Reconstruction project, Fritz Florin, Rothenburg ob der Tauber, Federal Republic of Germany, 1948–55

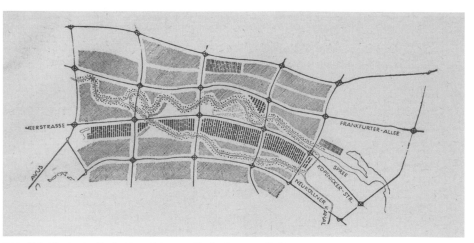

379 Kollektivplan for Berlin, Hans Scharoun, Berlin, Germany, 1946

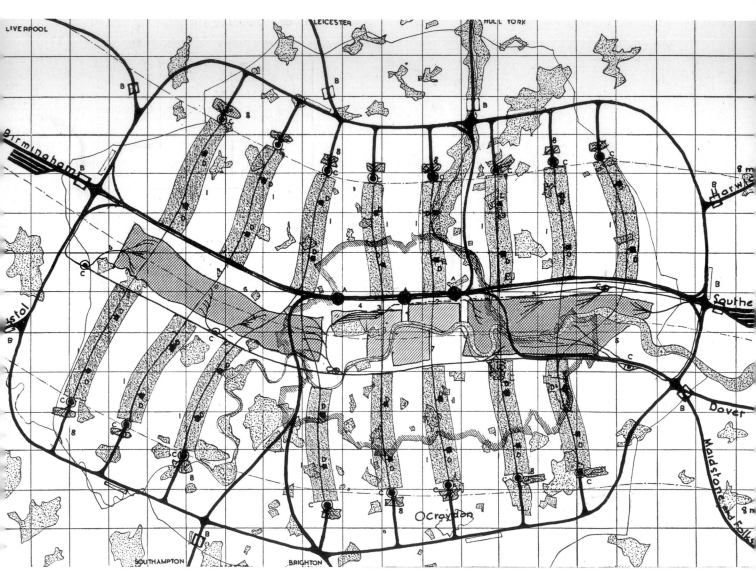

380 MARS Plan for London, Modern Architecture Research Society, London, United Kingdom, 1942

Chapter 23 | *Tabula rasa* to *horror vacui*: reconstruction and renaissance

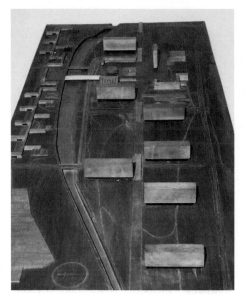

381 Reconstruction project, Le Corbusier, Saint-Dié, France, 1944

382 Reconstructed city center, Auguste Perret, Le Havre, France, 1945–55

completely replacing the preexisting layout of streets with a system applying the principles of the Athens Charter to the letter: factories were concentrated on the south bank of the river, a series of residential units on the north. The architect responded unsympathetically to the inhabitants' nostalgia for their old streets by insisting that "getting back in touch with nature, seeing beautiful landscapes, and access to sun and fresh air are the fundamental elements of urban planning." [11] But left-wing organizations and the local bourgeoisie fought the project, and Le Corbusier had to withdraw. His projects for La Rochelle and Saint-Gaudens likewise remained on paper, and his contribution to French reconstruction was ultimately limited to the painstaking realization of the Unité d'Habitation Apartment Building in Marseilles (1946–52).

Although the occupying administration of the French zone in Germany briefly believed it would be able to impose plans like the one for Saint-Dié, Marcel Lods failed to realize his project to move most of Mainz's population to large housing blocks (1946–7). In the Saarland, the Équipe des Urbanistes (Urban Planners' Team), headed by André Sive and Marcel Roux, produced a series of plans, but the only one implemented was in Saarbrucken (1946–9), the work of Georges-Henri Pingusson. [12] On the other side of the Alps, the Italian CIAM group gave its support to the AR Plan for Milan (1944–5), designed on functionalist principles by Franco Albini, the BPR group, and Piero Bottoni. The plan called for a business district separate from the historical center. The determining structure of the whole urban area was a highway intersection. The plan laid the groundwork for the theme of the 1948 Milan Triennale, an experimental residential district called QT8 to which the principal Milanese architects contributed.

The "neighborhood unit" as model

The grand modernizing schemes were quickly abandoned and the plans that were actually carried out were revised versions of systems that had been tested before the war. They combined regional expansion through new satellite cities and housing developments with urban renewal. At the same time, government intervention took place on an entirely new scale, through both the public financing of communication infrastructures and the creation of a hierarchical, continuous network of community facilities, calibrated for each population size according to the "neighborhood unit" scheme initially conceived by Clarence Perry and imported from the United States by way of England. This concept was disseminated in France through the writings of the urban planner Gaston Bardet and in Italy through the activities of the industrialist Adriano Olivetti. [13]

A unified vision of the city was more or less explicit in the European urban plans. Some favored a combination of axial compositions and modern buildings, as in the case of the reconstruction of Le Havre (1945–55) **382** under Auguste Perret's direction. Organized around a large avenue planted with greenery, the city was rebuilt with reinforced concrete by a team of architects who ensured that the high-quality buildings and their details achieved a degree of variety. The coherence of the overall design was guaranteed by the use of a single building module. This made it possible to erect both low buildings and a few high-rises, which, together with the city hall belfry and the openwork concrete tower of the Church of Saint-Joseph, created a new skyline. In his project for Maubeuge (1945–54), André Lurçat gained the trust of the war-battered inhabitants, something Le Corbusier was unable to do at Saint-Dié, and succeeded in creating a layout of streets

383 Reconstruction project, Georgui Goltz, Smolensk, USSR (Russia), 1944

and squares that retained echoes of the city center entirely destroyed in 1940. He coordinated his team's work by providing standardized elements – prefabricated stairs and window frames, for example – which the architect of each project could use in his own way. → 14 Louis Arretche rebuilt the residential buildings in the citadel city of Saint-Malo in concrete, then clad them in granite and slate to echo the prewar texture. Like a few other waterfronts, Marseilles's old port was treated with grandeur: Fernand Pouillon framed the surviving city hall between two stately housing projects in load-bearing stone. In Japan, where American bombs had flattened every city except Kyoto, the plans for rebuilding Tokyo and Osaka called for broad thoroughfares lined by new construction in concrete and later steel, in a vocabulary adapted from traditional wood structures. Urban planner Hideaki Ishikawa's War Damage Rehabilitation Plan for Tokyo (1946) called for the land in burned-out areas to be rezoned and a green belt to be created, but this was only minimally realized. A plan for Osaka by Toshihisa Kozu (1945) recommended replacing the city's old structure with a taller and denser urban area built on a grid pattern. → 15

The traditionalists at work

Traditionalism remained well established and in some cases strongly asserted itself. Under Franco's regime, the reconstruction of towns demolished during the Spanish civil war – whether flattened by Nazi bombs, like Guernica, or destroyed in combat, as Belchite had been – combined moderately modern approaches to housing with a historicist treatment of public buildings. Those in charge of the modernization of Madrid had difficulty dispelling the archetype of the Escorial. Agricultural villages were built according to plans assimilating ideas from both

the Weimar *Siedlungen* and the new cities of Italian Fascism. → 16 In the Soviet Union, the reconstruction of nearly the entire European section of the country was incorporated into a triumphant representation of victory. This yielded a number of large-scale compositions, sometimes making emphatic use of topography, as in Lev Rudnev's plan for Stalingrad. The historical arteries of demolished cities were rebuilt and expanded, as with Kiev's Kreshchatik, which Georgui Goltz envisaged (unsuccessfully) turning into an ingenious and elegant monumental concourse. But in cities with less complex sites and histories, such as Smolensk **383** and Minsk, the reconstruction of the urban form was reduced to a single axial intersection around which was assembled a system of large closed blocks. These blocks were in turn faced with eclectic facades in which classicism coexisted with decorative elements from local and national history.

In search of a British model

At the other end of the spectrum, the postwar reconstruction confirmed Great Britain's conversion to modernism, despite the country's widespread hostility to it before the war. → 17 Three major plans were conceived even before the fighting ended. The plan for the bombed city of Coventry, **384** designed by the city architect Sir Donald Evelyn Edward Gibson in 1942, called for the total expropriation of the city center and the creation of a modern urban form. In the middle of it, Basil Spence rebuilt the destroyed cathedral, erecting a new concrete and stone structure (1951–62) next to the historical nave, which was left as a gaping, symbolic shell. Patrick Abercrombie and J. Paton Watson's plan for the port town of Plymouth (1943) required a complete overhaul of the city center, which was considered

384 Reconstruction project, Sir Donald Evelyn Edward Gibson, Coventry, United Kingdom, 1942

unsanitary; it was restructured on a rigid axial system, around which a development of eighteen neighborhood units was built. Abercrombie and J. H. Forshaw's County of London Plan (1943) **385** covered a far greater area. Widely disseminated in book form, it became a key reference for the postwar debate through-out Europe. → 18 London was presented as a collection of "social communities" whose identities were determined by means of in-depth social and functional analysis. The plan provided specific recommendations for each area, clearly differentiating between the densest communities, located in the city center, and those in the more sparsely populated periphery. The London of the future was designed not by imposing a totally new grid but by adjusting the existing urban plan, in which historical hubs were confirmed and new roadways inserted. On a local level, neighborhood units of six to ten thousand inhabitants were meant to constitute the basic structure for the distribution of collective facilities such as schools and shops. The County of London Plan, which was the principal document of Abercrombie and Forshaw's larger project, was accompanied by F. J. Forty's plan for the City, the most heavily affected part of the urban center, and by a plan for Greater London that encompassed the surrounding area within a range of thirty miles. Although the architectural prescriptions tended toward an uncompromising modern style, the plans presented a vivid image of a city composed of clusters of different social groups. It could not have been more clearly opposed to the modernist – or the academic – idea of the city as a single, vast, sculptural composition.

The most original component of postwar British planning, the New Towns, relied on the schema laid out in the London plans. The New Towns were complete urban entities, composed of a cluster of neighborhood units assembled on the periphery of a central area that included public services and shopping. First envisaged in the 1940 report on the Distribution of the Industrial Population put together by Sir Anderson Montague-Barlow's Royal Commission, → 19 the New Town policy was inscribed in the Town and Country Planning Act of 1944. It created ten cities between 1945 and 1951 mostly located in a circle centered on London; among them were Harlow, Stevenage, Crawley, Basildon, and Bracknell. Places of pilgrimage for scores of architects and local administrators up to the 1970s, they showcased a moderate, even sedate, modernist architectural language combined with refined urban planning. The policy was soon codified in a handbook published by Frederick Gibberd, the planner of Harlow. → 20

German debates

The County of London Plan had a highly favorable reception in West Germany. It was essential in shaping Rudolf Schwarz's reflections on the Stadtlandschaft – the city as a landscape. In his book *Von der Bebauung der Erde* (On Building the Earth; 1949), Schwarz published diagrams of organic and decentralized territorial planning. → 21 His plan for the "new Cologne" (1950) **386** called for an urban area divided into two sections, one of which was a new entity built as a counterpart to the historical city. Reconstruction of the center of Cologne led to the creation of many new buildings hidden behind old facades along fluidly sequenced *Stadträume* (city spaces). In Frankfurt am Main, the dialectic between the center and the periphery and between restoration and reconstruction came to characterize the postwar discussions. Whereas Goethe's birthplace was restored with American subsidies (1951), Römerberg Square was rebuilt beginning in 1952 according to a scheme alternating

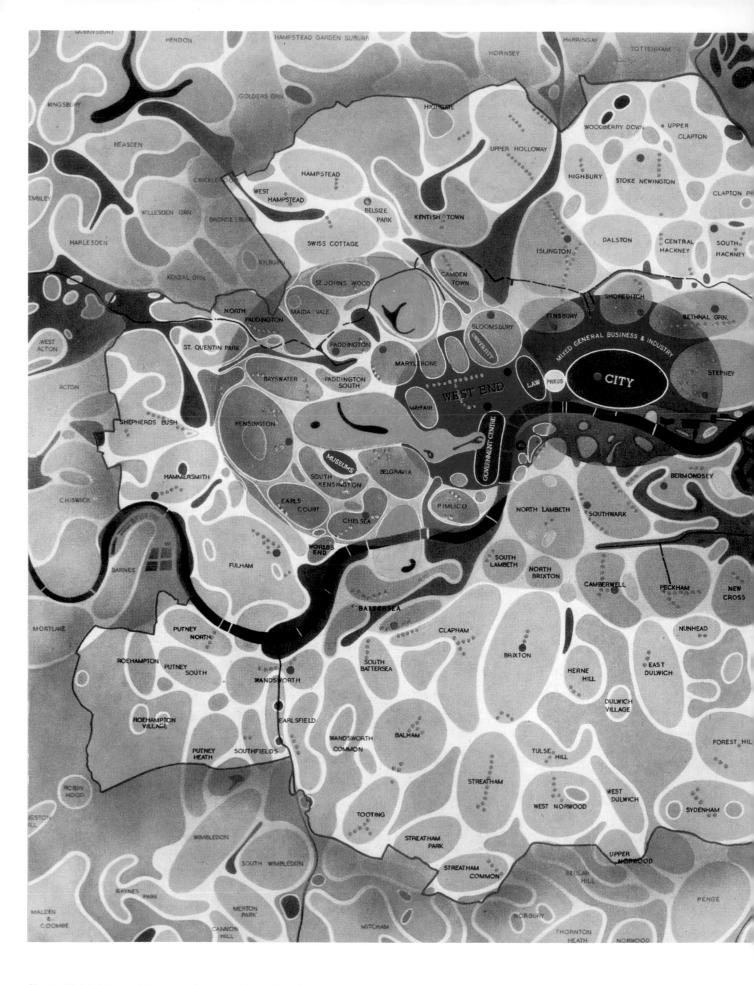

385 "Social and Functional Analysis of London," from *County of London Plan*, Patrick Abercrombie and J. H. Forshaw, London, United Kingdom, 1943

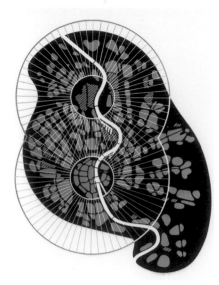

386 Reconstruction and Extension Plan for
Cologne, Rudolf Schwarz, Cologne, Federal Republic
of Germany, 1950

restored facades concealing new construction with entirely
new buildings adapted to the scale of their old surroundings. To the west of this city center – whose history was more
evoked than faithfully reconstituted – a business district was
created. The appearance of skyscrapers in Frankfurt beginning in the 1950s turned the city into a kind of "Mainhattan."
On the outskirts of the center, Ernst May's satellite city policy
was resurrected, with the Nordweststadt designed by the functionalist planner Walter Schwagenscheidt (1959).

The reconstruction of Hamburg, heavily damaged in 1942
following a particularly destructive air raid on its central area,
was planned according to the double criteria of the modernization of the city center – where thoroughfares were widened,
notably with the opening of a major east-west axis – and the
creation of new suburbs. Initially designed to house British
occupying forces, the first great collective buildings of the
postwar period were the Grindelhochhäuser housing projects
built by Bernhard Hermkes's team (1946–56). Architecturally,
one of the most effective projects undertaken in Germany was
Hans Döllgast's rebuilding of the Alte Pinakothek in Munich,
with an austere facade made out of salvaged brick (1946–57);
Döllgast refused to reproduce the museum's destroyed historicist ornamentation, leaving evidence of the bombing explicit.
During the same period, architects in Germany's Soviet
zone were brought into line ideologically with their colleagues in the USSR, and the Soviet model was exported to
the German Democratic Republic, created in 1949. The GDR
implemented a conservative program based on a set of sixteen principles aimed at re-creating compact cities. → 22 In
the port city of Rostock, for which Heinrich Tessenow had
designed an initial plan in 1946, interpretations of Hanseatic
buildings were erected on Neue Markt square, and Joachim

Näther's oversized Magistrale, or main thoroughfare (1953–9),
replaced the medieval Lange Straße. In Dresden, which had
also been burned to the ground, the Frauenkirche was deliberately left in ruins. A project for a skyscraper on the Altmarkt
was considered in 1953 before Herbert Schneider built a
vast neo-Baroque edifice (1954–5) there. Its arcade on the
new east-west Magistrale provided access from the historical center to neighborhoods to the south. The culmination of
the GDR's program of urban planning focused on major arteries was East Berlin's Stalinallee, **387** constructed from 1951 to
1957. Stretching between two thresholds, each marked by a
pair of vertical elements – towers with an Art Deco accent on
the Strausberger Platz, a tempietto motif at the Frankfurter Tor
– the extremely wide avenue was lined with two walls of buildings whose historicist ornamentation symbolized the desire to
insert housing for workers (or those purporting to represent
them) into the very heart of the city. → 23

The final act of German reconstruction took place in West
Berlin. Thirty years after the Weißenhof housing exhibition
in Stuttgart, and also following the *Constructa* exhibition in
Hanover of 1951, which marked a genuine revival of public reflection on urban planning and construction, a model
neighborhood in the Hansaviertel district **388** was built for
the *Interbau* exhibition of 1957. Embracing the slogan of the
"free world" promoted by the Atlantic Alliance, it proposed an
urban "free plan." Buildings designed by Alvar Aalto, Walter
Gropius, Oscar Niemeyer, Jacob Bakema, and other architects were located in a densely planted and informal urban
landscape that contrasted starkly with the axial structure of
the Stalinallee. A year later the Hauptstadt Berlin (Capital
Berlin) competition integrated the question of Berlin into the
European debate on a broader scale: the entire city center,

387 Planning the Stalinallee: Hermann Henselmann, Dr. Otto John and Erich Correns (foreground, left to right) in front of the model, East Berlin, German Democratic Republic, 1951–7

388 Hansaviertel, West Berlin, Federal Republic of Germany, 1957

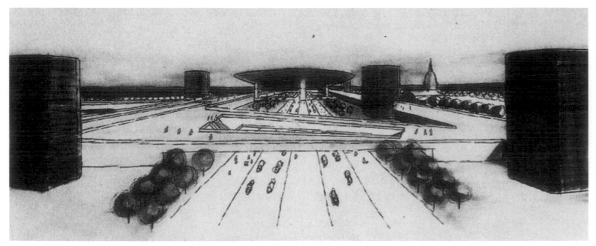

389 Hauptstadt Berlin competition project, Alison Smithson and Peter Smithson, with Peter Sigmund, West Berlin, Federal Republic of Germany, 1957

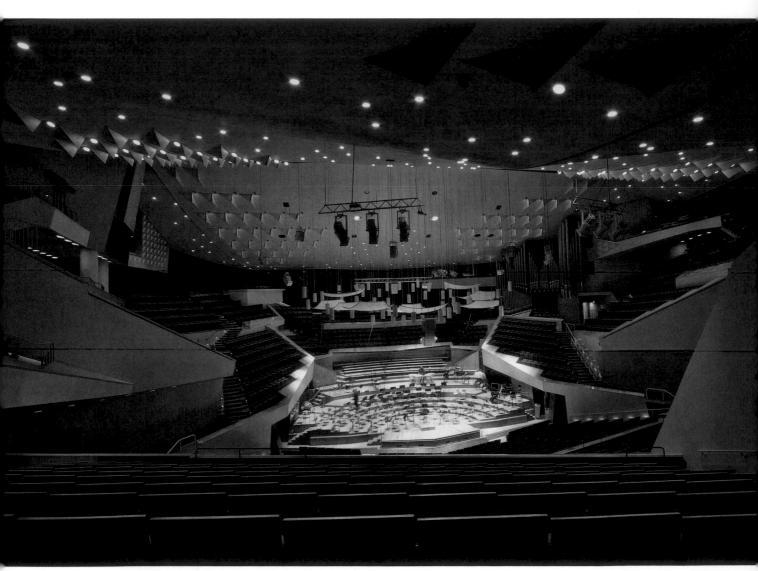

390 Philharmonie, Hans Scharoun, West Berlin, Federal Republic of Germany, 1956–63

391 *L'Art sacré* (Sacred Art), with church by Emil Steffan on the cover, published in Paris, France, 1959

including the portion of the city in East Berlin, was the object of an urban-design competition that proved a turning point with respect to the generational conflicts within the Modern Movement. Highway projects and housing blocks designed in a rigid and academic modernist style confronted the by now well-established Corbusian system. Peter and Alison Smithson's project with Peter Sigmund, **389** based on an organicist vision of the city, received third prize but, like the other innovative entries, had no impact locally, even though the Smithsons' ideas were to transform the vision of a generation. → 24 Overall, most of the Hauptstadt competitors seemed to envisage an open metropolis lacking any street grid and verging on the kind of vacuous stretches found in the British New Towns.

Without waiting for the impossible implementation of these plans for a reunified city, the crowning accomplishment of the new West Berlin was the gold-colored polyhedron of the Philharmonie (1956–63) **390** by Hans Scharoun. Built just a few steps from the Berlin Wall, which was erected in 1961, it formed the first component of a Kulturforum (Cultural Forum) that was intended to return the city to cultural preeminence. With its interior landscape of suspended foyers and boxes disposed throughout the cavernous space of the auditorium, it revolutionized the conception of music venues.

A modernist triumph?

Although an advanced level of modernity did not characterize every European plan conceived during the fifteen years following the war, the process of modernization was manifest. Whether buildings were aligned in rows or freely disposed, whether they had sloping or flat roofs, the priority accorded to the technical infrastructure, the emphasis on functional zoning,

the accommodation of the automobile, and the exploitation of industrial building techniques were nearly universal. The best proof of this universality was the ease with which even the architects who had forcefully endorsed socialist realism were able to reintegrate their work with modern architecture in just a few years. It is also important to note the role played, in a society shocked by war, by theologians and architects affiliated with the Catholic Church during the reconstruction period. A vision of a modern Catholicism was fundamental to Rudolf Schwarz's interest in creating harmonious urban communities. The periodical *L'Art sacré* (Sacred Art) **391** played an essential role in the Franco-German reconciliation of the 1950s and in the promotion of a modern style of religious edifices. Later, Father Pierre Teilhard de Chardin's attempts to reconcile Christianity with Darwin's theory of evolution would have considerable impact in Italy on figures such as the industrialist Adriano Olivetti and the architect Paolo Soleri. The reconstruction projects brought prominent architects and urban planners into close contact with both local and central governments, clearly illustrating the opposition between an architecture of "genius" and one of "bureaucracy," as the American architectural historian Henry-Russell Hitchcock suggested in 1947. → 25 The former was at best an "artistic gamble," like Frank Lloyd Wright's Solomon R. Guggenheim Museum, the design of which was made public at this time, while the latter, usually produced by the kind of large offices that had come into prominence during the war, lacked any symbolic resonance. Clearly, the emotion provoked by the ruins had left a certain scope for the impulses of "geniuses," but it also laid the groundwork for bureaucracies, whose dominance would increase in the transition from the reconstruction period to the mass-housing programs of the 1950s.

The fatal crisis of the Modern Movement, and the alternatives

The postwar era saw the consolidation of modern architecture everywhere except in the "people's democracies" of the Soviet Bloc. But even behind the Iron Curtain, the eclipse of modernism was brief, with socialist realism being called into question as early as 1954. This global diffusion of modernism was in no way homogeneous, though; it was accompanied by endless debates, controversies, and conflicts. The fifteen years that followed the war cannot be characterized as merely continuing the experimental episodes of the 1920s and 1930s. Not only did modern architecture spread at a scale unprecedented before 1939, but a new geography began to take shape in which places such as Brazil shifted from marginal to central importance. At the same time, confrontations between generations of architects led to sometimes fatal ruptures within modernism's existing networks and organizations.

The Festival of Britain

One of the most striking examples of modern architecture's postwar triumph was the 1951 Festival of Britain, **392** centered on the redevelopment of the South Bank of the Thames in London. Initiated by Clement Atlee's Labour government, it was the first international exposition since the 1939 New York World's Fair, and it commemorated the centennial of the Great Exhibition of 1851 and its Crystal Palace. Powell and Moya's Skylon, a steel mast floating above the skyline and tethered by cables, exemplified the progress made toward lightness and an elegant use of technology since the days of the more static Trylon at the New York fair. Yet, to many, this "tall thin structure with no visible means of support" seemed a metaphor for the state of the British economy. [1] In comparison, Leslie Martin's Royal Festival Hall, the only edifice standing today, seemed quite earthbound. Between these polar opposites, a series of pavilions built under the direction of Hugh

Casson to tell the history of the British Isles demonstrated the vigor of the period's various interpretations of modernism. Ralph Tubbs's Dome of Discovery was one of the first large constructions in aluminum, while the restaurant built on the riverbank by Maxwell Fry and Jane Drew used sandwich panels of light metal and insulating materials comparable to those employed by Jean Prouvé in Clichy. As at the 1948 Milan Triennale, the exhibition was complemented by a housing development. Built downstream in the borough of Poplar, it was designed by Frederick Gibberd with the firm of Yorke Rosenberg Mardall, and the landscape designer Geoffrey Jellicoe and represented a significant application of the concept of the "neighborhood unit."

In 1951 the *Architectural Review* lauded the care devoted to every aspect of this "modern version of the Picturesque" as "an object lesson to town-planners, borough engineers and others responsible for the design of roads and their furniture, public spaces and their layouts." [2] Under the editorship of Hubert de Cronin Hastings (alias Ivor de Wolfe), the *Review* engaged in these years in a passionate critique of the deteriorating landscape of Great Britain's cities and countryside. A year earlier, its criticism had been directed to the other side of the Atlantic, where the lack of "design" and professional engagement by architects was demonstrated by "the mess that is man-made America," and it was condemned by the editors as the work of a nation that had rejected a visual ideal in favor of "a universe of uncontrollable chaos sparsely inhabited by happy accidents." [3] The analyses by Hastings and the seductive sketches of urban spaces by Gordon Cullen suggested the alternative of visual scenography, or "Townscape," a neo-Picturesque fusion of architecture with such components of the urban environment as paving stones, plantings, signs, lighting, and the multifarious elements making up the built fabric. [4]

393 *Metron*, edited by Bruno Zevi, published in Rome, Italy, 1949

394 *Domus*, edited by Ernesto Nathan Rogers, published in Milan, Italy, 1947

395 *Spazio*, edited by Luigi Moretti, published in Rome, Italy, 1950

Italian Neorealism

In Italy, competition among the modern architectural factions intensified after a very brief phase of cooperation. The rivalry between periodicals reveals the geographical and doctrinal diversity of the forces at work, but also a distinctive feature of Italian architectural culture as compared to that elsewhere in Europe, namely the architect's self-acknowledged role as intellectual, capable of functioning consistently within a given ideological context. →[5] In Rome, Bruno Zevi edited *Metron* **393** from 1945 to 1954, while using an organization that he established, the Associazione per l'architettura organica, or APAO (Association for Organic Architecture), to propagate Frank Lloyd Wright's ideas. The shorter-lived *Spazio* **395** (Space; 1950–3), edited by Luigi Moretti, opposed Zevi's organicism and supported an alliance of art, architecture, and science. In Milan, Ernesto Nathan Rogers ran *Domus* **394** from 1946 until 1948, when it was taken back by its founder, Gio Ponti, who had left to set up *Stile* (1941–7) during the war. In 1953 Rogers relaunched the magazine *Casabella* as *Casabella-continuità* and embarked on an intense critical examination of the Modern Movement.

The immediate postwar years were also marked by a significant American presence in Italy. In 1946 the United States Information Service financed the *Manuale dell'architetto* (Architect's Handbook), in which a team headed by Mario Ridolfi provided a systematic survey of Italian and American dimensional standards and construction details. The UNRRA-CASAS program, developed under the aegis of the United Nations with Adriano Olivetti, provided new dwellings for villages like Matera in the south of the country. The various projects made use of economic and sociological research

carried out with American methods and financing. In literature and film, an interest in the United States of the 1930s and its novelists was one of the sources of Neorealism, the first examples of which – Elio Vittorini's novel *Conversazione in Sicilia* (translated as *Conversations in Sicily*) and Luchino Visconti's film *Ossessione* (Obsession) – were completed as early as 1942. Neorealism continued to develop on screen with Roberto Rossellini's *Rome, Open City* (1945) and Vittorio De Sica's *Bicycle Thief* (1948).

Roman architects became involved in the first projects of INA-Casa, founded in 1949 by the Christian Democrat minister Amintore Fanfani. The project most closely identified with Neorealism was the Tiburtino Housing, (1949–54) **396** built by Ludovico Quaroni, Mario Ridolfi, and many young Roman architects. Employing the "neighborhood unit" concept in spirit, it mixed streets of regularly spaced buildings with detached apartment blocks comparable in size to large houses. The tile roofs, brick screen-walls, and wrought-iron details evoked rural buildings, as if to re-create a familiar setting for the recently relocated inhabitants who came from Italy's agricultural areas. It would later be inhabited by refugees from Istria after that region became part of Yugoslavia. For UNRRA-CASAS, Quaroni collaborated with Federico Gorio to design the village of La Martella (1951–4), **397** to which the inhabitants of the Sassi, the cavelike dwellings of Matera, were relocated. He applied guidelines proposed by Olivetti – whose planning model in turn was the Tennessee Valley Authority – to a scheme combining the informal structure of the caves with garden city precepts. The houses in La Martella had a geometric simplicity based on an analysis of vernacular dwellings that Giuseppe Pagano and Guarniero Daniel had exhibited in 1936, while the stone and concrete church tower employed

396 Tiburtino Housing, Ludovico Quaroni, Mario Ridolfi, et al., Rome, Italy, 1949–54

397 La Martella village, Ludovico Quaroni and Federico Gorio, Matera, Italy, 1951–4

398 Prefeito Mendes Moraes Building, Affonso Eduardo Reidy, Rio de Janeiro, Brazil, 1946–52

399 Ibirapuera Park, Oscar Niemeyer, São Paulo, Brazil, 1951–5

400 Apartment Buildings, Park Guinle, Lucio Costa, Rio de Janeiro, Brazil, 1948–54

a purer language with its cubic volume. →6 Foreign visitors to these projects, among them the American G. E. Kidder Smith, emphasized the way they linked modern architecture and tradition. →7 But those who were actually responsible for realizing this housing soon provided their own evaluations. Quaroni pulled no punches in criticizing the Tiburtino in an article of 1957 entitled "Il paese dei barocchi" (The Land of Baroque), a play on *paese dei balocchi* – the land of toys inhabited by Pinocchio in the children's story. The Roman architect not only regretted the Tiburtino's intentionally naive appearance but also its evocations of Baroque Rome.

Planet Brazil

The postwar discovery of buildings erected in Brazil since 1940 opened new horizons for European and North American architects as well as for those working in Africa and the Middle East. The visibility of Brazilian architecture beyond its national borders began with the exhibition *Brazil Builds* at the Museum of Modern Art in 1943 and was amplified by special issues of the leading international periodicals. →8 The appeal of the Brazilian forms was in their fluency and elegance as well as in their technical boldness, which gave a look of lightness to the most complex structures. They appeared as pure articulations of the skeleton and the shell, two techniques integral to the development of reinforced-concrete buildings. In 1955 Henry-Russell Hitchcock noted that there was "more innate sympathy for the vault-like shapes of shell concrete construction" south of the Rio Grande than anywhere else in the world. →9 Brazilian inventiveness was also visible in new incarnations of Le Corbusier's *pilotis*, which were no longer simple cylinders but V or Y shapes with tapered extremities.

After the completion of Oscar Niemeyer's buildings in Pampulha and of the Ministry of Education and Health in Rio, which was correctly perceived as owing more to the young Brazilians than to Le Corbusier, an entire generation of Brazilian architects suddenly rose to prominence. →10 In Rio, the winding Prefeito Mendes Moraes Building (1946–52), **398** built in Pedregulho by Affonso Eduardo Reidy, seemed a runaway fragment of Le Corbusier's Obus Plan for Algiers with its horizontal profile playing visually with the surrounding *morros* (hills). It was designed with maisonette units, as was Reidy's Marquês de São Vicente Building (1952), which was built with a similar profile and which replaced a shantytown in Gávea. →11 Jorge Moreira was responsible for the definitive layout of Rio's University City (for which Le Corbusier had also designed a project) and built its Early Childhood Institute (1949–53), a low building on *pilotis* with an orthogonal geometry. He then undertook a series of large housing projects seemingly floating in a sea of gardens by Roberto Burle Marx. The latter's curvilinear landscape designs accompanied most of the major modern projects in Brazil, beginning with the terraces of the Ministry of Education and Health, and found their fullest development in Flamingo Park on the shores of Guanabara Bay in Rio. Lucio Costa's residential buildings around a large garden in the same city's Park Guinle (1948–54) **400** explore the principle of the housing slab on *pilotis* with a roof terrace, although on a less expansive scale than the Unité d'Habitation being built by Le Corbusier at the same date in Marseilles. Costa's design combined the Corbusian principles with the terracotta trellis screens of Brazilian vernacular architecture, successfully giving a tactile quality to a type of building usually treated schematically.

402 Niemeyer House, Oscar Niemeyer, Canoas, Rio de Janeiro, Brazil, 1953–4

401 Copan Building, Oscar Niemeyer, São Paulo, Brazil, 1951–3

Once his career was fully established by the international impact of his buildings, Niemeyer began working on large-scale projects in São Paulo and in Rio, such as the Hospital Sul-América (1952), where he inaugurated his V-shaped supports. In Burle Marx's Ibirapuera Park (1951–5), **399** built for the four hundredth anniversary of São Paulo, Niemeyer designed a series of large white domes connected to one another and to slabs on *pilotis* by serpentine galleries, reinterpreting elements from his Casa do Baile Dance Hall in Pampulha in a central block reached by interior ramps. At a time when North American models were beginning to proliferate in Brazil, Niemeyer took on the challenge of designing large urban buildings, the overall shapes of which he modulated through the play of shadow and light on linear balconies. His Niemeyer Building in Belo Horizonte (1954–5) is an isolated sculpture on the Praça da Libertade, one of the city's central squares. Competing with the sinuous developments that Reidy had built in Rio, though in a denser context, the gigantic Copan Building in São Paulo (1951–3) **401** plays with a complex urban program, including shopping arcades that cleverly connect to the neighboring streets by means of a sloping floor.

In 1954 a group of important European and American architects visited Brazil on the occasion of the first São Paulo Biennale. The "Report on Brazil" issued by Max Bill, Ernesto Nathan Rogers, and Walter Gropius, among others, upon their return criticized the lack of structural logic in Niemeyer's architecture, comparing it unfavorably to Reidy's Pedregulho Housing. → [12] But Niemeyer's own house at Canoas, a southern neighborhood of Rio (1953–4), **402** was remarkable for its simplicity: a concrete slab roof with a curvaceous outline covers a single open space in which individual areas are defined only by furniture. The house's position, overlooking a leafy

403 Villa Suissa, Jean-François Zevaco, Casablanca, Morocco, 1947

404 Housing for Muslim Workers, ATBAT-Afrique (Vladimir Bodiansky, Georges Candilis and Shadrach Woods), Casablanca, Morocco, 1952

405 Aérohabitat Housing, Louis Miquel, Algiers, Algeria, 1950–9

valley descending to the ocean, and the wooden wall into which the family dining table is integrated suggest a tropical Tugendhat House, while the rock jutting into the house and the mirroring of the house and pool seem to challenge Wright's Fallingwater.

Niemeyer, who in 1947 was a member of the initial design team for the United Nations Headquarters in New York, began to design other projects abroad. For Inocente Palacios, a left-wing Venezuelan political figure and collector, he projected a museum of modern art in Caracas in 1954; an inverted pyramid perched on a steep slope, it was apparently prompted by Wright's Solomon R. Guggenheim Museum in New York. In 1955 Niemeyer was invited to design a building in Berlin in the Hansaviertel model housing district. He ultimately felt that the building's execution was compromised by the contractors and local architects, but this structure with its elegant V-shaped *pilotis* represented a milestone: other than the pavilions produced for international expositions, it was the first permanent edifice built in Europe by an architect from a former colony.

Housing and innovation in North Africa

Niemeyer's forms had a significant impact in North African countries still under French rule, where a new golden age of architecture seemed to reign until the mid-1950s. In Casablanca, Jean-François Zevaco, an alumnus of the Paris Beaux-Arts, drew on Niemeyer's approach in his charming air terminal in Tit Mellil (1951). He was best known for his Villa Suissa (1947), **403** a compact block given great expansive presence by the outward cant of its *brise-soleil*. Élie Azagury was more sensitive to Scandinavian architecture and, particularly, to Richard Neutra's California villas, to which he paid

homage in his Schulmann House (1952). Gaston Jaubert, a former student of Auguste Perret (as was Azagury), created a sculptural facade for the Brami Building, which contained studio apartments (1952).

The most crucial problem stemming from Morocco's rapid urbanization was that of the shantytowns, which kept growing as a result of an inexorable exodus from the rural areas to the cities. Responding to a housing crisis that affected both the European working class and poor Muslim and Jewish Moroccans, the protectorate's urban planner, Michel Écochard, began designing a ring of large housing projects on the outskirts of Casablanca, each one assigned to a specific social group. Segregation thus became the basis of a project that was both rational and generous but unable to transcend colonial categories. The gigantic Carrières Centrales *bidonville*, the biggest and most politically turbulent in the country, was replaced by the first of a series of "satellite" settlements comprising several neighborhood units. On a grid of 8-by-8 meter (24¼-by-26¼-foot) lots, the "model cells" consisted of one or two rooms opening onto a patio, with a kitchen-shed and a bathroom. The development was dominated by three buildings designed by Georges Candilis and Shadrach Woods, **404** who had formerly worked for Le Corbusier, in collaboration with the engineer Vladimir Bodiansky. They created public housing, based on their study of Berber Casbahs in southern Morocco, adapted to the recent arrivals from the countryside. By stacking up patio dwellings, they produced a particularly striking sculptural effect. → 13

The projects carried out during the first half of the 1950s in Algiers, where Pierre Dalloz and Gérald Hanning's planning office produced urban plans respectful of the city's exceptional topography, represented a somewhat different approach.

406 Climat de France Housing, Fernand Pouillon, Algiers, Algeria, 1953–7

407 Tuscolano Housing, Adalberto Libera, Rome, Italy, 1950–4

The Algiers group of CIAM, led by Roland Simounet and Louis Miquel, carefully investigated the Mahieddine shantytown in order to design dwellings responsive to the local population's everyday life, which they sympathetically assessed. For the Aérohabitat (1950–9), **405** a large building on the slopes overlooking the sea, Miquel echoed Le Corbusier's urbanistic approach in his Obus Plan (to which Miquel had contributed two decades earlier), but used a language closer to that of the Unité d'Habitation in Marseilles. The Aérohabitat's interior street served as an urban passerelle connecting two levels of the steep hillside city. Simounet used his research to create the Djenan el-Hassan housing development (1958), which was positioned along the slope of a hill under concrete vaults, much like Le Corbusier's Roq project on the French Riviera. On the invitation of Algiers's mayor, the Marseilles architect Fernand Pouillon built three housing projects, largely in structural stone, in just a few months. The most spectacular of them, the Climat de France Housing (1953–7), **406** also known as the "Two Hundred Columns," towered above the city and was ringed with arcades sheltering stores. Pouillon gave each of the three projects, in contrast to many of his colleagues' housing complexes, and despite their modest construction budget, a clear gestalt that made them easily identifiable to their inhabitants. [14]

CIAM in turmoil

The North African projects had an immediate impact in Europe. In the Tuscolano Housing in Rome, **407** built by Adalberto Libera in 1950–4 for the INA-Casa, a building on *pilotis* dominated an expanse of courtyard houses, as if inspired by Écochard's housing projects. Libera, on the back of a postcard mailed from Morocco, ironically referred to it as "INA-Casbah." [15] The

research carried out in Algiers and in the housing projects in Casablanca, illustrated in *L'Architecture d'aujourd'hui* as early as 1952, created a sensation a year later at CIAM's meeting in Aix-en-Provence, France, where, according to Alison Smithson, participants were "seized" by these new developments. [16] During the twelve years between the sixth CIAM, held in Bridgwater, England, in 1947, and the eleventh and last CIAM, held in Otterlo in the Netherlands in 1959, generational conflicts led to a crisis and ultimately to the organization's demise. This internal strife took place at the same moment that CIAM was attracting increasing participation by Latin American, North African, and Japanese groups. [17] The Bridgwater congress had reunited the members in their first meeting after the war. It was organized by the local branch, the MARS, and groups "in training" from outside Europe were only provisionally allowed to take part in the proceedings. At the meeting the organization's objectives were reformulated in light of the changes in sensibility brought about by the war; as the Dutch contingent declared, "We come from countries which were occupied during four years, and during this time it was said too that we had to satisfy man's material and emotional needs, but now we have to do something more: we have to stimulate man's spiritual growth." [18] The young Aldo van Eyck criticized CIAM for its emphasis on machine civilization and invited the members to reclaim their avant-garde roots again – to the strong approbation of Le Corbusier, who cried out, "Finally imagination has entered CIAM!" [19] The congress that followed, held in Bergamo in 1949, dedicated itself principally to a discussion of the "CIAM grid." As initially envisioned at Bridgwater, this was a standard graphic layout that was supposed to "encourage CIAM groups to keep in touch with public needs and observe the progress of the public's understanding of CIAM principles, with the object

408 "Urban Reidentification," Alison Smithson and Peter Smithson, Aix-en-Provence, France, 1953

of assisting modern architecture to develop in sympathy with the aspirations of the people it serves." → 20 Subsequently it became a device used more for CIAM's internal purposes – and a bone of contention for the younger generation.

In Hoddesdon, England, in 1951, CIAM's discussions centered on the notion of the "core" of cities. **409** The concept of the core was, according to Le Corbusier, richer than the American idea of the "civic center" and encompassed it. The debate begun in 1943 regarding a "new monumentality" thus continued with this introduction of a symbolic and humanistic dimension missing from CIAM's early doctrine. Sigfried Giedion stated: "Our present interest in the core is part of this humanizing process or, if you prefer, the return to the human scale and the assertation [sic] of the rights of the individual against the tyranny of the mechanical tools." → 21 Yet the meeting was not marked by unanimity. Inspired by the presentation of student projects, the Latin American members at Hoddesdon criticized the organization's apolitical posture. More importantly, there were clear signs of a split between generations. Jacob Bakema and José Luís Sert contradicted the majority by favoring designs based on formal and compositional principles rather than zoning, while van Eyck expressed his interest in the systems of enclosures used in African villages and their anthropological meaning. The question of the urban context came to the fore in Ernesto Nathan Rogers's reminder of the importance of *preesistenze ambientali* (preexisting conditions), which, he argued, had to be taken into account to avoid a "vague and indeterminate" architecture. → 22 Two years after Hoddesdon, the CIAM congress in Aix-en-Provence (1953) marked a decisive turning point. The rebels – Bakema, van Eyck, Georges Candilis, Alison and Peter Smithson, and Giancarlo De Carlo – used sociological and ethnological research conducted in the Maghreb to call into

question the "universalist" approach of past congresses. After the obsession with the hygiene of European cities, which had dominated CIAM's previous urban thinking, and the fixation on biological and medical metaphors, the social sciences became the compass of the new generation. → 23 Through their own ironic twist on the sacrosanct "grid," the Smithsons proposed the concept of "urban reidentification," **408** which they illustrated with photographs taken by Nigel Henderson of London's working-class East End, reminding CIAM's members of the human context of urban planning. Following Aix and in preparation for CIAM's tenth congress, the homonymous Team 10 – consisting of Bakema, van Eyck, Candilis, and the Smithsons – proposed new strategies for overcoming what Rogers called "the greatest peril" for architecture: "modern conformism." → 24

The end of CIAM

The tenth CIAM took place in Dubrovnik in 1956 in an atmosphere of general dissension. The focus was the drafting of a "Charter of Habitat," a project that was supposed to complete the Athens Charter. The initiative failed, and the national groups were dissolved the following year, with Bakema appointed as secretary general of the organization. With his recognition of the importance of the element of play in human culture – a subject introduced by the Dutch historian Johan Huizinga in his book *Homo Ludens* (originally published in Dutch in 1938) – Bakema ceased to uphold the rigidity that had long dominated CIAM. → 25 The organization's official death took place on the occasion of its "reunion" congress held in September 1959 in Otterlo in the Netherlands. It was exactly thirty years old. The illusions of the founders about modern architecture's capacities to create productive relations had

409 "Core," illustration from the "Heart of the City," publication from CIAM 8, Hoddesdon, United Kingdom, 1951

410 "Tree Is Leaf Is Tree," Aldo van Eyck, 1959

by this time been dispelled by the inexorable course of modernization itself and by the younger generation's pursuit of less abstract, more complex solutions to environmental problems. In a characteristically provocative statement, van Eyck **410** declared: "When are architects going to stop fondling technology for its own sake – stop stumbling after progress? … They have betrayed society in betraying the essence of contemporary thought. Nobody can really live in what they concoct, although they may think so." [26]

In 1954 Team 10 had issued a statement known as the "Doorn Manifesto" in which it put forward its own position. Stressing the notion of "community," it insisted on the relationships of dwellings to each other and to other scales of social organization. Continuing to meet regularly but informally, Team 10 adopted a less rigid form of interaction than CIAM. Most significantly, it used its members' highly diverse projects to emphasize principles of complexity, local specificity, growth, and – especially – change and user participation, all notions that had largely been absent from the CIAM's linear vision of progress. [27] Beginning in 1963 and for the next ten years, under the aegis of Constantinos A. Doxiadis, a Greek architect who tried to establish his theory of "Ekistics" as a replacement dogma for CIAM's precepts, discussions of a parallel agenda took place every summer on the Aegean island of Delos. [28] Concurrent with the crisis of CIAM in the 1950s, other forums began to appear and to continue the reflection on the heritage of interwar modernism. Such critical premises did not, however, underpin the gatherings of the Union internationale des architectes (UIA). An outgrowth of the international meetings organized by Pierre Vago in the 1930s, the Union was founded in 1948. Aside from sponsoring a few competitions, it served mainly to justify travel by the profession's bureaucrats to its various meetings. [29] Nevertheless, it remained the standard context for academic debates between architects from the two Cold War blocs – the "free" world and the socialist camp. Gatherings like the *Darmstädter Gespräche* (Darmstadt Conversations), founded immediately after the war by the architects Otto Bartning and Theodor Heuss (the first president of the Federal Republic of Germany), were the UIA's polar opposite. In 1951 the Gespräche invited the philosopher Martin Heidegger to speak. Heidegger gave a seminal lecture entitled "Bauen, Wohnen, Denken" (Building, Dwelling, Thinking), which helped to launch a consequential encounter between phenomenology and architecture and offered a critical context for reconsidering the ideals of the Bauhaus. [30]

Le Corbusier reinvented and reinterpreted

In 1961 Le Corbusier wrote to thank the publisher Karl Krämer for sending him the proceedings of the final CIAM, held in Otterlo two years before. He said he was "happy" that "each generation takes its place in due time." But when he sent a copy of this same letter to Walter Gropius, Jacob Bakema, and other colleagues, he scrawled a caricature **414** on it of a young man brandishing a "freedom" flag and trampling the "bullshit" that had allegedly come from the "thirty years of work" by the older generation of "pains in the ass." In the margin, he commented: "They climb on your shoulders, but they don't say thanks!" [1] Yet the gratitude of the Team 10 generation toward their predecessor was apparent in their projects, which were sometimes less critical of Le Corbusier's work than he was himself in the postwar period. Indeed, no one was less "Corbusian" than Le Corbusier, particularly when he stunned his most stalwart supporters with the totally unexpected solutions of Ronchamp and the Jaoul Houses.

The Unité d'Habitation

The Unité d'Habitation in Marseilles (1946–52) **411** was the culmination of the research that Le Corbusier began with his *immeuble-villas* of 1922. He had clearly formulated the principle of the "standard-size housing unit" – or the "vertical garden city," to use one of Le Corbusier's favorite oxymorons – as early as 1942 in his book *La maison des hommes* (The Home of Man). Raoul Dautry, the French Minister of Reconstruction and Urbanism, accepted this principle as the basis for a rental building that was initially intended to be temporary accommodation for residents of Marseilles left homeless by the war. Built on thick *pilotis* that housed the building's utility pipes, the Unité was constructed like a reinforced-concrete "bottle rack." It contained 337 apartments, each spanning the full width of the building from one facade to the other and featuring a double-height living room. The apartments are entered from "streets in the air" located every three floors; a "main street" on the seventh floor originally offered shops and services. The roof, overlooking the landscape of Provence, has a running track and a kindergarten and resembles the deck of the transatlantic liners celebrated in his book *Vers une architecture*. [2]

Le Corbusier designed the Unité's components using the "Modulor," a system of proportions he had devised in 1945 based on a combination of the ancient golden section with the "average" statistical height of a human being: initially 1.75 meters (5 feet 9) inches and subsequently 1.83 meters (6 feet). His design was indebted to the research of the aesthetician Matila Ghyka and the mathematician Elisa Maillart, who had introduced him to the Fibonacci series, in which each number is the sum of the previous two. In contrast to this markedly intellectual approach, the rough surfaces and traces left on the concrete by the formwork planks and successive pourings – necessitated by an underfunded and overlong construction process – led Le Corbusier to proclaim the beauty of raw concrete. Although the failure of his plans to build entire neighborhoods of *unités* in southern Marseilles, Strasbourg, and Meaux prevented him from serializing the overall principles of his housing unit, he did succeed in building four more – in Nantes (1948–55), West Berlin (1955–8), Briey-en-Forêt (1955–60), and Firminy (1964–7).

Of palaces and houses

Le Corbusier's National Museum of Western Art in Ueno Park, Tokyo (1957–9), was the result of research he had begun with his Mundanéum project and continued with the Museum of Unlimited

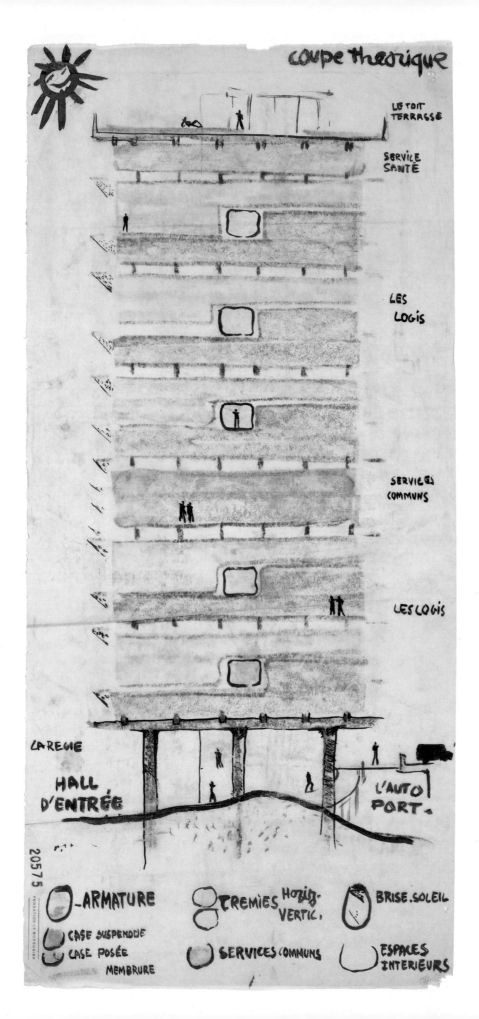

412 Jaoul Houses, Le Corbusier, Neuilly-sur-Seine, France, 1951–5

413 Chapel of Notre-Dame-du-Haut, Le Corbusier, Ronchamp, France, 1951–5

Growth in the early 1930s. The spiral of the galleries unfurls on a square plan raised on *pilotis* along an architectural ramp that ensures a progressive discovery of the interior space. The building volume is wrapped in a wall of heavily textured aggregate concrete. Le Corbusier's museums in Ahmedabad (1951–7) and Chandigarh (1964–8) in India explored different versions of the same principle, which would also serve as the basis for the Museum of the Twentieth Century, an unbuilt design of 1965 in Nanterre for the French Minister of Culture André Malraux. Le Corbusier had used concrete vaults and rubble walls for his Petite Maison de Weekend (Little Weekend House) in La Celle-Saint-Cloud, France, in 1934–5. He returned to the same motifs, but using exposed brick, for the houses he built for André and Michel Jaoul in Neuilly (1951–5). **412** In these dwellings made of rough brick, concrete, and plywood, he left behind the spartan interiors of his stark white villas of the 1920s, providing more comfortable areas with fireplaces and brightly colored walls. The storage niches integrated into the walls and the windows opening onto pleasant views and allowing ample light inside made the houses "inhabitable volumes rich in potential" – the polar opposite of the notion of the "machine for living in" he had famously coined earlier. →3 In 1955 the young British architect James Stirling declared that the Jaoul Houses had made Le Corbusier "the most regionalist of architects." In fact, Le Corbusier pursued this line of research in a remote location, in a house designed for Manorama Sarabhai, head of one of the most powerful Jain dynasties in Ahmedabad. Conceived as a series of parallel load-bearing brick walls, the house, completed in 1955, had vaulted ceilings of tiles set in cement that were carried by concrete lintels and ran perpendicular to the longitudinal walls. His Roq et Rob project in Roquebrune Cap-Martin (1950), in the south of France, was a variation on the principle of the

Jaoul Houses and also echoed designs he had originally conceived for Algeria. Intended to stand on a slope below the village, it returned to the idea of a series of vaulted cells.

The surprise of Ronchamp

In contrast to these buildings and designs, which reflected a gradual process of maturation, Le Corbusier's design for a new chapel at Ronchamp **413** in the Vosges, replacing an earlier church destroyed in 1944, shocked both his admirers and his detractors. Its startling sculptural form draws on the structural principle of the airplane wing as well as on organic metaphors – its roof evoking a crab shell, one of those "objects of poetic reaction" so dear to him. But the chapel also brought together a wealth of memories: of the gargoyles at Topkapi Palace in Constantinople, which he had seen in 1911; of the Serapeum in Hadrian's Villa; and of the honeycombed wall of the small Sidi Brahim Mosque in El Atteuf in the M'Zab, which he had come upon in 1931. Pilgrims making their way up the hill of Bourlémont to Notre-Dame-du-Haut – much as the young Jeanneret had climbed to the Acropolis in 1911 – initially encounter the concrete chapel's eastern wall with its sculptural altar. The pleasant, simple nave brings worshipers together in a space bathed in colored light entering through holes in the thick south wall. In 1955 Le Corbusier described it to the archbishop of Besançon as a "chapel of dear, faithful concrete, shaped perhaps with temerity but certainly with courage." →4 With this project, Le Corbusier drew on creative discoveries he had made during four decades of experience, and transcended them. The Philips Pavilion at the 1958 Brussels World's Fair, **415** which had a structure designed by Iannis Xenakis, a Greek engineer and musical composer working in Le Corbusier's office, went in

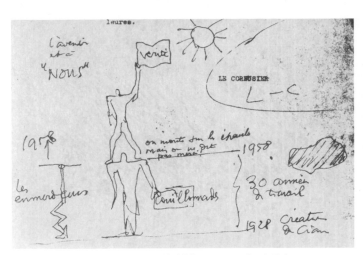

414 Caricature on copy of letter to Karl Krämer sent to Jacob Bakema, Le Corbusier, 1961

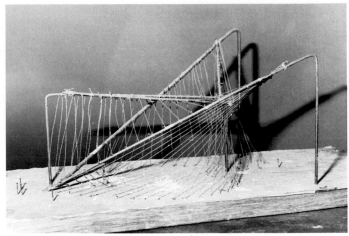

415 Philips Pavilion, Le Corbusier with Iannis Xenakis, Brussels, Belgium, 1957–8

a completely different direction. Chordal progressions from the musical score of Xenakis's 1954 piece *Metastasis* determined the hyperbolic paraboloid geometry of the pavilion's surfaces. On a plan in the shape of a stomach a framework of inverted V-shaped concrete ribs was erected to support the double-curved surfaces of precast concrete panels, which were in turn held in place by a network of cables. The pavilion housed Le Corbusier's *Poème électronique*, an innovative multimedia spectacle with music by Edgard Varèse that combined projected images of abstract color motifs, natural phenomena, folkloric creations, and frightening visions of technology. [5]

Indian adventures

During the last fifteen years of his life, Le Corbusier traveled to India twice a year to carry out the largest building project of his career. The government of Jawaharlal Nehru – which had launched a program of creating new cities, including Bhubaneswar, designed by German émigré Otto Koenigsberger – commissioned Le Corbusier to design what would be his only realized master plan for a city. To build the new Punjabi capital of Chandigarh – which Nehru described as "a new town symbolic of the freedom of India, unfettered by traditions of the past" – Le Corbusier transformed a plan that had been previously prepared by the American architect Albert Mayer in collaboration with the Polish émigré Matthew Nowicki and in consultation with Clarence Stein. Le Corbusier enlarged Mayer and his team's residential neighborhoods, which he dismissed as "fake modern," into "sectors" of 400 by 1,200 meters (1,300 by 3,900 feet). Most importantly, he used the principle of the "seven ways" he had earlier proposed in a plan for Bogotá to distinguish footpaths, roads, and avenues, adjusting each type of route to specific speeds and

usages. His mandate included the design of the master plan and the construction of the buildings in the capitol complex, the city's political center. The commission for shopping, university, and residential districts was entrusted to the British architects Jane Drew and Maxwell Fry and to Le Corbusier's former associate, Pierre Jeanneret, whom he recruited to represent him on site and take charge of the housing construction. In these districts, brick houses were aligned in staid rows according to a rigid hierarchy, from the luxurious residences of the ministers to the modest but highly functional single-story houses of the lowest-level employees. [6] The principal administrative buildings were concentrated in the capitol complex according to a refined and subtle composition that avoids any overall symmetry but plays with axes to create relationships between buildings despite the vast distances separating them. Le Corbusier derived this composition by inflecting his precise proportional plan for the capitol with features of Mughal gardens, which he had visited in northern India. Many of the buildings' details grew out of his observations of traditional Indian architecture and everyday life. The High Court was designed to house the principal legal institutions of the new Indian state under a large overhanging roof, which provided shaded passages to create an extraordinary *promenade architecturale*. The Palace of the Assembly (1955–64) **416** faces the High Court across a grand esplanade. The Assembly's main hall is lit by a hyperboloid light well inspired by the cooling towers of a power plant in Ahmedabad, and possibly also by the pyramidal form of the *chambre du tué*, a type of smokehouse with an oversized chimney stack that had made an impression on the young Jeanneret in the farmhouses of his native Jura. On the horizon beyond is the long slab of the Secretariat, where the ministries' offices are located. Between the main hall and the facades, circulation ramps rise through a dark space intersected by a dense

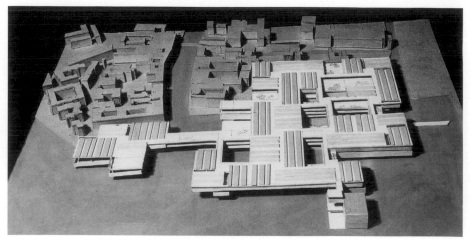

416   Palace of the Assembly, Le Corbusier, Chandigarh, India, 1955–64

417   Venice Hospital, project, Le Corbusier, Venice, Italy, 1962–5

418   Millowners' Association Building, Le Corbusier, Ahmedabad, India, 1951–4

419 ▶   Sainte Marie de la Tourette Convent, Le Corbusier, Eveux-sur-l'Arbresle, France, 1953–60

forest of columns. Le Corbusier also designed a Governor's Palace for the head Punjab official and a Monument of the Open Hand, laden with symbolic meanings. Although intended to dominate the complex, the Governor's Palace was never built, even after its program was transformed into a "Museum of Knowledge." The Open Hand was erected long after Le Corbusier's death. ↦ 7

Invention and introspection

After visiting monasteries in the Val d'Ema in Italy and Mount Athos in Greece as a young man, Le Corbusier had declared monastic life to be "heroic." Much later, the success of his chapel at Ronchamp brought him a commission from the Dominican denomination to build "a place of meditation, study, and prayer for the preaching friars." This became the Sainte Marie de la Tourette Convent (1953–60) **419** in Eveux-sur-l'Arbresle, near Lyons. Inverting the figure of the perimeter colonnade he had seen at the Cistercian monastery of Le Thoronet, he designed a cruciform ambulatory that cuts through the central courtyard space formed by the building's four main components: the large solid box of the chapel; two communal facilities, the library and the refectory, the latter opening toward the downslope of the site; and, on the upper levels, the monks' cells, which run along three sides of the square plan. The raw material of the convent is not just concrete but light. Channeled into the church by "light cannons," illumination pours onto the altar in beams of color. Sculpted by the ambulatory's glass walls – which Le Corbusier described as "undulating" because the spacing of the mullions varies rhythmically according to Modulor-based measurements – light shapes and reshapes the experience of the volumes of the central cloister at every hour of the day. ↦ 8

In designing the Villa Shodhan (1951–6) and the Millowners' Association Building (1951–4) **418** in Ahmedabad Le Corbusier rediscovered the virtues of the "free plan" he had first conceived in the 1920s. He similarly took advantage of the commission for Harvard University's Carpenter Center for the Visual Arts (1958–64) to return to his early theme of the *promenade architecturale*. Faced with critics who referred to him as "the brute of reinforced concrete," he insisted that his only American building have an "extremely elegant and very clean" finish, like that on the UNESCO Headquarters in Paris. Upon being invited to build a hospital in the Cannaregio neighborhood of Venice (1962–5), **417** Le Corbusier undertook to verify the analysis he had made of that city in 1935, according to which "Venice [was] a perfectly conceived machine, a clever set of precision instruments, an accurate product of true human dimensions." ↦ 9 Respecting the city's "physiology," he used the branching grid of his project to reinterpret the Venetian network of *calli* (alleys), *fondamente* (quays), and *campielli* (small squares) in a master plan with multiple specialized levels accessible by boat. Efforts to continue the project after his death in 1965 were ultimately abandoned. ↦ 10

Corbusian mannerisms

Depending on the commission, Le Corbusier might invent a completely new approach or pick up on themes from his previous work, but whatever type, theme, or material texture resulted inevitably received widespread attention. Although vehemently criticized by Lewis Mumford and Frank Lloyd Wright, the Unité d'Habitation in Marseilles inspired many subsequent buildings, which often adjusted its scale up or down without achieving its complexity. The Greater London Council architects studied the *unité* typology in depth, and their housing blocks in Roehampton (1959) aspire

420 Park Hill Housing Estate, Lewis Womersley, Sheffield, United Kingdom, 1953–61

421 Siedlung Halen, Atelier 5, Bern, Switzerland, 1955–61

to be reductions of the Marseilles building. → 11 The huge slab built by Andrei Meerson's team on Begovaia Street in Moscow (1965–78) is one of several inflated variations on the theme. Many of the buildings in Berlin's Hansaviertel model housing district also derived from it, and Bernhard Hermkes adopted its basic principle in his design of the architecture department of Berlin's Technical University on Ernst-Reuter-Platz (1965–7).

The commission for the Paris Headquarters of UNESCO (1953–8), the cultural arm of the United Nations, was awarded to Marcel Breuer, Pier Luigi Nervi, and Bernard Zehrfuss after a battle lost by Le Corbusier. Yet the UNESCO design borrowed many of his ideas – notably, the use of *pilotis*, the free plan, and visible concrete. Nervi's overhanging canopies, shells, and folded concrete slab responded to the rather superficial interpretation of Corbusian themes that Breuer brought to the Y-shaped structure of the main building.

Elsewhere, a kind of coupling of the Unité d'Habitation with the *redent* facades of Corbusier's Ville Contemporaine spawned elevated streets that stretched from building to building. This is evident in Lewis Womersley's Park Hill Housing Estate (1953–61), **420** in Sheffield but also in the original center of the Le Mirail neighborhood built in Toulouse by Georges Candilis, Alexis Josic, and Shadrach Woods (1962–72). These variants, however unlike their original model, reinforced the idea that Le Corbusier was the prime source of all dense high-rise housing projects. His cascading Roq et Rob project was the inspiration for Atelier 5's Siedlung Halen (1955–61) **421** in Bern, a concrete housing development built in tiers on a hillside and centered on a small square. Halen would have significant reverberations throughout Europe. → 12 The French resort villages built on the Riviera by the Atelier de Montrouge at Cap Camarat (1963–5) and by the Atelier d'urbanisme et d'architecture in Gassin (1967–70) continued this line of

research, replicating Le Corbusier's Mediterranean barrel vaults. Le Corbusier's architecture was also disseminated by countless other architects who displaced, combined, and deformed his signature elements, much as Mannerist architects had done with Filippo Brunelleschi's and Leone Battista Alberti's forms in the early sixteenth century. *Pilotis* got larger and smaller in endless variations, while the *brise-soleil*, which Le Corbusier had originally developed in dialogue with Brazilian architects, became a kind of cliché of southern buildings. The sculptural rooftop elements of Chandigarh's Secretariat were reiterated by José Luís Sert at the Maeght Foundation (1958–71) **424** in Saint-Paul de Vence, and the sculptural forms of La Tourette and Ronchamp also inspired scores of projects around the world.

Anglo-American Brutalism

The third manifestation of late Corbusianism was literally a superficial phenomenon, predominantly concerned with surfaces. The rough textures of the Unité d'Habitation in Marseilles and of La Tourette, the former revealing the traces of its wood formwork and joints and the latter deliberately finished with a coarse grain, became a hallmark of modern architecture after World War II. The British New Brutalism, whose semantic origins are blurry – do they stem from *brut* (raw, rough) concrete, or from Brutus, Peter Smithson's nickname in the 1950s? – explored the use of industrial materials and bare finishings, exposing the evidence of concrete's formwork and pouring, and sometimes collaging discrepant materials. → 13 The first building that was claimed to be New Brutalist was Alison and Peter Smithson's Hunstanton Secondary School near Norfolk (1949–54). **425** While the starting point for the project was Mies van der Rohe's Minerals and Metals Research Building in Chicago, the Smithsons' building

422 Leicester Engineering Laboratories, James Stirling and James Gowan, Leicester, United Kingdom, 1959–63

423 Simon Fraser University, Arthur Erickson, Burnaby, Canada, 1963–5

425 ▶ Hunstanton Secondary School, Alison Smithson and Peter Smithson, Norfolk, United Kingdom, 1949–54

424 Maeght Foundation, José Luis Sert, Saint-Paul de Vence, France, 1958–71

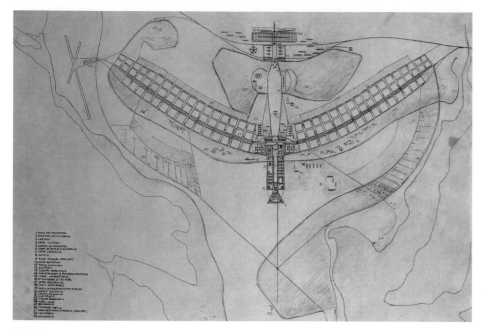

426   Pilot Plan, Lucio Costa, Brasília, Brazil, 1956

exposed its anatomy – steel structural members, glass and brick facades, roof trusses – which served as a backdrop for a dialogue between elements like sinks and radiators, whose pipework was also left visible. The critic Reyner Banham, a friend of the Smithsons, saw in their approach the premises of an "other architecture," an echo of the *art autre* (other art) put forward by the French critic Michel Tapié in 1952. → 14 Similarly combining vernacular sources and a technical aesthetic, James Stirling and James Gowan's residences in Ham Common (1955–8) and Colin St. John Wilson's extension to the Cambridge School of Architecture (1957–9) returned to the Corbusian dialectic of brick and concrete, recalibrating the balance of materials achieved by the Paris architect in his Jaoul Houses. Stirling's buildings erected on English campuses in the early 1960s continued to reflect his awareness of Le Corbusier's work but were also inspired by a rediscovery of Russian Constructivism. The University of Leicester's Engineering Labs (1959–63) **422** may be interpreted as a parody of the Dessau Bauhaus, with each volume adjusted to its specific function. But the English architect arrived at an entirely different level of complexity with his use of glass. The banal windows of the office tower serve as a counterpoint to the strip windows that illuminate the labs and to the extraordinary glass roof of the workshops, which echoes the diagonal pattern made by the rows of workers' housing on the edge of the campus. The building's handrails and air shafts brought ocean liner fetishism up to date in what Banham considered the first "world class" English building in many years. → 15 Stirling's subsequent Cambridge History Faculty (1964–7) is static in external appearance only. Its classrooms are divided between two perpendicular wings clad in brick, while the library, at the intersection of the two wings and covered in double-glass walls that expose the structure's ductwork,

is the institution's true center. Areas for group conversation and individual study are linked in a visual dialectic reinforced by the contrast of transparency and opacity. → 16

In the United States, Paul Rudolph used coarse textures in buildings that revisit methods invented by Auguste Perret and his contemporaries at the beginning of the century. → 17 Farther north, the Canadian architect Arthur Erickson used concrete in projects that operate on a grand scale, like the campus of Simon Fraser University 1963–7), **423** in Burnaby (or rely on symbolic elements, as in Vancouver's Museum of Anthropology (1971–4), which responds to Native American totems. → 18

The saga of Brasília

The biggest undertaking to carry forward many of Le Corbusier's ideas in the 1950s was undoubtedly the construction of Brasília, the new Brazilian capital, beginning in 1956. Here Corbusian concepts were applied at almost every level. Elected in 1954, President Juscelino Kubitschek resurrected the nineteenth-century idea of creating a "new Lisbon," a capital in the heart of the country. Selected after a public competition, Lucio Costa's simple "pilot plan" **426** resembles a distorted image of Le Corbusier's Ville Radieuse (Radiant City), the components of which are condensed, stretched, and rearranged into a basic figure resembling a bird. Brasília's wings consist of a 13-kilometer (8-mile) residential axis. This is intersected by a 6-kilometer (3.75-mile) monumental axis leading to the bird's "head," which consists of an equilateral triangle where the country's legislative, executive, and judiciary seats are concentrated.

These buildings were designed by Oscar Niemeyer. Despite the rhetorical effect of their elongation, they marked a shift to a somewhat more rationalist phase in the architect's career, at a

427 Superquadras Housing Blocks, Lucio Costa, Brasília, Brazil, 1960

time when he was reconsidering his approach. Regretting the excessive "originality" of his early work, Niemeyer declared that he was seeking greater simplicity by looking for the "beautiful, unhoped-for, and harmonious" forms made possible by modern technology. → 19 The axis at the heart of Brasília's pilot plan ends at the double verticals of the Secretariat, which dominates the interplay between the reversely curving domes of the Chamber of Deputies and the Senate. **428** The latter two buildings stand on a long platform, which seems to rise out of nowhere at the end of a lightly inclined passage along the Planalto, a plateau dominating a spacious landscape with an artificial lake as its horizon line. Visually connected to the Parliament, the Presidential Palace and the Supreme Court to its right mirror each other with porticoes featuring slender concrete members, on which Niemeyer collaborated with the engineer Joaquim Cardoso.

Both sides of the central axis are lined with the massive low-rise buildings of the ministries. Only the Itamaraty Palace, built for the Ministry of Foreign Affairs, was given special treatment: it is located at right angles to the other buildings, and its main structure – remarkable for its golden, swiveling *brise-soleil* – serves as a backdrop to a more solid block of offices and reception rooms fronted by an imposing concrete portico. Niemeyer also built the Cathedral (1959–70), a bundle of twenty-one concrete arches supporting a sky-lit atrium, the power of which is immediately evident upon entering the building through an underground ramp opening into a great circular room. Pursuing his search for forms specific to each program, Niemeyer went on to build the serpentine Federal University (1959–70), where pairs of classrooms are juxtaposed in two parallel sinuous lines facing a sequence of patios. During the interlude from 1964 to 1985 when Brazil was under military dictatorship, Niemeyer carried out previously approved projects and lost a commission to build

Brasília's airport. Afterward he continued to be awarded numerous projects into the beginning of the third millennium. Beyond the government center, the core of each of the city's "sectors" (the term over preferred over "zones" in Brasília) of twelve thousand inhabitants comprises four *superquadras*. **427** These contain housing complexes designed by Costa and conceived in the spirit of the neighborhood unit, the concept of which was brought to Brazil by José Luís Sert and Paul Lester Wiener in their project for the Cidade dos Motores (City of Motors; 1942–7). The buildings consist of six-story slabs on *pilotis*, roughly as tall as the buildings of Haussmann's Paris (as Costa pointed out), and without the streets in the air of their Corbusian model. Grouped in pairs with their rear facades facing each other and openwork walls reprising the theme of Costa's Park Guinle in Rio de Janeiro, they float above uninterrupted pedestrian walkways planted with trees. The sectors are subdivided by short shopping streets, while the rows of residential buildings along their periphery resemble the *Siedlungen* of Frankfurt transported to a tropical landscape. A hierarchical system of thoroughfares reserved for automobiles interconnects the sectors of this city of private transportation.

Brazil's new capital was inaugurated on April 24, 1960. Throughout its realization, construction work went on twenty-four hours a day. The project employed sixty thousand workers, most of whom would remain after the city was completed. It was for them that a string of "satellite cities," including Taguatinga, Nucleo Bandeirantes, Sobradinho, Planaltina, and Paranoa, were developed around the pilot plan. With the passage of time, what was intended to be an autonomous and self-sufficient city has become the administrative center and elite neighborhood at the heart of a sprawling urban area. The people of Brasília remain deeply attached to it, refuting the predictions of its strongest critics. → 20

The shape of American hegemony

429 Lever House, Gordon Bunshaft
for SOM, New York City, USA, 1950–2

430 ▶ Planning the United Nations
Building: Wallace K. Harrison,
Le Corbusier and Vladimir Bodiansky
(left to right) in front of one of the
models, New York City, USA, 1947

While the rest of the world was drained of its resources, the
United States came out of World War II as a creditor to most
of the combatants, holding an unprecedented amount of economic and symbolic power. Thanks to the general admiration for
American technology and culture and to the effect of U.S. foreign
policies, the appreciation of American culture that had prevailed
during previous decades now fed into a more or less potent
process of Americanization, as countries were transformed
by American cultural models and capital. [1] But in the United
States itself, the hopes for a continuation of the kind of socially
oriented policies that had characterized the Depression and the
war years were dashed. With the Cold War and McCarthyism,
progressive and dissident voices in the field of architecture were
silenced and public housing programs were sometimes suspended; in Los Angeles, such programs were brought to a halt
after being denounced as Communist inspired. [2]

The second skyscraper age

After a hiatus of two decades, skyscrapers reappeared on
Manhattan's skyline in the early 1950s. The first building project to symbolize American hegemony to the world was the
Headquarters of the United Nations, an institution created by
the Allies in 1945. The following year an international advisory
committee was established under the direction of Wallace K.
Harrison, composed of Le Corbusier, Josef Havliček, Oscar
Niemeyer, Ernest Cormier, Sven Markelius, and Max Abramovitz
(as Harrison's assistant). **430** Once the Rockefellers donated a
site along New York's East River, the team got down to work.
The committee ended up adopting Niemeyer's project, which
was based on a scheme by Le Corbusier, who was offended
in turn by what he felt was insufficient recognition of his

contribution. [3] Harrison designed the details of the office tower
as well as the low-rise General Assembly Building (1948–52).
No newcomer to the New York scene, Harrison was able to
win other significant commissions as well. He built the Alcoa
Building in Pittsburgh (1949–53) **437** with Abramovitz and Oscar
Nitzchké, creating the first curtain wall made of aluminum panels. Its rounded windows, punched into the panels and similar to those used in railroad cars, made the skyscraper look
like a stack of television sets. MoMA's curator Arthur Drexler
described the play of light across these panels, which were
stamped with a lozenge pattern, as "a shifting diagonal movement" giving the building "a sculptural interest reminiscent of,
say, the rustications of the Czernin Palace in Prague." [4]
The modern office building found one of its first West Coast
incarnations in Pietro Belluschi's Equitable Building in Portland,
Oregon (1944–8) – the first anywhere to be fully air conditioned. [5] The firm of Skidmore, Owings and Merrill (SOM) also
played a key role in the development of the postwar office building. With Gordon Bunshaft as chief designer, SOM built Lever
House (1950–2) **429** on New York's Park Avenue. The building
broke with the principle of setbacks mandated by the zoning
regulations of 1916 and established a new norm with a rectangular tower standing asymmetrically on a low plinth occupying the entire area of the site. The lightness of its glass facade
and the airiness of its interior volumes made it the prototype
for a new generation of modern open workplaces. With Natalie
de Blois's more modest building for Pepsi-Cola (1956–60), the
"Park Avenue School of Architecture" ushered in what critic Ada
Louise Huxtable described as nothing less than a "a post-war
miracle." [6] SOM also built the five-story Manufacturers Hanover
Bank Building on Fifth Avenue, with an entirely glazed facade
that made it into a giant light box when illuminated at night. Park

431 Minerals and Metals Research Building, Illinois Institute of Technology, Ludwig Mies van der Rohe with Holabird and Root, Chicago, Illinois, USA, 1942–3

432 Farnsworth House, Ludwig Mies van der Rohe, Plano, Illinois, USA, 1945–51

433 Apartment Buildings, 860–880 Lake Shore Drive, Ludwig Mies van der Rohe, Chicago, Illinois, USA, 1948–51

Avenue was also the site of the next significant reconceptualization of the office building when Mies van der Rohe, collaborating with Philip Johnson, put up the Seagram Building (1954–8) there. Located diagonally across from Lever House, it culminated thirty years of thought that began in Germany with Mies's theoretical projects for glass skyscrapers and a concrete office building.

Mies the American

On the campus of the Illinois Institute of Technology (IIT), Mies was responsible not only for the master plan of 1940–1, laid out on a strict spatial module, but also for several significant buildings that used a language derived from German industrial architecture. The first, the Minerals and Metals Research Building (1942–3), **431** defined the language of steel elements and brick or glass infill for almost all those that followed. His Alumni Memorial Hall (1945–6) was remarkable for its elegant metallic staircase and for the corner treatment of its steel frame. Projects for a library and an administrative building never got off the drawing board. Mies also developed in the early 1940s his vision of large, flowing spaces in projects for a Museum for a Small City and for a concert hall, in which the play of freestanding planes defined the space. His Farnsworth House (1945–51) **432** in Plano, Illinois, was the prototype for a transparent pavilion entirely open to the landscape. Enveloped in the largest panes of plate glass then available, it was supported by steel I-beams. For the first time, Mies placed the vertical supports outside the building volume, accentuating the impression that the house was levitating. Using the same principle of a space free of any internal supports, he built Crown Hall, a 120-by-220-foot (36.6-by-67-meter) rectangular box on IIT's campus; he considered it "the clearest structure we have done, the best to express our philosophy." [7]

Starting in the 1940s Mies constantly refined and designed, along with the large space free of any interior supports, variations on one other type of building: the high-rise with a steel frame. After using exposed concrete to build the Promontory Apartments in Chicago (1946–9), he returned to that city to put up his first two towers with steel structures and aluminum-and-glass facades, at 860–880 Lake Shore Drive (1948–51). **433** With his neighboring complex at 900–910 Lake Shore Drive (1953–6), it was the first convincing formulation of the concept of the high-rise apartment building in steel and glass, and it would be reproduced in many subsequent buildings. Yet Mies succeeded in building only one entire neighborhood, Lafayette Park in Detroit (1955–60), with a master plan designed by Ludwig Hilberseimer and landscape design by Alfred Caldwell. The towers of this residential project for the upper middle class were complemented by row houses and patio units. The Seagram Building (1954–8) **434** was an indisputable landmark in the development of the skyscraper. Rather than building it out to the edge of Park Avenue and using the entire area of the block, Mies chose to set it in the middle of the lot, providing a new type of urban plaza. The brown facades are particularly complex, offering the city a dark reflection of itself. Subdivided by bronze mullions, the glass curtain wall stops at the corners, where the vertical supports are enveloped in a concrete crust covered with steel. Uncharacteristically positive in respect to a skyscraper, Lewis Mumford wrote: "Out of the surrounding stalled, rush-hour clutter of new structures, brightly sordid, meretriciously up-to-date, the Seagram building has emerged like a Rolls Royce accompanied by a motorcycle escort." [8] The building's aura extended far beyond New York, to the point that it joined Le Corbusier's Unité d'Habitation as one of the architectural types most often imitated – and most misunderstood and cheapened – during the postwar era.

435 New National Gallery, Ludwig Mies van der Rohe, West Berlin, Federal Republic of Germany, 1962–8

434 Seagram Building, Ludwig Mies van der Rohe, with Philip Johnson, New York City, USA, 1954–8

With his Federal Center (1959–64) and later IBM Regional Headquarters (1966–9) Mies brought his industrial-order architecture to the Chicago skyline. The Toronto-Dominion Center in Toronto (1963–9) and the Westmount Square complex in Montreal (1965–9) demonstrate the urban potential of this aesthetic in their combination of towers with clear horizontal volumes. [9] He continued his work on large spatial containers, reaching a culmination with the New National Gallery in West Berlin (1962–8), **435** a symbol of his recovered prestige in Germany. The thousand-ton steel plate of its roof, which was raised in a single operation, is attached to eight perimeter columns with pin joints reminiscent of those in Peter Behrens's Turbine Factory. This great pavilion accomplished Mies's lifelong ambition: to achieve the vast scale and visual unity of the Gothic cathedral.

Wright's last return

As Le Corbusier had done with his chapel of Ronchamp, Frank Lloyd Wright unsettled his staunchest supporters with his Solomon R. Guggenheim Museum, **436** which he began working on in 1943 but which was not completed until 1959, after his death. An "inverted ziggurat" in Wright's own description, the museum has a white concrete shell that stands out against Manhattan's predominantly brick background. Its interior is traversed by a spiral ramp like the one Wright used in his V. C. Morris Shop in San Francisco (1949). The galleries' steep slope and unaccommodating curves led Franz Kline, Willem de Kooning, Robert Motherwell, and other artists to deplore the loss of a "rectilinear frame of reference" for the art on view there and to reject the structure as "not suitable for a sympathetic display of painting and sculpture." [10]

Wright continued to work late in his career on the idea of Broadacre City. Invigorated by the sight of multiplying American suburbs, he did not hesitate to claim paternity for them, telling Alvar Aalto on one occasion while driving the Finnish architect around the outskirts of Boston: " 'Unity in diversity': All this I have made possible." [11] Renaming his scheme "The Living City," he updated it in the mid-1950s to incorporate new technical developments and redid the drawings in a postwar graphic idiom. He also built variations on the principle of his Usonian houses, using triangular or circular geometries, as in the Friedman House in Pleasantville, New York (1950), which represents a tiny embryo of the overall project.

Striving for the sensational, Wright proposed a mile-high skyscraper for Chicago in 1956, but he actually built only two modest high-rises during his career: the Johnson Wax Administrative Building in Racine, Wisconsin (1936–9), notable for its concrete core, cantilevered floors, and double-height offices; and Price Tower in Bartlesville, Oklahoma (1955), a belated realization of his 1929 project for St. Mark's-in-the-Bouwerie in New York. These two buildings stood in vivid contrast to the orthogonal geometry and delicate tectonics adopted by Mies and, even more, to the frame structures favored by SOM. The Marin County Civic Center in San Rafael, California (1959–62), completed after Wright's death, was one of his rare public buildings among the roughly 430 structures he realized in a career spanning more than seventy years. [12] It was also one of the strangest – a long structure stretching across a rolling landscape of small valleys like a Roman aqueduct, combining Oriental touches and details seemingly borrowed from science-fiction comics. Wright's practice was carried forward in North America by the dozens of "apprentices" he had trained, while his discourse of organic architecture found its European agent and proselytizer in the tireless Bruno Zevi.

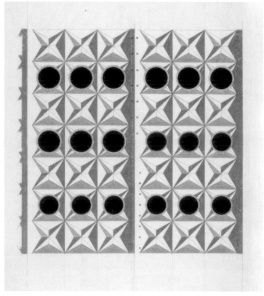

436 Solomon R. Guggenheim Museum, Frank Lloyd Wright, New York City, USA, 1943–59

437 Alcoa Building, Wallace K. Harrison, Max Abramovitz and Oscar Nitzchké, Pittsburgh, Pennsylvania, USA, 1949–53

Research out west

Wright's approach was carried on in the California houses of his son, Lloyd, whose major work is the Wayfarers Chapel (1949–51) **438** in Palos Verdes, near Los Angeles, with a glass nave that seems to merge with the surrounding trees. Bruce Goff's surprising structures throughout the Midwest, often built with salvaged materials, were an original extension of the individualism at the heart of Wright's Usonian houses. Wright's work was also the starting point for the Los Angeles projects of his former apprentice John Lautner, whose technical prowess and geometrical inventiveness gave each of his houses a unique aspect. Having served as Wright's assistant on the Sturges House (1939), with its large cantilevered deck hovering above a hillside, Lautner maintained the same sense of dynamism in the three suspended cylindrical forms of his Sheats Apartments in Westwood (1949). With Silvertop (1957) and the Garcia House (also known as the Rainbow House, 1962), he displayed a lyrical approach that exploits the potential of thin concrete shells. The strange Malin House, or Chemosphere (1960), **442** commissioned by an aeronautical engineer, looks like a flying saucer perched on a tall column. → 13

The dominant architect in postwar Southern California was Richard Neutra, whose international stature was such that in 1946 the first postwar monographic issue of *L'Architecture d'aujourd'hui* was dedicated to him. According to Marcel Lods, Neutra's work was the essence of "freshness, novelty, originality," and the man himself embodied nothing less than the "architect of today." → 14 Neutra's new directions were summed up in three important buildings. The cruciform plan of the single-story Tremaine House in Montecito, California (1946–50), **441** exemplified what remained the fundamental compositional device

in his projects: a rather simple longitudinal space facing in a single direction, which could be reoriented using similar spatial elements into a variety of different compositions. Openness to the outside bordered on total porosity in the spectacular house he built in 1946 in Palm Springs, California, for Edgar Kaufmann, Jr., **439** who had previously commissioned Wright's Fallingwater. This "desert house," sheathed in glass from floor to ceiling, suggested a hedonistic lifestyle in the open air and became world renowned through Julius Shulman's photographs. With the Moore House in Ojai, California (1952), Neutra created a landscape based on the play of water and glass. In each of his projects, he sought to develop a personal relationship with his clients, contributing the knowledge of psychoanalysis he had gained from his friendships with his former classmate Ernst Freud (son of Sigmund) and Wilhelm Reich. → 15 Neutra's domestic architecture was disseminated far beyond the United States – probably farther than that of any other American architect – both through his own projects around the world and through imitations in Latin America, North Africa, and Europe. In Los Angeles, Neutra participated in the Case Study House program launched by John Entenza's magazine *California Arts and Architecture*. From 1945 to 1962, twenty-four innovative houses were built as part of the program, each expressing the victory of the new taste for transparency and industrial materials. In the shade of the eucalyptus trees of Pacific Palisades, Charles Eames, who had been taught by Eliel Saarinen at Cranbrook Academy in Michigan, and his wife Ray built House #8 (1945–9), **440** the first genuine architectural manifesto of postwar Los Angeles. Divided into two boxes devoted to a studio and living space respectively, the Eames House is like an étagère enlarged to the scale of a house and opened to the exterior, a kind of ready-made of preexisting steel components.

438 Wayfarers Chapel, Lloyd Wright, Palos Verdes, California, USA, 1949–51

439 Kaufmann House, Richard Neutra, Palm Springs, California, USA, 1946, photograph by Julius Schulman

441 Tremaine House, Richard Neutra, Montecito, California, USA, 1946–50

440 Eames House (Case Study House #8), Charles Eames and Ray Eames, Pacific Palisades, California, USA, 1945–9

442 Malin House (Chemosphere), John Lautner, Los Angeles, California, USA, 1960

With Eero Saarinen, the Eameses also built House #9 (1949), intended for John Entenza himself, on a nearby lot. Neutra designed several Case Study houses; #20, the Bailey House (1947–48), a few steps from the Eames and Entenza houses, is made of brick and wood. The Case Study program introduced several locally trained architects, among them Craig Ellwood, who built House #16 in Bel Air (1952–3) and #17 in Beverly Hills (1954–5), using a seemingly weightless framework of slender steel components and thin panels and playing on the contrast between solid boxes and open patios. Shulman's photographs would also immortalize the image of the houses designed by Pierre Koenig, the youngest of the program's architects. His House #21, located in the Hollywood Hills (1958), consists of a skillfully put-together assembly of commercially available steel elements floating visually in a body of water. His House #22 (1959–60), which cantilevers over the Hollywood palisade, creates a duality between its picturesque entry from above and the sublime view to which it opens out over the endless grid of the city. → 16

Gropius and Breuer: the assimilation of the Bauhaus

Walter Gropius, active on the East Coast of the United States, played a role far different from that of Neutra. His contribution, founded on a mythical history of the Bauhaus (of which he was the principal propagator), was more methodological than architectural. With The Architects Collaborative (TAC), founded in 1945, he created a model for collective work, the first project of which was the Harvard University Graduate Center (1950). A complex of buildings clustered around courtyards and reiterating the established pattern of the campus, it introduced a

vocabulary of ramps and *pilotis* that clearly stood out from the nineteenth-century structures by Charles Bulfinch and Henry Hobson Richardson. From then on TAC worked on major projects such as the urban renewal of Boston's Back Bay (1953) and the University of Baghdad (1957), one of the first exemplars of an orientalizing modernist kitsch, a style that would meet with great success in the Middle East. In New York, TAC collaborated with Emery Roth Associates and Pietro Belluschi to build the Grand Central City Building (1958–63) – subsequently known as Pan Am after its airline company owner, then as MetLife – which borrowed heavily from Le Corbusier's skyscraper for Algiers. The building was widely criticized for brutally closing off the perspective down Park Avenue. Invited to Germany, Gropius built social housing in Berlin and, most significant, the modular whitish volumes of the Bauhausarchiv (1964–76), a building devoted to conserving the relics of his glory years. → 17

Marcel Breuer, Gropius's associate at the beginning of their American period, developed a more expressive approach. His houses differed markedly from Neutra's in their more solid appearance and in the way they invited their inhabitants to gather around a focal fireplace. They sometimes included audacious elements, such as the cantilevered floors and balcony of Breuer's own residence in New Canaan, Connecticut (1947–8). After his UNESCO Headquarters in the center of Paris, the buildings he put up in less urban areas, including the IBM Research Center in La Gaude, near Nice (1960–70), which looks ready to rear up on its legs and stalk away, responded strongly to the natural landscape. The Flaine Ski Resort (1960–9) features a starker play of contrasts, opposing the right angles of its volumes to the curvaceous Alpine slopes. In contrast, the Whitney Museum of American Art in New York (1963–6) **443** is introverted, inserting an alien modernist object – an opaque

444 TWA Terminal, Idlewild (John F. Kennedy) Airport, Eero Saarinen, Queens, New York City, USA, 1957–62

443 Whitney Museum of American Art, Marcel Breuer, New York City, USA, 1963–6

stack of cubes pierced by odd-shaped windows – into a genteel neighborhood. In the facade rhythms of his major projects as well as the materiality of the Whitney, Breuer explored the varied possibilities of exposed concrete. [18]

Saarinen's lyricism and Johnson's anxiety

Eero Saarinen's career, which abruptly ended with his early death in 1961, was characterized by buildings that each proposed a unique and powerful idea, taking into account function, overall image, and structural invention. After beginning his career working with his father Eliel, he designed the General Motors Technical Center in Warren, Michigan (1948–56), as an upbeat campus where offices and lab buildings with steel structures were disposed around a large lake and brought to life by vividly colored glazed brick. The potential value to major corporations of building monumental complexes was confirmed by Saarinen's office headquarters for the tractor manufacturer John Deere in Moline, Illinois (1957–63). The slab construction utilizes COR-TEN steel for the first time, exploiting its rusty, weathered coloration against the pastoral green of the landscape. At the Massachusetts Institute of Technology, Saarinen juxtaposed two ideas: Kresge Auditorium (1950–5) is a thin-shell structure resting on three points – the very embodiment of lightweight construction, like an "eighth of an orange," in Saarinen's description – while the adjacent chapel (1952–4) is a solid cylinder of brick into which sunlight is directed through an oculus so as to strike the altar vertically, evoking the theatrical devices of Gianlorenzo Bernini in Baroque Rome. These two contradictory orientations – light and heavy – would determine Saarinen's major projects. Among his other light-weight structures were the thin barrel vaults of the TWA

Terminal (1957–62) **444** at Idlewild (now John F. Kennedy) Airport in New York. In 1959 he wrote that he intended the architecture of this terminal to be not just "distinctive and memorable" among the others at Idlewild, but also a "place of movement and of transition," "a building in which the architecture itself would express the drama and specialness and excitement of travel." [19] His terminal at Dulles Airport, near Washington, D.C., has a cable-supported roof that evokes the pitch of an airplane wing and looks ready to lift the building off the ground. Among his more solid structures are the Ezra Stiles and Samuel Morse colleges at Yale (1958–62), **445** a labyrinthine complex evoking Italian hill towns, and the granite-covered "black rock" of the CBS Tower in New York (1960–4), in which he rejected glass curtain walls to return to the idea of a concrete load-bearing facade, as expressive as it is thick. [20]

A diversity of responses to specific functional and symbolic programs was also characteristic of the work of Philip Johnson, who followed architectural shifts more than he generated them. His work often appeared an anxious reaction to the new paradigms emerging around him. The Glass House he built for himself in New Canaan, Connecticut (1949), was an effete echo of Mies's Farnsworth House as well as a frontal and static one. It does not achieve Mies's sophisticated three-dimensional play despite the fact that it is built on a more spectacular site, dominating an idyllic valley. Johnson would erect a series of playful pavilions on his property at regular intervals, like an eighteenth-century British aristocrat building temples and pagodas. Responding anxiously as well as methodically to architecture's successive changes in orientation he would cast a long shadow over the American profession as well as its cultural institutions. [21]

445 Ezra Stiles and Samuel Morse colleges, Yale University, Eero Saarinen, New Haven, Connecticut, USA, 1958–62

446 Richards Medical Research Laboratories, University of Pennsylvania, Louis Kahn, Philadelphia, Pennsylvania, USA, 1957–60

In 1954 Johnson distanced himself from the precepts of functionalism in a lecture whose title alluded to John Ruskin's *Seven Lamps of Architecture* (1849). The "seven crutches of modern architecture," he argued, were history, "pretty drawing," utility or usefulness, comfort, cheapness, service to the client, and structure. → 22 In his professional practice, he gravitated to a lightweight classicism, as in his boxlike Kneses Tifereth Synagogue in Port Chester, New York (1954), which is bathed in colored light but could hardly be further from Le Corbusier's contemporary Ronchamp. His contribution to the performing arts complex at Lincoln Center in Manhattan, the overall plan of which was coordinated by Wallace K. Harrison, was the New York State Theater (1964), a drab volume with concrete columns; its principal attribute is a vast four-story foyer. The Kline Biology Tower at Yale (1962–5) is probably Johnson's most original building of the period. Like Saarinen's CBS Building, it returns solidity and tectonic power to the skyscraper, with brick cladding covering both the pilasters at the top of the building and the columns at its base.

The solitude of Kahn

Unlike most of his contemporaries, Louis Kahn was preoccupied with architecture's relationship to history. Although active in Philadelphia since the 1930s, he was the most conspicuous American architect to emerge in the 1950s. A student of Paul Philippe Cret, he had been an associate of George Howe and Oscar Storonov before designing his first major building, the Yale University Art Gallery (1951–3). Its floor levels are discreetly marked on the blank exterior brick surface with horizontal stone coursing, while inside the ceiling and floor-slab system consists of hollow concrete tetrahedrons that accommodate the buildings' utilities. The structural span allows for the partitions to be freely

rearranged within the galleries, while the stairs are enclosed in solid concrete volumes. The differentiation between the "served" rooms and their "servant," or subordinate, spaces – a principle derived from Julien-Azaïs Guadet's theories – is resolved clearly and compactly. This differentiation would become one of the cornerstones of Kahn's discourse, along with his idea of "order" and his insistence on the civic value of public buildings. → 23 The Richards Medical Research Laboratories (1957–60), **446** a biology center built on the campus of the University of Pennsylvania in Philadelphia, was an evocation of the towers of the medieval French city of Carcassonne, which Kahn particularly admired. Made of precast and prestressed concrete elements, the building was designed in collaboration with the engineer August Komendant; born in Estonia like Kahn, Komendant had designed innovative structures in Tallinn in the 1930s. The "served" spaces of the labs contrast with the "servant" spaces of the brick towers, which contain both staircases and utilities. The Richards Center marked a decisive turning point both in campus architecture and in Kahn's career, leading to Kahn's commission by Jonas Salk, developer of the polio vaccine, to build his institute in La Jolla, California in 1959–65. **449** Here the served spaces are the open expanses of the laboratory floors, which alternate with the servant floors through which the utilities pass. The scientists' studies, which are separated from the labs and staggered with them in level, appear opaque from outside but have an angled view of the Pacific Ocean. The Institute seems to reach out to this distant horizon as its two symmetrical wings face each other on either side of a travertine-covered esplanade like temples on a Greek acropolis. Visitors approaching from the direction of the city enter through an orange grove. The stone and unfinished concrete of the walls and the teak woodwork weathered by the sea breezes give the

447 Kimbell Art Museum, Louis Kahn, Fort Worth, Texas, USA, 1967–72

448 Indian Institute of Management, Louis Kahn, Ahmedabad, India, 1962–74

449 ▶ Salk Institute for Biological Studies, Louis Kahn, La Jolla, California, USA, 1959–65

overall complex a material texture on which time seems to have had nothing but poetic effects. With its orthogonal volumes and restrained geometry, the Salk Institute appears more than any other of Kahn's buildings to establish a dialogue with the emerging work of the Minimalist artists, even if Kahn did not necessarily share their theoretical views on art.

At the Kimbell Art Museum in Fort Worth, Texas (1967–72), Kahn collaborated again with Komendant to integrate support, lighting, and technical systems into the building's structure. **447** Daylight enters the space through slits at the apexes of the museum's self-supporting elliptical barrel vaults, then is reflected against the underside of the vaults by suspended troughs holding light fixtures. Thanks to the limited number of columns, the space from one gallery to the next is totally fluid, allowing diagonal views that create visual relationships relating the works of art to each other. The walls are faced with travertine, and on the entrance side the vaults become porticoes that interact with the surrounding trees to offer soothing shade to visitors.

The campus of the Indian Institute of Management in Ahmedabad has a far more complex composition. **448** Built with the support of the Ford Foundation in 1962–74, its elaborate master plan clusters classrooms and student residences around the library through an intricate play of modular elements and axes. Brick is the dominant material. Reinforced concrete, which was more expensive, is used only sparingly, for the elements in tension, which paradoxically are framed on the facades as if they were ornamental. Kahn's practice of treating the joints between materials as both functional and decorative was never clearer than in this project. In East Pakistan, which became the country of Bangladesh in 1971, Kahn put up the Parliament Building, his most ambitious public edifice, in the capital, Dhaka, in 1962–74. The main assembly chamber has an octagonal plan: it is

surrounded with passageways, then a series of concrete boxes and cylinders used as offices and meeting rooms. Partly covered in marble, these volumes have openings that allow beams of light to filter into the building, which Kahn compared to a many-faceted precious stone.

From experimentation to commerce

For a moment the quality of Kahn's work seemed to be equaled by that of his contemporary Paul Rudolph. Educated at Harvard in an architecture department entirely dedicated to modernism, Rudolph began his career in Florida with designs that play with elementary structural principles, like the Healy Guest House cottage in Sarasota (1948–50). In his subsequent senior high school for the same city (1957–9), he used concrete in thin folded planes. Like Kahn, Rudolph continued to work in concrete, but tried every means he could think of to make his surfaces "interesting." Many of his buildings are on campuses, among them the Jewett Arts Center at Wellesley College (1956–8) in Massachusetts, which features an ingenious interplay of concrete and brick. In New Haven, he handled both a housing complex for Yale's married students (1958–61) and Crawford Manor (1962–6), a residence for the elderly, with an acute sculptural sense, playing with a set of gesturally projecting elements. This approach would be widely publicized – and roundly criticized by Robert Venturi. Built across from Kahn's gallery, the powerful verticality and rather hostile facades of Yale's Art and Architecture Building (1959–63) belie the interesting relationships between the different levels in the building's interior. Damaged by fire in 1968 (and restored in 2008), the interior spaces gave the institution an unexpectedly amiable personality.

The American architectural scene was not limited to the work of
recognized and inventive professionals. In the two decades that
followed the war, the country was profoundly transformed by the
forces of both modernization and suburban sprawl. The
horizontal expansion of cities resulted from the popularity of the
automobile and especially from the passage of the G.I. Bill of
Rights in 1944, which made it possible for millions of returning
American soldiers to buy houses. The opening of this significant market, which launched builders such as Levitt on the East
Coast and, a little later, Kauffman & Broad in the West, resulted
in the vulgarization and ultimately demise of the garden city
model. Increased commerce was responsible for metastasizing
supermarkets, motels, and gas stations lining roads and highways. Yet repetition and aesthetic mediocrity were not inevitable.
At the Northland Shopping Center (1952–4) **450** in Detroit, Victor
Gruen built the prototype of the large shopping mall: a box
accessible from large highways in the middle of a huge parking
lot. Gruen built variations on the type, including some that were
even more enclosed and isolated, such as his air-conditioned
Southdale Center in Minneapolis (1952–6), but which occasionally led to complex and surprising solutions. →24 Morris Lapidus,
on the other hand, built hedonistic hotels like the Fontainebleau
(1954) on the beaches of Miami, updating the architecture of
tourism to flaunt an ostentatious but playful modernism. →25
American architecture was spread through the trade magazines
and other media communicating the images of these buildings
around the world. In addition, it circulated through the official
architecture of government embassies as well as unofficial networks like the Hilton Hotel chain, which from Havana to Istanbul
gave a tangible – and at the time often locally detested – form to
the economic and cultural expansion of the United States. →26

Repression and diffusion of modernism

451 Residential High-Rise Building, Dmitri Chechulin and Andrei Rostkovsky, Moscow, USSR (Russia), 1948–53, as shown on the cover of *L'Union Soviétique,* 1953

The breaking of ground in Brasília coincided with Nikita Khrushchev's secret speech to the Twentieth Congress of the Communist Party in Moscow condemning Stalinism, which had an immediate impact on Eastern European architecture. Whether promoted in Brazil thanks to the energy of a new president or rediscovered in Russia after twenty years of eclipse, modern architecture never severed its intimate ties with politics. After 1948 the Soviet Union had imposed socialist realism on the art and architecture of all the countries now under its power; they, in turn, applied those precepts with varying and short-lived enthusiasm. → 1 In the USSR, where reconstruction of the European part of the country went on long after the war, the compromises made with the Constructivists in the mid-1930s had been forgotten, and historicism ruled unchallenged. Columns, cornices, and capitals were standardized and prefabricated, while industrialization in architecture remained marginal. This reaction contrasted with the dominant postwar phenomena elsewhere in the world, where strong personal interpretations of modernist principles reigned.

Seven Sisters in Moscow

In 1948 the Moscow government decided to erect "tall buildings" – not "skyscrapers," since that term was considered capitalist – in order to create a new urban skyline around Boris Iofan's Palace of Soviets, the protracted construction of which was, in fact, soon to be abandoned. Although the campaign against "cosmopolitanism" and Western values was operating at full force, the project's chief technical adviser, Vyacheslav Oltarzhevsky, who had lived in New York between the wars, distanced himself from his American experience and insisted that in a city like Moscow, which was immune from the pressures of the real-estate market, there could be a "free composition" of buildings throughout the urban fabric, without consideration for the "exasperated capitalist competition." → 2 Dmitri Chechulin coordinated the construction of six of the "Seven Sisters," as they are known in the West, at strategic points in Moscow: the Ukraina and Leningradskaia hotels plus two residential buildings on Kotelnicheskaia Embankment, **451** the Ministry of Foreign Affairs on Smolenskaia Square, and Vosstaniia Square, and a mixed-used building for offices and residences at the Krasnie Vorota metro stop. Plans for another building to be erected at Zariadie, next to the Kremlin, were abandoned. This network of towers built along a curve roughly following the Garden Ring was supplemented by Lev Rudnev's State University, a monolithic block that was relegated to the southwest of the city, where it stood isolated and became the dominant element in a new neighborhood already envisioned in the 1935 plan. Although these buildings – built in part by German prisoners – had steel frames, their stone and terracotta cladding and some of their sculptured ornamentation evoked pre-1914 New York skyscrapers like McKim, Mead and White's Municipal Building; meanwhile their spires referred to those atop the historical edifices of Saint Petersburg. Similar spires soon appeared in other countries of the socialist bloc, to which the Soviet "big brother" exported the Moscow model of tall buildings: Rudnev built the Palace of Culture in Warsaw (1952–5); František Jerabek, the International Hotel in Prague (1953–9); and Horia Maicu, the Casa Scînteii in Bucharest (1950–6). Hans Hopp's project for East Berlin remained on the drawing board, but the idea of a dominant structure in the city center led to the awkward Palace of the Republic, built in the 1970s.

453 Beijing Exhibition Center, Dai Nianci, Mao Ziyao and Zhou Yongyuan, Beijing, China, 1954

452 House for Collective Services, Václav Hilsky and Evžen Linhart, Litvínov, Czechoslovakia (Czech Republic), 1946–8

Socialist realism exported

The USSR exercised its hegemony by example, organizing study trips for professionals from the various "people's republics." This approach extended to urban planning, with the creation of new cities associated with industrial complexes, including Stalinstadt in East Germany, Sztálinvaros in Hungary, Nowa Huta in Poland, and Dimitrovgrad in Bulgaria. The new cities' plans were based on a system of closed blocks and grandiose thoroughfares – for example, Kurt W. Leucht's Leninallee in Stalinstadt. [3] In Czechoslovakia, the rejection of modern architecture was less extreme than elsewhere, no doubt because the heads of the state architectural agency, which was established in 1946 to operate on a national scale, had formerly been functionalists. The agency's first director was Jiři Voženilek, who had previously worked for Bat'a as an urban planner. Josef Havliček's residential towers in Kladno-Rozdelov (1952) and Václav Hilsky and Evžen Linhart's House for Collective Services (1946–8) **452** in Litvínov carried the experiments of the 1930s into the 1950s. New neighborhoods were created in the Czechoslovak towns of Ostrava, Nová Dubnica, and Poruba, crossing Scandinavian precedents with the classical compositional principles of *sorela*, or socialist realism. The primary exponent of *sorela* was the former modernist Jiři Kroha, who studied traditional rural homes to find motifs that could be used in the new developments.

In East Berlin, Richard Paulick returned from China to build the Deutsche Sporthalle, the city's first socialist realist building (1950–1), while Hermann Henselmann's housing on the Weberwiese (1951–2) used a historicist language in which certain references to Karl Friedrich Schinkel could be identified. The Hungarians often used architectural elements borrowed from northern European traditionalists, as with Gyula Rimanóczy's

buildings in Várpalota (1953). In Sztálinvaros, where the former Bauhaus student Tibor Weiner worked after having lived in the Soviet Union and Chile, the city hall combines Venetian-inspired elements and a belfry with Slavic accents.

After Mao Zedong's victory in 1949, architecture in the People's Republic of China exemplified both the continuation of Beaux-Arts methods and the application of principles imported from the USSR. A debate over Beijing's new city center developed between the views of Liang Ssu Ch'eng – a graduate of the Beaux-Arts pedagogy at the University of Pennsylvania, who had nonetheless built modernist buildings such as the student residence at the University of Beijing (1935) – and those of Léon Hoa, a former student at the Paris Beaux-Arts and of André Lurçat. Hoa's ideas carried the day: the seat of power was built not outside the historical city but at the very gates of the Forbidden City on Tiananmen Square. [4] Buildings of the 1950s such as Zhang Bo's Friendship Hotel (1954) and Cheng Dengao's government complex in Beihai (1955) were built on Beaux-Arts plans but topped with the Chinese-style tiled "big roofs" characteristic of this idiom. Other buildings were erected in a more literal Soviet spirit, like the Beijing Exhibition Center (1954) **453** by Dai Nianci, Mao Ziyao, and Zhou Yongyuan. [5] A slightly modernized language was employed later in the decade in two massive buildings on Tiananmen Square: Zhang Bo's Hall of the People (1958) and Zhang Kaiji's Museum of the Revolution (1959).

Khrushchev's critique

In December 1954, barely a year after Stalin's death, Nikita Khrushchev used architecture as a pretext to launch an attack on his predecessor's "cult of personality." Prompted by the architect Georgi Gradov, he denounced the "excesses" of tall

454 Novye Cheremushki Housing, Moscow, USSR (Russia), 1956

455 Palace of Pioneers, Viktor Egerev, Valery Kubasov, Felix Novikov, et al., Moscow, USSR (Russia), 1959–62

456 ▶ Säynätsalo Town Hall, Alvar Aalto, Säynätsalo, Finland, 1949–52

buildings, softened the ban against Constructivism, and called for industrial methods of construction. → 6 Beginning in 1955, Soviet missions were sent abroad to study the solutions being adopted elsewhere, and starting at the end of the decade, the Camus system of prefabricating heavy concrete panels was imported from France to the Soviet Union and East Germany. The *kvartal*, a residential quarter with a built-out perimeter, was replaced by the *mikroraion*, or microquarter, which was comparable to the neighborhood unit. After being tested at Novye Cheremushki (1956) **454** in Moscow, the *mikroraion* began to spread and became the standard component of new city extensions across the country. A second competition to build a Palace of the Soviets was held in 1958, twenty-five years after the first. Boris Iofan submitted a project similar to his original one, but without the monumental statue of Lenin. The winner was Yuri Vlasov, who designed a large glass box, a version of which would be built inside the Kremlin by Mikhail Posokhin in 1961. These new orientations resulted in buildings with more flexible plans, modern volumes, and airy interiors, among them the Moscow Palace of Pioneers (1959–62) **455** by Viktor Egerev, Valery Kubasov, Felix Novikov, and others.

The urban fabric of other countries in the socialist bloc was similarly transformed. The prismatic volumes on Wolfgang Hänsch's new Prager Straße in Dresden (1958–62), lined by a lengthy housing slab in the Corbusian spirit, stood out from previously rebuilt structures in the area, while the new city of Halle-Neustadt paralleled French *grands ensembles*, or large housing developments. In the 1960s the massive concrete-panel buildings originally designed to fend off the Siberian cold were even "tropicalized" for use in Cuba. In Czechoslovakia, the *panelák*, or prefabricated panel building, was put into widespread use on the basis of research carried out during the war. Yet even

though the post-Stalin architectural language in the Soviet Bloc often borrowed from Le Corbusier and sometimes from Oscar Niemeyer, the architect most frequently referred to throughout Eastern Europe and Russia was Alvar Aalto.

Aalto's eminent position

During his stays in the United States, beginning in 1939, Aalto was exposed to the regionalist discourse of the critic Lewis Mumford and his circle. After 1945 Aalto began to explore the simplicity of Finnish vernacular architecture and to contest the dominant orthogonal logic of functionalism. He declared that "every commission is different and so solutions to problems cannot be stereotyped," insisting that "nothing is more dangerous than to separate analysis and synthesis: they inevitably belong together." → 7 Although Aalto accepted the principle of standardization, he found it best exemplified in biological systems, not automobile production lines: "the purpose of architectural standardization is not to produce types, but instead to create variety and richness which could, in the ideal case, be compared with nature's unlimited capacity to produce variation." → 8

Aalto won the commission of Baker House (1947–8), a student dormitory at Massachusetts Institute of Technology on the banks of the Charles River in Cambridge, when he was a visiting professor there. The building reaches toward the river in waves of brick, deploying the same curves that he had used in his furniture designs since the 1920s. The facade that opens onto the campus undulates around a stair tower set obliquely to the main volume. By comparison, the town hall of the small Finnish city of Säynätsalo (1949–52) **456** is so introverted that it practically huddles around its courtyard; here the play of materials is freer than at Baker House but still dominated by

457 Auditorium, Helsinki University of Technology, Alvar Aalto, Espoo, Finland, 1949–54

458 Vuoksenniska Church, Alvar Aalto, Imatra, Finland, 1956–9

459 St. Mark Parish Church, Sigurd Lewerentz, Stockholm, Sweden, 1956–63

brick walls. The tower maintains the tradition of municipal belfries, while the clustered form of the wood trusses in the council chamber may be seen as a metaphor for the relationship between the individual and the collective. → 9

Aalto continued his research into buildings representing collective values on a larger scale with the National Pensions Institute in Helsinki (1948–56). Here he adjusted Le Corbusier's ribbon windows to the local customs and climate. The library evokes Aalto's library in Viipuri, which had been annexed by the Soviet Union and renamed Vyborg. The material textures, the extensive use of tiles, and the complexity of the modes of lighting in this publicly accessible administrative building combine to provide a more sensuous experience than the offices of countless programs of the European welfare state. For Aalto, each office building was an opportunity to undertake new experiments. The Rautatalo Building in Helsinki (1951–60), designed for the Finnish ironmakers union, is an office block with an austere facade, but its courtyard is rougher and more engaging. It marked a turning point in Aalto's use of overhead lighting, adding to the solution pioneered in Viipuri's external projectors. The copper on the facade and the care devoted to the metal detailing served to promote the union's trade.

Beginning in 1949, Aalto spent twenty years working on the campus of the Helsinki University of Technology, for which he devised what he described as an "elastic plan," a "constantly moving instrument with which we strive consciously to increase man's freedom of movement and other forms of freedom, too." → 10 The campus terraced down from hills to a plateau, with courtyards surrounded by granite, red brick, and copper buildings. The crescent-shaped auditorium (1949–54), **457** conceived as the intersection of a cylinder and a cone, stands out from the orthogonal buildings around it. Its highly original

roof, supported by curved concrete beams, serves as both open-air stepped seating and a source of light. Aalto continued to develop his urban planning principles with the Jyväskylä Teachers' College (1951–5), where he evoked nineteenth-century educational buildings. In his dynamically composed city center at Seinäjoki (1953–60), a reference to the Greek Acropolis blends with memories of Italian hill towns, an image dear at this date to the British proponents of Townscape. Aalto's most unexpected building of this period was the Vuoksenniska Church (Church of the Three Crosses; 1956–9) **458** near Imatra. It was many ways his Ronchamp. Its three parts – nave, altar, and chancel – are autonomous but they are also fluidly integrated into the overall composition. The interior has a flexible plan, with retractable partitions allowing for multiple configurations. The exterior comprises three undulating bulges that allude to the rapids of the nearby Vuoksi River. The subtle interplay of acoustics, direct light, and light reflecting off the white walls makes the church a radiant yet comforting place of prayer. Aalto's more rigid projects of the 1960s drew criticism from young Finnish architects, whose assaults he had mocked in 1954 in naming his boat *Nemo propheta in patria* (No one is a prophet in his own country). He devoted himself to two private residences. His own summer house, on a granite island in Lake Päijänne near Muuratsalo (1953), has guest rooms and a sauna made of logs. With its brick walls of heavily contrasting textures forming a U around a Mediterranean-style courtyard centered on an open fireplace, the house is reminiscent of the *tupa*, or communal space, of traditional Finnish farms. A house for the art dealer Louis Carré in Montfort l'Amaury, south of Paris (1956–9), is nearly an inverted version of the Muuratsalo summer house; organized around a terraced entrance hall with a vaulted wood ceiling, its plan extends each room to the outdoors.

460 Museum of Modern Art, Junzo Sakakura, Kamakura, Japan, 1951

461 Kagawa Prefectoral Offices, Kenzo Tange, Takamatsu, Japan, 1955–8

Other representatives of Finnish architecture met success abroad. Viljo Revell won the competition for Toronto City Hall in 1957, and subsequently built a sculptural assembly consisting of a flying-saucerlike central building flanked by two curved office slabs (1959–65). Its "space-age modernism" changed the Canadian city's image. More generally Northern European architecture was preoccupied with issues of materiality. For instance, in Sigurd Lewerentz's Saint Mark Parish Church (1956–63) **459** in Björkhagen, Stockholm, a severe box in exposed brick, the interior wall surfaces carry on a tense dialogue with the elements in wood. On the Danish scene, where the accent was on interiors and furniture design, the work of Arne Jacobsen aimed at a harmonious continuity at all scales, from the chair to the skyscraper, as epitomized by the SAS Hotel in Copenhagen (1958–60). With his Søholm Housing Development in Gentofte (1950–5), Jacobsen gave a refined reinterpretation of the row house, using subtle variations on brick walls.

Japan's new energy

While Aalto's work continued prewar modernist experiments but transfigured them, Japanese modern architecture of the same era made a new departure. The Reader's Digest Headquarters (1949–51, demolished) located directly across from Tokyo's Imperial Palace, built by Antonin Raymond upon his return to Japan, was emblematic of postwar reconstruction. A slab balanced on *pilotis*, it transposed the principles of wood construction to a concrete structure whose technical systems – fluorescent lighting, air conditioning – were new to the country. For the small town of Kamakura, Junzo Sakakura designed the Museum of Modern Art (1951); **460** a building based on a square plan, it was supported on steel *pilotis* standing on

rocks in a body of water, with the galleries arranged around a square courtyard. Sakakura subsequently distanced himself from the Corbusian spirit of this museum in complexes in both Shibuya, which included a train station and department store (1954–6), and in Shinjuku (1966–7). The building systems of these two major projects evidenced his familiarity with Jean Prouvé's work. → 11 Kunio Maekawa, another disciple of Le Corbusier, built a concert hall and a library in Yokohama (1954) and offered his interpretation of the Unité d'Habitation in Marseilles with a ten-story apartment house on Harumi Island (1956–8, demolished), the massiveness of which was underscored by its powerful exposed-concrete framework. Apartments in the Harumi building were organized in blocks of three levels that were entered by a skip-stop elevator arrangement and rose from piers at ground level. Maekawa's Metropolitan Festival Hall (1957–61), built across from Le Corbusier's National Museum of Western Art in Ueno Park, was both an extrapolation based on the forms of Ronchamp and a development of Le Corbusier's unbuilt design for a cultural center that would have complemented his museum. → 12 The principal figure to emerge in Japan during this period was Kenzo Tange. While working on the Hiroshima Peace Center, he built his own house in Tokyo (1951–3) using traditional techniques – wood framing, *tatami* (straw mats), and *shoji* (sliding screens of rice paper) – within a modern building volume. He won the competition to design Tokyo City Hall, but built only a third of the project (1952–7, demolished 1995), consisting of a large office slab standing on two-story *pilotis* through which the building was entered. His offices in Takamatsu for the Kagawa Prefecture (1955–8) **461** were a milestone in national production for the way they transposed wood construction techniques to concrete while also defining an open public space beneath the

462 Extension Plan for Tokyo, project, Kenzo Tange, Tokyo, Japan, 1959–60

463 Centro Urbano Presente Alemán, Mario Pani, Mexico City, Mexico, 1947–9

buildings. Tange followed this project with an audacious pro-posal for the expansion of Tokyo (1959–60). **462** Reorganizing the city around a double linear axis leading to new structures built out into Tokyo Bay to the southeast, he designed sinu-ous office slabs and large A-shaped residential buildings with open cores, which were connected to a highway system run-ning above the water. A participant in the Otterlo CIAM in 1959, Tange was the first Japanese architect to receive significant commissions outside the country. Notable among them was his plan for the reconstruction of the Macedonian capital of Skopje following the 1963 earthquake, in which he proposed a monumental symbolic scheme centered about a "city gate" and a "city wall." → 13 In the eyes of the world, however, his cathe-dral and two stadiums for the Tokyo Olympics in 1964 were his most significant buildings, thanks to their recycling of elements of Japanese material culture – from the samurai's armor to pleated textiles – at a grand scale.

Latin Americanisms

The west-east relationship connecting Europe, the United States, and Japan was not the only geocultural configuration shaping architectural production in the 1950s. On the north-south axis, Latin America gave rise to significant and remarkably varied buildings, often designed by architects trained in Europe. The frequent trips of critics like Bruno Zevi did not define the range of homegrown Latin American inventiveness, nor did the echo of works by Frank Lloyd Wright, Le Corbusier, and Richard Neutra. In Mexico, large projects built in the capital had a unifying effect. These included Mario Pani's Centro Urbano Presidente Alemán (1947–9), **463** a complex of Corbusian *redent* housing, and espe-cially the Ciudad Universitaria (University City; 1950–4), whose

plan was produced by Pani and Enrique Del Moral. → 14 The painter David Alfaro Siqueiros and his fellow artists, in a local variation of a program spreading throughout Latin America at this time, decorated the university with murals in the spirit of the 1930s. Dominating the campus is the library **464** by the painter and architect Juan O'Gorman, who covered the building in mosaics of his own design, re-creating the history of Mexico. O'Gorman's own house-grotto in Pedregal de San Angel (1956, demolished) featured extensive sculptures and mosaic fig-ures, revealing the distance he had traveled from his modernist projects of the 1930s and marking his withdrawal into paint-ing. The Spanish architect Félix Candela turned Mexico into a testing ground for audacious concrete structures. After build-ing the parabolic arch of the modest Cosmic Ray Pavilion at the university (1952), he designed the umbrella roofs of the Cabero Warehouses in the Vallejo part of Mexico City (1955) and the intersecting hyperbolic paraboloids forming the octag-onal groined vault of the circular Los Manantiales Restaurant (1958) **465** in Xochimilco, in the south of Mexico City. Candela's experiments culminated in the hyperbolic paraboloids shells of the Lomas de Cuernavaca (1958) and San Pedro Martir (1965) churches, which are supported at no more than a few key points. In the stunning lava-flow landscape of the El Pedregal neigh-borhood, Luis Barragán built several residences, including the Eduardo Prieto López House (1948), a complex of cubic vol-umes inserted into a continuous landscape linking patios and gardens. Beginning in 1947, he used his own house there as a testing ground to refine a language stripped of the deco-rative excess of his early architecture, developing an idiom that was full of Mediterranean and sometimes African refer-ences and eventually evolved toward an aesthetic of minimal-ism. The Antonio Gálvez House in El Pedregal (1955) was the

464 University Library, University City, Juan O'Gorman, Mexico City, Mexico, 1950–4

465 Los Manantiales Restaurant, Félix Candela, Mexico City, Mexico, 1958

466 Cuadra San Cristobál, Los Clubes, Luis Barragán, Mexico City, Mexico, 1966–8

467 Pompéia Cultural Center, Lina Bo Bardi, São Paulo, Brazil, 1977

468 ▶ Aula Magna, Ciudad Universitaria de Caracas, Carlos Raúl Villanueva, with sculpture by Alexander Calder, Caracas, Venezuela, 1952–3

first manifestation of this new approach, although the Capuchin Chapel in Tlalpan (1952–5) had introduced a new way of using light, creating an interplay between painted surfaces and colored glass. The five towers of Satellite City (1957), erected by the sculptor Mathias Goeritz at a Mexico City traffic intersection, are a colorful monument designed for the gaze of passing motorists. Their total abstraction foreshadowed Barragán's projects in Las Arboledas (1958–61) and Los Clubes (1966–8), **466** landscape projects where space is defined exclusively by large colored walls and reflecting pools. → 15

The oil-rich economy of Venezuela made it possible to carry out major programs there. The plans for Caracas by the French city planner Maurice Rotival in the late 1930s led to the creation of grand thoroughfares and ambitious housing developments. Carlos Raúl Villanueva, who built the modernist El Silencio Residences in 1942–5, a decade later designed the Olympic Stadium (1950–1) and was responsible for a series of housing complexes funded by the Banco Obrero. These large housing slabs perching on the hillsides of Caracas include Cerro Piloto, El Paraíso, and 23 de Enero (1954–7). Villanueva's major project was the campus of the Ciudad Universitaria in Caracas (1952–3), remarkable for its covered square connecting its various buildings. Jean Arp and Fernand Léger, among many other artists, contributed works. The Aula Magna, **468** or great amphitheater, with its hovering mobile by Alexander Calder, is the dominant structure. → 16 In general, architecture in Venezuela seemed to be open to a more lyrical modernism than elsewhere outside of Brazil. The Milanese architect Gio Ponti proposed an overall vision for Caracas → 17 and built two elegant houses there – the Planchart Villa (1957), which would remain the most spectacular accomplishment of his postwar production, and the Arreaza Villa (1958).

Cuba was closely allied with the United States in the 1950s, and an inventive architecture spread through Havana and along Varadero Beach. After the revolution in 1959, Fidel Castro's administration undertook numerous projects for housing and schools. Fernando Salinas, who had been active before the revolution, collaborated with Raúl Gonzalez Romero to design the new city of Habana del Este (1959–60) and worked on industrialized building systems for the Ciudad Universitaria (1961–9). Ricardo Porro collaborated with Roberto Gottardi and Vittorio Garatti on an extraordinary sequence of brick domes, vaults, and arcades for the National School of Art in Havana (1961–3). → 18 **471**

The architectural flowering of Brazil was not limited to Rio. Lucio Costa and Oscar Niemeyer were busy building Brasília, and there were remarkable developments in the economic center of São Paulo, including Rino Levi's inventive apartment buildings. Though João Batista Vilanova Artigas, a leftist, criticized Le Corbusier's theories from his own political perspective, he continued to borrow elements of his architecture, which he and his colleagues revised and transformed in their projects in Rio. → 19

The two slabs of Artigas's Louveira Housing Development (1946–9) created a microcosm of rationality and poetry in the urban chaos of São Paulo. Under Brazil's military dictatorship, Artigas was able to complete the large concrete hall of the University of São Paulo's School of Architecture (1966–9). Lina Bo, who arrived from Milan after the war with her husband Pietro Maria Bardi, built residences like the couple's own "glass house" on *pilotis* (1951) as well as the São Paulo Museum of Modern Art on Avenida Paulista (1957–68), a large volume in concrete and glass suspended within a powerful structural frame. A decade later she transformed an oil drum factory into Pompéia Cultural Center (1977), **467** working with the existing concrete

470 Bank of London, Clorindo Testa, Buenos Aires, Argentina, 1960–6

471 National School of Art, Ricardo Porro, with Roberto Gottardi and Vittorio Garatti, Havana, Cuba, 1961–3

472 ▶ Bus Station, Eladio Dieste, Salto, Uruguay, 1973–4

469 Makdisi Building, Karol Schayer, Beirut, Lebanon, 1954

workshops and silos to create a place both truly sculptural and open to the modifications of its users. → 20

In the southern portion of the continent, several figures rose to prominence. Among them was the Uruguayan engineer Eladio Dieste, who spent five decades building brick structures with impressive sculptural qualities derived from his mastery of structural geometry. His notable achievements included the Church of Christ the Worker in Atlántida (1958–60), several markets, and numerous public transportation buildings such as the Salto Bus Station (1973–4), **472** which combines brick and concrete. → 21

But the most varied and intense production was in Argentina, where the effects of Le Corbusier's work were as evident as in Brazil. The young Amancio Williams, proponent of a laconic and minimalist interpretation of Le Corbusier's projects, designed an astonishing house in Mar del Plata for his father, the composer Alberto Williams. An inhabitable bridge in the spirit of Maillart, it consists of a glazed orthogonal volume supported by a thin concrete arch straddling a stream (1943–5). In Buenos Aires, Mario Roberto Alvarez explored various avenues of modernism, from concrete frames to steel-and-glass prisms, in buildings like the Teatro General San Martín (1953–60). Clorindo Testa's Bank of London (1960–6) **470** broke the stereotype of the office tower. A large hollow volume in concrete, it features a central hall that brings illumination to all the levels and contains a sculptural cylinder housing the circulation core. The exterior curtain wall is protected by a deep concrete *brise-soleil* that makes it stand out from the rest of the buildings in the city's financial district.

Archipelagoes of invention

A few pages hardly suffice to take stock of all the different national and urban cities around the world in which fruitful interpretations of modern architecture emerged. Yet certain local situations such as the one in Beirut, the financial capital of the Middle East since Lebanese independence in 1946, deserve special attention. There Edward Durell Stone built the Phoenicia Hotel (1954–62) and Michel Écochard put up several complexes with Claude Le Coeur, including the Protestant School (1953–7), a serene bar built with meticulous attention to circulation and lighting. Karol Schayer, a Pole who had lived in Lebanon since the war, designed elegant office and residential buildings such as Dar Assayad and the Makdisi Building **469** (both 1954). → 22 Another Middle Eastern capital, Baghdad, welcomed many key architects of the period: José Luís Sert built the American Embassy (1955–60) and Walter Gropius the University of Baghdad (1958–70). Le Corbusier designed an athletic complex (1956–64), small parts of which were built. Among unbuilt projects, Aalto projected a fine arts museum (1957–63), and Wright drafted one of his last major projects – a cultural center on the Isle of Edena in the middle of the Tigris River (1957–9). In the city's residential neighborhoods, the first generation of formally trained Iraqi architects attempted to interpret and adapt the elements of Western modernism. The major contribution was that of Rifat Chadirji, who reinterpreted archetypes and historical forms taken from a wide range of sources, from Babylonian walls to vernacular reed huts to Baghdad's typical urban dwellings. → 23

Somewhat outside the major architectural tendencies being exported at this time was Athens, which had a more pluralistic reception of the modern European movements. At one end, Dimitris Pikionis remodeled the landscape of the Acropolis and of Philopappos Hill with a network of footpaths (1954–7) **473** made of found stones that he assembled in mysterious and fascinating patterns, proposing a sort of imaginary archaeology

473 Pedestrian promenade on Philopappos Hill, Dimitris Pikionis, Athens, Greece, 1954–7

474 Sydney Opera House, Jørn Utzon, Sydney, Australia, 1957–73

in answer to the ubiquitous scientific digs going on in Greece in these years. At the opposite extreme from this personal response to the genius loci was the complex of concrete-frame slabs built on Mount Lycabettus by Constantinos Doxiadis, whose firm was at the time working on urban studies of a number of cities around the world, from Baghdad to Rio de Janeiro, with the support of the Ford Foundation in the United States. [24] Responding to the incline of the site, the elegant volumes of the complex appear simply to be adaptations of a global stereotype. Aris Konstantinidis's houses and hotels also brought widely disseminated themes to Greece, combining a type of Brutalism derived from Le Corbusier and Marcel Breuer with almost Miesian accents in his modular plans. The interior street and patios of his archaeological museum in Ioannina (1965–6) lend a kind of urban complexity to the overall structure. [25]

Beginning in the 1950s, certain cities used great cultural projects to assure themselves a place on the world map. This was certainly the aim of the Australian port city of Sydney when it launched a competition to build an opera house in 1957. Designed by the Danish architect Jørn Utzon and finally inaugurated in 1973, the Sydney Opera House **474** became the unrivaled heart of the city and its bay. In a collaboration with Ove Arup's engineering office, Utzon designed the shells that cover the structure as sections of a sphere, unmistakably alluding to the sails of the ships that first linked Australia with Europe. Their forms may also be likened to experiments by German Expressionists like Hermann Finsterlin. The opera house marked the true beginning of the global architectural phenomenon of the modern cultural building as an urban attractor. [26]

Over the course of two decades – even a single decade in the case of the socialist countries – resistance to modern architecture significantly diminished, and without resulting in homogeneity across the board. Modern architecture in all its variations proved capable of giving form, whether grandiloquent or intimate, to most of its clients' needs. But its adaptation to programs serving the "greater number" – whether mass housing or commercial projects – as well as its mainstream acceptance eventually led to repetitiveness and finally formal exhaustion, as well as to a disarming of serious critical discourse.

Toward new utopias

In the late 1950s it became increasingly unclear in which direction architectural culture was headed. The interest in history partly shared by Louis Kahn and Philip Johnson led those two architects to diametrically opposed conclusions. In Europe, other divides manifested themselves, for example between architects aspiring to root modern forms in the historical context of cities and those exploring the shift from the technologies that had coincided with early modernism – concrete and steel construction – to emerging technological systems related to a new age of space exploration and mass communications. The latter, with their open frames, their emphasis on networks, and their flexible character, especially fueled the imagination of younger architects.

Ernesto Nathan Rogers and Reyner Banham argued fervently about this changed, and highly charged, relationship between architecture and technology. Their argument was sparked by a series of Italian buildings, most notably the Bottega d'Erasmo apartment building by Roberto Gabetti and Aimaro d'Isola in Turin (1953–7) **476** and BPR's Torre Velasca in Milan (1957). **475** Brutally attacked in the Paris magazine *L'Architecture d'aujourd'hui* in 1958 as "reneging" on the ethos of modernism, these buildings are tinged by a nostalgia for historical forms and accused by Banham of representing "the Italian retreat from modern architecture." [1] The Bottega d'Erasmo, built out to the street edge, has a brick facade with vertical windows and sits on a stone base against which the concrete lintels and loggias and the wrought-iron railings stand out, explicitly recalling the formal play of pre-1914 structures. [2] The same architects echoed the ribbed vaulting of Anatole de Baudot's Church of Saint-Jean de Montmartre in Paris in the interior of their Turin Stock Exchange (1952–7), whose angular concrete frame combines with zigzag glass facades to create a crystalline continuity.

Standing high above downtown Milan, the Torre Velasca entered into a dialogue with Gio Ponti and Pier Luigi Nervi's contemporary Pirelli Tower (1956–60). The Pirelli – at the time the tallest skyscraper in Europe – is a tapered slab of concrete whose symmetry and prismatic simplicity illustrate Ponti's notion of a "finished form." [3] BPR's Torre Velasca is an entirely different affair: its concrete structure is exposed and its profile anything but smooth. With vertical windows and an upper structure resting on the rectangular shaft of the lower stories, it evokes the medieval Castello Sforzesco but perhaps also a Milanese palazzo, reflecting Rogers's concern with *preesistenze ambientali*. Abandoning the established modern tropes of the flat roof and the horizontal window, he mocked Banham as a "custodian of Frigidaires," declaring that while the modern movement was "not dead at all" in his eyes, it was necessary "to be sensitive to the beautiful (and not only to the value of documenting it) in some manifestations that are no longer sufficiently appreciated." He added: "It is respectable to historicize and update certain values left hanging because of the need for other struggles." [4] As editor of *Casabella-continuità* he defended this simultaneously orthodox and heterodox program.

Italy: critical continuity

Italian architecture of the 1950s was driven by contradictory tendencies. In Rome the scene had long revolved around Luigi Moretti, whose residential buildings, beginning with the Casa del Girasole (Sunflower House; 1947–50), **479** in which local rationalism inherited from the 1930s took on a Baroque flavor, offered a modern interpretation of Mediterranean themes. The two wings of this U-shaped building are separated by a narrow courtyard and hidden behind a thin facade cleaved in

477 House on the Zattere, Ignazio Gardella, Venice, Italy, 1953–8

476 Bottega d'Erasmo, Roberto Gabetti and Aimaro d'Isola, Turin, Italy, 1953–7

478 Museum of the Treasure of San Lorenzo, Franco Albini and Franca Helg, Genoa, Italy, 1952–6

half. Moretti's design aimed to accentuate the natural variations in light so as to give the wall "the continual palpitation of an antique facade, which changes every hour as the sun travels its course in harmony with the world." → 5

In Milan, Ignazio Gardella was a protagonist. He incorporated echoes of Piedmontese urban architecture into his apartment buildings for employees of the Borsalino Company in Alessandria (1950–2); this housing is remarkable for its play of windows and shutters and its projecting eaves. In Venice he carried out another meditation on urban context in his House on the Zattere (1953–8). **477** Here he added balconies to the vertical elements used for the Borsalino buildings, delicately adjusting the facade to the other palazzi overlooking the Giudecca Canal.

The Milanese firm of Franco Albini and Franca Helg worked on several projects in Genoa that made a decisive contribution to a new definition of museography. Albini renovated the White Palace (1949–51) and Red Palace (1952–62) on Via Garibaldi and built a crypt for the Museum of the Treasure of San Lorenzo (1952–6) **478** – a sequence of circular galleries with stone walls and ribbed-concrete ceilings that concentrate visitors' attention on skillfully illuminated artifacts. The confrontation with history took an entirely different turn in his extension to the Genoa City Hall (1950–62); here the stone and concrete terraces of the new municipal offices seem to be climbing to the top of the hill while below the scale of the courtyards of the original Palazzo Tursi remains intact.

In Rome, his Rinascente Department Store (1957–61) consists of a volume like that of a Renaissance palazzo but with a visible steel structure. The structural components recall the pilasters and cornices of historical buildings, while concrete panels enfold the air-conditioning ducts. Although the building is located in a historical setting, all of its internal elements are visible from the exterior, as if in a cutaway view. With the Dutch designer Bob Noorda, Albini and Helg fitted out the stations of the Milan subway (1964), using a modular system of steel and concrete panels against which the graphic signage and the colorful tubes of the handrails stand out.

Independent together

The technological questions dividing Rogers and Banham in the late 1950s had initially preoccupied Sigfried Giedion in his book *Mechanization Takes Command* (1948). Illustrated with a rich selection of striking images, the book traces the "anonymous history" of machines, furniture, and rationalized production. → 6 Meanwhile Buckminster Fuller continued to design lightweight, transportable structures, abandoning sheet metal in favor of tubular elements that allowed for larger and lighter domes, both for military purposes – for example, a geodesic dome for the U.S. Marine Corps (1954) – and civilian ones, such as the Climatron in Saint Louis, Missouri (1960) and the Union Tank Car Maintenance Facility in Baton Rouge, Louisiana (1958–60; destroyed 2007). A question Fuller liked to ask – "Madam, do you know how much your house weighs?" – summed up the problem that led him to propose a dome with a diameter of 1.8 miles (2.9 kilometers) but a total weight of only 80,000 tons to be installed by helicopters over much of Manhattan (1960). **481** Fuller's United States Pavilion at the Montreal World's Fair of 1967, gutted by fire in 1976, encapsulated the basic idea of his scheme for the Manhattan dome. The issues investigated and illustrated by Giedion and the excitement provoked by Fuller's projects contributed to the creation in London of the Independent Group, an informal collective of artists and architects founded in 1951 under the

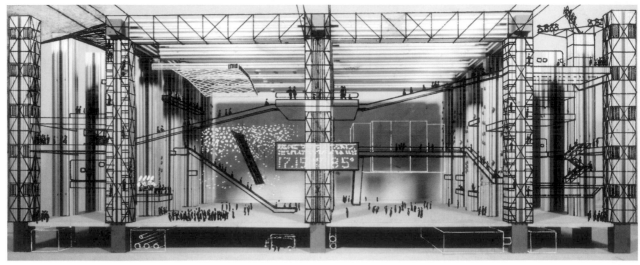

480   The Fun Palace, project, Cedric Price, 1961–70

481   Dome over Manhattan, project, Buckminster Fuller, New York City, USA, 1960

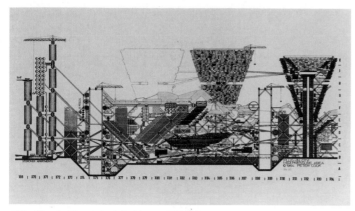

482 Plug-in City, project, Archigram, 1962–4

483 Instant City, project, Archigram, 1968–70

auspices of the Institute of Contemporary Arts. It included Alison and Peter Smithson, John McHale, Magda Cordell, Richard Hamilton, Nigel Henderson, Eduardo Paolozzi, Lawrence Alloway, and Reyner Banham. In a period cheered by the end of wartime shortages and a sort of neo-Futurism propagated by the Conservative government, which favored new technologies, the events staged by the group presented an optimistic vision of both technology and popular culture that was centered on America. Books like László Moholy-Nagy's *Vision in Motion* (1947) and Marshall McLuhan's *The Mechanical Bride: Folklore of Industrial Man* (1951) were significant sources for an approach in which advertisements were as important to the group as silos and planes had once been to Gropius and Le Corbusier. [7] In 1951 the Independent Group organized the exhibition *Growth and Form*, inspired by D'Arcy Wentworth Thompson's early-twentieth-century writings on biological morphology. *Parallel of Life and Art* (1953) explored ideas of kinetics, drawing on Futurism and the history of photography as well as Giedion's *Mechanization Takes Command*. Finally, the science fiction atmosphere and social criticism of *This Is Tomorrow* (1956), held at the Whitechapel Art Gallery, brought the Independent Group together with other architects on the British scene, including Colin St. John Wilson, whose group created a sculptural environment that paid homage to Le Corbusier's recently completed Ronchamp. [8]

Technology: ethos or icon?

The world envisaged by the Independent Group stimulated the imagination of the upcoming generation of British designers. In 1961 the Archigram collective was founded and published the first of its eponymous telegrammatic brochures.

Peter Cook, Warren Chalk, Ron Herron, David Greene, Mike Webb and Dennis Crompton met while working with Theo Crosby to modernize Euston Station in London. They developed an interest in the expendability of buildings, affirming that "the home, the whole city and the frozen pea pack are all the same." [9] Mike Webb's Sin Centre for London (1959–62), with its suspended cable structure and "drive-in galleria," inaugurated Archigram's series of theoretical projects. More representative of the expendability theme was Herron and Cook's Plug-in City (1962–4), **482** a system of technological components implemented "by applying a large scale network structure, containing access ways and essential services, to any terrain." According to its description, "[I]nto this network are placed units which cater for all needs. These units are planned for obsolescence. The units are served and manoeuvred by means of cranes operating from a railway at the apex of the structure. The interior contains several electronic and machine installations intended to replace present-day work operations." [10] Following this nearly literal re-creation of Sant'Elia's Città Nuova, Herron devised the Walking City (1964), a flock of insectlike buildings on long legs poised to stride across the terrain.

Archigram's proliferating urban machines took on their full implications only after being equipped with spacecraft-inspired capsules, which could be added, removed, or replaced at will. Chalk devised the Capsule Homes (1964) and the Montreal Tower (1963), the latter a treelike structure carrying changeable capsules. Greene's house project of 1965, including "a living pod and attached machines," seemed to respond to a provocative article by Banham, the group's mentor, entitled "A Home Is Not a House." Published in 1965, Banham's article set forth a radical program: "When your house contains such a complex

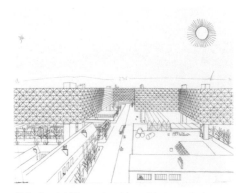

484 Spatial City, project, Yona Friedman, Paris, France, 1959

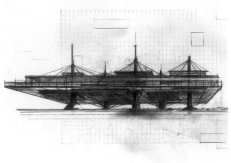

485 New Babylon, project, Constant Nieuwenhuis, 1957–74

486 Cluster City, project, Arata Isozaki, 1960–2

487 Nagakin Capsule Tower, Noriaki (Kisho) Kurokawa, Tokyo, Japan, 1970–2

of piping, flues, ducts, wires, lights, inlets, outlets, ovens, sinks, refuse disposer, hi-fi reverberators, antennae, conduits, freezers, heaters – when it contains so many services that the hardware could stand up by itself without any assistance from the house, why have a house to hold it up? When the cost of all this tackle is half of the total outlay (or more, as it often is) what is the house doing except concealing your mechanical pudenda from the stares of folks on the sidewalk?" [11] With one of its late projects, Instant City (1968–70), **483** Archigram proposed the creation of inflatable cities whose components would be delivered by dirigible. [12]

In contrast to Archigram's rather apolitical fantasies, the projects by their contemporary Cedric Price engaged in a dialogue with reformist forces in British society. Collaborating with Lord Snowdon and the engineer Frank Newby, Price built the aviary at the London Zoo (1961), a polyhedral steel-mesh structure. His project of 1964 for the Potteries Thinkbelt in the depressed industrial region of Staffordshire – designed in close contact with the local Labour Party and intended to provide a county-wide infrastructure for education using mobile modules and lightweight constructions – remained on the drawing board. The same fate befell his Fun Palace, **480** a collaborative project with the theater director Joan Littlewood, on which he worked for several years beginning in 1961. Still rather enigmatic, this project – for which no facade was ever designed – was intended to be both a theater space, convertible into any configuration through a system of gantry cranes and servicing towers, and a place of learning. Projecting a use of computers that was far ahead of its time, the Fun Palace was probably the first attempt to apply research on cybernetics and information technology to an architectural design. Despite the fact that it was never built, Price's theoretical reflections had considerable impact. [13]

Hovering cities of indeterminacy

On the Continent, the notion of an imaginary city constantly changing in response to play and other creative activities led to the concept of the New Babylon (1957–74), **485** a long-term project by the Dutch painter Constant Nieuwenhuis, known as Constant. A founding member of the CoBrA group, Constant was inspired, like Jacob Bakema, by Johan Huizinga's book *Homo Ludens* to construct a vibrant critique of Fordism. His thinking was expressed most clearly in a series of drawings and, especially, three-dimensional models depicting a network of loosely connected buildings hovering over existing urban areas. [14]

The "spatial urbanism" developed in Paris by the Hungarian-born architect Yona Friedman between 1958 and 1965 shared certain aspects with Constant's project. It was founded both on a reading of Huizinga and on a concept of uncertainty borrowed from the physicist Werner Heisenberg, whose lectures Friedman had attended in Budapest. Friedman's aerial cities were potentially unlimited developments; they were based on permanent change and the coexistence of variable daily activities. Among the different types of "mobile architecture" that he designed was a Spatial City (1959) **484** whose residential cells, floating above the Seine and the Champs-Élysées, were reminiscent of the interlocking houses of a North African medina. [15] The space-frame structure of the Paris project derived from the theoretical projects of Konrad Wachsmann, with whom Friedman had studied at the Technion in Haifa, while its housing capsules were related to research by Jean Prouvé, for whom Friedman had briefly worked.

488   *Airplane Carrier in Landscape*, collage, project, Hans Hollein, 1964

Metabolism in Japan

While Archigram dreamed up apolitical schemes and Friedman optimistically devised cities in the air, somewhat ironic uses of naval and aeronautical technologies were under development by the younger generation in Japan. In reaction to both Corbusian modernism and the celebration of Japanese tradition epitomized by the Katsura Imperial Villa, the critic Noboru Kawazoe and the radical young architects Kiyonori Kikutake, Masato Ohtaka, Fumihiko Maki, and Noriaki (Kisho) Kurokawa put forward the doctrine of Metabolism at the World Design Conference in Tokyo in 1960, drawing on biological references and Friedman's work. These left-leaning proponents of a revival of Constructivism sought to create meaningful projects by abandoning the Japanese obsession with memory and identity. Kawazoe wrote: "Our constructive age will be the age of high metabolism. Order is born from chaos, and chaos from order. Extinction is the same as creation. … We hope to create something which, even in destruction, will cause a subsequent new creation. This 'something' must be found in the form of the cities we are going to make – cities constantly undergoing the process of metabolism." → 16

Kikutake conceived his City on the Sea (1958–9) as a floating development with concrete pontoons that could sink into the ocean to become underwater constructions or serve as the base for slender skyscrapers. His Sky House in Tokyo (1958) was a radical caricature of Japanese construction, with a living space supported by four robust concrete *pilotis*. Kurokawa responded to Kikutake's ideas with the Ocean City project (1960), then with Helix City (1964), whose towers resembled giant-scale double spirals of DNA. He succeeded in building the Nagakin Capsule Tower in Tokyo (1970–2), **487** one of the rare structures in which

the Metabolist fantasy of minimal residential capsules was realized, appropriately enough for a short-stay hotel.

Though not a member of the Metabolist group, Arata Isozaki offered a more intellectualized interpretation of some of its themes with his Cluster City project (1960–2), **486** a perfect illustration of the metaphor of the city as a tree, and with his project for Shinjuku, Tokyo (1960–1), which featured buildings suspended between massive cylindrical towers. Kenzo Tange too began to venture in the same direction as the Metabolists, though he was a generation older than the group. His Tsukiji Development in Tokyo (1960) consisted of an assemblage of slabs suspended in space, while his programs for media centers like the Yamanashi Communication Center in Kofu (1960) and the Shizuoka Press and Broadcasting Corporation headquarters in Tokyo (1966–7) featured load-bearing stems with cantilevered volumes, bristling with antennas.

Megastructures and global agitation

Though Archigram's projects differed from those of the Metabolists – the latter being far more architectural in their composition and more conservatively rendered – both belonged to the wider category of the megastructure, which Maki defined as "a large frame in which all the functions of a city or part of a city are housed." Noting that this concept was made possible by present-day technology, he called it "a man-made feature of the landscape. … like the great hill on which Italian towns were built." → 17 Hans Hollein's collage **488** depicting a nuclear aircraft carrier run aground on – incidentally – a hill represented a variation on the theme of the large building integrating complex functions. The idea was realized in exemplary form in Hugh Wilson and Geoffrey Copcutt's

489 Cumbernauld City Centre, Geoffrey Copcutt and Hugh Wilson, Cumbernauld, United Kingdom, 1960–8

490 Habitat 67, Moshe Safdie, Montreal, Canada, 1964–7

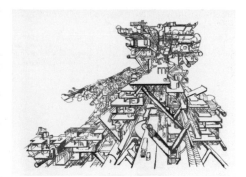

491 Ideal Communist City, project, NER (New Settlement Elements) Group (Alexei Gutnov, Ilya Lezhava, et al.), 1965–7

492 ▶ Church of Sainte-Bernardette, Claude Parent and Paul Virilio, Nevers, France, 1963–6

plan for the center of the New Town of Cumbernauld, Scotland (1960–8). **489** It also found expression in Peter Hodgkinson's stepped double slab built on artificial ground at Brunswick Square in London (1962–70), which makes a brief appearance in Michelangelo Antonioni's film *The Passenger*; and especially in Moshe Safdie's Habitat 67 housing complex in Montreal (1964–7), **490** an accumulation of factory-produced cubic volumes. Each of these projects created a landscape of multilayered inhabitation. [18] In the Netherlands, Herman Hertzberger's Central Beheer Office Block in Apeldoorn (1967–72) operated with a germane principle, in echo to Team 10 principles, deploying inside its assembled blocks nooks and balconies allowing for a new, more convivial, type of working experience. Subversive groups also proliferated in the mid-1960s, each seeking, often with undisguised irony, a formal or structural principle or a graphic style to serve as its own trademark. [19] In Moscow, the NER (New Settlement Elements) Group led by Alexei Gutnov conceived an ideal communist city (1965–7) **491** that was a hybrid of Archigram's technological forms and the Metabolists' organic networks. [20] Yona Friedman, Paul Maymont, Walter Jonas, Georges Patrix, Ionel Schein, and Nicolas Schoeffer formed the Groupe international d'architecture prospective (International Group of Perspective Architecture) in 1965 to "anticipate and organize the future instead of being subjected to it," working to conceive a "spatial" urban planning free from the constraints of commercial real-estate transactions and the burden of history. [21] Two years earlier, the architect Claude Parent and the urbanist Paul Virilio established a collaboration in Paris called Architecture principe (Architecture Principle) to explore both their fascination with abandoned World War II bunkers and the idea of an "oblique function." The former led them to design the

concrete forms of the Church of Sainte-Bernadette in Nevers (1963–6), **492** while they visualized the latter in models and sketches representing structures without any horizontal or vertical surfaces, featuring vast inclined planes and inhabitable stairs. [22] Meanwhile Maymont designed conical cities and floating islands. His most notable contribution was a plan to bury a ten-level city beneath the riverbed of the Seine (1962). The Florentine groups Archizoom and Superstudio proposed even more outrageous projects, abandoning even the feigned realism still present in Maymont's schemes. Archizoom (1966–74), founded by Andrea Branzi and his associates with a name that paid homage to Archigram, displayed its work at the *Superarchitettura* exhibitions in Pistoia (1966) and Modena (1967). The group created provocative furniture, designs for consumer products, and urban schemes ridiculing mass-produced housing. These included No Stop City (1969), **493** Wind Town (1969), and Homogeneous Quarters with Clouds (1970). Superstudio (1966–76), another promoter of "anti-design," was headed by Adolfo Natalini and Cristiano Toraldo di Francia, among others. It mocked the architecture of glass prisms with its Continuous Monument (1969), **495** a grid that extended across the entire planet, from Saint-Moritz in Switzerland to Manhattan. [23]

Technology and its double

The conventional range of techniques used to build high-density housing projects and central business districts was far more limited than that imagined in the projects of radical architects. Real-life technical innovation seemed to be focused essentially on improving productivity. The dominance of the prefabricated concrete panel and the modular steel structure appeared unshakable, and research on construction seemed

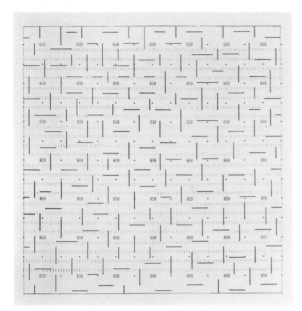

493 No Stop City, project, Archizoom, 1969

494 Inflatable Structure, Utopie Group, 1968

495 The Continuous Monument, project, Superstudio, 1969

entirely geared to increasing the efficiency of mass produc-tion. In this context, Jean Prouvé's work is all the more remark-able. Operating almost solo following the bankruptcy in 1953 of the workshops he had created after the war in Nancy, Prouvé projected lightweight metal houses and designed simple, ele-gant details for glass and aluminum curtain walls. The sys-tems he elaborated both in his commissions for the architects who employed him and in his classes from 1967 to 1971 at the Arts et Métiers technical school in Paris – the only alter-native with some intellectual legitimacy to the Beaux-Arts – pointed the way to a flexible and creative use of indus-trial techniques. The other pole of European invention was in Stuttgart, where the engineer Frei Otto opened the Institut für leichte Flächentragwerke (Institute for Lightweight Structural Structures) in 1964. Here Otto developed tensile structures of cables and fabric and pneumatic constructions that made some of the utopian groups' wildest ideas seem feasible. Experiments of his like the tent for the Germany Pavilion at the 1967 Montreal World's Fair were a major source of the bubble projects and other inflatable schemes by international archi-tects that proliferated in the second half of the 1960s.
On the other hand, groups of the 1960s most staunchly opposed to the capitalist order dismissed the irony wielded by radical architects as too weak a weapon. In 1958 Guy Debord founded the Situationist International, which vaunted the merits of the *derive*, or drift, through city streets as an alternative form of urbanism. He urged a move away from "the old monumental architecture's spectacular preoccupation with beauty in favor of topological organizations demanding general participation." In order to create a new "topophilia" – a concept borrowed from the philosopher Gaston Bachelard – he proposed the *détournement* (derailment or reappropriation) of products and

objects, "liberating existing desires at once, and deploying them within the new dimensions of an unknown actualization." → 24
In 1967 Debord denounced the "society of spectacle" in a global critique of capitalism. → 25 Another radical group, Utopie – founded the same year by Jean Aubert, Jean Baudrillard, Jean-Paul Jungmann, Antoine Stinco, and Hubert Tonka – was largely inspired by the sociologist Henri Lefebvre's Marxist cri-tique. Through its eponymous publication, it contested the illusions of Archigram and others who sought to counter a class-based society with a world of unbuildable fantasies. Given their positions, it was surprising – and even poignant – that a few of the ingenious inflatable structures **494** designed by Utopie's founders were exhibited in Paris in the spring of 1968, at a time when criticism of dominant urban policies and distrust of large-scale construction became themes of the stu-dent revolts that shook all of Europe and the Americas. → 26

Between elitism and populism: alternative architecture

The architectural revolutions that took place in 1968 were not a direct outgrowth of earlier utopian impulses, nor were they a simple projection of generational protests against the American war in Vietnam, racial segregation, and capitalist exploitation. This was particularly true in France and Italy, where unrest was not limited to university campuses but mobilized significant forces throughout society. Besides general anger over the overwhelming power of the military-industrial complex in the United States, the perceived authoritarianism of de Gaulle's regime in France, and the conservatism of Konrad Adenauer's followers in Germany, however, hostility was generated by the programs for urban renewal and mass housing implemented by technocrats, without democratic checks and balances. The widespread rejection of the political positions embodied in the dominant urban development and housing policies not only fueled outbursts of dissent but galvanized a range of alternative strategies that went well beyond the aspirations of a few individuals to an intellectually renewed architecture.

Research and technocracy

For architects, the main issue became the elaboration of an alternative form of practice, one opposed to that of the major firms, which were so often complicit in the destructive development projects. This search went in two opposite directions: a determined populism and an intellectualized elitism. These reciprocal trends coexisted throughout the 1960s. While Lewis Mumford's essays had long been critical of commercial American firms, it was Jane Jacobs's book *The Death and Life of Great American Cities*, published in 1961, that brought to a critical mass the outcry against brutal urban renewal and technocratic policies such as those carried out by Robert Moses in New York. [1]

In contrast to citizen-launched urban movements like that of Jacobs against the alliance between big architectural firms and top-down planning programs, the other force was intellectual and methodological. It was couched in a new concept of "urban design," generally accepted as an alternative to the notion of "planning" in academic and professional circles following a conference organized by José Luís Sert at Harvard in April 1956, and it coalesced a new disciplinary culture encompassing architects, landscape architects, and city planners. [2] Studies dealing with everyday urban experience as well as urban design primers quickly proliferated. [3] Harvard and MIT established a joint urban studies laboratory headed by Kevin Lynch, who investigated the way inhabitants perceived the space of their cities, **496** with the aim of using behavioral findings to produce a more satisfying urban landscape. Lynch also tried to imagine design strategies that would improve the landscape of urban highways, whose construction in American cities often contributed to the destruction of working-class neighborhoods. [4] His work was symptomatic of larger transformations taking place throughout American universities, characterized by an emphasis on scientifically based research on urban planning and manifesting itself in new doctoral programs in urban planning and architecture as well as greater emphasis on campus-based laboratories. For the first time since the Bauhaus, a new type of school emerged in which both theoretical work and research played an essential role. While the English, French, and Italian utopian movements derided the projects and clichés of commercial architecture, the North American scene was dominated by a certain academicism, sometimes expressed with borrowed forms. With the exception of Louis Kahn's buildings, few interesting projects saw the light of day during the 1960s. Wallace K. Harrison

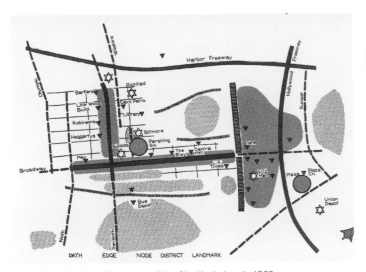

496 Illustration from *The Image of the City*, Kevin Lynch, 1960

497 Ford Foundation, John Dinkeloo and Kevin Roche, New York City, USA, 1963–8

built the Albany Mall (1962–5) in the state capital of New York for Governor Nelson Rockefeller, using belabored sculptural forms derived from Oscar Niemeyer's Brasília. →5 Boston City Hall (1963–8), by Kallmann, McKinnell, and Knowles, recycled devices found in Le Corbusier's monastery of La Tourette. Projects by I. M. Pei's firm also tended to adapt rather than to transform existing building types, often giving them a more elaborate concrete surface. The team of Kevin Roche and John Dinkeloo carried on Eliel Saarinen's legacy after his death. Their Ford Foundation in New York (1963–8), **497** however, was exceptional. More than just a simple adjustment of the traditional office building, it was a genuinely alternative solution. A twelve-story L-shaped tower built of COR-TEN steel wrapped around a tropical garden sheltered by a 130-foot-tall (40-meter) atrium, it provided the city with a large covered public space. In contrast, Minoru Yamasaki's twin towers for Manhattan's World Trade Center (1962–77; destroyed 2001) dissimulated the innovation of their load-bearing structural envelope, which permitted a layout of free-planned floors. The metallic walls rose from narrow "Gothic" arches at plaza level. Yamasaki claimed that his medieval-inspired tracery humanized what most people at the time saw as abstract and scaleless monoliths.

Venturi's critique

Museums came to play a parallel role in architectural discourse to that of universities. In 1966 the Museum of Modern Art published Robert Venturi's *Complexity and Contradiction in Architecture*, one of the most contentious books of the second half of the century. →6 Written during a stay at the American Academy in Rome and enthusiastically endorsed by the Yale architectural history professor Vincent Scully, the book

was a head-on attack on modernist clichés. Venturi made an exception for a few projects by Le Corbusier and Alvar Aalto, the latter of whom he considered to be the "Palladio of the Modern Movement." Drawing his examples largely from the Renaissance and the Baroque, he pleaded for greater ambiguity, a richer mix of form and meaning, and the juxtaposition of contradictory elements in response to both architectural context and urban scale. With his wife Denise Scott Brown, Venturi enjoyed popular roadside culture and visual heterogeneity and aspired to turn it into usable material in his designs. To the "magnificent paradox" of Ludwig Mies van der Rohe's statement "less is more," he countered "less is a bore" and "more is more," arguing for the rehabilitation of a more historicist perspective and the rediscovery of the value of ornament. →7 Venturi did not limit himself to architectural discourse in arguing for greater semantic liveliness. His own first buildings provided an effective demonstration of his positions. The house he built for his mother (1962) **498** in the Chestnut Hill section of Philadelphia was an architectural manifesto by virtue of the heterogeneity of its facade, which counterposed a square window to a Corbusian ribbon window, and its self-assured play with architectural conventions. The nonliteral symmetry of the principal facade displays every aspect of classical balance while in no way corresponding to the house's asymmetrical interior. Venturi's Guild House (1960–3), **499** on the other hand, a senior citizens' home in downtown Philadelphia, is completely symmetrical in both plan and elevation. The facade displays signs of the building's function: a large arched window recalling Roman baths gives central importance to the television room behind it – a function whose importance was further reinforced originally by a symbolic television antenna rising above it – while the institution's name is inscribed on the facade in

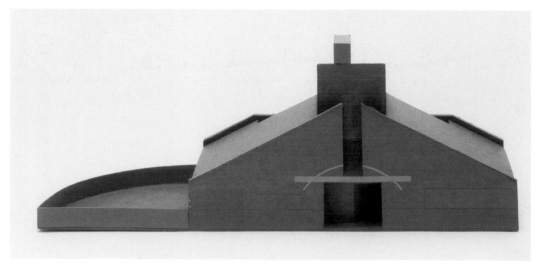

498 Vanna Venturi House, Robert Venturi, Philadelphia, Pennsylvania, USA, 1962

supergraphics much like an advertising billboard. Later Venturi ironically manipulated the stereotypes of vernacular architecture with his Trubek and Wislocki houses on the island of Nantucket (both 1970).

In clear opposition to the legion of critics denouncing the bad taste of the American suburbs, among them Peter Blake in his book *God's Own Junkyard*, → 8 Venturi wondered: "Is not Main Street almost all right?" → 9 He set about proving his point in a 1968 workshop, conducted with Scott Brown and a group of Yale University students, which aimed at a detailed study of the commercial strip in Las Vegas, and culminated in the pubication of a book, *Learning from Las Vegas* (1972). **500** Through an analysis both "open-minded" and "non-judgmental," they studied a "new type of urban form emerging in America and Europe, radically different from that we have known; one we have been ill-equipped to deal with and that, from ignorance, we define today as urban sprawl." → 10 Using a rich variety of graphic and photographic approaches, they dissected the intense spatial relationships among street, buildings, and advertising signs. Although the methodology they developed was for an extreme case – Las Vegas – it was meant to be applicable to the built-up environment of any suburb anywhere in the world.

Grays and Whites

Charles W. Moore, a professor at the University of California, Berkeley, and later at the University of California, Los Angeles, Yale, and the University of Texas at Austin, also studied vernacular types and proposed to replace the moderns' reflections on "space" by taking into account "place" and its specificities. → 11 Sea Ranch, (1964–5) **501** which he built with

his associates Donlyn Lyndon, William Turnbull, and Richard Whitaker on a cliff overlooking the Pacific in Sonoma County, was a revelation for an entire generation. On a wild terrain landscaped by Lawrence Halprin, Moore assembled clusters of houses ingeniously protected from the wind and echoing the volumes of nineteenth-century vernacular wood buildings, but with interiors of surprising complexity. The development received immediate, extensive attention throughout the world, as it seemed to promise a more site-sensitive architecture and a rediscovered sense of materiality. For the University of California, Santa Barbara, Moore designed a faculty club (1967–8) adhering to a more Mediterranean image, deemed appropriate to Southern California.

Subsequently dubbed by critics the "Grays" – for the weathered color that the Douglas pine exteriors of their houses took on after exposure to the elements – Venturi, Moore, and their followers were considered originators of a new "Shingle Style," a reference to Vincent Scully's label for a series of American buildings constructed in the second half of the nineteenth century. → 12 The Grays were polemically opposed to the "Whites" – a group of young New York architects eager to revive theories and forms from the radical modernism of the 1920s. It was the latter who most defined the elitist wing of the anti-corporate opposition. They were under the spell of the ideas of the British architect and historian Colin Rowe, then teaching at Cornell University in upstate New York, whose analyses of "literal" and "phenomenal" transparency had been formulated with his coauthor, the painter Robert Slutzky, at the University of Texas at Austin in the mid-1950s. These analyses together with Rowe's writing on the similarities between the geometric underpinnings of Le Corbusier's and Palladio's villas proved seminal. → 13

499 Guild House, Robert Venturi, Philadelphia, Pennsylvania, USA, 1960–3

501 ▶ Sea Ranch, Charles W. Moore, Donlyn Lyndon, William Turnbull and Richard Whitaker, landscape by Lawrence Halprin, Sonoma County, California, USA, 1964–5

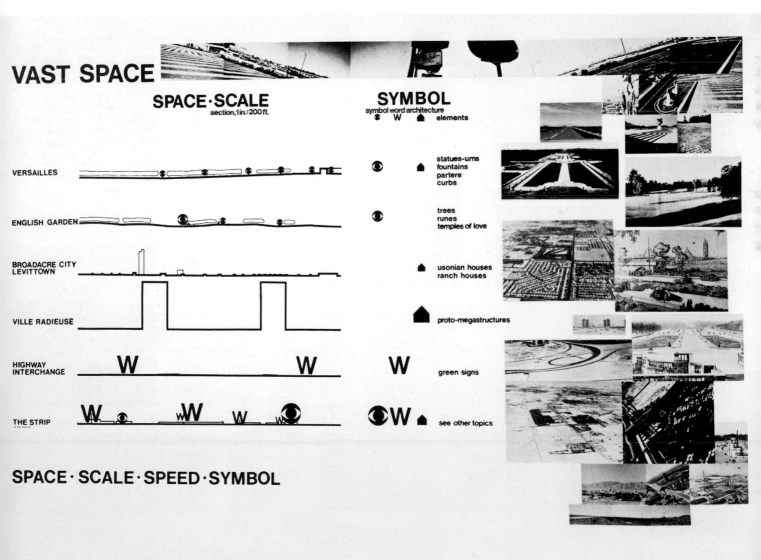

500 Page from *Learning from Las Vegas,* Robert Venturi, Denise Scott Brown and Steven Izenour, 1972

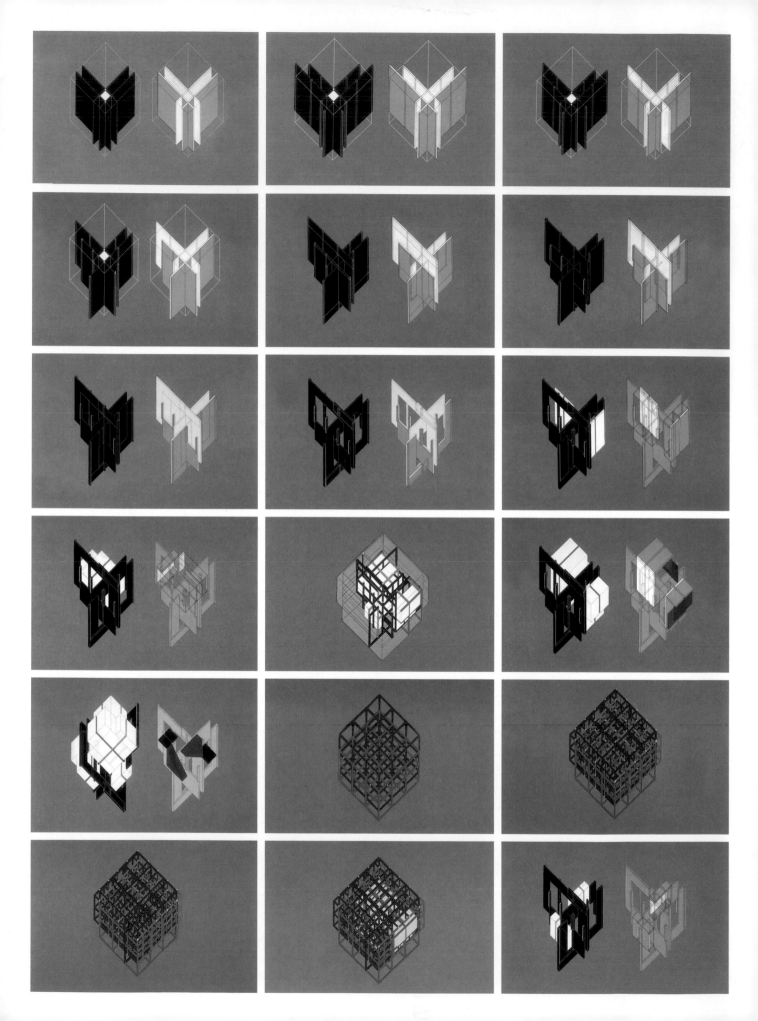

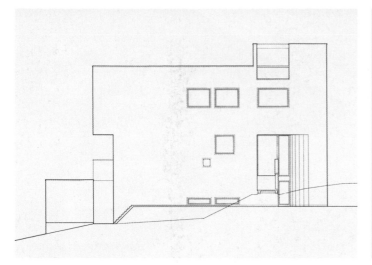

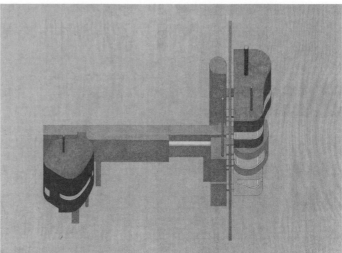

503 Smith House, Richard Meier, Darien, Connecticut, USA, 1965–7

502 Frank House (House VI), Peter Eisenman, Cornwall Bridge, Connecticut, USA, 1972–5

504 Wall House, project, John Hejduk, 1966–73

Peter Eisenman, the most theoretically motivated of the Whites, reflected on key projects of modernism, approaching them as independent of their social or political meaning and deriving from them formal strategies that he was able to realize only occasionally. Between designing the Falk House, or House II, in Hardwick, Vermont (1969–70), and the Frank House, or House VI (1972–5) **502** in Cornwall Bridge, Connecticut, he developed a vocabulary based on geometric grids that interacted in a series of arcane operations, eschewing, however, any purely literal imitation of modernist examples. In 1967 Eisenman founded the Institute for Architecture and Urban Studies in New York, establishing a place for theoretical and critical debate as well as experimental design that was deliberately outside of the established academy. These contributions played an essential role in the construction of a more intellectual approach to architecture.

Together with John Hejduk, **504** Michael Graves, Charles Gwathmey, and Richard Meier, Eisenman also belonged to a group that came to be known as the New York Five. Their work, which the New York-based English critic Kenneth Frampton described in 1971 as the product of an informal but important allance, had a major impact when it was published the following year. → 14 Each of the Five in his own way appropriated fragments of early twentieth-century modernism, restoring its relevance to current design theory and practice. Between Hejduk's approach, which was aesthetically the most experimental, and Gwathmey's, the most commercially oriented, the spectrum of attitudes and ambitions suggests the somewhat arbitrary nature of this grouping of architects. Graves applied his acute sense of decoration to designing house extensions and later buildings of increasing scale, sometimes closer to Le Corbusier's Purist paintings than to his

Paris villas. Meier interpreted more directly architectural elements from Le Corbusier in his residential projects. His Smith House (1965–7) **503** in Darien, Connecticut, a wood structure painted white, intensifies the play of the "free facade" and double-height rooms; it is inserted into its rocky site like an alien artifact, much like the Villa Savoye. Another white volume contrasting with the surrounding woods is Meier's Douglas House (1971–3) in Harbor Springs, Michigan, divided into served spaces facing the lake and servant spaces to the rear, replicating one of the organizational devices Le Corbusier himself borrowed from eighteenth-century French planning.

From functionalism to advocacy planning

While the Five attempted to create an American avant-garde from scratch, although not without a certain nostalgia for the avant-garde theories and designs of the 1920s, in Europe one of the rare institutions directly extending the experiments of those early years – principally those of the Bauhaus – suffered a terminal crisis. The Hochschule für Gestaltung (College of Design) in Ulm, West Germany, opened in 1954 on the initiative of Otl Aicher and Inge Aicher-Scholl, the sister of two young members of the resistance movement executed by the Nazis. The following year the school settled into facilities designed by Max Bill, its first director. For fifteen years, the school trained meticulous professionals, often working closely with industrial corporations such as Braun and Kodak as well as Lufthansa Airlines in the spirit of interwar functionalism. It focused on promoting the field of visual communication and, under the influence of Claude Schnaidt, advocated an architecture with close ties to industry and a predilection for prefabrication. The focus on an education linked to real-world commissions, an orientation

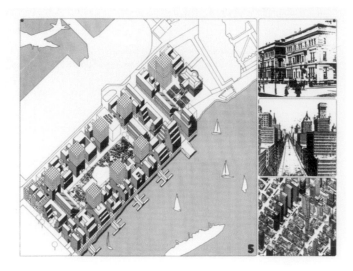

505 Roosevelt Island competition project, Oswald Mathias Ungers, New York City, USA, 1975

506 Municipal Orphanage, or Children's House, Aldo van Eyck, Amsterdam, Netherlands, 1955–60

inherited from the Bauhaus, became a subject of contestation within the school, notably by the Argentine Tomás Maldonado, who elaborated a critical theory of product design. Ultimately, the Hochschule's political leanings toward the Marxist Left served as a pretext for the local government to mandate its closure in 1968 – a fate also reminiscent of the Bauhaus history. Oswald Mathias Ungers, a German architect who taught first in Berlin and then at Cornell University before returning to his native country, took a totally different approach. Downplaying the political dimension in favor of urban morphology as the most determining factor in architectural design, he proposed that building forms be composed according to a very rigorous methodology. Yet the apparently rigid geometry of his projects did not preclude attention to their topographic specificity, while simultaneously updating – at least in the 1960s – the ideas of the *Neues Bauen* as well as the methods of the Russian avant-garde. [15] As dean of the architecture school at Cornell from 1969 to 1975, Ungers became an active participant on the North American scene, taking part, for instance, in the Roosevelt Island competition in New York (1975). **505**

The contradiction between scholarly, highly intellectualized architecture (as exemplified by the New York Five) and architectural styles deemed "popular" was among the factors that led to a global revolt by architecture students. Returning to the initial experiences of the Modern Movement, less in a celebratory than a critical mode now, and reevaluating which of its buildings and designs warranted careful reexamination, the younger generation aimed to recover a lost dimension of architectural experimentation. The question of the user and of the transformation of buildings over time had been raised since the 1950s in the work of Aldo van Eyck, one of Team 10's founding members. A devotee of Symbolist poetry, van Eyck was also interested in Surrealism, and he imagined a multicentered universe in which relationships took precedence over objects. Like Moore, he countered Sigfried Giedion's "space-time" with concepts of place and experience. After designing playgrounds in Amsterdam, van Eyck built the city's Municipal Orphanage, or Children's Home, in 1955–60. **506** A building without a facade, it consisted of a layer of dormitories and playrooms arranged mainly on one level, organized apparently according to a system of square modules and giving the impression of limitless horizontal extension. Every space is tailored to a different age group and keyed to the children's daily activities. [16] Hostile to both the forms of the modern masters and the celebration of technology, van Eyck was drawn to the settlement patterns of African and Oceanic houses and villages.

The move away from elite European and North American architecture undertaken by van Eyck was paralleled by Bernard Rudofsky in his exhibition *Architecture without Architects*, first shown at the Museum of Modern Art in New York in 1964 before touring the world for another decade. The exhibition revealed a treasure trove of native habitats found on the five continents and displayed dozens of surprising structures realized without professional designers. Rudofsky, who was aware of Giuseppe Pagano and Guarniero Daniel's 1936 *Architettura moderna in Italia* exhibition, used the photographic archive of the Musée de l'homme in Paris to carry out his research, aiming to give visual expression to the idea that "the philosophy and know-how of the anonymous builders presents the largest untapped source of architectural inspiration for industrial man." [17]

In 1971, ten years after the publication of Jane Jacobs's landmark book, Robert Goodman published *After the Planners*, a denunciation of the authoritarian urban planning practiced by an arrogant bureaucracy and compliant professionals. Propounding

507 Drop City, Gene Bernofsky, JoAnn Bernofsky, Clark Richert and Richard Kallweit, Trinidad, Colorado, USA, 1965–8

the ideal of advocacy, or of putting planning at the service of inhabitants, Goodman echoed the antiwar movement in criticizing the "urban-industrial complex" and the "architecture of counter-revolution" and proposed methods of working directly with the local population. In contrast to scholarly models, he invited readers fighting for the "liberation" of architecture to learn from "what we tend to call primitive cultures," where "people are indeed capable of making more personally meaningful connections with their environment." He also encouraged people to "sense they can begin to act on their needs without waiting for the government or its experts to take care of them." → 18

The temptation was great at this juncture for students and young intellectuals to break all ties with established society and the conventional practices of architecture and urban planning. Some became involved in building marginal communities in the American West, joining Paolo Soleri's Arcology movement, for example, to create autonomous dwelling schemes in Phoenix and the Arizona desert. Others, inspired by Buckminster Fuller, built geodesic domes and "zomes." The latter – its name combines "domes," "homes," and "zonahedrons" (a variety of polyhedron) – were derived from the former, but used salvaged materials, as in Drop City **507** in Colorado, founded by Clark Richert, Richard Kallweit, and Gene and JoAnn Bernofsky in 1965. → 19 The first experiments with solar power appeared in these unofficial settlements, as did the first signs of an environmental approach going beyond the critique of traditional urban planning to call into question industrial society's relationship to the natural environment. → 20

After 1968: architecture for the city

Besides the return to modernist design principles and the escape to alternative communities outside the city, there were other strategies that emerged from the 1968 student and social movements. [1] These had less to do with buildings than with decision-making processes and, above all, with the question of urbanity itself. The search for a response to the global crisis in the design disciplines that had affected Europe, North America, and Japan led to new alliances among architects, activists, and intellectuals. Among the offshoots of these new alliances in both academic circles and political and cultural groups were influential critical journals and magazines such as the New York–based *Oppositions*, the French *Architecture, Mouvement, Continuité*, the Italian *Contropiano*, and book series like *Pamphlet Architecture*, initially published out of San Francisco, which communicated new intellectual thinking throughout the 1970s. [2]

1968, annus mirabilis

Architecture schools around the world were among the most visible battlegrounds between young people and the establishment. In New York, students protested Columbia University's dealings as the main real-estate holder of property in Harlem. In Rome and Florence, universities were occupied by protesters from the fall of 1967 to the winter of 1968. At the École des Beaux-Arts in Paris, students and professionals contested the French and American political systems and in particular the unethical policies affecting the *bidonvilles* (shantytowns) and *"villes-bidons"* ("phony cities" – i.e., the French New Towns) in a great happening that lasted through the months of May and June 1968. **508** Reform of the Paris school's curriculum, which had become increasingly divorced from social and professional realities, had been under discussion since 1965, and social science courses were now among the offerings. But the aging system, discredited by its refusal to address the question of housing, was ultimately rejected and the architecture department dissolved. [3] Beginning in the fall of 1969, the former system was replaced by new schools representing a broad spectrum of divergent architectural doctrines and rival political affiliations.

Reverberations of the unrest in Paris – which with its barricades and prolonged occupation of the Sorbonne was the most spectacular of the '68 events – were heard around the world. In late May 1968, before the fourteenth Triennale in Milan was even inaugurated, it was occupied by rebellious artists. Devoted to the issue of the "Great Number" (a concept proposed by Team 10 members, who thus defined the mass user of their projects), the exhibition turned out to be Team 10's swan song. The Triennale's program had been the subject of heated confrontations between the Milanese architect Aldo Rossi, who had argued for an exhibition asserting the autonomous value of architectural projects in themselves, and the exhibition's chief curator, Giancarlo De Carlo. A member of Team 10, De Carlo was working at the time on a meticulously planned transformation of the historical city of Urbino, calibrated to the needs of the local university. Creating new, partly buried spaces in the city's fragile historic center, he built colleges and dormitories on the surrounding hills, with clusters of volumes carefully placed on the slopes. [4] The Triennale program, carried out under De Carlo's direction, featured a series of rooms comprising self-contained exhibitions by the Smithsons, Shadrach Woods, and György Kepes. Nothing but printed evidence attested to it, however, since in the climate of protest the show remained open only for a couple of hours. [5]

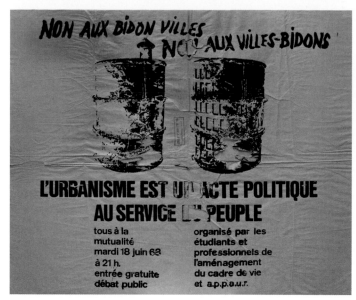

508 Non aux Bidon Villes, Non aux Villes-Bidon (No to Shantytowns, No to Phoney Towns), Paris, France, June 1968, poster

509 *Playtime*, Jacques Tati, 1967, film still

Observing the extended city

The fourteenth Triennale was intended to restore the social, sensuous, and semantic richness of urban space, impoverished by the modernization policies applied both to the renovation of city centers and to the building of massive housing developments in the suburbs. The initially favorable reception of larger and better-equipped housing had quickly been succeeded by a sense of isolation among displaced urban populations as well as those in exile from their native countries, and the lack of social diversity in the suburbs was increasingly deplored. Sociologists like Paul-Henry Chombart de Lauwe and Henri Lefebvre described the marginalization of the working classes, [6] while contemporary films denounced urban renewal policies and revealed the vacuousness of the architecture of commercial modernization. The Italian film director Francesco Rosi criticized Neapolitan real-estate promotion in *Hands over the City* (1963), while in France Jean-Luc Godard transformed the towers of the La Défense area of Paris into the capital of a distant, depersonalized planet in *Alphaville* (1965) and then evoked the alienation of women in the Paris suburbs in *Two or Three Things I Know about Her* (1967). Jacques Tati, who had skewered the gadgetry of modern houses in his film *Mon Oncle* (1958), hilariously attacked the repetitive spaces of the modern city and the ridiculous mishaps unleashed by a fashionable glass architecture in *Playtime* (1967). **509**

A few groups of architects attempted to produce dwellings and collective buildings that gave suburban space greater material and formal complexity. This was the case with the Atelier d'urbanisme et d'architecture (AUA), based in the Paris suburbs, which built the Bagnolet Towers (1968–71) **511** as well as residential buildings in Saint-Ouen and in the Arlequin development in Grenoble. AUA's leading figure, Paul Chemetov, pursued an astute interpretation of the suburban context during the following decades before winning larger commissions for public buildings such as the French Ministry of Finance in Paris (1981–8, with Borja Huidobro). The position he articulated in his copious writings combined the rationalist tradition of Viollet-le-Duc with the critical theater of Bertolt Brecht. [7]

In Barcelona, the Martorell Bohigas Mackay firm operated on the existing urban situation with their Pallars Housing Complex (1958–9), a clever arrangement of brick volumes within the envelope of the urban blocks of Ildefons Cerdà's 1859 extension plan for the city. Also in Barcelona, Josep Antoni Coderch designed housing developments like Les Cotxeres (1968), featuring new combinations of buildings with deep, expressive facades. In Milan, Carlo Aymonino responded to the repetitive nature of the suburbs with the Gallaratese Housing (1972–6), **512** a new interpretation of Le Corbusier's Unité d'Habitation. In contrast to these solid buildings exhibiting an inventive spatiality and robust plasticity, Aldo Rossi, then teaching in Venice with Aymonino, built an austere white slab supported on an elongated concrete colonnade evoking late-nineteenth-century Lombardian workers' lodgings.

The shape of the city

With his book *L'architettura della città* (The Architecture of the City; 1966), Rossi made a fundamental contribution to the definition of the city not as a transportation network or a set of functional zones but as an product of human culture. He drew on the work of historians such as Marcel Poëte, geographers such as Georges Chabot, and sociologists such as Maurice Halbwachs, seeking to counter a reductive functionalism.

510 *La Città analoga* (The Analogous City), collage, Aldo Rossi, 1973

Exploring the theme of "collective memory," and defining the city as a complex artifact, he focused on the different roles within the city of the continuous residential districts, "primary elements" such as urban infrastructure and places of public aggregation, and in particular monuments. →[8] In so doing, he rejected the idea that residential buildings could, by themselves, serve as the city's major spaces; the latter, he argued, could only be constituted by monumental buildings. Rossi's study of the specificity of forms led him to elaborate a theory of the *locus*, based in part on his reading of the French writer Raymond Roussel's enigmatic texts. Rossi understood urban building types as the expression of both individual and collective memory. The latter term he owed to Halbwachs, and it led him to adopt a repertory of forms that alluded to past structures while subjecting them to expressive changes of scale and materiality.

Taking the analysis of medieval building types in Venice and Rome by the Roman architect Saverio Muratori as the basis of an "operative history" to be used to design architectural projects in these cities, Rossi and Aymonino developed a theory based on the study of urban forms (morphology), individual building types, and their analysis of the interrelationship. As they demonstrated in the case of Padua, these factors were distinctive to each city. →[9] In 1973 the fifteenth Milan Triennale was devoted to the theme of *architettura razionale* (Rationalist architecture), and it proved to be more than just a vindication of Rossi's position over De Carlo's: it marked a turning point in the architectural conception of the city, which, after half a century, was again considered a composition of blocks, monuments, and streets. Rossi's *La Città analoga* (The Analogous City) **510** collage comments upon this strategy. The Triennale also reconnected with the experience of the Modern Movement, but

identified less with the brilliance of designs by Le Corbusier or Mies now than with the reformist urban projects developed from Frankfurt to Vienna during the interwar period. Despite the nostalgic gaze focused on the European complexes of the 1920s, the projects at the Triennale, whether rediscovered or new, proposed strategies to reinvest contemporary urban space with meaning. →[10]

Vittorio Gregotti, who had been Ernesto Nathan Rogers's assistant at *Casabella-continuità*, garnered attention for his design of several projects in Novara and Milan. In a variety of articles, notably those published in a 1966 issue of the journal *Edilizia moderna* (Modern Construction), he suggested that architecture could no longer limit its focus to urban space but had to concern itself with the potential to transform entire regions. →[11] In *Il territorio dell'architettura* (The Territory of Architecture), which appeared the same year as Rossi's *L'architettura della città*, he surveyed a variety of disciplines relevant to architecture including sociology, literary criticism, and semiotics, reflecting his broader disciplinary perspective. (In 1964 Gregotti had headed the thirteenth Milan Triennale with the semiologist Umberto Eco.) Yet he placed greatest emphasis on the idea of a "willed geography" *(geografia volontaria)* through which the "construction of the landscape becomes a field of expertise specific to architecture." His 1.8-km long (1.25-mile) project for the University of Calabria in Cosenza (1973–85) **513** illustrates this ambition. Skeptical of the notion of typology, which he considered conservative, Gregotti noted that "architectural organisms are constituted like the expansion of a continuous flow, the coagulation of a tight network of superimposed functions that can constantly take on new configurations, according to a mutation that tends to make the urban fabric, the structure of the organism, and the nature

511 Bagnolet Towers, Atelier d'Urbanisme et d'Architecture (Paul Chemetov and Jean Deroche), Bagnolet, France, 1968–71

512 Gallaratese Housing, Carlo Aymonino, Milan, Italy, 1972–6

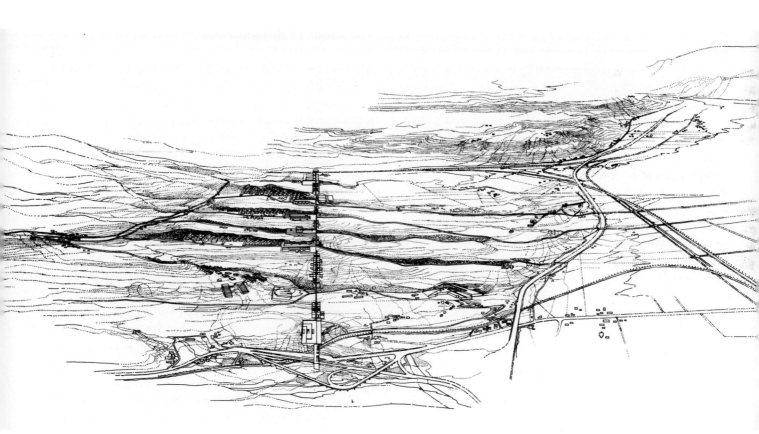

513 University of Calabria, Vittorio Gregotti, Cosenza, Italy, 1975–85

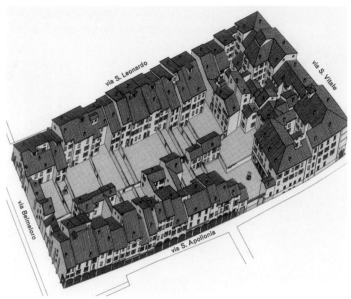

514 San Leonardo Quarter, Pierluigi Cervellati, Bologna, Italy, 1974–9

of the territory continuous." → 12 Gregotti later proposed seeing these mutations in the landscape as "modifications," in
the belief that no architectural or territorial situation was ever
completely new. → 13
Echoing the theories being developed in universities and
exhibitions, reforms occurred in the 1970s that gave greater
planning power to local authorities, allowing Italian cities
to implement their own programs and develop innovative
building strategies. In Bologna, the restoration of the historic
center was accomplished without displacing any of the area's
inhabitants. Pierluigi Cervellati comissioned buildings according to types derived from the study of medieval houses, **514**
seeking to avoid creating a soulless museum-city. The French
emissary of the Italian theorists, Bernard Huet, described
Bologna as the city where architects relearn how to become
modest – in other words, to sublimate their desire for innovation in favor of greater sensitivity to history and to the continuities inherent in building types considered obsolete by
modernist designers. The Italian projects contributed to a
new architectural discourse in which the primary issues
became the city and the study of building types, from housing to schools, hospitals, and other institutions. An example
of the success – and of the polysemous character – of the
notion of type and the study of typology is found in 1977 in
the Anglo-American theorist Anthony Vidler's notion of a "third
typology" based on the city, replacing previous paradigms
based successively on man and on the machine. Through an
intellectual dialogue with Vidler, the Madrid architect Rafael
Moneo placed the analysis of building types at the core of
a new theory of architecture, rejecting the simplifications of
functionalism and challenging the excesses that the modernist search for originality had engendered. → 14

The input of the user

A rather different concept of type took into account the uses
of buildings, opening a fruitful dialogue between architects
and sociologists that encouraged a second wave of populism.
Architects now focused their technical expertise – no longer
dismissed by critics celebrating the spontaneous creativity of
inhabitants – on clarifying the relationships between spaces
and their uses. These relationships could be addressed in
theoretical terms by a language of "patterns," as Christopher
Alexander, a professor at the University of California, Berkeley,
attempted to do in describing a wide spectrum of configu-
rational patterns, from the macroscopic scale of urban settlements to the microscopic one of everyday life, taking in
spaccs such as the front porch. → 15 On a practical level, inhabitants became actively involved in architecture projects like
the one carried out in Terni by Giancarlo De Carlo, who from
1970 to 1975 engaged the future inhabitants of the Matteotti
Neighborhood **516** in an intensive process of reflection on the
configuration of their future homes without surrendering his
own prerogatives as designer.
De Carlo was able to create the conditions for a participa-
tory housing project using sophisticated materials and building techniques. Meanwhile a similar concern with participation
surfaced in Europe and North America with the publication
in 1970 of *Construire avec le peuple* (issued in England in
1973 as *Architecture for the Poor*), an influential book that
related an experiment with preindustrial materials. Its author,
the Egyptian architect Hassan Fathy, described the construction of the village of New Gourna (1948–60), **515** near Luxor, by
its own inhabitants according to plans based on a historical
typology of local structures and the use of low-tech materials

515 New Gourna Village, Hassan Fathy, Luxor, Egypt, 1948–60

like unfired brick. → 16 In opposition to the myth of the "barefoot" architect, voluntarily relinquishing all his knowledge to serve the people – to which many young Western architecture graduates, enrolled in the American Peace Corps and similar European assistance programs, fell prey – the Cairo-trained Fathy worked with the village's inhabitants by applying solutions he had observed in existing cities and then configured for the local context through his mastery of composition, geometry, and construction. → 17

Rejecting both the temptation to populism and that of technocratic architecture to collaborate blindly with capitalist modernization, Manfredo Tafuri, a professor of history at the Architecture Institute in Venice, developed a radical critique of "architectural ideology" during these years. Inviting a reconsideration of the entire modern experience, Tafuri sought not to contest modernism's aesthetic innovations but rather to lay bare its illusions, beginning with the belief that a "good" city plan could guarantee a harmonious society. Considering "utopian" designs to be little more than a mask for capitalist reorganization, he pointed out the failure of the avant-gardes to sway those in power to adopt their positions. → 18 He also denounced the "operative criticism" of architectural writers like Bruno Zevi and Leonardo Benevolo, whose historical interpretations aimed to provide useful ballast for contemporary projects. The "historical project" that Tafuri set out was by no means a justification for a nostalgic use of the forms of the past, but rather an exercise in exposing the motivations and rhetorical strategies of architecture through an application of techniques of psychoanalysis and literary criticism. Tafuri compared the labor of writing history, as exemplified by the work of the Italian historian Carlo Ginzburg, to a meticulous detective investigation while questioning its compulsion to try to "find the

murderer." → 19 The subtlety of Tafuri's interpretations of architectural projects and buildings provided inspiration not just for theorists but also for practicing architects throughout Europe, America, and Japan, notwithstanding the often botched translations of his arduous books.

The postmodern season

Despite its wide diffusion, Manfredo Tafuri's skeptical approach remained marginal in impact compared to the almost fetishistic use of history that began to spread in response to what he and others acknowledged to be the exhaustion of modern architectural languages. Starting in the early 1970s, a new cycle of reaction set in, as if echoing the previous "returns to order" that had taken place throughout Europe in the early 1920s, again in the 1930s, and once more behind the Iron Curtain during the first decade of the Cold War. Remarkably, the first act of this massive rejection of modern architecture took place exactly where modernism had once triumphed, at the Museum of Modern Art in New York. The 1975 exhibition *The Architecture of the École des Beaux-Arts* **517** – a project Robert Venturi had proposed in the 1960s – rehabilitated the art of architectural composition and gave the now defunct institution of the Beaux-Arts a more complex and creative image. [1]

That exhibition was followed in 1979 by *Transformations in Modern Architecture*, in which the same curator, Arthur Drexler illuminated the crisis in modern architecture through a provocative juxtaposition of photographs articulated according to such categories as structure, vocabulary (e.g., "windows", "parapets," and "detachable parts"), and aesthetic attitudes (e.g., "sculptural form" and "the vernacular"). [2]

From nostalgia to play

Another school of thought based on historical precedent took shape in several new projects. The resort town of Port-Grimaud (1963–70), **520** built from the ground up by François Spoerry on the Côte d'Azur, proposed a "culinary" populism, to borrow Bertolt Brecht's term for the complacency of bourgeois theater. This cute rendition of Venice in Provence sought to give the illusion of organic, cumulative growth, imitating the cliché of Mediterranean villages. In Brussels, Maurice Culot, with his Archives d'architecture moderne, proposed an "anti-industrial resistance" to urban renewal, advocating a return to streets, squares, and motifs from local history. The Luxembourg-born architect Léon Krier's drawings of imaginary cities buttressed these explicitly political activities, which found their manifesto in the 1978 "Palermo Declaration" signed by Krier, Culot, Antoine Grumbach, Pierluigi Nicolin, and Angelo Villa. Declaring that "the separation of functions has led to an absurd extension of the city and urban areas," the authors diagnosed "the resulting slavery of modernity" as responsible for destroying "the social and physical cohesion of the European city." [3]

Several months later, the group was joined by Bernard Huet, Philippe Panerai, and François Loyer in issuing the "Brussels Declaration," which recommended banishing "urban clearways and motorways, mono-functional zones and residual green space," and postulated that "All intervention in the European city must necessarily focus on what the city has always been, that is: streets, squares, avenues, blocks, gardens … and [residential] quarters." [4]

Along with the nostalgia for historical cities, there was also a rejection by some of professional control of architectural and urban form. In the Mémé Medical School Dormitories in Woluwé-Saint-Lambert, near Brussels (1970–2), **518** Lucien Kroll denied the architect's exclusive mastery of aesthetics. Working with the users, he combined the informality of the design process with a looseness in the design verging on the formless. Drawing on Gaston Bardet's teachings on the social morphology of neighborhoods and the contributions of their inhabitants, he accepted the attendant diminution of some of architecture's creative ambition. [5]

517 The *Architecture of the École des Beaux-Arts* exhibition, curator Arthur Drexler, New York City, USA, 1975–6

518 Mémé Medical School Dormitories, Lucien Kroll, Woluwé-Saint-Lambert, Belgium, 1970–2

Other contemporary architectural transformations, which the American critic Charles Jencks surveyed in *The Language of Post-Modern Architecture* (1977), →6 seemed to echo the theories of sociologists like Alain Touraine and Daniel Bell, who predicted the advent of a "post-industrial society" that went beyond Fordist principles and was based largely on a service economy. →7 In *La condition postmoderne* (The Postmodern Condition; 1979), the philosopher Jean-François Lyotard announced the end of the great legitimating myths of the French Revolution and Hegelianism. →8 He argued that if the preceding period of modernity was the age of "master narratives" in its advocacy of the emancipation of the rational or working subject, then postmodernity was the age of "incredulity." But he also conceived of this postmodern condition as temporary, part of a crisis or cyclical moment within the ongoing trajectory of a revolutionary modernity, predicting that it would be succeeded by a fresh outpouring of formal innovation. Subsequent events would prove him right.

The "end of prohibitions"

Postmodern architecture was introduced to the world at large at the 1980 Venice Biennale with La Strada novissima (The Newest Street), installed in the Arsenale's Corderie by Paolo Portoghesi for the exhibition *La presenza del passato* (The Presence of the Past). **519** The facades of this mock street were designed by Léon Krier, Venturi/Scott Brown, Hans Hollein, the Roman GRAU group, and a then-unknown Californian, Frank Gehry, among others. The Biennale asserted the role of the street as an essential urban form and heralded what Portoghesi called the "end of prohibitions" – an emancipatory return to ornament, historical quotations, and monumental or playful

gestures. →9 For his part, Jencks argued for a return to drawing and for recovering the semantic and poetic values deemed lost by the Modern Movement. Failing to distinguish clearly between indisputable flaws in the moderns' methods and the process of modernization in general, Jencks celebrated the coexistence of extremely diverse approaches, which he attempted to classify into categories.

During this period, architects around the world were stricken with a sort of contagious anxiety. Finally freed of social responsibilities, architecture could at last escape the "moralism" that, according to the English historian David Watkin, had plagued design reformers since John Ruskin and irredeemably corrupted the Modern Movement, →10 but had to make difficult choices as for the most legitimate precedents to be used. Architecture could achieve this new freedom through a profusion of historical references and an efflorescence of ornament, both of which were favored by contemporary building technologies that, for instance, permitted facades to be non-load-bearing. While the "liberation" of architecture from its burdensome social responsibilities coincided with the election of Margaret Thatcher as British prime minister in 1979 and of Ronald Reagan to the White House in 1980, it would be simplistic to read the transformation of the discipline solely as the expression of an ascendant neoconservatism. →11 Reformist policies aimed at creating a more just society continued to make use of modern architectural forms and, conversely, postmodern projects continued to be driven on occasion by noncommercial motivations. Nonetheless, the crucial difference between these approaches and the "postmodern" return to order that manifested itself in the 1930s was that the phenomenon of the 1970s and 1980s, which produced playful objects and buildings that simulated historicity, was the product of the market, rather than that of state policies.

520 Port-Grimaud Resort, François Spoerry, Saint-Tropez, France, 1963–70

521 First La Villette competition project, Léon Krier, Paris, France, 1976

519 Hans Hollein installation, The Newest Street, *The Presence of the Past* exhibition, Venice Biennale, Italy, 1980

Retrieving urbanity's figures

The urge to monumentality may be seen in the inflated classical repertory featured in the designs of Ricardo Bofill. The Catalan architect's first major projects were driven by a utopian spirit. For example, his Walden 7 Complex (1970–4) in Sant Just Desvern, near Barcelona, is a labyrinthine sixteen-story megastructure indebted to Yona Friedman's spatial urbanism, with collective spaces stacked up to dizzying heights. Bofill was subsequently commissioned to design a project for the center of Paris on the site of the recently demolished Les Halles Marketplace. However, the project was cancelled and the partially-completed construction was torn down by Jacques Chirac after his election as mayor in 1977. Bofill's most ambitious built projects were for several new towns in France, in which he employed monumental metaphors. In Saint-Quentin-en-Yvelines, he built a housing development initially dubbed Versailles pour le peuple (Versailles for the People) and later renamed Les Arcades du Lac (The Arcades of the Lake; 1972–5), a vast composition of industrially constructed buildings forming closed blocks and extended by a "viaduct," a promontory built over the water. In Noisy-le-Grand, Les Espaces d'Abraxas (Spaces of Abraxas; 1978–83) **526** play with classical models based on the theater and the triumphal arch. In both cases, the technical research that Bofill put into prefabrication was as extensive as the ingenuity he invested in his oversize ornaments, from gigantic hollow columns containing staircases to exaggerated triglyphs. [12]

Léon Krier's drawings created a more familiar world, in which classical architectural elements were combined with references from the vernacular to create a recognizable landscape of streets and blocks. His Paris projects for the first Parc de la Villette competition (1976) **521** and for Les Halles (1978) provided a reassuring image of a dense, continuous city in which the public spaces were not less megalomaniacal than those of the public projects then under construction. For Berlin's Tegel neighborhood, he designed a housing development in 1980–3 on the scale of a small town and reminiscent in some ways of a seaside resort. His brother Rob Krier took a more didactic position in his book *Stadtraum in Theorie und Praxis* (1975; translated as *Urban Space*), a guide to the composition of squares and streets. [13] Rob Krier's apartment buildings in West Berlin, including one on Ritterstraße (1977–82), **524** re-created the continuous fabric of closed blocks that had been absent from Berlin since 1945 and opened the possibility of a different reconstruction of the city: one that was meant to be "critical," far from literal, and capable of resuscitating forgotten languages such as Karl Friedrich Schinkel's.

These ideas together with Aldo Rossi's theories led to a new Internationale Bauausstellung (International Building Exposition), or IBA. **522** Originally planned for 1984, it was eventually held in West Berlin in 1987. The preparatory work for this fourth large-scale housing and urban-planning exhibition held in Germany since 1910 zeroed in on the reconstruction of central neighborhoods and the rehabilitation of tenements inhabited by squatters and immigrant workers. Curated by Josef Paul Kleihues, the program led to the construction of rows of apartment houses and "urban villas" in the Tiergarten and the south of Friedrichstadt, both parts of the city still in ruins. A deep sensitivity to real and virtual traces of the past city suddenly emerged, inspiring projects commissioned for the exhibition from members of Europe's architectural elite – Krier, Rossi, Gregotti – as well as a few Americans, including Charles Moore and Peter Eisenman. In the Kreuzberg neighborhood,

522 Internationale Bauausstellung, Josef Paul Kleihues, West Berlin, Federal Republic of Germany, 1984–7, general plan of the areas for new construction

JANUARY 8, 1979 $1.25

TIME

IRAN
Violence and Chaos

U.S. Architects

Doing
Their Own
Thing

Philip Johnson

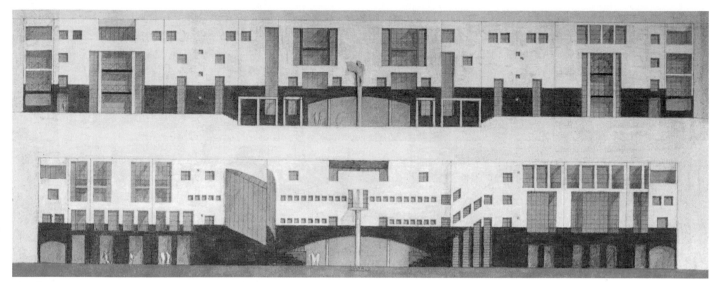

524 Ritterstraße Apartment Building, Robert Krier, West Berlin, Federal Republic of Germany, 1977–82

523 AT&T Building, John Burgee and Philip Johnson, New York City, USA, 1978–84, as seen on the cover of *Time* magazine of January 8, 1979

Hardt-Waltherr Hämer implemented simultaneously a "behutsame Stadtserneuerung" (gentle renewal), which permitted the conservation of mundane but appealing buildings that would have been condemned under a more systematic imposition of strict regulations. This policy made it possible to avoid displacing the inhabitants of blocks that were only minimally modernized. → 14

America turns postmodern

In the United States, the spread of the postmodern discourse provided second-rate proponents of a literal neoclassicism with immediate visibility. It also consolidated the position of Robert Venturi and Denise Scott Brown, who had been the first to play with popular stereotypes and historical precedents but whose aims were more sophisticated. For example, the chimney opening in their Brant-Johnson House in Vail, Colorado (1975), echoes the shape of the windows as well as the wood cladding of the house. In their exhibition *Signs of Life* (1976), held at the Renwick Gallery of the Smithsonian Institution in Washington, D.C., they proposed a radical critique of the semantics of suburban houses, manipulating classical signs and ornaments with a perfectly lucid sense of excess. They noted "a radical discrepancy between the needs, tastes, and preferences of the professionals – the urban designers, architects and planners, and the decision-makers whose policies they inform – and the people whose lives they influence." → 15 In their institutional buildings, they used oversized classical elements explicitly as nonstructural cladding, as on the facade of Gordon Wu Hall at Princeton University (1980–3). The extension of the National Gallery in London (1985–92) **525** is one of their most successful works, with its play of colonnades outside, and inside a progression

to the galleries by way of a grand staircase that reinterprets the perspectival illusionism of Baroque architecture.

Philip Johnson, who paid nearly obsessive attention to the shifting architectural currents, had long anticipated the return to classical elements and was also the first to use them at the scale of the skyscraper. In New York, his AT&T Building (1978–84; now Sony Plaza), **523** includes an arcade at ground level that creates a new urban space on the Manhattan avenue, while at the top it is crowned with an ornamental emblem resembling a Chippendale dresser. The shape of his Gerald D. Hines College of Architecture at the University of Houston (1985), with its four identical facades, is taken from Claude-Nicolas Ledoux's visionary drawings. Johnson was not the only architect to play with such nostalgic motifs. Michael Graves borrowed and magnified themes from the same French Enlightenment architect in many of his projects. One of them, the Public Services Building in Portland, Oregon (1979–82), is a large blocklike building whose front facade is treated as an arch of triumph with a disproportionately large keystone. Although his library in San Juan Capistrano, California (1981–3), continued to use Mediterranean themes recalling those of Léon Krier's watercolors, Graves was soon taking delight in an *architecture parlante* featuring zoomorphic figures, as in the Swan and Dolphin hotels he designed for Disney in Orlando, Florida (1990), **527** and in his Team Disney Building in Burbank, California (1985–91), **528** whose caryatids represent Snow White's seven dwarfs. Graves's architectural lexicon of pilasters, plinths, and moldings trickled down to the most commercial firms and for a while was ubiquitous. Robert A. M. Stern, another favored architect of the Walt Disney Company, began his career building houses characterized by a mannerist play with modernist forms before gradually introducing elements from American vernacular and classical

525 Sainsbury Wing, National Gallery, Robert Venturi and Denise Scott Brown, London, United Kingdom, 1985–92

526 Spaces of Abraxas, Ricardo Bofill and Taller de Arquitectura, Noisy-le-Grand, France, 1978–83

buildings. Enlarged to the scale demanded by his wealthy clients, these devices followed principles less explicitly decorative than those informing Graves's projects though no less ostentatious. Among public buildings, Thomas Beeby's Chicago Public Library of 1991–2 deployed similarly hybrid strategies, mixing motifs from the granite base of the nearby Monadnock Building, the windows of the demolished Marshall Field Store, and the large glass walls of Chicago industrial buildings. In all these structures, the quotation of fragments from history served as the starting point of the architectural conception.

The uncertain front of postmodernism

It was little surprise that architects like Johnson and Graves rallied to postmodernism. Yet the postmodern trend also attracted others who had previously embraced the techniques and ideas of modernism but now found themselves seduced by the dubious delights of historical or pop-cultural quotation. The British architect James Stirling, in whose office Léon Krier had worked, radically changed his design approach, especially in the context of programs involving expansions of existing structures. At the School of Architecture at Rice University in Houston (1980), Stirling concealed new galleries behind a facade that was an understated pastiche of the original neo-Romanesque building by Cram, Grosvenor and Ferguson while also allowing beautiful light to enter the interior through conical skylight towers, which are the only modern elements of the building's exterior. His extension to the Staatsgalerie in Stuttgart (1977–84) **530** was the most ambiguous product of this period of his work. Built on a site that slopes from an upper street to an avenue four levels below, the building is at once a solid – a representation of the cultural institution itself – and a void – an urban space linking

the two street levels by way of a ramp curling within a cylinder around which the galleries are organized. Although the stone cladding has Romanesque accents and there is no shortage of historicist quotations, including Egyptian-style cornices, the configuration of the interior and exterior circulation paths and the range of natural lighting devices make the gallery a unique cultural landscape. Stirling studied the circulation paths in inverted axonometric drawings done in the manner of Auguste Choisy, whose analyses he bore in mind during the design process. [16] Arata Isozaki's interest in the assembly of large geometric modules manifested itself in the 1970s in the Museum of Modern Art in Takasaki (1971–4) and the Fujimi Country Club (1973–4), whose cylindrical roof has a section evoking Ledoux's House of the Surveyors of the Loue River. His civic center for the new city of Tsukuba (1979–82) **529** also borrows formally from Ledoux, but more significantly its plan is based on a reproduction of Rome's Campidoglio, as if to insinuate that modern society is incapable of producing new collective spaces of its own that have a similar density of meaning. In the Museum of Contemporary Art in Los Angeles (1982–5), a building introduced into the heart of a city still searching for its own form after undergoing the trauma of slum clearance, he returned to a system of platonic volumes, each of which fulfills a role according to the principles of *architecture parlante*. By comparison with the brutal office towers surrounding it, the building looks like a fragile crystal. [17] Like Isozaki, the Viennese architect Hans Hollein had already embarked on an original direction prior to the advent of postmodernism. The series of tiny boutiques he designed had never neglected ornament, but with the second Schullin Jewelry Store (1981–2), he introduced classical themes into his decoration. His travel agencies (1976–8) brought a touch of comforting exoticism to the Vienna climate, featuring metal palm trees

527 Swan and Dolphin hotels, Walt Disney World, Michael Graves, Orlando, Florida, USA, 1990

528 Team Disney Building, Michael Graves, Burbank, California, USA, 1985–91

530 ▶ Extention to the Staatsgalerie, James Stirling, Stuttgart, Federal Republic of Germany, 1977–84

529 Tsukuba Civic Center, Arata Isozaki, Tsukuba, Japan, 1979–82

531　Cité de la Musique, Christian de Portzamparc, Paris, France, 1984–95

under a luminous glass ceiling. As it had been for Stirling, it was a German museum – in Mönchengladbach in the Ruhr (1975–82) **532** – that gave Hollein the opportunity to set forth most clearly the principles of an architecture based on the theme of circulation. Eschewing any one unifying path through the building as a whole, Hollein encouraged visitors to discover the museum as if they were undertaking a subterranean journey. In contrast, his Museum of Modern Art in Frankfurt am Main (1982–91) seems to be compressed into the envelope of a triangular block, with symmetrical galleries that become somewhat labyrinthine.

The Strada novissima set up at the 1980 Venice Biennale became a polygonal square when the exhibition traveled to Paris, where it was held under the dome of La Salpêtrière. The young Paris architect Christian de Portzamparc was added to roster of participants. Portzamparc's poetic sense of urbanity distinguishes him from others in his generation. In contrast to the then-dominant ideology of cascading housing complexes with a remote ancestor in Moshe Safdie's Habitat in Montreal, Portzamparc's competition project for the site of the former jail of La Roquette in Paris (1974) announced a suggestive return to monumentality. His apartment houses on Rue des Hautes Formes (1976–9) updated the scale of small Parisian squares and the material qualities of buildings of the faubourgs. In the Conservatoire de Musique (1984–90), also in Paris, he showed himself tempted by classical pediments, but he returned to greater plasticity with the volumes and voids of the École de Danse in Nanterre (1984–90). The campus of the Cité de la Musique at La Villette in Paris (1984–95) **531** was an expansion on his previous work, combining a main block devoted to music education with a spiral complex at the heart of which nestles a remarkable egg-shaped auditorium, whose

constantly changing color scheme resonates with the music. Increasingly active internationally, Portzamparc pursued his search for a poetic relationship between volume and materials, as well as his sensitivity to urban issues, in his LVMH Tower in midtown Manhattan (1995–9).

Beyond its application in this limited number of successful buildings, postmodernism was disseminated commercially as a cliché, on a scale comparable to that of the most banal forms of the postwar International Style. In a regression harking back to their eclectic forerunners, skyscrapers were made more visually "interesting" through the transformation of their outer layers, with solutions ranging from pure nostalgia to experiments with crystalline forms, like those of Helmut Jahn in Chicago. The commercialization of postmodernism transcended all political divides and geographic boundaries.

The city – composition or collage?

This new traditionalism managed to impose its agenda through the early 1990s. Drawing on a variety of historical references, the American theorists of the "New Urbanism" proposed an urban expression of postmodernism. But they were less obstinately conservative than the Prince of Wales, an architectural enthusiast who broke ground on Poundbury, near Dorchester, in 1989, a regressive development designed by Léon Krier, one of the most ardent architectural devotees of the past. In the United States, the New Urbanists, led by Andres Duany and Elisabeth Plater-Zyberk, were inspired by the reissues of Raymond Unwin's *Town Planning in Practice* (1909) and by handbooks of traditionalist urban planning such as Werner Hegemann and Elbert Peets's *The American Vitruvius* (1922). In Seaside, Florida (1983–90), **533** Duany

532 Städtisches Museum Abteiberg, Hans Hollein, Mönchengladbach, Federal Republic of Germany, 1975–82

533 Seaside City Center, Andres Duany and Elisabeth Plater-Zyberk, Seaside, Florida, USA, 1983–90

and Plater-Zyberk built a small resort town using a restrictive typology-based code according to a plan developed with advice from Léon Krier. Their discourse involved a validation of the qualities of the American and British garden city and a critique of the car-reliant postwar North American suburb. → 18 In preparing their master plans, Duany and Plater-Zyberk placed equal importance on the design of urban spaces and the formulation of new regulatory strategies intended to reestablish hierarchy and legibility in the service of the middle class. → 19 Inevitably, their ideas converged with Disney's commercial strategies and proved crucial in the invention of Celebration, a suburban development built near Orlando, Florida, during the 1990s on a plan by Jaquelin Robertson. Unlike the neo-traditionalist position of the New Urbanists, Colin Rowe and Fred Koetter's arguments in *Collage City* (1978) were not nostalgic. In this book, dense with allusions to the contemporary city, historical cases were used to criticize both Gordon Cullen's *Townscape* and Kevin Lynch's *Image of the City*. The authors reflected on what they called the crisis of the architectural object and its relationship to the urban fabric, as well as on the "reconquest of time" necessary for understanding the collage processes that constitute cities. The new order they proposed eschewed both utopian fantasy and historical precedent – with the exception of Hadrian's Villa. They recommended a design methodology similar to that of the *bricoleur*, or handyman, who makes do with what is available, as opposed to the top-down, scientific approach of the engineer – a distinction borrowed from Claude Lévi-Strauss's *La pensée sauvage* (The Savage Mind; 1962). → 20 Rowe and Koetter's ideas advanced a freer and more dynamic way of thinking about architecture's urban dimension without sinking to the saccharine prettiness of postmodern decoration. They

had durable effects on the design of cities, becoming particularly influential in shaping urban strategies of the 1980s from Barcelona to Berlin.

From regionalism to critical internationalism

In the 1980s, exhibitions and publications aggrandized post-modernism, giving it a dominance that was as superficial as the thin layer of historicist ornament its architects were wrapping around their structures. At the same time, a groundswell of ideas led to a genuine intellectual renewal in architecture without the total rejection of modernist discourse preached by the postmodernists. This renewal manifested itself in a wide variety of locations, in a kind of expanding archipelago around the world. It included university campuses such as Cornell in the early 1970s – where Colin Rowe taught alongside Oswald Matthias Ungers and where Rem Koolhaas was a student – and forums like the Institute for Architecture and Urban Studies in New York and the Architectural Association in London. It extended to cities such as Barcelona as well as to countries and cultural areas like Portugal and the Swiss canton of Ticino. These places became sites of intensive thinking and building, with an importance whose magnitude had little relationship to their sometimes minuscule size. The impact of dozens of alternative journals and "little" magazines published since the mid-1960s also began to be felt, as their contributors became recognized architects and teachers. [1]

Scarpa, or the rediscovery of craft

After being shaken by the social movements and populism of the 1960s, then encouraged to indulge in the decorative practices of postmodernism, architects began to regain a degree of self-confidence, whether they defined themselves purely as practitioners or as theorists or refused to be pigeonholed into a single role. The renaissance of architectural culture sprang initially from the rediscovery of its very materiality, after decades of faith in the products of industry. In this context, the subtle work of the Venetian architect Carlo Scarpa took on its full meaning only after his death in 1978. Indeed, his activity over half a century had not resulted in any single major autonomous building. [2] Scarpa was the designer of many exhibitions for the Venice Biennale, notably the ones dedicated to modern painters. He was also responsible for the Pavilion of the Book and the Venezuela Pavilion in the Biennale Gardens in 1950. [3] After meeting Frank Lloyd Wright during the American architect's trip to Europe the following year, Scarpa borrowed certain geometric concepts from him and combined them with elements that bore an affinity to De Stijl. It was his restoration of the Palazzo Abatellis in Palermo (1953–4), where he altered the Gothic windows to allow a soft light to fall on the paintings by Antonello da Messina, that first garnered attention. In Possagno, near Treviso, he expanded on this approach in 1955–7 with a gallery dedicated to the neoclassical sculptures of Antonio Canova. Each three-dimensional window became a volume of blue sky standing out against the white walls, along which Scarpa devised an elegant language of display cases and metallic supports. In Venice he designed the Olivetti Store on the Piazza San Marco (1957–8), a bright grotto under the arcades with floor patterns evoking Paul Klee. Also in Venice was Scarpa's complexly conceived restoration and extension of the Querini Stampalia Foundation (1961–3). **535** Its ingenious and somewhat mysterious treatment of a canal, which infiltrates the building's ground floor, and the resonance between its garden and galleries, marked a high point in his work. In Verona Scarpa worked for two decades with the museum director Liscisco Magagnato on the Castelvecchio Museum (1957–75). **534** Inspired by Luca Beltrami's restoration of the Castello Sforzesco in Milan at the turn of the twentieth century, he designed a circulation path through the museum featuring

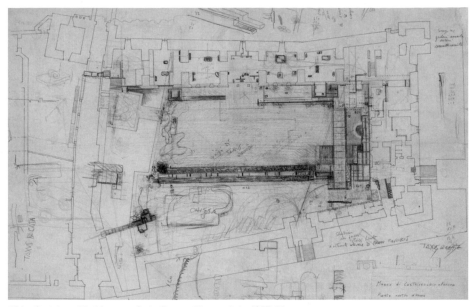

534 Castelvecchio Museum, Carlo Scarpa, Verona, Italy, 1957–75

535 Querini Stampalia Foundation, Carlo Scarpa, Venice, Italy, 1961–3

536   Bouça Low-income Housing, Alvaro Siza, Porto, Portugal, 1975–7

537   Galician Center of Contemporary Art, Alvaro Siza, Santiago de Compostela, Spain, 1988–93

contrasts and surprises. The castle's structural elments are exposed, sometimes to dramatic effect, as in the case of the setting for the equestrian statue of Cangrande della Scala, and each type of artwork is illuminated by meticulously sculpted light. [4]

Scarpa's last major work was the Brion Tomb in the cemetery of San Vito d'Altivole (1969–78). Its generous spaces bring together three autonomous objects, as if to constitute a small *campo santo* within a larger enclosure: the pavilion on water, which serves as an outdoor room for meditation; the chapel, whose roof is a masterpiece of abstract sculpture in wood; and the arcosolium, an arched concrete canopy sheltering the tombs, illuminated by light reflected from its enameled underside. In Louis Kahn's view, Scarpa's work represented "the inner realization of 'Form' " through its "symphony of the selected shapes of the elements." Chief among these elements were the joint, which "inspires ornament, its celebration," and the detail, which reflects "the adoration of nature." [5]

Siza's poetic rigor

In 1974 Portugal opened to the world as the Carnation Revolution put an end to Europe's oldest dictatorship. It revealed the work of the Porto architect Alvaro Siza and brought him new opportunities. From his first houses, his swimming pool in Matosinhos (1958–65), and his Pinto and Sotto Mayor Bank (1971–4) in the small town of Oliveira de Azeméis, Siza had paid close attention to the fragility of his buildings' sites while playing freely with modernist forms, which frequently evoked those of Adolf Loos and Alvar Aalto. After the revolution he designed two low-income housing projects in Porto, São Vitor (1974–9) and Bouça (1975–7) **536**. Both were commissioned by the SAAL, or

Serviço de apoio ambulatório local (Local Ambulatory Support Service), an agency founded by Nuno Portas, an architect whose appointment as minister of housing spurred the construction of new projects throughout the country. Siza's exploration of repetition and variation as well as of the economics of construction continued in the city of Evora with the Barrio da Malagueira (1977–97), a large-scale residential development. Here he displayed great understanding of place, echoing the ruins of a Roman aqueduct by creating a water distribution network connecting the rows of courtyard houses, and suggesting a cross between Mediterranean dwellings and the *Siedlungen* of Weimar Germany.

Berlin was the first city in which Siza would build outside Portugal. In 1980–84 he designed a public housing block commissioned by the IBA at Schlesisches Tor. Located on a corner site, its prowlike facade wraps a typical interior courtyard, while its repetitive punched windows led locals, in an eloquent commentary, to spray-paint the eloquent title of Françoise Sagan's novel *Bonjour tristesse* on its surface. [6] Siza was active in the Netherlands, then returned to Porto to build the architecture school there (1985–96). He would have a significant influence on its curriculum as well. The school buildings sit on a cliff overlooking the Douro River, engaged in a poetic dialogue among themselves. After a major fire in Lisbon on 25 August, 1988, Siza designed and coordinated the reconstruction of the Chiado neighborhood (1988–97), giving his buildings a flat, sober modernity in scale with the old city. [7] In Santiago de Compostela in Spain the stone facing of his Centro Galego de Arte Contemporánea (Galician Center of Contemporary Art; 1988–93) **537** responds to the medieval monuments of the town's center. A surprising sequence of galleries, lit from above unfolds from within.

538 Swimming Pool, Aurelio Galfetti with Flora Ruchat and Ivo Trümpy, Bellinzona, Switzerland, 1967–70

539 Medici House (Casa Rotonda), Mario Botta, Stabio, Switzerland, 1980–2

540 Apartment Buildings St. Alban-Tal, Diener & Diener, Basel, Switzerland, 1982–6

541 ▶ Public Buildings in Monte Carasso, Luigi Snozzi, Monte Carasso, Switzerland, 1977–2000

The wide reception of Siza's work in Europe is an indication of the global significance that approaches deeply rooted in local contexts were beginning to have in the late 1970s. Scholars Alex Tzonis and Liane Lefaivre interpreted this emerging tendency in an essay based on a reinterpretation of arguments made earlier by Lewis Mumford against International Style modernism. In a related argument, Kenneth Frampton invoked Paul Ricoeur's philosophical ideas to formulate a notion of "critical regionalism," describing the new architectural stance as an act of resistance to cultural homogenization. [8] Responding to the discourse of postmodernism, Frampton as well as a number of European architects also drew on the work of the German philosopher Jürgen Habermas, who affirmed in 1980 that modernity, far from being a conspiracy to standardize and destroy cultural values, was actually "an incomplete project" whose emancipatory potential was not yet exhausted. [9] Starting from the premise that modern architecture had produced positive social results, these critics strove to identify a coherent pattern in design strategies from Switzerland to the Iberian Peninsula. In fact, these lines of development were more parallel than convergent.

Collective endeavor in the Ticino

The work of architects who resisted both state and commercial standardization as well as the superficial devices of postmodernism needs, therefore, to be situated in its specific local context. One such group of professionals emerged out of the local realities of the Ticino, a Swiss canton that was close to the Milan scene and had served as an international launching pad for architects ever since Francesco Borromini. Architects there often operated as part of an informal collective and they were also involved in the area's social issues. Luigi Snozzi, initially in partnership with Livio Vacchini, shaped the village of Monte Carasso, **541** which was discreetly but thoroughly modernized over the course of a series of buildings begun in 1977. [10] In Bellinzona, in response to government support for building athletic facilities, Aurelio Galfetti designed a swimming pool (1967–70) **538** as the central element of a long linear complex that crosses the valley between the road and the river; boxes housing the program's multiple facilities adhere to its sides. In the same town he restored the Castelgrande, a castle dominating the landscape (1981–8), penetrating its base with large underground rooms sculpted in concrete.

The Ticinese architect Mario Botta made his reputation on a series of houses designed in the 1970s and 1980s. Rejecting any regionalist imitation, he conceived them as autonomous entities often illuminated by light entering through a glass roof. The volumes took geometric different shapes: rectangular in Ligornetto (1975–6), cubic in Pregassona (1979–80), and cylindrical in Stabio (1980–2). **539** All of Botta's subsequent architecture developed from this domestic typology, which served as the basis for a variety of compositional transformations. The Morbio Inferiore High School (1972–7), a slab lit from the sides and overhead, resembles a series of large houses arranged *enfilade*. Many of its details evoke the work of Louis Kahn, with whom Botta had earlier collaborated on a convention center project for Venice. The underground extension of the Capuchin Convent in Lugano (1976–9) centers on a library resembling a large living room. The State Bank in Fribourg (1977–82) is more ambitious. It inaugurated an approach based on the combination of heterogeneous forms – in this case a cylinder fitted into a massive orthogonal block – with a strong tectonic sensibility, even if here and in other major projects this sensibility

543 Museum of Roman Art, Rafael Moneo, Mérida, Spain, 1980–6

542 Thermal Baths, Peter Zumthor, Vals, Switzerland, 1986–96

544 Cathedral of our Lady of the Angels, Rafael Moneo, Los Angeles, California, USA, 1996–2002

sometimes seems to be contradicted by Botta's treatment of surfaces as colored bands lacking any structural role. [11] Beginning in the 1980s, other centers of activity emerged in the Swiss cantons. The Diener & Diener firm in Basel reinterpreted the modernist structures of the 1930s, borrowing their orthogonal volumes and the play between smooth surfaces and thin metallic elements. These hard-edged geometric buildings led the firm to gain commissions in Basel's old city, as in the case of their Architecture Museum (1984), a renovation of a modernist office building from the 1950s; and, in a medieval setting along the Rhine, the apartment houses of St. Alban-Tal (1982–6). 540 On the other side of the Rhine, the stuccoed and brick facades of the Warteck-Hof Housing Development (1996) create an urban quality at the scale of an industrial quarter. Roger Diener demonstrated his ability to work in different architectural idioms. While the Migros Shopping Center in Lucerne (1995–2000), lining a historical street, plays on the contrast between the reflections in the windows and the matte metallic panels, the Swiss Embassy in Berlin is at the opposite end of the spectrum from the firm's resolutely unmonumental projects. Combining a historical building and a bunkerlike concrete box, it is as mute as it is compact, inevitably recalling the tragic events often passively witnessed by Swiss diplomats during World War II.

Peter Zumthor's work is distinguished not by its quantity but by the strong tectonic presence of each of his buildings. All of his work is based on the logical deployment of a single dominant material. Stone walls line every room of the cavernous, severe Thermal Baths (1986–96), 542 in Vals in the canton of Graubünden whose dark interior is striated with beams of light. His single-family house of 1997–2003 in the same canton is a rustically articulated wood dwelling on the inside and out, while his

Sound Box, built as the Switzerland Pavilion at the 2000 World's Fair in Hanover, resembled a woodpile at a sawmill colonized by musicians. Zumthor's Kunsthalle in Bregenz (1989–97) differs from all these buildings in appearing to be built out of the light enveloping it. A translucent box by day, a lantern at night, it seems to be supported by its luminous wall, while its actual structural elements paradoxically appear almost ornamental. Closely attuned to a building's sensuous effects, Zumthor has stated that he pays strict attention to "thresholds, passages, and limits," balancing "serenity and seduction." [12]

Moneo and Iberia

In Madrid, another center of activity, the pivotal figure was Rafael Moneo. His critical writings and teaching also played a role beyond Spain, notably through his reflections on the permanence of architectural form, something exemplified, in his view, by the architectural palimpsest of the Great Mosque of Córdoba. [13] His first large buildings had to do with the massiveness of their walls, continuing Kahn's legacy. They explored the resources of materials like brick, which he used to cover the simple volumes of the Bankinter in Madrid (1973–8) and the halls of the Museum of Roman Art in Mérida (1980–6). 543 The bays of the latter straddle the ancient ruins and shelter the archaeological pathway. Moneo also transformed infrastructure projects into authentic urban complexes: the Atocha Station in Madrid (1984–92), built for the high-speed train to Seville, links clearly differentiated spaces and treats the station's most mundane components – parking lots, for instance – as architecture in their own right. At the San Pablo Airport in Seville (1987–92) Moneo provided a roof alluding to the Córdoba mosque. Together with city halls, museums have been among Moneo's

545 Moll de la Fusta (Timber Wharf), Manuel de Solà-Morales, Barcelona, Spain, 1981–7

546 Lyttos Hotel, Dimitris Antonakakis and Suzana Antonakakis, Anissaras, Crete, Greece, 1974–6

primary building types. He created original combinations of building envelope and natural lighting systems for the Miró Foundation in Palma de Mallorca (1987–92); the Davis Museum in Wellesley, Massachusetts (1989–93); and the Museum of Modern Art and Architecture in Stockholm (1998). The openness of his approach can be measured in his vastly different solutions for the Kursaal Cultural Center in San Sebastián (1990–9), a large lantern illuminating the Basque port that has come to represent the town much as Jørn Utzon's Opera House represents Sydney, and the Catholic cathedral in downtown Los Angeles (1996–2002), **544** an edifice infused with a spirit more Benedictine than Baroque and kept serenely bright by light falling through alabaster windows. → [14]

Elsewhere on the Iberian Peninsula, the architects of northern Portugal formed a cohesive group centered around Siza and Fernando Távora, who carried out refined restorations and extensions. → [15] Beginning with his market in Braga (1980–4), Eduardo Souto de Moura built many dwellings in harmony with the area's agricultural landscape, as well as public projects, including the Braga Stadium, erected on the dramatic site of a former quarry (2000–3). → [16] Among the most powerful works of the Portuguese group were Gonçalo Byrne's housing for SAAL South in Setúbal (1974–9), Alcino Soutinho's Matosinhos City Hall (1981–7), and João Luis Carrilho da Graça's Institute of Social Communication in Lisbon (1988–93). → [17]

Besides the cluster around Moneo in Madrid, centers of urban-architectural production emerged in several other Spanish regions, including Andalusia, the Basque Country, and Catalonia. A rich and diverse architectural culture developed in Barcelona, both in continuity with and in reaction against the work of the earlier generations represented by Josep Antoni Coderch and Oriol Bohigas. Following the post-Franco return to democracy, the latter took advantage of his tenure as deputy mayor for planning to launch a program for public spaces that gave younger architects a chance to assert themselves. The opening up of the city to the port, carried out by Manuel de Solà-Morales with an ingenious assembly of sunken roads and pedestrian walkways, **545** and the Plaça dels Països Catalans, by Albert Viaplana and Helio Piñon, announced an authentic urban and architectural renaissance that the 1992 Olympics would reveal to the world.

Europe as a field of experience

It is impossible to take note of all the design strategies that carried the agenda of a "critical" regionalism in the last decades of the twentieth century, yet a few others should be mentioned in passing. Though certain neo-modern – or "late modern," to use Charles Jencks's taxonomy – currents remained focused on Corbusian or Constructivist themes, others took more liberties with a heritage to which they nonetheless laid full claim. In Greece, this was the case with Suzana and Dimitris Antonakakis, whose vacation house in Euboea (1973–4) and Lyttos Hotel (1974–6), **546** in Anissaras, Cretewere designed in relation to the site and, like many of their other projects, play with local vernacular themes. Nicos Valsamakis's Amalia Hotel in Olympia (1976–9), built with white orthogonal forms, was closer to the work of the Porto School. In nearby Turkey, the work of Turgut Cansever followed parallel lines, negotiating between Brutalist poetics and the vernacular landscape. Dominated by a stifling mass production that crushed most creative impulses, the socialist countries of Eastern Europe and the USSR seemed oblivious to the questions preoccupying Western architecture. The most subtle approaches took shape on the

547 Sangath, Balkrishna Doshi, Ahmedabad, India, 1979–81

548 Triton Hotel, Geoffrey Bawa, Ahungalla, Sri Lanka, 1981

periphery of the Soviet Union, notably in school buildings and other constructions on the collective farms in the small nation of Estonia, where an architecture emerged that was sensitive to place and dense with references to local prewar functionalism, Aalto, and even to Robert Venturi. In Hungary, Imre Makovecz managed to build extravagant wood structures (1977–9); their exposed timberwork and roofs that seem to be made of wooden "scales" gave his biomorphically shaped buildings a baroque spatiality. → 18 In Czechoslovakia, the Stavoprojekt Liberec team, led by John Eisler, Emil Přikryl, and Jiři Suchomel, designed projects both conceptually clear and technologically advanced, returning to the creative achievements of the 1920s and 1930s while using the language of the space age.

Research in South Asia

Concurrently, unprecedented developments took place in countries that had reclaimed their independence after 1945. The case of India was remarkable, with several architects accomplishing a mediation between the local culture and the experience of modern architects in the West. In Ahmedabad, Balkrishna Doshi, formerly an assistant to Le Corbusier on the Shodhan and Sarabhai houses and to Kahn on the Indian Institute of Management, built social housing complexes, public buildings, and even new cities whose compositions went well beyond the models provided by his mentors. His Sangath, a studio for collective architectural research (1979–81), **547** is organized like an urban complex. Like many of his other projects, it is roofed with concrete vaults derived from Le Corbusier's Jaoul Houses, but they are clad in white tiles, providing Doshi with a unique workplace. The Madhya Pradesh Electricity Board in Jabalpur (1979–87) displays a more Kahnian logic with its polygonal plan.

The work of Delhi-based Raj Rewal tapped into the same sources, but also sprang from his experience working with Michel Écochard in Paris. Rewal's complex urban developments integrate elements and materials from Mughal architecture such as red sandstone. Notable examples of this approach include his Athletes' Village for the Asian Games (1980–2) and his Headquarters for the World Bank (1993), both in New Delhi. Charles Correa began his career by building the Gandhi Ashram in Ahmedabad (1963), with a plan and architectural vocabulary that evoke Aldo van Eyck's Municipal Orphanage in Amsterdam. Correa proposed refined solutions for modernizing India's slums, and then realized some of his original ideas for conventional building types, as in his Kanchanjunga Tower in Mumbai (1970–83), which cleverly deploys the principle of villa apartments on a vertical scale. → 19

In Sri Lanka, Geoffrey Bawa took a freer approach to designing structures and gardens, beginning with his own house in Colombo (1969) and institutions like the Yahapath Endera Farm School in Hanwella (1966). His tourist complexes, such as the Triton Hotel in Ahungalla (1981), **548** are inhabitable landscapes – hedonistic, luxurious microcosms inserted into the island's natural sites – in which the galleries and roofs of the local architecture are reinterpreted in new combinations. → 20

Also on the other side of the world from Europe, Harry Seidler began designing architecture in the 1950s responding to Australia's need for modernization. More radical propositions rooted in the country's building culture came from Glenn Murcutt, whose corrugated metal buildings, like the Nicholas House (1979–80, enlarged 2001), and the Simpson-Lee House (1989–94), **551** both located in the Australian bush country, transformed a common material used in vernacular structures into inhabitable sculpture. → 21

549 Torres del Parque Housing, Rogelio Salmona, Bogotá, Colombia, 1964–70

Latin American personalities

Latin American architecture cannot be summed up with generalizations. It has followed a process of national and regional diversification in which cultures and schools of thought have formed around dominant figures in different cities, much as in Europe. In Colombia, where José Luis Sert's plans for Medellín, Cali, and Bogotá had an impact, Rogelio Salmona's contribution was also central. A former assistant to Le Corbusier and Jean Prouvé, Salmona collaborated with the former on the plan for Bogotá. He studied art history with Pierre Francastel in Paris and was a reformer of architectural education. His Torres del Parque Housing (1964–70) **549** is a complex of three curvilinear brick towers connected to the ground by low structures; the towers' helical movement responds to a nearby bullring. At the Casa de Huéspedes Ilustres (House of Eminent Guests; 1978–9) in Cartagena, Salmona reinterpreted the colonial courtyard house in stone masonry. In other houses, he followed Doshi's example of using barrel vaults, but in exposed brick. Salmona used brick more decoratively in the Archivo General (1990–2) in Bogotá. [22]

In Brazil, the triumphal construction of Brasília by two Rio architects, Lucio Costa and Oscar Niemeyer, did not overshadow other centers of cultural activity. In São Paulo, a neo-Brutalist idiom found a local outlet in the work of Paulo Mendes da Rocha, whose own house (1964) is a remarkable statement, rough but warm, in which even the sliding partitions are made of concrete. After a near total interruption of his professional life during fifteen years of military dictatorship, Mendes da Rocha built complexes designed in relationship to the city such as the Museum of Contemporary Art (1975) and the Brazilian Museum of Sculpture (1988–94). **550** While displaying a certain minimalism

and linear simplicity in their overall composition, their material texture – concrete – is elegantly expressive. [23] João Filgueiras Lima (better known as Lelé) worked at the other end of the spectrum from Niemeyer's beloved large shells. He used prefabrication methods to construct the *Colina Velha* (Old Hill, 1963) faculty residences at the Brasília University as well as buildings at both the Taguatinga hospital in Brasília (1968) and the Administrative Center in Salvador (1973–2000). [24]

A critical internationalism

In the case of many of the architects discussed in this chapter, it would perhaps be more appropriate to speak of a "critical internationalism" than a critical regionalism. Rather than reacting defensively to the threat of a homogenizing modernization or espousing utopian positions, these architects made a cautious, calculated decision to respond to the market. Addressing themselves to the global scene, and inserting themselves into the network of professional and cultural relationships existing between different cities, they responded to the conservatism and vulgarity of postmodernism by claiming to return to the Modern Movement, a return that was sometimes accompanied nonetheless by some simplifications and distortions. Occasionally fetishistic – as when the range of references was reduced to Le Corbusier's *pilotis* or the free plan – but for the most part sincere, this look backward favored an architecture attuned to the rhythms and materials of the early twentieth century while eschewing the postmodern nostalgia for the medieval or classical city. [25]

At the same time, in an unsolved dialectic, the new internationalists cultivated a realistic and pragmatic relationship with their cities and regions, resisting the stark simplifications of modern functionalism. They took issues of landscape more into

550 Brazilian Museum of Sculpture, Paulo Mendes da Rocha, São Paulo, Brazil, 1988–94

551 Simpson-Lee House, Glenn Murcutt, Mount Wilson, Australia, 1989–94

553 Kiasma Museum of Contemporary Art, Steven Holl, Helsinki, Finland, 1998

account in keeping with a preference for incorporating architecture into the existing milieu, and they did not completely reject the architecture of the two generations preceding their own. In fact, it was not unusual for Spanish, Swiss, or French designers to acknowledge the quality of the vernacular structures built by anonymous postwar commercial architects producing "B" or "C" buildings. Nor did they struggle like their predecessors to intellectualize the architectural process as such; even if sometimes self-serving, the relationship between architecture and intellectual culture was now largely taken for granted thanks to radical changes in the training of architects. The cultural renewal that had taken place since 1968 was thus internalized rather than manifested as a demonstrative attempt to theorize the contemporary situation (with a few exceptions in the American context). An interest in film (seen, for instance, in the work of Fumihiko Maki) and in issues of contemporary art through the recycling of minimalist concepts (in Ticino) or Arte Povera (in the case of Murcutt) also contributed to the architect's new professional identity.

The relationship of architecture to politics, which had been defined in such explicit and polarized terms in the early 1970s, took on an aspect both more diffuse and more concrete once architects working in various national and regional settings turned to actual questions of housing and began actively pursuing alternatives to the monotonous towers and slabs emblematic of state modernization programs. With the waning of the illusory utopia of the megastructure, intensive typological research led to the invention of alternative housing forms, thanks to the support of experimental public programs, the best example of which was the PAN (Programme architecture nouvelle) in France. This entailed an updating of modernist themes in some cases, such as the Corbusian *immeuble-villas*,

revisited by Yves Lion in his Villejuif housing (1992–3). It also included an exploration of the potential of row houses as well as medium-density schemes — an intermediary scale between the large multifamily dwelling and the individual house. This widespread collective endeavor of the 1980s yielded its most interesting results in schemes built in the Netherlands, Iberia, and France.

Many architects now aimed their criticism not at the global conditions of modernization but at local situations, programs, technologies, and usages, considered as so many thematic avenues of attack. Siza and Moneo, for example, responded to one another through their respective positions regarding the permanence of historical urban traces and archetypes. A critical but sometimes intuitive reinterpretation of 1930s rationalism was undertaken by the Basel architects, as well as certain Dutch professionals, many Parisians, and even the Irish architects Sheila O'Donnell and John Tuomey 552 and the Norwegian firm Snøhetta. Tadao Ando, Yves Lion, and the Portuguese architects active around Porto demonstrated their shared penchant for abstract geometrism, working with a degree of autonomy that varied with the site. Dutch architect Jo Coenen developed surprising typological inventions. Finally, the work of Steven Holl 553 focused on the importance of walls and light, bringing him much closer to his European peers than to other Americans of his generation and revealing the crisscrossing vectors linking the work of individuals separated by no more than a plane flight. This informal international community of architects, many of whom tended to take to an ethical stance with respect to the profession's obligation toward society and the city while accepting the economic conditions of late capitalism, also reflected the constantly shifting boundaries of architecture in a world that was becoming ever smaller.

The neo-Futurist optimism of high tech

One position that remained immune to the contagion of post-modernism was that of those who dedicated themselves to exploring new technologies. Having persisted even during decades when such a position was out of step with dominant cultural developments, these architects were inspired by the examples of Buckminster Fuller, Jean Prouvé, and Frei Otto, as well as by the heroic phase of aerospace research, from the Sputnik launch in October 1957 to Neil Armstrong's walk on the moon in July 1969. They rejected the flying, or oblique, cities of the new utopians and the contextualism of those decrying standardization. These proponents of high-tech architecture created autonomous objects, but ones that internalized the tensions of the city and ingeniously fulfilled functional requirements.

Beaubourg establishes a canon

In 1971 the high-tech attitude emerged victorious in a competition to build a center for modern art and culture in a neighborhood of central Paris that had been cleared of slums in the 1930s. Presided over by Jean Prouvé, **560** the jury for the first architectural competition in Paris since the seventeenth century to be open to foreigners chose the Italian Renzo Piano and the British Richard Rogers, two unknown young architects, in partnership with the established engineer Ove Arup. Reyner Banham described their project for Centre Pompidou **554** – subsequently named after its staunch supporter, President Georges Pompidou – as "the most complete monument" to the concept of the megastructure, the first that "answers the ultimate acid-test of looking like one." With its "structural framework into which smaller structural units can be built" giving it "a useful life much longer than that of the smaller units which it may support," [1] the Pompidou did indeed appear to be the embodiment of Banham's highly elastic concept. The large, compact exoskeleton – so compact that it left room on the site for a large sloping public plaza that had not been called for in the competition brief – was also the progeny of Cedric Price's Fun Palace, Archigram's Plug-in City, and, sixty years after the fact, Antonio Sant'Elia's dream of elevators swarming up the facade like "glass serpents." [2] A gigantic erector set whose parts were transported to the site on trucks, the building was supposed to be totally flexible and convertible.

Yet the writer Georges Perec conveyed his sense of it as "a fat extraterrestrial creature, who seems unable to survive after having shed his space suit and his collection of ducts." [3] Equally skeptical of the museum's claim to real flexibility, the architect Alan Colquhoun voiced the fear that the building would only foster the "*Gesamtkunstwerk* of bureaucracy" that had already been set up to operate it. Discussing the "Beaubourg effect," the critic Jean Baudrillard for his part predicted that Pompidou would become "at the level of culture what the supermarket is at the level of the commodity." [4] Several decades later, however, the building seems to have delivered on its promise of flexibility, allowing modifications to be made to the library and the ground-floor "forum," the latter initially intended to be an open area for spontaneous events. The original Miesian free plan of the galleries on the upper floors has also undergone a series of transformations, notably in the 1990s when Gae Aulenti restructured the circulation as a conventional suite of rooms. Meanwhile, even before construction was completed in 1977, Rogers and Piano split up, while Peter Rice, the principal project engineer at Arup on the museum, opened his own firm. From this point on, the architects identified with high tech followed divergent paths, but their work stuck to what Banham defined in his last, unfinished book as the "canonical characteristics"

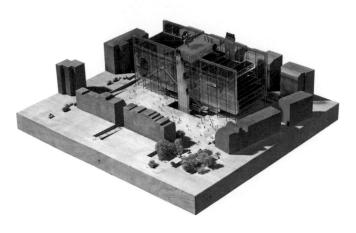

554 Centre Pompidou, Renzo Piano, Richard Rogers and Ove Arup, Paris, France, 1971–7, first model

555 Terminal 4, Barajas Airport, Richard Rogers, Madrid, Spain, 1997–2005

established by the Centre Pompidou: "a. large, open, clear-span spaces on all floors; b. high level of mechanical servicing; c. clear exhibition of metallic structure; d. clear exhibition of mechanical services; e. aesthetic derived from (or enhancing) c. and d." While in Banham's eyes high tech shared with the Modern Movement the cult of "high finish and meticulous detailing," it had one essential new feature: "the dominant visual elements in architecture are, for the first time in history, not structural." These dominant elements were the mechanical systems. → 5

Composition according to Rogers

Richard Rogers's first residential projects possessed great conceptual clarity. He alluded to Mies van der Rohe with his House in Wimbledon (1968–9) and evoked the settlements then being imagined for distant planets with his project for the Zip-up House (1969–71). Imbuing his designs with a sense of modular composition no matter the scale, he continued to leave all the pipes exposed on the exterior as at the Centre Pompidou. (The British television program *Spitting Image* satirized him with a puppet whose intestines were hanging out.) This approach led him to build hangars with cable-stiffened structures such as those for the Fleetguard Factory in Quimper, France (1979–81), the INMOS Microprocessor Factory in Gwent, Wales (1982–7), and the PA Technology Center in Princeton, New Jersey (1982–5). All displayed a certain classicism by virtue of their symmetry, the similarity between their front and back elevations, and the rigorous treatment of their corners. The Lloyd's Building (1978–86) **556** in the City of London marked a significant change of scale in Rogers's work. This large structure was conceived by Rogers as an open space with floors branching out from a central atrium. At its heart is

the insurance company's famous Lutine Bell, surrounded by the servant spaces of the circulation cores and utilities. The building recalls nineteenth-century department stores and, even more literally, Joseph Paxton's Crystal Palace, especially with its semicircular tympanums. From this building on, Rogers has worked mostly on large public buildings, abandoning any residual classicism in favor of more expressive solutions, as in the European Court of Human Rights in Strasbourg (1989–95) and his courthouse in Bordeaux (1993–6), whose chambers are located in rooms evoking oversized wine vats. Rogers designed the gigantic Millennium Dome in Greenwich, England (1995–9), a fabric membrane suspended from a network of steel cables and masts, which long failed to find a use commensurate with its structural ambitions. Richard Rogers's general method is first to work out his projects in section, next to define a basic modular unit to be repeated according to a grid or linear sequence, and then to generate the complete building, as exemplified in his terminal at Barajas Airport in Madrid (1997–2005) **555** with its wave-shaped roof.

Experimentation according to Piano

Renzo Piano followed a rather different path, taking less interest in composition per se than in devising distinctive details characteristic of each project. His work started with the polyester panels and steel braces of his Italy Pavilion at the Osaka World's Fair (1970). Then, at the Centre Pompidou, he developed the "gerberette" – a cantilevered arm connecting the steel columns to the floor-carrying trusses and wind bracing – which condensed the spatial and technical solution into a single component. His simplest museum to date, and one of his most successful, is the Menil Collection in Houston (1982–6), a one-story

box with opaque elevations, top-lit by a network of three hundred adjustable "leaves" in glass-reinforced concrete that serve to temper the bright Texas light.

The experimental research of Piano's architectural firm – RPBW, or Renzo Piano Building Workshop – has been carried out with full scale models, leading to several different families of buildings and to structural solutions that have usually been defined by a guiding metaphor. The Kansai International Airport on an artificial island in Osaka Bay (1988–94) **557** resembles a wave extending along the runways for just over a mile, although it may also be compared to the wing of a glider, beneath which the terminal's operations are carried out. In the Jean-Marie Tjibaou Cultural Center in Nouméa, New Caledonia (1991–8), arches of laminated wood reinterpret native Kanak huts, and they also give the complex the appearance of a group of masks, especially when viewed straight-on from the water. The same laminated wood concept was used for the tall arches of the Bercy II Shopping Center in Paris (1987–90), over which a metal skin is stretched, resulting in a structure whose interior resembles that of the whale in Walt Disney's *Pinocchio*. Piano has approached the question of cladding from several different angles. For his residential complex on Rue de Meaux in Paris (1988–91), he used prefabricated "leaves" in fiberglass-reinforced concrete to which a terra-cotta facing was clipped. He further developed this system for his first skyscraper, the DEBIS tower on Berlin's Potsdamer Platz (1992–9). In Berlin as well as in subsequent skyscrapers, like Aurora Place in Sydney (1996–2000) and the New York Times Building in Manhattan (2000–8), Piano extended the principle of servant and served spaces vertically, at the same time giving a genuine tectonic complexity to the building skins. With his conversions of industrial sites such as the Schlumberger

Factory in Montrouge (1981–4) and the Lingotto Factory in Turin (1983–2002), Piano endeavored to clarify the process of transformation by preserving the original buildings' spatial and structural qualities. This attention to the relationship between building components has also been characteristic of his many projects for cultural institutions in Europe and, increasingly, the United States, where he developed a reputation as *deus ex machina*, able to solve the most complicated problems. The Beyeler Foundation Museum in Riehen, near Basel (1992–7), in which opaque walls divide up a space underneath a floating roof, further elaborates the theme of the Menil Collection. The small Nasher Sculpture Center in Dallas, with its five parallel bays, derives from the same approach. In the Parco della Musica Auditorium in Rome (1994–2002), the walls enveloping the lobbies and auditoriums express a sort of "wallness" that seems inspired by antiquity, while the lead-coated wood shells sheltering the three music spaces are in an Expressionist vein, reminiscent of Hermann Finsterlin's mysterious animal-like fantasies.

Structure according to Foster

Norman Foster, a third seminal figure in the constellation of leading high-tech architects, has created a repertory of astonishing forms over four decades. Keenly aware of the large structures designed by Ludwig Mies van der Rohe and by Fuller, with whom he worked in the 1970s, he extended an invitation to Prouvé to come to London to discuss his projects. Large-span bridges and Japanese tatami mats are part of the repertory with which Foster has tackled programs of an ever-increasing scale. From 1963 to 1967 he was associated with Wendy Cheesman Foster and Richard and Su Rogers in Team 4, collaborating on the Reliance Controls Factory in Swindon, England (1965–6).

560   Jean Prouvé lecturing at the Conservatoire National des Arts et Métiers, Paris, France, 1969

That factory owes its near-classical unity to the repetition of its metal-and-glass bays, which are braced by Saint Andrew's crosses that stand out from the truss rods. The offices of Willis Faber and Dumas (1971–5) in Ipswich, England, abandoned all such static propriety. Here Foster created a tension between the building's dark reflective glass perimeter and the surrounding low buildings of the urban context while organizing the interior around a bank of escalators that rise to floors of open-plan offices. Following Willis Faber, the architect has offered with each new project a solution in which structure and mechanical elements combine without forced exhibitionism. The Sainsbury Centre for the Visual Arts (1974–8) **558** on the campus of the University of East Anglia in Norwich incorporates thematic galleries and classrooms under a single large roof, allowing for a flexible arrangement of partitions and installations. Its two layers of cladding, made of industrially produced components, are separated by a 2.4-meter (almost 8-foot) space, through which both utilities and daylight pass.

Several programs have given Foster an opportunity to develop modular systems. These have generated layered buildings that begin from a basic element and have the potential for unlimited growth. The Renault Distribution Centre (1980–2) **559** in Swindon is composed of alternating open and closed bays that are square in plan; the roof structure, held up by a grid of steel masts and beams stayed by tensile cables, creates an undulating landscape contrasting with the horizontals of the site. At Stansted Airport (1981–91) a different system was employed: each module is supported by a treelike column composed of several tubes. Sunlight diffuses into the space from overhead, making the roof appear lighter than it is. The terminal is a large unbroken space with all the technical support systems installed below the main level. Foster has continued to develop these principles in increasingly vast airport projects, such as Chek Lap Kok in Hong Kong (1992–8), where parallel barrel vaults support the roof floating above the terminals.

Beginning in the 1980s, Foster completely reexamined the typology of the skyscraper. The Hong Kong and Shanghai Bank (1979–86), **561** erected in the heart of the British colony, realized an idea that Prouvé had devised in 1970 for an unbuilt project for the French Ministry of Education at La Défense: an imaginative office tower with a hollow core. Foster broke not only with the central-core skyscraper but also with the traditionally opaque image of the bank. The office floors are suspended from the external structure, leaving the underlying plaza completely open; an escalator provides access to the vast interior space above, which is illuminated by a "sun-scoop" reflecting daylight into the atrium. Offices are disposed around the interior in constantly changing configurations, suggesting a cluster of villages arranged into a rational structure. Produced in Europe, the bathroom modules and technical systems were delivered by ship and hoisted into place during construction, as if the thesis of Archigram's Plug-in City had finally become reality. → 6

Based on a more ecological principle, the headquarters of the Commerzbank in Frankfurt am Main (1991–7) expanded on the idea of the village, gathering groups of offices around large suspended garden patios. A triangular plan made it possible to locate the vertical circulation in the corners of the atrium and to create clear-span office floors. The ovoid Swiss Re Tower in London (1997–2004) incorporates the complexity of earlier projects within a single tapered cylinder. Its lozenge-shaped structure, visible from the inside, supports a series of spiraling atriums, which are key to controlling the indoor climate and minimizing energy loss.

562 Eurostar Terminal, Waterloo Station, Nicholas Grimshaw, London, United Kingdom, 1993

561 Hong Kong and Shanghai Bank, Norman Foster, Hong Kong, (China), 1979–86

563 BCE Place, Santiago Calatrava, Toronto, Canada, 1987–92

Also involved in the design of civil engineering structures, Foster built the Millau Viaduct (1993–2004), whose curved roadway stretching over the valley of the Tarn in France is supported by cables anchored to pylons as tall as the Eiffel Tower. Foster's work on existing buildings has tended to confront the original construction with a new technical component. In the Reichstag in Berlin, he built a glass dome (1992–9), instead of the large glass roof initially proposed. The dome directs light into the assembly chamber while housing an encircling helical ramp open to the public. The roof over the Great Court of the British Museum (1994–2000) is a canopy elegantly connecting the building's wings, although the stonework enveloping the historical rotunda, now reduced to a sort of parody of itself, is pompous and disappointing. The global success of Foster + Partners, which developed into a truly multinational firm in the 1990s, has led to high-quality projects, yet the conceptual power of Foster's early buildings seems sometimes to have been lost in the transition.

Architects and engineers

Nicholas Grimshaw has also explored the potential of lightweight structures in metal and glass. His Grand Union Walk, a housing development in London's Camden Town (1985), with metallic panels enveloping the facade of the houses on the canal, projected the image of a machine for living in but without sacrificing comfort to a technical solution. Like so many other buildings of the high-tech sensibility, the glass roof of the Eurostar Terminal at London's Waterloo Station (1993) **562** can be likened to the visions of the Futurists. Mimicking the linear shape of the train cars, it resembles a huge serpent in the city. In France, Dominique Perrault's Bibliothèque Nationale,

the winning entry in a competition held in 1989, combines a central garden and four glazed L-shaped towers housing the book stacks in a simple rectangular composition. An autonomous object inserted into a redeveloped area of Paris, it has remained, despite its aspiration to transparency, a somewhat introverted institution. By contrast, Perrault's Olympic Swimming Pool and Velodrome (1992–7) **564** in reunified Berlin, which appear as two shallow volumes when seen from the exterior, strongly express the materiality of their steel skeleton. Following his early work on the Sydney Opera House and a decade later at the Centre Pompidou, and prior to his premature death in 1992, the engineer Peter Rice went on to invent a remarkable series of technical solutions for projects ranging from the Menil Collection in Houston to the Lloyd Building in London. With his partners in the RFR office, he devised new techniques for constructing large curtain-wall facades and long-span structures like Terminal 2F at Roissy–Charles de Gaulle Airport (1999), where he and the architect Paul Andreu collaborated on a visually complex metal roof that makes ingenious repetition of a single element. → 7

Other engineers working independently have designed buildings utilizing advanced technology. The Spanish engineer Santiago Calatrava, whose first projects displayed a certain biomorphism, has come up with schemes displaying an audacity due not only to his technical knowledge but also to his sculptural vision of engineering. This vision has sometimes inspired oversized structures whose lyricism has been achieved at the cost of economy. The Saint-Exupéry Airport Railway Station in Lyons (1989–94), for example, looks like a gigantic dinosaur skeleton half-buried beneath a roof that in turn resembles a bird poised to take flight. Calatrava's work is rich in metaphors, evoking forests at BCE Place in Toronto (1987–92) **563** and at

564 Olympic Velodrome, Dominique Perrault, Berlin, Germany, 1992–7

Orient Train Station in Lisbon (1993–8), for example, or a harp in his series of suspension and cable-stayed bridges. Drawing on Frei Otto's research, the Munich engineer Thomas Herzog has subtly integrated elegant solutions to energy issues in his buildings – with a certain dissimulation of their technological features – and also created technically innovative and aesthetically resolved forms for covering large volumes, such as the undulating landscape of the Expodach (1999–2000), an intricate double-curved wood latticework stretching over the pavilions of the 2000 world's fair in Hanover, Germany. Also in Germany, sometimes claimed to be the very motherland of engineering, Jürgen Schlaich's metal structures and Werner Sobek's research into energy use in buildings have opened new avenues for contemporary work.

New geometries

When some of the utopian thinkers of the 1960s belatedly succeeded in bringing their ideas to fruition, their designs at times benefited, in a generational reversal, from the work of younger architects whom they had previously inspired. Peter Cook and Colin Fournier's Kunsthaus in Graz, Austria (1999–2003), looks like a body part left behind by some mysterious giant animal, but its perforated skin also makes it a machine for emitting beams of light to the city. Although its load-bearing concrete structure is very conventional, its overall form recalls the experiments of groups such as Future Systems, a British office led by the Czech Jan Kaplicky, whose imaginative vision explicitly derived from aerospace construction. The group designed a space station for NASA in 1983 before producing their Doughnut House (1986), which was inspired by hypotheses for houses on the moon. Future Systems challenged the

stereotypical skyscraper with its Coexistence Tower (1985), a stack of large capsules held in place by a system of cables. In their Blob (1985), **565** a competition project for an office building in Trafalgar Square designed in collaboration with Frank Newby of Samuely and Partners, they proposed a thick, self-supporting skin that abandoned the standard orthogonal shape of the office building to explore the potential of an organically inspired membrane and envelope. They arrived at a convincing formulation of this concept in their Selfridges Store in Birmingham, England (1999–2003), which is covered in thousands of aluminum disks resembling fish scales. While these designers sought to challenge the mainly orthogonal geometry of twentieth-century architecture, the most advanced techniques in metal and glass construction were more frequently put to conventional use. In Paris the major projects, or *grands travaux*, that originated during François Mitterrand's two terms as French president (1981–95) launched a resurgence of commissions for cultural buildings, not just in France but in cities around the world, and opened a field of negotiation between advanced technology and more traditional modes of composition. To some extent, technology was domesticated, with the details treated more experimentally than the whole. → 8 The Institut du Monde Arabe (Arab World Institute; 1981–7) **567** by Jean Nouvel, Gilbert Lézénès, Pierre Soria and Architecture Studio is significant for its ingenious integration into the Parisian urban landscape but even more so for its southern facade, which contains a system of metal diaphragms that are opened and closed by photoelectric cells and regulate the interior illumination. The ungainliness of Johan Otto von Spreckelsen's Grande Arche in La Défense (1983–9) is partly counterbalanced by a canopy designed by Peter Rice in the shape of "clouds," although

565 Blob, project, Future Systems (Jan Kaplicky and David Nixon), London, United Kingdom, 1985

566 Embryological House, project, Greg Lynn, 1998–9

567 ▶ Arab World Institute, Jean Nouvel, Gilbert Lézénès, Pierre Soria and Architecture Studio, Paris, France, 1981–7

they are thicker as built than the diaphanous version Rice proposed in the competition. Another structure by Rice, the greenhouses of the Cité des Sciences at Parc de la Villette (1982–6), represents the most daring component of a museum built inside an obsolete slaughterhouse.

After 1973, the growing concern with energy consumption led initially to the invention of passive systems relying on the thickness of insulating walls, and subsequently to increasingly elaborate devices for thermal exchange and storage, which made it possible to produce totally self-sufficient and even energy-producing buildings. The movement toward lightweight structures inaugurated by Buckminster Fuller and continued by Frei Otto slowed down only temporarily before picking up again with the emergence of computer technology. The latter made it possible to calculate and build the "free" forms that previously had to be conceived and designed intuitively. Computer-assisted fabrication of double-curved elements was made possible by software like CATIA, an acronym for Computer-Aided Three-Dimensional Interactive Application, initially invented for Dassault fighter planes and adapted to architecture by Frank Gehry's team of designers. As a result, many architectural fantasies derived from machines and biomorphic forms but previously consigned to paper have now become reality. Greg Lynn's research on structures similar to embryonic organisms 566 and Bernard Cache's on the generation of complex geometric forms have provided just a first glimpse of the potential unleashed by the encounter between new materials and new methods of computing. Work has developed along these lines in engineering firms like Arup, where Cecil Balmond has investigated a range of innovative structures. It has also been embraced by architectural offices like the Rotterdam-based UN Studio, directed by Ben van

Berkel and Caroline Bos, which has explored new inhabitable geometries, as in the Moebius House in Het Gooi (1993–8), where the cycle of daily activities served as the prime generator of space and restored excitement to infrastructure works, with the dynamic tension of their Erasmus bridge in Rotterdam (1990–6). 577

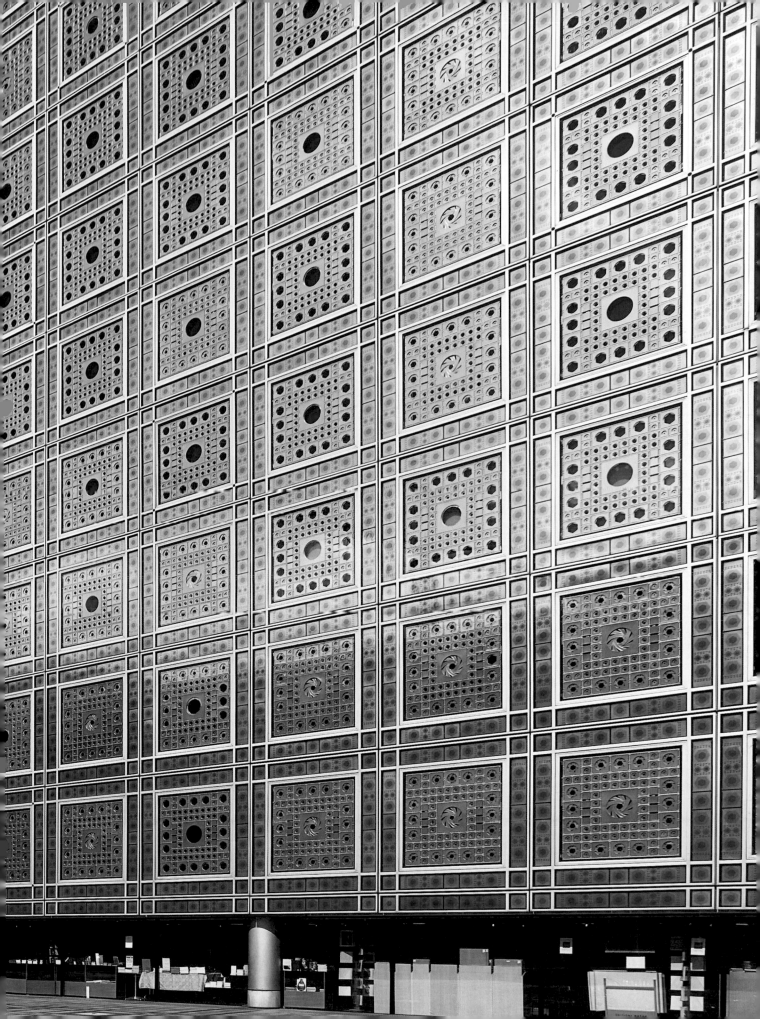

Architecture's outer boundaries

While certain architects were stimulated during the last two decades of the twentieth century by technological challenges and by questions concerning the future form of the city, many others focused their thinking on the discipline's own aims, distinguishing characteristics, and degree of autonomy. Active in the changing market for an architecture that was both technically expert and formally experimental – a marginal segment of building production, but one with increasing visibility – they predicated their practices less on revolutionary new theories than on the shared conviction that a critical practice was possible.

This analytical approach was encouraged by several centers of architectural thought that emerged in the 1970s. The first was the Architectural Association in London, a "finishing school" under Alvin Boyarsky's direction that was open to talented students from around the world. It produced the intellectual culture that subsequently allowed Rem Koolhaas, Bernard Tschumi or Zaha Hadid to shape their individual approaches. → [1] Another essential center was the Institute for Architecture and Urban Studies in New York and its journal *Oppositions* (1973–84), which introduced a critical vision of modernity to the United States that was notably indebted to Manfredo Tafuri's writings and teaching, but also propagated ideas coming out of emerging design practices in Spain and Japan. → [2]

Some of the orientations arising at this time may be seen as a continuation of the Modern Movement by other means, so to speak, and they have been labeled (among other things) "supermodern." → [3] Yet these were actually new strategies, which led to a redefinition of the architectural field and its objects. Despite the fears of the critics of globalization, the results have been extraordinarily varied, and they can be identified not only with the architects who have been in the forefront of the international scene since the 1980s but also with innovative design strategies that have permeated wider professional circles.

Gehry, or the seduction of art

Certain architects modeled their strategies on those of Pop, Minimalist, and Conceptual artists, no longer viewing the relationship between art and architecture in terms of a "synthesis of the arts" dominated by the architect. The most remarkable such strategy was developed by Frank Gehry in Los Angeles. At the beginning of his practice, Gehry integrated elements from early modernist houses in Los Angeles, as in his Danziger Studio and House (1964–5). But beginning with the Ron Davis Studio and House in Malibu (1972), he took advantage of the freedom permitted by wood structures to deform and then shatter the obligatory "box." The addition to his own house in Santa Monica (1977–8) **568** was a revelation to many not only for the way it exposed the wood framing of the existing volume but for its addition of peripheral structures made of everyday materials usually suppressed by architects, such as corrugated aluminum siding and chain-link fence. He continued to play with these materials in Venice, California, with the Indiana Avenue Studios (1979–81) and the Norton House (1982–4). Gehry also designed many museum installations. While a new building for the Museum of Contemporary Art in Los Angeles was under construction, he converted a warehouse for the museum to use as temporary quarters; the Temporary Contemporary (1982–3) was such a success that it became a permanent part of the museum.

During the 1980s Gehry investigated questions of diversity and unity, but his design method always remained rooted in

569 Chiat/Day Building, Frank Gehry, Los Angeles, California, USA, 1985–91

570 ▶ Guggenheim Museum, Frank Gehry, Bilbao, Spain, 1991–7

568 Gehry House, Frank Gehry, Santa Monica, California, USA, 1977–8

an acute awareness of the building's uses, to the point that it would not be incorrect to call him a functionalist. He reinterpreted conventional programs such as the shopping center, at Santa Monica Place (1972–80, demolished 2008), and the university campus, at Loyola University Law School in Los Angeles (1978–84). He also rethought the private house, treating it as an assemblage of disparate elements or a villagelike entity, in the Winton Guest House in Wayzata, Minnesota (1982–7) and later the Schnabel House in Los Angeles (1986–9).

Although also in the category of projects composed of fragments, Gehry's Edgemar complex in Santa Monica (1986–7) and Chiat/Day Building in Los Angles **569** (1985–91) were based on a different principle — that of a rapid reading from the street. The placement of the buildings' distinguishing features was thus calibrated to the glance of passing motorists. Gehry made humorous use of the culture of advertising in structures such as the parking lot at Santa Monica Place, where he incorporated supergraphics into the chain-link fence. The ironic presence of these unconventional buildings close to neighboring property lines and within prosaic subdivisions reflected his subtle attention to urban rhythms. Each project created its own context, with certain repetitive or "calming" elements acting as a backdrop. In the Chiat/Day complex, a copper-clad facade evoking a petrified forest and a pair of giant black binoculars that Gehry invited the sculptor Claes Oldenburg to reinterpret from a 1984 Conceptual Art project interact with a third element, the facade of a more abstract, curved white building. At Santa Monica Place, the shopping center's skewed planes and outriggers contrasted with the solid geometry of the block. The Vitra Design Museum of 1988–94 in the German city of Weil am Rhein is characterized by the clash of the metallic volumes of its roof and the white walls of its free-form envelope

against the green surrounding meadow, distantly echoing Lyubov Popova and Alexander Vesnin's Cubo-Futurist compositions. This project proved to be a decisive step for Gehry in arriving at a design strategy based more on integration than fragmentation. This change in strategy did not preclude him from continuing to insert his buildings thoughtfully into their urban context, as may be judged from the siting of his Guggenheim Museum Bilbao (1991–7). **570** Dominating the Nervión River Valley and visible from the grid of the city's streets, the museum has become the symbol and fulcrum of the Basque capital's renaissance, catalyzing the valley's transformation from shipbuilding to culture industry. In contrast to the artists who greeted Frank Lloyd Wright's museum in New York with hostility, artists received the Guggenheim Bilbao without protest; Gehry had long maintained a dialogue with them and, despite the museum's curvaceous exterior, half the galleries are reassuringly orthogonal. Yet there are similarities between Gehry's museum and the Wright's spiral building in New York, most significant of which is the architectural promenade leading to the upper galleries, which in both cases revolves around a central atrium. The Bilbao museum recycles themes from Gehry's earlier work, such as the torquing tower he used in his "Fred and Ginger" office building erected on a corner site in Prague in 1992–6.

Despite its unsettling image, the Guggenheim Bilbao nonetheless quickly found an enthusiastic audience. So did the Walt Disney Concert Hall in Los Angeles (1989–2003), whose design was governed by a search for optimal acoustics, harking back to precursors like Hans Scharoun's Philharmonie in Berlin. It also reflected the city's desire to rework a site marred by the awkward edifices of the Music Center, a West Coast counterpart to New York's Lincoln Center. Gehry did his best to engage

571 Parc de la Villette competition project, Rem Koolhaas, Paris, France, 1982–3

572 Kunsthal, Rem Koolhaas, Rotterdam, Netherlands, 1988-92

the existing buildings by pulling them into the turbulence of the new concert hall, whose auditorium is housed within the structure as tightly as a violin in its case. In the Ray and Maria Stata Research Center at Massachusetts Institute of Technology (2000–4), he opted for the creation of a continuous landscape of diversified volumes with contrasted cladding. The juxtaposition of the two vertical complexes containing the laboratories creates a kind of cliff surrounding smaller volumes arranged on a plinth. This plinth cascades by way of an outdoor amphitheater down to the rest of the campus and invites students in. The interior of the plinth contains an "endless corridor" that connects the researchers' trajectories with MIT's broader circulation routes, further contributing to the urban character of the scheme. → 4

Koolhaas, or fantastic realism

Beginning in the 1970s, the Dutch architect Rem Koolhaas sparked a revolution, one indebted to the conceptual approach of Oswald Mathias Ungers and the legacy of Russian Constructivism. With Elia Zenghelis, Koolhaas founded the Office for Metropolitan Architecture, or OMA, in 1975, after elaborating a series of fictional projects such as "Exodus, or the Voluntary Prisoners of Architecture" and "The City of the Captive Globe" (1972). The program denoted by OMA's name was made explicit in the text and illustrations of Koolhaas's 1978 book *Delirious New York* – an ironic and innovative reading of "Manhattanism." → 5 A plea for both architectural imagination and urban congestion, the book brought to light forgotten but meaningful buildings through the formulation of a "retroactive" theory of urbanism that had determined New York's skyscrapers without ever having been enunciated.

Dissecting examples from the entire corpus of the city's architectural history, the book created a narrative in which the flagrant errors of "proper" history were corrected. This imaginary museum was the source of certain elements in OMA's entry to the Parc de la Villette competition (1982–3). 571 Although inhibited by the rigid demands of the program, the office nonetheless conceived a structure based on the frequency and interrelationship of various activities, coming up with mathematic algorithms for space allocation in order to assign bands of landscape to sports or leisure activities.

In a similar vein, OMA reexamined the paradigm of the 1920s *Siedlungen* in its IJ-Plein Social Housing project in Amsterdam (1980–9), where a slab resembling an ocean liner dominates a development of row houses. In the Kunsthal in Rotterdam (1988–92) 572 the floors are disposed along a spiral circuit whose intersection with a public ramp running straight through the building becomes the project's central theme. OMA's enigmatic competition project for the new Bibliothèque Nationale in Paris (1989), with volumes hovering in a translucent white cube according to a kind of three-dimensional "free plan" indebted to Paul Nelson's Suspended House, was unsuccessful. But the office's winning scheme for the Euralille competition (1989–94), Koolhaas's first large-scale commission, extended his work on circulation to an entire urban area – a new center grafted onto the French city of Lille – and celebrated the programmatic diversity of retail, offices, housing, entertainment, and transportation in a single complex. The architect's study of the superimposition of networks and activities yielded the spatial complexity of an "invisible metropolis," with highways serving as Euralille's primary materials. Koolhaas effectively orchestrated the weblike system of movement, diffracting it into distinct programmatic and architectural sequences while exploring

573 House in Floirac, Rem Koolhaas, Bordeaux, France, 1994–8

574 Public Library, Rem Koolhaas, Seattle, Washington, USA, 1999–2004

themes of spatial variety and the links between diverse entities. The ovoid Grand Palais, the only building in the complex designed by Koolhaas himself, condensed the architect's ambitions. Presented by him as functionally innovative in terms of the connections among its different components, the building is actually characterized by the distinctness of its spaces: the large exhibition area of the main hall opening to the exterior, a complex circulation space, whose hallways and stairs offer a varied sequence of experiences, and the efficient curve of the amphitheater, used for rock concerts, whose form generated the building's overall envelope.

As suggested by the title of his second book, *S, M, L, XL*, [6] Koolhaas's work continued at an extremely diverse range of scales, from the domestic to the urban. For the Villa dall'Ava in Saint-Cloud (1984–92) and the House in Floirac, near Bordeaux (1994–8), **573** he designed surprising domestic spaces for enthusiastic clients. The former plays with Corbusian images, stretching between two volumes and culminating in a rooftop swimming pool that rests on the structure of the glass pavilion below it. The latter, centered on an elevator installed to accommodate its handicapped owner, constantly confronts its inhabitants with vertiginous situations and is in itself the very image of a delicate balance. The McCormick Tribune Campus Center in Chicago at the Illinois Institute of Technology (1997–2003), located across from Ludwig Mies van der Rohe's canonical buildings and inserted beneath an elevated rail track that Koolhaas encased in a stainless steel cylinder for acoustic insulation, is a vast cavern with distinct levels streaked with diagonal circulation routes in a configuration determined by the spontaneous paths blazed by the students. In opposition to the otherwise staid arrangement of the campus's functions and circuits, the center creates constant friction between activities and users.

Koolhaas's fascination with large-scale projects throughout the 1990s may have been a rhetorical ploy intended to attract grander commissions or else a commentary upon such commissions. But it came to fruition with the construction of the Seattle Public Library (1999–2004) **574** on a sloping downtown site. Elaborating on a circulation concept developed in his rejected project for the Jussieu Library in Paris (1993), the architect superimposed five principal levels, linking them by a spiral ramp and escalators and wrapping their obliquely angled spaces in a glass facade. The interior circuits pass from corridors to cantilevered balconies and turn the path from reading rooms to shops into an exciting *promenade architecturale* in which the potential of the multifunction skyscrapers studied in *Delirious New York* was finally exploited. Parallel to this long-awaited materialization of his theories, Koolhaas's ideas and methods began to be widely disseminated by the large number of young architects who passed through his office from the early 1980s onward and who contributed to an intellectual renovation of Dutch architecture. [7]

Nouvel, or mystery recovered

Jean Nouvel followed a track to prominence parallel to that of Rem Koolhaas. But while Koolhaas's approach involved incessant questioning of modern architecture's ideas in order to distance himself from them, Nouvel's constant search has been for striking yet complex visual effects, a preoccupation that has led him to take inspiration from cinema and from places like airports and nocturnal urban landscapes. Concurrent with the construction of his Institut du Monde Arabe in Paris, Nouvel designed projects remarkable for their conceptual clarity and close attention to the urban environment.

575 Cultural and Convention Center, Jean Nouvel, Lucerne, Switzerland, 1993–2000

576 Nemausus Social Housing, Jean Nouvel, Nîmes, France, 1985–7

577 Erasmus Bridge, UN Studio (Ben van Berkel and Caroline Bos), Rotterdam, Netherlands, 1990–6

The Nemausus complex in Nîmes (1985–7) **576** turned low-income housing into a structure resembling a parking garage with a very elaborate metal facade, using an industrial aesthetic and providing apartments twice the usual size. In the Saint-James Hotel in Bouliac, near Bordeaux (1987–9), Nouvel's frame of reference was rural: he shaped the building from volumes similar to those of the region's tobacco drying-houses, replacing the wood cladding of the kilns with COR-TEN steel. Often subverting programmatic stereotypes, Nouvel gave his Euralille Shopping Center (1995) a certain urban quality. For another example, he used large mirrored cones inside the Galeries Lafayette in Berlin (1991–5) to create anamorphic-type images in a changing scenography. His unrealized project for the Tour sans Fins (Tower without Limits) at La Défense (1990) was intended to dissolve into the sky with the increasing transparency of its upper levels; meanwhile its lateral load-bearing frame would have created an open volume accommodating multistory rooms. Nouvel returned to these ideas ten years later in the Agbar Tower in Barcelona.

In the Fondation Cartier in Paris (1991–4) Nouvel again played with the aesthetics of disappearance, or rather with the illusionism produced by a mirrorlike glass facade, conjuring up film metaphors like depth of field and framing. In a conversation with Jean Baudrillard he described the play of the building's three vertical planes of glass – the first appearing to prolong the boulevard's urban facade, the other two enclosing the actual building and visually dilating its volume: "The viewers never know if they're seeing the sky or its reflection. Generally you see both and that ambiguity creates an interplay of multiple appearances. At the same time, the building makes use of the most trivial function of transparency for the exhibition space. … Walking in front of the building you see the display." → 8

In other projects, Nouvel's volumes appear solid. The Cultural and Convention Center in Lucerne (1993–2000) **575** transformed the view of the city's lakefront through the framing effect of its overhanging roof, which appears more lightweight owing to the reflection of the water on its underside. Beneath this great visor, the volumes of the concert hall, auditorium, and exhibition space coexist harmoniously. In the law courts built on the banks of the Loire across from the historical center of Nantes (1993–2000), the broad black coffered roof supported by freestanding columns, between which the courtrooms are inserted, seems an idiosyncratic realization of Auguste Perret's ideal of the "sovereign shelter."

Herzog and de Meuron, or the principle of the collection

Sharing Gehry's fascination with contemporary art, the Basel architects Jacques Herzog and Pierre de Meuron have created visual effects that sometimes rely on figurative patterns, although without sacrificing tectonic rigor. They have also redefined the typological principle of each of their buildings, ignoring received ideas and avoiding clichés. In contrast to the ubiquitous and boring "big boxes" of commercial architecture, the polycarbonate facade of their warehouse for Ricola on the outskirts of Mulhouse (1992–3) is decorated with a leaf motif whose visibility shifts radically from day to night. Ricola in turn inspired solutions such as the one for the library at the Eberswalde Technical School (1993–6), where photographic motifs are engraved on the concrete panels, establishing the facade's rhythm and conveying the purpose of the structure. Elsewhere, the duo used quarried stone as a primary material. Their Stone House in Tavole, Italy (1982–8), opened a dialogue

578 Dominus Winery, Jacques Herzog and Pierre de Meuron, Yountville, California, USA, 1995–7

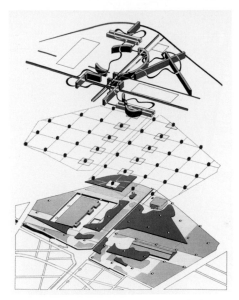

579 Parc de la Villette, Bernard Tschumi, Paris, France, 1982–98

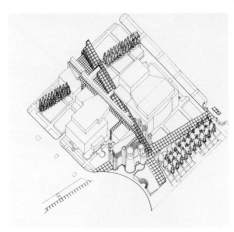

580 Wexner Center for the Arts, Peter Eisenman, Columbus, Ohio, USA, 1985–9

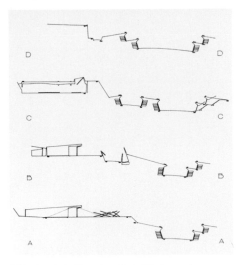

581 Igualada Cemetery, Enric Miralles and Carme Pinós, Barcelona, Spain, 1984–93

with traditional construction, while their Dominus Winery (1995–7) **578** in Yountville, California, uses gabion cladding cages in a technique adapted from the retaining walls put up along river banks and hillsides. The central Signal Box at the Basel Train Station (1994), which breaks with the conventional opaque base and glazed volume of this type of structure, is a concrete container covered in bands of copper, a poetic cladding that serves as both electrostatic shield and visual filter. At the Goetz Collection in Munich (1989–92), the architects worked in a subtle way with natural light. They then extrapolated the idea of its glazed surface to create the "lightbeam," the superstructure of the Tate Modern (1995–2000) **582** in London. With their renovation of the interior of Sir Giles Gilbert Scott's power station for the same client they pursued a different effect; here the great Turbine Hall becomes the unifying space of the entire program, the center from which all the galleries are reached. Herzog and de Meuron's connection to contemporary art is also explicit in their Schaulager in Münchenstein (1998–2003), near Basel, a storage and exhibition facility that consists of a rough box with a stack of open floors. The vertiginous interior clearly resembles an Andreas Gursky photograph. Each of the team's successive buildings seems to be a new formulation of the relationship between materials and space. [9]

The elective affinities between architecture and art exemplified by Herzog and de Meuron's practice led to the modification of the public image of the architect and his or her production. Architects sometimes appeared to be emulating artists in trying to create works that photographed well in catalogs rather than functioned as real buildings. But this position seemed inherently short-lived: once having graduated to more important programs, even the most radical architects tended to conform to more conventional professional models. This was the case with

Bernard Tschumi, who explored the relationship of architecture to dance and film in his *Manhattan Transcripts* before winning the competition for Parc de la Villette in Paris in 1982. [10] **579** Once he began actually building the project, he found himself obliged to abandon a few of his utopian objectives for it, retaining only the grid of Constructivist "follies," whose functions remain rather enigmatic.

Deconstructivists and rationalists

Peter Eisenman's development has been characterized by his dogged determination to maintain a critical stance. He was in large part responsible for the Museum of Modern Art's exhibition dedicated to *Deconstructivist Architecture* in 1988, in which the reference to the experiments of the Russian Constructivists, considered solely in terms of their formal "instability," was crossed with a Freudian concept of deconstruction read through Jacques Derrida. The group of architects who took part included Gehry, Eisenman, Tschumi, Koolhaas, Coop Himmelb(l)au, Daniel Libeskind, and Zaha Hadid. [11] **584** Eisenman has had few opportunities to realize his almost Talmudic strategies for combining grids and systems of geometric coordinates. The most convincing realization of his approach is the Wexner Center for the Arts (1985–9) **580** in Columbus, Ohio, whose structure he determined by overlaying a Mercator grid on the main axis of the campus. [12] Eisenman subsequently abandoned the exploration of grids to study other modes of generating form, particularly the notion of folding as derived from his reading of Gilles Deleuze's theory of the Baroque, [13] and of topographic inscription, a strategy he used to design his Ciudad de Cultura de Galicia (City of Culture of Galicia) in Santiago de Compostela (1999–2011), which seems to be an extension of the natural terrain.

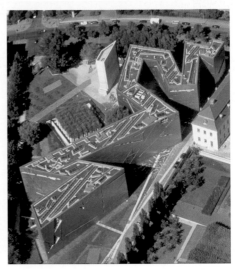

583 Slow House, project, Diller Scofidio, Long Island, New York, USA, 1988–90

582 Tate Modern, Jacques Herzog and Pierre de Meuron, London, United Kingdom, 1995–2000

584 The Peak, project, Zaha Hadid, Hong Kong, China, 1983

585 Jewish Museum, Daniel Libeskind, Berlin, Germany, 1990–5

The architectural scene in the 1990s appeared to be extremely diverse, but certain principles were shared by geographically remote architects and, on occasional, by regional and national clusters of practitioners. With the rapid shattering of the artificial unity of Deconstructivism, each of its initial representatives went on to pursue his or her own work, while the next generation came up with new themes. [14] In Los Angeles, after a phase in which Frank Gehry strongly dominated the local scene, Thom Mayne's firm Morphosis, Eric Owen Moss, and the Craig Hodgetts/Ming Fung partnership opened a new dialogue with projects anchored in that city. Meanwhile Gehry himself became increasingly active on other continents. Whatever the personal orientations of their designers, the Los Angeles projects displayed a deliberate complexity, resulting both from their geometric conceptions and from the use of building systems pushed to the limits of existing technology and used as expressive devices. In particular, Mayne succeeded in renewing the image of both public institutions, with the interlocked volumes of his Diamond Ranch High School in Pomona (1994–9), and corporate high-rises, with his Sun Tower in Seoul (1995–7). Designers like the Catalan architects Enric Miralles and Carme Pinós joined Eisenman and the southern Californians in their ambition to rethink the architectural object in its totality. Their intriguing projects include the Igualada Cemetery near Barcelona (1984–93) **581** and the Archery Range built for the Barcelona Olympics (1989–91). In partnership with Benedetta Tagliabue, Miralles designed Scotland's Parliament in Edinburgh (1998–2004), completed after his death; in its imaginative combination of linear and sculptural shapes it renews the very concept of the public building. Built several years before, Daniel Libeskind's Jewish Museum in Berlin (1990–5) **585** challenged existing representations of the typology of the museum and developed essentially out of an intricate graphic investigation. In New York the team of Elizabeth Diller and Ricardo Scofidio developed a design strategy that was an echo of Conceptual Art. It only came to fruition after 2000 once they began receiving commissions for substantial buildings, but they succeeded in making their mark earlier with provocative projects like the Slow House on Long Island (1988–90), **583** which made ironic use of technology and media.

A different group of designers remained committed to a certain constructive rationality, an urban integration of buildings, and a search for poetic forms. This group included within its rather porous boundaries the Swiss architect Roger Diener and the British David Chipperfield. The latter designed many museums, including the master plan and the Neues Museum (1998–2011) for the Museum Island complex in Berlin and public edifices such as the law courts in Salerno, Italy (1999–2011). Sharing many of Chipperfield's positions, particularly the clarity and order of his compositions, was the French architect Yves Lion, who designed a conference center in Nantes (1992) as well as a delicate extension to the Museum of French-American Cooperation in Blérancourt (1992). Sometimes built in difficult locations, as in the case of the French embassy in Beirut (1998–2002), Lion's architecture engaged in a dialogue with the existing structures. [15] Another Parisian, Patrick Berger, proved himself an expert above all in the use of materials. Particularly fond of wood, he featured it in his architecture school in Rennes (1990) and his UEFA Headquarters in Nyon, located between Lausanne and Geneva (1994–9), creating a subtle relationship with both the nearby bank and the lake.

587 Hillside Terrace, Fumihiko Maki, Tokyo, Japan, 1969

Despite the frenzy of production that followed Germany's reunification in 1990, the German scene has remained hard to define. Hans Kollhoff abandoned the rationalist orientation of his earlier buildings, like the housing on KNSM Island in Amsterdam (1994), for an explicit neo-traditionalism. This was evident in his projects for Berlin, newly reinstated as Germany's capital. Among these are his belt of skyscrapers around Alexanderplatz (1993) and his brick-faced triangular-plan tower on Potsdamer Straße (1997–2000). Alongside the generation of major firms that emerged in the 1950s – Günter Behnisch's, for example – and in the 1960s – like Meinhard von Gerkan & Volkwin Marg – new architectural teams appeared. Partnerships like that of Matthias Sauerbruch and Louisa Hutton have put emphasis on techniques for addressing climate issues while also proposing typological and formal innovations. Their GSW Building in Berlin (1992–9), **586** a sculpturally inventive addition to a mundane 1950s building, offers a complex approach to climate control with its electronically regulated facade, while the colorful, sinuous facade of their Adlershof Research Center (1995–8) evokes the waves of the light spectrum.

Fragmentation and poetry in Japan

In Japan the effects of postmodernism were relatively superficial and its principal representative, Arata Isozaki, quickly moved on to other pursuits. A critical relationship with modernist design developed along several axes. In his Hillside Terrace apartment complex in the Daikanyama neighborhood of Tokyo (1969), **587** Fumihiko Maki inflected urban architecture with picturesque elements as well as with what he called an "aesthetic of fragmentation." → 16 His campus for Keio

University in Shonan-Fujisawa (1992–4) ingeniously assimilated Le Corbusier's Villa Savoye and Giuseppe Terragni's Casa del Fascio, while his 1990s buildings in Tokyo adapted images from film. Maki's Tokyo Metropolitan Gymnasium (1990), Fujisawa Municipal Gymnasium (1984), and Makuhari Fairgrounds (1986–9) all feature metal skins that allude to Samurai armor.

Based in Osaka, Tadao Ando has created a more sensuous architecture, playing with light, sound, and tactility. His intimate single-family houses of the 1970s and 1980s and his Rokko 1 apartment complex (1981), which steps down a hill, combine Corbusian sources like the Roq et Rob development with a special concern for the solidity of walls and the different qualities of light. In his smallest structures, Ando interpreted the minimalist aesthetics of the Japanese tea house, while in his most complex works he skillfully adjusted his design to the existing commercial context or urban neighborhood, as in his Galleria Akka in Osaka (1985–8) **588** and Collezione Building in Tokyo (1985–9). Gradually he began building projects on less constricted sites. This allowed him to make poetic gestures that magnify every facet of the natural environment while maintaining his buildings' hermeticism, as in the chapel on Mount Rokko (1985–6), the Church of the Light in Ibaraki (1987–9), **590** and the Church on the Water in Tomamu on the island of Hokkaido (1985–8). **589** Originally developed in relation to traditional Japanese concepts of space, his idiom has opened up to a more complex geometry, while his activity has extended to Europe with the Conference Pavilion at the Vitra Design Museum (1993) and the Benetton Factory in Treviso (2000) and to the United States with the Pulitzer Foundation for the Arts (1991–2001) in St. Louis, Missouri, and the Modern Art Museum of Fort Worth in Texas (1997–2002).

588 Galleria Akka, Tadao Ando, Osaka, Japan, 1985–8

589 Church on the Water, Tadao Ando, Tomamu, Japan, 1985–8

590 Church of the Light, Tadao Ando, Ibaraki, Japan, 1987–89

591　Cardboard Building, Shigeru Ban, Kobe, Japan, 1995

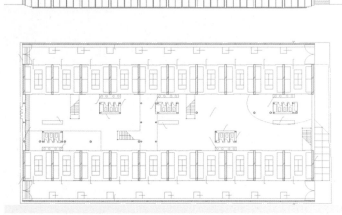

592　Saishunkan Seiyaku Women's Dormitory, Kazuyo Sejima, Kumamoto, Japan, 1991

593 ▶　Sendai Mediatheque, Toyo Ito, Sendai, Japan, 1995–2001

Toyo Ito's career reveals a more intellectualized, often ironic approach aimed at the creation of floating or transparent spaces. His Silver Hut in Tokyo (1984) was based on a composition of aluminum vaults covering a spare interior. He returned to this idea on an expanded scale with the floating roofscape of the Yatsushiro Museum (1991). Ito's investigations into materials and light culminated with the Sendai Mediatheque (1995–2001), **593** a program in which cultural activities were integrated into a seven-story volume with a square plan and entirely glazed facades. Its structure consists of a forest of "trees" – thin steel tubular columns clustered in lattices that take different configurations at each level; the public circulates among them with great fluidity. → [17] Ito was a participant in Art Polis, a public architecture program of the Kumamoto Prefecture of Kyushu Island initiated by Isozaki and overseen by Hajime Yatsuka. Kazuyo Sejima was another participant and received the opportunity to build her Saishunkan Seiyaku Women's Dormitory (1991) **592** there, an ethereal construction that updated the theme of the collective house by placing it into a diaphanous envelope. A partner with Ryue Nishizawa in the SANAA firm since 1995, Sejima further developed her aesthetic in two museums, in Nagano (1995–9) and Kanazawa (1999–2004), fashioning an elegant, minimalist language that plays with filtered, reflected, and diffracted light. She adapted this dialectic of transparency and opalescence in the De Kunstlinie Cultural Center in the Dutch New Town of Almere (1998–2006), creating a halo of hope at one extremity of an otherwise rather oppressive complex. → [18]

Although several of the architects whose early work has been described in this chapter evolved during the last decade of the twentieth century into firms operating on a global scale, they managed to retain an experimental attitude in at least a portion of their production. To be sure this was sometimes obscured by the intense media hype surrounding their buildings. Under the pressure of a new period in which architecture regained the prestige it lost during the 1960s and 1970s, interest in architectural research remained fragile but was nonetheless sustained by the creative anxiety and intellectual acuity of a handful of designers.

Vanishing Points

As the twentieth century came to an end, architecture seemed fully recovered as a discipline from the crisis that beset the Modern Movement after World War II and from the period of soul-searching of the 1980s. Nearly 120 years after the Paris and Chicago world's fairs unveiled their grand spectacles for visitors from the Old World and the New, innovative projects reestablished the image of the architect as a major public figure in dialogue with politicians, business leaders, and those in the world of art and fashion. At the same time, many of the issues that characterized the previous decades were, and still are, under discussion, albeit at a new global scale. A decade into the third millennium, these tensions appear to have made architecture a more open and plural field of cultural production.

Tourism and construction, two dominant components of the global economy, seem once again to be converging, with the emergence of an architecture defined primarily by its appeal as a monument, with usefulness sometimes remaining only a secondary consideration. →1 The proving grounds for the spectacle of architectural kitsch have expanded. In the early 1990s, in many of the former Soviet republics, for instance, a major model for architectural production seemed to be Las Vegas. In Moscow, nostalgia for the Stalin-era "Seven Sisters" lingered after the dissolution of the USSR and led to the construction of buildings like the Triumf Palace, a naive copy of 1950s towers. Only recently has an interest in the language of high-tech architecture begun to emerge, reflecting the taste of a more cosmopolitan neo-capitalist ruling class. →2 Chinese and Southeast Asian cities have tried out architectural idioms ranging from the most exhibitionist high tech to the most awkwardly historicist. Both Russia and China, with their respective forms of state capitalism, have put governmental and administrative structures in the service of economic oligarchies that have opened themselves up to the global circulation of architectural forms and professionals. European and North American architects have built some of their largest projects in these countries, while local architects have gradually entered the scene by associating with their Western counterparts. In Moscow, where the utopians of the 1970s once devised viable alternatives to neo-Stalinist colonnades, the spread of the new stereotypes of the tower and the big box shopping center has been unlimited, as it also has been in Latin America, Southeast Asia, and the Middle East.

A century after the early modernists overturned the eclecticism of historicist architecture and rejected monumental rhetoric as well as applied ornament, these repressed approaches seem to be returning. Meanwhile some of the landmarks of modern architecture are threatened by real-estate speculation. The proliferation of large and spectacular buildings expresses the aspiration of modern cities to be characterized by gigantic signs, but with the replication of similar gestures throughout the world their individuality eventually dissolves. Ironically this is a repetition of a phenomenon that occurred with premodern buildings, for instance the Beaux-Arts opera houses erected worldwide during the early twentieth century. Tectonic rigor – or asceticism – has been replaced by a play of surface ornament that, when employed by designers like Herzog and de Meuron, can sometimes be ingenious and experimental. A backlash against the standardization unleashed by mass production can be seen in these new decorative orders, which are sometimes based purely on technological protocols and mathematical algorithms. But nothing would be further from the truth than to ascribe this return to a simple regression or some inevitable cyclical movement.

Monumental and sometimes ornamental, architecture at the beginning of the third millennium has shifted the stakes by virtue of its scale, its enlarged urban and territorial scope, its materiality, and the ways it is communicated. Paradoxically, the widespread search for singular and "original" forms has led to the creation of generic spaces that are certainly more elaborate than those of earlier standardized housing projects and business centers, but equally banal, as the juxtaposition of too many singular, provocative, forms produces in the end an effect of boredom.

Strategic geographies

Half a century after the dismantling of the colonial empires and twenty years after the collapse of "real" socialism and of South African apartheid, a multipolar world has emerged whose fragility and interdependence were revealed in 2008–9 by an international economic depression. This new world is dominated not by nations or states but by cities and their specific contexts: in New York there is a concentration of skyscraper specialists; in London, of engineers; in Barcelona, of urban designers. Often these specialists are active thousands of miles from their home bases. Massive construction projects are underway in the former countries of the Soviet Bloc as well as in the Persian Gulf states where the future of the oil economy creates high stakes, providing work for European, North American, and Japanese architects. The impetuous development of a Chinese architecture in dialogue with the rest of the world no longer depends exclusively on foreign architects, but also on rising young professionals like Yung Ho Chang, who became head of MIT's Department of Architecture in 2005, and Ma Qingyun, appointed dean of the University of Southern California's School of Architecture in 2007. The global circulation of architects now leads in many directions.

Although still only partially reflected in the list of winners of the Pritzker Prize – awarded to the profession's most significant figures every year since 1979 – the map of global architecture has become more complex. Alongside the projects of truly multi- or transnational architectural firms operating throughout the world, such as the American practices of Kohn Pedersen Fox and DMJM (formerly Daniel, Mann, Johnson and Mendenhall), or of the British Foster + Partners, are architectural activities that do not emanate from either major firms or the figures whose trademark styles are recognized and glorified by the media. Medium-size and small firms now work on a transcontinental scale to survive, and few architects are able to resist the temptation to operate remotely, even on terrain with which they are unfamiliar, not to mention at times for clients with suspect or openly repressive political ambitions. This kind of architecture often falls back on a sort of oversimplification, even an iconic primitivism, which allows it to be instantly intelligible on television screens and the front pages of newspapers. → 3

The strategic alliances established among major architecture firms, corporations, and developers represent another important facet of the contemporary picture. These configurations tend to upset the architect's traditional role as the client's representative in dealing with builders and budgets. Through conscientious attention to urban integration and programmatic function, however, as well as kitsch-free interpretation of local cultures, the kind of critical internationalism described previously may offer a potential alternative to the pervasive tyranny of the image and the generalized indifference to local specificities.

594 A member of Gehry Partners'
studio works on an early model for
8 Spruce Street, New York City,
USA, 2011

Reinvented materials

Recent scientific and technological breakthroughs have given back to architecture its ability to surprise. The greatest power of such innovations is less in achieving an impressive span or a towering height than in facilitating fresh and counterintuitive uses of familiar materials. Glass – since the nineteenth century necessarily combined with a primary structure of steel or concrete – has now acquired its own insulating and load-bearing capacities. Its transparency can now be modulated by electronic devices to the point of opacity. [4] Concrete is being reconceived by the science of nanotechnology to resist bending – and therefore to be able to have the thinness of steel; it can also be poured in the most complex forms and even made translucent. [5] Meanwhile, resins, carbon, and metals like titanium have found ever more constructional possibilities. At the other extreme, plaster, raw clay – long considered a primitive material – and stone, which had become a mere veneer, are being given advanced uses. [6]

The digital revolution has made it possible to transcend the mass production logic inherited from Fordism, making it possible to adjust procedures to local conditions and users' requirements, leading to serial but "non-standard" projects. [7] Most importantly, new mathematical concepts have made it possible to calculate innovative forms, and complex shapes previously impossible to model have become constructible. Difficult questions in fields as challenging as concert acoustics seem at last to be finding scientific solutions. A new relationship is being defined between design and construction, with architects participating in research on new materials and how to put them to use. With the opportunity to control the fabrication of building elements, architects are regaining – at least partially – the authority of medieval master builders. [8] Yet their competence does have limits, and their collaboration with engineers is necessarily a dialogue of equals. Among many others, Cecil Balmond, Marc Mimram, or Guy Nordenson have made fundamental contributions to the conception of buildings, going far beyond technical calculations. [9]

Sustainable buildings

The growing attention to sustainable development addresses complex problems involving many elements of the design process, extending not just to construction but also to building management. Not only does the production of construction materials utilize a significant amount of energy; the operation of buildings is even more wasteful and needs to be rethought from scratch. The rediscovery of the value of the earth's natural resources – including straw, bamboo, and, of course, wood, which has been used in unusual ways by architects in regions such as the Vorarlberg in Austria – has contributed to global awareness of the importance of sustainability. But the demand for sustainability has not necessarily implied the rejection of industrial materials; the work of architects like Norman Foster in Frankfurt and elsewhere and certain projects by Glenn Murcutt, for example, have incorporated advanced technological components and elaborate climate-control devices. The Malaysian architect Ken Yeang has contributed to an environmental renovation of the design principles of the skyscraper, while Thomas Herzog and Werner Sobek have based their work on a comprehensive approach to energy conservation and even energy generation. [10] The demand for a sustainable architecture has also impelled a reconsideration of existing building types and their envelopes.

It has returned attention to fundamental building components related to the installation and orientation of buildings and their relationship to the natural resources of water, air, and light – matters that modern architects had addressed essentially from a hygienic rather than an ecological point of view. The object-like nature of buildings has been challenged by an approach more attentive to relationships among structures; for example, the need to produce shade in hot climates has encouraged a new look at certain historical urban forms.

The city reborn yet threatened

The trend toward disurbanization, which was a powerful force in certain contexts and periods during the twentieth century, has been called into question, and ideas of density recuperated. Just as new relationships have evolved between architectural objects and building technologies, relationships between the building and the city have also been updated through design practices that understand urban projects not simply as large-scale compositions but as the product of complex patterns of interaction among decision makers, designers, and citizens. Rem Koolhaas has dramatized the relationship between forms specifically invented by architects and those engendered by the "generic city" or the "junkspace" associated with the market. → [11] Christian de Portzamparc has detected an "age three" of the city that goes beyond the traditional city (age one) and the modern utopian city (age two), calling on urban designers to fulfill their "obligation to come together to invent new forms of the city, new groupings, assemblages, networks, and places." → [12] The examples in previous chapters have demonstrated that this type of speculation (despite its perennial claim to be radically new) has

actually been a recurrent force for change. This was notably so in the context of the urban-extension projects of the 1930s as well as in certain postwar reconstruction programs. The "third strategy" promoted by Portzamparc – undoubtedly the most efficient didactically – has its limits. Indeed, concepts that emerged during the age of modern social reform, which might be defined as "age one and a half," are probably not exhausted and can still deliver useful models for the large city. Promoted by democratic movements, the civic strategy of the urban project remains one of the most pertinent answers to the "obligation to invent" confronting contemporary architecture. → [13] The urban policies implemented in Barcelona, Berlin, and Genoa since the 1980s have engendered architectures attuned to these cities' social and spatial contexts, opposing attempts to reduce the discipline to the production of "bachelor machines" indifferent to their setting (to use a term Marcel Duchamp coined in 1913). Such an urban sensibility, while initially focused on public space, can also be applied to infrastructures and, most importantly, be made adaptable to rules governing the coexistence of buildings, even when these hold the individual architect's ego in abeyance.

One problem inherited from twentieth-century forms of urbanization still remains difficult to solve: that of the new peripheries, the areas no longer suburban but exurban, produced by sprawl. The new French housing estates, the Dutch VINEX developments (an acronym for Vierde Nota Ruimtelijke Ordening Extra, or Supplement to the Fourth Report on Development) of 1993, → [14] and the North American exurbs necessitate expanded highway networks and services, while the spread of gated communities and fortified developments has shattered the relationship between housing complexes and collective urban spaces. → [15]

Landscape as horizon

The search for a new urbanity and the aspiration to greater site-specificity have necessarily implicated architecture's relationship to the landscape. For a long time landscape designers were reduced to the marginal role of architects' collaborators – despite their significant contribution to the evolution of the great modern cities. Yet since the 1970s European and North American landscape designers have developed approaches to urban sites and the natural environment that revive the holistic methods of Frederick Law Olmsted, Jean Claude Nicolas Forestier, and Leberecht Migge. [16] Whether designed in close contact with architects or autonomously, the recent landscape projects involve a more modest definition of architectural intervention. [17] In the Ruhr Valley in Germany, Peter Latz has transformed industrial ruins into recreational landscapes that express the region's industrial identity. [18] In the United States, Peter Walker's work has evolved from simply accompanying architecture to engaging in a conversation about urban grids, architectural axes, and topographic features. In the Netherlands, Adriaan Geuze's West 8 firm has come up with imaginative responses to urban sites involving water. In France, research by landscape designers has come to be a genuinely collective discourse contributing to architectural reflection. Michel Corajoud's projects for urban parks, Alexandre Chemetoff's city plans based on in-depth studies of specific local conditions, Michel Desvigne's ingenious compositions, and Gilles Clément's botanical meditations have outlined a new field of thought and practice in which landscape designers play an expanded role. [19]

Through their detailed attention to sites – both their historical background and ecological systems – landscape designers are suggesting modes of urban development and renewal that avoid the narcissism of overpowering edifices, and they are establishing rules ensuring that buildings are properly integrated into their surroundings. They are making fundamental contributions by striking a delicate balance between development and preservation and by reformulating local specificities related not just to the built heritage but also to the very structure of natural and artificial landscapes. The application of landscape precepts to urban and regional infrastructures, including highway, air, and rail networks, is a particularly fruitful avenue of development. [20]

Hypermodern media

Until the 1980s, twentieth-century architecture was marked by the publication of theoretical and critical books, by the life cycles of journals, and by the opportunities for social exchange provided by conferences and professional associations. Along with political criticism and discussions of colonialism and postcolonialism, the study of race and gender, which emerged initially on North American campuses and then everywhere else, reshaped the accepted discourse of architecture. More recently, with the explosion of an image-hungry culture that favors instant availability on the Internet, journals have been dealt a hard, sometimes fatal blow. Books seem to be surviving, but often reduced to volumes of glossy images or catalogs. This state of affairs raises the question of what will become of architectural criticism. Traditionally a generally friendly if sometimes irritating force, professional journals and illustrated newspapers, ever since their establishment at the end of the nineteenth century, have been responsible for judging, praising, and contesting the work of architects.

Is criticism fated to be replaced by a form of communication controlled by architects themselves, paralleling the transformations that have taken place in the political sphere in an era of the spectacle? What will become of architectural history in this context?

Along with the wider audience taking interest in architecture since the 1990s, a new populism seems to be manifesting itself in a spectacular architecture whose models can be traced to the mass media. The proliferation of museums and athletic, cultural, and bureaucratic monuments has made architecture's ultimate goal the creation of big objects. Architecture commissioned by the world's leading powers now suffers from what Deyan Sudjic has brilliantly dubbed the "edifice complex." → 21 The architect has concurrently emerged as an *auteur*, a figure whose identity lies somewhere between the glamorous movie star and the anonymous technician.

The forms of interaction between architects have also changed. International organizations, which in the post-World War II period became gatherings of adherents who held like positions and were controlled by architect-bureaucrats, are now little more than tourist clubs, while most academies tend to be dens of self-congratulation. In many ways, the cycle of ten ANY (Architecture New York) conferences held from 1991 to 2000, each in a different city, was a terminal moment for the generation that was responsible for renewing architectural discourse after 1970. That discourse was characterized by real exchanges among designers, critics, intellectuals, and artists. → 22 Today the model for architectural debate appears to be closer to that of the art world, which moves from biennial to triennial according to a principle that has its precedents in the exhibitions of the early twentieth-century avant-gardes.

Persistent social expectations

A final, and disturbing, consideration is that of the relatively marginal status of research programs and experimental projects devoted to housing for the vast majority of the population. The Europan, a housing design competition for young architects founded in 1988 that has allowed emerging professionals both geographic mobility and access to commissions, remains a fruitful exception. → 23 The commitment of architects like Shigeru Ban, **591** Rural Studio, and Patrick Bouchain as well as a number of less conspicuous designers also remains exceptional. Otherwise there has been meager response to the needs of the poorer segments of society. The commitment to society that characterized architectural practice in the first part of the twentieth century, when the profession rose to meet the challenges of modern urbanization and played a leading role in movements for social reform, have largely been abandoned. Over the years the percentage of architect-designed buildings has diminished, with massive urban developments subject to little or no regulation. Facing a housing crisis as vast as the ever-growing cities of the third millennium, professionals no longer seem able to offer solutions to the problem of affordable housing, which rampant urbanization is making ever more urgent. → 24 Since the market rarely solicits these solutions, the limited number of buildings designed by architects tend generally to be spectacular high-budget productions rather than answers to the needs of the majority of people. What still deserves to be called "architecture" would seem to amount to little more than a handful of diamonds amid the rubble of the planet. From this perspective, the socially engaged experiences of the twentieth century may prove to have been just a brief interlude in history's ongoing drama.

Notes

Sources are usually cited in both the original language of publication and in English translation, where existing. Where noted, translations have been modified for accuracy or clarity. Quotations from untranslated sources have been rendered in English by the author.

Introduction

1 → Nikolaus Pevsner, *An Outline of European Architecture* (Harmondsworth, UK: Penguin Books, 1963), 15.

2 → I am alluding here to Rosalind Krauss's seminal essay "Sculpture in the Expanded Field," *October* 8 (Spring 1979): 30–44.

3 → Adrian Forty, "Of Cars, Clothes and Carpets: Design Metaphors in Architectural Thought," *Journal of Design History* 2, no. 1 (1989): 1–14.

4 → Eric Hobsbawm, *The Age of Extremes: A History of the World, 1914–1991* (New York: Pantheon Books, 1994).

5 → Fernand Braudel, "Preface," in *La Méditerranée et le monde méditerranéen à l'époque de Philippe II* (Paris: Armand Colin, 1949), 14; English: *The Mediterranean and the Mediterranean World in the Age of Philip II*, trans. Siân Reynolds (New York: Harper & Row, 1972), 21.

6 → Nikolaus Pevsner, *Pioneers of the Modern Movement from William Morris to Walter Gropius* (London: Faber & Faber, 1936).

7 → Henry-Russell Hitchcock and Philip Johnson, *The International Style: Architecture since 1922* (New York: W. W. Norton, 1932).

8 → See Eric Hobsbawm and Terence Ranger, eds., *The Invention of Tradition* (Cambridge: Cambridge University Press, 1983).

9 → I use here the term "hegemony" according to the meaning given by Antonio Gramsci, i.e., as a system of attitudes, beliefs, and values allowing domination: Antonio Gramsci, *Prison Notebooks*, vols. I and II., ed. and trans. Joseph A. Buttigieg (New York: Columbia University Press, 1992–96); see also Chantal Mouffe, "Hegemony and Ideology in Gramsci," *Research in Political Economy* 2 (1979), 1–31.

10 → Henry Luce, "The American Century," *Life Magazine*, February 7, 1941.

11 → See Jean-Louis Cohen, *Scenes of the World to Come: European Architecture and the American Challenge, 1893–1960* (Paris: Flammarion; Montreal: Canadian Centre for Architecture, 1995).

12 → See Jean-Louis Cohen, "Le culture della modernizzazione: il balletto delle egemonie," in Maria Luisa Scalvini and Fabio Mangone, eds., *Immagini e temi*, thematic volume of *Dizionario dell'architettura del XX secolo* (Rome: Istituto della Enciclopedia italiana, 2004), 21–31.

13 → See Anthony D. King, *Colonial Urban Development: Culture, Social Power, and Environment* (London: Routledge & Paul, 1976); and Mercedes Volait and Joe Nasr, eds., *Urbanism: Imported or Exported?* (West Sussex, UK: Wiley-Academy, 2003).

14 → Pierre Bourdieu, *Le sens pratique* (Paris: Éditions de Minuit, 1980); English: *The Logic of Practice*, trans. Richard Nice (Cambridge, UK: Polity, 1990).

15 → Hans Robert Jauss, *Toward an Aesthetic of Reception*, trans. Timothy Bahti (Minneapolis: University of Minnesota Press, 1982). In the architectural field, see Jean-Yves Andrieux and Fabienne Chevalier, eds., *La réception de l'architecture du mouvement moderne: image, usage, héritage* (Saint-Étienne: Publications de l'Université de Saint-Étienne), 2002.

16 → Bruno Fortier, *L'amour des villes* (Liège: Mardaga; Paris: Institut français d'architecture, 1994).

17 → See Maria-Luisa Scalvini and Maria-Luisa Sandri, *L'immagine storiografica dell'architettura moderna da Platz a Giedion* (Rome: Officina edizioni, 1984); Panayotis Tournikiotis, *The Historiography of Modern Architecture* (Cambridge, Mass.: MIT Press, 1999); and Anthony Vidler, *Histories of the Immediate Present: Inventing Architectural Modernism* (Cambridge, Mass.: MIT Press, 2008).

18 → Sigfried Giedion, "Nationalitätskonstante," in *Bauen in Frankreich, Bauen in Eisen, Bauen in Eisenbeton* (Leipzig: Klinkhardt & Biermann, 1928), 68; English: *Building in France, Building in Iron, Building in Ferroconcrete*, trans. J. Duncan Berry (Santa Monica: Getty Center for the History of Art and the Humanities, 1995), 152.

19 → Sigfried Giedion, *Space, Time and Architecture: The Growth of a New Tradition* (Cambridge, Mass.: Harvard University Press, 1941), 18; Henry-Russell Hitchcock, *Modern Architecture: Romanticism and Reintegration* (New York: Payson and Clarke, 1929), 77–149.

20 → Bruno Zevi, *Storia dell'architettura moderna* (Turin: Einaudi, 1951).

21 → Henry-Russell Hitchcock, *Architecture: Nineteenth and Twentieth Centuries* (Harmondsworth, UK: Penguin Books, 1958).

22 → Leonardo Benevolo, *Storia dell'architettura moderna* (Bari, Italy: Laterza, 1960); English: *History of Modern Architecture*, trans. H. J. Landry (Cambridge, Mass.: MIT Press, 1966).

23 → Kenneth Frampton, *Modern Architecture: A Critical History* (London: Thames & Hudson, 1980).

24 → William J. R. Curtis, *Modern Architecture since 1900* (London: Phaidon, 1982).

25 → Alan Colquhoun, *Modern Architecture* (Oxford: Oxford University Press, 2002).

26 → Reyner Banham, *Theory and Design in the First Machine Age* (London: Architectural Press, 1960).

27 → Manfredo Tafuri and Francesco Dal Co, *Storia dell'architettura contemporanea* (Milan: Electa, 1976). English [with a somewhat misleading title] *Modern Architecture*, trans. Robert Erich Wolf (New York: Rizzoli, 1986).

28 → Adrian Forty, *Words and Buildings: A Vocabulary of Modern Architecture* (London: Thames & Hudson, 2000); Anthony Vidler, *Histories of the Immediate Present: Inventing Architectural Modernism* (Cambridge, Mass.: MIT Press, 2008).

29 → Cf. Peter Blake, *The Master Builders* (New York: Knopf, 1960).

30 → Bruno Latour, *Nous n'avons jamais été modernes. Essai d'anthropologie symétrique* (Paris: La Découverte, 1991); English: *We Have Never Been Modern*, trans. Catherine Porter (Cambridge, Mass.: Harvard University Press, 1993).

01 Sheds to rails: the dominion of steel

1 → Lewis Mumford, *Technics and Civilization* (New York: Harcourt, 1934).

2 → Nikolaus Pevsner, *High Victorian Design: A Study of the Exhibits of 1851* (London: Architectural Press, 1951).

3 → Gottfried Semper, *Der Stil in den technischen und tektonischen Künsten, oder praktische Aesthetik, Ein Handbuch für Techniker, Künstler und Kunstfreunde* (Frankfurt: Verlag für Kunst und Wissenschaft, 1860–63), 11; English: *Style in the Technical and Tectonic Arts, or, Practical Aesthetics*, trans. Harry Mallgrave (Los Angeles: Getty Research Institute, 2004).

4 → Gottfried Semper, *Über Baustyle: Ein Vortrag gehalten auf dem Rathaus in Zürich am 4. März 1869* (Zurich: Friedrich Schulthess, 1869); English in *Gottfried Semper: The Four Elements of Architecture and Other Writings*, ed. and trans. Harry Francis Mallgrave and Wolfgang Herrmann (Cambridge: Cambridge University Press, 1988), 269.

5 → Eugène Emmanuel Viollet-le-Duc, *Entretiens sur l'architecture* (Paris: Vve A. Morel, 1863–73), Lecture 6, 191; English: *Discourses on Architecture*, trans. Henry Van Brunt (Boston: J. R. Osgood and Company, 1875), 189. Translation slightly modified.

6 → Eugène Hénard, *Exposition universelle de 1889. Le Palais des Machines (architecte M. F. Dutert). Notice sur l'édifice et sur la marche des travaux* (Paris: Librairies-Imprimeries réunies, 1891).

7 → John Ruskin, "The Lamp of Truth" [1849] in *The Seven Lamps of Architecture* (London: George Allen, 1880), 35.

8 → Karl Bötticher, *Die Tektonik der Hellenen* (Potsdam: Riegel, 1852). See also Werner Oechslin, *Stilhülse und Kern: Otto Wagner, Adolf Loos und der evolutionäre Weg zur Modernen Architektur* (Zurich: gta Verlag; Berlin: Ernst & Sohn, 1994).

9 → Walter Benjamin, *The Arcades Project*, trans. Howard Eiland and Kevin McLaughlin (Cambridge, Mass.: Belknap Press of Harvard University Press, 1999), 858.

10 → Arthur Drexler, ed., *The Architecture of the École des Beaux-Arts* (New York: Museum of Modern Art, 1977); Jean-Pierre Epron, *Comprendre l'éclectisme* (Paris: Norma, 1997).

11 → Ernest Flagg, "The École des Beaux-Arts," *Architectural Record* 3, no. 3 (January–April 1894): 302–13; no. 4 (April–June 1894): 419–28.

12 → Frantz Jourdain, "La décoration et le rationalisme architecturaux à l'Exposition Universelle," *Revue des arts décoratifs* 10 (1889): 37.

13 → Nikolai Gogol, "Ob arkhitekture nyneshnego vremeni" (1831). Cited in Anne Nesbet, " 'The Building to Be Built': Gogol, Belyi, Eisenstein, and the Architecture of the Future," *Russian Review* 65 (July 2006): 499.

14 → Joris-Karl Huysmans, "Le salon officiel de 1881," in *L'art moderne* (Paris: Plon, 1883), 220.

15 → Henry James, "New York Revisited," *Harper's Magazine* 12 (February 1906): 401–2.

16 → Pieter van Wesemael, *Architecture of Instruction and Delight: A Socio-Historical Analysis of World Exhibitions as a Didactic Phenomenon (1798–1851–1970)* (Rotterdam: 010 Publishers, 2001).

17 → Émile François Zola and Massin, eds., *Zola Photographer*, trans. Liliane Emery Tuck (New York: Seaver Books / Henry Holt, 1988); Melanie Birke, ed., *Frank Lloyd Wright's Fifty Views of Japan: The 1905 Photo Album* (New York: Pomegranate Books, 1996).

18 → Juliet Wilson-Bareau, *Manet, Monet, and the Gare Saint-Lazare* (New Haven: Yale University Press, 1998).

19 → Charles Garnier and Auguste Ammann, *L'habitation humaine* (Paris: Hachette, 1892).

20 → Otto Wagner, "Preface," *Moderne Architektur. Seinen Schülern ein Führer auf diesem Kunstgebiete*

(Vienna: Anton Schroll, 1898), 2–3; English: *Modern Architecture*, trans. Harry Francis Mallgrave (Santa Monica: Getty Center for the History of Art and the Humanities; Chicago: University of Chicago Press, 1988), 60.

02 The search for modern form

1 → Friedrich Nietzsche, *Thus Spoke Zarathustra*, trans. Walter Kaufmannn (New York: Penguin Books, 1978), 23. See also Alexandre Kostka and Irving Wohlfarth, eds., *Nietzsche and "An Architecture of our Minds"* (Los Angeles: Getty Research Institute for the History of Art and the Humanities, 1999).

2 → Harald Szeemann, ed., *Der Hang zum Gesamtkunstwerk: Europäische Utopien seit 1800* (Aarau, Switzerland: Sauerländer, 1983).

3 → *L'art moderne. Revue critique des arts et de la littérature* (Brussels) 1 (1881).

4 → Jean Jaurès, "Pâques rouges," [2 April 1899], in Jean Delhaye, *La Maison du Peuple de Victor Horta* (Brussels: Atelier Vokaer, 1987), 9.

5 → Henry van de Velde, *Les formules de la beauté architectonique moderne* (Brussels: L'Équerre, 1923), 7.

6 → Henry van de Velde, "Das neue Ornament," in *Die Renaissance im modernen Kunstgewerbe* (Berlin: Bruno & Paul Cassirer, 1901), 103.

7 → Van de Velde, *Formules*, 82.

8 → August Endell, "Möglichkeit und Ziele einer neuen Architektur," *Deutsche Kunst und Dekoration* 1 (1897–98): 144. English in Otto Wagner, *Modern Architecture*, trans. Harry Francis Mallgrave (Santa Monica: Getty Center for the History of Art and the Humanities; Chicago: University of Chicago Press, 1988), 44.

9 → William A. Lethaby, *Architecture, Mysticism and Myth* (London: Percival, 1892), 1.

10 → Anon., "Thoughts for the Strong," *Architectural Review* 17 (July 1905): 27. Cited in Reyner Banham, *Theory and Design in the First Machine Age* (London: Architectural Press, 1960), 46–47.

11 → David Gebhard, *Charles F. A. Voysey Architect* (Los Angeles: Hennessey & Ingalls, 1975), 15.

12 → Charles Robert Ashbee, *Should We Stop Teaching Art?* (London: B. T. Batsford, 1911), 7.

13 → William Buchanan, ed., *Mackintosh's Masterwork: The Glasgow School of Art* (Glasgow: Richard Drew, 1989).

14 → Salvador Dalí, "The Cylindrical Monarchy of Guimard" (1929), trans. Albert Field, in *Arts Magazine* 44 (March 1970): 42.

15 → René Binet to Ernst Haeckel, 21 March 1899, Haeckel Correspondence, Haeckel-Haus, Jena, Germany. See Robert Proctor, "Architecture from the Cell-Soul: René Binet and Ernst Haeckel," *Journal of Architecture* 11 (2006): 407–24.

16 → Frantz Jourdain, "La villa Majorelle à Nancy," *L'art décoratif* 5 (August 1902): 204–5.

17 → Paul Souriau, *La beauté rationnelle* (Paris: Félix Alcan, 1904).

18 → Marcello Piacentini, "L'opera di Raimondo d'Aronco," *Emporium* 36, no. 220 (1913): 244.

19 → Ugo Monneret de Villard, *L'architettura di Giuseppe Sommaruga* (1908), cited in Carol L. V. Meeks, *Italian Architecture, 1750–1914* (New Haven: Yale University Press, 1966), 428.

20 → William Craft Brumfield, *The Origins of Modernism in Russian Architecture* (Berkeley: University of California Press, 1991).

21 → Juan José Lahuerta, *Universo Gaudí* (Barcelona: Centre de Cultura Contemporània de Barcelona; Madrid: Museo Nacional Centro de Arte Reina Sofía, 2002).

03 Domestic innovation and tectonic expression

1 → Paul Sédille, *L'architecture moderne en Angleterre* (Paris: Librairie des bibliophiles, 1890).

2 → Monique Eleb with Anne Debarre, *L'invention de l'habitation moderne, Paris, 1880–1914* (Paris: Hazan, 1995).

3 → Hermann Muthesius, *Das englische Haus, Entwicklung, Bedingungen, Anlage, Aufbau, Einrichtung und Innenraum*, 3 vols. (Berlin: Wasmuth, 1908–11).

4 → Adolf Loos, *Das Andere: Ein Blatt zur Einführung abendländischer Kultur in Österreich*, vols. 1–2 (1903). See Massimo Cacciari, *Adolf Loos e il suo Angelo. "Das Andere" e altri scritti* (Milan: Electa, 2002).

5 → F. Rudolf Vogel, *Das amerikanische Haus, Entwicklung, Bedingung, Anlage, Aufbau, Einrichtung, Innenraum und Umgebung* (Berlin: Wasmuth, 1910).

6 → Eleb and Debarre, *L'invention de l'habitation*, 215–49.

7 → Randolph W. Sexton, *American Apartment Houses, Hotels and Apartment Hotels of Today; Exterior and Interior Photographs and Plans* (New York: Architectural Book Publishing, 1929).

8 → Günther Uhlig, *Kollektivmodell "Einküchenhaus": Wohnreform und Architekturdebatte zwischen Frauenbewegung und Funktionalismus 1900–1933* (Giessen, Germany: Anabas-Verlag, 1981).

9 → Louis Bonnier, *Les règlements de voirie* (Paris: C. Schmid, 1903); Walter-Curt Behrendt, *Die einheitliche Blockfront als Raumelement im Stadtbau: Ein Beitrag z. Stadtbaukunst d. Gegenwart* (Berlin: B. Cassirer, 1911).

10 → Richard Plunz, *A History of Housing in New York City: Dwelling Types and Social Change in the American Metropolis* (New York: Columbia University Press, 1990).

11 → Marie-Jeanne Dumont, *Le logement social à Paris 1850–1930: Les habitations à bon marché* (Liège: Mardaga, 1991).

12 → Peter Behrens, "Kunst und Technik," *Elektrotechnische Zeitschrift* 31 (2 June 1910): 552–55; address given at the Verband der deutschen Elektrotechniker in Braunschweig on 26 May 1910; English: "On Art and Technology," in Tilmann Buddensieg, ed., *Industriekultur: Peter Behrens and the AEG, 1907–1914* (Cambridge, Mass.: MIT Press, 1984), 218.

13 → Sigfried Giedion, "Nationalitätskonstante," in *Bauen in Frankreich, Bauen in Eisen, Bauen in Eisenbeton* (Leipzig: Klinkhardt & Biermann, 1928); English: *Building in France, Building in Iron, Building in Ferroconcrete*, trans. J. Duncan Berry (Santa Monica: Getty Center for the History of Art and the Humanities, 1995).

14 → Cyrille Simonnet, *Le béton, histoire d'un matériau* (Marseilles: Parenthèses, 2005).

15 → Gwénaël Delhumeau, *L'invention du béton armé: Hennebique, 1890–1914* (Paris: Norma, 1999).

16 → Anatole de Baudot, *L'architecture, le passé, le présent* (Paris: Librairie Renouard, 1916), 171. See also Marie-Jeanne Dumont, ed., *Anatole de Baudot, Rassegna 68* (Bologna: Editrice Compositori, 1996).

17 → Peter Collins, *Concrete, the Vision of a New Architecture: A Study of Auguste Perret and His Precursors* (New York: Horizon Press, 1959).

18 → Arthur C. David, "Innovations in the Street Architecture of Paris," *Architectural Record* 24 (August 1908): 125.

19 → Christian Freigang, *Auguste Perret, die Architekturdebatte und die "Konservative Revolution" in Frankreich 1900–1930* (Munich: Deutscher Kunstverlag, 2003).

20 → Jean-Michel Nectoux, ed., *1913: Le théâtre des Champs-Élysées* (Paris: Musée d'Orsay, 1987).

21 → Amy E. Slaton, *Reinforced Concrete and the Modernization of American Building, 1900–1930* (Baltimore: Johns Hopkins University Press, 2001).

22 → Robert Maillart, "Aktuelle Fragen des Eisenbetonbaues," *Schweizerische Bauzeitung* 111 (1 January 1938): 1; English: "Design in Reinforced Concrete," in Max Bill, *Robert Maillart* (Zurich: Verlag für Architektur, 1949), 17. Translation modified.

23 → José Antonio Fernández Ordóñez, *Eugène Freyssinet* (Barcelona: 2c Editions, 1979).

24 → Mart Kalm, *Eesti 20. Sajandi arhitektuur* (Tallinn: Sild, 2002), 17.

25 → François Hennebique, address at the Third Congress of Reinforced Concrete, 24 January 1899, in *Le béton armé* 2, no. 11 (1899): 4.

26 → Jeanneret's domino metaphor may have been inspired by his 1915 reading of Eugène Hénard's *Études sur les transformations de Paris*, vol. 2, *Les alignements brisés, la question des fortifications et le boulevard de grande-ceinture* (Paris: Librairies-imprimeries réunies, 1903), 39.

27 → Gottfried Semper, ms. 181, fol. 47, Semper Archive, Eidgenössische Polytechnische Hochschule, Zurich; English: Wolfgang Herrmann, *Gottfried Semper, In Search of Architecture* (Cambridge, Mass: MIT Press, 1984), 151.

04 America rediscovered, tall and wide

1 → Alexis de Tocqueville, *De la démocratie en Amérique, 1835–40* (Paris: Garnier-Flammarion, 1981), 2: 304; English: *Democracy in America*, trans. Henry Reeve (Cambridge, Mass.: Sever and Francis, 1863), 303.

2 → David E. Nye, *American Technological Sublime* (Cambridge, Mass.: MIT Press, 1994).

3 → See Sigfried Giedion, *Mechanization Takes Command: A Contribution to Anonymous History* (New York: Oxford University Press, 1948), 209–46.

4 → Paul Bourget, *Outremer, notes sur l'Amérique* (Paris: Plon, 1894), 1: 160; English: *Outre-Mer: Impressions of America* (New York: Charles Scribner's Sons, 1896), 117.

5 → A., "L'organisation des bureaux d'architectes aux Etats-Unis," *La semaine des constructeurs*, 2nd ser., 4 (8 and 15 March 1890): 436–38, 453; plan, 437.

6 → Daniel Bluestone, *Constructing Chicago* (New Haven: Yale University Press, 1991), 104–51.

7 → Louis Sullivan, "Ornament in Architecture," *Engineering Magazine* 3 (August 1892): 634; cited in Robert Twombly, ed., *Louis Sullivan: The Public Papers* (Chicago: University of Chicago Press, 1988), 80.

8 → Louis Sullivan, *A System of Architectural Ornaments According with a Philosophy of Man's Power* (New York: Eakins Press, 1967); written in 1922.

9 → Louis Sullivan, "The Tall Office Building Artistically Considered," *Lippincott's Magazine* 57 (March 1896): 408; 406.

10 → David van Zanten, "Sullivan to 1890," in Wim de Wit, ed., *Louis Sullivan: The Function of Ornament* (Chicago: Chicago Historical Society, 1986), 12–63.

11 → Kevin Nute, *Frank Lloyd Wright and Japan: The Role of Traditional Japanese Art and Architecture in the Work of Frank Lloyd Wright* (New York: Van Nostrand Reinhold, 1993).

12 → Frank Lloyd Wright, *The Future of Architecture* (New York: Horizon Press, 1953), 188.

13 → Gwendolyn Wright, *Moralism and the Model Home: Domestic Architecture and Cultural Conflict in Chicago, 1873–1913* (Chicago: University of Chicago Press, 1980).

14 → Robert C. Spencer, Jr., "The Work of Frank Lloyd Wright," *Architectural Review* 7 (June 1900): 72; 62.

15 → William C. Gannett, *The House Beautiful* (River Forest: Auvergne Press, 1897), n.p.

16 → Frank Lloyd Wright, "In the Cause of Architecture," *Architectural Record* 23 (March 1908): 3.

17 → Jean Castex, *Le printemps de la Prairie House* (Liège: Pierre Mardaga, 1987).

18 → Reyner Banham, *The Architecture of the Well-Tempered Environment* (London: Architectural Press, 1969), 115–21.

19 → Frank Lloyd Wright, *An Autobiography* (New York: Duell, Sloan and Pearce, 1943), 150.

20 → Neil Levine, *The Architecture of Frank Lloyd Wright* (Princeton: Princeton University Press, 1996), 40–46; Joseph Siry, *Unity Temple: Frank Lloyd Wright and Architecture for Liberal Religion* (Cambridge: Cambridge University Press, 1996).

21 → Anthony Alofsin, *Frank Lloyd Wright, the Lost Years, 1910–1922: A Study of Influence* (Chicago: University of Chicago Press, 1993).

22 → Frank Lloyd Wright, *Ausgeführte Bauten und Entwürfe von Frank Lloyd Wright* (Berlin: Wasmuth, 1910; reprint, New York: Horizon Press, 1968). Frank Lloyd Wright, *Frank Lloyd Wright, Chicago, Sonderheft der Architektur des XX. Jahrhunderts* 8 (Berlin: Wasmuth, 1911); English: *The Early Work of Frank Lloyd Wright: The "Ausgeführte Bauten" of 1911*, intro. by Grant Carpenter Manson (New York: Dover, 1982).

23 → See Leonard Eaton, *American Architecture Comes of Age: European Reaction to H. H. Richardson and Louis Sullivan* (Cambridge, Mass: MIT Press, 1972). For Berlage's accounts, see Hendrik Petrus Berlage, "Neuere amerikanische Architektur," *Schweizerische Bauzeitung* 60 (September 14 and 21, 1912): 148–50; 165–67; and Hendrik Petrus Berlage, *Amerikaansche Reisherinneringen* (Rotterdam: W. L. & J. Brusse, 1913).

24 → Sarah Bradford Landau and Carl W. Condit, *Rise of the New York Skyscraper, 1865–1913* (New Haven: Yale University Press, 1996).

25 → Alfred Stieglitz quoted in Dorothy Norman, *Alfred Stieglitz, an American Seer* (New York: Random House, 1973), 45. For a new aesthetic, see also Sidney Allan, "The 'Flat-Iron' Building –An Esthetical Dissertation," *Camera Work* 1 (October 1903): 36–40.

26 → Carol Willis, *Form Follows Finance* (New York: Princeton Architectural Press, 1995).

27 → Louis-Ferdinand Céline, *Voyage au bout de la nuit* (Paris: Denoël, 1932), 185; English: *Journey to the End of the Night*, trans. Ralph Manheim (New York: New Directions Books, 2006), 159.

05 The challenge of the metropolis

1 → Friedrich Nietzsche, *Thus Spoke Zarathustra*, trans. Walter Kaufmann (New York: Penguin Books, 1978), 177.

2 → August Endell, *Die Schönheit der grossen Stadt* (Stuttgart: Strecker & Schröder, 1908), 23.

3 → Anthony Sutcliffe, ed., *Metropolis 1890–1940* (London: Mansell, 1984).

4 → Thierry Paquot and Marcel Roncayolo, eds., *Villes et civilisation urbaine, XVIIIe–XXe siècle* (Paris: Larousse, 1992).

5 → See Hans Christian Nussbaum, *Die Hygiene des Städtebaus* (Leipzig: G. J. Göschen, 1907).

6 → François Loyer and Hélène Guéné, *Henri Sauvage: Set-Back Buildings*, trans. Charlotte Ellis (Liège: Pierre Mardaga, 1987).

7 → Anthony Sutcliffe, *Towards the Planned City: Germany, Britain, the United States and France, 1780–1914* (Oxford: Basil Blackwell, 1981).

8 → Franco Mancuso, *Le vicende dello zoning* (Milan: Il Saggiatore, 1978).

9 → Werner Hegemann, *Der Städtebau nach den Ergebnissen der allgemeinen Städtebau-Ausstellung in Berlin, nebst einem Anhang: Die Internationale Städtebau-Ausstellung in Düsseldorf* (Berlin: Wasmuth, 1911 and 1913).

10 → Josef Stübben, *Der Städtebau* (Darmstadt: A. Bergsträsser, 1890); Raymond Unwin, *Town Planning in Practice: An Introduction to the Art of Designing Cities and Suburbs* (London: Allen & Unwin, 1909; reprint, New York: Princeton Architectural Press, 1994).

11 → Camillo Sitte, *Der Städtebau nach seinen künstlerischen Grundsätzen* (Vienna: Graeser, 1889); English: *The Art of Building Cities; City Building according to its Artistic Fundamentals*, trans. Charles T. Stewart (New York: Reinhold, 1945). See also Christiane Crasemann Collins and George Collins, *Camillo Sitte: The Birth of Modern City Planning* (New York: Rizzoli, 1986).

12 → Albert Erich Brinckmann, *Platz und Monument: Untersuchungen zur Geschichte und Ästhetik der Stadtbaukunst in neuerer Zeit* (Berlin: Wasmuth, 1908).

13 → William H. Wilson, *The City Beautiful Movement* (Baltimore: Johns Hopkins University Press, 1989).

14 → [Daniel H. Burnham and Edward H. Bennett], *Plan of Chicago Prepared under the Direction of the Commercial Club during the Years 1906, 1907 and 1908* (Chicago: The Commercial Club, 1909; reprint, New York: Princeton Architectural Press, 1993).

15 → See Giuliano Gresleri and Dario Matteoni, eds., *La città mondiale: Andersen, Hébrard, Otlet, Le*

Corbusier (Venice: Marsilio, 1982). See also Wolfgang Sonne, *Representing the State: Capital City Planning in the Early Twentieth Century* (Munich: Prestel, 2003).

16 → See *Transactions of the Town Planning Conference, London, 10–15 October 1910* (London: Royal Institute of British Architects, 1911); and Eugène Hénard, *Études sur les transformations de Paris* (Paris: Librairies-imprimeries réunies, 1903–1909; new edition with intro. by Jean-Louis Cohen, Paris: Éditions de la Villette, 2011).

17 → Otto Wagner, *Die Großstadt, eine Studie über diese* (Vienna: A. Schroll, 1911); English: "The Development of a Great City," *Oppositions* 17 (Summer 1979): 103–16.

18 → Émile Verhaeren, *Les villes tentaculaires* (Brussels: E. Deman, 1895).

19 → Georges R. Collins and Carlos Flores, *Arturo Soria y la Ciudad Lineal* (Madrid: Revista de Occidente, 1968); Arturo Soria y Mata, *La cité linéaire, nouvelle architecture de villes* [1926] (Paris: CERA/ENSBA, 1979).

20 → Morton White and Lucia White, *The Intellectual versus the City: From Thomas Jefferson to Frank Lloyd Wright* (Cambridge, Mass.: Harvard University Press, 1962).

21 → Ebenezer Howard, *Garden-Cities of To-morrow* (1898 [*To-morrow: A Peaceful Path to Real Reform*]; 2nd edition, London: S. Sonnenschein, 1902; reprint with intro. by Lewis Mumford, Cambridge, Mass.: MIT Press, 1965).

22 → Stephen V. Ward, *The Garden-City: Past, Present, and Future* (London and New York: E. & F. N. Spon, 1992).

23 → Ferdinand Tönnies, *Gemeinschaft und Gesellschaft. Abhandlung des Communismus und des Socialismus als empirischer Culturformen* (Leipzig: Reisland, 1887).

24 → Tony Garnier, *Une cité industrielle* (Paris: Vincent & Fréal, 1917; reprint; New York: Princeton Architectural Press, 1989).

25 → Commission d'extension de Paris (Louis Bonnier and Marcel Poëte), *Considérations techniques préliminaires* (Paris: Imprimerie Chaix, 1913).

26 → Patrick Geddes, *Cities in Evolution: An Introduction to the Town Planning Movement and to the Study of Civics* (London: Williams & Norgate, 1915).

27 → Robert Grant Irving, *Indian Summer: Lutyens, Baker, and Imperial Delhi* (New Haven: Yale University Press, 1981).

28 → Jean Dethier and Alain Guiheux, eds., *La ville, art et architecture en Europe, 1870–1993* (Paris: Éditions du Centre Georges Pompidou, 1994), 166–68.

29 → Karl Scheffler, *Die Architektur der Großstadt* (Berlin: B. Cassirer, 1913).

06 New production, new aesthetic

1 → Lewis Mumford, *Technics and Civilization* (New York: Harcourt, 1934).

2 → See Tilmann Buddensieg and Hennig Rogge, *Industriekultur: Peter Behrens und die AEG 1907–1914* (Berlin: Gebr. Mann Verlag, 1979); English: *Industriekultur: Peter Behrens and the AEG, 1907–1914*, trans. Iain Boyd White (Cambridge, Mass.: MIT Press, 1984).

3 → Walther Rathenau, "Die schönste Stadt der Welt," *Die Zukunft* 7 (1899): 39.

4 → See Jean-Louis Cohen, *"France ou Allemagne?" Un livre inécrit de Le Corbusier* (Paris: Éditions de la Maison des sciences de l'homme, 2009).

5 → See Fritz Hoeber, *Peter Behrens* (Munich: Georg Muller & Eugen Rentsch, 1913), 172; and Peter Behrens, *Zur Erinnerung an die Einweihung des Verwaltungsgebäudes des Mannesmannröhren-Werke in Düsseldorf, 10. Dezember 1912* (Düsseldorf: Mannesmann, 1913).

6 → Walter Gropius, "Die Entwicklung moderner Industriebaukunst," in *Die Kunst in Industrie und Handel. Jahrbuch des deutschen Werkbundes 1913* (Jena, Germany: Eugen Diederichs, 1913), 21–22; English: Charlotte Benton, Tim Benton, and Dennis Sharp, eds., *Architecture and Design, 1890–1939: An International Anthology of Original Articles* (New York: Whitney Library of Design, 1975), 54–55.

7 → Federico Bucci, *L'architetto di Ford, Albert Kahn, e il progetto della fabbrica moderna* (Milan: Città Studi, 1991); English: *Albert Kahn, Architect of Ford* (New York: Princeton Architectural Press, 1993).

8 → See Matthias Schirren, "Sachliche Monumentalität, Hans Poelzigs Werk in den Jahren 1900–1914," in Vittorio Magnago-Lampugnani and Romana Schneider, eds., *Moderne Architektur in Deutschland 1900–1950, Reform und Tradition* (Stuttgart: Gerd Hatje, 1992), 79–103.

9 → See Mark Jarzombek, "The *Kunstgewerbe*, the Werkbund, and the Aesthetics of Culture in the Wilhelmine Period," *Journal of the Society of Architectural Historians* 54 (March 1994): 7–19; and John V. Maciuika, *Before the Bauhaus: Architecture, Politics, and the German State, 1890–1920* (Cambridge: Cambridge University Press, 2005).

10 → Fritz Schumacher, "Rede zur Gründung des deutschen Werkbundes," in Kurt Junghanns, *Der Deutsche Werkbund: Sein erstes Jahrzehnt* (Berlin: Henschelverlag, 1982), 141.

11 → Friedrich Naumann, *Deutsche Gewerbekunst* (Berlin-Schöneberg: Buchverlag d. Hilfe, 1908), 39.

12 → Bruno Paul, "Passagierdampfer und ihre Einrichtungen," in *Der Verkehr, Jahrbuch des deutschen Werkbundes 1914* (Jena, Germany: Eugen Diederichs, 1914), 55–58. See John Malcolm Brinnin, "The Decoration of Ocean Liners: Rules and Exception," *Journal of Decorative and Propaganda Art* 15 (Winter–Spring 1990): 38–47.

13 → Joseph August Lux, *Ingenieur-ästhetik* (Munich: Verlag Gustav Lammers, 1910).

14 → See Jeffrey Herf, *Reactionary Modernism: Technology, Culture, and Politics in Weimar and the Third Reich* (Cambridge: Cambridge University Press, 1984).

15 → See Norbert Elias, *Über den Prozess der Zivilisation: Soziogenetische und psychogenetische Untersuchungen* (Basel: Haus zum Falken, 1939); English: *The History of Manners*, trans. Edmund Jephcott (New York: Pantheon Books, 1982).

16 → See Wulf Herzogenrath, Dirk Teuber, and Angelika Thiekötter, eds., *Die Deutsche Werkbund-Ausstellung Cöln 1914* (Cologne: Kölnischer Kunstverein, 1984).

17 → Hermann Muthesius quoted in Reyner Banham, *Theory and Design in the First Machine Age* (London: Architectural Press, 1960), 75–76.

18 → See Angelika Thiekötter, *Kristallisationen, Splitterungen. Bruno Tauts Glashaus* (Basel: Birkhäuser Verlag, 1993).

19 → See Leo Ikelaar, ed., *Paul Scheerbart und Bruno Taut: Zur Geschichte einer Bekanntschaft. Scheerbarts Briefe der Jahre 1913–1914 an Gottfried Heinersdorff, Bruno Taut und Herwarth Walden* (Paderborn: Igel-Verlag, 1996).

20 → Paul Scheerbart, *Das graue Tuch und zehn Prozent Weiß: Ein Damenroman* (Munich: Müller, 1914); English: *The Gray Cloth: Paul Scheerbart's Novel on Glass Architecture*, trans. with intro. by John A. Stuart (Cambridge, Mass.: MIT Press, 2001).

21 → Filippo Tommaso Marinetti, "Manifeste du Futurisme," *Le Figaro*, 20 February 1909; English: *Marinetti Selected Writings* (New York: Farrar, Straus and Giroux, 1971), 42.

22 → Umberto Boccioni, "Architettura futurista manifesto" (1914), Getty Research Institute, Boccioni papers. See Esther Da Costa Meyer, *The Work of Antonio Sant'Elia: Retreat into the Future* (New Haven: Yale University Press, 1995), 162–64.

23 → Antonio Sant'Elia, "L'architettura futurista, manifesto," 11 July 1914; English: Luciano Caramel and Alberto Longatti, *Antonio Sant'Elia: The Complete Works* (New York: Rizzoli, 1988), 302. Translation modified.

24 → Antonio Gramsci, *Note sul Machiavelli. Americanismo e fordismo* (Rome: Editori riuniti, 1975), 435–76; English: *Selections from the Prison Notebooks of Antonio Gramsci*, trans. and ed. Quintin Hoare and Geoffrey Nowell Smith (New York: International Publishers, 1971), 287.

07 In search of a language: from classicism to Cubism

1 → See Arthur Drexler, ed., *The Architecture of the École des Beaux-Arts* (London: Secker & Warburg, 1977); and Donald Drew Egbert, *The Beaux-Arts Tradition in French Architecture* (Princeton: Princeton University Press, 1980).

2 → Patrice L. R. Higonnet, *Paris: Capital of the World* (Cambridge, Mass.: Belknap Press of Harvard University Press, 2002).

3 → Julien-Azaïs Guadet, *Éléments et théorie de l'architecture* (Paris: Librairie de la construction moderne, 1901–1904); English: *Elements and Theory of Architecture* trans. N. Clifford Ricker (Urbana: University of Illinois Press, 1916).

4 → Edwin L. Lutyens to Herbert Baker, 1930; in A. S. G. [Arthur Stanley George] Butler, *The Architecture of Sir Edwin Lutyens* (London: Country Life, 1950), 135.

5 → Paul Mebes, *Um 1800, Architektur und Handwerk im letzten Jahrhundert ihrer traditionellen Entwicklung* (Munich: F. Bruckmann, 1908).

6 → Paul Schultze-Naumburg, *Kulturarbeiten* (Munich: G. D. W. Callwey, 1902–17).

7 → Heinrich Tessenow, *Hausbau und dergleichen* (Berlin: B. Cassirer, 1916).

8 → Adolf Loos, "Ornement et crime," *Les Cahiers d'aujourd'hui* 2 (June 1913): 247–56.

9 → Adolf Loos, "Das Prinzip der Bekleidung," *Neue freie Presse*, 4 September 1898; and "Damenmode," *Neue freie Presse*, 1 August 1898; English: "The Principle of Cladding" and "Ladies' Fashion," in Adolf Loos, *Spoken into the Void: Collected Essays 1897–1900*, trans. Jane O. Newman and John H. Smith (Cambridge, Mass.: MIT Press, 1982), 66–67 and 99–103. On this theme, see Mark Wigley, *White Walls, Designer Dresses: The Fashioning of Modern Architecture* (Cambridge, Mass.: MIT Press, 1995).

10 → Adolf Loos, "Architektur" (1910), in *Sämtliche Schriften* (Vienna: Herold, 1962), 315; English: Charlotte Benton, Tim Benton, and Dennis Sharp, eds., *Architecture and Design, 1890–1939: An International Anthology of Original Articles* (New York: Whitney Library of Design, 1975), 339.

11 → Adolf Loos, "Heimatkunst" (1914), in *Sämtliche Schriften*, 339; English: Benedetto Gravagnuolo, *Adolf Loos: Theory and Works* (New York: Rizzoli, 1982), 22.

12 → Arnold Schönberg, *Adolf Loos zum 60. Geburtstag am 10. Dezember 1930* (Vienna: Buchhandlung Richard Lanyi, 1930), 60; English: Gravagnuolo, *Adolf Loos*, 25.

13 → Hendrik Petrus Berlage, *Grundlagen und Entwicklung der Architektur: Vier Vorträge gehalten im Kunstgewerbemuseum zu Zürich* (Rotterdam: W. L. & J. Brusse; Berlin: Justus Bard, 1908); English: *Thoughts on Style 1886–1909*, trans. Iain Boyd Whyte and Wim de Wit (Santa Monica: Getty Center for the History of Art and the Humanities, 1996), 185.

14 → Berlage, *Thoughts on Style*, 185, 192.

15 → Berlage, *Thoughts on Style*, 249.

16 → Hendrik Petrus Berlage, "Beschouwingen over Stij," in *Studies over bouwkunst stil en samenleving* (Rotterdam: W. L. & J. Brusse, 1908), 60.

17 → Aldo Rossi, "Berlage," in *Hendrik Petrus Berlage disegni* (Venice: Arsenale Editrice, 1986), 18.

18 → Eve Blau and Nancy Troy, eds., *Architecture and Cubism* (Cambridge, Mass.: MIT Press, 1997).

19 → Raymond Duchamp-Villon to Walter Pach, 16 January 1916, in Walter Pach, *Queer Thing, Painting: Forty Years in the World of Art* (New York: Harper and Brother, 1938), 18.

20 → Pavel Janák, "Od moderní architektury k architektuře," *Styl* 2 (July 1910): 109.

21 → Josef Chochol, "K funkci architektonického článku," *Styl* 5 (1913): 93.

22 → Karel Teige, *Moderní architektura v Československu, Mezinárodní soudobá architektura* 2 (1930), 91–92; English: *Modern Architecture in Czechoslovakia*, trans. Irena Murray with intro. by Jean-Louis Cohen (Los Angeles: Getty Research Institute for the History of Art and the Humanities, 2000), 142.

08 The Great War and its side effects

1 → Albert Scheibe, "Das Kriegschiff," in *Der Verkehr, Jahrbuch des deutschen Werkbundes 1914* (Jena, Germany: Eugen Diederichs, 1914), 59–66.

2 → Filippo Tommaso Marinetti, "Manifeste du Futurisme," *Le Figaro*, February 20, 1909; English: *Marinetti: Selected Writings* (New York: Farrar, Straus and Giroux, 1971), 42.

3 → See Robert Wohl, *The Generation of 1914* (Cambridge, Mass.: Harvard University Press, 1979).

4 → Nicole Zapata-Aubé, ed., *André Mare, cubisme et camouflage 1914–1918* (Bernay, France: Musée des Beaux-Arts, 1998).

5 → Karl Kiem, "Die Gartenstadt Staaken als Prototyp der modernen deutschen Siedlung," in Vittorio Magnago-Lampugnani and Romana Schneider, eds., *Moderne Architektur in Deutschland 1900-1950, Reform und Tradition* (Stuttgart: Gerd Hatje, 1992), 133–49.

6 → Frederick Winslow Taylor, *Principles of Scientific Management* (London: New York: Harper, 1911).

7 → See Adrian Forty, *Objects of Desire* (New York: Pantheon Books, 1986); and Mauro F. Guillén, *The Taylorized Beauty of the Mechanical: Scientific Management and the Rise of Modernist Architecture* (Princeton: Princeton University Press, 2006).

8 → Jacques Gréber, *Organisation des travaux d'architecture aux États-Unis* (Paris: Librairie Centrale des Beaux-Arts, 1919).

9 → *Kriegergräber im Felde und daheim. Jahrbuch des deutschen Werkbundes 1916/1917* (Munich: F. Bruckmann, 1917). See also George L. Mosse, *Fallen Soldiers: Reshaping the Memory of the World Wars* (New York and Oxford: Oxford University Press, 1990).

10 → Timothy John Skelton and Gerald Gliddon, *Lutyens and the Great War* (London: Frances Lincoln, 2008).

11 → Jay Winter and Jean-Louis Robert, eds., *Capital Cities at War: London, Paris, Berlin, 1914–1919* (Cambridge: Cambridge University Press, 1997).

12 → Georges B. Ford, *Out of the Ruins* (New York: Century, 1919); William MacDonald, *Reconstruction in France* (New York: Macmillan, 1922); Victor Cambon, *États-Unis–France* (Paris: Roget, 1917).

13 → Hartmut Frank, "Heimatschutz und typologisches Entwerfen. Modernisierung und Tradition beim Wiederaufbau von Ostpreußen 1915–1927," in Magnago-Lampugnani and Schneider, *Moderne Architektur*, 105–31.

14 → Friedrich Ostendorf, *Sechs Bücher vom Bauen, enthaltend eine Theorie des architektonischen Entwerfens*, 3 vols. (Berlin: W. Ernst & Sohn, 1914–20).

15 → *Le logis et la maison des champs: Exposition de l'architecture régionale dans les provinces envahies* (Paris: Goupil, 1917). See Jean-Pierre Epron, ed., *Les trois reconstructions 1918, 1940, 1945* (Paris: Institut français d'architecture, 1984).

16 → *National Conference on Housing after the War, Organising Committee Report* (Manchester, 1917); *A Million Homes after the War: Statement on the Housing Problem as Affected by the War and Some Suggestions* (London: Cooperative Printing Society Ltd, 1917). See Mark Swenarton, *Homes Fit for Heroes: The Politics and Architecture of Early State Housing in Britain* (London: Heinemann Educational Books, 1981).

17 → Henri Barbusse, *Le Feu* (Paris: Flammarion, 1917); English: *Under Fire*, trans. W. Fitzgerald Wray (London: Dent, 1917); Ernst Jünger, *In Stahlgewittern* (Berlin: E. S. Mittler & Sohn, 1920); English: *The Storm of Steel*, trans. Michael Hoffmann (London: Penguin Classics, 1975).

18 → Oswald Spengler, *Der Untergang des Abendlandes: Umrisse einer Morphologie der Weltgeschichte* (Munich: Beck, 1920); English: *The Decline of the West*, trans. Charles Francis Atkinson, 2 vols (New York: A. A. Knopf, 1926–1928). Jean Cocteau, *Le coq et l'arlequin* (Paris: Éditions de la Sirène, 1918); English: *Cock and Harlequin*, trans. Rollo H. Myers (London: Faber & Gwyer, 1926).

19 → Victoria de Grazia, *Irresistible Empire: America's Advance through Twentieth-Century Europe* (Cambridge, Mass.: Belknap Press of Harvard University Press, 2005).

20 → Beatriz Colomina, *Privacy and Publicity: Modern Architecture as Mass Media* (Cambridge, Mass.: MIT Press, 1994).

21 → Hans Richter, "Der neue Baumeister," *Qualität* 4 (January-February 1925): 3–9.

22 → Moisei Ginzburg, "Mezhdunarodny front sovremennoi arkhitektury," *Sovremennaia Arkhitektura* 1, no. 2 (1926): 42; English: Jean-Louis Cohen, *Le Corbusier and the Mystique of the USSR: Theories and Projects for Moscow 1928–1936* (Princeton: Princeton University Press, 1992), 35.

09 Expressionism in Weimar Germany and the Netherlands

1 → Bruno Taut, "Architektur-Programm" (Berlin: Arbeitsrat für Kunst,1919); English: Ulrich Conrads, *Programs and Manifestoes on 20th-Century Architecture*, trans. Michael Bullock (Cambridge, Mass.: MIT Press, 1970), 44.

2 → Taut, "Architektur-Programm," in Conrads, *Programs*, 45.

3 → Walter Gropius, *Ausstellung für unbekannter Architekten* (Berlin: Arbeitsrat für Kunst, 1919), n.p.; in Conrads, *Programs*, 46–47.

4 → Bruno Taut, *Ausstellung für unbekannter Architekten*, in Conrads, *Programs*, 47.

5 → Ernst Haeckel, *Kunstformen der Natur* (Leipzig and Vienna: Bibliographisches Institut, 1899–1904); Ernst Haeckel, *Kristallseelen, Studien über das anorganische Leben* (Leipzig: Alfred Kroner Verlag, 1917). Bruno Taut, *Alpine Architektur* (Hagen: Folkwang-Verlag, 1919); English: *Glass Architecture by Paul Scheerbart and Alpine Architecture by Bruno Taut*, trans. Shirley Palmer (New York: Praeger, 1972).

6 → See Wolfgang Pehnt, *Die Architektur des Expressionismus* (1973; reprint, Stuttgart: Gerd Hatje, 1998); English: *Expressionist Architecture*, trans. J. A. Underwood and Edith Küstner (New York: Praeger, 1973).

7 → Hans Poelzig, "Lecture Held on the Occasion of the Revival of the Werkbund," in *Mitteilungen des deutschen Werkbundes*, 4 (1919); English: Julius Posener, *Hans Poelzig: Reflections on his Life and Work*, trans. Christine Charlesworth (New York: Architectural History Foundation; Cambridge, Mass.: MIT Press, 1992), 133. Translation slightly modified.

8 → Erich Mendelsohn, "Gedanken zur neuen Architektur (im Felde 1914–1917)," *Wasmuths Monatshefte für Baukunst* 8 (January 1924): 3; English: *Erich Mendelsohn: Structures and Sketches* (London: Ernest Benn, 1924), 3.

9 → See Herman George Scheffauer, "Dynamic Architecture: New Forms of the Future," *The Dial* 70 (March 1921): 323–28.

10 → Erich Mendelsohn, *Amerika, das Bilderbuch eines Architekten* (Berlin: R. Mosse, 1926); English: *Erich Mendelsohn's "Amerika": 82 Photographs* (New York: Dover, 1993).

11 → Regina Stephan, ed., *Erich Mendelsohn, Dynamik und Funktion* (Osfildern-Ruit: Hatje Cantz Verlag, 1999).

12 → Claudia Turtenwald, ed., *Fritz Höger (1877–1949), Moderne Monumente* (Munich: Dölling und Galitz Verlag, 2003).

13 → See Helen Searing, "With Red Flags Flying: Politics and Architecture in Amsterdam," in Henry A. Millon and Linda Nochlin, eds., *Arts and Architecture in the Service of Politics* (Cambridge, Mass.: MIT Press, 1978), 230–70; and Maristella Casciato, *The Amsterdam School* (Rotterdam: 010 Publishers, 1996).

14 → Jeroen Schilt and Jouke van der Werf, *Genootschap Architectura et Amicitia* (Rotterdam: 010 Publishers, 1992).

15 → Manfred Bock, Sigrid Johannisse, and Vladimir Stissi, *Michel de Klerk: Architect and Artist of the Amsterdam School, 1884–1923* (Rotterdam: NAI Publishers, 1997).

10 Return to order in Paris

1 → Paul Boulard [Le Corbusier], "Allemagne…," *L'Esprit nouveau* 5 (November 1924): n.p.

2 → Kenneth E. Silver, *Esprit de Corps: The Art of the Parisian Avant-Garde and the First World War, 1914–1925* (Princeton: Princeton University Press, 1989).

3 → Guillaume Apollinaire, *Les peintres cubistes, méditations esthétiques* (Paris: E. Figuière, 1913; repr., Paris: Hermann, 1980), 114–15; English: *The Cubist Painters,* trans. Patricia Roseberry (Harrogate: Broadwater House, 2000), 109.

4 → Paul Dermée, "Quand le symbolisme fut mort," *Nord-Sud* 1 (15 March 1917): 3; English: Silver, *Esprit de Corps,* 89.

5 → Charles-Édouard Jeanneret and Amédée Ozenfant, *Après le cubisme* (Paris: Éditions des Commentaires, 1918), 28, 53; English: "After Cubism," in Carol S. Eliel, ed., *L'Esprit nouveau: Purism in Paris, 1918–1925* (Los Angeles: Los Angeles County Museum of Art; New York: Harry N. Abrams, 2000), 143, 160.

6 → See Carlo Olmo and Roberto Gabetti, *Le Corbusier e "L'Esprit nouveau"* (Turin: Einaudi, 1975); Stanislaus von Moos, ed., *L'Esprit nouveau: Le Corbusier et l'industrie 1920–1925* (Strasburg: Musées de la Ville, 1987).

7 → Le Corbusier, *Vers une architecture* (1923; repr., Paris: G. Crès, 1924), 53–64, 123–40; English: *Toward an Architecture,* trans. John Goodman with intro. by Jean-Louis Cohen (Los Angeles: Getty Research Institute, 2007), 133–44, 195–212.

8 → Bruno Reichlin and Yve-Alain Bois, eds., *De Stijl et la France* (Liège: Mardaga, 1985).

9 → Tim Benton, *The Villas of Le Corbusier and Pierre Jeanneret, 1920–1930* (Basel: Birkhäuser, 2007).

10 → Colin Rowe, *The Mathematics of the Ideal Villa and Other Essays* (Cambridge, Mass.: MIT Press, 1976). See also Dan Sherer, "Le Corbusier's Discovery of Palladio in 1922 and the Transformation of the Classical Code," *Perspecta* 36 (2005): 20–39.

11 → The "Five Points of a New Architecture" were first enunciated as "Fünf Punkte zu einer neuen Architektur" in Alfred Roth, *Zwei Wohnhäuser von Le Corbusier und Pierre Jeanneret* (Stuttgart: F. Wedekind, 1927), 5–7. See Werner Oechslin's analysis in Jacques Lucan, ed., *Le Corbusier 1887–1965, une encyclopédie* (Paris: Centre George Pompidou, 1987), 92–94.

12 → Le Corbusier, *Une maison, un palais* (Paris: G. Crès, 1928).

13 → Karel Teige, "Mundaneum," *Stavba* 7, no. 10 (1928–9): 145–55.

14 → Jean-Louis Cohen, *Le Corbusier and the Mystique of the USSR: Theories and Projects for Moscow 1928–1936* (Princeton: Princeton University Press, 1992).

15 → See Marcel Zahar, *D'une doctrine d'architecture. Auguste Perret* (Paris: Vincent, Fréal et Cie., 1959), 15; and Bruno Reichlin, "The Pros and Cons of the Horizontal Window: The Perret-Le Corbusier Controversy," *Daidalos* 13 (1984): 65–78.

16 → Paul Valéry, "Eupalinos, ou l'architecte," in Louis Süe and André Mare, *Architectures* (Paris: Éditions de la Nouvelle revue française, 1921), 9–58. See also Massimo Cacciari, "Eupalinos, or Architecture," *Oppositions* 21 (Summer 1980): 106–16.

17 → Auguste Perret, *Contribution à une théorie de l'architecture* (Paris: Cercle d'études architecturales chez A. Wahl, 1952), n.p.

18 → Nancy J. Troy, *Modernism and the Decorative Arts in France: Art Nouveau to Le Corbusier* (New Haven: Yale University Press, 1991); Tag Gronberg, *Designs on Modernity: Exhibiting the City in 1920s Paris* (Manchester: Manchester University Press, 1998).

19 → See Yvonne Brunhammer, ed., *Les années UAM 1929–1958* (Paris: Musée des Arts Décoratifs, 1989); and Arlette Barré-Despond, *Union des Artistes Modernes* (Paris: Éditions du Regard, 1887).

20 → Olivier Cinqualbre, ed., *Robert Mallet-Stevens, l'oeuvre complète* (Paris: Centre Georges Pompidou, 2005).

21 → Rob Mallet-Stevens, "Notre enquête chez les cubistes," *Bulletin de la vie artistique* 5 (1 December 1924): 533; English: Jean-François Pinchon, ed., *Rob Mallet-Stevens, Architecture, Furniture, Interior Design* (Cambridge, Mass.: MIT Press, 1990), 27.

22 → Man Ray, quoted in Jean-Michel Bouhours and Patrick de Haas, ed., *Man Ray, directeur du mauvais movies* (Paris: Éditions du Centre Pompidou, 1997), 93.

23 → See Marie Dormoy, "Le faux béton," *L'Amour de l'art* 10 (April 1929): 128.

24 → Tony Garnier, *Les grands travaux de la ville de Lyon, études, projets et travaux exécutés* (Paris: Charles Massin, 1919).

11 Dada, De Stijl and Mies: from subversiveness to elementarism

1 → Leah Dickerman, ed., *Dada: Zurich, Berlin, Hanover, Cologne, New York, Paris* (Washington, D.C.: National Gallery of Art, 2005).

2 → Nancy J. Troy, *The De Stijl Environment* (Cambridge, Mass.: MIT Press, 1983).

3 → See Giovanni Fanelli, *De Stijl* (Rome and Bari: Laterza, 1983).

4 → Theo van Doesburg to J. J. P. Oud, 23 December 1919, in Evert van Straaten, *Theo van Doesburg: Painter and Architect* (The Hague: SDU Publishing, 1988), 66.

5 → Theo van Doesburg, "Tot een beeldende architectuur," *De Stijl* 6, no. 6–7 (1924): 80; English: "Toward Plastic Architecture," in Joost Baljeu, *Theo van Doesburg* (London: Studio Vista, 1974), 144.

6 → Theo van Doesburg, "Vers une construction collective," *De Stijl* 6, no. 6–7 (1924): 89; English: Baljeu, *Theo van Doesburg,* 147.

7 → Theo van Doesburg, "Notices sur l'Aubette à Strasbourg," *De Stijl* 10, no. 87–89 (1928): 7–8; English: Troy, *The De Stijl Environment,* 170.

8 → J. J. P. Oud, "Kunst en machine," *De Stijl* 1 (January 1918): 25; English: *De Stijl* (Amsterdam: Stedelijk Museum, 1951), 75.

9 → Gerrit Rietveld, interview filmed by Piet van Mook, 1963; English: István L. Szénássy, ed., *G. Rietveld, Architect* (Amsterdam: Stedelijk Museum, 1971), cat. entries 11, 12.

10 → See Theodore M. Brown, *The Work of G. Rietveld, Architect* (Utrecht: Bruna & Zoon, 1958); Ida van Zijl, *Gerrit Rietveld* (London: Phaidon, 2010).

11 → Lisa Phillips, ed., *Frederick Kiesler* (New York: Whitney Museum of American Art and W. W. Norton, 1989).

12 → *KI, Konstruktivische Internationale schöpferische Arbeitsgemeinschaft 1922–1927, Utopien für eine europäische Kultur* (Stuttgart: Gerd Hatje, 1992).

13 → Ludwig Mies van der Rohe, "Bürohaus," *G* 1 (July 1923): 3; English: Fritz Neumeyer, *The Artless Word: Mies van der Rohe on the Building Art,* trans. Mark Jarzombek (Cambridge, Mass.: MIT Press, 1991), 241. The quotation by Behrens appears as an epigraph in Fritz Hoeber, *Peter Behrens* (Munich: G. Müller und E. Rentsch, 1913).

14 → Juan Antonio Ramírez, *The Beehive Metaphor: From Gaudí to Le Corbusier* (London: Reaktion Books, 2000).

15 → Carl Gotfrid, "Hochhäuser," *Qualität* 3 (August 1922–March 1923): 63–66.

16 → Ludwig Mies van der Rohe, "Bauen," *G* 1 (September 1923): 1; English: Jean-Louis Cohen, *Mies van der Rohe* (London: Spon, 1996), 34.

17 → Ludwig Mies van der Rohe, manuscript for a lecture on 19 June 1924, Library of Congress, Mies van der Rohe Archive, Box 61; English: Neumeyer, *The Artless Word,* 250.

18 → Robin Evans, "Mies van der Rohe's Paradoxical Symmetries," *AA Files* 19 (Spring 1990): 56–68.

19 → Paul Westheim, "Mies van der Rohe, Entwicklung eines Architekten," *Das Kunstblatt* 11 (February 1927): 57–58.

12 Architecture education in turmoil

1 → Antonio Brucculeri, "L'École des beaux-arts de Paris saisie par la modernité," in Jean-Louis Cohen, ed., *Les années 30: l'architecture et les arts de l'espace entre industrie et nostalgie* (Paris: Éditions du Patrimoine, 1997), 219–24.

2 → Isabelle Gournay, "L'École des Beaux-Arts e la modernità: il 'grand tour' americano (1926–1939)," *Casabella* 493 (July–August 1983): 40–47.

3 → Joseph Abram, *Perret et l'école du classicisme structurel (1910–1960)* (Nancy: École d'architecture de Nancy, 1985); Jean-Louis Cohen, *André Lurçat, 1894–1970: l'autocritique d'un moderne* (Liège: Pierre Mardaga, 1995), 165–75.

4 → Isabelle Gournay, "Architecture at the Fontainebleau School of Fine Arts, 1923–1939," *Journal of the Society of Architectural Historians* 45 (September 1986): 270–85.

5 → Rolf Bothe and Hans Maria Wingler, eds., *Kunstschulreform 1900–1933* (Berlin: Gebr. Mann, 1977).

6 → See Bauhaus-Archiv Berlin, Klassik Stiftung Weimar, and Stiftung Bauhaus Dessau, *Bauhaus. A Conceptual Model* (Ostfildern, Germany: Hatje Cantz Verlag, 2009).

7 → Walter Gropius, *Programm des Staatlichen Bauhauses in Weimar* (Weimar: Staatliches Bauhaus, 1919), 1; English: Hans Maria Wingler, *The Bauhaus: Weimar, Dessau, Berlin, Chicago,* trans. Wolfgang Jabs and Basil Gilbert (Cambridge, Mass.: MIT Press, 1979), 32.

8 → Ibid.

9 → *Staatliches Bauhaus, Weimar, 1919–1923* (Weimar and Munich: Bauhausverlag, 1923).

10 → Walter Gropius, *Bauhausbauten Dessau* (Munich: A. Langen, 1930).

11 → Winfried Nerdinger, *The Architect Walter Gropius* (Berlin: Gebr. Mann, 1985).

12 → Hannes Meyer, "Bauen," *Bauhaus* 2, no. 4 (1928): 12; English: Wingler, *Bauhaus*, 153–54.

13 → Christian Wohlsdorf, *Mehr als das blosse Zweck: Mies van der Rohe am Bauhaus 1930–1933* (Berlin: Bauhaus-Archiv, 2001).

14 → See the works discussed in Selim O. Khan-Magomedov, *Vkhoutémas*, vol. 2 (Paris: Éditions du Regard, 1990), 467–555. See also Alexander Kudriavstev and Natalia Duskhkina, eds., *From Vkhutemas to Markhi 1920–1936* (Moscow: A-Fond, 2005).

15 → Le Corbusier, handwritten note on page 37 of Agenda 7, 1928, Fondation Le Corbusier, Paris; English: Jean-Louis Cohen, *Le Corbusier and the Mystique of the USSR: Theories and Projects for Moscow 1928–1936* (Princeton: Princeton University Press, 1992), 46.

16 → Xing Ruan, "Accidental Affinities: American Beaux-Arts in Twentieth-Century Chinese Architectural Education and Practice," *Journal of the Society of Architectural Historians* 61 (March 2002): 30–47.

17 → Margret Kentgens-Craig, *The Bauhaus and America, First Contacts 1919–1936* (Cambridge, Mass.: MIT Press, 1999).

18 → Herbert Bayer, Walter Gropius, and Ise Gropius, *Bauhaus 1919–1938* (New York: Museum of Modern Art, 1938).

19 → Franz Schulze, "How Chicago Got Mies—and Harvard Didn't," *Inland Architect* 21 (May 1978): 23–24.

20 → Wolfgang Thöner and Peter Müller, eds., *Bauhaus-Tradition und DDR-Moderne: Der Architekt Richard Paulick* (Munich: Deutscher Kunstverlag, 2006).

13 Architecture and revolution in Russia

1 → See Rainer Graefe, Murat Gappoev, and Ottmar Pertschi, eds., *Vladimir Suchov 1853–1939: Die Kunst der sparsamen Konstruktion* (Stuttgart: Deutsche Verlags-Anstalt, 1990); Rainer Graefe and Ottmar Pertschi, "Un ingegnere rivoluzionario: Vladimir Grigor'evič Šuchov, 1853–1939," *Casabella* 573 (1990): 8–58, 61–63.

2 → Nikolai Punin, *Pamiatnik III Internatsionala* (Petrograd: Izdanie otdela izobrazitelnykh iskusstv NKP, 1920), n.p.

3 → See Christina Lodder, *Russian Constructivism* (New Haven: Yale University Press, 1983).

4 → Moisei Ginzburg, *Stil i epokha, problemy sovremennoi arhitektury* (Moscow: Gosudarstvennoe izdatelstvo, 1924); English: *Style and Epoch*, trans. with intro. by Anatole Senkevitch, Jr. (Cambridge, Mass.: MIT Press, 1982).

5 → See the partial reprint: Guido Canella and Maurizio Meriggi, eds., *SA, Sovremennaia Arkhitektura 1926–1930* (Bari, Italy: Dedalo, 2007).

6 → S. Frederick Starr, *Le pavillon de Mel'nikov, Paris, 1925* (Paris: L'Équerre, 1981).

7 → Richard Pare and Jean-Louis Cohen, *The Lost Vanguard: Russian Modernist Architecture 1922–1932* (New York: Monacelli Press, 2007).

8 → See Victor Buchli, *An Archaeology of Socialism* (Oxford and New York: Berg, 1999).

9 → See S. Frederick Starr, "Visionary Town Planning during the Cultural Revolution," in Sheila Fitzpatrick, ed., *Cultural Revolution in Russia, 1928–1931* (Bloomington: Indiana University Press, 1978), 207–40.

10 → Carlo Olmo and Alessandro de Magistris, eds., *Iakov Chernikhov* (Paris: Somogy; Turin: Allemandi, 1995).

11 → Joseph Stalin, letter to Lazar Kaganovich, Klim Voroshilov, and Vyacheslav Molotov, 7 August 1932; quoted in Elisabeth Essaian, "Le plan général de reconstruction de Moscou de 1935; la ville, l'architecte et le politique, héritages culturels et pragmatisme économique" Ph.D. diss., Université de Paris 8, 2006, 337–38.

12 → See Hugh D. Hudson, Jr., "Terror in Soviet Architecture: The Murder of Mikhail Okhitovich," *Slavic Review* 51 (Autumn 1992): 448–67; Hugh D. Hudson, Jr., *Blueprints and Blood: The Stalinization of Soviet Architecture* (Princeton: Princeton University Press, 1994); and Vladimir Paperny, *Architecture in the Age of Stalin: Culture Two* (Cambridge: Cambridge University Press, 2002).

14 The architecture of social reform

1 → See *Architecture et politiques sociales, les principes architecturaux à l'âge du réformisme*, triple issue of *Les Cahiers de la recherche architecturale*, no. 15, 16, 17 (1985).

2 → Richard Pommer, David A. Spaeth, and Kevin Harrington, *In the Shadow of Mies: Ludwig Hilberseimer: Architect, Educator, and Urban Planner* (Chicago: Art Institute of Chicago; New York: Rizzoli, 1988).

3 → See Manfredo Tafuri, *Vienna Rossa* (Milan: Electa, 1980); and Eve Blau, *The Architecture of Red Vienna 1919–1934* (Cambridge, Mass.: MIT Press, 1999).

4 → See Rosemarie Hopfner and Volker Fischer, eds., *Ernst May und das Neue Frankfurt, 1925–1930* (Berlin: Ernst & Sohn, 1986).

5 → Jean Castex, Philippe Panerai, and Jean-Charles Depaule, *Formes urbaines: de l'îlot à la barre* (Paris: Dunod, 1977); English: *Urban Forms: Death and Life of the Urban Block*, trans. Olga Vitale Samuels (Oxford: Architectural Press, 2004).

6 → Leberecht Migge, *Der soziale Garten. Das grüne Manifest* [1926] (Berlin: Gebr. Mann, 1999). See David H. Haney, *When Modern Was Green: Life and Work of Landscape Architect Leberecht Migge* (London: Routledge, 2010).

7 → Iain Boyd Whyte, *Bruno Taut and the Architecture of Activism* (Cambridge: Cambridge University Press, 1982).

8 → Christine Mengin, *Guerre du toit et modernité architecturale: loger l'employé sous la république de Weimar* (Paris: Publications de la Sorbonne, 2007).

9 → Hartmut Frank, ed., *Fritz Schumacher; Reformkultur und Moderne* (Stuttgart: Gerd Hatje, 1994).

10 → Robert Koch and Eberhard Pook, eds., *Karl Schneider Leben und Werk (1892–1945)* (Hamburg: Dölling & Galitz Verlag, 1992).

11 → Henri Sellier, *Réalisations de l'Office public d'habitations de la Seine* (Paris: OPH de la Seine, 1933). On Sellier's work, see Katherine Burlen and Bernard Barraqué, *La "Banlieue Oasis." Henri Sellier et les cités-jardins 1900–1940* (Saint-Denis: Presses universitaires de Vincennes, 1987).

12 → Anne-Sophie Clémençon, ed., *Les gratte-ciel de Villeurbanne* (Paris: Éditions de l'imprimeur, 2004).

13 → Ken Oshima, "Denenchōfu: Building the Garden City in Japan," *Journal of the Society of Architectural Historians* 55 (March 1996): 140–51.

14 → Marco Pompili, *Dojunkai Apartments, Tokyo 1924–1934: Collective Housing in Japan and the Modern City* (Milan: Dedalo, 2001).

15 → Catherine Bauer, *Modern Housing* (Boston: Houghton Mifflin, 1934).

16 → Clarence Stein, *Towards New Towns for America* (Liverpool: University Press of Liverpool, 1951).

17 → Clarence A. Perry, "The Neighborhood Unit," in *Neighborhood and Community Planning* (New York: Regional Plan of New York and Its Environs, 1929), 22–140.

18 → Anne-Marie Châtelet, Dominique Lerch, and Jean-Noël Luc, eds., *L'école de plein air: une expérience pédagogique et architecturale dans l'Europe du XXe siècle* (Paris: Éditions Recherches, 2003).

19 → Jean-Louis Cohen, *André Lurçat, 1894–1970: l'autocritique d'un moderne* (Liège: Pierre Mardaga, 1995).

20 → Bruno Schwann, ed., *Städtebau und Wohnungswesen der Welt* (Berlin: Verlag Ernst Wasmuth, 1935); Irenio Diotallevi and Francesco Marescotti, *Ordine e destino della casa popolare* (Milan: Editoriale Domus, 1941).

15 Internationalization, its networks and spectacles

1 → Walter Gropius, *Internationale Architektur* (Munich: A. Langen, 1925).

2 → See Hélène Jannière, *Politiques éditoriales et architecture "moderne": l'émergence de nouvelles revues en France et en Italie, 1923–1939* (Paris: Arguments, 2002).

3 → Alvar Aalto, "The Stockholm Exhibition: Summary of an Interview," in *Åbo Underrättelser*, 22 May 1930; English: Göran Schildt, *Alvar Aalto in His Own Words* (New York: Rizzoli, 1998), 73.

4 → Walter Curt Behrendt, *Der Sieg des neuen Baustils* (Stuttgart: Fr. Wedekind, 1927); English: *The Victory of the New Building Style*, trans. Harry Francis Mallgrave with intro. by Detlef Mertins (Los Angeles: Getty Research Institute for the History of Art and the Humanities, 2000).

5 → See Johannes Cramer and Niels Gutschow, *Bauausstellungen: Eine Architekturgeschichte des 20. Jahrhunderts* (Stuttgart: Kohlhammer, 1984).

6 → Paul Overy, *Light, Air and Openness: Modern Architecture between the Wars* (London: Thames & Hudson, 2007).

7 → Henry-Russell Hitchcock and Philip Johnson, *The International Style: Architecture since 1922* (New York: W. W. Norton, 1932). See also Terence Riley, *The International Style: Exhibition 15 and the Museum of Modern Art* (New York: Rizzoli, 1992).

8 → See Lewis Mumford, "Housing," in Hitchcock and Johnson, *Modern Architecture*, 1932), 179–89.

9 → CIAM, "Declaration of La Sarraz, 1928." English: Le Corbusier, *The Athens Charter*, trans. Anthony Eardley (New York: Grossmann Publishers, 1973), 6–7. See also Jacques Gubler, *Nationalisme et internationalisme dans l'architecture moderne de la Suisse* (Lausanne: Éditions L'Âge d'homme, 1975).

10 → See Le Corbusier, *La charte d'Athènes, avec un discours liminaire de Jean Giraudoux* (Paris: Plon, 1943), 43; English: *The Athens Charter*, 20.

11 → Nader Vossoughian, *Otto Neurath: The Language of the Global Polis* (Rotterdam: NAi Publishers, 2008).

12 → Fernand Léger, "Discours aux architectes," *Tekhnika Kronika* 44–45–46 (1933): 1160. See also Paola di Biagi, ed., *La Carta d'Atene, manifesto e frammento dell'urbanistica moderna* (Rome: Officina Edizioni, 1998).

13 → Bernard Huet, "The City as Dwelling Space: Alternatives to the Charter of Athens," *Lotus International* 41 (1984): 6–17.

14 → Le Corbusier, *Athens Charter*, 61, 65, 76, 85.

15 → Ibid., 88.

16 → Jean-Louis Cohen, "Il nostro cliente è il nostro padrone, Le Corbusier e Baťa," *I clienti di Le Corbusier, Rassegna* 3 (June 1980): 47–60.

17 → Pierre Vago, *Une vie intense* (Brussels: AAM éditions, 2000).

18 → These books are discussed in Maria-Luisa Scalvini and Maria-Luisa Sandri, *L'immagine storiografica dell'architettura moderna da Platz a Giedion* (Rome: Officina Edizioni, 1984); and Panayotis Tournikiotis, *The Historiography of Modern Architecture* (Cambridge, Mass.: MIT Press, 1999).

19 → Sigfried Giedion, *Space, Time and Architecture: The Growth of a New Tradition* (Cambridge, Mass.: Harvard University Press, 1941).

16 Futurism and Rationalism in Fascist Italy

1 → See Carlo Olmo, ed., *Il Lingotto, 1915–1939: l'architettura, l'immagine, il lavoro* (Turin: Umberto Allemandi, 1994).

2 → Blaise Cendrars, "F.I.A.T.," *Avanscoperta* 2 (25 February 1917); English: Blaise Cendrars, *Complete Poems*, trans. Ron Padgett (Berkeley: University of California Press, 1992), 71.

3 → See Enrico Crispolti, *Attraverso l'architettura futurista* (Modena: Galleria Fonte d'Abisso, 1984), 30.

4 → Virgilio Marchi, *Architettura futurista* (Foligno, Italy: Franco Campitelli, 1924), 46.

5 → See Stefano de Martino and Alex Wall, eds., *Cities of Childhood: Italian Colonies of the 1930s* (London: Architectural Association, 1988).

6 → Giorgio de Chirico, "Sull'arte metafisica," *Valori plastici* 1 (April–May 1919): 37. On this journal, see Paolo Fossati, *"Valori Plastici," 1918–1922* (Turin: Giulio Einaudi, 1981).

7 → Benito Mussolini, "Alla mostra del Novecento," speech given on 26 March 1923, published in *Il Popolo d'Italia*, 27 March 1923; trans. in Emily Braun, *Mario Sironi and Italian Modernism: Arts and Politics under Fascism* (Cambridge: Cambridge University Press, 2000), 1.

8 → Alberto Savinio, *Ascolto il tuo cuore* (Milan: Bompiani, 1944), 161.

9 → Paolo Mezzanotte, "Edilizia milanese," *Architettura e arti decorative* 2 (1922–23): 84.

10 → Giovanni Muzio, "Alcuni architetti d'oggi in Lombardia," *Dedalo* 9 (August 1931): 1107; English: Dennis Doordan, *Building Modern Italy: Italian Architecture, 1914–1936* (New York: Princeton Architectural Press, 1988), 30.

11 → Gio Ponti, "La casa all'italiana," *Domus* 1, no. 1 (1928): 7.

12 → See Paolo Nicoloso, *Mussolini architetto* (Turin: Einaudi, 2008).

13 → See Claudia Conforti, Roberto Dulio, and Marzia Marandola, *Giovanni Michelucci 1891–1990* (Milan: Electa, 2006).

14 → Gruppo 7, "Architettura," *Rassegna italiana* 103 (December 1926): 849.

15 → Jean-Paul Sartre, *Lettres au Castor et à quelques autres*, vol. 1 (Paris: Gallimard, 1983), 74; English: Jean-Paul Sartre, *Witness to My Life: The Letters of Jean-Paul Sartre to Simone de Beauvoir, 1926–1939*, trans. Lee Fahnestock and Norman MacAffee (New York: Charles Scribner's Sons, 1992), 59–60.

16 → See Giorgio Ciucci, ed., *Giuseppe Terragni: opera completa* (Milan: Electa, 1996); and Attilio Terragni, Daniel Libeskind, and Paolo Rosselli, *Atlante Terragni*, Architetture costruite (Milan: Skira, 2004).

17 → Giuseppe Terragni, "La costruzione della casa del Fascio di Como," *Quadrante* 4 (October 1936): 6; English: Doordan, *Building Modern Italy*, 137.

18 → Giulio Carlo Argan, Carlo Levi, and Matteo Marangoni, eds., *Dopo Sant'Elia*, (Milan: Edizioni Domus, 1935); Edoardo Persico, "L'esempio di Sant'Elia," *Casabella* 7 (October 1934): 2.

19 → See Peter Eisenman, *Giuseppe Terragni: Transformations, Decompositions, Critiques* (New York: Monacelli Press, 2003).

20 → MIAR, "L'architettura razionale italiana," *Casabella* 4, no. 40 (1931): 82; cited in Silvia Danesi Squarzina, "Aporie dell'architettura italiana in periodo fascista—mediterraneità e purismo," in Silvia Danesi Squarzina and Luciano Patetta, eds., *Il razionalismo e l'architettura in Italia durante il fascismo* (Venice: La Biennale di Venezia, 1976), 21.

21 → Enrico Peressutti, "Architettura mediterranea," *Quadrante* 3 (January 1935): 40.

22 → See Monika Platzer, ed., *Lessons from Bernard Rudofsky: Life as a Voyage* (Basel: Birkhäuser, 2007); Alfredo Buccaro and Giancarlo Mainini, eds., *Luigi Cosenza oggi, 1905–2005* (Naples: CLEAR, 2006).

23 → Marida Talamona, *Casa Malaparte* (New York: Princeton Architectural Press, 1992).

24 → Agnoldomenico Pica, *Nuova architettura italiana* (Milan: U. Hoepli, 1936); Agnoldomenico Pica, *Nuova architettura nel mondo* (Milan: U. Hoepli, 1938); Giuseppe Pagano and Guarniero Daniel, *Architettura rurale italiana* (Milan: U. Hoepli, 1936); Michelangelo Sabatino, *Pride in Modesty: Modernist Architecture and the Vernacular Tradition in Italy* (Toronto: University of Toronto Press, 2010).

25 → See Carlo Olmo, ed., *Costruire la città dell'uomo: Adriano Olivetti e l'urbanistica* (Milan: Edizioni di Comunità, 2001).

26 → Paolo Nicoloso, *Gli architetti di Mussolini: scuole e sindacato, architetti e massoni, professori e politici negli anni del regime* (Milan: Franco Angeli, 1999).

17 The spectrum of classicisms and traditionalisms

1 → Bruno Zevi, *Il linguaggio moderno dell'architettura. Guida al codice anticlassico* (Turin: Einaudi: 1973); English: *The Modern Language of Architecture* (Seattle: University of Washington Press, 1978). John Summerson, *The Classical Language of Architecture* (London: Methuen, 1964; rev. ed., London: Thames & Hudson, 1980).

2 → This thesis is attested to by many authors in Dawn Ades, Tim Benton, et al., eds., *Art and Power: Europe under the Dictators, 1930–1945* (London: Hayward Gallery, 1995).

3 → Deyan Sudjic, "The Long March to the Leader's Desk," in *The Edifice Complex: How the Rich and Powerful Shape the World* (New York: Penguin Press, 2005), 19–61.

4 → Jean-Richard Bloch, "Le peuple a droit à des colonnes" (1937), in *Moscou-Paris* (Paris: Éditions Raisons d'être, 1947), 148–53. On the theory of "socialist" realism see Régine Robin, *Le réalisme socialiste, une esthétique impossible* (Paris: Payot, 1986); English: *Socialist Realism: an Impossible Aesthetic*, trans. Catherine Porter (Stanford: Stanford University Press, 1992).

5 → Paul Philippe Cret, "Can Modern Architecture Be Good?," *Federal Architect* 1 (October 1930): 6.

6 → See Wolfgang Voigt and Hartmut Frank, eds., *Paul Schmitthenner 1884–1972* (Tübingen: Wasmuth, 2003).

7 → See Hartmut Frank, "La loi dure et la loi douce: monument et architecture du quotidien dans l'Allemagne nazie," in Jean-Louis Cohen, ed., *Les années 30: l'architecture et les arts de l'espace entre industrie et nostalgie* (Paris: Éditions du Patrimoine, 1997), 200–06.

8 → See Jean-Louis Cohen, *André Lurçat (1904–1970), autocritique d'un moderne* (Liège: Pierre Mardaga, 1995), 189–94.

9 → See Ed Taverne and Dolf Broekhuizen, *Het Shell-Gebouw van J. J. P. Oud, ontwerp en receptie* (Rotterdam: NAi Uitgevers, 1995).

10 → N. B. Sokolov, *A. V. Shchusev* (Moscow: Gosudarstvennoe izdatelstvo literatury po stroitelstvu i arkhitekture, 1952).

11 → See Mario Lupano, *Marcello Piacentini* (Rome and Bari, Italy: Laterza, 1991).

12 → See Bertrand Lemoine, ed., *Paris 1937: Cinquantenaire de l'Exposition Internationale des Arts et Techniques dans la Vie Moderne* (Paris: Institut français d'architecture and Paris-Musées, 1987).

13 → See Paolo Nicoloso, *Mussolini architetto* (Turin: Einaudi, 2008).

14 → See Vieri Quilici, *E 42–EUR: Un centro sulla metropolis* (Rome: Olmo, 1996).

15 → See Romy Golan, "From Monument to Muralnomad: The Mural in Modernist Architecture," in Karen Koehler, ed., *The Built Surface: Architecture and Pictures from Antiquity to the Millenium*, vol. 2 (London: Ashgate Press, 2002), 186–208; and Romy Golan, *Muralnomad: The Paradox of Wall Painting, Europe 1927–1957* (New Haven: Yale University Press, 2009).

18 North American modernities

1 → See David G. De Long, ed., *Frank Lloyd Wright: Designs for an American Landscape* (New York: Harry N. Abrams, 1996).

2 → Frank Lloyd Wright, *Modern Architecture: Being the Kahn Lectures for 1930* (Princeton: Princeton University Press, 1931); facsimile ed., intro. by Neil Levine (Princeton: Princeton University Press, 2008).

3 → Frank Lloyd Wright, "Broadacre City: A New Community Plan," *Architectural Record* 77 (April 1935): 247, 254.

4 → See Thomas S. Hines, *Architecture of the Sun: Los Angeles Modernism, 1900-1970* (New York: Rizzoli, 2010).

5 → See Thomas S. Hines, *Irving Gill and the Architecture of Reform* (New York: Monacelli Press, 2000).

6 → See Elizabeth A. T. Smith and Michael Darling, eds., *The Architecture of R. M. Schindler* (New York: Abrams, 2001).

7 → Richard Neutra, *Wie baut Amerika?* (Stuttgart: Julius Hoffmann, 1927); Richard Neutra, *Amerika: Die Stilbildung des neuen Bauens in den Vereinigten Staaten* (Vienna: Anton Schroll, 1930).

8 → David Gebhard and Harriette von Breton, *Los Angeles in the Thirties: 1931–1941* (Los Angeles: Hennessey & Ingalls, 1989).

9 → Giuseppe Pagano, "Impressioni d'America," *Casabella* 10 (December 1937): 2–4.

10 → See Albert Christ-Janer, *Eliel Saarinen: Finnish-American Architect and Educator* [1948] (Chicago: University of Chicago Press, 1979).

11 → See Carol Willis, *Form Follows Finance* (New York: Princeton Architectural Press, 1995).

12 → See Robert A. M. Stern, *Raymond M. Hood* (New York: Rizzoli, 1982).

13 → See Carol Herselle Krinsky, *Rockefeller Center* (New York: Oxford University Press, 1978); and Rem Koolhaas, "How Perfect Perfection Can Be: The Creation of Rockefeller Center," in *Delirious New York: A Retroactive Manifesto for Manhattan* (New York: Rizzoli, 1978), 161–233.

14 → See Grant Hildebrand, *Designing for Industry: The Architecture of Albert Kahn* (Cambridge, Mass.: MIT Press, 1974); Federico Bucci, *Albert Kahn, Architect of Ford* (New York: Princeton Architectural Press, 1993).

15 → See Richard S. Tedlow, *New and Improved: The Story of Mass Marketing in America* (New York: Basic Books, 1990).

16 → Secretary of Commerce Herbert Hoover, telephone address to the 4th Annual Exposition of Women's Arts and Industries, 1925, quoted in Arthur J. Pulos, *American Design Ethic: A History of Industrial Design to 1940* (Cambridge, Mass.: MIT Press, 1983), 304.

17 → See Jeffrey Meikle, *Twentieth Century Limited: Industrial Design in America 1925–1939* (Philadelphia: Temple University Press, 1979); and Ariane Lourie, "L'invention de l'industrial designer aux États-Unis," in Jean-Louis Cohen, ed., *Les années 30: l'architecture et les arts de l'espace entre industrie et nostalgie* (Paris: Éditions du Patrimoine, 1977), 232–39.

18 → Norman Bel Geddes, *Horizons* (Boston: Little, Brown, 1932). On the Futurama, see Adnan Morshed, "The Aesthetics of Ascension in Norman Bel Geddes's Futurama," *Journal of the Society of Architectural Historians* 63, no. 1 (March 2004): 74–99.

19 → Walter Lippmann. "Today and Tomorrow," *New York Herald Tribune*, 6 June 1939. See Robert F. Rydell, *World of Fairs: The Century-of-Progress Expositions* (New York: University of Chicago Press, 1993); and Donald Bush, "Futurama: World's Fair as Utopia," *Alternative Futures* 4 (1979): 3–20.

20 → Keller Easterling, *Organization Space: Landscapes, Highways, and Houses in America* (Cambridge, Mass.: MIT Press, 1999).

21 → See Gail Radford, *Modern Housing for America: Policy Struggles in the New Deal Era* (Chicago: University of Chicago Press, 1996).

22 → Serge Chermayeff, "Telesis: The Birth of a Group," *New Pencil Points* 23 (July 1942): 45–48. See Marc Treib, ed., *The Architecture of Landscape, 1940–1960* (Philadelphia: University of Pennsylvania Press, 2002).

19 Functionalism and machine aesthetics

1 → "Warum sind unsere Maschinen schön?" *ABC: Beiträge zum Bauen 1*, no. 3–4 (1925): 8; "ABC fordert die Diktatur der Maschine," *ABC Beiträge zum Bauen* 3, no. 4 (1927–28): 1–2.

2 → On the concept of *Sachlichkeit* see Francesco Passanti, "The Vernacular, Modernism, and Le Corbusier," *Journal of the Society of Architectural Historians* 56 (December 1997): 448–49; Stanford Anderson, "*Sachlichkeit* and Modernity, or Realist Architecture," in Harry Francis Mallgrave, ed., *Otto Wagner: Reflections on the Raiment of Modernity* (Santa Monica: Getty Research Center in the History of Art and the Humanities, 1993), 323–62; and Rosemary Haag Bletter, introduction to Adolf Behne, *The Modern Functional Building*, trans. Michael Robinson (Santa Monica: Getty Research Center for the History of Art and the Humanities, 1996), 1–83.

3 → Adolf Behne, *Der moderne Zweckbau* (Munich: Drei Masken Verlag, 1923); English: Behne, *The Modern Functional Building*, trans. Michael Robinson (Santa Monica: Getty Research Center for the History of Art and the Humanities, 1996).

4 → Henry-Russell Hitchcock and Philip Johnson, *The International Style: Architecture Since 1922* (New York: W. W. Norton, 1932), 35.

5 → Alberto Sartoris, *Gli elementi dell'architettura funzionale: sintesi panoramica dell'architettura moderna* (Milan: U. Hoepli, 1932).

6 → See Adrian Forty, "Function," in *Words and Buildings: A Vocabulary of Modern Architecture* (London: Thames & Hudson, 2000), 174–95; and Bruno Reichlin, "L'infortune critique du fonctionnalisme," in Jean-Louis Cohen, ed., *Les années 30: l'architecture et les arts de l'espace entre industrie et nostalgie* (Paris: Éditions du Patrimoine, 1977), 186–95.

7 → Christine Frederick, *The New Housekeeping: Efficiency Studies in Home Management* (Garden City, N.Y.: Doubleday, Page, 1913). See Janice Williams Rutherford, *Selling Mrs. Consumer: Christine Frederick and the Rise of Household Efficiency* (Athens, Ga.: University of Georgia Press, 2003).

8 → Moisei Ginzburg, "Tselevaia ustanovka v sovremennoi arkhitekture," *Sovremennaia Arkhitektura* 2, no. 1 (1927): 4.

9 → See Claude Schnaidt, *Hannes Meyer: Bauten, Projekte und Schriften* (Teufen: Niggli, 1965); and Matthias Schirren, ed., *Hannes Meyer, 1889–1954: Architekt, Urbanist, Lehrer* (Berlin: Ernst & Sohn, 1989).

10 → Alexander Klein, "Versuch eines graphischen Verfahrens zur Bewertung von Kleinwohnungsgrundrissen," *Wasmuths Monatshefte für Baukunst* 22, no. 7 (1927): 296–98; Alexander Klein, "Grundrissbildung und Raumgestaltung von Kleinwohnungen und neue Auswertungsmethoden," *Zentralblatt der Bauverwaltung* 48, no. 34 (1928): 541–49.

11 → Ernst Neufert, *Bauentwurfslehre* (Berlin: Bauwelt-Verlag, 1936); English: *Architects' Data* (New York: Halsted Press, 1980). See Walter Prigge, ed., *Ernst Neufert: normierte Baukultur im 20. Jahrhundert* (Frankfurt am Main: Campus-Verlag, 1999).

12 → Jan Mukařovský, "K problému funkcí v architektuře," *Stavba* 14 (1937–38): 5–12. See also Jan Mukařovský, *Estetická funkce, norma a hodnota jako sociálne fakty* (Prague: F. Borový, 1936); English: *Aesthetic Function, Norm and Value as Social Facts*, trans. Mark E. Suino (Ann Arbor: University of Michigan Press, 1970), 95; and Jan Mukařovský, *Structure, Sign, and Function: Selected Essays*, trans. John Burbank and Peter Steiner (New Haven: Yale University Press, 1978).

13 → See Paulette Bernège, *Si les femmes faisaient les maisons* (Paris: À mon Chez-moi, 1928).

14 → Marie Dormoy, "Les intérieurs à l'Exposition Internationale des Arts Décoratifs," *L'Amour de l'art* 5 (August 1925): 315.

15 → See Marc Vellay, *Pierre Chareau: Architect and Craftsman, 1883–1950* (New York: Rizzoli, 1985).

16 → See Terence Riley and Joseph Abram, eds., *The Filter of Reason: Work of Paul Nelson* (New York: Rizzoli, 1990).

17 → Gus Dudley, ed., *Oscar Nitzchké, Architect* (New York: Irwin S. Chanin School of Architecture of the Cooper Union, 1985).

18 → See Bruno Reichlin, "Maison du Peuple at Clichy, a Masterpiece of 'Synthetic' Functionalism?" *Daidalos* 18 (December 1985): 88–99; and Catherine Dumont d'Ayot and Bruno Reichlin, eds., *Jean Prouvé, the Poetics of the Technical Object* (Weil am Rhein: Vitra Design Museum, 2006).

19 → See Marc Dessauce, "Contro lo Stile Internazionale: Shelter e la stampa architettonica americana," *Casabella* 57 (September 1993): 46–53, 70–71.

20 → See Joachim Krausse and Claude Lichtenstein, *Your Private Sky: R. Buckminster Fuller, the Art of Design Science* (Baden: Lars Müller, 1999), 202–11.

21 → Knud Lonberg-Holm, "Time Zoning as a Preventive of Blighted Areas" *Architectural Record* 74 (November 1933): 340–41. See Marc Dessauce, "Les Structural Studies Associates et la poursuite du bonheur," in Jean-Louis Cohen, *Les années 30*, 154–61.

20 Modern languages conquer the world

1 → Alberto Sartoris, *Encyclopédie de l'architecture nouvelle*, 3 vols. (Milan: U. Hoepli, 1948–54).

2 → For a new perspective, see Alan Powers, *Britain: Modern Architecture in History* (London: Reaktion Books, 2007).

3 → Berthold Lubetkin, "The Builders," *Architectural Review* 71 (May 1932), 201–14.

4 → See James Dunnett and Gavin Stamp, eds., *Ernö Goldfinger* (London: Architectural Association, 1983).

5 → See Charlotte Benton, ed., *A Different World: Émigré Architecture in Britain 1928–1938* (London: RIBA Publications, 1995).

6 → See Claes Caldenby, Jöran Lindvall, and Wilfried Wang, eds., *Twentieth-Century Architecture: Sweden* (Munich: Prestel, 1998).

7 → See Eva Rudberg, *The Stockholm Exhibition 1930: Modernism's Breakthrough in Swedish Architecture* (Stockholm: Stockholmia, 1999); and Eva Rudberg, *Sven Markelius, Architect* (Stockholm: Arkitektur Förlag, 1989).

8 → See Gustav Holmdahl, Sven Ivar Lind, and Kjell Ödeen, eds., *Gunnar Asplund, Architect, 1885–1940* (Stockholm: Byggförlaget, 1981); and Peter Blundell Jones, *Gunnar Asplund* (London: Phaidon, 2006).

9 → See Göran Schildt, *Alvar Aalto: The Decisive Years* (New York: Rizzoli, 1986).

10 → See Rostislav Švacha, *The Architecture of New Prague, 1895–1945* (Cambridge, Mass.: MIT Press, 1995).

11 → Karel Teige, *Moderní architektura v Československu, Mezinárodní soudobá architektura 2* (1930); English: *Modern Architecture in Czechoslovakia*, trans. Irena Murray, intro. Jean-Louis Cohen (Los Angeles: Getty Research Institute for the History of Art and the Humanities, 2000), 142.

12 → See Ladislava Horňáková, ed., *Fenomén Baťa, zlínská architektura 1910–1960* (Zlín: Krajská galerie výtvarného umění v Zlíně, 2009); and Winfried Nerdinger, Ladislava Horňáková, and Radomíra Sedláková, eds., *Zlín—Model Town of Modernism* (Munich: Jovis Verlag, 2009).

13 → See Ákos Moravánszky, *Die Erneuerung der Baukunst: Wege zur Moderne in Mitteleuropa 1900–1940* (Salzburg: Residenz Verlag, 1988); and Wojciech Lesnikowski, ed., *East European Modernism: Architecture in Czechoslovakia, Hungary and Poland between the Wars, 1919–1939* (New York: Rizzoli, 1996).

14 → See Silvia Parlagreco, ed., *Il costruttivismo in Polonia, percorsi e deviazioni di un avanguardia* (Milan: Bollati Boringhieri, 2005).

15 → See Adam Milobedzki, ed., "Architecture and Avant-Garde in Poland 1918–1939," thematic issue, *Rassegna* 65 (1996).

16 → See Ljiljana Blagojević, *Modernism in Serbia: The Elusive Margins of Belgrade Architecture* (Cambridge, Mass.: MIT Press, 2003).

17 → See Peter Krečič, *Plečnik: The Complete Works* (New York: Whitney Library of Design, 1993); and Damjan Prelovšek, *Jože Plečnik, 1872–1957: Architectura Perennis* (New Haven: Yale University Press, 1997).

18 → See Luminiţa Machedon and Ernie Scoffham, *Romanian Modernism: The Architecture of Bucharest, 1920–1940* (Cambridge, Mass.: MIT Press, 1999); and Ana-Maria Zahariade, *Centenar Horia Creangă 1892–1992* (Bucharest: Simmetria, 1992).

19 → See Savas Condaratos and Wilfried Wang, eds., *Twentieth-Century Architecture: Greece* (Munich: Prestel, 1999).

20 → See Carlos Flores, *Arquitectura española contemporánea* (Madrid: Aguilar, 1961); and Oriol Bohigas, *Arquitectura española de la Segunda República* (Barcelona: Tusquets, 1970).

21 → See Antonio Pizza and Josep M. Rovira, eds., *GATCPAC: Una nova arquitectura para una nova ciutat 1928–1939* (Barcelona: Col·legi Oficial d'Arquitectes de Catalunya, 2006).

22 → See David B. Stewart, *The Making of a Modern Japanese Architecture, 1868 to the Present* (Tokyo: Kodansha International, 1987); and Ken Tadashi Oshima, *International Architecture in Interwar Japan: Constructing Kokusai Kenchiku* (Seattle: University of Washington Press, 2009).

23 → See Kurt G. F. Helfrich and William Whitaker, eds., *Crafting a Modern World: The Architecture and Design of Antonin and Noémi Raymond* (New York: Princeton Architectural Press, 2006).

24 → See Angela Schneider, Gabriele Knapstein, David Elliott, and Mami Kataoka, eds., *Berlin–Tokyo/Tokyo–Berlin, die Kunst zweier Städte* (Berlin: Staatliche Museen zu Berlin; and Ostfildern, Germany: Hatje Cantz, 2006).

25 → Bruno Taut, *Houses and People of Japan* (Tokyo: Sanseido, 1937).

26 → See Philip Goodwin, with photographs by G. E. Kidder Smith, *Brazil Builds: Architecture New and Old, 1652–1942* (New York: Museum of Modern Art, 1943).

27 → See Geraldo Ferraz, *Warchavchik e a introdução da nova arquitetura no Brasil: 1925 to 1940* (São Paulo: MASP, 1965); and José Talvares Correia de Lira, "Ruptura e construção: a obra de Gregori Warchavchik," *Novos Estudos* 78 (July 2007): 145–67.

28 → On Kalnay, see Ramon Gutierrez, ed., *Andrés Kálnay: Un húngaro para la renovación arquitectónica argentina* (Buenos Aires: Cedodal, 2002).

29 → See Jorge Francisco Liernur, *La arquitectura en la Argentina del siglo XX: la construcción de la modernidad* (Buenos Aires: Fondo Nacional de las Artes, 2001); and Jorge Francisco and Fernando Aliata, eds., *Diccionario de Arquitectura en la Argentina: estilos, obras, biografías, instituciones, ciudades*, 6 vols. (Buenos Aires: Clarín/Arquitectura, 2004).

21 Colonial experiences and new nationalisms

1 → Mark Crinson, *Modern Architecture and the End of Empire* (Aldershot, UK: Ashgate, 2003).

2 → See François Béguin, *Arabisances: décor architectural et tracé urbain en Afrique du Nord, 1830–1950* (Paris: Dunod, 1983); and Catherine Bruant, Sylviane Leprun, and Mercedes Volait, eds., *Figures de l'orientalisme en architecture*, special issue of *Revue du monde musulman et de la Méditerranée*, no. 73-74 (1996).

3 → Le Corbusier, "Louanges à l'Algérie," *Journal general Travaux publics et Bâtiment*, 25–27 June 1931, 1; Georges Duhamel, "Considérations … poligéognostiques," *Les nouvelles littéraires*, 9 March 1935.

4 → Manfredo Tafuri, *Progetto e utopia: architettura e sviluppo capitalistico* (Bari, Italy: Laterza, 1973), 117; English: *Architecture and Utopia: Design and Capitalist Development*, trans. Barbara Luigia La Penta (Cambridge, Mass.: MIT Press, 1976), 127.

5 → See Jean-Louis Cohen, Nabila Oulebsir, and Youcef Kanoun, eds., *Alger, paysage urbain et architecture 1800–2000* (Paris: Éditions de l'Imprimeur, 2003).

6 → See Jean-Louis Cohen and Monique Eleb, *Casablanca: mythes et figures d'une aventure urbaine* (Paris: Hazan, 1998); English: *Casablanca: Colonial Myths and Architectural Ventures*, trans. Sarah Parsons (New York: Monacelli Press, 2002).

7 → Robert Saliba, *Beirut 1920–1940: Domestic Architecture between Tradition and Modernity* (Beirut: Ordre des Architectes et Ingénieurs de Beyrouth, 1998).

8 → See Jade Tabet, ed., *Beyrouth: Portrait de ville* (Paris: Institut français d'architecture, 2001).

9 → See Gilbert Herbert, *Rex Martienssen and the International Style: The Modern Movement in South African Architecture* (Cape Town: Balkema, 1975); and Clive M. Chipkin, *Johannesburg Style: Architecture & Society, 1880s–1960s* (Cape Town: D. Philip Publishers, 1993).

10 → See Huib Akihary, *Architectuur en stedebouw in Indonesië, 1870–1970* (Zutphen, Netherlands: De Walburg Pers, 1990); and Peter J. M. Nas, ed., *The Past in the Present, Architecture in Indonesia* (Rotterdam: NAi Publishers, 2007).

11 → See Mercedes Volait, *Le Caire–Alexandrie, architectures européennes, 1850–1950* (Cairo: CEDEJ/IFAO, 2001).

12 → See Robert Ilbert, *Héliopolis 1905–1922: la genèse d'une ville* (Paris: Éditions du CNRS, 1981).

13 → See Mercedes Volait, *L'architecture moderne en Egypte et la revue "Al-'Imara"* (Cairo: CEDEJ/IFAO, 1987).

14 → See Dario Matteoni, ed., "Architecture in the Italian Colonies in Africa," thematic issue, *Rassegna* 51 (September 1992); Giuliano Gresleri, Pier Giorgio Massaretti, and Stefano Zagnoni, eds., *Architettura italiana d'oltremare: 1870–1940* (Venice: Marsilio, 1993); and Ruth Ben-Ghiat and Mia Fuller, eds., *Italian Colonialism* (New York: Palgrave Macmillan, 2005).

15 → Ottavio Cabiati, statement made in 1936; cited in Vassilis Kolonas, *Italian Architecture in the Dodecanese Islands, 1912–1943* (Athens: Olkos, 2002) 23–24.

16 → See Edward Denison, Guang Yu Ren, and Naigzy Gebremedhin, *Asmara: Africa's Secret Modernist City* (London and New York: Merrell, 2003).

17 → Le Corbusier's drawings for Addis Ababa were kept for many years in the archives of Giuseppe Bottai. See Giorgio Ciucci, "A Roma con Bottai," *Rassegna* 2, no. 3 (July 1980): 66–71.

18 → See Sibel Bozdoğan, *Modernism and Nation Building: Turkish Architectural Culture in the Early Republic* (Seattle: University of Washington Press, 2001).

19 → See Bernd Nicolai, "Der neue Bruno Taut, die neue Türkei," in Manfred Speidel, ed., *Bruno Taut, Natur und Fantasie 1880–1938* (Berlin: Ernst & Sohn, 1995), 317–25; and Bernd Nicolai, *Moderne und Exil: deutschsprachige Architekten in der Türkei 1925–1955* (Berlin: Verlag für Bauwesen, 1998). See also Esra Akcan, *Çeviride Modern Olan–Çehir ve Konutta Türk-Alman İlişkileri* (Istanbul: Yapı Kredi Yayınları, 2009); and Esra Akcan, *Modernity in Translation: Intertwined Histories of Residential Architecture* (Durham, NC: Duke University Press, 2011).

20 → See Mina Marefat, "Building to Power: Architecture of Tehran 1921–1941" (Ph.D. diss., Massachusetts Institute of Technology, 1988); and Elisabeth Vitou, with Dominique Deshoulières and Hubert Jeanneau, *Gabriel Guévrékian, 1900–1970: une autre architecture moderne* (Paris: Connivences, 1987).

21 → See Jeffrey W. Cody, *Exporting American Architecture, 1870–2000* (London: Routledge, 2003).

22 → See Jeannine Fiedler, ed., *Social Utopias of the Twenties: Bauhaus, Kibbutz and the Dream of the New Man* (Wuppertal, Germany: Müller & Busman Press, 1995).

23 → Erich Mendelsohn, letter to Oskar Beyer, 30 April 1935, in Oskar Beyer, ed., *Eric Mendelsohn: Letters of an Architect*, trans. Geoffrey Strachan, intro. Nikolaus Pevsner (London: Abelard-Schuman, 1967), 142.

24 → See Michael Levin, *White City: International Style Architecture in Israel: Portrait of an Era* (Tel Aviv: Tel Aviv Museum, 1984); Nitza Metzger-Szmuk, *Dwelling on the Dunes, Tel Aviv: Modern Movement and Bauhaus Ideals*, trans. Vivianne Barsky (Paris and Tel-Aviv: Éditions de l'Éclat, 2004); and Catherine Weill-Rochant, *L'Atlas de Tel-Aviv, 1908–2008* (Paris: CNRS Editions, 2008).

25 → Emil Kaufmann, *Von Ledoux bis Le Corbusier: Ursprung und Entwicklung der autonomen Architektur* (Vienna and Leipzig: Verlag Dr. Rolf Passer, 1933).

26 → Sharon Rotbart, "Wall and Tower (Homa Oumigdal): The Mold of Israeli Architecture," in Eyal Weizman and Rafi Segal, eds., *A Civilian Occupation: The Politics of Israeli Architecture* (New York: Verso; and Tel Aviv: Babel, 2004), 39–56.

22 Architecture of a total war

1 → See Jean-Louis Cohen, *Architecture in Uniform: Designing and Building for World War II* (Paris: Hazan, 2011).

2 → Filippo Tommaso Marinetti, *Poema africano della divisione "28 ottobre"* (Milan: Mondadori, 1937), 28. The original text has no punctuation marks. The passage is quoted here following the English in Walter Benjamin, "The Work of Art in the Age of Mechanical Reproduction," in *Illuminations*, trans. Harry Zohn (New York: Schocken, 1968), 241–42.

3 → Benjamin, "The Work of Art," 242.

4 → See Paul Virilio, *Bunker archéologie* (Paris: Centre Georges Pompidou, 1975); English: *Bunker Archeology*, trans. George Collins (New York: Princeton Architectural Press, 1994).

5 → See Jun Sakudo and Takao Shiba, eds., *World War II and the Transformation of Business Systems*, vol. 20 of *The International Conference on Business History: Proceedings of the Fuji Conference* (Tokyo: University of Tokyo Press, 1994).

6 → See "Producer of Production Lines," *Architectural Forum* 91 (June 1942): 39–42. See also Federico Bucci, *Albert Kahn: Architect of Ford* (New York: Princeton Architectural Press, 1993), 105–16.

7 → See "Windowless Defense Plant," *Pencil Points* 24 (February 1943): 107–10; and "War Requirements to Accelerate Progressive Design," *Architectural Record* 91 (January 1942): 65–68.

8 → See Winfried Nerdinger and Ute Brüning, eds., *Bauhaus-Moderne im Nationalsozialismus: zwischen Anbiederung und Verfolgung* (Munich: Prestel, 1993);

and Ulrich Brinkmann. "Luftwaffen-Moderne: Herbert Rimpls Flugzeugwerke in Oranienburg," *Archithese* 29 (September–October 1999): 24–29.

9 → Le Corbusier, *Sur les quatre routes* (Paris: Gallimard, 1941), 18; English: *The Four Routes*, trans. Dorothy Todd (London: Dennis Dobson, 1947), 15.

10 → See Thomas S. Hines, *Richard Neutra and the Search for Modern Architecture: A Biography and History* (New York: Oxford University Press, 1982), 175–80.

11 → See David S. Geer, "Oak Ridge: A World War II New Town," *American Institute of Architects Journal* 15 (January 1951): 16–20. See also Nicholas Adams, *Skidmore, Owings & Merrill: The Experiment since 1936* (Milan: Electa, 2006), 23–24.

12 → See Robert Jan van Pelt and Deborah Dwork, *Auschwitz: 1270 to the Present* (New Haven: Yale University Press, 1996).

13 → See "Biggest Office Building," *Architectural Forum* 75 (September 1941): 2, 4; "Pentagon Building," *Architectural Forum* 78 (January 1943): 37–52; and "The Army's Pentagon Building," *Architectural Record* 93 (January 1943): 63–70.

14 → See Marlene P. Hiller, Eberhard Jäckel, and Jürgen Rohwer, eds., *Städte im Zweiten Weltkrieg: Ein internationaler Vergleich* (Essen, Germany: Klartext Verlag, 1991). See also the essays by the novelist W. G. Sebald, *On the Natural History of Destruction* (New York: Random House, 2003).

15 → Lieutenant-Colonel [Arsène Marie Paul] Vauthier, *Le danger aérien et l'avenir du pays* (Nancy, Paris, and Strasbourg: Berger-Levrault, 1930). Giulio Douhet's seminal text is *Il dominio dell'aria: saggio sull'arte della guerra aerea* (Rome: Stabilimento poligrafico per l'amministrazione della guerra, 1921); English: *The Command of the Air* (New York: Coward-McCann, 1942).

16 → Hans Schoszberger, *Bautechnischer Luftschutz* (Berlin: Bauwelt-Verlag, 1934).

17 → See Koos Bosma, *Schuilstad: Bescherming van de bevolking tegen luchtaavallen* (Amsterdam: SUN, 2006); English: *Shelter City: Protecting Citizens against Air Raids* (Amsterdam: Amsterdam University Press, 2011).

18 → Tecton, *Planned A.R.P.: Based on the Investigation of Structural Protection against Air Attack in the Metropolitan Borough of Finsbury* (London: Architectural Press, 1939).

19 → See Timothy Newark, *Camouflage: Now You See Me, Now You Don't* (London: Thames & Hudson, 2007).

20 → See Henrietta Goodden, *Camouflage and Art: Design and Deception in World War 2* (London: Unicorn Press, 2007). See also John L. Scott, László Moholy-Nagy, and György Kepes, "Civilian Camouflage Goes into Action," "A Bird's-Eye View of Camouflage," and "Materials for the Camoufleur," in *Civilian Defense* 1 (June 1942): 7–11; (July–August 1942): 10–14 and 37; (September 1942): 13–16.

21 → See Wolfgang Voigt, "Standardization, War and Architecture: The Work of Ernst Neufert," *Archis* 10 (October 1995): 58–65.

22 → See Mike Davis, "Berlin's Skeletons in Utah's Closet," in *Dead Cities and Other Tales* (New York: W. W. Norton, 2002), 64–83; and Enrique Ramirez, "Erich Mendelsohn at War," *Perspecta* 41 (2008): 83–91; Enrique Ramirez, "Fata Morgana", *Thresholds* 33 (2008): 51–60.

23 → See Max Mengeringhausen, *Die MERO-Bauweise* (Berlin: self-published, 1942); and Max Mengeringhausen, *Komposition im Raum: die Kunst individueller Baugestaltung mit Serienelementen*. (Gütersloh, Germany: Bertelsmann, 1983). See also Karl-Eugen Kurrer, "Ingenieurportrait: Max Mengeringhausen, ein Komponist von Raumfachwerken," *Deutsche Bauzeitung* 138 (October 2004): 88–95.

24 → See Gilbert Herbert, *The Dream of the Factory-Made House: Walter Gropius and Konrad Wachsmann* (Cambridge, Mass.: MIT Press, 1984), 243–325.

25 → See Julie Decker and Chris Chiei, *Quonset Hut: Metal Living for a Modern Age* (New York: Princeton Architectural Press, 2005).

26 → See Nicholas Bullock, "New Ways of Building for Houses and Schools," in *Building the Post-War World: Modern Architecture and Reconstruction in Britain* (London: Routledge, 2002), 169–98.

27 → Le Corbusier. *Sur les quatre routes*, 18; *The Four Routes*, 15.

28 → Carl von Clausewitz, *On War*, ed. and trans. Michael Howard and Peter Paret (Princeton: Princeton University Press, 1984).

29 → Jean-Louis Cohen and Hartmut Frank, eds., *Les relations franco-allemandes 1940–1950 et leurs effets sur l'architecture et la forme urbaine* (Hamburg: Hochschule für bildende Künste; and Paris: École d'Architecture Paris-Villemin, 1989).

30 → See Niels Gutschow and Barbara Klain, *Vernichtung und Utopie: Stadtplanung Warschau 1939–1945* (Hamburg: Junius Verlag, 1994).

31 → See Werner Durth, *Deutsche Architekten: biographische Verflechtungen, 1900–1970* (Braunschweig: F. Vieweg & Sohn, 1988).

32 → See Andrew M. Shanken, *194X: Architecture, Planning, and Consumer Culture on the American Home Front* (Minneapolis: University of Minnesota Press, 2009).

33 → Eric Mumford, *The CIAM Discourse on Urbanism, 1928–1960* (Cambridge, Mass.: MIT Press, 2000).

34 → José Luís Sert, Fernand Léger, and Sigfried Giedion, "Nine Points on Monumentality" (1943), in *S. Giedion, Architecture, You and Me: The Diary of a Development* (Cambridge, Mass.: MIT Press, 1950), 49, 50.

35 → See "Spitfires to Saucepans," in *Britain Can Make It*, supplement to the *Board of Trade Journal*, 28 September 1946, 4–5; and "War to Peace," in Council of Industrial Design, *Britain Can Make It* (London: His Majesty's Stationery Office, 1946), 217–20.

36 → See Joachim Krausse and Claude Lichtenstein, *Your Private Sky: R. Buckminster Fuller, the Art of Design Science* (Baden: Lars Müller, 1999), 228–49; Michael John Gorman, *Buckminster Fuller, Designing for Mobility* (Milan: Skira, 2005), 70–78; and Federico Neder, *Fuller Houses: R. Buckminster Fuller's Dymaxion Houses and Other Domestic Adventures* (Baden: Lars Müller, 2008), 61–85.

37 → See Gunnar Brand, "Bekenntnisse eines Angepaßten: der Architekt Wilhelm Kreis als Generalbaurat für die Gestaltung der deutschen Kriegerfriedhöfe," in Ulrich Kuder, ed., *Architektur und Ingenieurwesen zur Zeit der nationalsozialistischen Gewaltherrschaft* (Berlin: Gebrüder Mann Verlag, 1997), 124–56.

38 → Hideto Kishida, *Kako no kôsei* (Tokyo: Kôseisha, 1929).

39 → See Adachiara Zevi, *Fosse Ardeatine, Roma* (Turin: Testo e Immagine, 2000).

40 → See Bruno Reichlin and Ulrike Jehle-Schulte Strathaus, "Parole di pietra—architettura di parole," in Marco Pogačnik, ed., *BBPR: Monumento ai caduti nei campi nazisti—1945-1995, il segno della memoria* (Milan: Electa, 1995), 11–53.

23 Tabula rasa to horror vacui: reconstruction and renaissance

1 → See Tony Judt, *Postwar: A History of Europe since 1945* (New York: Penguin, 2006); and Henry Heller, *The Cold War and the New Imperialism: A Global History, 1945–2005* (New York: Monthly Review Press, 2006).

2 → See Elizabeth Mock, ed., *Built in USA, 1932–1944* (New York: Museum of Modern Art, 1944). The catalog also appeared in German, French, and Italian editions.

3 → See Victoria de Grazia, *Irresistible Empire: America's Advance through Twentieth-Century Europe* (Cambridge, Mass.: Belknap Press of Harvard University Press, 2005), 336–75.

4 → See Ruth Oldenziel and Karin Zachmann, eds., *Cold War Kitchen: Americanization, Technology, and European Users* (Cambridge, Mass.: MIT Press, 2009).

5 → See Dominique Barjot, Rémi Baudouï, and Danièle Voldman, eds., *Reconstructions en Europe 1945–1949* (Brussels: Éditions Complexe, 1997).

6 → Max Bill, *Wiederaufbau: Dokumente über Zerstörungen, Planungen, Konstruktionen* (Zurich: Verlag für Architektur, 1945).

7 → See Boleslaw Bierut, *The Six-Year Plan for the Reconstruction of Warsaw* (Warsaw: Książka i Wiedza, 1951).

8 → See Jean-Charles Moreux, "Quelques considérations sur l'aménagement des villes," *L'illustration*, 24 May 1941, n.p.

9 → See Werner Durth and Niels Gutschow, *Träume in Trümmern: Planung zum Wiederaufbau zerstorter Städte im Westen Deutschlands 1940-1950* (Braunschweig: F. Vieweg & Sohn, 1988).

10 → See Anatole Kopp, Frédérique Boucher, and Danièle Pauly, *L'architecture de la reconstruction en France, 1945–1953* (Paris: Éditions du Moniteur, 1982); and Danièle Voldman, *Reconstruction des villes françaises de 1940 à 1954: histoire d'une politique* (Paris: L'Harmattan, 1997).

11 → Le Corbusier to the inhabitants of Saint Dié, 27 October 1945; quoted in Édouard Mure and Nathalie Régnier, "Saint-Dié: chronique d'un échec," in Jacques Lucan, ed., *Le Corbusier 1887–1965, une encyclopédie* (Paris: Centre Georges Pompidou, 1987), 363.

12 → See Jean-Louis Cohen and Hartmut Frank, eds., "Architettura dell'occupazione: Francia e Germania 1940–1950," *Casabella* 567 (April 1990): 40–58.

13 → See Patrizia Bonifazio, "La rivista 'Comunità': il territorio e i suoi confini intellettuali," in Carlo Olmo, ed., *Costruire la città dell'uomo: Adriano Olivetti e l'urbanistica* (Milan: Edizioni di Comunità, 2001), 113–43; and Jean-Louis Cohen, "Le 'nouvel urbanisme' de Gaston Bardet," *Le Visiteur* 2 (Spring 1996): 134–47.

14 → See Jean-Louis Cohen, *André Lurçat (1904–1970), autocritique d'un moderne* (Liège: Pierre Mardaga, 1995), 252–59; and Paul Hilaire, "Maubeuge ville neuve: la reconstruction de la ville par André Lurçat" (diploma thesis, École d'Architecture de Lille et des régions Nord, 1988).

15 → Carola Hein, Jeffry M. Diefendorf, and Ishida Yorifusa, eds., *Rebuilding Urban Japan after 1945* (Houndmills: Palgrave Macmillan, 2003).

16 → Carlos Sambricio, *Cuando se quiso resucitar la arquitectura* (Murcia: Comisión de cultura del colegio oficial de aparejadores y arquitectos técnicos, 1983).

17 → Nicholas Bullock, "The Search for New Directions after 1945," in *Building the Post-War World: Modern Architecture and Reconstruction in Britain* (London: Routledge, 2002), 39–60.

18 → *County of London Plan: Prepared for the London County Council by J. H. Forshaw and Patrick Abercrombie* (London: Macmillan, 1943).

19 → Royal Commission on the Distribution of the Industrial Population, *Report* (London: HMSO, 1940).

20 → Frederick Gibberd, *Town Design* (New York: Reinhold; and London: Architectural Press, 1953).

21 → Rudolf Schwarz, *Von der Bebauung der Erde* (Heidelberg: L. Schneider, 1949).

22 → "Die 16 Grundsätze des Städtebaus," in Lothar Bolz, *Von deutschem Bauen: Reden und Aufsätze* (Berlin: Verlag der Nation, 1951), 32–52; English: in Joan Ockman with Edward Eigen, ed., *Architecture Culture 1943–1968: A Documentary Anthology* (New York: Rizzoli, 1993), 125–28.

23 → See Bernhard Schulz, ed., *Grauzonen, Farbwelten: Kunst und Zeitbilder; 1945–1955* (Berlin: Medusa, 1983); Klaus von Beyme, Werner Durth, Niels Gutschow, Winfried Nerdinger, and Thomas Topfstedt, eds., *Neue Städte aus Ruinen: deutscher Städtebau der Nachkriegszeit* (Munich: Prestel, 1992); and Jeffry M. Diefendorf, *In the Wake of War: The Reconstruction of German Cities after World War II* (New York: Oxford University Press, 1993).

24 → See Helmut Geisert and Carola Hein, eds., *Hauptstadt Berlin: Internationaler städtebaulicher Ideenwettberb 1957/1958* (Berlin: Argon Verlag, 1990).

25 → Henry-Russell Hitchcock, "The Architecture of Bureaucracy and the Architecture of Genius," *Architectural Review* 101 (January 1947): 3–6.

24 The fatal crisis of the Modern Movement, and the alternatives

1 → Sir Philip Powell, quoted in Elain Harwood and Alan Powers, eds., *Festival of Britain* (London: Twentieth Century Society, 2001), 85; see also the London Observer film *Brief City: The Story of London's Festival Buildings* (1952), released by the Twentieth Century Society in connection with this book; and Becky E. Conekin, *"The Autobiography of a Nation": The 1951 Festival of Britain* (Manchester: Manchester University Press, 2003).

2 → See "Foreword" and Anon., "The Exhibition as a Town Builder's Pattern Book," *Architectural Review* 110 (August 1951): 75, 107.

3 → Introduction to thematic issue "Man Made America," *Architectural Review* 108 (December 1950): 339, 343.

4 → Gordon Cullen, *Townscape* (London: Architectural Press, 1961).

5 → See Jean-Louis Cohen, *La coupure entre architectes et intellectuels, ou les enseignements de l'italophilie* (Paris: École d'architecture Paris-Villemin, 1984).

6 → See Maristella Casciato, "On Neorealism in Italian Architecture," in Sarah Williams Goldhagen and Réjean Legault, eds., *Anxious Modernisms* (Cambridge, Mass.: MIT Press; and Montreal: Canadian Centre for Architecture, 2000), 25–53.

7 → G. E. Kidder Smith, *Italy Builds: Its Modern Architecture and Native Inheritance* (New York: Reinhold, 1954).

8 → Philip L. Goodwin, with photographs by G. E. Kidder Smith, *Brazil Builds: Architecture New and Old, 1652–1942* (New York: Museum of Modern Art, 1943); "Architecture of Brazil," *Architectural Record* 93 (January 1943): 34–56; "Brazil," *Architectural Review* 95 (March 1944): 58–84; "Brazil Still Builds," *Progressive Architecture* 28 (April 1947): 1–64; and "Brésil," thematic issue, *L'architecture d'aujourd'hui* 13–14 (1947).

9 → Henry-Russell Hitchcock, *Latin American Architecture since 1945* (New York: Museum of Modern Art, 1955), 26.

10 → See Henrique E. Mindlin, *Modern Architecture in Brazil* (London: Architectural Press, 1956).

11 → See Nabil Bonduki and Carmen Portinho, *Affonso Eduardo Reidy* (São Paulo: Editorial Blau; Instituto Lina Bo e P. M. Bardi, 2000).

12 → Max Bill, Peter Craymer, Walter Gropius, Hiroshi Ohye, and Ernesto Rogers, "Report on Brazil," *Architectural Review* 116 (October 1954): 235–40.

13 → See Jean-Louis Cohen, "Le Groupe des Architectes Modernes Marocains et l'habitat du plus grand nombre," *Rassegna* 14 (December 1992): 58–69; and Monique Eleb, "An Alternative to Functionalist Universalism: Ecochard, Candilis and ATBAT-Afrique," in Goldhagen and Legault, *Anxious Modernisms*, 55–73.

14 → See Zeynep Çelik, *Urban Forms and Colonial Confrontations: Algiers under French Rule* (Berkeley: University of California Press, 1997); and Jean-Louis Cohen, Nabila Oulebsir, and Youcef Kanoun, eds., *Alger, paysage urbain et architecture 1800–2000* (Paris: Éditions de l'Imprimeur, 2003).

15 → Adalberto Libera to Arnaldo Foschini, 1951, quoted in Letizia Capannini, "Habitat collectif méditerranéen et dynamique des espaces ouverts," in *Le logement et l'habitat comme objet de recherche,* conference proceedings (Paris: Université de Paris 1, 2005), 12.

16 → Alison Smithson, *Team 10 Meetings* (New York: Rizzoli, 1991), 20.

17 → See Jos Bosman, ed., "Gli ultimi CIAM," *Rassegna* 14 (December 1992).

18 → Jacob Bakema, "Introductory Talk," in Oscar Newman, ed., *CIAM '59 in Otterlo* (Stuttgart: Karl Kramer Verlag, 1961), 22.

19 → Le Corbusier, quoted by Francis Strauven in "The Dutch Contribution: Bakema and van Eyck," *Rassegna* 52 (December 1992): 52. See also Francis Strauven, *Aldo van Eyck: The Shape of Relativity* (Amsterdam: Architectura & Natura, 1998), 118.

20 → "Reaffirmation of the Aims of CIAM," in Sigfried Giedion, ed., *A Decade of Contemporary Architecture* (Zurich: Girsberger, 1951), 17.

21 → Sigfried Giedion, "The Historical Background of the Core," in J. Tyrwhitt, J. L. Sert, and E. N. Rogers, eds., *The Heart of the City: Towards the Humanisation of Urban Life* (New York: Pellegrini and Cudahy, 1952), 17.

22 → See Ernesto N. Rogers, "Le preesistenze ambientali e i temi pratici contemporanei." *Casabella-continuità* (February–March 1955): 3–6; English in Joan Ockman with Edward Eigen, ed., *Architecture Culture 1943–1968: A Documentary Anthology* (New York: Rizzoli, 1993), 200–4.

23 → See Eleb, "An Alternative."

24 → Ernesto N. Rogers, "Pour une déclaration sur le logis," talk given at La Sarraz, Switzerland, 1953, quoted in "Gli ultimi CIAM," *Rassegna* 14 (December 1992): 37.

25 → Johan Huizinga, *Homo ludens: proeve eener bepaling van het spel-element der cultuur* (Haarlem: H.D. Tjeenk Willink, 1938). English: *Homo Ludens: A Study of the Play Element in Culture* (London: Routledge & K. Paul, 1949).

26 → Aldo van Eyck, "Is Architecture Going to Reconcile Basic Values?" talk at the Otterlo CIAM, September 1959, in Aldo van Eyck, *Writings*, ed. Vincent Ligtelijn and Francis Strauven (Amsterdam: SUN, 2008), 202.

27 → See Max Risselada and Dirk van den Heuvel, eds., *Team 10: 1953–1981: In Search of a Utopia of the Present* (Rotterdam: NAi Publishers, 2005).

28 → See Constantinos A. Doxiadis, *Ekistics: An Introduction to the Science of Human Settlements* (New York and Oxford: Oxford University Press, 1968).

29 → See Aymone Nicolas, *L'apogée des concours internationaux d'architecture: l'action de l'UIA, 1948–1975* (Paris: Picard, 2007).

30 → See Otto Bartning, ed., *Darmstädter Gespräch: Mensch und Raum* (Darmstadt: Neue Darmstädter Verlagsanstalt, 1952).

25 Le Corbusier reinvented and reinterpreted

1 → Le Corbusier, letter to Karl Krämer, 5 July 1961, copy sent to Jacob Bakema, Fondation Le Corbusier, Paris, Box G1-20.

2 → Jacques Sbriglio, *Le Corbusier, l'Unité d'habitation de Marseille* (Marseilles: Parenthèses, 1992).

3 → James Stirling, "Ronchamp: Le Corbusier's Chapel and the Crisis of Rationalism," *Architectural Review* 118, no. 3 (September 1955): 155–161. See also Caroline Maniaque, *Le Corbusier and the Maisons Jaoul* (New York: Princeton Architectural Press, 2009).

4 → Le Corbusier, speech delivered at Ronchamp's consecration, 25 June 1955; quoted in Le Corbusier, *The Chapel at Ronchamp* (New York: Frederick A. Praeger, 1957), 25.

5 → Le Corbusier and Jean Petit, *Le poème électronique de Le Corbusier* (Paris: Éditions de Minuit, 1958). See also Marc Treib, *Space Calculated in Seconds: The Philips Pavilion, Le Corbusier, Edgard Varèse* (Princeton: Princeton University Press, 1996).

6 → Kiran Joshi, *Documenting Chandigarh: The Indian Architecture of Pierre Jeanneret, Edwin Maxwell Fry, Jane Beverly Drew* (Ahmedabad: Mapin; and Chandigarh: Chandigarh College of Architecture, 1999).

7 → For critical commentary on Chandigarh see Vikramaditya Prakash, *Chandigarh's Le Corbusier:*
The Struggle for Modernity in Postcolonial India (Seattle: University of Washington Press, 2002); and Charles Correa, "Chandigarh, the View from Benares," in H. Allen Brooks, ed., *Le Corbusier: the Garland Essays* (New York: Garland, 1987), 197–202.

8 → See Sergio Ferro, *Le Corbusier: le couvent de la Tourette* (Marseilles: Parenthèses, 1987).

9 → Le Corbusier, "Je prends Venise à témoin," in *La ville radieuse* (Boulogne-Billancourt: Éditions de l'Architecture d'aujourd'hui, 1935), 269; English in *The Radiant City*, trans. Pamela Knight, Eleanor Levieux, and Derek Coltman (New York: Orion Press, 1967), 269.

10 → Hashim Sarkis, ed., *CASE: Le Corbusier's Venice Hospital and the Mat Building Revival* (Munich, London, and New York: Prestel, 2001).

11 → See the discussion among several members of the London County Council Architects' Department, "Le Corbusier's Unité d'Habitation," *Architectural Review* 109 (May 1951): 293–96.

12 → See Friedrich Achleitner, *Atelier* 5 (Basel: Birkhäuser, 2000).

13 → Reyner Banham, *The New Brutalism: Ethic or Aesthetic* (London: Architectural Press, 1966).

14 → Reyner Banham, "The New Brutalism," *Architectural Review* 118 (December 1955): 355–61.

15 → Reyner Banham, "The Word in Britain: 'Character,' " *Architectural Forum* 121 (August–September 1964): 118–24.

16 → *James Stirling: Building and Projects 1950–1974*, intro. John Jacobus (New York: Oxford University Press, 1975).

17 → Réjean Legault, "The Semantics of Exposed Concrete," in Jean-Louis Cohen and G. Martin Moeller, Jr., eds., *Liquid Stone: New Architecture in Concrete* (New York: Princeton Architectural Press, 2006), 46–56.

18 → See Nicholas Olsberg and Ricardo L. Castro, eds., *Arthur Erickson: Critical Works* (Vancouver: Douglas McIntyre, 2006).

19 → Oscar Niemeyer, "Depoimento," *Módulo* 9 (February 1958): 3–6; quoted in Ugo Segawa, *Arquiteturas no Brasil: 1900–1990* (São Paulo: Editora da Universidade de Saõ Paulo, 1998), 143.

20 → See James Holston, *The Modernist City: An Anthropological Critique of Brasília* (Chicago: University of Chicago Press, 1989).

26 The shape of American hegemony

1 → See, for example, the case of the Netherlands in Hans Ibelings, *Americanism: Dutch Architecture and the Transatlantic Model* (Rotterdam: NAi Publishers, 1997).

2 → Paul Boyer, *By the Bomb's Early Light: American Thought and Culture at the Dawn of the Atomic Age* (New York: Pantheon, 1985); and Tom Vanderbilt, *Survival City: The Architecture of the Cold War* (New York: Princeton Architectural Press, 2002).

3 → See George A. Dudley, *A Workshop for Peace: Designing the United Nations Headquarters* (New York: Architectural History Foundation; and Cambridge, Mass.: MIT Press, 1994).

4 → Arthur Drexler, "Post-War Architecture," in *Built in USA: Post-War Architecture* (New York: Museum of Modern Art, 1952), 26.

5 → See Meredith Clausen, "Belluschi and the Equitable Building in History," *Journal of the Society of Architectural Historians* 50 (June 1991): 109–29.

6 → Ada Louise Huxtable, "Park Avenue School of Architecture," *New York Times Magazine*, 15 December 1957, 30–31.

7 → "Mies' Enormous Room," *Architectural Forum* 105 (August 1956): 105.

8 → Lewis Mumford, "The Lesson of the Master," *New Yorker*, 13 December 1958, 141.

9 → Detlef Mertins, ed., *The Presence of Mies* (Princeton: Princeton Architectural Press, 1994).

10 → Sanka Knox, "21 Artists Assail Museum Interior; Object to Showing Pictures on Spiraling Ramp in Frank Lloyd Wright Building," *New York Times*, 12 December 1956, 46.

11 → Frank Lloyd Wright, quoted in Herbert Muschamp, *Man about Town* (Cambridge, Mass.: MIT Press, 1983), 185.

12 → William Allin Storer has identified 433 structures built during Wright's lifetime; see William Allin Storer, *The Architecture of Frank Lloyd Wright: A Complete Catalogue* (Cambridge, Mass.: MIT Press, 1974).

13 → See Frank Escher, ed., *John Lautner, Architect* (London: Artemis, 1994); Frank Escher, and Nicholas Olsberg, eds., *Between Earth and Heaven: The Architecture of John Lautner* (Los Angeles: Armand Hammer Museum; and New York: Rizzoli, 2008).

14 → Alexandre Persitz, "Un architecte d'aujourd'hui," *L'Architecture d'aujourd'hui* 6 (May–June 1946): 9.

15 → See Sylvia Lavin, *Form Follows Libido: Architecture and Richard Neutra in a Psychoanalytic Culture* (Cambridge, Mass.: MIT Press, 2004); and David Leatherbarrow, *Uncommon Ground: Architecture, Technology, and Topography* (Cambridge, Mass.: MIT Press, 2000).

16 → On the Case Study program, see Elisabeth A. T. Smith, ed., *Blueprints for Modern Living: History and Legacy of the Case Study Houses* (Los Angeles: Museum of Contemporary Art, 1989); and Ethel Buisson and Thomas Billard, *Presence of the Case Study Houses* (Basel and Boston: Birkhäuser, 2004).

17 → See Winfried Nerdinger, *The Architect Walter Gropius* (Berlin: Gebr. Mann, 1985); and Reginald R. Isaacs and Georg G. Meerwein, *Walter Gropius: der Mensch und sein Werk*, 2 vols. (Berlin: Mann, 1983).

18 → See Marcel Breuer and Cranston Jones, *Marcel Breuer: 1921–1962.* (Stuttgart: Gerd Hatje, 1962); Alexander von Vegesack and Mathias Remmele, eds., *Marcel Breuer: Design and Architecture* (Weil am Rhein: Vitra Design Museum, 2003); and Réjean Legault, "The Semantics of Exposed Concrete," in Jean-Louis Cohen and G. Martin Moeller, Jr., eds., *Liquid Stone: New Architecture in Concrete* (New York: Princeton Architectural Press, 2006), 76–95.

19 → Statement by Eero Saarinen, January 1959, quoted in Aline B. Saarinen, ed., *Eero Saarinen on His Work* (New Haven: Yale University Press, 1968), 68.

20 → See Donald Albrecht and Eeva-Liisa Pelkonen, eds., *Eero Saarinen: Shaping the Future* (New Haven: Yale University Press, 2006).

21 → On Johnson's relationship to power and the way he wielded it, see Franz Schulze, *Philip Johnson: Life and Work* (New York: Knopf, 1996).

22 → Philip Johnson, "The Seven Crutches of Modern Architecture," transcript of a lecture given at Harvard University in 1954, *Perspecta* 3 (1955): 41–43.

23 → See Richard Saul Wurman, *What Will Be Has Always Been: The Words of Louis I. Kahn* (New York: Access Press and Rizzoli, 1986); David B. Brownlee and David G. De Long, eds., *Louis I. Kahn: In the Realm of Architecture* (New York: Rizzoli, 1991); and Sarah Williams Goldhagen, *Louis Kahn's Situated Modernism* (New Haven: Yale University Press, 2001).

24 → Victor Gruen and Larry Smith, *Shopping Towns USA: The Planning of Shopping Centers* (New York: Reinhold, 1960). See also Alex Wall, *Victor Gruen: From Urban Shop to New City* (Barcelona: Actar, 2005).

25 → See Morris Lapidus, *Too Much Is Never Enough* (New York: Rizzoli, 1996).

26 → See Jane C. Loeffler, *The Architecture of Diplomacy: Building America's Embassies* (New York: Princeton Architectural Press, 1998); and Annabel Jane Wharton, *Building the Cold War: Hilton International Hotels and Modern Architecture* (Chicago: University of Chicago Press, 2001).

27 Repression and diffusion of modernism

1 → See Anders Åman, *Architecture and Ideology in Eastern Europe during the Stalin Era: An Aspect of Cold War History* (New York: Architectural History Foundation; and Cambridge, Mass.: MIT Press, 1992); and Carmen Popescu, ed., "Behind the Iron Curtain: Architecture in the Former Communist Bloc, between Isolation and Fascination," thematic issue, *Journal of Architecture* 14, nos. 1 and 2 (2009).

2 → Vyacheslav K. Oltarzhevsky, *Stroitelstvo vysotnykh zdanii v Moskve* (Moscow: Gosusdartvennoe izdatelstvo literatury po stroitelstvu i arkhitekture, 1953).

3 → Edmund Goldzamt, *Urbanistyka krajów socjalistycznych: problemy spoleczne* (Warsaw: Arkady, 1971).

4 → See Wilma Fairbank. *Liang and Lin: Partners in Exploring China's Architectural Past* (Philadelphia: University of Pennsylvania Press, 1994); and Léon Hoa, *Reconstruire la Chine: trente ans d'urbanisme, 1949–1979* (Paris: Éditions du Moniteur, 1981).

5 → See Peter G. Rowe and Seng Kuan, *Architectural Encounters with Essence and Form in Modern China* (Cambridge, Mass.: MIT Press, 2002).

6 → See Catherine Cooke, "Modernity and Realism: Architectural Relations in the Cold War," in Susan E. Reid, ed., *Russian Art and the West: A Century of Dialogue in Painting, Architecture and the Decorative Arts* (DeKalb: Northern Illinois University Press, 2007), 172–94.

7 → Alvar Aalto, "Esipuheena keskustelu," in Leonardo Mosso, *Alvar Aalto, teokset 1918–1967* (Helsinki: Otava, 1967), 5; English: "Conversation as Preface," in Aarno Ruusuvuori, ed., *Alvar Aalto 1898–1970* (Helsinki: Museum of Finnish Architecture, 1978), 167.

8 → Alvar Aalto, "Euroopan jälleenrakentaminen tuo pinnalle aikamme rakennustaiteen keskeisimmän probleemin," *Arkkitehti* 5 (1941): 78–80; English: "The Reconstruction of Europe Is the Key Problem for the Architecture of Our Time," in Göran Schildt, ed., *Alvar Aalto in His Own Words* (New York: Rizzoli, 1998), 154.

9 → See Göran Schildt, Alvar Aalto, *The Mature Years* (New York: Rizzoli, 1991); Peter Reed, ed., *Alvar Aalto: Between Humanism and Materialism* (New York: Museum of Modern Art, Harry N. Abrams, 1998); and

Eeva-Liisa Pelkonen, *Alvar Aalto: Architecture, Modernity, and Geopolitics* (New Haven: Yale University Press, 2009).

10 → Alvar Aalto, "Valtakunnansuunitellu ja kulttuurimme tavoitteet," *Suomalainen Suomi*, 1949; English: "National Planning and Cultural Goals," in Ruusuvuori, *Alvar Aalto*, 142.

11 → See "Sakakura Associates: Half a Century in Step with Postwar Architectural Modernism," thematic issue, *Process Architecture* 110 (1993).

12 → See Jonathan M. Reynolds, *Maekawa Kunio and the Emergence of Japanese Modernist Architecture* (Berkeley: University of California Press, 2001).

13 → See Udo Kultermann, *Kenzo Tange 1946–1969; Architecture and Urban Design* (Zurich: Artemis, 1970); and Ines Tolic, "Skopje 1963–1966: politica, città e memoria in (ri)costruzione" (Ph.D. diss., Scuola Studi di Avanzati di Venezia, 2009).

14 → See Edward R. Burian, ed., *Modernity and the Architecture of Mexico* (Austin: University of Texas Press, 1997); and Valerie Fraser, *Building the New World: Studies in the Modern Architecture of Latin America 1930–1960* (London: Verso, 2000).

15 → See Raúl Rispa, ed., *Barragán: The Complete Works* (New York: Princeton Architectural Press, 1996); Federica Zanco, ed., *Luis Barragán: The Quiet Revolution* (Milan: Skira, 2001); and Danièle Pauly with Jérôme Habersetzer, *Barragan: Space and Shadow, Walls and Colour* (Basel: Birkhäuser, 2002).

16 → See Carlos Brillembourg, "Architecture and Sculpture: Villanueva and Calder's Aula Magna," in Carlos Brillembourg, ed., *Latin American Architecture 1929–1960: Contemporary Reflections* (New York: Monacelli Press, 2004), 61–73.

17 → See Gio Ponti, "Coraggio del Venezuela" and "Idea per Caracas," *Domus* 295 (June 1954): 1–7; 8–13. See also Mónica Ponce de León, "Gio Ponti: Snapshots from Caracas," *Journal of the Society of Architectural Historians* 57 (December 1998): 460–63.

18 → See Roberto Segre. *Cuba, l'architettura della rivoluzione* (Padua: Marsilio, 1970).

19 → See Hugo Segawa, *Arquiteturas no Brasil: 1900–1990* (São Paulo: Editora da Universidade de São Paulo, 1998).

20 → See Marcelo Carvalho Ferraz, ed., *Lina Bo Bardi* (Milan: Editions Charta; and São Paulo: Instituto Lina Bo e P. M. Bardi, 1994).

21 → See Stanford Anderson, ed., *Eladio Dieste: Innovation in Structural Art* (New York: Princeton Architectural Press, 2004).

22 → See Georges Arbid, "Practicing Modernism in Beirut: Architecture in Lebanon, 1946–1970" (Ph.D. diss., Graduate School of Design, Harvard University, 2002).

23 → See Rifat Chadirji, *Concepts and Influences: Towards a Regionalized International Architecture, 1952–1978* (London and New York: KPI, 1986).

24 → See Alexandros-Andreas Kyrtsis, *Constantinos A. Doxiadis: Texts, Design Drawings, Settlements* (Athens: Ikaros, 2006).

25 → See Yannis Aesopos and Yorgos Simeoforidis, eds., *Landscapes of Modernisation: Greek Architecture 1960's and 1990's* (Athens: Metapolis, 1999).

26 → See Françoise Fromonot, *Jørn Utzon et l'Opéra de Sydney* (Paris: Gallimard, 1998); English: *Jørn Utzon: The Sydney Opera House*, trans. Christopher Thompson (Corte Madera, CA: Gingko Press, 2008).

28 Toward new utopias

1 → Reyner Banham, "Neo-Liberty: The Italian Retreat from Modern Architecture," *Architectural Review* 125 (April 1959): 231–35.

2 → See Paolo Portoghesi, "Dal neorealismo al neoliberty," *Comunità* 65 (1958): 65–79.

3 → See Gio Ponti, *Amate l'architettura: l'architettura è un cristallo* (Genoa: Società editrice Vitali e Ghianda, 1957), 51; English: *In Praise of Architecture*, trans. Giuseppina and Mario Salvadori (New York: F. W. Dodge, 1960), 55.

4 → Ernesto N. Rogers, "L'evoluzione dell'architettura, risposta al custode dei frigidaires," *Casabella-continuità* 228 (June 1959): 2; English: "The Evolution of Architecture: Reply to the Custodian of Frigidaires," in Joan Ockman with Edward Eigen, ed., *Architecture Culture 1943–1968: A Documentary Anthology* (New York: Rizzoli, 1993), 303.

5 → Luigi Moretti, "Valori della modanatura," *Spazio* 6 (December 1951–April 1952): 12.

6 → Sigfried Giedion, *Mechanization Takes Command: A Contribution to Anonymous History* (New York: Oxford University Press, 1948).

7 → See Alison Smithson and Peter Smithson, "But Today We Collect Ads," *Ark* 18 (November 1956): 49–53.

8 → See David Robbins, ed., *The Independent Group: Postwar Britain and the Aesthetics of Plenty* (Cambridge, Mass., and London: MIT Press, 1990).

9 → *Archigram* 3 (Autumn 1963).

10 → Peter Cooke, ed., *Archigram* (London: Studio Vista, 1973), 39.

11 → Reyner Banham, "A Home Is Not a House," *Art in America* 53 (April 1965): 70.

12 → On the end of Archigram, see Martin Pawley, " 'We Shall Not Bulldoze Westminster Abbey': Archigram and the Retreat from Technology," *Oppositions* 7 (Winter 1976): 25–33.

13 → See Cedric Price, *Works II* (London: Architectural Association, 1984). See also Mary Louise Lobsinger, "Cybernetic Theory and the Architecture of Performance: Cedric Price's Fun Palace," in Réjean Legault and Sarah Williams Goldhagen, eds., *Anxious Modernisms* (Cambridge, Mass.: MIT Press; and Montreal: Canadian Centre for Architecture, 2000), 119–40.

14 → Mark Wigley, *Constant's New Babylon: The Hyper-Architecture of Desire* (Rotterdam: Witte de With Center for Contemporary Art and 010 Publishers, 1998).

15 → See three books by Yona Friedman: *L'architecture mobile: vers une cité conçue par ses habitants* (Tournai, Belgium: Casterman, 1970); *Toward a Scientific Architecture*, trans. Cynthia Lang (Cambridge, Mass: MIT Press, 1975); and *Yona Friedman: Structures Serving the Unpredictable* (Rotterdam: NAi Publishers, 1999).

16 → Noburo Kawazoe, "Metabolism 1960: The Proposal for a New Urbanism," *Bijutsu shuppansha* (April 1960): 49; English: in Cherie Wendelken, "Putting Metabolism Back in Place," in Legault and Goldhagen, *Anxious Modernisms*, 287.

17 → Fumihiko Maki, *Investigations in Collective Form* (St. Louis: Washington University School of Architecture, 1964), 8.

18 → See Reyner Banham, *Megastructure: Urban Futures of the Recent Past* (London: Thames & Hudson, 1976).

19 → See Dominique Rouillard, *Superarchitecture: le futur de l'architecture, 1950–1970* (Paris: Éditions de la Villette, 2004).

20 → Alexei Gutnov, *The Ideal Communist City* (New York: G. Braziller, 1971).

21 → See Lawrence Busbea, *Topologies: The Urban Utopia in France, 1960–1970* (Cambridge, Mass.: MIT Press, 2007).

22 → See Pamela Johnston, ed., *The Function of the Oblique: The Architecture of Claude Parent and Paul Virilio, 1963–1969* (London: AA Publications, 1996).

23 → See Terence Riley, ed., *The Changing of the Avant-Garde: Visionary Architectural Drawings from the Howard Gilman Collection* (New York: Museum of Modern Art, 2002).

24 → Guy Debord, "La frontière situationniste," *Internationale situationniste* 5 (December 1960): 9; English: in Libero Andreotti and Xavier Costa, eds., *Theory of the Dérive and Other Situationist Writings on the City* (Barcelona: Actar, 1996), 107.

25 → Guy Debord, *La société du spectacle* (Paris: Éditions Champ Libre, 1967); English: *The Society of Spectacle*, trans. Fredy Perlman and Jon Supak (1970; rev. ed., New York: Black & Red, 1977).

26 → See Marc Dessauce, ed., *The Inflatable Moment: Pneumatics and Protest* (New York: Princeton Architectural Press, 1999).

29 Between elitism and populism: alternative architecture

1 → Jane Jacobs, *The Death and Life of Great American Cities* (New York: Random House, 1961).

2 → See "Urban Design," *Progressive Architecture* 37 (August 1956): 97–141.

3 → See Paul D. Spreiregen, *Urban Design: The Architecture of Towns and Cities* (New York: McGraw Hill, 1965).

4 → See Kevin Lynch, *The Image of the City* (Cambridge, Mass.: MIT Press, 1960); and Kevin Lynch, Donald Appleyard, and John R. Myer, *The View from the Road* (Cambridge, Mass.: MIT Press, 1964).

5 → Deyan Sudjic, *The Edifice Complex: How the Rich and Powerful Shape the World* (New York: Penguin Press, 2005), 228–34.

6 → Robert Venturi, *Complexity and Contradiction in Architecture* (New York: Museum of Modern Art, 1966).

7 → Ibid., 16.

8 → Peter Blake, *God's Own Junkyard: The Planned Deterioration of America's Landscape* (New York: Holt, Rinehart, and Winston, 1964).

9 → Venturi, *Complexity and Contradiction*, 104.

10 → Robert Venturi, Denise Scott Brown, and Steven Izenour, *Learning from Las Vegas* (Cambridge, Mass.: MIT Press, 1972), 9.

11 → Charles Moore, Gerald Allen, and Donlyn Lyndon, *The Place of Houses* (New York: Holt, 1974); and Charles Moore and Gerald Allen, *Dimensions: Space, Shape & Scale in Architecture* (New York: Architectural Record Books, 1976).

12 → Vincent Scully, *The Shingle Style: Architectural Theory and Design from Richardson to the Origins of Wright* (New Haven: Yale University Press, 1955).

13 → See Colin Rowe and Robert Slutzky, "Transparency: Literal and Phenomenal (Part I)," *Perspecta* 8 (1963): 45–54; and Colin Rowe, *The Mathematics of the Ideal Villa and Other Essays* (Cambridge, Mass.: MIT Press, 1976).

14 → *Five Architects: Eisenman, Graves, Gwathmey, Hejduk, Meier*, intro. Colin Rowe and critical essay by Kenneth Frampton (New York: Wittenborn, 1972).

15 → See Heinrich Klotz, *O. M. Ungers, 1951–1984; Bauten und Projekte* (Braunschweig: Vieweg, 1985). For the publication of a series of lectures given by Ungers at Technische Universität Berlin in the mid-1960s, see Oswald Mathias Ungers, "Architekturlehre: Berliner Vorlesungen 1964–65," thematic issue, *Archplus* 179 (2006).

16 → See Francis Strauven, *Aldo van Eyck: The Shape of Relativity* (Amsterdam: Architectura & Natura, 1998); and Raphaël Labrunye, "Médiatisation, réinterprétations et analyse d'un édifice-événement: l'orphelinat d'Aldo van Eyck à Amsterdam (1955–1960)," Ph.D. diss., Université de Versailles-Saint-Quentin en Yvelines, 2008.

17 → Bernard Rudofsky, *Architecture without Architects: A Short Introduction to Non-Pedigreed Architecture* (New York: Museum of Modern Art, 1965), 16. See also Monika Platzer, ed., *Lessons from Bernard Rudofsky: Life as a Voyage* (Basel, Berlin, and Boston: Birkhäuser Verlag, 2007).

18 → Robert Goodman, *After the Planners* (New York: Simon & Schuster, 1971), 199, 206.

19 → See Caroline Maniaque, *Alternative Architecture: French Encounters with the American Counterculture (1960–1980)* (Farnham, UK: Ashgate, 2011).

20 → See Giovanna Borasi and Mirko Zardini, eds., *Sorry, Out of Gas: Architecture's Response to the 1973 Oil Crisis* (Montreal: Canadian Centre for Architecture; and Mantua: Corraini Edizioni, 2007).

30 After 1968: architecture for the city

1 → For background and itineraries of the "generation of 1968," see Paul Berman, *A Tale of Two Utopias: The Political Journey of the Generation of 1968* (New York: W. W. Norton, 1996); and Morris Dickstein, *Gates of Eden: American Culture in the Sixties* (New York: Basic Books, 1977).

2 → See K. Michael Hays, ed., *Oppositions Reader: Selected Readings from a Journal for Ideas and Criticism in Architecture, 1973–1984* (New York: Princeton Architectural Press, 1998); Steven Holl and William Stout, eds., *Pamphlet Architecture 1–10* (New York: Princeton Architectural Press, 1998); and Beatriz Colomina and Craig Buckley, eds., *Clip, Stamp, Fold: The Radical Architecture of Little Magazines, 196X–197X* (Barcelona: Actar, 2010).

3 → See Jean-Louis Violeau, *Les architectes et mai 68* (Paris: Éditions Recherches, 2004).

4 → Giancarlo De Carlo, *Urbino: The History of a City and Plans for Its Development*, trans. Loretta Schaeffer Guarda (Cambridge, Mass.: MIT Press, 1970).

5 → See Triennale di Milano, *Quattordicesima Triennale di Milano* (Milan: Arti Grafiche Crespi & Occhipinti, 1968).

6 → See Paul-Henry Chombart de Lauwe, ed., *Famille et habitation* (Paris: Centre national de la recherche

scientifique, 1959–60), and Henri Lefebvre, *Le droit à la ville* (Paris: Anthropos, 1967).

7 → See Jean-Louis Cohen, "Actions de parole," foreword to *Paul Chemetov, un architecte dans le siècle* (Paris: Éditions du Moniteur, 2002), 8–11.

8 → Aldo Rossi, *L'architettura della città* (Padua: Marsilio, 1966), 66–65 and 91–93; English: *The Architecture of the City*, trans. Diane Ghirardo and Joan Ockman, intro. Peter Eisenman (Cambridge, Mass.: MIT Press, 1982), 65, 86.

9 → Carlo Aymonino, ed., *La città di Padova: saggio di analisi urbana* (Rome: Officina Edizioni, 1970).

10 → Ezio Bonfanti et al., *Architettura razionale, XV Triennale di Milano* (Milan: Franco Angeli, 1973).

11 → Vittorio Gregotti, ed., "La forma del territorio," thematic issue, *Edilizia moderna* 87–88 (1965).

12 → Vittorio Gregotti, *Il territorio dell'architettura* (Milan: Feltrinelli, 1966), 157–58.

13 → Vittorio Gregotti, "Modificazione," *Casabella* 498–99 (1984): 2–7.

14 → See Anthony Vidler, "The Third Typology," *Oppositions* 7 (Winter 1977): 1–4; and Rafael Moneo, "On Typology," *Oppositions* 13 (Summer 1978): 23–45.

15 → Christopher Alexander et al., *A Pattern Language: Towns, Buildings, Construction* (New York: Oxford University Press, 1977).

16 → Hassan Fathy, *Construire avec le peuple: histoire d'un village d'Égypte: Gourna* (Paris: Sindbad, 1970); English: *Architecture for the Poor: An Experiment in Rural Egypt* (Chicago: University of Chicago Press, 1976; originally published as *Gourna: A Tale of Two Villages* (Cairo: Ministry of Culture, 1969).

17 → See James Steele, *An Architecture for People: The Complete Works of Hassan Fathy* (London: Thames & Hudson, 1997).

18 → Manfredo Tafuri, *Progetto e utopia: architettura e sviluppo capitalistico* (Rome and Bari, Italy: Laterza, 1973); English: *Architecture and Utopia: Design and Capitalist Development*, trans. Barbara Luigia La Penta (Cambridge, Mass.: MIT Press, 1976).

19 → See Manfredo Tafuri, "Introduzione: Il 'progetto storico,' " in *La sfera e il labirinto: avanguardie e architettura da Piranesi agli anni '70* (Turin: Giulio Einaudi, 1980), 6; English: "Introduction: The Historical 'Project,' " in *The Sphere and the Labyrinth: Avant-Gardes and Architecture from Piranesi to the 1970s*, trans. Pellegrino D'Acierno and Robert Connolly (Cambridge, Mass.: MIT Press, 1987), 3.

31 The postmodern season

1 → See Arthur Drexler, ed., *The Architecture of the École des Beaux-Arts* (New York: Museum of Modern Art, 1977). Among the studies published in the wake of this show, see Donald Drew Egbert, *The Beaux-Arts Tradition in French Architecture* (Princeton: Princeton University Press, 1980); and Robin Middleton, ed., *The Beaux-Arts and Nineteenth-Century French Architecture* (Cambridge, Mass.: MIT Press, 1982).

2 → Arthur Drexler, *Transformations in Modern Architecture* (New York: Museum of Modern Art, 1979), 112–55. See also Felicity D. Scott, "When Systems Fail: Arthur Drexler and the Postmodern Turn," *Perspecta* 35 (2004): 134–53; and Felicity D. Scott, *Architecture or Techno-Utopia: Politics after Modernism* (Cambridge, Mass.: MIT Press, 2007).

3 → "Déclaration de Palerme," *Archives d'architecture moderne* 14 (1978): 7.

4 → "Déclaration de Bruxelles," in André Barey, *Déclaration de Bruxelles 1980: propos sur la reconstruction de la ville européenne* (Brussels: Archives d'Architecture Moderne, 1980), 17; English in Charles Jencks and Karl Kropf, eds., *Theories and Manifestoes of Contemporary Architecture* (London: Academy Editions, 1997), 176.

5 → Gaston Bardet, *Le nouvel urbanisme* (Paris: Vincent & Fréal, 1948).

6 → Charles Jencks, *The Language of Post-Modern Architecture* (London: Academy Editions, 1977).

7 → See Alain Touraine, *La société postindustrielle* (Paris: Denoël, 1969); English: *The Post-Industrial Society*, trans. Leonard F. X. Mayhew (New York: Random House, 1971); and Daniel Bell, *The Coming of Post-Industrial Society: A Venture in Social Forecasting* (New York: Basic Books, 1973).

8 → See Jean-François Lyotard, *La condition post-moderne: rapport sur le savoir* (Paris: Éditions de Minuit, 1979); English: *The Postmodern Condition: A Report on Knowledge*, trans. Geoff Bennington and Brian Massumi, foreword Fredric Jameson (Minneapolis: University of Minnesota Press, 1984). See also Fredric Jameson, *Postmodernism, or, The Cultural Logic of Late Capitalism* (Durham, NC: Duke University Press, 1991).

9 → See Paolo Portoghesi, *Postmodern: l'architettura nella società post-industriale* (Milan: Electa, 1982).

10 → David Watkin, *Morality in Architecture: The Development of a Theme in Architectural History and Theory from the Gothic Revival to the Modern Movement* (Oxford: Clarendon Press, 1977).

11 → See Martin Pawley, "Economic Foundations of Postmodernism," *Architectural Review* 176 (August 1994): 63; and Mary McLeod, "Architecture and Politics in the Reagan Era: From Postmodernism to Deconstructivism," *Assemblage* 7 (February 1989): 22–59.

12 → See Christian Norberg-Schulz, *Ricardo Bofill: Taller de Arquitectura* (New York: Rizzoli, 1985).

13 → Rob Krier, *Stadtraum in Theorie und Praxis* (Stuttgart: Krämer, 1975); English: *Urban Space*, trans. Christine Czechowski and George Black (London: Academy Editions, 1979).

14 → Dankwart Guratzsch, ed., *Das Neue Berlin: Konzepte der Internationalen Bauausstellung 1987 für einen Städtebau mit Zukunft* (Berlin: Gebr. Mann, 1987).

15 → Robert Venturi and John Rauch, *Signs of Life: Symbols in the American City* (Washington, D.C.: Aperture, 1976), n.p. [p.4]

16 → See Peter Arnell and Ted Bickford, eds., *James Stirling, Buildings and Projects*, intro. Colin Rowe (London: Architectural Press, 1984); Claire Zimmerman, "James Stirling Reassembled," *AA Files* 56 (2007): 30–41; "The Architecture of James Stirling 1964–1992," thematic issue, *OASE* 79 (2009); and Anthony Vidler, *James Frazer Stirling: Notes from the Archive* (New Haven: Yale University Press, 2010).

17 → See Hajime Yatsuka, "Architecture in the Urban Desert: A Critical Introduction to Japanese Architecture after Modernism," *Oppositions* 23 (Winter 1981): 3–35.

18 → See Robert A. M. Stern and John Montague Massengale, *The Anglo-American Suburb* (London: Academy Editions, 1981).

19 → See Andres Duany, Elisabeth Plater-Zyberk, and Alex Krieger, *Towns and Town-Making Principles* (New York: Rizzoli, 1991); David Mohney and Keller Easterling, eds., *Seaside: Making a Town in America*

(New York: Princeton Architectural Press, 1991); and Andres Duany, Elizabeth Plater-Zyberk, and Robert Alminana, *New Civic Art: Elements of Town Planning* (New York: Rizzoli, 2003).

20 → Claude Lévi-Strauss, *La pensée sauvage* (Paris: Plon, 1962), 26–44; English: *The Savage Mind* (London: Weidenfeld and Nicholson, 1966), 16–36.

32 From regionalism to critical internationalism

1 → See Alexis Sornin, Hélène Jannière, and France Vanlaethem, eds., *Architectural Periodicals in the 1960s and 1970s* (Montreal: Institut de recherche en histoire de l'architecture, 2008); and Beatriz Colomina and Craig Buckley, eds., *Clip, Stamp, Fold: The Radical Architecture of Little Magazines 196X–197X* (Barcelona: Actar, 2010).

2 → Francesco Dal Co and Giuseppe Mazzariol, eds., *Carlo Scarpa: Complete Works* (Milan: Electa, 1984); and Nicholas Olsberg et al., *Carlo Scarpa Architect* (Montreal: Canadian Centre for Architecture, 1999).

3 → Orietta Lanzarini, *Carlo Scarpa, l'architetto e le arti: gli anni della Biennale di Venezia 1948–1972* (Venice: Marsilio, 2003).

4 → See Richard Murphy, *Scarpa and the Castelvecchio* (London: Butterworth, 1980).

5 → Louis I. Kahn, foreword to *Carlo Scarpa: architetto poeta* (London: Royal Institute of British Architects, 1974), n.p.

6 → Alvaro Siza, "Bonjour Tristesse: Story of a Project," *Lotus* 41 (1984): 50–71.

7 → Kenneth Frampton, *Alvaro Siza: Complete Works* (London: Phaidon, 2000).

8 → See Alex Tzonis and Liane Lefaivre, "The Grid and the Pathway," in Kenneth Frampton, ed., *Atelier 66: The Architecture of Dimitris and Suzana Antonakakis* (New York: Rizzoli, 1985), 14–25; and Kenneth Frampton, "Towards a Critical Regionalism: Six Points for an Architecture of Resistance," in Hal Foster, ed., *The Anti-Aesthetic: Essays on Postmodern Culture* (Port Townsend, Wash.: Bay Press, 1983), 16–30.

9 → Jürgen Habermas, "Modernity versus Postmodernity," *New German Critique* 22 (1981): 3–14. On this debate, see Richard Rorty, "Habermas and Lyotard on Postmodernism," in Richard Bernstein, ed., *Habermas and Modernity* (Cambridge, Mass: MIT Press, 1985), 161–75.

10 → See Peter Disch, *Luigi Snozzi: costruzioni e progetti 1958–1993* (Lugano, Switzerland: ADV Publishing House, 1994).

11 → Francesco Dal Co, ed., *Mario Botta: architetture 1960–1985* (Milan: Electa, 1987).

12 → Peter Zumthor, *Penser l'architecture* (Basel: Birkhäuser, 2008), 86.

13 → See Rafael Moneo, "La vida de los edificios," *Arquitectura* 256 (1985): 26–36.

14 → See Cecilia Fernando Márquez and Richard Levene, *Rafael Moneo 1967–2004* (Madrid: El Croquis, 2004).

15 → See Antonio Esposito and Giovanni Leoni, eds., *Fernando Távora: opera completa* (Milan: Electa, 2005).

16 → Antonio Esposito and Giovanni Leoni, eds., *Eduardo Souto de Moura* (Milan: Electa, 2003).

17 → See Nuno Portas and Manuel Mendes, *Portugal Architecture 1965–1990* (Paris: Éditions du Moniteur,

1992); and Annette Becker, Ana Tostões, and Wilfried Wang, eds., *Architektur im 20. Jahrhundert Portugal* (Munich: Prestel, 1997).

18 → See János Gerle, *Architecture as Philosophy: The Work of Imre Makovecz* (Stuttgart: Edition Axel Menges, 2005).

19 → See William J. R. Curtis, *Balkrishna Doshi: An Architecture for India* (New York: Rizzoli, 1988); Brian Brace Taylor, *Raj Rewal* (Ahmedabad: Mapin, 1992); and Kenneth Frampton, *Charles Correa* (London: Thames & Hudson, 1996).

20 → See Brian Brace Taylor, *Geoffrey Bawa* (London: Thames & Hudson, 1995); and David Robson, *Geoffrey Bawa: The Complete Works* (London: Thames & Hudson, 2002).

21 → See Françoise Fromonot, *Glenn Murcutt: Buildings & Projects 1962–2001* (London: Thames & Hudson, 2003).

22 → See Germán Téllez, *Rogelio Salmona: arquitectura y poética del lugar* (Bogotá: Facultad de Arquitectura, Universidad de los Andes and Editorial Escala, 1991); and Ricardo L. Castro, *Rogelio Salmona* (Bogotá: Villegas Editores, 1998).

23 → Helio Piñón, *Paulo Mendes da Rocha* (Barcelona: Universitat Politècnica de Catalunya and Ediciones UPC, 2003); Rosa Artigas and Guilherme Wisnik, *Paulo Mendes da Rocha: Projects 1957–2007* (New York: Rizzoli, 2007).

24 → Marcelo Carvalho Ferraz, ed., *João Filgueiras Lima: Lelé* (Lisbon: Editora Blau; and São Paulo: Instituto Lina Bo Bardi, 2000).

25 → Jean-Louis Cohen, "Alla ricerca di una pratica critica," *Casabella* 630–631 (January–February 1996): 20–27.

33 The neo-Futurist optimism of high tech

1 → Reyner Banham, *Megastructure: Urban Futures of the Recent Past* (London: Thames & Hudson, 1976), 212–14.

2 → Antonio Sant'Elia, "Manifesto dell'architettura futurista, 1914", English: in Luciano Caramel and Alberto Longatti, *Antonio Sant'Elia: The Complete Works* (New York: Rizzoli, 1987), 302.

3 → Georges Perec, *L'infra-ordinaire* (Paris: Seuil, 1989), 76.

4 → Alan Colquhoun, "Critique," *Architectural Design* 47 (February 1977): 116; and Jean Baudrillard, *L'effet Beaubourg: implosion et dissuasion* (Paris: Galilée, 1977), 33; English: in Jean Baudrillard, *Simulacra and Simulations*, trans. Sheila Faria Glaser (Ann Arbor: University of Michigan Press, 1994), 68.

5 → Reyner Banham, "High Tech Architecture: The Beginning of an Argument," unpublished manuscript, undated [c. 1986], Reyner Banham Papers, Getty Research Institute, Box 8, 1–3.

6 → Chris Seddon, "Hongkong Bank Revisited," in *Norman Foster: 1964–1987, Architecture & Urbanism* Extra Edition 5 (May 1988): 215.

7 → See Peter Rice, *An Engineer Imagines* (London: Artemis, 1994).

8 → See William J. R. Curtis, "Les grands projets parisiens: monumentalité et machines d'état," *Techniques et architecture* 385 (August–September 1989): 116–26. See also François Chaslin, *Les Paris de François Mitterrand, histoire des grands projets architecturaux* (Paris: Gallimard, 1985).

34 Architecture's outer boundaries

1 → See "Searching for the Subject: Alvin Boyarsky and the Architectural Association School," in Andrew Higgott, *Mediating Modernism: Architectural Cultures in Britain* (London and New York: Routledge, 2007) 153–88.

2 → See K. Michael Hays, ed., *Oppositions Reader: Selected Readings from a Journal for Ideas and Criticism in Architecture, 1973–1984* (New York: Princeton Architectural Press, 1998).

3 → Hans Ibelings, *Supermodernism: Architecture in the Age of Globalization* (Rotterdam: NAi Publishers, 1998).

4 → See Jean-Louis Cohen, "Frankly Urban: Gehry from Billboards to Bilbao," in J. Fiona Ragheb, ed., *Frank Gehry, Architect* (New York: Solomon R. Guggenheim Museum, 2001), 322–36.

5 → Rem Koolhaas, *Delirious New York: A Retroactive Manifesto for Manhattan* (New York: Oxford University Press, 1978).

6 → Rem Koolhaas, *S, M, L, XL* (New York: Monacelli Press, 1995).

7 → Bart Lootsma, *SuperDutch: New Architecture in the Netherlands* (London: Thames & Hudson, 2000).

8 → Jean Baudrillard and Jean Nouvel, *Les objets singuliers: architecture et philosophie* (Paris: Calmann-Lévy, 2000), 97; English: *The Singular Objects of Architecture*, trans. Robert Bononno (London and Minneapolis: University of Minnesota Press, 2002), 62.

9 → See Philip Ursprung, ed., *Herzog & de Meuron: Natural History* (Baden: Lars Müller; and Montreal: Canadian Centre for Architecture, 2002).

10 → Bernard Tschumi, *Manhattan Transcripts* (London: Academy Editions, 1981).

11 → See Philip Johnson and Mark Wigley, eds., *Deconstructivist Architecture* (New York: Museum of Modern Art, 1988).

12 → Jean-François Bédard, ed., *Cities of Artificial Excavation: The Work of Peter Eisenman, 1978–1988* (Montreal: Canadian Centre for Architecture; and New York: Rizzoli, 1994).

13 → Gilles Deleuze, *Le pli: Leibniz et le baroque* (Paris: Minuit, 1988); English: *The Fold: Leibniz and the Baroque*, trans. Tom Conley (Minneapolis: University of Minnesota Press, 1993).

14 → See Peter Noever, ed., *Architecture in Transition. Between Deconstruction and New Modernism* (Munich: Prestel, 1991); Peter Noever, *The End of Architecture? Documents and Manifestos: Vienna Architecture Conference* (Munich: Prestel, 1992).

15 → See Jean-Louis Cohen, *Urban Textures: Yves Lion* (Basel: Birkhäuser, 2005).

16 → See Serge Salat, *Fumihiko Maki: An Aesthetic of Fragmentation* (New York: Rizzoli, 1988).

17 → See Tomoko Sakamoto and Albert Ferre, eds., *Toyo Ito: Sendai Mediatheque* (Barcelona: Actar, 2003).

18 → See "Ocean of Air: SANAA Kazuyo Sejima & Ryue Nishizawa, 1998–2004," thematic issue, *El Croquis* 121–22 (2004).

35 Vanishing points

1 → See Joan Ockman and Salomon Frausto, eds., *Architourism: Authentic, Escapist, Exotic, Spectacular* (Munich: Prestel, 2005).

2 → See Bart Goldhoorn and Philipp Meuser, eds., *Capitalist Realism: New Architecture in Russia* (Berlin: DOM Publishers, 2008).

3 → See Charles Jencks, *The Iconic Building: The Power of Enigma* (New York: Rizzoli, 2005).

4 → See Michael Bell and Jeannie Kim, eds., *Engineered Transparency: The Technical, Visual, and Spatial Effects of Glass* (New York: Princeton Architectural Press, 2008).

5 → Jean-Louis Cohen and G. Martin Moeller, Jr., eds., *Liquid Stone: New Architecture in Concrete* (New York: Princeton Architectural Press, 2006); and Michael Bell and Craig Buckley, eds., *Solid States: Concrete in Transition* (New York: Princeton Architectural Press, 2010).

6 → See Jean Dethier, *Architectures de terre: atouts et enjeux d'un matériau de construction méconnu, Europe, Tiers-Monde, États-Unis* (Paris: Éditions du Centre Pompidou, 1986).

7 → See Frédéric Migayrou and Zeynep Mennan, eds., *Architectures non standard* (Paris: Centre Pompidou, 2003).

8 → See Mario Carpo, "Post-Hype Digital Architecture: From Irrational Exuberance to Irrational Despondency," *Grey Room* 14 (Winter 2004): 102–15; and Stephen Kieran and James Timberlake, *Refabricating Architecture: How Manufacturing Methodologies Are Poised to Transform Building Construction* (New York: McGraw-Hill, 2004).

9 → See Antoine Picon, *Marc Mimram Architect-Engineer: Hybrid[e]* (Gollion, Switzerland: Infolio, 2007); and Guy Nordenson, *Patterns and Structures: Selected Writings 1973–2008* (Basel: Lars Müller, 2010).

10 → Peter Buchanan, *Ten Shades of Green: Architecture and the Natural World* (New York: W. W. Norton, 2005); and Simon Guy and Steven Moore, eds., *Sustainable Architectures: Cultures and Natures in Europe and North America* (New York: Spon, 2005).

11 → Rem Koolhaas, *S, M, L, XL* (New York: Monacelli Press, 1995).

12 → Christian de Portzamparc, foreword to Olivier Mongin, *Vers la troisième ville?* (Paris: Hachette, 1995), 7–16.

13 → See David Mangin and Philippe Panerai, *Projet urbain* (Marseilles: Parenthèses, 1999); and Yannis Tsiomis, *Échelles et temporalités des projets urbains* (Paris: Jean-Michel Place, 2007).

14 → See Hans Ibelings, ed., *The Artificial Landscape: Contemporary Architecture, Urbanism, and Landscape Architecture in the Netherlands* (Rotterdam: NAi Publishers, 2000).

15 → Mario Gandelsonas, *X-Urbanism: Architecture and the American City* (New York: Princeton Architectural Press, 1999); Dolores Hayden and Jim Wark, A *Field Guide to Sprawl* (New York: W. W. Norton, 2004); and *VINEX!: Een morfologische verkenning* (Rotterdam: NAi publishers, 2006).

16 → See Peter S. Reed, ed., *Groundswell: Constructing the Contemporary Landscape* (New York: Museum of Modern Art, 2005); and Charles Waldheim, ed., *Landscape Urbanism Reader* (New York: Princeton Architectural Press, 2006).

17 → Anita Berrizbeitia and Linda Pollak, eds., *Inside Outside: Between Architecture and Landscape* (Gloucester, Mass.: Rockport Publishers, 1999); and Pierluigi Nicolin and Francesco Repishti, *Dizionario dei nuovi paesaggisti* (Milan: Skira, 2003).

18 → See Manfred Sack, *Siebzig Kilometer Hoffnung: die IBA Emscher-Park, Erneuerung eines Industriegebiets* (Stuttgart: Deutsche Verlags-Anstalt, 1999).

19 → See Sébastien Marot, "L'alternative du paysage," *Le visiteur* 1, no. 1 (October 1995): 54–81; and Alexandre Chemetoff, *Visits* (Paris: Archibooks, 2009).

20 → See Kelly Shannon and Marcel Smets, eds., *The Landscape of Contemporary Infrastructure* (Rotterdam: NAi Publishers, 2009).

21 → Deyan Sudjic, *The Edifice Complex: How the Rich and Powerful Shape the World* (New York: Penguin Press, 2005).

22 → The tenth and final volume in the ANY series was titled *Anything*; see Cynthia C. Davidson, ed., *Anything* (Cambridge, Mass.: MIT Press; and New York: Anyone, 2001).

23 → See Jean-Louis Violeau and Juliette Pommier, *Notre histoire: Europan à 20 ans: des architectes et d'Europan en France* (Paris: Archibooks & Sautereau, 2007).

24 → See Mike Davis, *Planet of Slums* (New York: Verso, 2006).

Bibliography

For practical reasons, the following bibliography has been limited to books and edited volumes. In addition some monographic journal issues and unpublished theses have been inserted. Whenever available, English editions are cited, with the initial publication date in brackets, and only works published in Western European languages have been mentioned.

The first section deals with 20th century architectural history and theory, followed by general issues relative to 20th century architecture, and finally sections focused on geographic or national areas, in which general works and books relative to single architects have been differentiated. The former follow the alphabetical order of the authors and the latter the order of the architects mentioned.

Dictionaries and Documentary Anthologies

Benton, Charlotte, Benton, Tim and Sharp, Dennis, eds., *Architecture and Design, 1890–1939: an International Anthology of Original Articles* (New York: Whitney Library of Design, 1975)

Conrads, Ulrich, *Programs and Manifestoes on 20th-century Architecture* [1964] (Cambridge, Mass.: MIT Press, 1970)

De Benedetti, Maria and Pracchi, Attilio, *Antologia dell'architettura moderna, Testi, manifesti, utopie* (Bologna: Zanichelli, 1988)

Jencks, Charles and Kropf, Karl, eds., *Theories and Manifestoes of Contemporary Architecture*, Second ed. (London: Wiley-Academy, 2006)

Noever, Peter, ed., *The End of Architecture? Documents and Manifestos: Vienna Architecture Conference, June 15, 1992 at MAK* (Munich: Prestel, 1992)

Magnago-Lampugnani, Vittorio, Frey, Katia and Perotti, Eliana, eds., *Anthologie zum Städtebau* (Berlin: Gebr, Mann Verlag, 2005)

Midant, Jean-Paul, ed., *Dictionnaire de l'architecture du XXe siècle* (Paris: Hazan, 1996)

Ockman, Joan and Eigen, Ed, eds., *Architecture Culture, 1943–1968: a Documentary Anthology* (New York: Rizzoli, 1993)

Olmo, Carlo, ed., *Dizionario dell'architettura del XX secolo* (Turin: U, Allemandi, 2000)

Histories of Architecture written before 1950

Behne, Adolf, *The Modern Functional Building* [1923] (Santa Monica: Getty Research Center for the History of Art and the Humanities, 1996)

Behrendt, Walter-Curt, *The Victory of the New Building Style* [1927] (Los Angeles: Getty Research Institute for the History of Art and the Humanities, 2000)

Choisy, Auguste, *Histoire de l'architecture* (Paris: Gauthier-Villars, 1899)

Giedion, Sigfried, *Space, Time and Architecture; the Growth of a New Tradition* (Cambridge: Harvard University Press, 1941)

Hitchcock, Henry-Russell, *Modern Architecture, Romanticism and Reintegration* (New York: Payson and Clarke Ltd., 1929)

Hitchcock, Henry-Russell and Johnson, Philip, *The International Style: Architecture Since 1922*, lst ed. (New York: W.W. Norton & Co, 1932)

Hitchcock, Henry-Russell and Johnson, Philip, *Modern Architecture, International Exhibition* (New York: Museum of Modern Art, 1932)

Kaufmann, Emil, *Von Ledoux bis Le Corbusier, Ursprung und Entwicklung der autonomen Architektur* (Vienna, Leipzig: Verlag Dr, Rolf Passer, 1933)

Mumford, Lewis, *Technics and Civilization* (New York: Harcourt, 1934)

Nelson, George, *Building a New Europe, Portraits of Modern Architects, Essays by George Nelson, 1935–1936* (New Haven: Yale University Press, 2007)

Pevsner, Nikolaus, *Pioneers of the Modern Movement from William Morris to Walter Gropius* (London: Faber & Faber, 1936)

Platz, Gustav Adolf, *Die Baukunst der neuesten Zeit* (Berlin: Propyläen-Verlag, 1927)

Sartoris, Alberto, *Gli elementi dell'architettura funzionale; sintesi panoramica dell'architettura moderna* (Milan: U. Hoepli, 1932)

Histories of Architecture written after 1950

Banham, Reyner, *Theory and Design in the First Machine Age* (London: The Architectural Press, 1960)

Banham, Reyner, *The New Brutalism, Ethic or Aesthetic* (London: The Architectural Press, 1966)

Banham, Reyner, *Megastructure: Urban Futures of the Recent Past* (London: Thames & Hudson, 1976)

Benevolo, Leonardo, *History of Modern Architecture* [1960], 2 vols (Cambridge, Mass.: MIT Press, 1960)

Benton, Tim, ed., *Modernism* (London: Victoria & Albert Museum, 2006)

Choay, Françoise, *The Invention of the Historic Monument* [1991] (Cambridge: Cambridge University Press, 2001)

Colomina, Beatriz, *Privacy and Publicity: Modern Architecture as Mass Media* (Cambridge, Mass.: MIT Press, 1994)

Colquhoun, Alan, *Modern Architecture* (Oxford: Oxford University Press, 2002)

Curtis, William J. R., *Modern Architecture since 1900* [1982] 3rd edition (London, New York: Phaidon, 1996)

Doordan, Dennis P., *Twentieth-Century Architecture* (New York, London: Harry N., Abrams, 2001)

Frampton, Kenneth, *Modern Architecture: a Critical History* (London: Thames & Hudson, 1980)

Frampton, Kenneth, *Studies in Tectonic Culture* (Cambridge, Mass.: MIT Press, 1995)

Frampton, Kenneth, ed., *World Architecture 1900–2000, A Critical Mosaic*, 9 vols (Vienna; New York: Springer, 2000)

Hatherley, Owen, *Militant Modernism* (Winchester: Zero Books, 2008)

Hitchcock, Henry-Russell, *Architecture: Nineteenth and Twentieth Centuries* (Harmondsworth, Middlesex: Penguin Books, 1958)

Ibelings, Hans, *European Architecture Since 1890* (Amsterdam: SUN, 2011)

Legault, Réjean and Williams Goldhagen, Sarah, eds., *Anxious Modernisms* (Cambridge, Mass., Montreal: MIT Press, Canadian Centre for Architecture, 2000)

Nuttgens, Patrick, *The Story of Architecture* (London, New York: Phaidon Press, 1983)

Overy, Paul, *Light, Air & Openness; Modern Architecture Between the Wars* (London: Thames & Hudson, 2007)

Pearman, Hugh, *Contemporary World Architecture* (London, New York: Phaidon Press, 1998)

Posener, Julius, *Anfänge des Funktionalismus; von Arts and Crafts zum Deutschen Werkbund* (Frankfurt/Main: Ullstein, 1964)

Ragon, Michel, *Histoire mondiale de l'architecture et de l'urbanisme modernes*, 3 vols (Tournai: Casterman, 1971-1978)

Sartoris, Alberto, *Encyclopédie de l'architecture nouvelle*, 3 vols (Milan: U, Hoepli, 1948-1954)

Steele, James, *Architecture Today* (London, New York: Phaidon Press, 1997)

Tafuri, Manfredo, *Architecture and Utopia, Design and Capitalist Development* (Cambridge, Mass.: MIT Press, 1976)

Tafuri, Manfredo, *The Sphere and the Labyrinth: Avant-Gardes and Architecture from Piranesi to the 1970s* [1980] (Cambridge, Mass.: MIT Press, 1987)

Tafuri, Manfredo and Dal Co, Francesco, *Modern Architecture* [1976] (New York: Electa/Rizzoli, 1986)

Zevi, Bruno, *Storia dell'architettura moderna* (Turin: Einaudi, 1951)

Zevi, Bruno, *The Modern Language of Architecture* [1973] (London, Seattle: University of Washington Press, 1978)

Historiography of Twentieth Century Architecture

Forty, Adrian, *Words and Buildings: a Vocabulary of Modern Architecture* (London: Thames & Hudson, 2000)

Frampton, Kenneth, *Labour, Work and Architecture: Collected Essays on Architecture and Design* (London, New York: Phaidon Press, 2002)

Georgiadis, Sokratis, *Sigfried Giedion: An Intellectual Biography* [1989] (Edinburgh: Edinburgh University Press, 1993)

Scalvini, Maria-Luisa and Sandri, Maria-Luisa, *L'immagine storiografica dell'architettura moderna da Platz a Giedion* (Rome: Officina edizioni, 1984)

Tournikiotis, Panayotis, *The Historiography of Modern Architecture* (Cambridge, Mass.: MIT Press, 1999)

Vidler, Anthony, *Histories of the Immediate Present: Inventing Architectural Modernism* (Cambridge, Mass.: MIT Press, 2008)

Watkin, David, *Morality in Architecture; the Development of a Theme in Architectural History and Theory from the Gothic Revival to the Modern Movement* (Oxford: Clarendon Press, 1977)

Whiteley, Nigel, *Reyner Banham: Historian of the Immediate Future* (Cambridge, Mass.: MIT Press, 2002)

Theories and Criticism

Alexander, Christopher, *Notes on the Synthesis of Form* (Cambridge, Mass.: Harvard University Press, 1964)

Colquhoun, Alan, *Collected Essays in Architectural Criticism* (London: Black Dog Pub, 2009)

Dessauce, Marc, ed., *The Inflatable Moment: Pneumatics and Protest* (New York: Princeton Architectural Press, 1999)

Guadet, Julien-Azaïs, *Elements and Theory of Architecture* [1901-04] (Urbana: University of Illinois Press, 1916)

Hays, K. Michael, ed., *Architecture Theory Since 1968* (Cambridge, Mass.: MIT Press, 1998)

Heynen, Hilde, *Architecture and Modernity: a Critique* (Cambridge, Mass.: MIT Press, 1999)

Ibelings, Hans, *Supermodernism: Architecture in the Age of Globalization* (Rotterdam: NAI Publishers, 1998)

Jencks, Charles, *The Language of Post-Modern Architecture* (London: Academy Editions, 1977)

Jencks, Charles, *The Iconic Building, the Power of Enigma* (New York: Rizzoli, 2005)

Johnson, Philip and Wigley, Mark, *Deconstructivist Architecture* (New York: Museum of Modern Art, 1988)

King, Anthony D., *Spaces of Global Cultures: Architecture, Urbanism, Identity* (London, New York: Routledge, 2004)

Kostka, Alexandre and Wohlfarth, Irving, eds., *Nietzsche and "An Architecture of Our Minds"* (Los Angeles: Getty Research Institute for the History of Art and the Humanities, 1999)

Migayrou, Frédéric and Mennan, Zeynep, *Architectures non standard* (Paris: Centre Pompidou, 2003)

Moneo, Rafael, *Theoretical Anxiety and Design Strategies in the Work of Eight Contemporary Architects* (Cambridge, Mass.: MIT Press, 2004)

Noever, Peter, ed., *Architecture in Transition, Between Deconstruction and New Modernism* (Munich: Prestel, 1991)

Oechslin, Werner, *Stilhülse und Kern: Otto Wagner, Adolf Loos und der evolutionäre Weg zur modernen Architektur* (Zurich: gta Verlag, Berlin: Ernst & Sohn, 1994)

Otero-Pailos, Jorge, *Architecture's Historical Turn: Phenomenology and the Rise of the Postmodern* (Minneapolis: University of Minnesota Press, 2010)

Portoghesi, Paolo, *Postmodern: l'architettura nella società post-industriale* (Milan: Electa, 1982)

Ramírez, Juan Antonio, *The Beehive Metaphor: from Gaudí to Le Corbusier* [1998] (London: Reaktion Books, 2000)

Rouillard, Dominique, *Superarchitecture: le futur de l'architecture, 1950–1970* (Paris: Editions de la Villette, 2004)

Rowe, Colin, *The Mathematics of the Ideal Villa and Other Essays* (Cambridge, Mass.: MIT Press, 1976)

Rowe, Colin and Slutzky, Robert, *Transparenz, Commentary by Bernhard Hoesli* (Basel, Stuttgart: Birkhäuser, 1968); originally: "Transparency: Literal and Phenomenal (Part 1)," *Perspecta* 8 (1963): 44–54.

Rykwert, Joseph, *The Necessity of Artifice* (London: Academy Editions, 1982)

Rudofsky, Bernard, *Architecture without Architects; a Short Introduction to Non-Pedigreed Architecture* (New York: Museum of Modern Art, 1965)

Ruskin, John, *The Seven Lamps of Architecture* (London: Smith, Elder, and Co, 1849)

Semper, Gottfried, *Style in the Technical and Tectonic Arts, or, Practical Aesthetics* [1860–1863] (Los Angeles: Getty Research Institute, 2004)

Viollet-le-Duc, Eugène-Emmanuel, *Lectures on Architecture* [1863–73] (London: Sampson Low, Marston, Searle, and Rivington, 1877-1881)

Architectural Education

Bauhaus-Archiv Berlin, Klassik Stiftung Weimar and Stiftung Bauhaus Dessau, *Bauhaus: A Conceptual Model* (Ostfildern: Hatje Cantz Verlag, 2009)

Bayer, Herbert, *Staatliches Bauhaus Weimar 1919–1923* (Munich, Weimar: Bauhausverlag, 1923)

Bayer, Herbert, Gropius, Walter and Gropius, Ise, *Bauhaus 1919–1928* (New York: Museum of Modern Art, 1939)

Bergdoll, Barry and Dickerman, Leah, eds., *Bauhaus 1919–1933: Workshops for Modernity* (New York: The Museum of Modern Art, 2009)

Bothe, Rolf and Wingler, Hans Maria, eds., *Kunstschulreform 1900–1933* (Berlin: Gebr, Mann Verlag, 1977)

Delevoy, Robert-L., Culot, Maurice and Loo, Anne van, *La Cambre 1928–1978* (Bruxelles: Archives d'architecture moderne, 1979)

Drew Egbert, Donald, *The Beaux-Arts Tradition in French Architecture* (Princeton: Princeton University Press, 1980)

Drexler, Arthur, ed., *The Architecture of the École des Beaux-Arts* (London: Secker & Warburg, 1977)

Droste, Madgalena, Nerdinger, Winfried, Strohl, Hilde and Conrads, Ulrich, *Die Bauhaus Debatte 1953: Dokumente einer verdrängten Kontroverse* (Braunschweig: Vieweg, 1994)

Epron, Jean-Pierre, *Comprendre l'éclectisme* (Paris: Norma, 1997)

Fiedler, Jeannine and Feierabend, Peter, *Bauhaus* (Cologne: Könemann, 1999)

Herdeg, Klaus, *The Decorated Diagram, Harvard Architecture and the Failure of the Bauhaus Legacy* (Cambridge, Mass.: MIT Press, 1983)

Kentgens-Craig, Margret, *The Bauhaus and America, First Contacts 1919–1936* (Cambridge, Mass.: MIT Press, 1999)

Khan-Magomedov, Selim O., *Vkhoutémas* (Paris: Éditions du Regard, 1990)

Kudriavtsev, Alexander and Duskhkina, Natalia, eds., *From Vkhutemas to Markhi 1920–1936* (Moscow: A-Fond, 2005)

Middleton, Robin, ed., *The Beaux-arts and Nineteenth-Century French Architecture* (Cambridge, Mass.: MIT Press, 1982)

Nicolaisen, Dörte and Wolsdorff, Christian, *Das andere Bauhaus: Otto Bartning und die Staatliche Bauhochschule Weimar 1926–1930* (Berlin: Bauhaus-Archiv, 1997)

Oliver, Richard, ed., *The Making of an Architect, 1881–1981, Columbia University in the City of New York* (New York: Rizzoli, 1981)

Pollak, Martha, ed., *The Education of the Architect* (Cambridge, Mass.: MIT Press, 1997)

Ungers, Oswald Mathias, "Architekturlehre; Berliner Vorlesungen 1964–65," *Archplus*, no. 179 (2006)

Wingler, Hans Maria, *The Bauhaus: Weimar, Dessau, Berlin, Chicago* (Cambridge, Mass.: MIT Press, 1979)

Wohlsdorf, Christian, *Mehr als das blosse Zweck, Mies van der Rohe am Bauhaus 1930–1933* (Berlin: Bauhaus-Archiv, 2001)

Architecture and the Arts

Celant, Germano, ed., *Architecture & Arts 1900/2004: a Century of Creative Projects in Building, Design, Cinema, Painting, Sculpture* (Milan: Skira, 2004)

Curtis, Penelope, *Patio and Pavilion, The Place of Sculpture in Modern Architecture* (Los Angeles, The J. Paul Getty Museum; London: Ridinghouse, 2008)

Damaz, Paul, *Art in European Architecture* (New York: Reinhold Pub, Corp., 1956)

Koehler, Karen, ed., *The Built Surface: Architecture and Pictures from Antiquity to the Millenium* (London: Ashgate Press, 2002)

Szeemann, Harald, *Der Hang zum Gesamtkunstwerk; europäische Utopien seit 1800* (Aarau: Sauerländer, 1983)

Building Types

Campi, Mario, *Skyscrapers, An Architectural Type of Modern Urbanism* (Basel, Berlin, Boston: Birkhäuser, 2000)

Châtelet, Anne-Marie, Lerch, Dominique and Luc, Jean-Noël, *L'École de plein air: une expérience pédagogique et architecturale dans l'Europe du XXe siècle* (Paris: Recherches, 2003)

Goldberger, Paul, *The Skyscraper* (New York: Knopf, 1981)

Lindner, Werner, *Die Ingenieurbauten in ihrer guten Gestaltung* (Berlin: E, Wasmuth, 1923)

Lindner, Werner, *Bauten der Technik: ihre Form und Wirkung: Werkanlagen* (Berlin: E, Wasmuth, 1927)

Meeks, Carroll L. V., *The Railroad Station; An Architectural History* (New Haven: Yale University Press, 1956)

Mujica, Francisco, *History of the Skyscraper* (Paris: Archeology and Architecture Press, 1929)

Nordenson, Guy, *Tall Buildings* (New York: Museum of Modern Art, 2003)

Parent, Véronique, *Enquête sur les sièges de l'info* (Paris: Pavillon de l'Arsenal, Hazan, 1994)

Roth, Alfred., *Das neue Schulhaus* (Zurich: Girsberger, 1950)

Wharton, Annabel Jane, *Building the Cold War: Hilton International Hotels and Modern Architecture* (Chicago: University of Chicago Press, 2001)

Winter, John, *Industrial Architecture: a Survey of Factory Building* (London: Studio Vista, 1970)

Zukowsky, John, ed., *Building for Air Travel: Architecture and Design for Commercial Aviation* (New York: Prestel, 1996)

City Planning and Urban Design

Abercrombie, Patrick and Forshaw, John H., *County of London Plan* (London: Macmillan, 1943)

Blake, Peter, *God's Own Junkyard, the Planned Deterioration of America's Landscape* (New York: Holt, Rinehart and Winston, 1964)

Bonnet, Michel, ed., *L'élaboration des projets architecturaux et urbains en Europe* (Paris: Plan Construction et Architecture, 1997)

Bonnier, Louis, *Les règlements de voirie* (Paris: C. Schmid, 1903)

Burdett, Ricky and Sudjic, Deyan, eds., *The Endless City* (London, New York: Phaidon Press, 2007)

Burdett, Ricky and Sudjic, Deyan, eds., *Living in the Endless City* (London, New York: Phaidon Press, 2011)

Castex, Jean, Panerai, Philippe and Depaule, Jean-Charles, *Urban forms: Death and Life of the Urban Block* [1977] (Oxford, Boston: The Architectural Press, 2004)

Choay, Françoise, *L'urbanisme, utopies et réalités; une anthologie* (Paris: Seuil, 1965)

Choay, Françoise, *The Modern City, Planning in the 20th Century* (New York: George Braziller, 1970)

Cullen, Gordon, *Townscape* (London: The Architectural Press, 1961)

Dethier, Jean and Guiheux, Alain, eds., *La Ville, art et architecture en Europe, 1870–1993* (Paris: Editions du Centre Georges Pompidou, 1994)

Di Biagi, Paola, *I classici dell'urbanistica moderna* (Rome: Donzelli, 2002)

Doxiadis, Constantinos, *Architecture in Transition* (London: Hutchinson, 1963)

Doxiadis, Constantinos, *Ekistics; an Introduction to the Science of Human Settlements* (New York; Oxford: Oxford University Press, 1968)

Duany, Andres, Plater-Zyberk, Elizabeth and Alminana, Robert, *New Civic Art: Elements of Town Planning* (New York, London: Rizzoli, Troika, 2003)

Duany, Andres, Plater-Zyberk, Elizabeth, Krieger, Alex and Lennertz, William R., *Towns and Town-Making Principles* (Cambridge, Mass., Harvard University Graduate School of Design, New York: Rizzoli, 1991)

Durth, Werner and Gutschow, Niels, *Träume in Trümmern: Planungen zum Wiederaufbau zerstörter Städte im Westen Deutschlands, 1940–1950*, 2 vols (Braunschweig: Friedr, Vieweg & Sohn, 1988)

Endell, August, *Die Schönheit der großen Stadt* (Stuttgart: Strecker & Schröder, 1908)

Feder, Gottfried, *Die neue Stadt: Versuch der Begründung einer neuen Stadtplanungskunst aus der sozialen Struktur der Bevölkerung* (Berlin: Springer, 1939)

Fortier, Bruno, *L'amour des villes* (Liège, Mardaga, Paris: Institut français d'architecture, 1994)

Gandelsonas, Mario, *X-Urbanism, Architecture and the American City* (New York: Princeton Architectural Press, 1999)

Goodman, Robert, *After the Planners* (New York: Simon & Schuster, 1971)

Gresleri, Giuliano and Matteoni, Dario, *La città mondiale: Andersen Hébrard Otlet Le Corbusier* (Venice: Marsilio, 1982)

Hall, Peter, *Cities of Tomorrow: an Intellectual History of City Planning in the Twentieth Century* (Oxford, New York: Blackwell, 1988)

Hayden, Dolores and Wark, Jim, *A Field Guide to Sprawl*, 1st ed. (New York: W. W. Norton, 2004)

Hegemann, Werner, *Der Städtebau nach den Ergebnissen der Allgemeinen Städtebau-Ausstellung in Berlin, nebst einem Anhang: Die Internationale Städtebau-Ausstellung in Düsseldorf* (Berlin: Wasmuth, 1911–1913)

Hein, Carola, "Hauptstadt Europa." Doctorate thesis, Hamburg, Hochschule für bildende Künste, 1995

Hilberseimer, Ludwig, *The New City, Principles of Planning,* introduction by Ludwig Mies van der Rohe (Chicago: Paul Theobald, 1944)

Howard, Ebenezer, *Garden Cities of To-Morrow* [1898] (London: Swan Sonnenschein & Co, Ltd, 1902)

Jacobs, Jane, *The Death and Life of Great American Cities* (New York: Random House, 1961)

Krier, Rob, *Urban Space* [1975] (New York: Rizzoli, 1979)

Lynch, Kevin, *The Image of the City* (Cambridge, Mass.: MIT Press, 1960)

Lynch, Kevin, Appleyard, Donald and Myer, John R., *The View from the Road* (Cambridge, Mass.: MIT Press, 1964)

Magnago Lampugnani, Vittorio, *Die Stadt im 20, Jahrhundert, Visionen, Entwürfe, Gebautes* (Berlin: Wagenbach, 2010)

Maki, Fumihiko, *Investigations in Collective Form* (Saint-Louis: Washington University School of Architecture, 1964)

Mangin, David and Panerai, Philippe, *Projet urbain* (Marseille: Parenthèses, 1999)

Miliutin, Nikolai, *Sotsgorod, the Problem of Building Socialist Cities* [1930] (Cambridge, Mass.: MIT Press, 1974)

Mohney, David and Easterling, Keller, eds., *Seaside: Making a Town in America* (New York: Princeton Architectural Press, 1991)

Mongin, Olivier, *Vers la troisième ville?*, preface by Christian de Portzamparc (Paris: Hachette, 1995)

Osborn, Frederic J., *New Towns after the War* (London: Dent, 1942)

Osborn, Frederic J., *New Towns: the Answer to Megalopolis* (London: Leonard Hill Books, 1963)

Rossi, Aldo, *The Architecture of the City* [1966] (Cambridge, Mass., London: MIT Press, 1982)

Scheffler, Karl, *Die Architektur der Großstadt* (Berlin: B. Cassirer, 1913)

Shannon, Kelly and Smets, Marcel, *The Landscape of Contemporary Infrastructure* (Rotterdam: NAi Publishers, 2010)

Sonne, Wolfgang, *Representing the State: Capital City Planning in the Early Twentieth Century* (Munich, New York: Prestel, 2003)

Spreiregen, Paul D., *Urban Design: the Architecture of Towns and Cities* (New York: McGraw Hill, 1965)

Stein, Clarence, *Toward New Towns for America* [1951] (New York: Reinhold Publishing Co., 1957)

Stern, Robert A. M. and Massengale, John Montague, *The Anglo-American Suburb* (London: Academy Editions, 1981)

Sutcliffe, Anthony, ed., *Metropolis 1890–1940* (London: Mansell, 1984)

Tagliaventi, Gabriele, ed., *Città Giardino, cento anni di teorie, modelli, esperienze* (Roma: Gangemi editore, 1994)

Tsiomis, Yannis, *Echelles et temporalités des projets urbains* (Paris: Jean-Michel Place, 2007)

Volait, Mercedes and Nasr, Joe, eds., *Urbanism: Imported or Exported?: Native Aspirations and Foreign Plans* (West Sussex, England: Wiley-Academy, 2003)

Ward, Stephen V., ed., *The Garden City: Past, Present, and Future* (London, New York: E & FN Spon, 1992), Reprint

Europe and the American Model

Banham, Reyner, *A Concrete Atlantis: U.S, Industrial Buildings and European Modern Architecture, 1900–1925* (Cambridge, Mass.: MIT Press, 1986)

Cody, Jeffrey W., *Exporting American Architecture, 1870–2000* (London: Routledge, 2002)

Cohen, Jean-Louis, *Scenes of the World to Come: European Architecture and the American Challenge, 1893–1960* (Paris, Montréal: Flammarion, Canadian Centre for Architecture, 1995)

Cohen, Jean-Louis and Damisch, Hubert, eds., *Américanisme et modernité, l'idéal américain dans l'architecture* (Paris: Flammarion, 1993)

De Grazia, Victoria, *Irresistible Empire: America's Advance Through Twentieth-Century Europe* (Cambridge, Mass.: Belknap Press of Harvard University Press, 2005)

Fraser, Murray and Kerr, Joe, *Architecture and the 'Special Relationship': The American Influence on Post-War British Architecture* (London, New York: Routledge, 2007)

Gréber, Jacques, *L'architecture aux États-Unis* (Paris: Payot, 1920)

Ibelings, Hans, *Americanism: Dutch Architecture and the Transatlantic Model* (Rotterdam: NAI Publishers, 1997)

Maniaque, Caroline, *Alternative Architecture: French Encounters with the American Counterculture (1960–1980)* (Farnham: Ashgate, 2011).

Vogel, F. Rudolf, *Das Amerikanische Haus, Entwicklung, Bedingung, Anlage, Aufbau, Einrichtung, Innenraum und Umgebung* (Berlin: Wasmuth, 1910)

Expositions and Exhibitions

Cramer, Johannes and Gutschow, Niels, *Bauausstellungen: eine Architekturgeschichte des 20, Jahrhunderts* (Stuttgart: Kohlhammer, 1984)

Hämer, Hardt-Waltherr and Kleihues, Josef P., *Idee, Prozess, Ergebnis: die Reparatur und Rekonstruktion der Stadt: Internationale Bauausstellung Berlin 1987* (Berlin: Frölich & Kaufmann, 1984)

Herzogenrath, Wulf, Teuber, Dirk and Thiekötter, Angelika, eds., *Der Westdeutsche Impuls 1900–1914: Kunst und Umweltgestaltung im Industriegebiet, Die Deutsche Werkbund-Ausstellung, Cöln 1914* (Cologne: Kölnischer Kunstverein, 1984)

Kleihues, Josef P., and Klotz, Heinrich, eds., *International Building Exhibition Berlin 1987: Examples of New Architecture* (New York: Rizzoli, 1986), Reprint

Kirsch, Karin, *Werkbund-Ausstellung "Die Wohnung": Stuttgart 1927: die Weissenhofsiedlung* (Stuttgart: Deutsche Verlags-Anstalt, 1993)

Pansera, Anty, *Storia e cronaca della Triennale* (Milan: Longanesi, 1978)

Pica, Agnoldomenico, *Storia della Triennale di Milano, 1918–1957* (Milan: Edizioni del Milione, 1957)

Pommer, Richard and Otto, Christian F., *Weissenhof 1927 and the Modern Movement in Architecture* (Chicago, London: University of Chicago Press, 1991)

Riley, Terence, ed., *The International Style: Exhibition 15 and the Museum of Modern Art* (New York: Rizzoli, 1922)

Rudberg, Eva, *The Stockholm Exhibition 1930: Modernism's Breakthrough in Swedish Architecture* (Stockholm: Stockholmia, 1999)

Rydell, Robert W., *World of Fairs, The Century of Progress Exhibitions* (Chicago: University of Chicago Press, 1993)

Sack, Manfred, *Siebzig Kilometer Hoffnung: die IBA Emscher-Park: Erneuerung eines Industriegebiets* (Stutgart: Deutsche Verlags-Anstalt, 1999)

Housing and Domestic Architecture

Baffa Rivolta, Matilde and Rossari, Augusto, eds., *Alexander Klein, Lo studio delle pianto e la progettazione degli spazi negli alloggi minimi* (Milan: Mazzotta, 1975)

Bauer, Catherine, *Modern Housing* (New York: Houghton Mifflin, 1934)

Davis, Mike, *Planet of Slums* (London, New York: Verso, 2006)

Diotallevi, Irenio and Marescotti, Francesco, *Ordine e destino della casa popolare* (Milan: Editoriale Domus, 1941)

Dumont, Marie-Jeanne, *Le logement social à Paris 1850–1930: les habitations à bon marché* (Liège: Mardaga, 1991)

Eleb, Monique and Debarre, Anne, *L'invention de l'habitation moderne, Paris, 1880–1914* (Paris: Hazan, 1995)

Frederick, Christine, *The New Housekeeping: Efficiency Studies in Home Management* (Garden City, N.Y.: Doubleday, 1913)

Klein, Alexander, *Étude rationnelle des plans de constructions* (Paris: Dunod, 1939)

Moore, Charles Willard, Allen, Gerald and Lyndon, Donlyn, *The Place of Houses* (New York: Holt, Rinehart and Winston, 1974)

Muthesius, Hermann, *Das englische Haus, Entwicklung, Bedingungen, Anlage, Aufbau, Einrichtung und Innenraum*, 3 vols (Berlin: Wasmuth, 1908–1911)

Oldenziel, Ruth and Zachmann, Karin, eds., *Cold War Kitchen, Americanization, Technology, and European Users* (Cambridge, Mass.; London: MIT Press, 2009)

Plunz, Richard, *A History of Housing in New York City: Dwelling Type and Social Change in the American Metropolis* (New York: Columbia University Press, 1990)

Radford, Gail, *Modern Housing for America: Policy Struggles in the New Deal Era* (Chicago: University of Chicago Press, 1996)

Rutherford, Janice Williams, *Selling Mrs. Consumer: Christine Frederick & the Rise of Household Efficiency* (Athens, GA: University of Georgia Press, 2003)

Schwann, Bruno, ed., *Städtebau und Wohnungswesen der Welt* (Berlin: Wasmuth, 1935)

Sherwood, Roger, *Modern Housing Prototypes* (Cambridge, Mass.: Harvard University Press, 1978)

Sexton, Randolph W., *American Apartment Houses, Hotels and Apartment Hotels of Today; Exterior and Interior Photographs and Plans* (New York: Architectural Book Pub, Co., 1929)

Uhlig, Günther, *Kollektivmodell « Einküchenhaus »: Wohnreform und Architekturdebatte zwischen Frauenbewegung und Funktionalismus 1900–1933* (Giessen: Anabas-Verlag, 1981)

Wright, Gwendolyn, *Moralism and the Model Home: Domestic Architecture and Cultural Conflict in Chicago, 1873–1913* (Chicago: University of Chicago Press, 1980)

Wright, Gwendolyn, *Building the Dream: a Social History of Housing in America* (New York: Pantheon Books, 1981)

Landscape

Berrizbeitia, Anita and Pollak, Linda, eds., *Inside Outside: Between Architecture and Landscape* (Gloucester, Mass.: Rockport Publishers, 1999)

Ibelings, Hans, ed., *The Artificial Landscape: Contemporary Architecture, Urbanism, and Landscape Architecture in the Netherlands* (Rotterdam: NAI Publishers, 2000)

Imbert, Dorothée, *The Modernist Garden in France* (New Haven: Yale University Press, 1993)

Migge, Leberecht, *Der soziale Garten, Das grüne Manifest* [1926] (Berlin: Gebr, Mann Verlag, 1999)

Nicolin, Pierluigi and Repishti, Francesco, *Dizionario dei nuovi paesaggisti* (Milan: Skira, 2003)

Racine, Michel, ed., *Créateurs de jardins et de paysages en France de la Renaissance au XXIe siècle* (Arles: Actes Sud, 2001), Reprint

Reed, Peter S., ed., *Groundswell, Constructing the Contemporary Landscape* (New York: Museum of Modern Art, 2005)

Spens, Michael, *Modern Landscape* (London, New York: Phaidon Press, 2003)

Treib, Marc, ed., *Modern Landscape Architecture, a Critical Review* (Cambridge, Mass.: MIT Press, 1993)

Treib, Marc, ed., *The Architecture of Landscape, 1940–1960* (Philadelphia: University of Pennsylvania Press, 2002)

Waldheim, Charles, ed., *The Landscape Urbanism Reader* (New York: Princeton Architectural Press, 2006)

Materials, Technology and Engineering

Balmond, Cecil and Smith, Jannuzzi, *Informal* (Munich, Berlin, London, New York: Prestel, 2002)

Baudot, Anatole de, *L'architecture, le passé, le présent* (Paris: Librairie Renouard, 1916)

Bell, Michael and Kim, Jeannie, eds., *Engineered Transparency: the Technical, Visual, and Spatial Effects of Glass* (New York: Princeton Architectural Press, 2009)

Bell, Michael and Buckley, Craig, eds., *Solid States: Concrete in Transition* (New York: Princeton Architectural Press, 2010)

Cohen, Jean-Louis and Moeller, G, Martin, Jr., eds., *Liquid Stone, New Architecture in Concrete* (New York: Princeton Architectural Press, 2006)

Collins, Peter, *Concrete, the Vision of a New Architecture; a Study of Auguste Perret and his Precursors* (New York: Horizon Press, 1959)

Dethier, Jean, *Architectures de terre* (Paris: Éditions du Centre Pompidou, 1986)

Forty, Adrian, *Objects of Desire* (New York: Pantheon Books, 1986)

Giedion, Sigfried, *Mechanization Takes Command, a Contribution to Anonymous History* (New York: Oxford University Press, 1948)

Guillón, Mauro F., *The Taylorized Beauty of the Mechanical: Scientific Management and the Rise of Modernist Architecture* (Princeton: Princeton University Press, 2006)

Guy, Simon and Moore, Steven, eds., *Sustainable Architectures: Cultures and Natures in Europe and North America* (New York: Spon, 2005)

Herbert, Gilbert, *The Dream of the Factory-made House: Walter Gropius and Konrad Wachsmann* (Cambridge, Mass.: MIT Press, 1984)

Hilberseimer, Ludwig and Vischer, Julius, *Beton als Gestalter, Bauten in Eisenbeton und ihre architektonische Gestaltung, Ausgeführte Eisenbetonbauten* (Stuttgart: Julius Hoffmann, 1928)

Hunt, Anthony and Macdonald, Angus, *The Engineer's Contribution to Contemporary Architecture* (London: Thomas Tolford, 2000)

Kieran, Stephen and Timberlake, James, *Refabricating Architecture: How Manufacturing Methodologies Are Poised to Transform Building Construction* (New York: McGraw-Hill, 2004)

Leatherbarrow, David, *Uncommon Ground: Architecture, Technology, and Topography* (Cambridge, Mass.: MIT Press, 2000)

Nye, David E, *American Technological Sublime* (Cambridge, Mass.: MIT Press, 1994)

Picon, Antoine, *Digital Culture in Architecture, An Introduction for the Design Professions* (Basel: Birkhäuser, 2010)

Picon, Antoine, ed., *L'Art de l'ingénieur: constructeur, entrepreneur, inventeur* (Paris: Centre Georges Pompidou, 1997), Reprint

Rice, Peter, *An Engineer Imagines* (London: Artemis, 1994)

Simonnet, Cyrille, *Le Béton, histoire d'un matériau* (Marseille: Parenthèses, 2005)

Slaton, Amy E, *Reinforced Concrete and the Modernization of American Building, 1900–1930* (Baltimore: Johns Hopkins University Press, 2001)

Taylor, Frederick Winslow, *Principles of Scientific Management* (London, New York: Harper, 1911)

Periodicals, Studies and Reprints

Baglione, Chiara, *Casabella 1928–2008* (Milan: Electa, 2008)

Canella, Guido and Meriggi, Maurizio, eds., *SA, Sovremennaia Arkhitektura 1926–1930* (Bari: Dedalo, 2007)

Colomina, Beatriz and Craig Buckley, eds., *Clip, Stamp, Fold: The Radical Architecture of Little Magazines 196x – 197x* (Barcelona: Actar, 2009)

Hays, K, Michael, ed., *Oppositions Reader: Selected Readings from a Journal for Ideas and Criticism in Architecture, 1973–1984* (New York: Princeton Architectural Press, 1998)

Holl, Steven and Stout, William, eds., *Pamphlet Architecture 1–10* (New York: Princeton Architectural Press, 1998)

Jannière, Hélène, *Politiques éditoriales et architecture « moderne », l'émergence de nouvelles revues en France et en Italie (1923–1939)* (Paris: Arguments, 2002)

Jennings, Michael and Mertins, Detlef, eds., *G: Elements for Elemental Form-Creation (1923–1926)* (Los Angeles: Getty Research Institute Press, 2010)

Rovira, Josep María, *A. C.: la revista del G.A.T.E.P.A.C., 1931–1937* (Madrid: Museo Nacional Centro de Arte Reina Sofía, 2008)

Sornin, Alexis, Jannière, Hélène and Vanlaethem, France, eds., *Architectural Periodicals in the 1960s and 1970s* (Montreal: Institut de recherche en histoire de l'architecture, 2008)

Volait, Mercedes, *L'architecture moderne en Egypte et la revue Al-'Imara (1939–1959)* (Le Caire: Cedej, 1988)

Africa

"Modern Heritage in Africa," thematic issue, *Docomomo Journal*, no. 28 (2003)

Béguin, François, *Arabisances: décor architectural et tracé urbain en Afrique du Nord, 1830–1950* (Paris: Dunod, 1983)

Çelik, Zeynep, *Urban Forms and Colonial Confrontations: Algiers under French Rule* (Berkeley: University of California Press, 1997)

Chipkin, Clive M., *Johannesburg Style: Architecture & Society, 1880s–1960s* (Cape Town: D, Philip Publishers, 1993)

Chipkin, Clive M., *Johannesburg Transition: Architecture & Society from 1950* (Johannesburg: STE Publishers, 2008)

Cohen, Jean-Louis and Eleb, Monique, *Casablanca, Colonial Myths and Architectural Ventures* [1998] (New York: The Monacelli Press, 2002)

Cohen, Jean-Louis, Oulebsir, Nabila and Kanoun, Youcef, eds., *Alger, paysage urbain et architecture 1800–2000* (Paris: Éditions de l'Imprimeur, 2003)

Culot, Maurice and Thiveaud, Jean-Marie, eds., *Architectures françaises outre-mer* (Paris: Institut Français d'Architecture, Liège Pierre Mardaga, 1992)

Denison, Edward, Guang Yu Ren and Gebremedhin, Naizgy, *Asmara, Africa's Secret Modernist City* (London, New York: Merrell, 2003)

Folkers, Antoni, *Modern Architecture in Africa* (Amsterdam: SUN, 2010)

Gresleri, Giuliano, Massaretti, Pier Giorgio and Zagnoni, Stefano, eds., *Architettura italiana d'oltremare: 1870–1940* (Venice: Marsilio, 1993)

Herbert, Gilbert, *Rex Martienssen and the International Style: The Modern Movement in South African Architecture* (Cape Town, Rotterdam: Balkema, 1975)

Ilbert, Robert, *Héliopolis 1905–1922: la genèse d'une ville* (Paris: Editions du CNRS, 1981)

Kultermann, Udo, *Neues Bauen in Afrika* (Tübingen: Wasmuth, 1963)

Asia and Australia

Crinson, Mark, *Modern Architecture and the End of Empire* (Aldershot: Ashgate, 2003)

Denison, Edward and Guang Yu Ren, *Modernism in China: Architectural Visions and Revolutions* (New York: Wiley, 2008)

Hoa, Léon, *Reconstruire la Chine: trente ans d'urbanisme, 1949–1979* (Paris: Editions du Moniteur, 1981)

Irving, Robert Grant, *Indian Summer: Lutyens, Baker, and Imperial Delhi* (New Haven: Yale University Press, 1981)

Joshi, Kiran, *Documenting Chandigarh: the Indian Architecture of Pierre Jeanneret, Edwin Maxwell Fry, Jane Beverly Drew* (Ahmedabad, Mapin Publishing; Chandigarh: Chandigarh College of Architecture, 1999)

Lee, Leo Ou-fan, *Shanghai Modern: the Flowering of a New Urban Culture in China, 1930–1945* (Cambridge, Mass.: Harvard University Press, 1999)

Rowe, Peter G, and Kuan, Seng, *Architectural Encounters with Essence and Form in Modern China* (Cambridge, Mass.: MIT Press, 2002)

Architects

Robson, David, *Geoffrey Bawa: the Complete Works* (London: Thames & Hudson, 2002)

Taylor, Brian Brace, *Geoffrey Bawa* (London: Thames & Hudson, 1995)

Frampton, Kenneth, *Charles Correa* (London: Thames & Hudson, 1996)

Curtis, William J. R., *Balkrishna Doshi, an Architecture for India* (New York: Rizzoli, 1988)

Fairbank, Wilma, *Liang and Lin: Partners in Exploring China's Architectural Past* (Philadelphia: University of Pennsylvania Press, 1994)

Fromonot, Françoise, *Glenn Murcutt: Buildings + Projects 1962–2001* (London: Thames & Hudson, 2003)

Tadgell, Christopher, *The History of Architecture in India* (London, New York, Phaidon Press, 1990)

Taylor, Brian Brace, *Raj Rewal* (Ahmedabad. Mapin Publications, 1992)

White, Stephen, *Building in the Garden: The Architecture of Joseph Allen Stein in India and California* (Oxford: Oxford University Press, 1993)

Austria

Blau, Eve, *The Architecture of Red Vienna 1919–1934* (Cambridge, Mass.: MIT Press, 1999)

Tafuri, Manfredo, *Vienna Rossa* (Milan: Electa, 1980)

Architects

Pozzetto, Marco, *Max Fabiani, Ein Architekt der Monarchie* (Vienna: Edition Tusch, 1983)

Sekler, Eduard P., *Josef Hoffmann, the Architectural Work* (Princeton: Princeton University Press, 1985)

Hans Hollein: eine Ausstellung (Vienna: Museen der Stadt Wien, 1995)

Loos, Adolf, *Spoken into the Void: Collected Essays, 1897–1900* (Cambridge, Mass.: MIT Press, 1982)

Cacciari, Massimo, *Adolf Loos e il suo Angelo, « Das Andere » e altri scritti* (Milan: Electa, 2002)

Gravagnuolo, Benedetto, *Adolf Loos, Theory and Works* (New York: Rizzoli, 1982)

Platzer, Monika, ed., *Lessons from Bernard Rudofsky, Life as a Voyage* (Basel, Berlin, Boston: Birkhäuser Verlag, 2007)

Wagner, Otto, *Modern Architecture* [1896] (Santa Monica, Chicago: Getty Center for the History of Art and the Humanities, University of Chicago Press, 1988)

Mallgrave, Harry Francis, ed., *Otto Wagner, Reflections on the Raiment of Modernity* (Santa Monica: Getty Research Center in the History of Art and the Humanities, 1993)

Belgium

Hennaut, Eric and Liesens, Liliane, *Cités-jardins 1920–1940 en Belgique* (Bruxelles: Archives d'architecture moderne, 1994)

Smets, Marcel, *L'avènement de la cité-jardin en Belgique: histoire de l'habitat social en Belgique de 1830 à 1930* (Liège: P, Mardaga, 1977)

Architects

Borsi, Franco and Portoghesi, Paolo, *Victor Horta* (New York: Rizzoli, 1991)

Pehnt, Wolfgang, *Lucien Kroll, projets et réalisations* (Teufen: Niggli, 1987)

Ploegaerts, Léon and Puttemans, Pierre, *L'œuvre architecturale de Henry Van de Velde* (Bruxelles: Vokaer, 1987)

Velde, Henry van de, *Vom neuen Stil* (Leipzig: Insel-Verlag, 1907)

Velde, Henry van de, *Les formules de la beauté architectonique moderne* (Bruxelles: L'Equerre, 1923)

Brazil

Andreoli, Elisabetta and Forty, Adrian, *Brazil's Modern Architecture* (London, New York: Phaidon, 2004)

Goodwin, Philip, *Brazil Builds, Architecture New and Old, 1652–1942,* photographs by G. E. Kidder Smith (New York: Museum of Modern Art, 1943)

Holston, James, *The Modernist City: an Anthropological Critique of Brasilia* (Chicago: University of Chicago Press, 1989)

Mindlin, Henrique E., *Modern Architecture in Brazil* (London: The Architectural Press, 1956)

Monnier, Gérard, ed., *Brasilia, l'épanouissement d'une capitale* (Paris: Picard, 2006)

Segawa, Hugo M., *Arquiteturas no Brasil: 1900–1990* (São Paulo: Editora da Universidade de Saõ Paulo, 1998)

Williams, Richard J., *Brazil* (London: Reaktion, 2009)

Architects

Ferraz, Marcelo Carvalho, *Lina Bo Bardi* (Milan: Editions Charta; São Paulo: Instituto Lina Bo e P. M. Bardi, 1994)

Ferraz, Marcelo Carvalho, *João Filgueiras Lima — Lelé* (Lisbon, São Paulo: Ed., Blau, Instituto Lina Bo Bardi, 2000)

Artigas, Rosa and Wisnik, Guilherme, *Paulo Mendes da Rocha: Projects 1957-2007*, 2 vols (New York: Rizzoli, 2007)

Piñón, Helio, *Paulo Mendes da Rocha* (Barcelona: Universitat Politècnica de Catalunya, 2003)

Niemeyer, Oscar, *The Curves of Time: the Memoirs of Oscar Niemeyer* (London, New York: Phaidon, 2000)

Philippou, Styliane, *Oscar Niemeyer: Curves of Irreverence* (New Haven: Yale University Press, 2008)

Bonduki, Nabil and Portinho, Carmen, *Affonso Eduardo Reidy* (São Paulo: Editorial Blau, Instituto Lina Bo e P. M. Bardi, 2000)

Puntoni, Alvaro, ed., *Vilanova Artigas* (São Paulo: Instituto Lina Bo e P. M. Bardi, Fundação Vilanova Artigas, 1997)

Eastern and Central Europe

Åman, Anders, *Architecture and Ideology in Eastern Europe during the Stalin Era: an Aspect of Cold War History* (New York: Architectural History Foundation, Cambridge, Mass.. MIT Press, 1992)

Bierut, Boleslaw, *The Six-Year Plan for the Reconstruction of Warsaw* (Warsaw: Ksiażka i Wiedza, 1951)

Blagojević, Ljiljana, *Modernism in Serbia, The Elusive Margins of Belgrade Architecture* (Cambridge, Mass.: MIT Press, 2003)

Blau, Eve and Platzer, Monika, eds., *Shaping the Great City, Modern Architecture in Central Europe, 1890-1937* (Munich, London: Prestel, 2000)

Goldzamt, Edmund, *Städtebau sozialistischer Länder: soziale Probleme* (Berlin (East): VEB Verlag für Bauwesen, 1974)

Kalm, Mart, *Eesti 20, sajandi architektuur* (Estonian 20th Century Architecture) (Tallinn: Sild, 2002)

Lesnikowski, Wojciech, ed., *East European Modernism; Architecture in Czechoslovakia, Hungary and Poland Between the Wars 1919–1939* (New York: Rizzoli, 1996)

Machedon, Luminiţa and Scoffham, Ernie, *Romanian Modernism: the Architecture of Bucharest, 1920–1940* (Cambridge, Mass: MIT Press, 1999)

Moravánszky, Ákos, *Die Erneuerung der Baukunst: Wege zur Moderne in Mitteleuropa 1900–1940* (Salzburg: Residenz, 1988)

Moravánszky, Ákos, *Competing Visions: Aesthetic Invention and Social Imagination in Central European Architecture, 1867-1918* (Cambridge, Mass.: MIT Press, 1998)

Nerdinger, Winfried, Horňáková, Ladislava and Sedláková, Radomíra, eds., *Zlín — Model Town of Modernism* (Munich: Jovis Verlag, 2009)

Parlagreco, Silvia, *Il costruttivismo in Polonia, percorsi e deviazioni di un avanguardia* (Milan: Bollati Boringhieri, 2005)

Popescu, Carmen, ed., "Behind the Iron Curtain: Architecture in the Former Communist Bloc, between isolation and fascination," thematic issue, *The Journal of Architecture* 13, no. 6 (2008)

Švácha, Rostislav, *The Architecture of New Prague, 1895–1945* (Cambridge: MIT Press, 1995)

Švácha, Rostislav, *Form Follows Science; Teige, Gillar, and European Scientific Functionalism, 1922–1948* (Prague: Obec architektů Praha, 2008)

Teige, Karel, *Modern Architecture in Czechoslovakia* [1930] (Los Angeles: Getty Research Institute for the History of Art and the Humanities, 2000)

Vegesack, Alexander von and Lamarova, Milena B., *Czech Cubism: Architecture, Furniture, and Decorative Arts, 1910–1925* (New York: Princeton Architectural Press, 1992)

Architects

Zahariade, Ana-Maria, *Centenar Horia Creangă 1892–1992* (Bucharest: Simmetria, 1992)

Bocănet, Anca, Lascu, Nicolae and Zahariade, Ana-Maria, eds., *Centenar Marcel Iancu 1895–1995* (Bucharest: Simmetria, 1996)

Gerle, János, *Architecture as Philosophy: The Work of Imre Makovecz* (Stuttgart: Edition Axel Menges, 2005)

Krečič, Peter, *Plečnik, the Complete Works* (New York: Whitney Library of Design, 1993)

Prelovšek, Damjan, *Jože Plečnik, 1872–1957: Architectura Perennis* (New Haven: Yale University Press, 1997)

Finland and Scandinavia

Caldenby, Claes, Lindvall, Jöran and Wang, Wilfried, eds., *Twentieth-century Architecture: Sweden* (Munich, New York: Prestel, 1998)

Connah, Roger, *Finland* (London: Reaktion Books, 2005)

Norri, Marja-Riitta, Standertskjöld, Elina and Wang, Wilfried, eds., *Finland* (Munich, New York: Prestel, 2000)

Architects

Fleig, Karl, *Alvar Aalto, Complete Works* (Zurich: Hans Girsberger, 1963)

Pelkonen, Eeva-Liisa, *Alvar Aalto: Architecture, Modernity, and Geopolitics* (New Haven: Yale University Press, 2009)

Reed, Peter S., ed., *Alvar Aalto: Between Humanism and Materialism* (New York: Museum of Modern Art, Harry N., Abrams, 1998)

Ruusuvuori, Aarno, *Alvar Aalto 1898–1970* (Helsinki: Museum of Finnish Architecture, 1978)

Schildt, Göran, *Alvar Aalto: the Early Years* (New York: Rizzoli, 1984)

Schildt, Göran, *Alvar Aalto: the Decisive Years* (New York: Rizzoli, 1986)

Schildt, Göran, *Alvar Aalto: the Mature Years* (New York: Rizzoli, 1991)

Schildt, Göran, *Alvar Aalto in his Own Words* (New York: Rizzoli, 1998)

Westen, Richard, *Alvar Aalto* (London, New York: Phaidon Press, 1995)

Blundell Jones, Peter, *Gunnar Asplund* (London, New York: Phaidon, 2006)

Holmdahl, Gustav, Lind, Sven Ivar and Ödeen, Kjell, *Gunnar Asplund, Architect, 1885–1940* (Stockholm: Byggförlaget, 1981)

Norberg-Schulz, Christian and Postiglione, Gennaro, *Sverre Fehn : opera completa* (Milan: Electa, 1997)

Thau, Carsten and Vindum, Kjeld, *Arne Jacobsen* (Copenhagen: Danish Architectural Press, 2001)

Flora, Nicola, Giardiello, Paolo and Postiglione, Gennaro, *Sigurd Lewerentz 1885–1976* (Milan: Electa, 2001)

Rudberg, Eva, *Sven Markelius, Architect* (Stockholm: Arkitektur Förlag, 1989)

Merkel, Jayne, *Eero Saarinen* (London, New York: Phaidon Press, 2005)

Christ-Janer, Albert, *Eliel Saarinen: Finnish-American Architect and Educator* [1948] (Chicago: University of Chicago Press)

Fromonot, Françoise, *Jørn Utzon: the Sydney Opera House* (Corte Madera, California: Gingko; Milan: Electa, 2008)

France

Borsi, Francesco and Godoli, Ezio, *Paris 1900, Architecture and Design* (New York: Rizzoli, 1978)

Burlen, Katherine and Barraqué, Bernard, eds., *La "Banlieue oasis"; Henri Sellier et les cités-jardins 1900–1940* (Saint-Denis: Presses universitaires de Vincennes, 1987)

Busbea, Larry, *Topologies: the Urban Utopia in France, 1960–1970* (Cambridge, Mass.: MIT Press, 2007)

Clémençon, Anne-Sophie, ed., *Les gratte-ciel de Villeurbanne* (Paris: Editions de l'Imprimeur, 2004)

Ford, Georges B., *Out of the Ruins* (New York: The Century Co., 1919)

Giedion, Sigfried, *Building in France, Building in Iron, Building in Ferroconcrete* [1928] (Santa Monica: Getty Center for the History of Art and the Humanities, 1995)

Higonnet, Patrice L. R., *Paris: Capital of the World* (Cambridge, Mass.: Belknap Press, 2002)

Kopp, Anatole, Boucher, Frédérique and Pauly, Danièle, *L'architecture de la reconstruction en France, 1945–1953* (Paris: Editions du Moniteur, 1982)

Monnier, Gérard, ed., *L'architecture moderne en France*, 3 vols (Paris: Picard, 1997–2000)

Monnier, Gérard, *Histoire critique de l'architecture en France 1918–1950* (Paris: Philippe Sers, 1990)

Silver, Kenneth, *Esprit de Corps: the Art of the Parisian Avant-Garde and the First World War, 1914-1925* (Princeton: Princeton University Press, 1989)

Silverman, Debora, *Art nouveau in Fin-de-Siècle France: Politics, Psychology, and Style* (Berkeley, Los Angeles: University of California Press, 1989)

Troy, Nancy J., *Modernism and the Decorative Arts in France: Art Nouveau to Le Corbusier* (New Haven: Yale University Press, 1991)

Vigato, Jean-Claude, *Le jeu des modèles, les modèles en jeu; doctrines architecturales dans l'entre deux guerres* (Villers-les-Nancy: CEMPA, 1980)

Vigato, Jean-Claude, *L'architecture régionaliste: France, 1890–1950* (Paris: Editions Norma, 1994)

Violeau, Jean-Louis, *Les architectes et mai 68* (Paris: éditions Recherches, 2004)

Violeau, Jean-Louis, *Les architectes et mai 81* (Paris: éditions Recherches, 2011)

Violeau, Jean-Louis and Pommier, Juliette, *Notre histoire: Europan à 20 ans: des architectes et d'Europan en France* (Paris: Archibooks + Sautereau, 2007)

Voldman, Danièle, *Reconstruction des villes françaises de 1940 à 1954: histoire d'une politique* (Paris: L'Harmattan, 1997)

Architects

Dumont, Marie-Jeanne, "Anatole de Baudot," thematic issue, *Rassegna*, no. 68 (1996)

Vellay, Marc, *Pierre Chareau: Architect and Craftsman, 1883–1950* (New York: Rizzoli, 1985)

Ordóñez, José Antonio Fernández, *Eugène Freyssinet* (Barcelona: 2c Ediciones, 1979)

Friedman, Yona, *L'architecture mobile: vers une cité conçue par ses habitants* (Tournai: Casterman, 1970)

Friedman, Yona, *Toward a Scientific Architecture* [1971] (Cambridge, Mass.: MIT Press, 1975)

Lebesque, Sabine, ed., *Yona Friedman, Structures Serving the Unpredictable* (Rotterdam: NAI Publishers, 1999)

Guiheux, Alain and Cinqualbre, Olivier, eds., *Tony Garnier, l'œuvre complète* (Paris: Centre Pompidou, 1990)

Vitou, Elisabeth, Deshoulières, Dominique and Jeanneau, Hubert, *Gabriel Guévrékian: 1900–1970: une autre architecture moderne* (Paris: Connivences, 1987)

Rheims, Maurice, *Hector Guimard* (New York: Harry N, Abrams, 1988)

Thiébaut, Philippe, ed., *Guimard* (Paris: Musée d'Orsay, Réunion des musées nationaux, 1992)

Barré-Despond, Arlette and Tise, Suzanne, *Jourdain: Frantz 1847–1935, Francis 1876–1958, Frantz-Philippe 1906–1990* (London: Academy Editions, 1988)

Clausen, Meredith L., *Frantz Jourdain and the Samaritaine: Art Nouveau Theory and Criticism* (Leiden: E, J, Brill, 1987)

Benton, Tim, *The Villas of Le Corbusier and Pierre Jeanneret 1920–1930* (Basel, Berlin, Boston: Birkhäuser, 2007)

Curtis, William J. R., *Le Corbusier: Ideas and Forms* (London, New York: Phaidon Press, 1986)

Le Corbusier, *Toward an Architecture* [1923] (Los Angeles: Getty Research Institute, 2007)

Le Corbusier, *The City of Tomorrow and its Planning* [1925] (Cambridge, Mass.: MIT Press, 1971)

Le Corbusier Le Grand (London, New York: Phaidon Press, 2008)

Le Corbusier, *Precisions on the Present State of Architecture and City Planning* [1930] (Cambridge, Mass.: MIT Press, 1991)

Le Corbusier, *The Athens Charter* [1943] (New York: Grossmann Publishers, 1973)

L'Œuvre complète de Le Corbusier et Pierre Jeanneret, 3 vols (Zurich: Girsberger, 1930 to 1938)

L'Œuvre complète de Le Corbusier, 5 vols (Zurich: Verlag für Architektur, 1938 to 1969)

Cohen, Jean-Louis, *Urban Textures: Yves Lion* (Basel, Berlin, Boston: Birkhäuser, 2005)

Cohen, Jean-Louis, *André Lurçat, 1894–1970: l'autocritique d'un moderne* (Liège: Mardaga, 1995)

Cinqualbre, Olivier, ed., *Robert Mallet-Stevens: l'œuvre complète* (Paris: Centre Pompidou, 2005)

Pinchon, Jean-François, ed., *Rob Mallet-Stevens, Architecture, Furniture, Interior Design* (Cambridge, Mass.: MIT Press, 1990)

Picon, Antoine, *Marc Mimram: Hybrid Architect Engineer* (Gollion: Infolio, 2007)

Riley, Terence and Abram, Joseph, *The Filter of Reason: Work of Paul Nelson* (New York: Rizzoli, 1990)

Dudley, Gus, *Oscar Nitzchké, Architect* (New York: Irwin S, Chanin School of Architecture of the Cooper Union, 1985)

Baudrillard, Jean and Nouvel, Jean, *The Singular Objects of Architecture* (Minneapolis: University of Minnesota Press, 2002)

Johnston, Pamela, ed., *The Function of the Oblique: the Architecture of Claude Parent and Paul Virilio, 1963–1969* (London: Architectural Assocation, 1996)

Abram, Joseph, *Perret et l'école du classicisme structurel (1910–1960)* (Nancy: École d'architecture de Nancy, 1985)

Britton, Karla, *Auguste Perret* (London, New York: Phaidon Press, 2001)

Culot, Maurice, Peyceré, David and Ragot, Gilles, eds., *Les Frères Perret, L'œuvre complète* (Paris: Institut français d'architecture/Norma, 2000)

Jamot, Paul A.-G., *Perret et l'architecture du béton armé* (Paris, Bruxelles: Van Oest, 1927)

Dumont d'Ayot, Catherine and Reichlin, Bruno, eds., *Jean Prouvé: the Poetics of the Technical Object* (Weil/Rhein: Vitra Design Museum, 2006)

Loyer, François and Guéné, Hélène, *Henri Sauvage: Set-Back Buildings* (Liège: P, Mardaga, 1987)

Minnaert, Jean-Baptiste, *Henri Sauvage, ou l'exercice du renouvellement* (Paris: Norma, 2002)

Germany

Bartning, Otto, ed., *Mensch und Raum, Darmstädter Gespräch* (Darmstadt: Neue Darmstädter Verlagsanstalt, 1952)

Beseler, Hartwig, Gutschow, Niels and Kretschmer, Frauke, *Kriegsschicksale deutscher Architektur* (Neumünster: K, Wachholtz, 1988)

Beyme, Klaus von, Durth, Werner, Gutschow, Niels, Nerdinger, Winfried and Topfstedt, Thomas, eds., *Neue Städte aus Ruinen: deutscher Städtebau der Nachkriegszeit* (Munich: Prestel, 1992)

Campbell, Joan, *The German Werkbund: the Politics of Reform in the Applied Arts* (Princeton: Princeton University Press, 1978)

Diefendorf, Jeffry M., *In the Wake of War: The Reconstruction of German Cities after World War II* (New York, Oxford: Oxford University Press, 1993)

Durth, Werner, *Deutsche Architekten: biographische Verflechtungen, 1900–1970* (Braunschweig: F. Vieweg & Sohn, 1988)

Durth, Werner, Düwel, Jorn and Gutschow, Niels, *Ostkreuz, Personen, Pläne, Perspektiven, Architektur und Städtebau der DDR*, 2 vols (Frankfurt/Main: Campus Verlag, 1999)

Frank, Hartmut and Hain, Simone, *Zwei deutsche Architekturen 1949–1989* (Stuttgart: Institut für Auslandbeziehungen, 2004)

Geisert, Helmut, *Hauptstadt Berlin; Internationaler städtebaulicher Ideenwetteberb 1957/1958* (Berlin: Argon-Verlag, 1990)

Gutschow, Niels and Klain, Barbara, *Vernichtung und Utopie: Stadtplanung Warschau 1939–1945* (Hamburg: Junius, 1994)

Junghanns, Kurt, *Der Deutsche Werkbund: sein erstes Jahrzehnt* (Berlin: Henschelverlag, 1982)

Maciuika, John V., *Before the Bauhaus: Architecture, Politics, and the German State, 1890–1920* (Cambridge: Cambridge University Press, 2005)

Magnago-Lampugnani, Vittorio and Schneider, Romana, eds., *Moderne Architektur in Deutschland 1900-1950, Reform und Tradition* (Stuttgart: Gerd Hatje, 1992)

Mengin, Christine, *Guerre du toit et modernité architecturale: loger l'employé sous la république de Weimar* (Paris: Publications de la Sorbonne, 2007)

Nerdinger, Winfried and Brüning, Ute, *Bauhaus-Moderne im Nationalsozialismus, zwischen Anbiederung und Verfolgung* (Munich: Prestel, 1993)

Nicolai, Bernd and Benton, Charlotte, *Architektur und Exil, Kulturtransfer und architektonische Emigration 1930 bis 1950* (Trier: Porta Alba, 2003)

Pehnt, Wolfgang, *Expressionist Architecture* (New York: Praeger, 1973)

Pehnt, Wolfgang, *Deutsche Architektur seit 1900* (Ludwigsburg, Munich: Wüstenrot-Stiftung, Deutsche Verlags-Anstalt, 2006)

Pelt, Robert Jan Van and Dwork, Deborah, *Auschwitz: 1270 to the Present* (New Haven, London: Yale University Press, 1996)

Schneider, Romana and Wang, Wilfried, eds., *Moderne Architektur in Deutschland 1900 bis 2000, Macht und Monument* (Stuttgart: Gerd Hatje, 1998)

Schulz, Bernhard, ed., *Grauzonen, Farbwelten: Kunst und Zeitbilder; 1945–1955* (Berlin: Medusa, 1983)

Schwartz, Frederic J., *The Werkbund: Design Theory and Mass Culture Before the First World War* (New Haven, London: Yale University Press, 1996)

Architects

Anderson, Stanford, *Peter Behrens and a New Architecture for the Twentieth century* (Cambridge, Mass.: MIT Press, 2000)

Sembach, Klaus-Jürgen and Haeseler, Gottfried von, *August Endell, der Architekt des Photoateliers Elvira 1871–1925* (Munich: Museum Villa Stück, 1977)

Hoeber, Fritz, *Peter Behrens* (Munich: G, Müller und E. Rentsch, 1913)

Buddensieg, Tilmann, ed., *Industriekultur; Peter Behrens and the AEG, 1907–1914* (Cambridge, Mass.: MIT Press, 1984)

Voigt, Wolfgang and May, Roland, eds., *Paul Bonatz 1877–1956* (Tübingen, Berlin: Wasmuth, 2010)

Sembach, Klaus-Jürgen and Haeseler, Gottfried von, *August Endell, der Architekt des Photoateliers Elvira 1871–1925* (Munich: Museum Villa Stück, 1977)

Nerdinger, Winfried, ed., *Theodor Fischer: Architekt und Städtebauer* (Berlin: Ernst & Sohn, 1988)

Gropius, Walter, *Internationale Architektur* (Munich: A. Langen, 1925)

Gropius, Walter, *Bauhausbauten Dessau* (Munich: A. Langen, 1930)

Isaacs, Reginald R., *Gropius: an Illustrated Biography of the Creator of the Bauhaus* [1983] (Boston: Little, Brown, 1991)

Nerdinger, Winfried, ed., *The Architect Walter Gropius* (Berlin: Gebr, Mann Verlag, 1985)

Blundell-Jones, Peter, ed., *Hugo Häring: the Organic versus the Geometric* (London, Stuttgart: Edition Axel Menges, 1999)

Schirren, Matthias, ed., *Hugo Häring, Architekt des Neuen Bauens 1882-1959* (Ostfildern-Ruit: Hatje Cantz Verlag, 2001)

Turtenwald, Claudia, ed., *Fritz Höger (1877-1949), Moderne Monumente* (Munich: Dölling und Galitz Verlag, 2003)

Hopfner, Rosemarie and Fischer, Volker, *Ernst May und das Neue Frankfurt, 1925-1930* (Berlin: Ernst & Sohn, 1986)

Bergdoll, Barry and Riley, Terence, eds., *Mies in Berlin* (New York: Museum of Modern Art, Abrams, 2001)

Neufert, Ernst, *Bauentwurfslehre* (Berlin: Bauwelt-Verlag, 1936)

Neufert, Ernst, *Bauordnungslehre* (Berlin: Volk und Reich, 1943)

Prigge, Walter, ed., *Ernst Neufert: normierte Baukultur im 20, Jahrhundert* (Frankfurt: Campus-Verlag, 1999)

Ostendorf, Friedrich, *Sechs Bücher vom Bauen, enthaltend eine Theorie des architektonischen Entwerfens* (Berlin: W. Ernst & Sohn, 1914-1920)

Thöner, Wolfgang and Müller, Peter, *Bauhaus-Tradition und DDR-Moderne, der Architekt Richard Paulick* (Munich: Deutscher Kunstverlag, 2006)

Posener, Julius, *Hans Poelzig; Reflections on his Life and Work* [1970] (Architectural History Foundation, Cambridge, Mass.: MIT Press, 1992)

Blundell-Jones, Peter, ed., *Hans Scharoun* (London, New York: Phaidon, 1995)

Pfankuch, Peter, *Hans Scharoun: Bauten, Entwürfe, Texte* (Berlin: Akademie der Künste, 1974)

Frank, Hartmut, ed., *Fritz Schumacher; Reformkultur und Moderne* (Stuttgart: Hatje, 1994)

Frank, Hartmut and Voigt, Wolfgang, *Paul Schmitthenner 1884-1972* (Tübingen: Wasmuth, 2003)

Koch, Robert and Pook, Eberhard, eds., *Karl Schneider, Leben und Werk (1892-1945)* (Hamburg: Dölling & Galitz Verlag, 1992)

Schultze-Naumburg, Paul, *Kulturarbeiten* (Munich: G. D. W. Callwey, 1902-1917)

Schwarz, Rudolf, *Von der Bebauung der Erde* (Heidelberg: L. Schneider, 1949)

Boyd Whyte, Iain, *Bruno Taut and the Architecture of Activism* (Cambridge, New York: Cambridge University Press, 1982)

Speidel, Manfred ed., *Bruno Taut, Natur und Fantasie 1880-1938* (Berlin: Ernst & Sohn, 1995)

Taut, Bruno, *Alpine Architektur* (Hagen: Folkwang-Verlag, 1919)

Taut, Bruno, *Die Auflösung der Städte, oder die Erde eine gute Wohnung* (Jena: Diederichs, 1920)

De Michelis, Marco, *Heinrich Tessenow, 1876-1950* (Milan: Electa, 1991)

Tessenow, Heinrich, *Hausbau und dergleichen* (Berlin: B, Cassirer, 1916)

Tessenow, Heinrich, *Handwerk und Kleinstadt* (Berlin: Bruno Cassirer, 1919)

Wangerin, Gerda, Weiss, Gerhard and Rasmussen, Steen Eiler, *Heinrich Tessenow Baumeister: 1876-1950: Leben, Lehre, Werk* (Essen: Bacht, 1976)

Klotz, Heinrich, *O.M, Ungers, 1951-1984: Bauten und Projekte* (Braunschweig: Vieweg, 1985)

Ungers, Oswald Mathias, *Architecture as Theme* (Milan: Electa, 1982)

Greece

Aesopos, Yannis and Simeoforidis, Yorgos, eds., *Landscapes of Modernisation, Greek Architecture 1960's and 1990's* (Athens: Metapolis, 1999)

Condaratos, Savas and Wang, Wilfried, eds., *Twentieth-century Architecture: Greece* (Munich, New York: Prestel, 1999)

Kolonas, Vasilis, *Italian Architecture in the Dodecanese Islands (1912-1943)* (Athens: Oikos, 2002)

Architects

Frampton, Kenneth, ed., *Atelier 66; The Architecture of Dimitris et Suzana Antonakakis* (New York: Rizzoli, 1985)

Kyrtsis, Alexandros-Andreas, *Constantinos A, Doxiadis: Texts, Design Drawings, Settlements* (Athens: Ikaros Publications, 2006)

Ferlenga, Alberto, ed., *Pikionis, 1887-1968* (Milan: Electa, 1999)

Italy

Aymonino, Carlo, ed., *La città di Padova, saggio di analisi urbana* (Rome: Officina Edizioni, 1970)

Belluzzi, Amedeo and Conforti, Claudia, *Architettura italiana: 1944-1984* (Rome, Bari: Laterza, 1985)

Bonfanti, Ezio, ed., *Architettura razionale, XV Triennale di Milano* (Milan: Franco Angeli, 1973)

Bossaglia, Rossana, *Il Novecento italiano: storia, documenti, iconografia* (Milan: Feltrinelli, 1979)

Cennamo, Michele, ed., *Materiali per l'analisi dell'architettura moderna, Il MIAR* (Naples: Società editrice napoletana, 1976)

Ciucci, Giorgo and Muratore, Giorgio, eds., *Storia dell'architettura italiana, Il primo Novecento* (Milan: Electa, 2004)

Ciucci, Giorgio, *Gli architetti e il fascismo: architettura e città, 1922-1944* (Turin: Einaudi, 1989)

Crispolti, Enrico, *Attraverso l'architettura futurista* (Modena: Galleria Fonte d'Abisso, 1984)

Danesi Squarzina, Silvia and Patetta, Luciano, eds., *Il Razionalismo e l'architettura in Italia durante il fascismo* (Venezia: La Biennale di Venezia, 1976)

De Carlo, Giancarlo, *Urbino; the History of a City and Plans for its Development* (Cambridge, Mass.: MIT Press, 1970)

De Martino, Stefano and Wall, Alex, eds., *Cities of Childhood, Italian Colonies of the 1930s* (London: The Architectural Association, 1988)

De Seta, Cesare, *Architettura e città durante il fascismo* (Roma, Bari: Laterza, 1976)

Doordan, Dennis P., *Building Modern Italy: Italian Architecture, 1914-1936* (New York: Princeton Architectural Press, 1988)

Freni, Vera and Vanier, Carla, *Raimondo D'Aronco: l'opera completa* (Padua: Centro grafico editoriale, 1983)

Irace, Fulvio, *Gio Ponti, La casa all'italiana* (Milan: Electa, 1988)

Gentile, Emilio, *Fascismo di pietra* (Rome, Bari: Laterza, 2007)

Gregotti, Vittorio, *Il territorio dell'architettura* (Milan: Feltrinelli, 1966)

Kidder Smith, George E., *Italy Builds; its Modern Architecture and Native Inheritance* (New York: Reinhold, 1954)

Mariani, Riccardo, *E 42: un progetto per l'"ordine nuovo"* (Milan: Edizioni di Comunità, 1987)

Melograni, Carlo, *Architettura italiana sotto il fascismo, L'orgoglio della modestia contro la retorica monumentale 1926-1943* (Turin: Bollati Boringhieri, 2008)

Nicoloso, Paolo, *Gli architetti di Mussolini: scuole e sindacato, architetti e massoni, professori e politici negli anni del regime* (Milan: Franco Angeli, 1999)

Nicoloso, Paolo, *Mussolini architetto; propaganda e paesaggio urbano nell'Italia fascista* (Turin: Giulio Einaudi, 2008)

Olmo, Carlo, ed., *Il Lingotto, 1915-1939: l'architettura, l'immagine, il lavoro* (Turin: U. Allemandi, 1994)

Olmo, Carlo, ed., *Costruire la città dell'uomo: Adriano Olivetti e l'urbanistica* (Milan: Edizioni di Comunità, 2001)

Pagano, Giuseppe and Daniel, Guarniero, *Architettura rurale italiana* (Milan: U. Hoepli, 1936)

Patetta, Luciano, *L'architettura in Italia 1919-1943, le polemiche* (Milan: Clup, 1972)

Pica, Agnoldomenico, *Nuova architettura italiana, Quaderni della Triennale* (Milan: U. Hoepli, 1936)

Quilici, Vieri, *E 42-EUR, Un centro sulla metropolis* (Rome: Olmo, 1996)

Tafuri, Manfredo, *History of Italian Architecture, 1944-1985* [1986] (Cambridge, Mass.: MIT Press, 1989)

Architects

Piva, Antonio and Prina, Vittorio, *Franco Albini, 1905-1977* (Milan: Electa, 1998)

Freni, Vera and Vanier, Carla, *Raimondo D'Aronco: l'opera completa* (Padua: Centro grafico editoriale, 1983)

Barillari, Diana, *Raimondo D'Aronco* (Rome: Laterza, 1995)

Sessa, Ettore, *Ernesto Basile: dall'eclettismo classicista al modernismo* (Palermo: Novecento, 2002)

Bonfanti, Ezio and Porta, Marco, *Città, museo e architettura: il gruppo BBPR nella cultura architettonica italiana 1932-1970* (Florence: Vallecchi, 1973)

Pogačnik, Marco, ed., *Il segno della memoria; BBPR, Monumento ai caduti nei campi nazisti - 1945-1995* (Milan: Electa, 1995)

Buccaro, Alfredo and Mainini, Giancarlo, *Luigi Cosenza oggi 1905/2005* (Neaples: Clear, 2006)

Gregotti, Vittorio and Marzari, Giovanni, eds., *Luigi Figini, Gino Pollini: opera completa* (Milan: Electa, 1996)

Guidarini, Stefano, *Ignazio Gardella nell'architettura italiana: opere 1929-1999* (Milan: Skira, 2002)

Talamona, Marida, *Casa Malaparte* (Princeton: Princeton Architectural Press, 1992)

Conforti, Claudia, Dulio, Roberto and Marandola, Marzia, *Giovanni Michelucci 1891–1990* (Milan: Electa, 2006)

Reichlin, Bruno and Tedeschi, Letizia, eds., *Luigi Moretti, Razionalismo e trasgressività tra barocco e informale* (Milan: Electa, 2010)

Lupano, Mario, *Marcello Piacentini* (Rome, Bari: Laterza, 1991)

Buchanan, Peter, *Renzo Piano Building Workshop: Complete Works*, 5 vols. (London, New York: Phaidon Press, 1993–2008)

Piano, Renzo, *On Tour with Renzo Piano* (London, New York, Phaidon Press, 2004)

Ponti, Gio, *In Praise of Architecture* [1957] (New York: F. W. Dodge, 1960)

Irace, Fulvio, *Gio Ponti, La casa all'italiana* (Milan: Electa, 1988)

Nicolini, Renato, *Mario Ridolfi architetto, 1904–2004* (Milan: Electa, 1989)

Rogers, Ernesto N., *Esperienza dell'architettura* (Milan: Skira, 1997)

Ferlenga, Alberto, *Aldo Rossi: tutte le opere* (Milan: Electa, 2000)

Argan, Giulio Carlo, Levi, Carlo and Marangoni, Matteo, *Dopo Sant'Elia* (Milan: Editoriale Domus, 1935)

Caramel, Luciano and Longatti, Alberto, *Antonio Sant'Elia, The Complete Works* (New York: Rizzoli, 1988)

Da Costa Meyer, Esther, *The Work of Antonio Sant'Elia: Retreat into the Future* (New Haven: Yale University Press, 1995)

Dal Co, Francesco and Mazzariol, Giuseppe, *Carlo Scarpa, Complete Works* (Milan: Electa, 1984)

Lanzarini, Orietta, *Carlo Scarpa, l'architetto e le arti: gli anni della Biennale di Venezia 1948–1972* (Venice: Marsilio, 2003)

Olsberg, Nicholas, ed., *Carlo Scarpa Architect* (Montréal: Canadian Centre for Architecture, 1999)

Bairati, Eleonora and Riva, Daniele, *Giuseppe Sommaruga: un protagonista del Liberty italiano* (Milan: Comune di Milano, Mazzotta, 1982)

Ciucci, Giorgio, ed., *Giuseppe Terragni: opera completa* (Milan: Electa, 1996)

Eisenman, Peter, *Giuseppe Terragni, Transformations Decompositions Critiques* (New York: The Monacelli Press, 2003)

Schumacher, Thomas L., *The Danteum, A Sudy in the Architecture of Literature* (Princeton: Princeton Architectural Press, 1985)

Terragni, Attilio, Libeskind, Daniel and Rosselli, Paolo, *Atlante Terragni, Architetture costruite* (Milan: Electa, 2004)

Japan

Bognar, Botond, *Beyond the Bubble: The New Japanese Architecture* (London, New York: Phaidon Press, 2008)

Hein, Carola, Diefendorf, Jeffry M., and Yorifusa Ishida, eds., *Rebuilding Urban Japan After 1945* (Houndmills, New York: Palgrave Macmillan, 2003)

Oshima, Ken Tadashi, *International Architecture in Interwar Japan: Constructing Kokusai Kenchiku* (Seattle: University of Washington Press, 2009)

Pollock, Naomi, *Modern Japanese House* (London, New York: Phaidon Press, 2005)

Schneider, Angela, Knapstein, Gabriele, Elliott, David and Kataoka, Mami, *Berlin-Tokyo/Tokyo-Berlin, die Kunst zweier Städte* (Berlin, Ostfildern: Staatliche Museen zu Berlin, Hatje Cantz, 2006)

Stewart, David B., *The Making of a Modern Japanese Architecture, 1968 to the Present* (New York, Tokyo: Kodansha International, 1987)

Taut, Bruno, *Houses and People of Japan* (Tokyo: Sanseido, 1937)

Architects

Dal Co, Francesco, *Tadao Ando, Complete Works* (London, New York: Phaidon Press, 1995)

Pare, Richard and Heneghan, Tom, *Tadao Ando, The Colours of Light* (London, New York: Phaidon Press, 1996)

McQuaid, Matilda, *Shigeru Ban* (London, New York: Phaidon Press, 2003)

Oshima, Ken Tadashi, ed., *Arata Isozaki* (London, New York: Phaidon, 2009)

Ito, Toyo, Yamamoto, Riken, Buntrock, Dana, and Igarashi, Taro, *Toyo Ito* (London, New York: Phaidon Press, 2009)

Maffei, Andrea, ed., *Toyo Ito : Works, Projects, Writings* (Milan: Electa, 2002)

Witte, Ron, ed., *CASE: Toyo Ito; Sendai Médiathèque* (London, Munich, New York: Prestel, 2002)

Reynolds, Jonathan M., *Maekawa Kunio and the Emergence of Japanese Modernist Architecture* (Berkeley: University of California Press, 2001)

Maki, Fumihiko, *Investigations in Collective Form* (Saint Louis: Washington University School of Architecture, 1964)

Maki, Fumihiko, Frampton, Kenneth, et al., *Fumihiko Maki* (London, New York: Phaidon Press, 2009)

Salat, Serge, *Fumihiko Maki: an Aesthetic of Fragmentation* (New York: Rizzoli, 1988)

Raymond, Antonin, *Architectural Details* (Tokyo: A, Raymond 1938)

Helfrich, Kurt G F, and Whitaker, William, eds., *Crafting a Modern World: the Architecture and Design of Antonin and Noémi Raymond* (New York: Princeton Architectural Press, 2006)

Ocean of Air: SANAA Kazuyo Sejima, Ryue Nizhizawa 1998–2004 (Madrid: El Croquis, 2004)

Kultermann, Udo, *Kenzo Tange 1946–1969, Architecture and Urban Design* (Zurich: Artemis, 1970)

Latin America

Anda Alanís, Enrique X. de, *Vivienda colectiva de la modernidad en México* (México: Universidad nacional autónoma de México, 2008)

Anda Alanís, Enrique X. de, *La arquitectura de la revolución mexicana, corrientes y estilos en la década de los veinte* (México: Universidad nacional autónoma de México, 2008)

Brillembourg, Carlos, ed., *Latin American Architecture 1929–1960: Contemporary Reflections* (New York: The Monacelli Press, 2004)

Burian, Edward R., ed., *Modernity and the Architecture of Mexico* (Austin: University of Texas Press, 1997)

Fraser, Valerie, *Building The New World, Studies in the Modern Architecture of Latin America 1930–1960* (London, New York: Verso, 2000)

Hitchcock, Henry-Russell, *Latin American Architecture since 1945* (New York: Museum of Modern Art, 1955)

Liernur, Jorge Francisco, ed., *America latina, architettura 1965–1990* (Milan: Electa, 1990)

Liernur, Jorge Francisco, *La arquitectura en la Argentina del siglo XX: la construcción de la modernidad* (Buenos Aires: Fondo Nacional de las Artes, 2001)

Liernur, Jorge Francisco and Aliata, Fernando, eds., *Diccionario de Arquitectura en la Argentina; Estilos, obras, biografías, instituciones, ciudades*, 6 vols (Buenos Aires: Clarín/Arquitectura, 2004)

Segre, Roberto, *Cuba, l'architettura della rivoluzione* (Padua: Marsilio, 1970)

Architects

Pauly, Danièle and Habersetzer, Jérôme, *Barragan: Space and Shadow, Walls and Colour* (Basel, Berlin, Boston: Birkhäuser, 2002)

Rispa, Raúl, *Barragán, the Complete Works* (New York: Princeton Architectural Press, 1996)

Zanco, Federica, ed., *Luis Barragán: the Quiet Revolution* (Milan: Skira, 2001)

Anderson, Stanford, *Eladio Dieste, Innovation in Structural Art* (New York: Princeton Architectural Press, 2004)

Gutiérrez, Ramon, *Andrés Kálnay, un húngaro para la renovación arquitectónica argentina* (Buenos Aires: Cedodal, 2002)

Noëlle, Louise, *Mario Pani* (Mexico, Universidad Nacional Autónoma de México, 2008)

Castro, Ricardo, *Rogelio Salmona* (Bogotá: Villegas Editores, 1998)

Téllez, Germán, *Rogelio Salmona: arquitectura y poética del lugar* (Bogotá: Facultad de Arquitectura, Universidad de los Andes, Escala, 1991)

Villanueva, Paulina and Pintó, Maciá, *Carlos Raúl Villanueva* (New York: Princeton Architectural Press, 2000)

Middle East

Akcan, Esra, *Modernity in Translation: Intertwined Histories of Residential Architecture* (Durham: Duke University Press, 2011)

Arbid, Georges, "Practicing Modernism in Beirut: Architecture in Lebanon, 1946-1970." Ph.D thesis, Harvard University, 2002

Barillari, Diana and Godoli, Ezio, *Istanbul 1900, Art Nouveau Architecture and Interiors* (New York: Rizzoli, 1996)

Bozdogan, Sibel, *Modernism and Nation Building: Turkish Architectural Culture in the Early Republic* (Seattle: University of Washington Press, 2001)

Bruant, Catherine, Leprun, Sylviane and Volait, Mercedes, eds., "Figures de l'orientalisme en architecture," thematic issue, *Revue du Monde musulman et de la Méditerranée*, no. 73/74 (1996)

Chadirji, Rifat, *Concepts and Influences: Towards a Regionalized International Architecture, 1952–1978* (London, New York: KPI, 1986)

Fiedler, Jeannine, ed., *Social Utopias of the Twenties: Bauhaus, Kibbutz and the Dream of the New Man* (Wuppertal: Müller + Busman Press, 1995)

Holod, Renata and Evin, Ahmet, *Modern Turkish Architecture* (Philadelphia: University of Pennsylvania Press, 1984)

Levin, Michael, *White City, International Style architecture in Israel, Portrait of an Era* (Tel Aviv: The Tel Aviv Museum, 1984)

Marefat, Mina, "Building to Power: Architecture of Tehran 1921-1941." Ph.D thesis, Massachusetts Institute of Technology, 1988

Metzger-Szmuk, Nitza, *Dwelling on the Dunes, Tel Aviv: Modern Movement and Bauhaus Ideals* (Paris, Tel-Aviv: Editions de l'Eclat, 2004)

Nicolai, Bernd, *Moderne und Exil: deutschsprachige Architekten in der Türkei 1925–1955* (Berlin: Verl, für Bauwesen, 1998)

Pieri Caecilia L., "La brique, la palme et le béton, Stratégies de la modernité urbaine à Bagdad, 1921–1958." Doctorate thesis, Paris: École des hautes études en sciences sociales, 2010

Saliba, Robert, *Beirut 1920–1940, Domestic Architecture Between Tradition and Modernity* (Beirut: Ordre des Architectes et Ingénieurs de Beyrouth, 1998)

Volait, Mercedes, *Le Caire — Alexandrie, architectures européennes, 1850–1950* (Cairo: Cedej/Ifao, 2001)

Volait, Mercedes, *Architectes et architectures de l'Egypte moderne (1830-1950): genèse et essor d'une expertise locale* (Paris: Maisonneuve et Larose, 2005)

Weill-Rochant, Catherine, *L'Atlas de Tel-Aviv, 1908–2008* (Paris, CNRS Éditions: 2008)

Weizman, Eyal, Segal, Rafi and Tartakover, David, eds., *A Civilian Occupation: the Politics of Israeli Architecture* (London; New York; Tel Aviv: Verso; Babel, 2004)

Architects

Bozdogan, Sibel, Özkan, Süha and Engin, Yenal, *Sedad Eldem: Architect in Turkey* (London: Butterworth, 1987)

Fathy, Hassan, *Architecture for the Poor, An Experiment in Rural Egypt* (Chicago: University of Chicago Press, 1976)

Richards, J. M., Serageldin, Ismail and Rastdorfer, Darl, *Hassan Fathy* (London: Architectural Press, Singapore: Concept Media Ltd., 1985)

Steele, James, *An Architecture for People; The Complete Works of Hassan Fathy* (London: Thames & Hudson, 1997)

Netherlands

Singelenberg, Pieter, *H. P. Berlage, Idea and Style: the Quest for Modern Architecture* (Utrecht: Haentjens Dekker & Gumbert, 1972)

Ibelings, Hans, *20th Century Architecture in the Netherlands* (Rotterdam: NAI Publishers, 1995)

Lootsma, Bart, *Superdutch: New Architecture in the Netherlands* (London: Thames & Hudson, 2000)

Migayrou, Frédéric, ed., *De Stijl, 1917–1931* (Paris: Centre Georges Pompidou, 2010)

Troy, Nancy J., *The De Stijl environment* (Cambridge, Mass.: MIT Press, 1983)

Architects

Haan, Hilde de, ed., *Jo Coenen: from Urban Design to Architectural Detail* (Basel: Birkhäuser, 1991)

Wigley, Mark, *Constant's New Babylon: the Hyper-Architecture of Desire* (Rotterdam: Witte de With Center for Contemporary Art, 010 Publishers, 1998)

Baljeu, Joost, *Theo van Doesburg* (London: Studio Vista, 1974)

Hoek, Els, ed., *Theo van Doesburg, Œuvre catalogue* (Utrecht, Otterlo: Centraal Museum, Kröller-Müller Museum, 2000)

Straaten, Evert van, *Theo van Doesburg Painter and Architect* (The Hague: SDU Publishing, 1988)

Bergeijk, Herman van, ed., *W. M. Dudok* (Rotterdam: 010 Publishers, 2001)

Bak, Peter et al., *J. Duiker bouwkundig ingenieur; constructeur in stuc en stal* (Delft: Stichting Bouw, 1982)

Jelles, E. J. and Alberts, C. A., *Duiker 1890–1935* (Amsterdam: Architectura ed Amicitia, 1972)

Bock, Manfred, Rossem, Vincent van and Somer, Kees, *Cornelis van Eesteren Architect Urbanist* (The Hague, Rotterdam: EFL Stichting, NAI Publishers, 2001)

Ligteljin, Vincent and Strauven, Francis, eds., *Aldo van Eyck: Writings* (Amsterdam: Sun, 2008)

Strauven, Francis, *Aldo van Eyck, The Shape of Relativity* (Amsterdam: Architectura & Natura, 1998)

Bergeijk, Herman van, *Herman Hertzberger* (Basel: Birkhäuser Verlag, 1997)

Bock, Manfred, Johannisse, Sigrid and Stissi, Vladimir, *Michel de Klerk, Architect and Artist of the Amsterdam School 1884–1923* (Rotterdam: NAI Publishers, 1997)

Koolhaas, Rem, *S, M, L, XL* (New York: The Monacelli Press, 1995)

Lucan, Jacques, ed., *OMA-Rem Koolhaas: Architecture 1970–1990* [1990] (New York: Princeton Architectural Press, 1991)

Taverne, Ed, Wagenaar, Cor and Vletter, Martien de, eds., *J. J. P. Oud, Poetic Functionalist: the Complete Works, 1890–1963* (Rotterdam: NAi Publishers, 2001)

Taverne, Ed and Broekhuizen, Dolf, *Het Shell-Gebouw van J. J. P. Oud, ontwerp en receptie* (Rotterdam: NAI Publishers, 1995)

Dettingmeijer, Rob, van Thoor, Marie-Thérèse and van Zijl, Ida, eds., *Rietveld's Universe* (Rotterdam: NAI Publishers, 2010)

Küper, Marijke and Zijl, Ida van, *Gerrit Th, Rietveld 1888–1964; the Complete Works* (Utrecht: Centraal Museum, 1992)

Zijl, Ida van, *Gerrit Rietveld* (London, New York: Phaidon Press, 2010)

Bergeijk, Herman van, *Jan Wils: De Stijl en verder* (Rotterdam: 010 Publishers, 2007)

Russia/USSR

Buchli, Victor, *An Archeology of Socialism* (London, New York: Berg, 1999)

Essaian, Elisabeth, "Le plan général de reconstruction de Moscou de 1935; la ville l'architecte et le politique, héritages culturels et pragmatisme économique." doctorate thesis, Université de Paris 8, 2006

Goldhoorn, Bart and Meuser, Philipp, eds., *Capitalist Realism: New Architecture in Russia* (Berlin: DOM Publishers, 2008)

Gutnov, Alexei, *The Ideal Communist City* (New York: G, Braziller, 1971)

Hudson, Hugh D., Jr, *Blueprints and Blood, the Stalinization of Soviet Architecture* (Princeton: Princeton University Press, 1994)

Khan-Magomedov, Selim O., *Pioneers of Soviet Architecture* [1983] (New York: Rizzoli, 1987)

Kopp, Anatole, *Town and Revolution, Soviet Architecture and City Planning, 1917–1935* [1967] (New York: Braziller, 1970)

Lodder, Christina, *Russian Constructivism* (New Haven: Yale University Press, 1983)

Paperny, Vladimir, *Architecture in the Age of Stalin: Culture Two* (Cambridge, New York: Cambridge University Press, 2002)

Pare, Richard and Cohen, Jean-Louis, *The Lost Vanguard: Russian Modernist Architecture 1922–1932* (New York: The Monacelli Press, 2007)

Reid, Susan E., ed., *Russian Art and the West, a Century of Dialogue in Painting, Architecture and the Decorative Arts* (DeKalb, Ill.: Northern Illinois University Press, 2007)

Architects

Ginzburg, Moisei, *Style and Epoch* [1924] (Cambridge, Mass.: MIT Press, 1982)

Cohen, Jean-Louis, *Le Corbusier and the Mystique of the USSR, Theories and Projects for Moscow 1928–1936* [1987] (Princeton: Princeton University Press, 1992)

De Magistris, Alessandro and Korobina, Irina, *Ivan Leonidov 1902–1960* (Milan: Electa Mondadori, 2009)

Graefe, Rainer, Gappoev, Murat and Pertschi, Ottmar, eds., *Vladimir Suchov 1853–1939; die Kunst der sparsamen Konstruktion* (Stuttgart: Deutsche Verlags-Anstalt, 1990)

Olmo, Carlo and De Magistris, Alessandro, eds., *Iakov Tchernikhov* (Paris: Somogy, Turin: Allemandi, 1995)

Kirichenko, Evgenia, *Fiodor Shekhtel* (Moscow: Stroiizdat, 1973)

Spain and Portugal

Becker, Annette, Tostões, Ana and Wang, Wilfried, eds., *Architektur im 20, Jahrhundert: Portugal* (Munich: Prestel, 1997)

Bohigas, Oriol, *Arquitectura española de la segunda República* (Barcelona: Tusquets, 1970)

Capitel, Antón and Wang, Wilfried, eds., *Twentieth-century Architecture: Spain* (Munich, New York: Prestel, 2000)

Flores, Carlos, *Arquitectura española contemporánea* (Bilbao: Aguilar, 1961)

Pizza, Antonio and Rovira, Josep M., eds., *GATCPAC, Una nova arquitectura para una nova ciutat 1928–1939* (Barcelona: Col-legi Oficial d'Arquitectes de Catalunya, 2006)

Portas, Nuño and Mendes, Manuel, *Portugal Architecture 1965–1990* (Paris: Éditions du Moniteur, 1992)

Sambricio, Carlos, *Cuando se quiso resucitar la arquitectura* (Murcia: Comisión de Cultura del Colegio Oficial de Aparejadores y Arquitectos Técnicos, 1983)

Architects

Norberg-Schulz, Christian, *Ricardo Bofill, Taller de Arquitectura* (New York: Rizzoli, 1985)

Lahuerta, Juan José, *Universo Gaudi* (Barcelona, Madrid: Centre de Cultura Contemporània de Barcelona, Museo Nacional Centro de Arte Reina Sofía, 2002)

Femando Márquez, Cecilia and Levene, Richard, *Rafael Moneo 1967–2004* (Madrid: El Croquis, 2004)

Castanheira, Carlos and Siza, Álvaro, *Álvaro Siza: The Function of Beauty* (London, New York: Phaidon Press, 2009)

Frampton, Kenneth, *Álvaro Siza, Complete Works* (London, New York: Phaidon, 2000)

Esposito, Antonio and Leoni, Giovanni, *Eduardo Souto de Moura* (Milan: Electa, 2003)

Esposito, Antonio and Leoni, Giovanni, *Fernando Távora: opera completa* (Milan: Electa, 2005)

Switzerland

Delizia, Ilaria, and Mangone, Fabio, *Architettura e politica, Ginevra e la Società delle Nazioni 1925–1929* (Rome: Officina Edizioni, 1992)

Gubler, Jacques, *Nationalisme et internationalisme dans l'architecture moderne de la Suisse* (Lausanne: Éditions L'Age d'homme, 1975)

Lucan, Jacques, ed., *A Matter of Art, Contemporary Architecture in Switzerland* (Basel: Birkhäuser Verlag, 2001)

Wörner, Hans Jakob, ed., *P. M.: Aufsätze von Peter Meyer, 1921–1974* (Zurich: Verlags AG der akademischen und technischen Vereine, 1984)

Architects

Achleitner, Friedrich, *Atelier 5* (Basel: Birkhäuser, 2000)

Dal Co, Francesco, *Mario Botta, architetture 1960–1985* (Milan: Electa, 1987)

Diener, Roger, Abram, Joseph and Steinmann, Martin, *Diener & Diener* (London, New York: Phaidon Press, 2011)

Zardini, Mirko, *Aurelio Galfetti* (Barcelona: Gustavo Gili, 1989)

Mack, Gerhard, *Herzog & de Meuron: das Gesamtwerk* (Basel, Berlin, Boston: Birkhäuser, 1996)

Ursprung, Philip, ed., *Herzog & de Meuron: Natural History* (Montréal, Canadian Centre for Architecture; Baden: Lars Müller, 2002)

Bill, Max, *Robert Maillart* (Erlenbach/Zurich: Verlag für Architektur, 1949)

Billington, David P., *Robert Maillart and the Art of Reinforced Concrete* (Zurich, Munich: Verlag für Architektur Artemis, 1990)

Schirren, Matthias, ed., *Hannes Meyer, 1889-1954: Architekt, Urbanist, Lehrer* (Berlin: Ernst & Sohn, 1989)

Schnaidt, Claude, *Hannes Meyer: Bauten, Projekte und Schriften* (Teufen: Niggli, 1965)

Croset, Pierre-Alain, ed., *Luigi Snozzi, progetti e architetture 1957–1984* (Milan: Electa, 1984)

Disch, Peter, *Luigi Snozzi, costruzioni e progetti 1958–1993* (Lugano: ADV Publishing House, 1994)

Zumthor, Peter, *Peter Zumthor, Works: Buildings and Projects, 1979–1997* (Baden: Lars Müller, 1998)

Zumthor, Peter, *Penser l'architecture* (Basel, Berlin, Boston: Birkhäuser, 2008)

United Kingdom and Ireland

Benton, Charlotte, ed., *A Different World: Emigré Architecture in Britain 1928–1938* (London: RIBA Publications, 1995)

Bullock, Nicholas, *Building the Post-War World; Modern Architecture and Reconstruction in Britain* (London, New York: Routledge, 2002)

Conekin, Becky E, *"The Autobiography of a Nation": the 1951 Festival of Britain* (Manchester, New York: Manchester University Press, 2003)

Davey, Peter, *Arts and Crafts Architecture* (London, New York: Phaidon Press, 1995)

Duff, Alan Colquhoun, *Britain's New Towns; an Experiment in Living* (London: Pall Mall Press, 1961)

Harwood, Elain and Powers, Alan, *Twentieth Century Architecture 5: Festival of Britain and Brief City: The Story of London's Festival Buildings (Engineering Happiness)* (London: Twentieth Century Society, 2001)

Higgott, Andrew, *Mediating Modernism: Architectural Cultures in Britain* (London; New York: Routledge, 2007)

Powers, Alan, *Britain* (London: Reaktion Books, 2007)

Powers, Alan and Von Sternberg, Morley, *Modern: the Modern Movement in Britain* (London, New York: Merrell, 2005)

Robbins, David, *The Independent Group: Postwar Britain and the Aesthetics of Plenty* (Cambridge, Mass.: MIT Press, 1990)

Swenarton, Mark, *Homes Fit for Heroes: The Politics and Architecture of Early State Housing in Britain* (London: Heinemann Educational Books, 1981)

White, R. B., *Prefabrication: A History of its Development in Great Britain* (London: Her Majesty's Stationery Office, 1965)

Architects

Cook, Peter, *Archigram* (London: Studio Vista, 1973)

Cantacuzino, Sherban, *Wells Coates, A Monograph* (London: Gordon Fraser, 1978)

Jenkins, David, *Norman Foster: Works*, 6 vols (Munich, Berlin, London, New York: Prestel, 2002-2011)

Sudjic, Deyan, *Future Systems* (London, New York: Phaidon Press, 2006)

Ernö Goldfinger (London: Architectural Association, 1983)

Constant, Caroline, *Eileen Gray* (London, New York: Phaidon Press, 2000)

Pearman, Hugh, *Equilibrium. The Work of Nicholas Grimshaw & Partners* (London, New York: Phaidon Press, 2000)

Curtis, William J. R., *Denys Lasdun: Architecture, City, Landscape* (London, New York: Phaidon Press, 1994)

Allan, John, *Berthold Lubetkin, Architecture and the Tradition of Progress* (London: RIBA Publications, 1992)

Skelton, Timothy John and Gliddon, Gerald, *Lutyens and the Great War* (London: Frances Lincoln, 2008)

Lethaby, William A., *Architecture, Mysticism and Myth* (London: Percival, 1892)

Rubens, Godfrey, *William Richard Lethaby, his Life and Work 1857-1931* (London: The Architectural Press, 1986)

Kaplan, Wendy, ed., *Charles Rennie Mackintosh* (New York: Abbeville Press, 1996)

Macleod, Robert, *Charles Rennie Mackintosh: Architect and Artist* (New York: E. P. Dutton, 1983)

Leatherbarrow, David and Campbell, Hugh, *O'Donnell + Tuomey: Selected Works* (New York: Princeton Architectural Press, 2006)

Cedric Price (London: Architectural Association, 1984)

Powell, Kenneth, *Richard Rogers: Complete Works*, 3 vols (London, New York: Phaidon Press, 1999–2006)

Arnell, Peter and Bickford, Ted, *James Stirling, Buildings and Projects: James Stirling, Michael Wilford and Associates*, introduction by Colin Rowe (London: The Architectural Press, 1984)

Jacobus, John, *James Stirling, Building and Projects 1950–1974* (New York: Oxford University Press, 1975)

Vidler, Anthony, *James Frazer Stirling: Notes from the Archive* (New Haven: Yale University Press, 2010)

Wilford, Michael and Muirhead, Thomas, *James Stirling, Michael Wilford and Associates, Building and Projects 1975–1992* (London: Thames and Hudson, 1994)

Tecton, *Planned A. R. P. Based on the Investigation of Structural Protection Against Air Attack in the Metropolitan Borough of Finsbury* (London: The Architectural Press, 1939)

Gebhard, David, *Charles F, A, Voysey Architect* (Los Angeles: Hennessey & Ingalls, 1975)

Hitchmough, Wendy, *C. F. A. Voysey* (London, New York: Phaidon, 1995)

USA and Canada

Bluestone, Daniel, *Constructing Chicago* (New Haven, London: Yale University Press, 1991)

Buisson, Ethel and Billard, Thomas, *Presence of the Case Study Houses* (Basel, Boston: Birkhäuser, 2004)

Davis, Mike, *Dead Cities and Other Tales* (New York: W. W. Norton, 2002)

Dickstein, Morris, *Gates of Eden: American Culture in the Sixties* (New York: Basic Books, 1977)

Drexler, Arthur and Hitchcock, Henry Russell, *Buit in USA: Post-War Architecture* (New York: Museum of Modern Art, Simon & Schuster, 1952)

Dudley, George A., *A Workshop for Peace: Designing the United Nations Headquarters* (New York, Cambridge, Mass.: Architectural History Foundation, MIT Press, 1994)

Easterling, Keller, *Organization Space: Landscapes, Highways, and Houses in America* (Cambridge, Mass.: MIT Press, 1999)

Frampton, Kenneth and Rowe, Colin, *Five Architects: Eisenman, Graves, Gwathmey, Hejduk, Meier* (New York: Wittenborn, 1972)

Gebhard, David and Von Breton, Harriette, *Los Angeles in the Thirties: 1931–1941* (Los Angeles: Hennessey & Ingalls, 1989)

Gruen, Victor and Smith, Larry, *Shopping Towns USA: the Planning of Shopping Centers* (New York: Reinhold, 1960)

Hines, Thomas S., *Architecture of the Sun: Los Angeles Modernism, 1900–1970* (New York: Rizzoli, 2010)

Koolhaas, Rem, *Delirious New York, A Retroactive Manifesto for New York* (New York: Rizzoli, 1978)

Krinsky, Carol Herselle, *Rockefeller Center* (New York: Oxford University Press, 1978)

Loeffler, Jane C., *The Architecture of Diplomacy: Building America's Embassies* (New York: Princeton Architectural Press, 1998)

Meikle, Jeffrey, *Twentieth Century Limited, Industrial Design in America 1925–1939* (Philadelphia: Temple University Press, 1979)

Mock, Elizabeth, *Built in USA, 1932–1944* (New York: Museum of Modern Art, 1944)

Neutra, Richard, *Wie baut Amerika?* (Stuttgart: Julius Hoffmann, 1927)

Neutra, Richard, *Amerika, Die Stilbildung des neuen Bauens in den Vereinigten Staaten* (Vienna: Anton Schroll Verlag, 1930)

Pulos, Arthur J., *American Design Ethic; A History of Industrial Design to 1940* (Cambridge, Mass.: MIT Press, 1983)

Shanken, Andrew M, *194X, Architecture, Planning, and Consumer Culture on the American Home Front* (Minneapolis: University of Minnesota Press, 2009)

Smith, Elisabeth A. T., ed., *Blueprints for Modern Living: History and Legacy of the Case Study Houses* (Los Angeles: Museum of Contemporary Art, 1989)

Vanderbilt, Tom, *Survival City: The Architecture of the Cold War* (New York: Princeton Architectural Press, 2002)

Venturi, Robert, Scott Brown, Denise and Izenour, Steven, *Learning from Las Vegas* (Cambridge, Mass.: MIT Press, 1972)

Wright, Gwendolyn, *USA* (London: Reaktion Books, 2008)

Zukowsky, John, ed., *Chicago Architecture 1872–1922; Birth of a Metropolis* (Munich: Prestel, 1987)

Architects

Driller, Joachim, *Breuer Houses* [1998] (London, New York: Phaidon Press, 2000)

Hyman, Isabelle, *Marcel Breuer, Architect: the Career and the Buildings* (New York: Harry N., Abrams, 2001)

Jones, Cranston, *Marcel Breuer: Buildings and Projects 1921–1962* (Stuttgart: G, Hatje, 1962)

Vegesack, Alexander von and Remmele, Mathias, eds., *Marcel Breuer: Design and Architecture* (Weil am Rhein. Vitra Design Museum, 2003)

Krinsky, Carol Herselle, *Gordon Bunshaft of Skidmore, Owings & Merrill* (New York, Cambridge, Mass.: Architectural History Foundation, MIT Press, 1988)

Olsberg, Nicholas and Castro, Ricardo L., eds., *Arthur Erickson, Critical Works* (Vancouver, Seattle: Douglas McIntyre, Vancouver Art Gallery, University of Washington Press, 2006)

Chu, Hsiao-Yun and Trujillo, Roberto G., eds., *New Views on R, Buckminster Fuller* (Stanford: Goldsmith, Myron, Buildings and Concepts (New York: Rizzoli, 1987)

Gorman, Michael John, *Buckminster Fuller, Designing for Mobility* (Milan: Skira, 2005)

Krausse, Joachim and Lichtenstein, Claude, *Your Private Sky: R, Buckminster Fuller, the Art of Design Science* (Baden: Lars Müller, 1999)

Pawley, Martin, *Buckminster Fuller* (London: Trefoil, 1990)

Ragheb, J. Fiona, ed., *Frank Gehry, Architect* (New York: Solomon R, Guggenheim Museum, 2001)

Hines, Thomas S., *Irving Gill and the Architecture of Reform* (New York: The Monacelli Press, 2000)

Bosley, Edward R., *Greene & Greene* (London, New York: Phaidon Press, 2000)

Mackinson, Randell L., *Greene & Greene; Architecture as a Fine Art* (Salt Lake City, Santa Barbara: Peregrine Smith, Inc., 1977)

Wall, Alex, *Victor Gruen: from Urban Shop to New City* (Barcelona: Actar, 2005)

Pommer, Richard, Spaeth, David A, and Harrington, Kevin, eds., *In the Shadow of Mies: Ludwig Hilberseimer, Architect, Educator, and Urban Planner* (Chicago, New York: Art Institute of Chicago, Rizzoli, 1988)

Waldheim, Charles, ed., *CASE: Hilberseimer/Mies van der Rohe, Lafayette Park Detroit* (Munich, Cambridge, Mass.: Prestel, Harvard University, Graduate School of Design, 2004)

Stern, Robert A. M., *Raymond M. Hood* (New York: Rizzoli, 1982)

Miller, Nory, *Helmut Jahn* (New York: Rizzoli, 1986)

Geddes, Norman Bel, *Horizons* (Boston: Little, Brown, and Company, 1932)

Petit, Emmanuel, ed., *Philip Johnson, The Constancy of Change* (New Haven; London: Yale University Press, 2009)

Schulze, Franz, *Philip Johnson: Life and Work* (New York: Knopf, 1996)

Bucci, Federico, *Albert Kahn: Architect of Ford* (New York: Princeton Architectural Press, 1993)

Hildebrand, Grant, *Designing for Industry, the Architecture of Albert Kahn* (Cambridge, Mass.: MIT Press, 1974)

Brownlee, David B, and De Long, David G., *Louis I, Kahn: in the Realm of Architecture* (Los Angeles, Museum of Contemporary Art, New York: Rizzoli, 1991)

Goldhagen, Sarah Williams, *Louis Kahn's Situated Modernism* (New Haven: Yale University Press, 2001)

McCarter, Robert, *Louis I. Kahn* (London, New York: Phaidon Press, 2005)

Wurman, Richard Saul, *What Will Be Has Always Been: the Words of Louis I. Kahn* (New York: Access Press, Rizzoli, 1986)

Phillips, Lisa, ed., *Frederick Kiesler* (New York: Whitney Museum of American Art, W, W, Norton, 1989)

Steele, James and Jenkins, David, *Pierre Koenig* (London, New York: Phaidon Press, 1998)

Düttmann, Martina and Schneider, Friederike, *Morris Lapidus, Architect of the American Dream* (Basel, Berlin, Boston: Birkhäuser, 1992)

Escher, Frank, *John Lautner, Architect* (London: Artemis, 1994)

Escher, Frank, and Olsberg, Nicholas, eds., *Between Earth and Heaven: The Architecture of John Lautner* (Los Angeles, New York: Hammer Museum, Rizzoli, 2008)

Lanmon, Lorraine Welling, *William Lescaze, Architect* (Philadelphia, London, Toronto: The Art Alliance Press, Associated University Press, 1987)

Cardwell, Kenneth H., *Bernard Maybeck; Artisan, Architect, Artist* (Salt Lake City, Santa Barbara: Peregrine Smith, Inc., 1977)

Carter, Peter, *Mies van der Rohe at Work* [1974] (London, New York: Phaidon Press, 1999)

Lambert, Phyllis, ed., *Mies in America* (Montreal: Canadian Centre for Architecture, New York: Whitney Museum for American Art, Abrams, 2001)

Mertins, Detlef, ed., *The Presence of Mies* (Princeton: Princeton Architectural Press, 1994)

Moore, Charles Willard and Allen, Gerald, *Dimensions: Space, Shape & scale in Architecture* (New York: Architectural Record Books, 1976)

Mayne, Thom and Warke, Val, *Morphosis* (London, New York: Phaidon, 2002)

Hines, Thomas S., *Richard Neutra and the Search for Modern Architecture: a Biography and History* (New York: Oxford University Press, 1982)

Lavin, Sylvia, *Form Follows Libido: Architecture and Richard Neutra in a Psychoanalytic Culture* (Cambridge, Mass.: MIT Press, 2004)

Monk, Tony, *The Art and Architecture of Paul Rudolph* (Chichester: Wiley-Academy, 1999)

Sheine, Judith, *R. M. Schindler* (London, New York: Phaidon Press, 2001)

Adams, Nicholas, *Skidmore, Owings & Merrill: SOM Since 1936* (Milan: Electa, 2007)

Wit, Wim de, ed., *Louis Sullivan: the Function of Ornament* (Chicago: Chicago Historical Society, 1986)

De Long, David G., ed., *Frank Lloyd Wright: Designs for an American Landscape* (New York: Harry N., Abrams, 1996)

Muschamp, Herbert and Walker, Donald D., *Man about Town: Frank Lloyd Wright in New York City* (Cambridge, Mass.: MIT Press, 1983)

Riley, Terence, ed., *Frank Lloyd Wright Architect* (New York: Museum of Modern Art, Harry N., Abrams, 1994)

Tschumi, Bernard, *Manhattan Transcripts* (London: Academy Editions, 1981)

Venturi, Robert, *Complexity and Contradiction in Architecture* (New York: Museum of Modern Art, 1966)

Venturi, Robert and Scott Brown, Denise, *A View from the Campidoglio: Selected Essays, 1953–1984* (New York: Harper & Row, 1984)

McCarter, Robert, *Frank Lloyd Wright* (London, New York: Phaidon Press, 1997)

Levine, Neil, *The Architecture of Frank Lloyd Wright* (Princeton: Princeton University Press, 1996)

Siry, Joseph, *Unity Temple: Frank Lloyd Wright and Architecture for Liberal Religion* (Cambridge, New York: Cambridge University Press, 1996)

Storer, William Allin, *The Architecture of Frank Lloyd Wright: A Complete Catalog* (Cambridge, Mass.: MIT Press, 1974)

Twombly, Robert C., *Frank Lloyd Wright: An Interpretive Biography* (New York: Harper & Row, 1973)

Twombly, Robert C., *Frank Lloyd Wright, His Life and His Architecture* (New York: John Wiley & Sons, 1979)

Wright, Frank Lloyd, *Modern Architecture; Being the Kahn lectures for 1930* (Princeton: Princeton University Press, 1931); fac-simile ed., with an introduction by Neil Levin (Princeton: Princeton University Press, 2008)

Wright, Frank Lloyd, *An Autobiography* (New York: Duell, Sloan and Pearce, 1943)

Index

Acknowledgments and credits

Acknowledgments

This book is an extension of the many courses taught since 1994 at New York University's Institute of Fine Arts, and retains from the sequence of the lectures it extends and concatenates both its strengths and its weaknesses. In order to morph the notes on which my oral discourse was based, with their often allusive character, into a structured volume, I have benefited from the help of many colleagues, friends and interlocutors.

My gratitude goes first all the persons who have guided and contributed to the project at Phaidon, on both sides of the Atlantic and of the Channel, from the initial commissioning to the final printing. In New York, Karen Stein and Valérie Breuvard, who initiated the endeavor, and Nancy Grubb who followed its preparation, before undertaking the reading of the first draft; in London, Emilia Terragni and Sara Goldsmith, the book's editor, who has led from the very beginning the layout, the picture research and the production; in Paris, Hélène Gallois-Montbrun and Dominique Leconte, patient editor of the French version. And credit is due to the picture researchers who transformed the illustrations featured in my initial database as an expression of my desire into a reality: Julia Rydholm, in New York, and in London, Anna Zizlsperger, Ashley Lumb and Emmanuelle Peri.

Concocted after many difficulties, the English text owes its quality to the knowledge, the consistency and the elegance of Joan Ockman, who has been able to shape a graceful final version. I also convey my thanks to all the readers of the manuscript, at various stages of its development, whose wise recommendations have been for the most part injected into the text: Esra Akcan, Maristella Casciato, Mary McLeod, Carlo Olmo, Danièle Pauly, Yannis Tsiomis, Anthony Vidler, Michael Webb and Claire Zimmerman, whose students at the University of Michigan served as guinea pigs, reading in class an early version. Esther Da Costa Meyer shared with me her translation of Umberto Boccioni and clarified another futurist mystery. Reflections and information by Caroline Maniaque, Benoît Jacquet and Liza Essaian have also been precious.

Finally, I want to thank most warmly all the persons who have contributed to the collection of illustrations, particularly George Arbid, Anya Bokov, Malik Chebahi, Alexandre Chemetoff, Sonja Ganne, Patrick Henry, Rachid Ouahès, Ilya Lejava, Mihajl Oroveanu and Carmen Popescu. And also Jacob Stewart Halevy, efficient research assistant at the Getty Research Institute in 2009, and the students of the Institute of Fine Arts for their help in researching and digitizing pictures: Luis Castañeda, Anna Jozefacka, Matico Josephson, Kat Koh and Anoo Siddiqi.

Picture credits

Every reasonable effort has been made to acknowledge the ownership of copyright images included in this volume. Any errors that may have occurred are inadvertent, and will be corrected in subsequent editions provided notification is sent in writing to the publisher.

© A + H van Eyck Architects: 506; Accademia Nazionale di San Luca, Archivio Storico, Fondo Ridolfi-Frankl-Malagricci: 256; © ADAGP, Paris and DACS, London 2011. BI, ADAGP, Paris / Scala, Florence: 560; © ADAGP, Paris and DACS, London 2011. Courtesy Shchusev Museum of Architecture, Moscow: 268; © ADAGP, Paris and DACS, London 2011. RIBA Library Photographs Collection: 226; akg-images: 6, 29, 51, 94, 104, 108, 138, 263; akg-images © Mario Sironi / VG Bild-Kunst © DACS 2011: 127; akg-images / Erich Lessing: 109, 141; akg-images / Hilbich: 272; akg-images / L. M. Peter: 219; akg-images / L. M. Peter © FLC / ADAGP, Paris and DACS, London 2011: 413; akg-images / RIA Novosti: 204; akg-images / Suzanne Held: 357; Albert Kahn Family of Companies, www.albertkahn.com: 297; Photograph by Jim Alinder: 501; Alvar Aalto Museo: 320, 321, 322; Amsterdam City Archives: 136; Peter Aprahamian: 449; Arata Isozaki Architects: 486; Georges Arbid: 469; Arbid: 348; Architectural Press Archive / RIBA Library Photographs Collection: 245, 259, 312, 374, 425, 489; Architecture Museum of Ljubljana: 15, 330; Architekturmuseum der Technischen Universität Berlin: 95; Architekturmuseum der TU München - Archiv: 107; Archives Communales / Châtenay-Malabry: 220; Archives d'Architecture Moderne, Brussels: 187; Archives municipales et communautaires de Reims: 123; Archivio Centrale dello Stato: 479; Archivio Fotografico © La Triennale di Milano: 234, 249, 260; Archivio Fotografico Fondazione Michelucci: 247; Archivio Storico Olivetti, Ivrea, Italy: 397; Arquivo Carmen Portinho: 398; © ARS, NY and DACS, London 2011 and 2010. The Frank Lloyd Wright Fdn, AZ / Art Resource, NY / Scala, Florence: 436; © ARS, NY and DACS, London 2011 and CORBIS: 280; © ARS, NY and DACS, London 2011 and Richard Bryant / Arcaid / Corbis: 279; © ARS, NY and DACS, London 2011. Courtesy Getty Images: 278; © ARS, NY and DACS, London 2011. Courtesy S C Johnson and Son inc: 283; © ART on File / Corbis: 569; Arts of the United States Collection, University of Georgia: 441; Arxiu Nacional de Catalunya / Catalonia National Archive: 33; Atelier 5 / Balthasar Burkhard: 421; Atelier Hollein, Vienna: 519; Ateliers Jean Nouvel / Philippe Ruault: 575, 576; © Atlantide Phototravel / Corbis: 35, 349;

AUA Paul Chemetov: 511; Chant Avedissian / Aga Khan Trust for Culture: 515; Kayoko Azami: 334; Balzerowitz: 37; © 2011 Barragan Foundation, Birsfelden, Switzerland / ProLitteris / DACS. Photograph by Armando Salas Portugal: 466; Photograph by Bastin & Evrard: 17; Bauhaus-Archiv Berlin: 90, 182, 192; Bauhaus-Archiv Berlin, Foto: Markus Hawlik: 91; Bauhaus-Archiv Berlin, Photo: Labor Petersen: 183; Bauhaus-Universität Weimar / Archiv der Moderne: 302; Baukunstarchiv, Akademie Der Kunste, Berlin: 97, 135; © Cezary M Bednarski, 2010: 471; Benaki Museum, Athens: 332, 473; Berlin Partner GmbH / FTB-Werbefotografie: 218; Bernard Tschumi Architects: 579; Bertram D Wolfe Collection, Hoover Institution Archives, Stanford University: 341; © Bettmann / CORBIS: 55, 122, 387, 443, 450; Giuseppe Bianco: 246; Biblioteca Nazionale, Rome: 255; Biblioteka Muzeum Sztuki: 327; Photo Dida Biggi / Courtesy Rafael Moneo: 543; Bildarchiv Foto Marburg: 22, 88, 96, 112, 132; Bitter Fotografie, Berlin: 586; © Chris Bland; Eye Ubiquitous / CORBIS: 562; Photograph by Peter Blundell-Jones: 318; Photograph by Richard Boutin: 403; Andrea Branzi: 493; Nicholas Breach / RIBA Library Photographs Collection: 102; Urs Buttiker: 448; Cadaval & Solà-Morales: 545; Valeria Carullo / RIBA Library Photographs Collection: 563; Casa Lucio Costa: 426; Andy Castro: 528; Cedric Price fonds / Collection Centre Canadien d'Architecture / Canadian Centre for Architecture, Montréal: 480; Centre Pompidou-Bibliothèque Kandinsky: 156, 307, 352, 389, 407, 408, 482; Pierluigi Cervellati: 514; Photograph by Martin Charles: 19, 153; Christian de Portzamparc / photo Nicolas Borel: 531; © Christian und Klaus Herdeg, Zurich / New York: 324; City of Milan: 248; Courtesy of Jean-Louis Cohen: 4, 8, 12, 25, 28, 67, 68, 70, 71, 72, 77, 78, 79, 80, 83, 84, 89, 93, 100, 103, 105, 106, 114, 115, 116, 119, 121, 128, 131, 151, 157, 158, 161, 162, 180, 186, 189, 190, 191, 194, 208, 209, 210, 229, 230, 235, 237, 242, 243, 252, 258, 266, 277, 294, 300, 301, 303, 304, 305, 326, 331, 344, 345, 346, 361, 363, 364, 367, 370, 371, 376, 377, 378, 385, 391, 393, 396, 405, 409, 410, 439, 451, 454, 494, 508, 512, 516; Photograph by Jean-Louis Cohen: 120, 193, 354, 464, 491; Collection Centre Canadien d'Architecture / Canadian Centre for Architecture, Montréal: 124, 309, 437; Collection Kröller-Müller Museum, Otterlo, The Netherlands: 113; Collection of the Library of FAU, University of Sao Paulo: 337; © Comune di Milano (all rights reserved), Archivio Storico Civico Biblioteca Trivulziana: 31; © CORBIS: 264, 296; Gianni Cosenza: 257; Cranbrook Archives: 291; CSAC Università di Parma. Sezione Progetto / Marco Pipitone: 477; © DACS 2011 and Bettmann / CORBIS: front cover,

Phaidon Press Limited
Regent's Wharf
All Saints Street
London N1 9PA

Phaidon Press Inc.
180 Varick Street
New York, NY 10014

www.phaidon.com

First published 2012
© 2012 Phaidon Press Limited

ISBN 978 0 7148 4598 2

A CIP catalogue record for this book is available
from the British Library.

Designed by Béla Stetzer

Printed in China

Front cover   Apartment Buildings, 860–880 Lake
Shore Drive, Ludwig Mies van der Rohe, Chicago,
Illinois, USA, 1948–51

Back cover   Guggenheim Museum, Frank Gehry,
Bilbao, Spain, 1991–7

Pages 2–3   Plan Voisin, project, Le Corbusier, Paris,
France, 1925

Pages 8–9   The City of the Captive Globe,
project, Rem Koolhaas, New York City, USA, 1972,
drawing by Madelon Vriesendorp